T0315811

EXCHANGE RATE POLICIES IN EMERGING ASIAN COUNTRIES

High-performing Asian currencies have until 1997 been pegged to the US dollar, around which a major currency bloc is based. However, the future emergence of a European monetary zone is set to transform the configuration of the international monetary system and the roles of the dollar, the Euro and the yen within this system. Consequently, the strategic orientations in Asian exchange rate policies must be thoroughly re-examined.

Exchange Rate Policies in Emerging Asian Countries addresses this issue with discussion of:

- exchange rate policies pursued in the principal Asian countries
- the measurement of equilibrium exchange rates for these countries
- the maintenance of the dollar peg by Asian currencies
- the absence of a trend to monetary regionalism based on the yen
- the outlook for regional monetary cooperation

Case studies pay particular attention to South Korea, Taiwan, Singapore and Thailand.

Written and edited by an international group of experts, this work makes a major contribution to the debate on the future of the Asian currencies in a changing monetary system.

Stefan Collignon is the Director of Research and Communication at the Association for the Monetary Union of Europe (AMUE), Paris. **Jean Pisani-Ferry** is a ministerial adviser in the French Ministry of Economy, Finance and Industry. **Yung Chul Park** is a Professor of Economics at Korea University, Seoul. He is also President of the Korea Institute of Finance and a member of the Ministry of Finance's Financial Development Committee.

ROUTLEDGE STUDIES IN THE GROWTH ECONOMIES OF ASIA

1 The Changing Capital Markets of East Asia
Edited by Ky Cao
2 Financial Reform in China
Edited by On Kit Tam
3 Women and Industrialization in Asia
Edited by Susan Horton
4 Japan's Trade Policy
Action or reaction?
Yumiko Mikanagi
5 The Japanese Election System
Three analytical perspectives
Junichiro Wada
6 The Economics of the Latecomers
Catching-up, technology transfer and institutions in Germany, Japan and South Korea
Jang-Sup Shin
7 Industrialization in Malaysia
Import substitution and infant industry performance
Rokiah Alavi
8 Economic Development in Twentieth Century East Asia
The international context
Edited by Aiko Ikeo
9 The Politics of Economic Development in Indonesia
Contending perspectives
Edited by Ian Chalmers and Vedi Hadiz
10 Studies in the Economic History of the Pacific Rim
Edited by Sally M. Miller, A. J. H. Latham and Dennis O. Flynn
11 Workers and the State in New Order Indonesia
Vedi R. Hadiz
12 The Japanese Foreign Exchange Market
Beate Reszat
13 Exchange Rate Policies in Emerging Asian Countries
Edited by Stefan Collignon, Jean Pisani-Ferry and Yung Chul Park
14 Chinese Firms and Technology in the Reform Era
Yizheng Shi
15 Japanese Views on Economic Development
Diverse paths to the market
Kenichi Ohno and Izumi Ohno
16 The Thai Economy
Uneven development and internationalization
Chris Dixon
17 Technological Capabilities and Export Success in Asia
Edited by Dieter Erust, Tom Ganiatsos and Lynn Mytelka
18 Trade and Investment in China
The European experience
Edited by Roger Strange, Jim Slater and Limin Wang
19 Technology and Innovation in Japan
Policy and Management for the 21st Century
Edited by Martin Hemmert and Christian Oberländer

EXCHANGE RATE POLICIES IN EMERGING ASIAN COUNTRIES

Edited by
Stefan Collignon, Jean Pisani-Ferry
and
Yung Chul Park

London and New York

First published 1999
by Routledge
2 Park Square, Milton Park, Abingdon, Oxon OX14 4RN
Simultaneously published in the USA and Canada
by Routledge
711 Third Avenue, New York, NY 10017
Routledge is an imprint of the Taylor & Francis Group

Typeset in Garamond by Pure Tech India Ltd, Pondicherry

British Library Cataloguing in Publication Data
A catalogue record for this book is available from the British Library

Library of Congress Cataloging in Publication Data
Exchange rate policies in emerging Asian countries / edited by Stefan
Collignon, Jean Pisani-Ferry, Yung Chul Park.
'Proceedings of a conference held in Seoul on 14–16 November
1996'—Added t.p.
Includes bibliographical references and index.
ISBN 0–415–17852–5
1. Foreign exchange rates—Government policy—Asia.
I. Collignon, Stefan   II. Pisani-Ferry, Jean.   III. Park, Yung Chul
HG3968.E944 1998
332.4'56'095—dc21   98–5915

ISBN 0–415–17852–5

CONTENTS

List of figures   xi
List of tables   xv
List of contributors   xviii
Editors' introduction   xx
Acknowledgements   xxviii

PART I
Exchange rate policies in Asia: the evidence   1

1   **Flexibility or nominal anchors?**   3
    RÜDIGER DORNBUSCH AND YUNG CHUL PARK

    1   The setting 4
    2   The convertibility issue 11
    3   Exchange rate choices: fixed rates 12
    4   Exchange rate choices: flexible rates 15
    5   Exchange rate choices: band-basket-crawl (BBC) 16
    6   Conclusion: nominal anchor or flexibility? 23
    Appendix: exchange rate regimes of East Asian countries 24

2   **Discussion**   35
    ANDRÉ ICARD

    1   The setting 35
    2   Convertibility 36
    3   Fixed rates 36
    4 and 5   Floating rates and band-basket-crawl 37

3   **Exchange rate regimes and policies: an empirical analysis**   40
    AGNÈS BÉNASSY-QUÉRÉ

    1   Introduction 40

CONTENTS

2 De facto exchange rate regimes in Asia 41
3 Rationale for exchange rate policies in Asia 49
4 Summary and concluding remarks 56
Appendix 1: computing long-run estimates 57
Appendix 2: unit root and cointegration analysis, 1973–93 58
Appendix 3: Asian external trade 59

4 Discussion   65
JANG-YOUNG LEE

5 Exchange Rate Policy and Effectiveness of Intervention:
   the case of South Korea   69
YEONGSEOP RHEE AND CHI-YOUNG SONG

1 Introduction 69
2 Exchange rate system and movement of the exchange rate in the
     1980s and 1990s 70
3 Current account, capital flows and exchange rate 80
4 Foreign exchange market intervention 89
5 Concluding remarks 99

6 Discussion   105
AGNÈS BÉNASSY-QUÉRÉ

7 Foreign Exchange Rate Fluctuations and Macroeconomic
   Management: the case of Taiwan   109
RAY B. DAWN AND GANG SHYY

1 Introduction 109
2 A review of Taiwan's exchange rate regime 110
3 The movement of REER index of NTD since 1980 116
4 Factors that affect the fluctuations of NTD 117
5 Consequences of NTD fluctuations 128
6 Macroeconomic policies regarding exchange rate
     fluctuations 132
7 Intermarket relationship between foreign exchange rate and
     interest rate 138
8 Concluding remarks 140

8 Discussion   143
MARTIN WEALE

CONTENTS

PART II

Exchange rates and economic development: long-run
views   147

9   Industrialization and the optimal real exchange rate
policy for an emerging economy   149
GUILLERMO LARRAÍN

    1   *Introduction 149*
    2   *Two approaches to industrialization: active and interventionist*
       (Asia) or passive and free-marketeer (Latin America) 152
    3   *The pitfalls of optimal industrialization policies 154*
    4   *The logic of price incentives and industrialization:*
       a model 155
    5   *Three complementary arguments to the optimal policy 159*
    6   *A view of two benchmark cases: Chile and South Korea 167*
    7   *Conclusions 176*

10   Discussion   185
JOHN WILLIAMSON

11   Asian currencies in the context of export-oriented
industrial development   188
LAM KEONG YEOH AND AI NING WEE

    1   *Introduction 188*
    2   *Typical stages of Asian industrial development 189*
    3   *Stages of industrial development, currency theory and*
       behaviour: a life cycle model of Asian currencies 191
    4   *Empirical methodology and results 193*
    5   *The life cycle model and selected Asian currencies 197*
    6   *The current life cycle stages of Asian currencies looking at*
       recent cross-section data 204
    7   *Medium-term outlook for Asian currencies based on life cycle*
       hypothesis: North-East Asia and ASEAN 204
    8   *Conclusion and implications of an Asian currency life cycle*
       model 211
    Appendix 1(a) 212
    Appendix 1(b) 214

12   Discussion   219
VIRGINIE COUDERT

13 Measuring exchange rate misalignments with
    purchasing power parity estimates   222
    FRANÇOIS BENAROYA AND DIDIER JANCI

    1   The Balassa–Samuelson effect and its application to measure
        exchange rate misalignments: a brief review 223
    2   An extended Balassa–Samuelson model 227
    3   Data and econometric estimates 230
    4   Implications for exchange rate levels in emerging Asia 234
    5   Conclusion 239

14 Discussion   243
    GANG SHYY

15 FEERs for the NICs: exchange rate policies and
    development strategies in Taiwan, South Korea,
    Singapore and Thailand   245
    RAY BARRELL, BOB ANDERTON, MELANIE LANSBURY AND
    JAMES SEFTON

    1   The growth experience of South Korea, Singapore, Taiwan
        and Thailand 245
    2   Exchange rate policies – the concept of equilibrium 249
    3   Econometric models of Singapore, Thailand, South Korea
        and Taiwan 252
    4   Exchange rates and development policies in East Asia 257
    5   Conclusions 270
    Appendix: the econometric models in detail 271

16 Discussion   280
    BENOÎT COEURÉ

    1   Defining the external balance: the case of NIEs 280
    2   The role of the US dollar and the need for a global approach 282

PART III
Regional monetary cooperation: rationale and effects   283

17 Bloc floating and exchange rate volatility: the causes
    and consequences of currency blocs   285
    STEFAN COLLIGNON

    1   Introduction 285

2 *Investment and exchange risk reduction: why currency blocs emerge 289*

3 *The consequences of bloc floating for equilibrium exchange rates in a bloc-floating regime 297*

4 *Empirical evidence of bloc-floating effects 307*

5 *Conclusion 317*

18 **Discussion** 323
RÜDIGER DORNBUSCH

19 **The case for a common basket peg for East Asian currencies** 327
JOHN WILLIAMSON

1 *Exchange rate policies 327*
2 *Evaluation 331*
3 *Selecting a peg 332*
4 *The constraints imposed by a common peg 340*

20 **Discussion** 344
JEAN PISANI-FERRY

21 **Is Asia an optimum currency area? Can it become one? Regional, global, and historical perspectives on Asian monetary relations** 347
BARRY EICHENGREEN AND TAMIM BAYOUMI

1 *How have Asian exchange rate arrangements evolved? 348*
2 *Regional perspectives 351*
3 *Historical perspectives 360*
4 *Conclusion 364*

22 **Discussion** 367
ADRIAAN DIERX

23 **Roundtable discussion: prospects for regional monetary cooperation** 369
JEAN PISANI-FERRY

Jean Pisani-Ferry 369
Masahiro Sugita 369
In June Kim 372

CONTENTS

André Icard 376
Toru Kusukawa 381
Adriaan Dierx 383

24 **The currency crisis in Thailand** 389
TOSHIYUKI KOBAYASHI

1 *The prelude to the currency crisis and the present state*
  of the Thai economy 390
2 *Factors behind Thailand's currency turmoil* 396
3 *Impact of Thailand's currency crisis* 408
4 *Conclusions* 414

Index 417

FIGURES

1.1	REERs of Asian countries	5–6
1.2	Shares of East Asian trade	8
1.3	Manufactures exports	9
1.4	South Korea–US relative deflators	13
1.5	Inflation rates of Asian countries	17
1.6	Chile's REER	19
5.1	Trend of daily won–dollar exchange rate	77
5.2	GARCH variance of daily won–dollar exchange rate	79
5.3	Exchange rates and cumulative current account balance in South Korea	82
5.4	Trend of daily won–dollar and yen–dollar exchange rates	84
5.5	Exchange rate and balance of payments in South Korea	88
5.6	Daily intervention in the foreign exchange market by the Bank of Korea	92
5.7	Responses of exchange rate to intervention	98–9
7.1	The movement of the exchange rate of NTD vis-à-vis US$	111
7.2	The means of standard deviations of NTD/US$ in four sub-periods	113
7.3	The annual means and standard deviations of NTD/US$ from 1980 to 1995	115
7.4	The movement of the REER index of NTD since 1980	118
7.5	The annual means and standard deviations of REER index of NTD	119
7.6	The growth rates of monetary aggregates from 1980 to June 1996	121
7.7	CPI growth rate, WPI growth rate and the interest rate of commercial papers from 1980 to June 1996	122
7.8	The movement of trade balance from 1980 to June 1996	123
7.9	The movement of NTD/US$, Canadian$/US$ and DM/US$ from 1980 to 1995	124
7.10	The real interest rate differentials from 1981 to June 1996	125
7.11	The movement of REER indices since 1980	127

7.12	The movement of NTD/US$ and net capital flows	130
7.13	The annual index and transaction volumes of Chinese Taipei's stock market	131
7.14	Instruments and goals of Chinese Taipei's monetary policy	133
7.15	The transmission process and effectiveness of Chinese Taipei's monetary policy	134
7.16	The decision-making process of Chinese Taipei's monetary policy	135
7.17	The changes in the required reserve ratios and liquidity ratios since 1980	137
9.1	Relative prices of exports in selected countries experiencing export booms	153
9.2	Entrepreneurial effort in the tradable sector and real exchange rate	161
9.3	Productivity and real exchange rate level in the tradable sector	163
9.4	Stimulation of the profit function	164
9.5	Impact of the Balassa–Samuelson effect on profits	165
9.6	A non-industrialization trap due to protectionism	167
9.7	Real exchange rate indices	169
9.8	Per capita growth since reform started (%)	171
9.9	Investment (% GDP)	171
9.10	Private and government consumption	172
9.11	Real wages (index, reform year = 100)	172
9.12	Exports (% GDP)	175
9.13	Sectoral composition of investment	176
9.14	Manufacturing value added	177
9.15	Manufacturing exports and income level in selected countries	177
11.1	Asian currencies and the Mexican peso	195
11.2	G-4 and Asia – currency versus economic performance	196
11.3	Japanese yen life cycle, 1961–95	198
11.4	Singapore dollar life cycle, 1975–95	199
11.5	Korean won life cycle, 1975–95	201
11.6	Indonesian rupiah life cycle, 1975–95	202
11.7	Thai baht life cycle, 1975–95	203
11.8	G-4 and Asian currencies life cycle behaviour (November 1996)	205
11.9	Taiwan dollar and Korean won life cycle and forecast	207
11.10	Malaysian ringgit and Thai baht life cycle and forecast	208
11.11	Indonesian rupiah and Philippine peso life cycle and forecast	210
13.1	Price level and income for selected countries in 1993	224
13.2	PPP over exchange rate, actual and predicted	235

13.3	PPP over exchange rate, actual and predicted (model 2)	236
15.1	Domestic saving ratios (% GDP)	246
15.2	Share of world exports of manufactures (%)	246
15.3	Share of manufacturing in output (%)	247
15.4	South Korea: FEER based on import prices	260
15.5	South Korea: current balance as a percentage of GDP	260
15.6	Singapore: FEER based on relative import prices	263
15.7	Singapore: current balance as a percentage of GDP	264
15.8	Taiwan: FEER based on relative import prices	266
15.9	Taiwan: current balance as a percentage of GDP	267
15.10	Thailand: FEER based on relative import prices	270
15.11	Thailand: current balance as a percentage of GDP	270
17.1	Share of currency zones in world exports	288
17.2	Expected and required returns and portfolio shares	296
17.3	Fundamental equilibrium	301
17.4	World exports and relative export shares with and without intra-EU trade in $ billion (1994)	306
17.5	Nominal exchange rate indices	309
17.6a	Volatility of real exchange rates, bilateral and effective, USA	309
17.6b	Volatility of real exchange rates, bilateral and effective, Japan	310
17.6c	Volatility of real exchange rates, bilateral and effective, Germany	310
17.7a	Relative volatility of bilateral real exchange rates to REER, USA	311
17.7b	Relative volatility of bilateral real exchange rates to REER, Japan	311
17.7c	Relative volatility of bilateral real exchange rates to REER, Germany	312
18.1	Iso-loss function and constraint diagram	324
24.1	Contribution to the growth of Thai GDP based on "growth accounting"	391
24.2	The exchange rate of the Thai baht against the US dollar	392
24.3	The Thai baht against the US dollar (January to August 1997)	394
24.4	Short-term interest rates in the ASEAN-4 countries in 1997	395
24.5	Sequence of events leading to the Thai currency crisis	397
24.6	Outstanding balance of loans via the BIBF	399
24.7	Foreign debt of Thailand	401
24.8	Thailand's current and capital accounts	402
24.9	The US and Thai consumer price indices (CPI)	404
24.10	The real exchange rate of the Thai baht and its real effective exchange rate	405

FIGURES

24.11   Total number of golf courses in Thailand   407
24.12   The exchange rates and real effective exchange rates of
        the ASEAN-4 currencies other than the Thai baht   414

TABLES

1.1	Asian currency arrangements	4
1.2	Stability of REER (coefficient of variation, %)	7
1.3	Correlations of REERs among Asian developing countries	7
1.4	Trade patterns of Asian economies (%)	8
1.5	Manufactures exports (% of total exports)	10
1.6	Regional and aggregate import demand	10
3.1	Exchange rate regimes in 1996	40
3.2	The relative volatility of monthly variations of nominal exchange rates against the US dollar	42
3.3	Estimates of the implicit nominal basket pegs (equation 3.2)	44
3.4	Estimates of the implicit nominal basket pegs (equation 3.3)	46
3.5	Estimates of the implicit real basket pegs (equation 3.4)	49
3.6	Some macroeconomic indicators in selected Asian countries	50
3.7	International bank liabilities by creditor country, at end 1994 (% of total external bank debt)	53
3.8	Currency composition of the long-term debt in selected Asian countries in 1993	53
A3.1	Unit roots	58
A3.2	Cointegration	59
A3.3	Orientation of exports by selected Asian countries	59
A3.4	Origin of imports of selected Asian countries	60
A3.5	Share of oil in the external trade of selected Asian countries	60
5.1	Volume of daily turnover in foreign exchange markets	75
5.2	Summary statistics of rate of changes in won–dollar exchange rate	77
5.3	GARCH estimation of won–dollar exchange rate	79
5.4	Test of random walk hypothesis	80
5.5	Effects of changes in yen–dollar rate on won–dollar rate	85

5.6	Effects of changes in yen–dollar rate on the volatility of won–dollar rate	86
5.7	Summary statistics of daily intervention	92
5.8	Degree of sterilization	93
5.9	Intervention effectiveness and reaction	96
5.10	Bank of Korea's credibility	97
7.1	The correlation coefficient matrix of the international and external factors that may influence NTD/USD	126
7.2	Correlation coefficients of REER indices	128
9.1	Share of imported inputs by sector in selected countries	162
9.2	Ratio of effective exchange rates for exports relative to imports in South Korea	170
9.3	R&D and its sources	173
11.1	Ranking of Asian currencies by total returns, spot returns and composite indicator readings, 1994–5	211
13.1	Changes in the manufacturing sector relative to the overall economy for selected Asian countries	226
13.2	Regressing e_{PPP-e} (logarithm of the exchange rate at PPP over the actual exchange rate)	231
13.3	Deviations from the standard and extended Balassa–Samuelson model, 1993	234
13.4	Deviations from the standard and extended Balassa–Samuelson model, 1996	238
17.1	Financial risk premia in Asian countries 1985–90	292
17.2	Volatility under bloc floating and basket pegs	294
17.3	Trade matrix in a three-country world	298
17.4	Openness of European Union	305
17.5	Normality test of monthly variations of logarithmic real exchange rates and REERs	313
17.6	GARCH (p,q) models of real exchange rates	316
19.1	Relative exchange rate volatility, 1992–5	328
19.2	Direction of trade of East Asian economies excluding intra-group trade (1994)	333
19.3	Export similarity indices for nine East Asian countries (1992)	336
19.4	Actual and hypothetical exchange rate changes, end 1994 to end April 1995	337
19.5	Export similarity indices for nine EU countries (1992)	341
20.1	Hypothetical effects of exchange rate changes	346
21.1	Exchange rate arrangements	349
21.2	Optimum currency area indices for Asian countries	353
21.3	OCA indices for bilateral relationships	354
21.4	Size and speed of adjustment to disturbances	355
21.5	Correlations of demand disturbances across different geographic regions	356

21.6	Correlations of supply disturbances across different geographic regions	357
24.1	Major political and economic events in Thailand over the last twelve months	393
24.2	Thailand's capital account	400
24.3	Ratio of FDI inflows to current account deficit	402
24.4	Pledges by the Thai government on 5 August 1997	408
24.5	The IMF financing package for Thailand	409
24.6	Volatility in ASEAN-4 currencies (January 1991 to August 1996)	412

CONTRIBUTORS

Bob Anderton, Research Fellow, National Institute of Economic and Social Research (NIESR), London, Great Britain.

Ray Barrell, Senior Research Fellow, NIESR, London, Great Britain.

Tamim Bayoumi, Senior Economist, International Monetary Fund, Washington, DC, USA.

François Benaroya, Foreign Economic Relations Department, Ministry of the Economy and Finance, Paris, France.

Agnès Bénassy-Quéré, Scientific adviser, Centre d'Études Prospectives et d'Informations Internationales (CEPII), Paris, France.

Benoît Coeuré, Deputy Head of the Treasury, Ministry of the Economy and Finance, Paris, France.

Stefan Collignon, Director, Research and Communication, Association for the Monetary Union of Europe, Paris, France.

Virginie Coudert, Economic Senior, CEPII[1], Paris, France.

Ray B. Dawn, Director of Financial Research Division, Taiwan Institute of Economic Research, Taipei, Taiwan.

Adriaan Dierx, Administrator, DG II, European Commission, Brussels, Belgium.

Rüdiger Dornbusch, Department of Economics, Massachusetts Institute of Technology, Cambridge, Mass., USA.

Barry Eichengreen, Department of Economics, University of California, Berkeley, USA.

André Icard, Assistant General Manager, The Bank for International Settlements, Basle, Switzerland.

Didier Janci, Head of General Studies and Country Risk Assessment, DREE, Ministry of the Economy, Finance and Industry, Paris, France.

In June Kim, Professor, Seoul National University, Seoul, South Korea.

Toshiyuki Kobayashi, Fuji Research Institute Corporation, Tokyo, Japan.

Toru Kusukawa, Chairman, Fuji Research Institute Corporation, Tokyo, Japan.

Melanie Lansbury, Research Officer, NIESR, London, Great Britain.

Guillermo Larraín Consultant, OECD,[2] Santiago, Chile.

Jang-Young Lee, Research Division Chief, International Finance Division, Korea Institute of Finance (KIF), Seoul, South Korea.

Yung Chul Park, President, KIF, Seoul, South Korea.

Jean Pisani-Ferry, Director, CEPII,[3] Paris, France.

Robert Raymond, Director General, European Monetary Institute, Frankfurt, Germany.

Yeongseop Rhee, Department of Foreign Trade, Sook Myung Women's University, Seoul, South Korea.

James Sefton, Senior Research Officer, NIESR, London, Great Britain.

Gang Shyy, Department of Finance, National Central University, Taiwan, Taiwan.

Chi-Young Song, Research Fellow, KIF,[4] Seoul, South Korea.

Masahiro Sugita, Director, International Department, Bank of Japan, Tokyo, Japan.

Martin Weale, Director, NIESR, London, Great Britain.

Ai Ning Wee, Research Manager, Economics Department, Government of Singapore Investment Corporation, Singapore.

John Williamson, Senior Fellow, The World Bank, Washington, DC, USA.

Lam Keong Yeoh, Senior Manager, Economics Department, Government of Singapore Investment Corporation, Singapore.

Notes

1 Now working as Economic Adviser at the Banque de France.
2 Now working as Macroeconomic Adviser, at the Ministero de Hacienda, Chile.
3 Now working as Economic Adviser at Ministère de l'Economie, des Finances et de l'Industrie, France.
4 Now working as Assistant Professor, Kookmin University.

EDITORS' INTRODUCTION

The monetary and financial crises in East Asia have put into question the policies of the emerging countries there. For decades, these policies had been considered a key component of the region's impressive development performance. Since September 1997, research has been started to investigate what went wrong and which policies should bear the blame for the collapse of what used to be considered one of the most remarkable economic achievements in modern history. Was the miracle a mirage? Asia's success was seen to spring from putting in place strong microeconomic incentives and getting macroeconomics right; its crisis is now explained by macroeconomic policy mistakes linked to micro inefficiencies.

As in the crisis of the European exchange rate mechanism (ERM) in 1992–3 or the Mexican crisis of 1995, there is controversy between those who stress 'fundamental' domestic factors causing an asset price bubble (in South-East Asia) or excessive business investment (in South Korea), and those who emphasize the self-fulfilling character of the financial panic that engulfed East Asia in the autumn of 1997. However, the turbulences started as a foreign exchange crisis in Thailand and then spilled over into other countries and the real economy. The comparison with the ERM crisis in Europe in 1992–3 is tempting: that crisis also spread from Italy and the UK to neighbouring countries, but the real effects were contained and the perspective of monetary union helped with the return to stability. Are there any lessons that Asia can learn from Europe? Research on these issues is still at an early stage, and the only firm conclusion one can draw at the time of writing is that the East Asian crises of 1997 will no doubt give birth to a new generation of exchange crisis models.

Whatever the analysis of the factors behind the crises, however, it is difficult not to include as one reason the specific monetary and exchange rate regimes of the East Asian countries. Three salient features of these regimes can be identified in this respect: (1) the prevalence of the US dollar as an anchor currency for most of the countries in the region, in spite of the relatively limited share of the United States in their foreign trade; (2) the relatively rigid and generally opaque character of the peg, in spite of an increasing liberalization of the capital account; (3) the still embryonic character of regional monetary cooperation, in spite of rapidly growing integration through trade and FDI flows. The weight of the US dollar in the region's implicit basket pegs facilitated its export drive from the mid-1980s until 1996, but it resulted in a significant real effective appreciation of the East Asian currencies in 1996–7, when the dollar started to appreciate against the yen and the European currencies. The rigidity of the peg prevented governments from reacting to the deterioration in the export performance of several countries, while its opaque character led market participants to question the strength of the governments' commitment to maintaining a fixed dollar link. Finally, the absence of an institutionalized monetary cooperation mechanism deprived the national central banks of the kind of (limited) assistance that their European counterparts could count on during the exchange crises of 1992–3.

The nature of, the rationale for and the problems connected with these exchange rate regimes were discussed in a seminar that took place in Seoul on 14–16 November 1996, only a few months before the crisis broke, with the participation of leading economists and policy makers from Asia, Europe and the USA. This seminar was jointly organized by three institutions: an association devoted to the promotion of European monetary union, which has for years aimed to foster research on European and more generally regional monetary integration, the AMUE (Association for the Monetary Union of Europe); France's major research institute in international economics, the CEPII (Centre d'Études Prospectives et d'Informations Internationales, Paris); and one of the top Korean research institutes, which is also actively involved in advising Korean policy makers, the KIF (Korea Institute of Finance, Seoul). At this conference leading economists from Asia, Europe and America discussed exchange rate policies in Asia and their potential consequences for the world economy. Nobody was able to forecast future events. But it quickly became apparent that the traditional policies of East Asian countries of pegging to the US dollar were a matter for discussion. New forms of foreign exchange management and new ideas for policy options were discussed, together with the outlook for cooperation in the region, possible alternatives for managing exchange rates (which are still relevant for the future monetary organization of East Asia) and the wider implications of East Asian currency arrangements for the world economy.

The debate is only starting. But it is obvious that much remains to be learned. This volume is a collection of the papers presented to the conference. They focus on four issues: evidence of exchange rate policy – how countries in East Asia have actually managed their exchange rates; country experiences which were not well known abroad and deserve analysis in detail; the link between the role of exchange rate policies and long-term economic development; and finally the future of regional monetary cooperation and the consequences of East Asia's policies for the world economy.

Exchange rate policies in Asia: the evidence

In Chapter 1 Rüdiger Dornbusch and Yung Chul Park start with a review of the exchange rate settings; they look at broad policy options and proceed to policy conclusions. At the start, they recommend a move towards current account convertibility, but the resulting stability issues which they noted in passing became more urgent than they expected at the conference. They do not recommend the formation of a yen bloc because they regard Japan as an unreliable anchor. Instead, they favour a more structured flexible exchange rate regime such as a band-basket-crawl (BBC). It would allow depreciations at a pace offsetting the countries' inflation differentials, thus maintaining competitiveness. The reference is a basket of currencies since the country does not have a single main trade partner. Third, the band aspect allows some room for domestic monetary policy. A BBC combines – even if imperfectly – the need for (limited) flexibility of *nominal* rates which matters in asset markets with the predictability of *real* exchange rates that matter in goods markets.

In the discussion in Chapter 2, André Icard points to the fragilities in the region's financial market developments. OECD experiences show that changes in the regulatory environment and the speed of deregulation should be determined case by case. As to the BBC proposal, the US dollar does not seem to be more suitable as an anchor currency than the yen. The yen should at least have a significant weight in the proposed basket. He criticizes the proposals' lack of practical detail such as the determination of the rate of crawl, and the transparency or elasticity of the band.

Agnès Bénassy-Quéré in Chapter 3 examines the *de facto* exchange rate regimes in the region as opposed to those reported by the IMF and tries to explain their rationales. Her central observation is a mismatch between trade blocs, capital blocs and currency blocs. A bloc in the sense of low exchange rate volatility vis-à-vis the yen is non-existent. Most countries pegged their currencies nominally either to the US dollar or to a basket in which the US dollar is predominant. In a second step she rationalizes these findings in a simple optimization model. The absence of a yen bloc is explained by a mismatch between the country distribution of trade and of external debt. The model shows that the development of trade between Asian NICs may favour either more stability towards the yen or generally a more flexible exchange rate regime.

In his comment in Chapter 4, Jang-Young Lee points out that the observed nominal pegs of some Asian countries against other currencies could also stem from the presence of a common economic shock rather than from a central bank's intervention. Likewise, the absence of an observable peg could also simply be the result of a failed attempt to influence the exchange rate.

Country experiences

In Chapter 5, Yeongseop Rhee and Chi-Young Song carefully describe the Korean exchange rate policy and its development since 1980. They explain the working of the multi-currency-basket-peg system (MCBP) which was used during the 1980s and the market average exchange rate system (MAR) to which Korean policy shifted in early 1990, as well as the objectives of foreign exchange rate policy. Their chapter illustrates the lack of transparency of the policy adopted by Korea in the 1980s and the 1990s, and the degree of discretion that the central bank sought to keep in spite of the adoption of a formal regime.

In Chapter 6, Agnès Bénassy-Quéré comments on official interventions. They have no lasting effect on the exchange rate, but provided they are not fully sterilized, they can influence long-run exchange rates over the mechanism of falling interest rates.

Ray B. Dawn and Gang Shyy in Chapter 7 review in their Taiwan case study the movements of the nominal exchange rate of the New Taiwan dollar (NTD) vis-à-vis the US dollar from 1963 to 1995 and the real effective exchange rate between 1980 and 1996, focusing on the associated changes in Taiwan's foreign exchange rate regime. The long-term trend of the NTD has been correlated with that of the yen and the DM. Volatile fluctuations of the NTD have produced several severe effects on the economy but have also provided an environment of stable prices.

In his comment in Chapter 8, Martin Weale claims that some important aspects such as relatively modest price level rises from the mid-1980s onwards or possible intervention during the floating exchange rate period have not been pursued.

Exchange rates and economic development: long-run views

East Asia's economic performance has been impressive and it has sometimes been argued that exchange rate policy was a key factor in it. In Chapter 9, Guillermo Larraín analyses how exchange rate policy in an emerging country can contribute to sustained growth in the presence of market failures and discusses in this respect the impact of exchange rate policy and that of targeted industrial policy. He compares the free-market approach as followed in Latin America with the interventionist approach followed in Asia. He concludes that the real exchange rate is the key relative price on which a non-interventionist approach to development must be based. Theoretically, industrialization may be achieved through real exchange rate undervaluation, creating profits in the tradable sector. However, difficulties could arise: first, an undervalued currency involves a worsening of income distribution. Second, a real devaluation might lead to intensive use of natural resources. Third, strong entrepreneurs' lobbies could obstruct a policy of slow real appreciation which should optimally follow a large initial real depreciation. Interventionist approaches could help to overcome some of these difficulties. Larraín proceeds to a comparison of two benchmark cases, Chile and South Korea. Regarding the composition of investment and exports, the South Korean interventionist approach seems to be more successful.

In his comment, Chapter 10, John Williamson criticizes the assumption of a large initial depreciation as well as the preference given to interventionist policies. A country does not necessarily need a depreciation to start the industrialization process, only an exchange rate that is sufficiently competitive to make the country an attractive platform from which to export manufactures. An interventionist policy should be favoured only if particular externalities concerning certain exports have to be offset.

In Chapter 11, Lam Keong Yeoh and Ai Ning Wee present a 'life cycle' model of East Asian currency behaviour: stage 1 usually shows a balance of payments crisis accompanied by exploding government and/or external debt burden and very high inflation. In stage 2, a labour-intensive export-oriented industry emerges. In stage 3, shortages of semi-skilled and even unskilled workers appear. Industry starts to shift to low but rising value-added per worker manufactures. In the fourth and final stage, industrial maturity with high value-added per worker is reached. The external deficit typically falls sharply, often turning into surplus. Skills and technology intensity account for an increasing share of productivity growth. A tendency to currency appreciation develops from this life cycle approach. Using econometric analysis, the East Asian countries are positioned in the cycle and their future perspectives outlined.

In her comment in Chapter 12, Virginie Coudert explains Ai Ning Wee and Lam Keong Yeoh's results of currency appreciation by the Belassa effect, resulting from productivity differentials in the traded and non-traded sector. Provided purchasing powers parity holds, a decrease in inflation then translates into a nominal *and* real appreciation.

In Chapter 13, François Benaroya and Didier Janci try to measure exchange rate misalignments using a Purchasing Power Parity model with a modified Balassa–Samuelson effect. They find that taking into account the US dollar's own undervaluation most Asian NICs appear to be slightly undervalued, even though the discrepancy seems to be gradually disappearing. The currency crisis since 1997 has obviously created a completely new position.

Gang Shyy, in Chapter 14, comments that the Balassa–Samuelson model is a long-run model with no explanatory power when long-run equilibrium is changing. He thereby questions the conclusion of a deliberately induced undervaluation.

Ray Barrell, Bob Anderton, Melanie Lansbury and James Sefton, in Chapter 15, examine exchange rate policies and development strategies in Taiwan, Korea, Singapore and Thailand using a FEER model. They conclude that the four countries have had very different experiences in terms of trade exchange rate and foreign investment policies. Only Thailand and Taiwan have at times pursued active exchange rate policies. In Taiwan's case, political reasons such as relations with mainland China may also have played a role. Recent currency turmoil has led to depreciations, but in the mid-1990s this has led to higher inflation rather than greater competitiveness.

In his comment, Chapter 16, Benoît Coeuré questions the FEER approach to estimate correct valuations of East Asian currencies. Defining a current account target poses theoretical difficulties since normative contents as well as precise previews are difficult to obtain in the fast-changing economies involved. Second, a possible misalignment of the US dollar with respect to European currencies puts into question the consistency of the resulting FEER estimates, given that many Asian currencies are pegged to the dollar.

Regional monetary cooperation: rationale and effects

Stefan Collignon, in Chapter 17, examines why countries form currency blocs and what consequences this has for the exchange rate between blocs. By pegging their currencies to an anchor, countries reduce exchange rate risk within the bloc. Risk premia in the return on investment consequently fall, and thereby boost investment. Thus, the emergence of currency blocs is the natural outcome when authorities aim at maximizing growth and risk-averse private investors maximize profits.

However, in a system of currency blocs, the exchange rate between the anchor currencies becomes the only adjustment tool to correct fundamental imbalances. The larger the regional currency zone, the larger will be the required shift in the flexible bilateral exchange rate between anchor currencies. Therefore, there exists a trade-off between intra-bloc stability and inter-bloc volatility. Collignon then compares bloc floating with a basket peg as advocated by Dornbusch, Park and Williamson. It is uncertain whether a change in Asian exchange rate policy towards a basket peg will improve their economic situation. The creation of European Monetary Union has very different effects, because a monetary union with a unified monetary policy and a single external exchange rate is very different from the logic of currency blocs. It would lower volatility between the key world currencies and stimulate economic growth.

In his comment in Chapter 18, Rüdiger Dornbusch asks for an exploration of the costs of pegging a currency to an anchor currency. He questions why flexibility in this context is valued so little. In addition, one has to distinguish between hubs, i.e. currency association around the dollar, and clubs such as the EMS in Europe. Clubs might do better if there is no dominant trade partner.

John Williamson's proposal in Chapter 19 of a basket peg for a group of East Asian currencies (China, Hong Kong, Indonesia, South Korea, Malaysia, the Philippines, Singapore, Taiwan and Thailand) is today more timely then ever. He first describes actual exchange rate policies as well as their problems and dangers. Most of them could be solved independently by the individual country by pegging its currency unilaterally to a trade-weighted basket. But, since trading patterns differ, these baskets would differ, leading to volatility in intra-East Asia exchange rates. Comparing the geographical distribution of their trade and competition in world markets, the East Asian countries in the group are more similar to each other than to any outside country with the exception of Indonesia. Three possible currency baskets are constructed and evaluated. Regarding changes in effective exchange rates, each of these arrangements would have allowed all of the countries to be vastly better off than with their actual policy. Williamson concludes that, although Asia might not be ready for an ERM-type system, it could benefit from greater exchange rate cooperation. A common basket peg seems to be the best solution.

In his comment, Chapter 20, Jean Pisani-Ferry emphasizes that cost-benefit analysis is not that simple. For Singapore, adopting a common basket peg would mean accepting that the yen–dollar exchange rate impacts on its exchange rate vis-à-vis the dollar and the Deutsche Mark although Japan is a minor trade partner and the USA and Europe are major ones. Hence, it is not obvious that all countries in the region would gain from adopting a common basket peg. However, it would increase the transparency of exchange rate policies within the region by making 'beggar-thy-neighbour' policies more observable.

In Chapter 21, Barry Eichengreen and Tamim Bayoumi analyse the economic and political prospects for monetary integration in East Asia. According to the standard criteria, the region qualifies as an optimum currency area as well as Western Europe. However, domestic financial systems are less well developed, the legacy of financial repression and capital controls limiting financial depth. Currency pegs are risky where governments are required to intervene in support of their banking system, even if the fluctuation of currencies is limited and the band is allowed to crawl. The events since the conference have proved these authors right. Moreover, the question remains whether Asia possesses the political will to operate a common basket peg successfully. Putting economic integration ahead of political integration might lead to the creation of an unstable and unsatisfactory arrangement which could set back the cause of regional economic cooperation for years to come.

In his comment, Chapter 22, Adriaan Dierx claims that East Asian banking problems are less pervasive than those in other emerging markets. Even if this were true, subsequent developments have shown them to be difficult enough.

The roundtable discussion presented in Chapter 23 concentrates on three issues: what scope is there for greater coordination among East Asian countries? Why is the international role of the yen so limited? What role might the introduction of the Euro have on future monetary relations with Asia? A consensus seems to emerge according to which the role of the yen depends on the interest shown in it by Japan's neighbours. Greater cooperation in Asia is found desirable and the events in 1997 have further underlined its necessity. As for the Euro, the proof of the pudding is in the eating, but its potential is recognized.

Chapter 24 was added after the 1997 crisis. Toshiyuki Kobayashi looks at the factors behind the currency crisis in Thailand. His preliminary conclusion is that in order to avoid a serious currency crisis in the future, an appropriate foreign exchange and macroeconomic policies must be employed. That, of course, is an eternal hope.

Stefan Collignon
Yung-Chul Park
Jean Pisani-Ferry

March 1998

ACKNOWLEDGEMENTS

We would like to thank the following companies and institutions for their support: Association for the Monetary Union of Europe (AMUE), Paris; Bank for International Settlements (BIS), Basle; Caisse des Dépôts et Consignations, Paris; Centre d'Études Prospectives et d'Informations Internationales (CEPII), Paris; Deutscher Sparkassen- und Giroverband, Bonn; European Commission (DG II), Brussels; European Monetary Institute (EMI), Frankfurt; Korea Institute of Finance (KIF), Seoul; Ministère de l'Industrie, Paris; OECD Development Centre, Paris. We also wish to thank Susanne Mundschenk who helped to organize the conference and Fabien Lim who helped to prepare this edition.

Part I

EXCHANGE RATE POLICIES IN ASIA

The evidence

1

FLEXIBILITY OR NOMINAL ANCHORS?

Rüdiger Dornbusch and Yung Chul Park

The issue of exchange rate policy in Asia comes up in a large variety of ways. In the past, being competitive was most of the message. Today, the range of challenges seems to have become far wider. And even if it has not, contrary to our contention, it is well worth reassessing whether past policies have been productive. In fact, though, new considerations come from all sides:

- Should we not expect a real appreciation of Asian New Industrial Economies' exchange rates relative to Japan to make a large contribution to the widening slack and structural depression in Japan?
- Is it helpful for Asian NIEs to use exchange rate policy to try and offset the sharply higher cyclical response of their export sectors to fluctuations in world industrial production?[1]
- If various Asian economies – Indonesia, Malaysia, Thailand – are becoming more vulnerable to speculative attacks, is it not appropriate to think of exchange rate regimes suitable for countries where macro instability predominates over trend growth influences?
- As Asia opens up to international capital flows, what is an exchange rate regime that goes with such a new and possibly dominant influence on the external balance and the financial sector?
- If US–Japan currency instability is a continuing feature, how should Asian NIEs respond, including the question of a yen bloc?
- How, if at all, does China figure in Asian NIEs' exchange rate policy?
- With Europe moving towards a monetary area, with Latin America increasingly moving to the dollar, should Asia form a yen bloc?

Our discussion starts with a review of the situation, including broad policy options, and proceeds from there to policy recommendations. To anticipate our conclusions: no to a yen bloc because Japan is an unreliable anchor; yes to a Williamson-style band crawl which brings together the notion of an exchange rate regime or policy rather than haphazard, opportunistic exchange market actions.[2] The combined band + basket + crawl (or BBC for short)

3

proposal offers, beyond sheer transparency, the desirable possibility of some (limited) flexibility of *nominal* rates (important from the perspective of asset markets) without sacrificing the predictability of *real* exchange rates (important matter for the goods market). Can it be done? Yes. Will it work perfectly? Probably not. Will it work better than other schemes? Yes.[3]

1 The setting

We can think of exchange rate regimes almost as a continuum from full dollarization, at one extreme, to fully flexible rates (with some monetary rules) at the other. Arrangements in between include currency boards, fixed rates, strict crawling pegs, crawling pegs with bands, and dirty floating. If this variety is not enough, an extra dimension for these arrangements can be added, since they may be defined (other than by dollarization or currency boards) relative to a reference currency or basket. It would be surprising if there were a simple answer to what regime to use.

In fact, barring the extreme of dollarization, just about every arrangement is being used somewhere at the present time. This is not surprising in view of differences in the composition of trade, in the diversification of trade, and in the extent of macroeconomic stability. Because key currencies in the world move relative to each other – the DM/US dollar and the yen/US dollar rate – there are trade-offs between various considerations and, as a result, in different countries there are different optimum currency arrangements (see Table 1.1; see Appendix for exchange rate regimes in Asia).

There is yet a further dimension in which regimes differ: the extent and the details of currency convertibility. Here, the range is from restricted current

Table 1.1 Asian currency arrangements

	Fixed		Floating		Convertibility	
	Dollar	Basket	Managed	Free	Partial	Full
Japan				*		*
China			*		*	
Indonesia			*		*	
Hong Kong	*					*
South Korea			*		*	
Malaysia			*		*	
Philippines				*	*	
Singapore			*			*
Thailand		*			*	
Vietnam			*		*	

Source: IMF, *International Financial Statistics and Handbook of Payments Restrictions*, Washington, DC.

account convertibility to full and unrestricted foreign exchange transactions for goods, services and assets. The striking evidence is that in these superperforming economies, even today currency convertibility is substantially restricted. Of course, across countries the extent of limitations differs substantially.

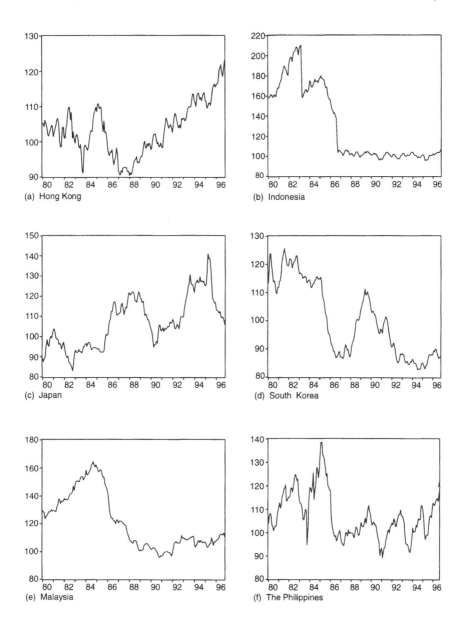

Figure 1.1 REERs of Asian Countries

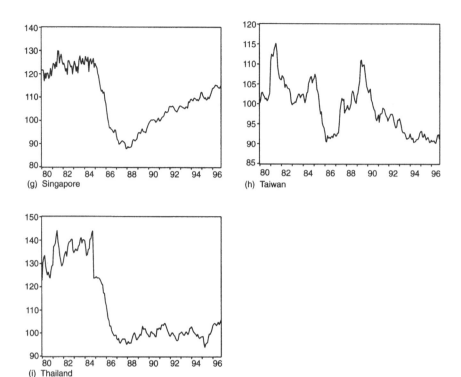

Figure 1.1 (continued)

Source: JPMorgan Internet web site.

Restrictions on the capital account predominate, but they are porous or entirely on the way out.

Whatever the nominal exchange rate regime, one important question is always the behaviour of the real effective exchange rate (REER). Figure 1.1 shows a sample of major East Asian economies using the data provided in JPMorgan's web site. The sample period is 1980 – July 1996, and the data refer to manufacturing. Interesting differences are immediately apparent; Hong Kong's steady real appreciation, the wide fluctuations in the Japanese real exchange rate (deriving from the movements in the yen/US dollar rate) with a resulting impact on all Asian economies, and the stability of Indonesia's real exchange rate since 1987.[4]

The extent of the stability of real exchange rates is reported in Table 1.2. We show the coefficient of variation for each country, and for two sample periods. We also aggregate Asia (as a simple weighted average) and compare it to Latin America. The results are striking.

In the 1990s, real exchange rates are more stable in almost all Asian economies than they are for the longer sample period. In Asia, real exchange rates

6

Table 1.2 Stability of REER (coefficient of variation, %)

	1980–96	1990–6
Asia	0.14	0.05
Hong Kong	0.30	0.09
Indonesia	0.13	0.03
South Korea	0.16	0.07
Malaysia	0.93	0.04
Philippines	0.11	0.06
Singapore	0.06	0.04
Thailand	0.15	0.04
Taiwan	0.12	0.02
Latin America	0.24	0.11

Source: Calculated by the authors using the JPMorgan data. Latin America refers to Argentina, Brazil, Chile, Peru and Venezuela.

are consistently far more stable than they are in Latin America. This does not in and of itself imply that the Asian exchange rate policy is 'better'. Asia's greater stability may reflect the fact that there have been more shocks in Latin America and hence greater volatility in equilibrium relative prices. This is true, but it would be a mistake to dispense with common sense. Asia's macro economy is more stable, and this is certainly partly due to a conscientious policy of stabilizing real exchange rates (around trend).

The analysis of real exchange rate volatility is supplemented in Table 1.3 which presents correlations of the REER across Asian economies. The striking point is that there is substantial correlation. This is largely explained by

Table 1.3 Correlations of REERs among Asian developing countries

		Hong Kong	Indonesia	Malaysia	Philippines	Singapore	Thailand
Hong Kong	1980–6	1.00	0.23	−0.03	0.56	−0.20	−0.30
	1990–6	1.00	0.41	0.76	0.61	0.95	0.27
Indonesia	1980–6		1.00	0.05	0.39	0.36	0.39
	1990–6		1.00	0.39	0.41	0.29	0.67
Malaysia	1980–6			1.00	0.58	0.11	0.07
	1990–6			1.00	0.55	0.71	0.06
Philippines	1980–6				1.00	−0.02	−0.15
	1990–6				1.00	0.64	0.17
Singapore	1980–6					1.00	0.68
	1990–6					1.00	0.17
Thailand	1980–6						1.00
	1990–6						1.00

Table 1.4 Trade patterns of Asian economies (%)

| | 1984 | | | 1994 | | |
| | Exp/GDP | Asia/Total | | Exp/GDP | Asia/Total | |
		Exp	Imp		Exp	Imp
China	9.6	37.7	16.0	22.7	40.3	33.6
Hong Kong	108.3	30.6	38.9	139.1	45.6	61.5
Indonesia	25.3	16.1	18.6	26.3	25.3	26.7
South Korea	37.4	13.8	11.2	30.6	32.2	15.9
Malaysia	56.4	39.3	26.7	95.4	44.2	32.6
Philippines	25.5	17.9	22.6	36.0	22.7	30.3
Singapore	169.6	39.8	28.3	192.3	50.6	37.6
Thailand	24.9	26.3	23.5	40.5	29.1	27.6
Taiwan	58.8	14.0	10.5	46.8	45.9	48.0

Source: IMF, *Directions of Trade Statistics, 1995*, Washington, DC.

Note
Exp and Imp refer to exports and imports while Total denotes the total exports or imports respectively.

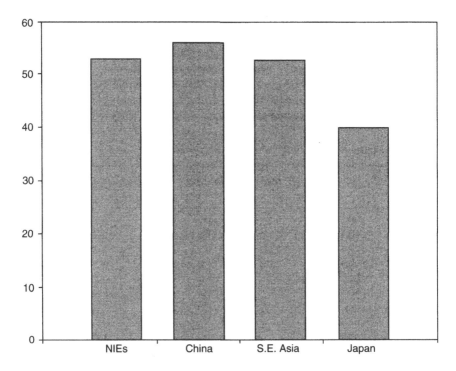

Figure 1.2 Shares of East Asian trade
Source: IMF, *Direction of Trade Statistics*, various issues.

exchange rate management that has one eye on the dollar and the other on the yen. But, clearly, the correlation is not complete, which suggests, reasonably, that different countries face different trade environments or pursue different targets and strategies.

Two crucial aspects of East Asian economies are their very substantial exposure to trade and the extent of intra-Asian trade. These aspects are highlighted in Table 1.4. Figure 1.2 picks up the same facts by including Japan in the set of export destinations. The simple message is this: intra-regional trade is now half or more of the region's total trade.

A final characteristic worth noting is trade structure. Over the past two decades, trade has increasingly shifted to manufactures. Countries which in the past were typical commodity exporters, say Indonesia or Malaysia, today show very substantial concentrations in manufactures as shown in Figure 1.3 and Table 1.5. For other countries such as South Korea, this was always the case.

The concentration on manufactures means two things. First, Asian economies are more nearly competitive with each other. Exchange rate policies that do not closely follow the same pattern have a major impact on the countries' relative competitiveness. Second, exports should be highly cyclically

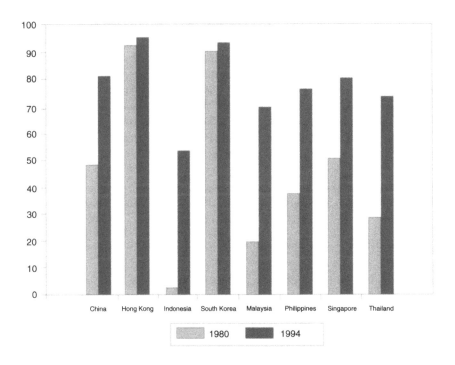

Figure 1.3 Manufactures exports (percentage of total exports)

Table 1.5 Manufactures exports (% of total exports)

	1980	1993
China	48	81
Hong Kong	92	95
Indonesia	2	53
South Korea	90	93
Malaysia	19	70
Philippines	37	76
Singapore	50	80
Thailand	28	73
Taiwan	94	96

Sources: World Bank, *World Development Report*, Washington, DC; Taiwan Ministry of Finance, *Monthly Bulletin of Statistics*, 1995.

correlated with the business cycle in advanced countries. This is more true, of course, the more Asian economies supply intermediate goods.

A final preliminary concerns the impact of exchange rates on trade flows. Since the policy discussion on the exchange regime assumes that exchange rates do matter, we should offer support for that premise before moving any further. An important body of evidence on the adjustment of trade flows has been brought together in a paper by Reinhardt (1994). Reinhardt shows that for developing countries, in the aggregate and by region, trade flows are significantly responsive to relative prices. The same is true for the import elasticities of industrial countries in their trade with emerging economies, which is reported on the right-hand side of Table 1.6. Note, however, that the elasticities shown by other studies are far smaller than those usually found in industrial countries, although relative prices are found to be statistically significant

Table 1.6 Regional and aggregate import demand

| | Developing countries | | Industrial countries | |
	Relative price	Income	Relative price	Income
Asia	−0.40	1.34	−0.40	2.49
	(0.07)	(0.05)	(0.09)	(0.14)
All developing countries	−0.53	1.22	−0.32	2.05
	(0.05)	(0.04)	(0.05)	(0.98)

Source: Reinhardt (1995, Table 6).

Note
The industrial countries' demand refers to their import demand from developing countries. Standard errors are in parentheses.

in most of the developing countries.[5] The reason for this finding still needs to be investigated, and there are not necessarily any grounds for pessimism about elasticity. Studies that focus on substitutability among alternative suppliers among emerging economies tend to find relatively high elasticities.

Of course, showing that trade flows respond to relative prices is not enough to make the case for the effectiveness of exchange rate changes. It must also be shown that nominal exchange rate changes translate substantially into real exchange rate movements. That is very often not the case. The more inflationary the economy, and the more it is indexed, the less likely that a devaluation has lasting real effects. Of course, this applies more to Latin America than to Asia. The fact that developing economies are very open increases the difficulty of making a major real depreciation stick since it is so obviously a cut in real wages.

2 The convertibility issue

Exchange rate policy has two dimensions: the extent of convertibility and the specific institutional arrangements that determine the day-to-day setting of exchange rates. We start with the issue of convertibility and move from there to exchange rate regimes.

Asia, including Japan, has a history of procrastination in freeing up trade in assets and financial services. This reluctance to some extent reflects the high degree of financial repression prevalent in Asian financial markets, the absence of effective sterilization tools, and the poor quality of balance sheets in the aftermath of a long period of mismanaged finance. The good macroeconomic performance of Asia has a surprising and perhaps strange counterpart in the neglect of financial markets as opposed to forced savings mechanisms. Thus, the lack of an open capital account also reflects a supporting policy for domestic management of the macro economy. It also, of course, reflects a determination to capture domestic savings for domestic investment.

It might perhaps be claimed that restrictions on convertibility have worked in the past – that there was more investment and growth, and fewer disturbances were imported via the capital account. That view, of course, expresses the underlying sense that capital movements are mostly a nuisance. If countries with high domestic saving rates had accompanying high rates of efficient investment, that would not be altogether implausible. Of course, if saving is inadequate or investment is inefficient, there can be little support for closing the capital account to the market.

Even where a country can plausibly claim high saving and efficient investment, failure to implement the decentralization required for an open capital account becomes increasingly difficult to defend. If transition to an open market is accepted in principle, steps should be taken to put it into practice. An appropriate regulatory structure has to be established and pre-emptive clean-up operations in the balance sheets of existing institutions have to be carried out. There seems little reason to delay an inevitable process.

For example, although membership in the OECD carries a commitment to an open capital account, South Korea is finding it difficult to take the plunge. Is it then surprising that China, for example, is postponing far more rudimentary reform towards current account convertibility?

The overriding presumption is that an early move to full and unrestricted convertibility will mean having to deal with a multitude of remnants from the previous intensely managed, repressed economies.[6] The accumulating evidence on inefficiency of the investment process, including overinvestment, reinforces the presumption that a more decentralized structure of decision making (the greater choice and freedom that come with markets) is highly desirable. Of course, there is a need to deal with the resulting question of stability. With substantially full convertibility, market factors become a significant source or amplification of disturbances. Here, the exchange rate regime, including regulation, must come into play to make the move to the market on a net calculation a beneficial experience. Above all, in opening the capital account, work on cleaning up the banking system will have to be complete. As is well known, bad banks get worse over time. There is therefore no excuse in delaying this preliminary step.[7]

3　Exchange rate choices: fixed rates

Just what to make of exchange rate policy depends on one's prior experience as to how the economy operates. At one extreme is a monetarist-equilibrium view: wages and prices are fully flexible so as to clear markets. What is left is the determination of the level of prices, the rate of inflation, the exchange rate and the rate of depreciation. The *real* exchange rate is not a policy variable in any sense.

This is indeed a useful starting point because it highlights two issues: one is the inflation implication of the currency regime; the second is the question of trend changes in the real exchange rate. Both issues have an important bearing on the choice of exchange rate regime.

Consider first the question of the national rate of inflation. Under fixed rates, assuming purchasing power parity (PPP), the rate of inflation is determined by the rate of increase of import prices. It is thus determined substantially by the rate of price increase experienced by the dominant partner country that anchors the home currency. Under the Bretton Woods system, for example, Germany experienced 'imported inflation' far in excess of what was domestically acceptable. The breakdown of the system can be partly attributed to precisely that issue.

The issue is somewhat complicated by combining PPP for traded goods with the existence of non-traded goods. As is well established from the Samuelson–Balassa–Komyia effect, the country with higher productivity growth (in the traded goods sector) will experience a rise in its relative price level over time. Thus, if the reference country has no inflation, the periphery and high productivity growth country will experience a rising price level over time. If the reference country has inflation, then the periphery country will have even more inflation. That was the experience, for example, of Japan in the years of the Bretton Woods system.

How does this consideration apply to Asian economies? Figure 1.4 shows the South Korea–US relative GDP deflators (measured in a common currency). It is apparent that from 1966 to 1995 there has been a pronounced real appreciation of the South Korean won. Such a real appreciation could occur under fixed rates by extra inflation relative to the anchor country or, under flexible or managed rates, by trend nominal appreciation. The equilibrium real appreciation will happen one way or another; the only relevant issue is whether appreciation of the nominal rate or of fixed rates and extra inflation are preferred ways of going about it.

A further complication in the choice between fixed or managed rates arises from the issue of a reference currency country. Often, there is a very simple answer: the Czech Republic, for example, will have no difficulty deciding that

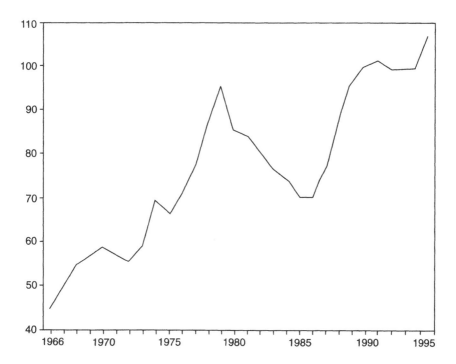

Figure 1.4 South Korea–US relative deflators (on a dollar basis, index 1990 = 100)
Source: IMF, *International Financial Statistics Yearbook, 1996*, Washington, DC.

the European Monetary Union (or failing that, Germany) is its natural reference country. The reason is both the relative financial stability of the anchor country as well as its dominance in the trade pattern. However, the same is not really true in a situation where countries' trade patterns straddle more than one reference country and where outside exchange rates are unstable. Fixing on one means large fluctuations of the national wage and price level in terms of the other. The benefits of stability are very limited. The simplicity of a fixed rate regime is lost and with it much of its appeal.

We saw above the trade pattern of Asian economies. Since half their trade or even somewhat more is intra-Asian, it would seem natural to focus on the yen. But since the other half is not with Asia, the immediate interest of a yen bloc scheme is limited.

But there is another way in which a yen bloc might be attractive. Increasingly, the Asian economies are competitive with each other and with Japan. It is therefore natural to ask whether a yen bloc strategy would not bring with it important strategic advantages by cutting out *easy* beggar-thy-neighbour strategies. In a fixed rate setting, there is still room for real appreciation or depreciation, but it has to come via wage and price movements, not by the stroke of a pen at the central bank.

The strategic advantage of a yen bloc depends critically on how much the exchange rate experience of the centre country fulfils the requirements of the partners. It is useful to remember the case of Germany in the exchange rate mechanism: German unification meant equilibrium real appreciation but the ERM framework did not admit nominal exchange rate changes. As a result, Germany was fighting inflation with high interest rates, and the partner countries went under. In the end, in 1992, the old-style ERM collapsed to give rise to major realignments. Is there a possibility of similar developments in the context of a yen bloc?

The immediate answer is yes. First, Japan is undergoing a dramatic structural change as it opens up its markets domestically and cross-border and, at the same time, relocates its industry offshore. Normally, such a process ultimately involves a significant real depreciation.[8] Real depreciation relative to what? In large part, the equilibrium real exchange rate relative to Asian partner countries will have to move. If the ERM experience is at all relevant, a fixed exchange rate setting is presumably an arrangement that makes it much harder to bring about the required changes in equilibrium relative prices.

If this consideration is not enough, it is worth adding two extra points. First, Japan has not clearly embarked on an identifiable prosperity policy. Over the past few years the country has mismanaged the response to dramatic balance-sheet problems and deflation. The lack of pragmatism, the institutional inflexibility and possibly incompetence make it unsuitable as a centre country. Another consideration is the medium-term trend imposed by dramatic social security problems. The required offset in terms of fiscal policies will almost surely call for major real exchange rate changes. Their timing and magnitude are hard to determine. These real exchange rate changes are presumably more easily achieved with managed rather than fixed rates. Surrounding countries' chances for prosperity are probably enhanced if they have at least a relatively flexible exchange rate to cope with the inevitable real disturbances.

It is worth concluding this consideration of fixed rates on the dominant note of scepticism that Obstfeld and Rogoff (1995: 94) bring to the topic:

> The choice between fixed and flexible exchange rates has long been one of the most fundamental issues in international finance. For most countries today, however, the choice between fixed and flexible rates is increasingly becoming moot. Aside from a few minor tourist economies, oil sheikdoms and heavily dependent principalities, only a very small number of fixed rates have survived the past few years intact.

A recent OECD study (Funke, 1996) strongly underlines the incompatibility of fixed rates and divergent fundamentals.

4   Exchange rate choices: flexible rates

Even in the mid-1980s, the idea of flexible rates for emerging economies was regarded as a non-starter. The assumption was that a flexible rate can only be a stable rate if markets are deep and institutions stable and predictable. None of the above seemed plausible. In fact, stabilizing speculation was still a key issue. And where would that come from in a world where portfolio capital did not readily reach emerging economies, if only because they did not even have domestic financial markets of any standing?

Today, the idea of flexible rates for emerging economies is certainly far easier to accept. A world capital market is undoubtedly in place. The only issue, then, is a hook-up for an emerging market. If there is a domestic money market there is no technical problem. The remaining issue is whether policies and institutions are sufficiently stable to generate a stable exchange rate.

The current issue, then, is not the availability of capital and speculators. The real question is whether the speculators are stabilizing. Here, there is a very clear divide in the profession. For some, in the tradition of Milton Friedman, the speculators are not the problem, the policies are. Don't blame the speculator who pushes down a currency because he sees deficits and inflation in the making. Others follow the school of Joan Robinson and Ragnar Nurkse for whom the inter-war experience bore the clear message that speculators make things worse or even create crises with no underlying reason.

In fact, there has already been limited experimentation with flexible rates in emerging economies.[9] In its most recent count, the IMF listed thirty-five countries as floating independently, most of them emerging economies. Of course, this does not mean a 'free float', since it may well involve intervention; even so, floating is certainly quite common. Nevertheless, while flexible rates have become far more plausible, a broad range of international economists view their credentials as incomplete. They mistrust the capital market and the far-sightedness of speculators even more than the good sense of policy makers. On balance, some form of managed rate is given preference, but it is also true that rates today would be given far more room to move and signal than used to be the case. In that sense, fixed rates have lost much of their attraction, and flexible rates have just broken the ice.

But there is a serious problem with flexible rates: the regime is not defined. A 'pure float' means presumably that the central bank does not intervene in the foreign exchange market. That is not the case, for example, for the USA, Germany and Japan. When central banks decide that a currency has gone too far, they do intervene, as in Japan in 1995. Thus it is surely duplicitous for new OECD members to be committed to a flexible rate if the centre countries in fact practise at least *ad hoc* target zones. But even if there was never any intervention, there is still a need to identify the monetary and fiscal setting in which rates are determined. It is obviously the case that a reduction in domestic credit leads to currency appreciation and an expansion leads to depreciation without any intervention taking place. Mexico, for example, maintained a constant nominal exchange rate in the face of 30 per cent inflation for an entire year and called the regime a 'flexible exchange rate'. Of course, the feat was accomplished by manipulation of the aggregates.

A flexible rate policy, then, is not fully specified unless there is an extra dimension such as an inflation target that governs monetary policy, an aggregate strategy or an interest rate policy. Countries with floating rates have a bit of everything and as a result the exchange rate regime adds to volatility and lacks transparency. For that reason we favour a more structured flexible rate regime in the form of the BBC scheme.

5   Exchange rate choices: band-basket-crawl (BBC)

The central focus of band-basket-crawl is threefold. First and foremost, it must maintain competitiveness. Over time, the exchange rate will depreciate at such a pace that the countries' inflation differential (beyond what is induced by the Balassa–Samuelson–Komyia effect) is offset by nominal depreciation. Second, because there is no dominant trading partner, the reference point is a basket of currencies rather than a single reference currency. Third, there is room for exchange rate fluctuations to free up, within limits, domestic monetary policy and to have some market-based signalling role for exchange rates.

The experience of Israel and Chile, both economies with inflation too high to be compatible with fixed rates, throws some light on these arrangements.

Both examples show that a country practising this kind of arrangement can have substantial integration in the world capital market, gradual disinflation, stable real exchange rates and a strongly performing real economy. Clearly, the regime is not a panacea: domestic monetary and fiscal policies matter for performance, but the arrangement is sufficiently stabilizing for capital markets to elicit substantially stabilizing speculation rather than wild gyrations and recurrent encounters with one-way speculators causing enormous losses to the central bank.

Figure 1.5 shows Asian inflation rates. While these are mostly moderate (compared to Latin America since the mid-1980s), the rates in some countries are sufficiently high to be patently incompatible with fixed or unchanging nominal exchange rates. This leads to the first part of the proposal: the crawl. Crawling was first practised in Latin America. It clearly involves a trade-off: indexing the exchange rate means inflation is more likely to perpetuate itself than to come down under the force of a (fixed) nominal exchange rate anchor. However, in exchange, there is no loss of competitiveness and the associated risk of recurrent devaluation crises declines. The higher the rate of inflation, the more important the emphasis on the crawl.

The second part of the scheme is the basket feature: because trade with the dollar bloc and with Europe is a significant portion of Asian commerce, the

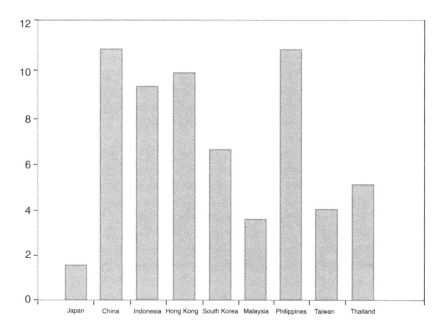

Figure 1.5 Inflation rates of Asian countries
Source: DRI, *World Market Executive Overview*, fourth quarter, 1996.

rate regime should be diversified. In that way another source of major swings in competitiveness – external currency movements rather than domestic inflation – is contained. Any trend inflation and productivity adjustment aside, external currency changes affect the central parity. Suppose we consider the South Korean won. Let the weights be 0.3 for the US dollar and the Ecu and 0.6 for the yen. Whenever the dollar appreciates 10 per cent on the yen and the Ecu, there is an offsetting 3 per cent appreciation of the won against these currencies. As a result, weighted average competitiveness is preserved: a gain in the dollar markets of 7 per cent and a loss in the Euro and yen markets of 3 per cent. The adjustment is clearly not neutral across firms, but it is the best that can be done under the circumstances. Firms can go further in seeking stability by using forward contracts. From an inflation point of view, the rule maintains the stability of the average price level.

The basket feature does not mean that there is a need to intervene in all reference currencies. In practice, the foreign exchange market is run in terms of one of the reference currencies, say the dollar. The central dollar rate is then adjusted in terms of the trend factors and the corrections deriving from external rate movements among the basket currencies.

The third feature involves the band aspect. The band is the result of a lesson drawn from experiments with flexible rates. The lesson is twofold. First, fully flexible rates may not be stable rates and, moreover, fundamentals (like monetary policy) are not fully exogenous. As a result, extreme moves like 80 yen to the dollar or 3.50 DM to the dollar emerge as market phenomena, unexplained and wildly counterproductive. Second, and in the other direction, market-determined rates may play a useful role in signalling the need for realignments of the central parity. Between the market signalling and policy makers learning and reacting, we have the potential for gradualist change in the central parity. That offers far more flexibility than a fixed rate and quite possibly a far more stable transition than a fully flexible rate. It thus tries to blend the best of both worlds.

There are two critical questions in the design of the target zone scheme. One is the issue of the band width. There is no scientific basis to determine a good band width. Williamson (1996) recommends a 7–10 per cent range on either side. His basis for these numbers is that less is too little and more is too much. Ultimately, that is a correct calculation, except that it has to be calibrated on the stability of the central parity real exchange rate and on the stability of the domestic financial policies. The more stable each of these is, the more stable the expected exchange rate and, hence, the narrower the plausible range of fluctuations and the defensible range. By contrast, if the equilibrium real rate is subject to substantial fluctuation and financial policies are all over the place, wide margins are essential, and even that is not enough. Clearly, in the latter case, there is an urgent need to bring financial policies under control since that, not intervention, is the only way to stabilize the foreign exchange market. An unstable equilibrium real exchange rate in

turn calls for an extra arrangement that makes the real central parity significantly flexible over time. Here is, in fact, a key challenge of the BBC
approach.

The story of Chile may be useful here. Figure 1.6 shows the real exchange
rate over the past decade. At the outset, the band was relatively narrow and
inflation near 30 per cent; real shocks were large, and the economy was emerging from a dramatic depression. By 1988–90, however, the economy had
been brought under control, growth was substantial, inflation more moderate, and international capital inflows more significant. The real effective
exchange rate shows minor fluctuations around a trend of steady real appreciation. The exchange rate strategy – avoiding major fluctuations with their
destabilizing impact on growth and inflation – was a complete success.[10]
Of course, along the way, it involved changes in band width and in operating
rules, including even an explicit provision for trend real appreciation deriving
from a favourable productivity growth differential.

A key ingredient in getting good performance is a realistic assessment of
the equilibrium real exchange rate. This is all the more important, the
more significant is structural change from trade and capital market opening.
The prevalent model for calculation of real equilibrium exchange rates takes
as given a current account target:

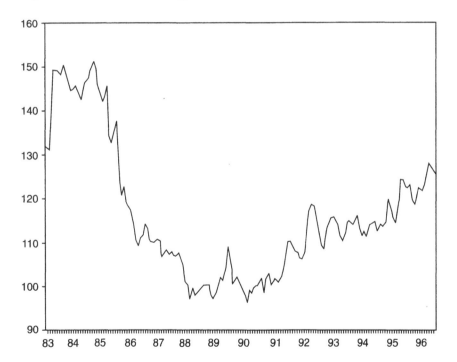

Figure 1.6 Chile's REER

$$x = f(R, Y, Y^* \ldots) \text{ or } R' = \lambda(x' \ldots) \tag{1.1}$$

where R is the real exchange rate, Y and Y^* are home and foreign output, x is the current account, and x' the target level. The dots represent other relevant policy variables. For given paths of output and policy variables that have a bearing on the current account, and for a given current account target, we arrive at the equilibrium real exchange rate, R'. The brief discussion makes clear two points: first, a current account target is needed to indicate what an equilibrium exchange rate is. Without a target, anything is possible – 5 per cent of GDP deficits or even 10 per cent. As the example of Mexico reminds us, what seems plausible one day – and is easily rationalized as the wonder of reform and modernization – the next day is called unsustainable.[11] Thus, the authorities must take a stance.

There are no hard and fast rules for allowable or sustainable deficits. The more a deficit reflects investment rather than consumption, the more plausible the case for allowing it to go forward. The more a deficit is financed by direct investment, the more plausible a larger number. But when everything is said and done, large deficits create vulnerability and that is why a target is appropriate.

The second point, which is just as important, is that the current account does not depend exclusively on the real exchange rate. Other policies need to be consistent to reflect the real exchange rate. Thus, we cannot have full employment, a large fiscal expansion and a small deficit without expecting high real interest rates and a major real appreciation. They might create the right size current account, but they are not sustainable because the real interest rate will attract an avalanche of capital and the real appreciation will destroy the traded goods sector. Since these outcomes are deeply inconsistent with medium-term stability, any target zone arrangement built around them is bound to be challenged. In that sense, BBC-style exchange rate arrangements – or any exchange rate arrangement for that purpose – are not a panacea for remedying bad policy.

Flexibility of the real rate

Over time, disturbances to the economy originating from policy or an evolving structure at home or abroad will necessitate a reassessment of the equilibrium real exchange rate. In other words, the underlying real exchange rate function $\lambda(x' \ldots)$ is not expected to be invariant. Thus, a trade opening, for example, will require a real depreciation in order to maintain the same current account imbalance. The same is true for a terms of trade deterioration or an investment boom. Also, important changes in a key competitor country cannot fail to have a bearing on a country's equilibrium real exchange rate. The case of China's integration in the world economy comes to mind, as do major structural changes in the Japanese integration in the world economy.

Hence, there is a need for adaptation. The central parity (adjusted for PPP and productivity drift) cannot be expected to be a constant. Generally, the changes in the environment tend to evolve gradually, and that means the market is learning at the same time as the authorities. Accordingly, a gradualist approach to revising the equilibrium real exchange rate is appropriate. This will not always be satisfactory. Some events might occur which very permanently change the equilibrium, literally from one day to the next. These events will be sufficiently dramatic to understand that the equilibrium real rate has changed and that an appropriate revision should be implemented.

The Chilean example shows that the BBC scheme is sufficiently flexible to accommodate changing real exchange rates. When the authorities are basically on the right lines, commonsense gradualism and some experimentation are totally acceptable. There is no presumption of a collapse from making a change too slow or too small because the presumption remains that the authorities watch the outcomes and have in mind a relatively elastic system. Moreover, there is no attempt to enforce an exact, by the month, external balance target. This is altogether different from systems that rely on the incantation of unbreakable rules cast in stone and credibility gained the hard way and for ever to be preserved. It is the latter kind of system that tends to crash in the midst of unsustainable ambitions and massive onslaughts of capital with a one-way bet.

Capital controls?

One cannot mention the Chilean example without returning to the issue of unimpeded capital mobility. In a situation of important structural change – say OECD membership for South Korea and unification prospects – capital flows may be overwhelming. How to react, how to keep the external deficit moderate? In Chile's case, shifting regulatory impediments to the free flow of capital have been found helpful. The underlying rationale is that the market also has to learn and that the long-run fundamental values of real exchange rates and external balances are likely to be far more stable than market-determined ones in a game of fashion. It is not at all easy to accept restrictions on capital flows, but it is equally hard to accept that market-assisted outcomes such as Mexico's rise and fall are to be accepted with the authorities standing by and taking for granted that everything is all right.

During times of surges in inflows, any government of a country facing potentially dangerous speculative attacks should, as the IMF (1995) suggests, consider implementing some of the following measures to influence the volume and characteristics of capital inflows such as reserve requirements against foreign borrowing, prudential limits on banks' offshore borrowing, and limits on consumption loans.

A practical, though imperfect answer, may be a tax applied to all cross-border transactions, a variant of a Tobin tax. As everybody knows, such a system is imperfect, but the Mexican experience was also flawed. As to which is the worse of the two evils, there is no question.[12]

The BBC proposal, assisted by a mechanism to stabilize capital flows such as a Tobin tax, is at the very least an effective learning mechanism and operating setting as economies are increasingly integrated in the world goods and capital market. That is a period of learning, and it helps for everybody to understand that they are unlikely to gain a lot by taking very contrary positions. As the system matures and economies settle down to lower inflation and more macroeconomic stability, it may become increasingly possible to give up the BBC mechanism.

Capital controls are always reprehensible since they involve clumsy bureaucratic interference with market forces and often go hand in hand with corruption. There is a need to use market forces to the greatest possible extent, but to supplement them with a clean-cut disincentive mechanism when capital flows create more excitement than the economy can plausibly digest. Speed limits are appropriate, not blanket bans.

Transition to an independently free-floating system

A number of East Asian countries may have to adopt a flexible exchange rate system earlier than expected as these economies' integration with each other and into Europe and North America could progress at a faster pace than in the past. Could these economies then structure and manage their BBC systems in a way that will facilitate such a transition?

It should be emphasized here that the BBC system is consistent with an independently free-floating system as it is a learning and adjustment process and hence an intermediate stage on the way to a more flexible system. As we noted, so far no country in the world, present or past, has actually practised a come-whatever free float!

One crucial element for the success of the BBC system is that it should be transparent and managed in a manner that will persuade market participants to accept it and to learn to expect changes in the equilibrium real exchange rate with changes in macroeconomic variables. If the market builds up its confidence in the BBC, speculation in the foreign exchange market will then become stabilizing.

A second element for success will hinge on the flexibility of the system in adjusting its central parity rate whenever the need for change arises. In many countries, the central bank preoccupied with price stability and the government more concerned with growth and employment could clash on the direction and extent of changes to the central rate. The lack of policy coordination between the central bank and the government could be damaging as Williamson (1996) points out and therefore should be avoided as much as possible.

Over time, as the misalignment between the central parity and the equilibrium real exchange rate and the volatility of the central rate are substantially reduced, the band width could gradually be expanded. And if the nominal and real exchange rates remain stable with this increase in the band width, and if stability of the financial system and lower rates of inflation are sustainable, setting and adjusting the central parity rate may no longer be necessary.

6 Conclusion: nominal anchor or flexibility?

We return here to where we started: should an exchange rate system be, above all, a nominal anchor or should it have substantial flexibility to accommodate a changing nominal exchange rate with a wide range of evolving influences on the equilibrium real exchange rate? Our answer is quite unambiguous: there is no overriding interest – in the East Asian context – in a nominal anchor strategy. That kind of consideration is suitable for economies which have a dramatic inflation problem – because they lack the institutions and record of moderate inflation.

The emphasis on nominal anchors is the legacy of inflation fighting in the major industrialized countries in the 1980s and the need to establish a modicum of stability in Latin America. It has relatively little relevance for East Asia today. The IMF in 1991 expressed the nominal anchor philosophy as follows:

> when the authorities are genuinely determined to establish financial discipline and price stability, but lack credibility because of their past record, a commitment to fix the nominal exchange rate for an extended period would help provide a strong anchor for price stability.
> (Aghevli et al., 1991: 21)

When inflation is not the number one problem – and it very rarely is or should be – then an exchange rate is a key tool in adjusting relative prices to their changing equilibrium levels. That is the old message of Milton Friedman's 'Case for Flexible Exchange Rates'. It is as important today as it ever was.

Asia's economies are in rapid growth with dramatically changing environments for trade in goods and services. A high degree of flexibility is desirable. The BBC approach offers that without throwing the baby out with the bath water. It allows virtually full flexibility of the real exchange rate over an extended period. In the short run, though, it focuses on the current account and takes for granted that massive shifts rarely have a sound underlying economic reason. By denying the existence of massive current account shocks – with exchange rate policy and supporting monetary and, in particular, fiscal policy – it reins in the economy. Above all, it avoids speculative bubbles that take a whole economy on a joy ride only to crash when it runs out of gas.

The BBC proposal is not a panacea, and it does not mean the end of all discussion about exchange rate policy. On the contrary, it is merely a formal method for evaluating which way the real rate should move, given a variety of news on the economy and on policy. By forcing a current account target to be set, it helps limit the risk of crashes. Capital flows have become dominant in the foreign exchange market, and they have become more short run-oriented; the BBC approach is a relatively flexible response to this basic change in countries' operating environments in the world economy.

APPENDIX: EXCHANGE RATE REGIMES OF EAST ASIAN COUNTRIES

1   Thailand: multiple currency basket peg system

Since November 1984, the baht has been linked to a multiple-currency basket. Previously, it had been pegged to the US dollar. The shift in exchange rate regime partly reflected the appreciation of the US dollar in the mid-1980s. Even though the composition of the basket is not disclosed to the public, higher weights are likely to be given to the currencies of Thailand's major trading partners – the United States, Japan and Germany. The weights are known to be adjusted according to developments in the foreign exchange markets. According to *Euromoney* (1995), the weights are 80–85 per cent for the US dollar, 8–15 per cent for the yen, and 4–10 per cent for the Deutsche Mark.

Each business day at 8 a.m., the Thai Exchange Equalization Fund (EEF) announces a basic exchange rate for the baht against the US dollar. The EEF will trade varying amounts of the dollar with the commercial banks within a 0.02 baht band around this rate until noon of each trading day. In the afternoon, the dollar is traded only in the interbank foreign exchange market, where the rate for the baht is largely dependent on expectations of the next day's basic rate.

In setting the basic rate each day, the EEF takes into account the current state and future prospects for exports, imports and domestic inflation, along with developments in the major currencies in the international foreign exchange markets. Most observers, however, conjecture that the current account balance plays a major role in deciding the basic rate. This is reflected in the fact that the nominal rate has been extremely stable since the late 1980s. In fact, during the period of 1990–4, the baht appreciated against the US dollar by only 0.3 per cent annually, despite the fact that the overall account had shown a large surplus – attributable to a substantial inflow of foreign capital which more than offset a large current account deficit.

2   Indonesia: managed floating system

The rupiah has been pegged to a basket of the currencies of Indonesia's major trading partners since 1978. (Before then, the rupiah had been pegged to the US dollar.) Each business day at 3 p.m., Bank Indonesia announces a selling and a buying rate for the rupiah against the US dollar. The rates are applied to commercial banks' same-day settlement and swap transactions and export draft rediscounting with the central bank. In 1994, the band was widened from 20 to 30 rupiahs. The market rate of the rupiah against the US dollar is determined in the interbank foreign exchange market, with its level reflecting expected changes in central bank rates. It normally fluctuates within the central bank's band set during the previous day.

The main factor which Bank Indonesia considers in setting its official rate has been the inflation differential between Indonesia and its major trading partners (*Bank Indonesia Annual Report* (1992/93) and *Euromoney* (1995)). Given that inflation has been persistently high in Indonesia relative to the industrial economies, the nominal exchange rate of the rupiah has persistently depreciated even when the overall balance was recording a surplus due to the large inflow of foreign capital. The nominal exchange rate of the rupiah showed a steady depreciation of about 4 per cent annually against the US dollar during 1990–4, while the CPI differential between Indonesia and the United States was 4.8 percentage points. The rupiah also depreciated sharply against the Japanese yen during the same period. The real effective exchange rate of the rupiah was therefore fairly stable.

3   Hong Kong: linked exchange rate system[13]

In 1982 and 1983 the Hong Kong financial sector confronted a severe test. Following then Prime Minister Margaret Thatcher's visit to Beijing in September 1982, a confidence crisis arose due to political uncertainty over the territory's future after 1997. The lack of confidence first triggered a collapse in the real estate market. Many real estate companies suffered severe liquidity problems; some were forced to close. The disaster promptly spread into the financial sector because more than 40 per cent of public companies listed on the stock market were heavily involved in real estate. The stock index fell from 1035.33 in August 1982 to 690 on 4 October 1983. At the same time, banks and deposit taking companies (DTCs) which had lent heavily to the real estate sector suffered great losses as many loans had to be written off. This naturally led other financial institutions to begin tightening credit lines to those banks and DTCs. In turn, this worsened the liquidity problems of some financial institutions. Tremendous concerns thus arose, not only about the political future, but also about the stability of the financial system. A rush ensued as crowds of people sought to withdraw money and convert it into foreign currencies. Some banks suffered runs on their deposits, and several DTCs became bankrupt. Many financial institutions which had previously been active in foreign exchange dealings were forced to withdraw from the market altogether.

Political uncertainty induced significant capital outflows. Pessimistic sentiment prevailed in both the foreign exchange (FX) market and the economy.

The currency depreciated from 6.10 against the US dollar at the end of August 1982 (before Mrs Thatcher's visit) to 7.595 on 31 August 1983, nearly 25 per cent in just twelve months. In an effort to halt and reverse the slide of the Hong Kong dollar, the government announced two measures on 15 October 1983. The first called for a revised arrangement for issuing notes, fixing the rate at HK$7.8 per US$1.0. That brought into existence what we call the linked exchange rate system. The second measure was the removal of a 10 per cent interest withholding tax on Hong Kong dollar deposits. Both of these measures were intended to restore confidence in, and the attractiveness of, the local currency, and they indeed seem to have been effective towards those ends. Under the new arrangement, the forces of competition and arbitrage have ensured that the market exchange rate fluctuates narrowly around the level of HK$7.8 most of the time.

The new arrangement centres on Certificates of Indebtedness (CIs), which are issued by the Exchange Fund to the two note-issuing banks (Bank of Hong Kong and Standard Chartered Bank), to be held as cover for the issue of Hong Kong dollar notes. Prior to 17 October 1983, the CIs were issued and redeemed against payments in Hong Kong dollars. Under the new arrangement, such payments are made in US dollars, at a fixed exchange rate of US$1 = HK$7.80. The Exchange Fund promises to issue and redeem the CIs at 7.80, and the note-issuing banks agree that they should provide notes to, and accept notes from, other banks on the same basis as in their dealings with the Exchange Fund (that is, against payments in US dollars at the rate of US$1 = HK$7.80). In other words, an interbank market for Hong Kong dollar notes at a fixed exchange rate was created. It can be seen that under the new arrangement, any rise in note circulation has to be matched by a US dollar payment to the Exchange Fund, and any fall in circulation is matched by a similar payment from the Fund.

It should be stressed that in the FX market, the exchange rate of the Hong Kong dollar is still allowed to float freely, so it theoretically should be determined by market supply and demand. The forces of competition and arbitrage between markets will ensure that the FX market exchange rate stabilizes at a level close to the fixed rate of 7.80 without intervention by the Exchange Fund in the market.

Of course, this process will hold only if the market obeys the laws of economics. Political factors might overshadow the normal workings of supply and demand. If people continue to be worried about the future and withdraw money from Hong Kong, it is inevitable that the government will have to spend heavily from its foreign exchange fund to buy up Hong Kong dollars in the market in an effort to defend the HK$7.80 rate.

The new scheme of linking the Hong Kong dollar to the US dollar transfers the impact of any adjustment to balance of payments pressures away from the exchange rate and onto the banking system, and more specifically onto the liquid reserve base of the banks and onto the level of Hong Kong dollar interest rates. In effect, the exchange rate is no longer an important variable in the economy's adjustment process. Factors such as interest rates, money supply and the level of economic activity, rather than the exchange rate, now adjust automatically to balance of payments pressure, without government intervention being necessary.

Further, the role of interest rates as an instrument of monetary policy has changed fundamentally. Interest rates now assume a more passive role, changing, more frequently perhaps, in response to balance of payments inflows and outflows. Under the new exchange regime it is neither so necessary nor so desirable for the government to influence interest rates through the Hong Kong Association of Banks or by direct intervention in the money market.

Under the linked rate system, as the market exchange rate of the Hong Kong dollar has been stabilized at the level of 7.80 against the US dollar – the major currency in international trade – external trade is facilitated. The adverse impact of exchange fluctuation on domestic prices, output, employment and so on can also be minimized.

The exchange rate of the Hong Kong dollar under this system is stable. However, without adjustment in the exchange rate as a protection, the economy is now more vulnerable to exogenous factors. The link with the US dollar is equivalent to a US dollar exchange standard, and the Hong Kong economy has in effect become dependent on the US economy. The international value of the Hong Kong dollar is now entirely dependent on the performance of the US dollar and the US economy rather than on its own.

4   Singapore: managed floating system[14]

The Singapore dollar (S$) is regulated under a managed floating system. It was linked to the Malaysian ringgit in the 1960s but currently trades against a basket of currencies which appears to be weighted towards the currencies of Singapore's major trade partners, especially the USA, Japan and Malaysia.

The Monetary Authority of Singapore (MAS) manages the trade-weighted value of the Singapore dollar with the primary objective of maintaining low and stable domestic inflation. However, the MAS is also watchful of the impact of the exchange rate on the country's export competitiveness. This targeting renders interest rate policy subordinate to exchange rate policy.

The MAS discourages destabilizing swings in both the exchange and interest rates and firmly discourages speculative activities and the internationalization of the Singapore dollar. Swaps cannot be undertaken in amounts greater than S$5 million. Loans in excess of S$5 million to non-residents or for use outside Singapore require authorization.

Following its 9 per cent appreciation against the US dollar in 1994, the Singapore dollar made further gains of 3 per cent in 1995. The currency draws much of its strength from its 'safe haven' status, having provided a shelter for capital inflows in times of currency turbulence, such as that surrounding the Mexican peso crisis in early 1995 or in March 1996 when tensions were running high in the Taiwan Straits. Many other factors also contribute to the strength and stability of the Singapore dollar, such as Singapore's political stability, developed infrastructure and sound economic fundamentals.

Singapore is increasingly challenged by rising costs and diminishing productivity gains, two developments which are in sharp contrast to previous years. Against such a backdrop, maintaining export competitiveness is assuming ever-growing importance. The MAS has capped gains by the Singapore dollar in recent months with this goal in view, as reflected in the rising foreign exchange reserves. It is likely that this trend will continue and that foreign reserves will top $80 billion by the end of 1996 compared with $68.7 billion at the end of 1995.

Soft domestic demand and a strong Singapore dollar contributed to the 1.7 per cent inflation rate in 1995, the lowest in seven years. Inflation is expected to remain benign this year by international standards, remaining under the 2 per cent level.

The economy's growth engine should slow further later in 1996, with GDP growth projected to fall to 8.5 per cent in 1996 from 8.9 per cent recorded in 1995. In view of the impressive economic growth but soft inflation data, the MAS will pursue a cautious 'strong currency' policy to counteract inflation.

5   Malaysia: managed floating system

Since 1975, the ringgit has been pegged to a basket of currencies of Malaysia's major trading partners – principally the United States, Japan, Singapore, Germany, Great Britain, and the Netherlands. Bank Negara Malaysia, the central bank, has intervened frequently in the interbank foreign exchange market to maintain the ringgit–dollar exchange rate within a target range. It has been widely believed that the bank's target rate has been determined by the movement of an undisclosed multiple-currency basket.

Bank Negara manages the ringgit to support the nation's export competitiveness and maintain monetary stability. Occasionally, it administers exchange controls on behalf of the Malaysian government.

A number of factors put tremendous pressure on the ringgit in 1995. The spillover from the Mexican peso crisis had an especially great impact as Malaysia, too, had a large and growing current account deficit. In time, however, Malaysia was able to shed all apparent indications of being another Mexico, and its burgeoning trade deficit came to be seen only as symptomatic of an overheating economy. The trade deficit drastically deteriorated from 1994's US$0.8 billion to US$3.7 billion in 1995. Coupled with the deficit in trade in services, the current account shortfall spiralled to a tremendous US$7.1 billion in 1995 (8.8 per cent of GNP). The ringgit nevertheless managed to hold up quite well to close the year at M$2.54–US$1, which represented an actual gain of 0.8 per cent in 1995. This was nevertheless much slower than the 1994 gain of more than 5 per cent.

Bank Negara has attempted to cool the economy since the fourth quarter of 1995 through a two-pronged approach. This has entailed selective credit controls (largely targeted at cars and speculative property investment) and a policy of higher interest rates.

Despite the general decline in global interest rates, the benchmark three-month interbank rate has moved up by some 100 basis points since October 1995, to its current level of 7.15 per cent. Also, to raise the cost of funds, the statutory reserve requirement (SRR) was hiked one percentage point to 12.5 per cent. However, this and the other measures have yet to rein in the buoyant economy. Real GDP growth of 8.5 per cent is expected in 1996, and although slower than 1995's 9.5 per cent expansion, this is a blistering pace by any standard.

Higher yields, attracting foreign fund inflows, are among the factors behind the ringgit's remarkable surge in April and May 1996. It strengthened sharply to trade at a nine-month high of M$2.4795–US$1 on 9 May 1996.

6 Taiwan: managed floating system

Market forces have been permitted to dictate the movements of the new Taiwanese dollar since 1987. The exchange rate is market-determined, but the Central Bank of China (CBC) regularly intervenes in the foreign exchange market to smooth out the day-to-day excess fluctuations.

Despite the authority's recent efforts to liberalize Taiwan's financial markets, a tight grip is still maintained on foreign exchange transactions. Offshore entities, for example, need to have the CBC's approval for both inward and outward remittances, and non-residents are excluded from the foreign spot and forward markets. In terms of product availability, the markets for currency and interest rate swaps/options are only in their nascent stages.

The New Taiwan dollar has appreciated significantly (about 30 per cent) against the US dollar since the mid-1980s, in line with the country's strong current account performance and rising international reserves. As a major exporting economy in the region, sustained trade surpluses (averaging more than $10 billion per year) have contributed significantly to Taiwan's foreign exchange reserves, which peaked in June 1995 at $100.4 billion.

The gradual appreciation of the currency stopped in mid-1995 following the heightened tensions between mainland China and Taiwan. Tensions in the Taiwan Straits reached a climax just before Taiwan's first presidential election on 23 March 1996, causing the currency to fall to a low of NT$27.50–US$1 in early March.

In an effort to minimize volatility in the depreciation of the currency, the central bank intervened heavily in the foreign exchange market throughout the turbulent period. This necessarily meant a significant depletion of the island's foreign exchange reserves. After peaking at a record high of US$100.4 billion in June 1995, reserves fell steadily to US$82.5 billion by the end of March 1996.

7 China: managed floating system

China's currency is the renminbi, which since its introduction in 1949 has been non-convertible. Before the 1970s, the renminbi's exchange rate was dictated by the Chinese government with little reference to market conditions.

In 1986, foreign trade corporations in China were allowed to buy back a certain amount of their foreign exchange earnings based on a retention quota. This spurred the establishment of foreign exchange adjustment centres (FEACs) where enterprises traded (or adjusted) their retention quotas. At the same time, China introduced a dual exchange rate system: an official exchange rate was fixed by the government and ran parallel to another market rate, determined by the FEACs.

Early in 1994, the foreign exchange retention and quota system was abandoned and the dual exchange rates were unified. With the subsequent opening of a national interbank foreign exchange trading centre in Shanghai (the China Foreign Exchange Trading System), the renminbi's exchange rate has since been determined by market supply and demand conditions. The central bank, the People's Bank of China (PBoC), however, has kept a close watch on the unitary managed floating rate to smooth out fluctuation. The PBoC uses discretion over policies on foreign exchange while the State Administration of Exchange Control, under the PBoC's supervision, implements those policies and regulations.

China has pledged that the renminbi will be convertible for current account transactions by the year 2000, or even earlier. Implementation of current account convertibility without effective macro control policies is likely to result in chronic current account problems and a sharp fall in the renminbi, which would thwart the pace of China's economic reform. At present, the only safeguard China has is its huge foreign exchange reserve of US$80.8 billion (in March 1996). To remedy these shortfalls, China has created indirect and market-based policy instruments, which are very different in nature from the previous administrative measures. A national renminbi interbank market was established in early 1996 by electronically linking thirty-five cities.

Since unification of the dual rates in early 1994, the renminbi has maintained a firm tone. While domestic inflation eroded the internal value of the unit substantially, the unit remained on a steady upward trend in 1994 and 1995 due to remarkable export performance and inflow of direct investment. This has led to a substantial currency appreciation in real terms. The trend also highlighted the dilemma faced by the PBoC in containing the expansion of the monetary base and keeping a lid on the currency's appreciation. However, the rising trend of the renminbi was reversed in late 1995 and early 1996 due mainly to the changing trade and investment environment in China.

In July 1995 and January 1996, the rate on export VAT rebates was reduced and import tariffs were slashed from April 1996. The hampering effect that this had on external trade was quickly reflected in the currency's external value. The gradual liberalization of the economy has attracted continued foreign capital inflows. As the government attempts to enter the OECD in 1996, more gradual economic deregulation will be planned. This will induce even greater flows of foreign capital, thereby increasing the upward pressure.

8 South Korea: managed floating system

South Korea's exchange rate system is a variant of the managed floating system which is known as the market average rate system (MARS) and in which the exchange rate of the won vis-à-vis the US dollar is primarily determined in an interbank foreign exchange market. At present, participants of the market comprise 110 banking institutions including the Bank of Korea; they are twenty-five domestic commercial banks, five specialized banks, three development banks, twenty-seven merchant banks, and forty-nine branches of foreign banks.

The market average rate, which is used as a daily basic rate for interbank transactions of the US dollar, is a weighted average of the market exchange rates related to all transactions of the previous day with the weight being the volume of each transaction. Each business day the interbank market rate of the won against the US dollar is allowed to fluctuate within a specified band of the basic rate which is revised daily.

When the MARS was first introduced, the market exchange rate was allowed to vary within ± 0.4 per cent of the basic rate. Since then, the band has been gradually widened. At present the band is ± 2.25 per cent of the basic rate. The South Korean government plans to widen further the band and to remove it entirely in the near future.

It should be noted that there are no commercial foreign exchange brokerage firms in South Korea. As a result, most of the interbank transactions are intermediated by a public brokerage house, the Fund Trading Center at Korea Financial Telecommunication and Clearing. The public foreign exchange brokerage system may help the Bank of Korea to monitor developments closely in the foreign exchange market and to maintain stability of the market through effective supervision. However, the supervision of the market is likely to create distortions because banks as market makers may be discouraged from active price quotations, and the Fund Trading Center, as a public institution, has little incentive to develop new products or in general to serve the market. Furthermore, the total volume of direct interbank foreign exchange transactions is trivial compared to the volume cleared through the

Fund Trading Center. Even in the case of direct interbank foreign exchange transactions, detailed information on each transaction must be reported to the Fund Trading Center after it is completed.

The exchange rates of the Korean won against currencies other than the US dollar are determined by the cross-rate. Assuming an arbitrage relation, they are calculated by multiplying the won/dollar exchange rate by the exchange rates of other currencies vis-à-vis the US dollar determined in the international foreign exchange market. The exchange rates quoted in the Tokyo foreign exchange market in the morning (8.00 a.m. of each business day) are used to calculate the official exchange rates of the won against the Japanese yen, British pound, German Mark, Swiss franc and Australian dollar. They are announced in the morning of each business day along with the basic won/dollar exchange rate.

The net foreign exchange position of market participants is subject to limits. For example, a spot over-sold position of each bank at the end of each business day should not exceed 2 per cent of its capital or $3 million, whichever is larger. Also, an overall over-sold position at the end of each business day is permitted up to $20 million or 30 per cent of its daily average of the amount of foreign exchange purchase in the previous month. An overall over-bought position is allowed up to $20 million or two times its daily average foreign exchange purchase in the previous month, whichever is larger. The position restriction is imposed in order to maintain stability of the foreign exchange market and to prevent excessive speculative foreign exchange trading.

The Bank of Korea often intervenes in the interbank market through the sale or purchase of the US dollar. It is conjectured that the main purpose of the intervention in the foreign exchange market is to stabilize the real effective exchange rate of the won in order to maintain the price competitiveness of South Korean exports. The central bank intervention has been effective due to the thinness of the domestic foreign exchange market, where the average volume of daily turnover in 1995 was only $2 billion.

Notes

1 Reference to Asia throughout means the relatively advanced East Asian economies, excluding in particular India, Pakistan and Bangladesh.
2 The seminal reference is Williamson (1996) which usefully illustrates the ideas not only conceptually but also with the policy experience of Israel, Colombia and Chile, as well as with commentary on a vast range of countries.
3 How can we be sure? We can't; that is the charm of the policy.
4 Unfortunately, JPMorgan does not provide, as yet, a real exchange rate measure for China. In the Appendix, we report a series calculated by the authors.
5 For those empirical studies examining the relations between trade flows and relative prices, see Rittenberg (1986), Faini *et al.* (1992), Muscatelli *et al.* (1994), Muscatelli *et al.* (1992) and Riedel (1988).

6 See Quirk (1994b) and the references given there for an evaluation of transition to convertibility. Even in the aftermath of the Mexican crash, the IMF remains firmly wedded to convertibility, full and immediate, as the right strategy.

7 See Caprio *et al.* (1994), Lingren *et al.* (1996) and Sundarajan and Balino (1991), as well as Goldstein and Turner (1996).

8 On long-run real equilibrium exchange rates see Williamson (1994), Faruquee (1995) and Macdonald (1995).

9 See Quirk (1994a and 1994b) for a survey.

10 For further discussion see Williamson (1996) and Dornbusch and Edwards (1994).

11 It would be interesting to explore the fate of all large deficits. We know from the work of Goldfajn and Valdes that large real appreciations have little chance of going away without a crash. One surmises that the same fate befalls their mirror image, large deficits. As the bankers say, it is not speed that kills, it is the sudden halt.

12 There are inherent dangers in imposing these control features unilaterally as they necessarily interfere with further global financial liberalization. There are also no workable international financial mechanisms in place which could help prevent a financial crisis in any one particular country from spilling over into other countries. Therefore, rather than the problem being left to individual countries, serious consideration should be given to supporting multilateral efforts to control speculative short-term capital movements by establishing a supranational monetary authority that could provide a safety net to those countries vulnerable to speculative attacks.

13 This section is based on Y.H. Lui (1991) 'The Foreign Exchange Market', in Richard Y. Ho, Robert H. Scott and Kie A. Hong (eds), *The Hong Financial System*, Hong Kong: Oxford University Press.

14 For Singapore, Taiwan, China and Malaysia, the details of their exchange rate regimes are excerpted from *The 1996 Guide to Emerging Market Currencies*, Euromoney, June 1966.

References

Aghevli, B., Khan, M. and Montiel, P.J. (1991) *Exchange Rate Policy in Developing Countries: Some Analytical Issues*, Occasional Paper No. 78, Washington, DC: IMF.

Caprio, G., Atiyas, I. and Hansop, J. (eds) (1994) *Financial Reform*, Cambridge: Cambridge University Press.

Dornbusch, Rüdiger and Edwards, S. (1994) 'Exchange Rate Policy and Trade Strategy', in Bosworth, B. *et al.* (eds) *The Chilean Economy*, Washington, DC: Brookings.

Faini, R., Clavijo, F. and Senhadji-Semlali, A. (1992) 'The Fallacy of the Composition Argument: Is It Relevant for LDCs' Manufactured Exports?', *European Economic Review*, Vol. 36.

Faruqee, H. (1995) 'Long Run Determinants of the Real Exchange Rate', *IMF Staff Papers*, March.

Funke, N. (1996) 'Vulnerability of Fixed Exchange Rate Regimes: The Role of Economic Fundamentals', *OECD Economic Studies*, No. 26, I.

Goldstein, M. and Turner, P. (1996) *Banking Crises in Emerging Countries: Origin and Policy Options*, Basle: Bank of International Settlements.

International Monetary Fund (1995a) *International Capital Markets*, Washington, DC: IMF.

—— (1995b) *World Economic Outlook*, Washington, DC: IMF.

Lingren, C., Garcia, G. and Sael, M. (eds) (1996) *Bank Soundness and Macroeconomic Policy*, Washington, DC: IMF.

Macdonald, R. (1995) 'Long Run Exchange Rate Modelling', *IMF Staff Papers*, September.

Muscatelli, V.A., Stevenson, A.A. and Montagna, C. (1994) 'Intra-NIE Competition in Exports of Manufactures', *Journal of International Economics*, Vol. 37.

Muscatelli, V.A., Srinivasan, T.G. and Vines, D. (1992) 'Demand and Supply Factors in the Determination of NIE Exports: A Simultaneous Error-correction Model for Hong Kong', *Economic Journal*, Vol. 102.

Obstfeld, M. and Rogoff, K. (1995) 'The Mirage of Fixed Exchange Rates', *Journal of Economic Perspectives*, Fall.

Quirk, P. (1994a) 'Recent Experience With Floating Exchange Rates in Developing Countries', in Barth, Richard and Wong, Chorng-Huey (eds) *Approaches to Exchange Rate Policy Choices for Developing and Transition Economies*, Washington, DC: IMF.

—— (1994b) 'Adopting Currency Convertibility: Experiences and Monetary Policy Considerations for Advanced Developing Countries', unpublished manuscript, IMF.

Reinhardt, Carmen (1994) *Devaluation, Relative Prices and International Trade: Evidence from Developing Countries*, IMF Working Paper WP/94/140/ Washington, DC.

Riedel, James (1988) 'The Demand for LDC Exports of Manufactures: Estimates from Hong Kong', *Economic Journal*, Vol. 98.

Rittenberg, L. (1986) 'Export Growth Performance of Less Developed Countries', *Journal of Development Economics*, Vol. 24.

Sundarajan, V. and Balino, T. (eds) (1991) *Banking Crises: Cases and Issues*, Washington, DC: IMF.

Williamson, J. (ed.) (1994) *Estimating Equilibrium Exchange Rates*, Washington, DC: Institute for International Economics.

—— (1996) *The Crawling Band as an Exchange Rate Regime*, Washington, DC: Institute for International Economics.

2

DISCUSSION

André Icard

For those of us who have had the privilege of reading work by Professor Dornbusch in the past, Chapter 1 comes as no surprise: it is fast-paced and
thought-provoking, it deals with important questions facing central banks
in Asia and elsewhere, and it alternates between careful analysis and poking
fun at policy makers.

In my comments, I would like briefly to go over Chapter 1 and bring out
the main message, and, in doing so, point to some questions that arose in my
mind as I read it. As I broadly share the main conclusions expressed, I will
concentrate on questions that I think deserve more attention than they were
given.

The authors start by listing on page 3 a number of issues that are of
importance to policy makers in the region. To mention but a few:

- How should Asian NIEs respond to US dollar–yen fluctuations?
- Should the Asian NIEs use exchange rate policy to shield their export sectors from fluctuations in world industrial production?
- What will the gradual liberalization of capital flows in the region imply
  for the choice of an appropriate exchange rate regime?

But the authors do not return to most of these interesting questions in the
rest of the chapter. We shall see later that answering these questions would
have clarified the final proposal.

1   The setting

In Section I of Chapter 1 the authors provide a brief overview of economic
conditions in the Asian NIEs, focusing on some of the considerations that
are of importance in selecting an exchange rate regime.

Here I found little to disagree with, but I had one small regret. While
there is a clear discussion of the importance of trade flows etc. for the choice
of exchange rate system, there was little mention of the growth and deepening of financial markets which these countries have experienced. Apart from

35

Japan, the region already contains two major international financial centres – Hong Kong and Singapore – and more are coming as liberalization of the financial sectors proceeds. We know from other parts of the world that the free flow of capital can have a large impact on the appropriate choice of exchange rate regime, and I think that some discussion of this issue would have been desirable.

2　Convertibility

In Section 2, the authors turn to a discussion of the convertibility issue. Their main argument here is that the Asian economies should be opened up to international capital flows, essentially as fast as possible. Here again, without disagreeing, I have some questions.

We know from the experiences of a number of OECD countries in Europe and elsewhere, which deregulated the financial sector in the 1980s, that rapid changes in the regulatory environment can lead to asset price booms and crashes, which can have very large real costs.

The reason these problems arise is clear: once the financial system is opened up, the past is no guide to the future. Credit expansion and thus credit risks rise dramatically, large positions may be taken in sophisticated financial instruments of which traders and managers alike have little experience, and so on. It becomes difficult for regulators and supervisors, monetary policy makers and managers of financial institutions to judge whether developments are too quick, and whether risks are accumulating excessively. In short, risk control at the macro and micro levels is difficult during and immediately after the deregulation.

I would like to emphasize that I am not arguing that deregulation should be delayed, only that determining the speed at which it should take place is difficult, and that the answer is likely to depend on the exact institutional arrangements in the country in question. Thus, different central banks are likely to have different answers. The answer in the chapter – 'the faster the better' – sounds a little too sweeping. It may be right, but further analysis seems warranted before we can conclude that this is the case in all Asian countries.

3　Fixed rates

Next, the authors turn to a discussion of the choice of exchange rate regime. However, they do not refer to the convertibility issue discussed in Section 2. This is surprising since it seems natural to ask how further financial deregulation will affect the choice of exchange rate regime. In particular, will the current managed float system adopted by many countries remain appropriate also in the case of highly integrated capital markets?

In Chapter 1, the authors argue that fixed rates are likely to be inappropriate, because:

- the rate of inflation is still somewhat too high in many of these countries;
- there is no single natural reference country, as, for instance, there is in Europe.

In particular, the authors argue that pegging to the yen would be inappropriate, for two main reasons:

- the exchange rate of the yen has experienced too large fluctuations for it to be a good anchor;
- trade with countries outside Asia is too extensive for a yen policy to be desirable, Japan not being an overwhelmingly dominant trading partner.

I found these arguments against pegging to the yen somewhat unconvincing for three reasons. First, trade in Asia and with Japan is undoubtedly very important for these countries. Second, while the yen has been subject to large movements in real effective terms over time, I am not sure that these movements have been markedly larger than those of the US dollar. Furthermore, one reason why they have been relatively large is that no currency is pegged against the yen. Third, one of the main difficulties in the Asian region is that since the dollar is being used as an anchor for several NIEs, the competitive positions between Japan and the other major Asian countries vary considerably in parallel with the US dollar/yen fluctuations. Unless we consider that the US dollar/yen parity should be closely monitored by the concerned central banks (an idea that I am not sure the authors will agree upon), I do not see any solution other than promoting the role of the yen in the Asian area, if not as a pegging reference at least as a significant element of the basket that the authors consider in Section 5.

4 and 5   Floating rates and band-basket-crawl

After a rapid review of flexible rates, which they consider as a possible arrangement, the authors turn to their proposal: that the countries in the region adopt a Williamson-style crawling band, which they call 'band-basket-crawl' (BBC). This proposal has three elements:

- First, the central exchange rate parity should be allowed to evolve gradually (or crawl) over time. This is important in the authors' opinion because the rate of inflation in the countries in question is still a bit too high to permit a fixed rate.
- Second, the parity should be expressed in terms of a basket and not a single foreign currency. The argument here is that there is no single currency (in particular not the yen) to which these countries can peg.
- Third, there should be a broad band around the parity in which the market-determined exchange rate may move. The authors give several reasons

why bands are desirable. They argue that the use of a band will provide the authorities with some flexibility to gear monetary policy to domestic economic conditions rather than solely to the exchange rate. Furthermore, they note that since the exchange rate is free to move within the band, observing the movements of the exchange rate provides the authorities with information about the strength of market forces, which can serve to guide policy. Finally, they are concerned that it may be difficult to determine the equilibrium real exchange rate precisely, so a broad band is desirable.

While agreeing with these arguments, I would like, at this stage, to express a reaction common among practitioners. I was somewhat surprised by the lack of detail in the authors' proposals. Indeed, there is little or no discussion of many questions that policy makers tend to attach considerable attention to, for instance:

- How should the rate of crawl be decided? (In economies undergoing rapid growth and structural change, price indices can diverge greatly, so that the success of a crawling peg regime will depend on selecting the 'right rate of crawl'.)
- Under what conditions should the rate of crawl be adjusted?
- Should the choice of parity and the exact form of the band be announced? (I note that central banks in the region typically do not announce the exact modalities of their exchange rate regimes.)
- Should the limits of the band be hard or soft?
- What criteria should be used to select the component currencies and their weights in the basket? This may be more difficult than is normally the case, in light of the fact that trade in the region is growing fast; that the countries compete directly in markets for manufactured goods in third countries; and that in some countries (especially China) complete convertibility on current account is still lacking. This, in fact, reopens the debate on the weight which should be given to the yen in the basket.

Behind these unanswered questions lie, in my view, two main ambiguities. First, the debate about rules versus discretion seems relevant, and could have been developed in the chapter. Second, the final proposal should be made clearer: are the authors aiming at a relatively binding system which only some selected countries will enter, that is a kind of 'Asian monetary system'? In this case, the membership, the conditions of access to the system and the technicalities would certainly have to be clarified. Or, alternatively, do the authors envisage a soft and open system to which a large number of Asian countries could have access and in which they will enjoy a large degree of liberty, especially for the conditions of adjustment of the rate of crawl, the length of the band, the nature of the limits, the choice of the basket?

If the second option is taken, it may not be globally advantageous. The merits of the system would have to be considered country by country, and there is no certainty that in all cases the BBC framework will be more desirable from a national point of view than the current foreign exchange regimes.

In conclusion, Chapter 1 implicitly views the Asian economies as identical, so that the same type of exchange rate regime could be appropriate for all. However, it is striking that, as indicated in Table 1.1, there are important differences in exchange rate regime between the different Asian countries. Thus, while Hong Kong fixes its exchange rate against the US dollar, others pursue different kinds of managed float. Furthermore, we know from the European experience that economies that appear to be quite similar sometimes opt for very different exchange rate regimes. For instance, Austria has pursued a DM peg since the early 1980s, while Switzerland has let the Swiss franc float since the early 1970s. Thus, I am less persuaded than the authors that the same framework is necessarily appropriate for all countries.

Accordingly, while I think that Chapter 1 raises some topics that require further debate, I would like to thank the authors for their very interesting and thought-provoking contribution.

3

EXCHANGE RATE REGIMES
AND POLICIES

An empirical analysis

Agnès Bénassy-Quéré

1 Introduction

The exchange rate policies of Asian countries have become a great concern in recent years. Specifically, Asian economies have been affected by dollar fluctuations.

However, the exchange rate regimes in Asian countries are not straightforward. Officially, only Hong Kong pegs its currency to the US dollar, whereas the exchange rate regimes of most countries are 'managed floats', i.e. flexible exchange rates with frequent, official interventions (Table 3.1). Thus, the official regimes are rather vague, and they include a wide range of *de facto* policies.

How is it possible to disentangle the *de facto* exchange rate regimes from the official regimes which are reported by the IMF? Two approaches may be taken. The first looks at official reserves as well as interest rate management, and tries to derive the preferences of the government. This approach was used by Popper and Lowell (1994) in the case of the United States, Canada, Australia and Japan. Studying official interventions assumes that they matter for

Table 3.1 Exchange rate regimes in 1996

Hong Kong	Peg to the US$ since October 1983	Indonesia	Managed float
South Korea	Managed float	Malaysia	Managed float
Singapore	Managed float	Philippines	Managed float
Taiwan	Managed float	Thailand	Peg to a basket
Bhutan	Peg to the Indian rupee	Pakistan	Managed float
China	Managed float	Sri Lanka	Managed float
India	Free float		

Sources: IMF, *Exchange Arrangements and Exchange Restrictions*, Washington, DC, 1995; Caisse des Dépôts et Consignations, *Zones Emergentes* 1, July 1996.

the evolution of exchange rates, but this assumption has been questioned.[1] The analysis of the interest rate management does not lead to clear-cut conclusions either, given the fragility of estimates for the reaction function of the monetary authorities.

The second approach looks at the results of the exchange rate policies, i.e. at the variations of exchange rates. This approach was initiated by Frankel and Wei (1992, 1993) and Frankel (1993) who found some evidence of an increasing influence of the yen in the nominal exchange rate policy of some Asian countries since the early 1980s.[2] Basically, this method looks at the results of exchange rate policies, instead of studying the instruments (official reserves, monetary policy). The main problem is that the stability of the exchange rate can be obtained without any will from the monetary authorities, if most shocks are common shocks. This problem can be avoided through comparing the results to the optimal basket pegs of Asian currencies.

The link between the short-run nominal volatility and the long-run real fluctuations depends on the drift of the nominal exchange rate compared to cumulated inflation differentials. Pegging a currency to an international anchor in nominal terms leads to a real appreciation if cumulated differentials are not compensated by nominal devaluations. But in pegging their nominal rate, monetary authorities hope that domestic inflation will converge with the foreign rate. Hence, nominal and real pegs should be consistent in the long run. In the short run, the two pegs are consistent if the nominal exchange rate is not devalued too frequently, or if it is devalued with great regularity. In brief, a real peg is related to some long-run stability in the real exchange rate, while a nominal peg is connected to some stability in the nominal exchange rate over short periods. Section 2 studies both types of pegs through measures of the volatility and econometric analysis, for eleven Asian currencies over the 1974–95 period.[3] Section 3 studies the rationale for exchange rate regimes in Asia. A simple optimization model is proposed to rationalize the choice of a foreign anchor. A quick look at some statistics on trade and capital flows in Asia provides some orders of magnitude which are introduced as parameters in the model. Concluding remarks are given in Section 4.

2   *De facto* exchange rate regimes in Asia

Suppose the monetary authorities of an inflationary country follow an implicit foreign peg in real as well as in nominal terms. The short-run evolution of the real exchange rate depends on the type of nominal peg. In the case of a constant nominal peg, the real exchange rate appreciates progressively, and then it is suddenly devalued. In the case of a crawling peg, the real exchange rate stays constant or appreciates slightly in the short run. In all cases, the real peg is characterized by the stability of the real exchange rate in the long run, while the nominal peg is defined either by a stability in the level of the nominal exchange rate or by a regularity of its variations in the short run. Hence, the methodology must differ when dealing with nominal pegs and with real pegs.

2.1 Nominal pegs

Nominal exchange rate policies can be examined first by comparing the volatility of monthly, nominal exchange rate variations against the US dollar and against the yen (Table 3.2).[4] The volatility in the value of Asian currencies is always smaller against the US dollar than it is against the yen. The implicit link to the dollar was reinforced in recent years in South Korea, Indonesia and Thailand, while it became looser for Bhutan, China and India.[5]

Table 3.2 The relative volatility of monthly variations of nominal exchange rates against the US dollar (as a % of their volatility against the yen)

	January 1974 – October 1978	November 1978 – February 1985	March 1985 – April 1990	May 1990 – May 1995
South Korea	73.1	49.3	27.0	21.1
Singapore	68.9	60.0	37.6	41.4
Indonesia	0.0	91.3	78.4	8.9
Malaysia	79.5	57.4	33.2	42.3
Philippines	39.3	73.9	28.2	51.7
Thailand	5.3	53.8	26.1	18.8
Bhutan	71.9	48.2	44.4	74.2
China	92.2	74.5	60.3	94.4
India	71.9	48.2	44.4	74.2
Pakistan	0.0	43.2	30.1	35.2
Sri Lanka	91.7	40.7	39.2	55.5

Source: Author's calculations based on IMF data (*International Financial Statistics*, line rf).

The problem with this analysis is that a relatively low volatility against the US dollar does not preclude Asian countries from trying to stabilize their nominal exchange rates against a *basket* of foreign currencies. Suppose the monetary authorities of country k wish to stabilize their currency against the US dollar, against European currencies (proxied by the DM) and against the yen, i.e. they try to limit the variations in the nominal exchange rates. They minimize the following loss function:

$$L = \alpha_0 \left(a(L) \Delta S_{k,\$} - \sigma_0 \right)^2 + \alpha_1 \left(b(L) \Delta S_{k,\mathrm{DM}} - \sigma_1 \right)^2$$
$$+ \alpha_2 \left(c(L) \Delta S_{k,\mathrm{Y}} - \sigma_2 \right)^2 \tag{3.1}$$

with $\alpha_0, \alpha_1, \alpha_2 \geq 0$ a(L), b(L) and c(L) are lagged polynomials.[6] $\Delta S_{k,i}$ stands for the monthly log-variation of the nominal exchange rate of currency k against i. $\sigma_0, \sigma_1, \sigma_2$ are the corresponding targets. $\sigma_i = 0$ in case of a fixed peg; $\sigma_{i>0}$ in case of a crawling peg. Given that $\Delta S_{k,DM} = \Delta S_{k,\$} - \Delta S_{DM,\$}$ and $\Delta S_{k,Y} = \Delta S_{k,\$} - \Delta S_{Y,\$}$, the optimal exchange rate policy is:

$$\Delta S_{k,\$} = D + A(L)\Delta S_{k,\$} + B(L)\Delta S_{DM,\$} + C(L)\Delta S_{Y,\$} + \varepsilon \qquad (3.2)$$

$$\text{with} \quad D = \frac{\alpha_0 a(0)\sigma_0 + \alpha_1 b(0)\sigma_1 + \alpha_2 c(0)\sigma_2}{\alpha_0 a(0)^2 + \alpha_1 b(0)^2 + \alpha_2 c(0)^2},$$

$$A(L) = \frac{\alpha_0 a(0)[a(0) - a(L)]}{\alpha_0 a(0)^2 + \alpha_1 b(0)^2 + \alpha_2 c(0)^2},$$

$$B(L) = \frac{\alpha_1 b(0)b(L)}{\alpha_0 a(0)^2 + \alpha_1 b(0)^2 + \alpha_2 c(0)^2},$$

$$C(L) = \frac{\alpha_2 c(0)c(L)}{\alpha_0 a(0)^2 + \alpha_1 b(0)^2 + \alpha_2 c(0)^2}.$$

The regression is carried out on the monthly average of nominal exchange rates for eleven Asian countries (IMF, *International Financial Statistics*). The behaviour of monetary authorities may be influenced by the fluctuations in the US dollar exchange rate against the yen and the DM. Here, four sub-periods are considered, matching the main turning points of the yen/US dollar exchange rate:

January 1974 – October 1978: the US dollar depreciated;
November 1978 – February 1985: the US dollar appreciated;
March 1985 – April 1990: the US dollar depreciated sharply, and then stabilized;
May 1990 – May 1995: the US dollar depreciated.

The nominal peg was defined above by the short-run stability of the nominal exchange rate, as opposed to the real peg which concerns long-term trends. Hence, only three lags are included in the regression of equation 3.2. More lags will be included for the analysis of the real pegs. The econometric results do not suffer from the small number of lags since the lagged variables are rarely significant.

The results are reported in Table 3.3. B(0) and C(0) represent the short-run coefficients. Levasseur and Serranito (1996) have shown that the monthly variations of the Asian nominal exchange rates against the US dollar are stationary over 1976–94. Our results are consistent with this finding since when they are significant, the 'long-run' estimates of A(L) (written A(1)) always

Table 3.3 Estimates of the implicit nominal basket pegs (equation 3.2)

May 1974 – October 1978

Country	B(0)	B̃(1)	C(0)	C̃(1)	$\bar{R}^2$	k†
Bhutan	0.419**	0.545**	-0.046	0.133	0.532	0
China	1.037*	0.890	-0.196	0.191	0.444	0
South Korea	Constant USD peg from 1975:01 to 1979:12					
India	0.419**	0.545**	-0.046	0.134	0.632	0
Indonesia	Constant USD peg until 1978:10					
Malaysia	0.385**	0.541**	0.180*	-0.012	0.428	12
Pakistan	Constant USD peg until 1981:12					
Philippines	0.081	0.126	-0.016	-0.148	0.092	10
Singapore	0.554**	0.559**	0.038	-0.065	0.639	12
Sri Lanka	0.127	0.420	-0.186	-0.286	0.278	0
Thailand	0.003	-0.007	0.013	0.029	0.282	12

March 1985 – April 1990

Country	B(0)	B̃(1)	C(0)	C̃(1)	$\bar{R}^2$	k†
Bhutan	0.246**	0.022**	0.026	-0.077	0.502	0
China	-0.229	-0.543	-0.018	0.334	0.135	0
South Korea	-0.038	-0.453*	0.092	0.519**	0.758	0
India	0.184**	0.432**	0.053	-0.054	0.525	0
Indonesia	-0.049	-0.115	0.122	-0.024	0.120	3
Malaysia	0.111*	0.124	0.056	-0.078	0.369	8
Pakistan	0.106*	0.135	0.055	-0.012	0.294	0
Philippines	-0.004	-0.052	-0.064	-0.019	0.035	0
Singapore	0.119*	0.158	0.126**	-0.014	0.409	0
Sri Lanka	0.098	0.252	0.004	0.097	0.355	0
Thailand	0.057**	0.073*	0.125**	0.028	0.760	0

November 1978 – February 1985

Country	B(0)	B̃(1)	C(0)	C̃(1)	$\bar{R}^2$	k†
Bhutan	0.278**	0.526**	0.039	-0.115	0.454	0
China	0.369**	0.483	0.147**	-0.073	0.615	0
South Korea	0.066	-0.132	0.026	0.066	0.174	12
India	0.284**	0.640**	0.007	0.121	0.511	0
Indonesia	0.118	-0.060	-0.046	-0.134	-0.118	4
Malaysia	0.178**	0.358**	0.211**	0.115*	0.681	0
Pakistan	0.110*	0.144	0.082	0.144	0.366	0
Philippines	-0.254	-0.009	-0.117	-0.322	-0.041	0
Singapore	0.162**	0.182**	0.244**	0.242	0.821	7
Sri Lanka	0.111*	0.238**	-0.023	-0.214	0.230	0
Thailand	-0.064	0.211	0.040	-0.005	0.124	0

May 1990 – May 1995

Country	B(0)	B̃(1)	C(0)	C̃(1)	$\bar{R}^2$	k†
Bhutan	0.095	0.809**	-0.125	-0.310	-0.011	5
China	0.184	0.234	0.072	0.344	-0.139	0
South Korea	-0.00	0.179	0.061	0.102	0.213	9
India	0.085	0.787**	-0.117	-0.265	-0.023	7
Indonesia	0.014	0.018	0.016	-0.015	0.143	0
Malaysia	0.081	0.122	0.026	0.132	0.250	0
Pakistan	0.155**	0.543**	-0.106*	-0.399**	0.540	0
Philippines	0.043	0.313	-0.210*	-0.678**	0.203	0
Singapore	0.211**	0.183*	0.096**	0.084	0.658	0
Sri Lanka	0.058	0.129*	0.020	-0.080	0.320	0
Thailand	0.075**	0.048**	0.103*	0.070**	0.946	0

Notes
* Significantly ≠ 0 at 10%.
** Significantly ≠ 0 at 5%.   † Highest order of autocorrelation of residuals (k = 0 to 12) at 5% (Breusch–Godfrey test).
Source: Author's calculations based on IMF data.

differ significantly from 1. When A(1) is significant, the other 'long-run' estimates are: $\tilde{B}(1) = B(1)/1 - A(1)$ and $\tilde{C}(1) = C(1)/1 - A(1)$.

Otherwise, we have $\tilde{B}(1) = B(1)$ and $\tilde{C}(1) = C(1)$. The 'long-run' estimates are computed using a Wold decomposition (see Appendix 1).

Surprisingly, several Asian countries have been weighting the DM in their implicit basket pegs for a long time. This is especially the case in Bhutan, India and Singapore. Only China, South Korea, Indonesia and the Philippines never stabilized their exchange rates against the DM, while Thailand has given only a small weight to the DM since 1985.[7]

Conversely, the yen appears quite infrequently in the implicit basket pegs, and this sort of peg is generally short-lived. Only Singapore weighted the yen over a long period (November 1978 – May 1995). But the peg concerns only the very short run ($\tilde{C}(1)$ is not significant), and the weight falls over time: C(0) = 0.244 over November 1978 – February 1985, 0.126 over March 1985 – April 1990, and 0.096 over May 1990 – May 1995. Thailand has been weighting the yen since March 1985, but the weight remains low (not exceeding 0.1). Finally, Pakistan and the Philippines cannot be considered as using the yen as a partial anchor over the last sub-period, since C(0) and $\tilde{C}(1)$ are negative.

It can be argued that the regression of equation 3.2 does not provide good estimates due to multicolinearity problems. In a second step, the DM/US dollar exchange rate is dropped, and the following regression is carried out:

$$\Delta S_{k,\$} = D + A(L)\Delta S_{k,\$} + C(L)\Delta S_{Y,\$} + u \qquad (3.3)$$

The results are reported in Table 3.4. Not surprisingly, C(0) and $\tilde{C}(1)$ partially catch the previous DM effect. But the yen does not completely make up for the DM, especially over the last sub-period where C(0) and $\tilde{C}(1)$ are not significant for Bhutan, India, Pakistan and Sri Lanka, while B(0) and/or $\tilde{B}(1)$ were significant for the corresponding countries in equation 3.2. Moreover, only Malaysia and, to a certain extent, South Korea appear to weight the yen in equation 3.3 while none of the estimates was significant for these countries in equation 3.2 (but the adjusted R^2 remains low).

The main conclusion that emerges is the absence of a yen bloc. In addition, the yen has not increased its role as a partial, nominal anchor in Asia since 1990. Our results confirm those of Frankel and Wei (1993) who found 'no special role for the yen' in South Korea, China, Thailand and Singapore, except in January 1988 – August 1992 where they found a statistically significant but low coefficient on the yen in Thailand and Singapore. But in contradiction with Frankel (1993), we cannot conclude that there is an increasing role of for the yen in the region.[8]

Table 3.4 Estimates of the implicit nominal basket pegs (equation 3.3)

Country	May 1974 – October 1978				Country	November 1978 – February 1985			
	C(0)	$\tilde{C}$ (1)	$\bar{R}^2$	$k^\dagger$		C(0)	$\tilde{C}$ (1)	$\bar{R}^2$	$k^\dagger$
Bhutan	0.096	0.407**	0.283	0	Bhutan	0.203**	0.035	0.248	0
China	0.283	0.435	0.081	0	China	0.371**	0.014	0.472	0
South Korea	Constant USD peg 1975:01 to 1979:12				South Korea	0.073	0.032	0.245	12
India	0.096	0.407	0.283	0	India	0.179**	0.085	0.345	0
Indonesia	USD peg until 1978:10				Indonesia	0.037	−0.159	0.044	3
Malaysia	0.323**	0.281	0.112	9	Malaysia	0.315	0.229	0.592	0
Pakistan	USD peg until 1981:12				Pakistan	0.153**	0.180	0.363	0
Philippines	0.013	0.189**	0.238	11	Philippines	−0.262	−0.326	−0.035	0
Singapore	0.256**	0.214	0.160	12	Singapore	0.350**	0.346**	0.742	0
Sri Lanka	−0.154	−0.220	0.301	0	Sri Lanka	0.040	−0.115	0.185	0
Thailand	0.015**	0.026**	0.317	3	Thailand	−0.009	0.059	−0.059	0

Country	March 1985 – April 1990				Country	May 1990 – May 1995			
	C(0)	$\tilde{C}$ (1)	$\bar{R}^2$	$k^\dagger$		C(0)	$\tilde{C}$ (1)	$\bar{R}^2$	$k^\dagger$
Bhutan	0.198**	0.131	0.283	0	Bhutan	−0.059	0.227	−0.084	0
China	−0.197	−0.063	0.134	0	China	0.272	0.705	−0.086	0
South Korea	0.071**	0.653**	0.757	0	South Korea	0.050**	0.158	0.224	0
India	0.174**	0.160	0.361	0	India	−0.070	0.292	−0.082	0
Indonesia	0.096	0.100	0.157	0	Indonesia	0.019	−0.005	−0.006	0
Malaysia	0.131**	0.030	0.356	8	Malaysia	0.090*	0.411**	0.256	0
Pakistan	0.127**	0.094	0.278	0	Pakistan	0.024	0.100	0.294	0
Philippines	−0.076*	−0.042	0.019	1	Philippines	−0.095	−0.477	0.146	0
Singapore	0.211**	0.066	0.410	0	Singapore	0.207**	0.170*	0.388	0
Sri Lanka	0.064	0.165**	0.347	0	Sri Lanka	0.107	0.105	0.224	0
Thailand	0.166**	0.109*	0.777	11	Thailand	0.137**	0.115**	0.795	0

Source: Author's calculations based on IMF data.

Notes

* Significantly $\neq$ 0 at 10%.

** Significantly $\neq$ 0 at 5%.

† Highest order of autocorrelation of residuals (k = 0 to 12) at 5% (Breusch–Godfrey test).

When B and C do not significantly differ from zero, and when the explanatory power of equations 3.2 and 3.3 is low (as is often the case over the last sub-period), the econometric analysis does not reveal whether Asian countries follow a US dollar peg, or whether they do not follow any peg. But Table 3.2 shows that over the last sub-period, the volatility of the nominal exchange rate against the US dollar is less than half its volatility against the yen in South Korea, Indonesia, Pakistan and Sri Lanka. It can be concluded that the latter countries follow a US dollar peg.[9] By contrast, Bhutan, China, India and, to a lesser extent, the Philippines would follow a floating regime.[10] Finally, only Singapore, Thailand and, to a lesser extent, Malaysia seemed to peg their currencies to a basket of international currencies over the last sub-period, although the weights of the yen and of the DM remained low.

2.2 Real pegs

Because the short-run volatility of prices is much lower than that of nominal exchange rates, the short-run volatility of real exchange rates is generally similar to that of nominal exchange rates. But the long-run volatility of both exchange rates differs since the nominal exchange rate can adjust in order to stabilize the real exchange rate. Thus, the analysis of real pegs must rely on the long-run evolution of real exchange rates. The usual approach to long-run economic relationships is the unit-root and cointegration analysis. In a first step, unit-root tests were carried out over the 1974–93 period. Real exchange rates are calculated with monthly output prices.[11] Though more reliable, consumer prices are not suited to the problem of measuring external competitiveness, because they include the prices of imported goods and of non-traded goods. Conversely, export prices are not available for most of the countries under review. Output prices are available for all countries but Bhutan, China and Malaysia.

Most Asian real exchange rates appear to be non-stationary in level, but stationary in first differences, both against the dollar and against the yen (Appendix 2). Only in Pakistan and Sri Lanka is the level of the real exchange rate stationary against the dollar: the news affecting both exchange rates does not have any lasting effect. This result can be interpreted as an attempt by the monetary authorities to compensate the news in order to control the evolution of the real exchange rate in the long run. Conversely, the only case of stationarity against the yen is that of the Philippines. But the real exchange rate of the Philippine peso against the US dollar is stationary too. Thus, it is not possible to draw any conclusion from the unit-root analysis for the Philippines. For all other currencies, the real exchange rate both against the dollar and against the yen is $I(1)$, which does not lead to any conclusion either.

In a second step, cointegration analysis was carried out for $I(1)$ currencies. The test consists in looking for a linear combination of the k/US dollar and the yen/US dollar exchange rates which may be stationary over 1974–93.[12] In fact, no cointegration relationship was found (see Appendix 2).

In brief, the unit-root analysis does not permit any conclusions about the real pegging behaviour of Asian currencies, except for Pakistan and Sri Lanka which appear to be US dollar peggers. The cointegration analysis shows that Asian currencies do not follow the yen in real terms in the long run. But the test is rather restrictive since it requires that the residuals of the regression be stationary, which will not be the case if some variables are omitted.

A less demanding test of real exchange rate policy consists in regressing equation 3.4 in order to measure the long-run impact of DM/dollar and yen/dollar variations on each real exchange rate against the dollar:

$$\Delta E_{k,\$} = F + G(L)\Delta E_{k,\$} + H(L)\Delta E_{DM,\$} + J(L)\Delta E_{Y,\$} + \varepsilon \qquad (3.4)$$

where $E_{k,i}$ is the logarithm of the real exchange rate of k against i, and L is the lag operator.[13] Equation 3.4 can be derived from the minimization of a loss function similar to equation 3.1. Additional lags (totalling twelve lags) are included here since monetary authorities generally adjust the nominal exchange rate with a lag when inflation differentials accumulate if they also have a nominal anchor (in this case, adjusting the nominal exchange rate in response to inflation is costly). This leads to short-run fluctuations in the real exchange rate that do not preclude the existence of a real anchor.

Following this analysis, only long-run estimates are of interest. As in the nominal case, they are calculated using a Wold decomposition (Appendix 1).

The regressions are carried out over the 1974–93 period, with seasonal dummies. The sum of the auto-regressive coefficients ($G(1)$) is always significantly different from one, which is consistent with I(1) or I(0) real exchange rates and allows to interpret $\tilde{H}(1) = H(1)/[1 - G(1)]$ and $\tilde{J}(1) = J(1)/[1 - G(1)]$. The two latter coefficients do not significantly differ from zero, except in Thailand where the adjusted R^2 is very low (Table 3.5). Other Asian countries do not give weight to the DM or to the yen in their implicit basket pegs. This can be interpreted as a peg to the US dollar (with an appreciation trend) in Singapore where the constant is highly significant and the adjusted R^2 not very low. For other countries, the results can be interpreted either as a peg to the US dollar or as no peg at all.[14]

In sum, Pakistan, Sri Lanka and, to a lesser extent, Singapore seem to peg the dollar in real terms. Other countries follow a US dollar real peg or no real peg at all. The results concerning nominal anchors differ according to the sub-periods considered. But over the last sub-period, only Thailand, Singapore and, to a certain extent, Malaysia weighted the yen in their implicit basket pegs. In the three cases, however, the US dollar remained prominent.

The evolution of nominal and real exchange rates evidenced above may reflect their free adjustment to nominal and real shocks rather than to exchange rate policies. In a second step, the optimal basket peg is studied and compared to the empirical results in order to see whether Asian countries had an interest in the observed exchange rate fluctuations.

Table 3.5 Estimates of the implicit real basket pegs (equation 3.4)

Country	F	G(1)	$\tilde{H}(1)$	$\tilde{J}(1)$	$\bar{R}^2$	$k^\dagger$
India	0.004	0.105	0.287	0.064	0.145	0
Indonesia	−0.010	−0.221	−0.127	−0.278	0.139	0
South Korea	0.007**	0.256	0.088	0.148	0.101	0
Singapore	−0.007**	0.265	0.188	−0.027	0.375	0
Thailand	0.000	0.103	0.372**	−0.088	0.098	0
Philippines[‡]	4.828**	0.901**	–	−0.040	0.960	3

Notes
* Significantly $\neq$ 0 at 10%.
** Significantly $\neq$ 0 at 5%.
† Highest order of autocorrelation of residuals (k = 0 to 12) at 5% (Breusch–Godfrey test).
‡ See end note 17.

3 Rationale for exchange rate policies in Asia

This section studies the rationale for the very modest role played by the yen as a regional anchor. For convenience, the term NICs (New Industrialized Countries) is used to refer to the group comprising Hong Kong, South Korea, Taiwan and Singapore; and ASEAN (Association of South-East Asian Nations) is used for the group including Indonesia, Malaysia, the Philippines and Thailand.

This section begins with the choice of an exchange rate regime in Asia (Section 3.1). Then, it turns to the choice between the dollar and the yen as foreign anchors (Section 3.2). A simple optimization model is proposed in Section 3.3 in order to rationalize the stylized facts presented in the previous section.

3.1 Choosing an exchange rate regime in Asia

The choice of an exchange rate regime in developing (or transition) countries can be viewed as a trade-off between the 'real target approach' and the 'nominal anchor approach' (see Corden, 1993). In theory, each approach excludes the other.

According to the former, nominal exchange rate fluctuations can have an impact on the real exchange rate, as in the Keynesian tradition. Conversely, the nominal anchor approach stipulates that a nominal exchange rate policy can help to reduce inflation without any lasting effect on real variables, as in the monetarist tradition. In practice, countries which peg their nominal exchange rate hope their inflation rate will converge towards the inflation rate in the anchor country. In the meantime, they allow for a real appreciation

Table 3.6 Some macroeconomic indicators in selected Asian countries

	CPI inflation % in 1995	Current account % GDP, 1995*	Export/GDP ratio, % in 1993**	Net external debt, % of GNP 1993	Long-term debt service, % of GDP, 1993[†]
Hong Kong	9.0	n.a.	26.1	n.a.	n.a.
South Korea	4.5	−2.0	24.9	14.4	2.5
Taiwan	3.7	1.6	38.6	n.a.	n.a.
Singapore	1.7	18.3	84.3	n.a.	n.a.
Indonesia	9.4	−3.7	25.7	65.9	8.6
Malaysia	3.4	−8.5	71.4	37.8	6.1
Philippines	8.1	−3.3	21.7	63.7	8.3
Thailand	5.8	−7.1	27.3	37.6	6.5
Bhutan	8.0	n.a.	n.a.	36.4	2.8
China	14.8	2.3	19.1	21.4	2.2
India	10.2	−1.5	8.8	37.3	3.2
Pakistan	12.3	−3.8	12.8	49.7	6.1
Sri Lanka	7.7	n.a.	n.a.	65.5	3.6

Sources: * IMF, *World Economic Outlook*, May 1996.
** CEPII-CHELEM Data Base, 1995.
† World Bank, *World Debt Tables*, 1994–5.

that helps to reduce inflation at the expense of external competitiveness. Discretionary or pre-announced devaluations help to reconcile the nominal objective with the real target during the disinflation process.

The NICs and the ASEAN countries have followed an export-oriented development strategy. India and China have turned to this strategy in recent years. This strategy is geared to the external world in order to promote exports and attract foreign direct investment. In recent years, NICs' current accounts (except that of South Korea) have gone into surplus, while ASEAN countries have run deficits (Table 3.6). Following the balance of payments cycle theory, the NICs may progressively allow for a real appreciation of their currencies, while the ASEAN countries would keep an objective of external competitiveness until they accumulate a positive net external position.

However, the current account is not just a question of external competitiveness, when there is an external debt denominated in foreign currencies: a depreciation in real terms improves the trade account if the Marshall–Lerner condition is verified, but the external debt is revalued. The net effect on the current account is uncertain. This argument applies especially to Indonesia and the Philippines where the external debt represents over 60 per cent of GNP. With a 10 per cent debt service/GDP ratio, a 10 per cent depreciation against the currency of denomination induces a rise in the debt service ratio by 1 percentage point.[15] On the other hand, a depreciation of the currency raises external competitiveness. With an export/GNP ratio of 25 per cent, the net effect of a depreciation on the current account is positive if the sum of the price elasticities of exports and imports exceeds 1.4 (instead of 1 if there is no external debt). Thus, the net effect of a currency depreciation on the balance of payments is ambiguous in a highly indebted country.[16]

3.2   Choosing a foreign anchor

Assuming that Asian countries wish to stabilize their real exchange rates, they still have to choose between various foreign anchors. Following the above analysis, the choice of a foreign anchor depends on the country and currency breakdown of trade and capital flows.

3.2.1   Trade flows

The breakdown of Asian external trade by country is detailed in Appendix 3 for 1973 and 1993.

For the NICs, the US market is not as important as it used to be, while Asian markets are developing. On the import side, Asian countries, including Japan, are larger suppliers than the USA, even though the latter represents 20–21 per cent of imports in South Korea and Taiwan.

The USA remains an important market *for the ASEAN countries* (especially for the Philippines), but an increasing share of exports is directed to the NICs. On the import side, the USA is a small partner compared to Japan and the NICs.

Lastly, the external trade of India and Pakistan is European Union-oriented. Chinese exports are diversified, while its imports come mainly from Asia.

Kwan (1994) makes a clear distinction between the NICs, which mainly compete between each other in the US market, and ASEAN countries, which have Japan as their main partner for imports. The analysis here shows that this distinction, while quite significant in 1973, is now vanishing due to two trends: (i) intra-NIC trade is developing at the expense of exports to the USA and Japan; and (ii) NICs have also become major suppliers for ASEAN countries, at the expense of Japan.[17]

It has become conventional wisdom to say that, unlike Europe, Asia is not a trade bloc. Maswood (1994) argues that such a bloc should include Japan. Yet Japan's trade intensity index declined between 1980 and 1991 for East Asia, while it increased for the United States:[18] the rising share of the Asian countries in total Japanese exports was more than explained by the dynamism of Asian countries as importing countries. In a similar way, Frankel and Wei (1993) and Frankel (1993) estimate a gravitational model of trade. They test whether trade bloc dummies are significant in explaining trade flows, even when distance and openness are included in the regressions. They conclude that unlike Europe and the Western Hemisphere, the Pacific and East Asian blocs seem to have weakened in the 1980s. The expansion of trade in these two blocs was simply in line with their economic development, their geographical proximity and their opening trend. But it is not important here to know whether or not intra-Asia trade expansion was due to a specific trade bloc effect. The important things are that: (i) there is a trade dynamism between Asian countries other than Japan; (ii) the role of Asia as a trading partner is growing for Japan; and (iii) the role of Japan as a trading partner is declining for most of the other Asian countries.

3.2.2   Capital flows

Capital flows between Asian countries are well described in Kwan (1994). Traditionally, Japan ran a trade deficit with the ASEAN countries because of large oil imports from Indonesia and Malaysia. But in recent years, the large flow of direct investment from Japan to the ASEAN countries has stimulated Japanese exports of investment goods. The trade deficit turned into surplus in 1992. The Asian NICs also provide foreign investment to the ASEAN countries (Taiwan is running a surplus vis-à-vis the ASEAN countries).

There is a long tradition of Japanese trade surpluses vis-à-vis the Asian NICs, and this surplus has increased in recent years. As a whole, in 1994, the Japanese surplus vis-à-vis Asia was $63 billion while its surplus vis-à-vis the USA was $61 billion.[19] But Japanese investment in ASEAN countries is being rivalled by the NICs, which are increasingly investing in the region. In fact, every stage of the balance of payments cycle is represented in Asia. Thus, there is a good basis for the further development of capital flows between Asian countries.

The role of Japan as a direct investor in Asia has been widely documented. In 1994, the stock of Japanese direct investment in Asia was $51 billion, while that of the USA amounted only to $46 billion.[20] However, Japanese direct investment to the NICs has been decreasing since 1989, while that to ASEAN countries has increased steadily since 1986 (see MITI, 1994). The NICs have also begun to invest massively in ASEAN countries, and the stock of direct investment amounted to $88 billion in 1994 (see Note 24).

The role of banks located in Japan is shown in Table 3.7. The share of Japan as a creditor is much larger than that of the United States throughout the region except in Thailand. Pakistan is another exception, with credits coming mainly from Europe. Finally, the yen is already the major currency for long-run debts in the ASEAN countries (Table 3.8).

Table 3.7 International bank liabilities by creditor country, at end 1994 (% of total external bank debt)

	United States	Japan		United States	Japan
South Korea	9.7	30.9	Indonesia	7.2	53.7
Taiwan	12.1	25.7	Malaysia	10.2	43.3
China	2.3	34.5	Philippines	14.7	39.3
India	8.1	28.7	Thailand	61.0	6.2
Pakistan	6.0	7.8			

Source: BIS, *Maturity, Sectoral and Nationality Distribution of International Bank Lending*, July 1995.

Table 3.8 Currency composition of the long-term debt in selected Asian countries in 1993

	US dollar	Yen	Multiple currency		US dollar	Yen	Multiple currency
China	54.2	21.0	20.6	Indonesia	13.2	40.7	30.6
India	55.0	12.8	14.6	Malaysia	25.1	37.5	21.8
Pakistan	34.5	14.2	32.4	Philippines	30.2	38.3	25.3
Sri Lanka	36.4	27.4	18.1	Thailand	21.8	52.1	18.6

Source: World Bank, *World Debt Tables*, 1994–5.

To summarize, three facts emerge from the above analysis of the Asian economies.

- First, there is an intra-regional trade dynamism among Asian countries other than Japan. Asia as a whole has also become a major partner for Japan, although the reverse is not true: the role of Japan as a trade partner has diminished for Asian countries since 1973.
- Second, Japan is the main foreign investor in Asia, although Asia is not the main destination for Japanese direct investments. The NICs play an increasing role in financing the ASEAN countries.
- Finally, the yen already plays a major role in the external debt of Asian countries. This feature is likely to be important for the exchange rate policy in countries which have a large debt/GNP ratio, i.e. in Indonesia and the Philippines.

The next section provides a simple model in order to infer the optimal foreign anchor of an Asian currency.

3.3 A simple model for the choice of a foreign anchor

3.3.1 The small country case

Suppose the public authorities of a small Asian country wish to minimize the squared discrepancies between the external account b and a target $\bar{b}$ (both as percentages of the nominal GDP):[21]

$$Min\ \Omega = \frac{1}{2}(b - \bar{b})^2 \tag{3.5}$$

For simplicity, we assume that the monetary authorities optimize over a single period. The external account considered here is the sum of the trade balance and of the debt service (interests + principal repayments). Thus, the external account represents the needs for additional foreign financings:

$$b = \eta\delta\,e - \sigma f + b_0 \tag{3.6}$$

Here e represents the logarithm of the real effective exchange rate corresponding to the country distribution of external trade;[22] f is the logarithm of the real effective exchange rate corresponding to the currency breakdown of the external debt; η is the export/GDP ratio; δ measures the impact of a depreciation on the trade account, through increased competitiveness (demand effect) or through a supply effect due to the rise in export profits; σ is the debt service/GDP ratio; and b_0 covers omitted variables.

The effective exchange rates can be defined as follows:

$$e = \varepsilon_\$ S_\$ + \varepsilon_Y s_Y \tag{3.7}$$

$$f = \varphi_\$ S_\$ + \varphi_Y s_Y \tag{3.8}$$

where s_i is the logarithm of the real bilateral exchange rate against currency $i(i = \$, Y)$, ϵ_i is the weight of currency i-country as a trade partner and φ_i is the weight of currency i in the denomination of the external debt. At this stage, we assume $\varepsilon_\$ + \varepsilon_Y = 1$ and $\varphi_\$ + \varphi_Y = 1$.[23]

With $S_{Y\$}$ standing for the real exchange rate of the yen against the dollar, the minimization of the loss function leads to the optimal reaction to yen/US dollar fluctuations:

$$\frac{\partial S_\$}{\partial S_{Y\$}} = \frac{\eta\delta\varepsilon_Y - \sigma\varphi_Y}{\eta\delta - \sigma} \tag{3.9}$$

With no external debt ($\sigma = 0$), the above solution simply becomes $\partial S_\$ / \partial S_{Y\$} = \varepsilon_Y$. When the yen appreciates by 1 per cent against the US dollar, the currency of the small Asian country appreciates by ε_Y per cent against the US dollar, so that its effective exchange rate e stays constant.

If the currency breakdown of the external debt fits the country distribution of trade ($\varphi_Y = \varepsilon_Y$), we also have $\partial S_\$ / \partial S_{Y\$} = \varepsilon_Y$, because keeping e constant leads to a constant f too.

If $\sigma \approx \eta \delta$, the optimal exchange rate policy is undetermined since an exchange rate variation has no net effect on the external account.

It was shown in Section 3.2 that in Asia, we have $\eta \delta > \sigma$ and $\varepsilon_Y < \varphi_Y$. The following orders of magnitude can be derived for ASEAN countries like the Philippines or Thailand: $\eta = 0.25$; $\varepsilon_Y = 0.2$; $\sigma = 0.08$; $\varphi_Y = 0.4$.

Finally, the price elasticities of external trade have been estimated by Mimosa (1996) for the NICs, implying $\delta = 1.4$.[24] With these figures, the optimal exchange rate policy is: $\partial S_\$ / \partial S_{Y\$} = 0.14$. When the yen appreciates by 1 per cent against the US dollar, the currency of the small country should appreciate by 0.14 per cent against the US dollar in order to keep the external account constant. This small weight attributed to the yen in the optimal basket peg comes from the facts that: (i) exchange rate fluctuations have a greater impact on the external account through trade flows than through the valorization of the external debt service ($\eta \delta > \sigma$); (ii) Japan plays a smaller role as a trade partner than the yen does as a creditor currency ($\varepsilon_Y < \varphi_Y$).

This result fits quite well the policies evidenced in Section 2. However, the small country framework hides the fact that a large part of the external trade of each Asian country is with Asian partners.

3.3.2 The two-country case

Suppose now that there are two identical ASEAN countries, called A and B, which carry out some trade with each other and compete on the same foreign markets (the USA and Japan). The bilateral trade between both countries represents $(1 - \varepsilon_\$ - \varepsilon_Y) = (1 - \varepsilon)\%$ of the total trade of each country. Their currencies are not used for debt denomination. The effective exchange rates of currency A must be redefined as:

$$e_A = \varepsilon_\$ S_{A\$} + \varepsilon_Y S_{AY} + (1 - \varepsilon) S_{AB} \tag{3.10}$$

$$f_A = \varphi_\$ S_{A\$} + \varphi_Y S_{AY} \tag{3.11}$$

where S_{Aj} stands for the exchange rate of currency A against currency j ($j = \$, Y, B$). Similar relations prevail for currency B. As in the small country case, each country minimizes the squared discrepancy of its external account from a target. If country A takes as given the exchange rate policy of its partner, its optimal exchange rate policy does not change compared to the small country case (equation 3.9). But if it knows that country B will follow the same exchange rate policy, then its reactions to yen/dollar fluctuations are modified:

$$\frac{\partial S_\$}{\partial S_{Y\$}} = \frac{\eta\delta\varepsilon_Y - \sigma\varphi_Y}{\eta\delta\varepsilon - \sigma} \qquad (3.12)$$

Now, when currency A depreciates against the US dollar, the effect on the trade account is reduced because currency B also depreciates. Thus, the optimal policy is rebalanced in favour of the yen. With $\varepsilon = 0.5$,[25] the optimal exchange rate policy is $\partial S_\$/\partial S_{Y\$} = 0.4$: when the yen appreciates by 1 per cent against the dollar, the optimal policy is to appreciate the currency against the dollar by 0.4 per cent. But the solution of the optimization problem becomes unstable for small values of ε. With $\varepsilon = 0.2$, we have $\eta\delta\varepsilon - \sigma \approx 0$: the variations in the exchange rate have little impact on the external account since the valuation effects make for the competitiveness effects. In this case, there may be no optimal basket peg, i.e. the floating regime may be optimal.[26]

Of course, this very simple model does not cover the whole rationale for the exchange rate policies in Asia. More specifically, this model does not describe the trade-off made by the monetary authorities between various objectives. Here, pegging the currency to the optimal basket makes it possible to reach a single objective. An interesting extension would be to introduce a second objective in the model. For instance, the monetary authorities may want a real appreciation in order to reduce the inflation rate. Then, targeting the external account would have a cost in terms of the second objective. Such an enriched model would probably show that Asian countries might be better off coordinating their exchange rate policies, because this would eliminate ineffective exchange rate fluctuations.

4 Summary and concluding remarks

The main finding of this chapter is that there is a mismatch between trade blocs, capital blocs and currency blocs in Asia. Trade flows are increasingly intensive between Asian countries other than Japan. Capital flows are especially dynamic between Japan (and, more recently, the NICs) and the ASEAN countries. Finally, there is no currency bloc in Asia in the sense of a stability of exchange rates vis-à-vis the yen, although there is an increasing use of the yen for denominating the debt and, to a lesser extent, for denominating trade transactions.

The absence of a yen bloc is evidenced through the econometric analysis of nominal and real exchange rates of eleven Asian currencies (nine for the real analysis) against the US dollar, the DM and the yen, over the January 1974–May 1995 period for the nominal analysis, January 1974–December 1993 for the real analysis.

For the nominal analysis, the 1974–95 period was divided into four sub-periods matching the main turning points of the yen/US dollar exchange rate. All over the period, the US dollar stayed prominent in the exchange rate regimes of Asian countries. Recent years have not seen a growing weight of the yen in the exchange rate policies: since May 1990 all countries but Bhutan, China, India and, to a lesser extent, the Philippines have pegged their currencies either to the US dollar or to a basket where the US dollar is prominent. In addition, over 1974–93, Pakistan, Sri Lanka and Singapore pegged their currencies to the US dollar in real terms,[27] while no country weighted the yen in its implicit real basket peg.

A simple optimization model is developed to rationalize these findings on the basis of a few statistics on regional flows of trade and capital. The absence of a yen bloc is explained by a mismatch between: (i) the country distribution of trade, and (ii) the currency distribution of the external debt. It shows that the development of trade between Asian countries other than Japan may rebalance the exchange rate strategies in favour of more stability against the yen, or push Asian countries towards more flexible regimes.

APPENDIX 1: COMPUTING LONG-RUN ESTIMATES

The long-run estimates are computed using the Wold lag formula, which makes it possible to test with a Student t for the significance of the sum of the coefficients estimated for the lags of each explanatory variable. Consider equation 3.2:

$$\Delta S_{k,\$} = D + A(L)\Delta S_{k,\$} + B(L)\Delta S_{DM,\$} + C(L)\Delta S_{Y,\$} + \varepsilon \qquad (3.2)$$

This equation can be rewritten as:

$$\Delta S_{k,\$}(t) = D + A(1)\Delta S_{k,\$}(t-1) + \sum_{i=1}^{11} A_i^* \Delta^2 S_{k,\$}(t-i)$$

$$+ B(1)\Delta S_{DM,\$}(t) + \sum_{i=0}^{11} B_i^* \Delta^2 S_{DM,\$}(t-i)$$

$$+ C(1)\Delta S_{Y,\$}(t) + \sum_{i=0}^{11} C_i^* \Delta^2 S_{Y,\$}(t-i) + \varepsilon$$

with $A_i^* = -\sum_{l=i+1}^{12} a_l, \quad B_i^* = -\sum_{l=i+1}^{12} b_l, \quad C_i^* = -\sum_{l=k+1}^{12} c_l.$

The same methodology is applied to the estimation of the implicit real basket pegs.

APPENDIX 2: UNIT ROOT AND COINTEGRATION ANALYSIS, 1973–93

Unit roots

Three regressions are carried out:

$$\Delta E_{i,j}(t) = \rho E_{i,j}(t-1) + \sum_{h=1}^{p} \gamma_h \Delta E_{i,j}(t-h) + u_t \tag{A3.1}$$

$$\Delta E_{i,j}(t) = c + \rho E_{i,j}(t-1) + \sum_{h=1}^{p} \gamma_h \Delta E_{i,j}(t-h) + v_t \tag{A3.2}$$

$$\Delta E_{i,j}(t) = c + \beta t + \rho E_{i,j}(t-1) + \sum_{h=1}^{p} \gamma_h \Delta E_{i,j}(t-h) + w_t \tag{A3.3}$$

where p stands for the last significant lag ($p \leq 12$) which is chosen by an optimizing procedure; c is a constant and u_t, v_t, w_t are the residuals. We test whether ρ differs significantly from zero using the augmented Dickey–Fuller test. If it does, than $E_{i,j}$ is stationary (I(0)), i.e. it tends in the long run to return to its past level (equation A3.1), to a constant (equation A3.2), or to an exogenous trend (equation A3.3). In all three cases, currency i can be said to use j as a real anchor.

Table A3.1 Unit roots

	Real exchange rate/US dollar			Real exchange rate/DM			Real exchange rate/yen		
	Equation	Lags p	Concl.*	Equation	Lags p	Concl.*	Equation	Lags p	Concl.*
India	A3.3	0	I(1)	A3.3	9	I(1)	A3.2	12	I(1)**
Indonesia	A3.3	3	I(1)	A3.3	0	I(1)	A3.3	9	I(1)
South Korea	A3.3	6	I(1)	A3.3	0	I(1)	A3.3	12	I(1)
Pakistan	A3.3	2	I(0)	A3.3	1	I(1)	A3.3	5	I(1)
Philippines	A3.3	10	I(0)	A3.3	10	I(1)	A3.3	5	I(0)
Singapore	A3.1	11	I(1)	A3.2	0	I(1)	A3.2	11	I(1)
Sri Lanka[a]	A3.2	8	I(0)	A3.3	12	I(1)	A3.3	11	I(1)
Thailand	A3.3	2	I(1)	A3.3	7	I(1)	A3.3	5	I(1)

Notes
*at 10 percent.
** Residuals auto-correlated.
[a] From January 1976.

Cointegration

The test consists in seeing whether a linear combination of $E_{i\$}$ and $E_{Y\$}$ (resp. $E_{DM\$}$) is stationary, i.e. I(0). Using the Engle–Granger (Engle and Granger, 1987) method, we regress:

$$E_{i,\$}(t) = c + \lambda E_{Y,\$}(t) + z(t) \tag{A3.4}$$

Then, the stationarity of the residuals z(t) is tested using an augmented Dickey–Fuller unit root test. If z(t) is stationary, then $E_{i,\$}$ and $E_{Y\$}$ (resp. $E_{DM\$}$) are cointegrated and λ is the cointegrating coefficient.

Cointegration tests are carried out over the whole 1973–93 period for I(1) currencies.

Table A3.2 Cointegration

Country i	Cointegration between $E_{i,\$}$ and $E_{Y,\$}$			Cointegration between $E_{i,\$}$ and $E_{DM,\$}$		
	Lags p	ADF	λ	Lags p	ADF	λ
India	3	−2.55	0.040	3	−2.71	−0.050
Indonesia	2	−2.70	0.301	2	−2.58	−0.213
South Korea	2	−1.62	0.199	2	−1.86	0.199
Thailand	3	−3.03	0.313	3	−2.37	0.292
Singapore	3	−2.65	−0.004	3	−2.58	0.063

Note
* 10 per cent rejection of the nul hypothesis of no cointegration.

APPENDIX 3: ASIAN EXTERNAL TRADE

Table A3.3 Orientation of exports by selected Asian countries (% of total exports of each country)

Exporting country	To the USA		To Japan		To NICs		To ASEAN		To the EU15		Elsewhere	
	1973	1993	1973	1993	1973	1993	1973	1993	1973	1993	1973	1993
Japan	27.7	29.4	–	–	13.5	19.1	7.4	9.2	14.3	16.2	37.1	26.1
Hong Kong	35.3	22.5	5.7	4.0	5.0	8.9	2.7	3.7	32.6	21.6	18.7	39.3
South Korea	33.6	21.3	37.8	14.3	5.7	11.1	2.0	7.7	10.7	12.1	10.2	33.5
Singapore	16.6	21.9	10.3	7.0	9.2	15.6	22.4	23.4	16.2	14.5	25.3	17.6
Taiwan	42.1	28.3	14.8	11.2	9.4	9.9	4.1	7.1	13.0	15.3	16.6	28.2
Indonesia	12.1	13.0	56.3	31.7	14.9	21.1	1.1	3.9	11.5	14.8	4.1	15.5
Malaysia	13.3	21.0	29.7	15.5	16.1	29.4	1.4	5.5	23.0	14.9	16.5	13.7
Philippines	35.2	38.2	40.4	18.9	4.7	12.2	1.2	3.5	13.0	16.4	5.5	10.8
Thailand	10.7	22.2	28.3	17.9	14.8	15.5	12.1	4.3	19.4	18.9	14.7	21.2
China	1.4	29.0	20.1	19.8	19.3	9.0	1.1	3.2	13.8	20.5	44.3	18.5
India	13.7	18.0	16.7	9.1	2.1	7.6	1.4	5.1	24.7	29.1	41.4	31.1
Pakistan	11.9	13.4	15.9	7.7	15.3	10.8	3.9	3.5	23.9	31.6	29.1	33.0

Source: CEPII-CHELEM data base.

Table A3.4 Origin of imports of selected Asian countries (% of total imports of each country)

Importing country	From the USA		From Japan		From NICs		From ASEAN		From the EU15		From Elsewhere	
	1973	1993	1973	1993	1973	1993	1973	1993	1973	1993	1973	1993
Japan	24.6	22.1	–	–	6.5	11.8	12.1	12.3	9.2	13.8	47.6	40.0
Hong Kong	13.4	9.1	21.1	18.7	10.3	23.3	3.3	6.0	18.7	22.0	33.2	20.9
South Korea	27.2	19.3	13.0	26.0	1.8	4.4	8.1	6.6	7.2	13.7	42.7	30.0
Singapore	15.5	14.3	20.6	22.6	5.9	9.6	17.1	21.5	15.9	13.1	25.0	18.9
Taiwan	22.4	20.5	38.8	32.8	4.4	7.3	4.5	6.3	13.9	14.5	16.0	18.6
Indonesia	17.4	10.8	36.5	23.6	9.4	20.5	2.6	3.0	20.5	21.6	13.6	20.5
Malaysia	8.2	16.0	22.1	26.7	13.9	26.1	7.7	5.3	22.0	14.1	26.1	11.8
Philippines	26.9	19.3	33.7	27.2	4.2	17.3	1.5	5.0	13.3	12.6	21.5	18.6
Thailand	13.1	9.1	38.3	31.2	8.1	17.2	1.3	5.7	20.4	16.6	18.8	20.2
China	13.8	11.6	20.3	26.7	3.7	27.7	1.7	3.1	16.3	14.5	44.2	16.4
India	16.5	11.3	10.5	6.5	0.9	11.0	1.0	1.9	29.4	31.3	41.7	38.0
Pakistan	29.8	8.6	13.3	15.0	1.7	8.3	0.8	6.8	26.2	27.6	28.2	33.7

Source: CEPII-CHELEM data base.

Table A3.5 Share of oil in the external trade of selected Asian countries

Importing country	% of total imports	Exporting country	% of total exports
South Korea	11.7	Indonesia	15.5
Singapore	10.0	Malaysia	9.0
Philippines	10.2		
India	15.8		

Source: CEPII-CHELEM data base.

Notes

This work was supported by the French Commissariat Général au Plan and by the European Commission (DGII). The author is grateful to V. Donnay for assistance, and to J.P. Azam, E. Benayoun, S. Collignon, V. Coudert, A. Dierx, F. Ilzkovitz, L. Fontagné, J.Y. Lee, C. Mathieu and J. Pisani-Ferry for their remarks.

1 On the basis of daily data, Weber (1995) shows that most interventions are sterilized and have no lasting effect on the exchange rates.

2 Haldane and Hall (1991) also used this method in order to investigate the pound sterling's transition from a dollar peg (in the mid-1970s) to a DM peg (in the late 1980s).

3 The methodology differs from Frankel and Wei (1993) and Frankel (1993) in that both nominal and real pegs are analysed. Moreover, the nominal and the real pegs are defined so as to be consistent. Finally, nearly three years (September 1992–May 1995) are added to the sample, and lagged adjustments are allowed. The methodology is not applied to Hong Kong which clearly pegs its currency to the US dollar in nominal terms.

4 The volatility is defined as the standard deviation of the first difference of the logarithmic exchange rate. With this definition, both a constant peg and a crawling peg imply a low volatility. For the choice of the sub-periods, see below.

5 Taiwan is not included since it is not an IMF member. Several Asian countries (for instance, Vietnam and Myanmar) are missing due to insufficient or uninformative data.

6 $a(L) = \sum_{i=0}^{l} a_i L^i$, $b(L) = \sum_{i=0}^{l} b_i L^i$, $c(L) = \sum_{i=0}^{l} c_i L^i$, where L is the lag operator.

7 $B(1)$ is negative for Korea over March 1985–April 1990, which means that the won depreciated against the US dollar when the DM appreciated. This behaviour is the opposite of a DM peg.

8 Frankel (1993) uses purchasing power over local goods (the inverse of the local price level) as the numeraire, while our results are based on nominal exchange rates against the US dollar. The difference in the results can be due to the choice of a numeraire, to the samples, or to the model specification (Frankel does not include lags in the regressions).

9 For Indonesia, Pakistan and Sri Lanka, this conclusion is reinforced by the fact that the constant is significant in equations 3.2 and 3.3.

10 This finding partially fits the official regimes which are a free float for India and the Philippines, and a peg to the Indian rupee for Bhutan.

11 Taken from IMF, *International Financial Statistics*, line 63 (wholesale prices).

12 The yen/US dollar exchange rate is also stationary in first difference, which allows to test for cointegration.

13 The exchange rates are first-differentiated because only their first differences are stationary. In the case of the Philippines, the real exchange rate is stationary both against the US dollar and against the yen. Thus, the following regression is carried out: $E_{k,\$} = F + G(L)E_{k,\$} + J(L)E_{k,Y} + \varepsilon$. The long-run estimate $\tilde{J}(1)$ does not significantly differ from 0 at 5 per cent, which means that the Philippines does not weight the yen in its implicit basket pegs. This can be shown by rearranging the above equation as: $E_{k,\$} = F + (G(L) - J(L))E_{k,\$} + J(L)E_{Y,\$} + \varepsilon$.

14 Due to lagged adjustments, the monthly volatility of the real exchange rate does not say anything about the real pegs. Over the whole 1974–93 period, the annual volatility of the real exchange rate against the US dollar typically represents 60–70 per cent of the annual volatility against the yen, which is less conclusive than the corresponding nominal figures. The only exception is the Singaporean dollar whose annual volatility against the US dollar is 44 per cent of its volatility against the yen.

15 In theory, indebted countries should be indifferent to the currency of denomination of their debt if the uncovered interest parity (UIP) holds, because any change in the exchange rate would be compensated by an interest differential. In fact, asset holders are risk-averse, and the UIP does not hold. In practice, exchange rates are much more volatile than interest rates, and the cost of the external debt is more dependent on valuation effects than on interest rates differentials.

16 In theory, the trade balance is influenced by the real exchange rate while re-evaluation effects are due to variations in the nominal exchange rate. But a developing country considers world inflation as exogenous. The evolution of its real exchange rate basically depends on that of its nominal exchange rate compared to domestic inflation. While the external debt is influenced by the nominal exchange rate, the nominal GDP depends on domestic inflation. Hence, the debt ratio rises when the real exchange rate depreciates.

17 Singapore is the only NIC whose exports to the USA have expanded faster than its total exports, while Malaysia is the only ASEAN country whose imports from Japan have expanded faster than its total imports.

18 The trade intensity index is defined as the ratio of the reporting country exports to total world exports, divided by the ratio of the target country imports to total world imports. Thus, the bilateral trade is corrected for the share of each partner in world trade.

19 Taken from CEPII-CHELEM data base.

20 CEPII calculations based on *World Investment Report, Survey of Current Business* and MITI data. In fact, Asia is not the main destination of Japanese direct investments (on this point, see de Laubier, 1995).

21 The squared formulation keeps the model tractable. The symmetry in the loss function is unrealistic since a country will generally prefer a positive current account. Nevertheless, this is not a big problem for developing countries in Asia where the current account is generally negative (see Table 3.6). Thus, the programme generally consists in minimizing the deficit.

22 The trade balance can be extended so as to include direct investment which responds to exchange rate variations in a similar way to trade flows.

23 More specifically, all trade flows with countries outside Japan are supposed to be with the USA, and the external debt that is not denominated in yen is assumed denominated in US dollars. The former assumption is relaxed in the two-country framework.

24 The estimates of the price elasticities are 1.9 for exports and 0.5 for imports; δ is the sum of the elasticities less one. This estimate is applied to ASEAN countries due to the lack of estimates for them.

25 As shown in Appendix 3, approximately 50 per cent of ASEAN countries' exports are directed to countries other than Japan or the USA.

26 The share of bilateral trade between A and B underestimates the extent of the competition between the two countries, because it does not consider competition on third markets. Considering the whole competition between both countries would lower ϵ.

27 In the case of Singapore, there was a trend in the exchange rate against the US dollar.

References

Argy, V. (1990) 'Choice of Exchange Rate Regime for a Smaller Economy: a Survey of Some Key Issues', in Argy, V. and De Grauwe, P., eds, *Choosing an Exchange Rate Regime*, International Monetary Fund, Washington, DC.

Balassa, B. (1964) 'The Purchasing Power Parity Doctrine: a Reappraisal', *Journal of Political Economy*, December, pp. 584–96.

Bank of International Settlements (1989, 1992) *Foreign Exchange Market Activity – International Banking Activity*, monthly reports, various issues.

Bénassy, A. and Deusy-Fournier, P. (1994) 'La Concurrence pour le statut de monnaie internationale depuis 1973', *Économie Internationale*, 59.

Corden, W.M. (1993) 'Exchange Rate Policy in Developing Countries', in Barth, R.C. and Wong, C.-H., *Approaches to Exchange Rate Policy*, IMF Institute, Washington DC.

Engle, R.F. and Granger, C.W.J. (1987) 'Co-Integration and Error Correction: Representation, Estimation and Testing', *Econometrica*, 55, 2.

Fouquin, M., Dourille-Feer, E. and Oliveira-Martins, J. (1991) 'Pacifique: le recentrage asiatique', *Economica*.

Frankel, J.A. (1993) 'Is Japan Creating a Yen Bloc in East Asia and in the Pacific?', in Frankel, J.A. and Kahler, M. eds, *Regionalism and Rivalry: Japan and the United States in Pacific Asia*, NBER, Cambridge, Mass.

——(1995) 'Still the Lingua Franca', *Foreign Affairs*, 74, 4, July/August.

Frankel, J.A. and Wei, S.J. (1992) 'Yen Bloc or Dollar Bloc? Exchange Rate Policies in the East Asian Economies', in Ito, T. and Krueger, A., eds, *Macroeconomic Linkage*, University of Chicago Press, Chicago.

——(1993) *Trade Blocs and Currency Blocs*, NBER Working Paper 4335, Cambridge, Mass.

Haldane, A.G. and Hall, S.G. (1991) 'Sterling's Relationship with the Dollar and the Deutschemark: 1976–89', *The Economic Journal*, 101, pp. 436–43.

International Monetary Fund, *Exchange Arrangements and Exchange Restrictions*, various issues, Washington, DC.

——*International Financial Statistics*, various issues, Washington, DC.

——(1994) *World Economic Outlook*, May and October, Washington, DC.

——(1995) *Annual Report*, Washington, DC.

Kwan, C.H. (1994) *Economic Interdependence in the Asia-Pacific Region*, Routledge, London.

de Laubier (1995) 'Les Investissements manufacturiers à l'étranger depuis 1980', *Économie Internationale*, 61, 1st quarter.

Levasseur, V. and Serranito, F. (1996) 'Formation d'un bloc yen dans la région asiatique: une approche par la cointégration', *Économie Internationale*, 66, 2nd quarter.

Loulergue, G. and Hatem, F. (1994) 'Intégration régionale en Asie', *Chroniques Économiques de la SÉDÉIS*, XLIII, 12, 15 December.

Maswood, S.J. (1994) 'Japan and East Asian Regionalism', *ASEAN Economic Bulletin*, 11, 1, July.

Mimosa team (1996) 'La Nouvelle Version du modèle MIMOSA', mimeo.

MITI (1994) 'The Role of Japan in Asia and the Internationalisation of the Yen', mimeo.

Popper, H. and Lowell, J. (1994) 'Officially Floating, Implicit Targeted Exchange Rates: Examples from the Pacific Basin', in Glick, R. and Hutchison M.M., *Exchange Rate Policy and Interdependence, Perspectives from the Pacific Basin*, Cambridge.

Touzard, C. (1995) 'Les Répercussions de la hausse du yen sur la dette des pays d'Asie', *Problèmes Économiques*, 2439, 27 September.

Turnovsky, S.J. (1994) 'Exchange Rate Management: a Partial View', in Glick, R. and Hutchison, M.M., eds, *Exchange Rate Policy and Interdependence*, Cambridge University Press, Cambridge.

Weber, A. (1995) 'Exchange Rates and the Effectiveness of Central Bank Intervention: New Evidence for the G3 and the EMS', in Bordes, C., Girardin, E. and Mélitz J., eds, *European Currency Crises and After* Manchester University Press, Manchester.

World Bank (1995) *World Debt Tables, 1994–95*, Washington, DC.

4

DISCUSSION

Jang-Young Lee

Chapter 3 by Agnès Bénassy-Quéré provides valuable information and insight into the role of the Japanese yen and other major currencies in the formulation and execution of the exchange rate policies of Asian countries. The first half of the chapter investigates the so-called '*de facto* exchange rate regimes', as opposed to the official regimes reported by the IMF, by empirically estimating the weights given to the yen, dollar and other major currencies in the implicit basket pegs of eleven Asian economies.

A body of literature already exists on similar topics, such as Frankel and Wei's 1993 paper entitled *Trade Blocs and Currency Blocs* or Kawai's 1996 paper on 'The Japanese Yen as an International Currency'. For the most part, a common theme that comes out of this literature is that there is no noticeable evidence of the emergence of a so-called yen bloc outside the national boundary of Japan. Some of the literature focused on the trade aspect of the yen bloc, while others looked at the currency aspect of the yen bloc, which carries a financial/monetary connotation. Chapter 3 examines the currency links directly in terms of exchange rate policies, and it shows similar results on the absence of a yen bloc.

At the same time, however, Chapter 3 can be distinguished from earlier studies in the following two respects: first, larger and updated sample data are used, so the empirical analysis is more comprehensive; and second, the analytical framework or model specification adopted is more rigorous, if not perfect. For example, the regression technique employed in Chapter 3 seems appropriate for the analysis of both nominal and real exchange rate pegs. This methodology has additional merit in that, as emphasized by the author, the nominal and real exchange rate pegs are defined in such a way that they are consistent in the long run. In other words, the real peg is defined by the stability of the real exchange rate in the long run, while the nominal peg is characterized by either stability in the nominal exchange rate in the short run or regularity of its variation in the short run. The underlying assumption here is that the monetary authorities seek to reduce the gap between the domestic and foreign inflation rates by devaluing their currencies gradually or at a regular intervals so that the nominal pegging to a foreign anchor may not lead to real appreciation in the long run. While there may be some exceptions, this assumption seems quite relevant to most Asian countries' cases.

Nevertheless, there are a few drawbacks I would like to point out in connection with the approach adopted in Chapter 3.

First, the same results on exchange rate links can be obtained regardless of the policy intention and actual exchange rate policies implemented by the authorities. In other words, the observed nominal peg of a certain Asian country to a foreign anchor currency can be detected, whether or not the country in question has actually tried to stabilize the bilateral exchange rate. In some cases, the observed correlation between any two currencies may simply reflect the presence of a common economic shock that hit the financial markets in two countries at the same time. For example, the positive and statistically significant coefficient on the yen/US dollar exchange rate in the regression of Singapore's nominal exchange rates (which is reported in Table 3.3.) could simply be the result of increased Japanese direct investment in these countries whenever the yen becomes stronger in relation to other major currencies. Indeed, those sub-periods when Singapore and Thailand increased their links to the yen (i.e. 1985–90 and 1990–95) seem to match the periods of yen appreciation against the US dollar. Thus, the observed peg has little to do with the authorities' intention to follow a certain peg in their exchange rate policies. Likewise, the absence of the nominal peg to a certain currency may simply be the result of unsuccessful exchange rate policies, even in cases where the authorities tried very hard to move the exchange rate in certain directions. The latter point would particularly be true for those countries where the authorities' ability to intervene in the foreign exchange market is often limited by the inadequate conditions of the local foreign exchange markets. All of this implies that the empirical results should be more cautiously interpreted.

A second point that deserves attention here is whether the monthly average data used in this study are appropriate for identifying short-term movements in the exchange rates. Obviously, low-frequency data such as the monthly data do not reveal valuable information as to how the week-to-week or the day-to-day variations in the nominal exchange rates are correlated with other anchor currencies.

Third, I also have a comment on the result of the estimation reported in Table 3.5. This concerns the test of real exchange rate policy. The two coefficients representing the long-run impact of DM/dollar and yen/dollar variations on each country's real exchange rate movements are not significantly different from zero for all countries except Thailand, meaning that most Asian countries, except Thailand, do not give any weight to real fluctuations in the DM/dollar or yen/dollar rates in their implicit basket peg in the long run. Here, I wonder whether Thailand's behaviour can also be explained by the fact that it is the only country in the sample that officially maintains the 'basket peg' exchange rate system. Obviously, the maintenance of the official basket peg system is likely to add credibility to the exchange rate policies and thereby may have strengthened the effectiveness of any exchange rate links in the long run.

Fourth, I wonder how the regression results on real pegging behaviour of Asian currencies will change if additional lags are included. The twelve lags seem rather too short in light of the fact that the monetary authorities in this region are often very slow in adjusting their nominal exchange rates to changes in inflation differential. It is not unusual for them to wait and delay the adjustment of the nominal rates until huge inflation differentials, and therefore tremendous depreciatory pressure, have already accumulated in the system.

The second half of the chapter provides a theoretical framework for the optimal choice of exchange rate regime (or to use a more accurate term, the choice of a foreign anchor currency) in developing countries. A nice theoretical model is developed here to support the empirical evidence presented in earlier sections of the chapter, especially on the small weight given to the yen in the optimal basket peg of the ASEAN countries. According to this model, it is justifiable by the stylized fact that the impact of yen–dollar exchange rate fluctuation on the current account balance through revaluation of external debt service is small as compared to the effect of exchange rate change on the trade flow. Another rationale is that the role of Japan as a trading partner is declining among Asian countries, while the share of Japan as a direct foreign investor and as a creditor is increasing in these countries.

I only have two comments on this part of the chapter.

First, as Agnès Bénassy-Quéré admits, the model does not allow for the multiple policy objectives that are usually pursued by the monetary authorities. The assumption that the Asian authorities are concerned only about the external current account balance is somewhat unrealistic. It is well known that some Asian monetary authorities have pursued the domestic price stability instead of the external account balance as the dominant policy objective. Singapore is one example.

Second, the functional form of the authorities' objective function, expressed in the squared deviation of the actual from the target current account balance, assumes that a country reacts to the deficit or surplus in the current account in the same manner in terms of the exchange rate adjustment. This assumption, however, seems rather restrictive. This is because those Asian countries with current account surpluses must have been less inclined to adjust their exchange rates than have those countries that experienced current account deficits. As is well documented in other studies, some Asian NICs are known to be quite hesitant to allow their currencies to appreciate in the face of rising current account surpluses.

References

Frankel, J.A. and Wei, S.J. (1993) *Trade Blocs and Currency Blocs*, NBER Working Paper 4335, Cambridge, Mass.

Kawai, Masahiro (1996) 'The Japanese Yen as an International Currency: Performance and Prospects', in Ryuzo Sato, Rama V. Ramachandran and Hajime Hori (eds) *Organisation, Performance and Equity: Perspectives on the Japanese Economy*, Kluwer Academic Publishers, pp. 305–55.

5

EXCHANGE RATE POLICY AND EFFECTIVENESS OF INTERVENTION

The Case of South Korea

Yeongseop Rhee and Chi-Young Song

1 Introduction

The movement of the exchange rate is one of the most important issues in policy discussions in South Korea today. Exchange rate policy seems to have been considered an independent policy for affecting the current account, which has been one of the main engines of economic growth in South Korea. Whenever its economy has been in recession, many have blamed overvaluation of the Korean won, in turn faulting the monetary authorities for pursuing an inappropriate exchange rate policy. Indeed, similar complaints can be heard today with the present recession taking hold. Firms and politicians alike are renewing their demands for a cheaper won. It is not so clear, however, that exchange rate policy has done anything to reverse the current account deficit or to correct other economic problems. Obviously, this is something which merits closer examination.

What is also not clear is whether or not the central bank still has the power to affect the exchange rate as it desires. South Korea made the shift in its exchange rate regime from a multiple currency basket peg system to the market average exchange rate system in early 1990. Even though a number of regulations are in force in the local foreign exchange market, the current system is not unlike those used by developed countries, and the central bank's ability to set the exchange rate at some arbitrary level is now limited. The Bank of Korea (BOK) still has the capability to control exchange rates, but not nearly so easily as before because, under the current system, it is only one of many foreign exchange market participants.

Much attention has been given to the implementation of proper foreign exchange rate policies by the Korean policy makers. In particular, as the South Korean economy has become more exposed to external factors such as the increase in cross-border capital movements after its financial opening, it has become more difficult for the country's monetary authorities to determine what exactly constitutes a proper foreign exchange rate policy and to implement that policy.

This chapter intends to examine the objectives of foreign exchange rate policy in South Korea during the 1980s and 1990s and, by looking at the mechanisms of the exchange rate system and the movements of economic fundamentals, investigate whether the monetary authorities have achieved their objectives. It also investigates whether central bank intervention is effective in moving the exchange rate in the desired direction under the current market-based exchange rate system. On the basis of the empirical results we obtained, we suggest how exchange rate policy should be coordinated with other policies to achieve economic objectives more easily in the future, considering the rapid change in the Korean financial markets.

In Section 2, we describe the development of the exchange rate system in Korea during the 1980s and 1990s and explain the mechanism of each system. We also analyse the behaviour of the exchange rate. In Section 3, we examine the objectives of the foreign exchange rate policies and investigate the economic factors which had the greatest bearing in determining the objectives. We also examine how these policies were adjusted in response to changes in the economic fundamentals and how successful they have been. In Section 4, we explain the mechanics of foreign exchange market intervention by the BOK and investigate the effectiveness of the central bank's intervention under the current exchange rate system. In Section 5, we conclude with a brief summary of the previous sections and make some suggestions for future exchange rate policy.

2 Exchange rate system and movement of the exchange rate in the 1980s and 1990s

2.1 *Multiple currency basket peg system (March 1980–February 1990)*

The multiple currency basket peg (MCBP) system was introduced in March 1980. Previously, the exchange rate of the Korean won had been pegged to the US dollar according to the single currency peg (SCP) system. This system had been established in May 1964, and while it was in effect, the Korean government set the lower limit of the won's exchange rate vis-à-vis the US dollar and did not allow commercial banks to trade foreign exchange certificates below this limit.[1] The lower limit was originally set at 255 won per dollar in 1964, although the won was devalued in later years. Mainly because of the government's expansionary monetary and fiscal policy and the oil shocks in 1974 and 1979, inflation was running apace and eroding the competitiveness of South Korea's exports. The government was therefore obliged to devalue the won on four occasions, the last being January 1980 by which time the won stood at 580 per dollar.

It can hardly be denied that the US dollar peg system contributed meaningfully to the rapid growth of the South Korean economy. Because it guaranteed an extremely stable won–dollar exchange rate and the USA was South Korea's major trade partner, it encouraged trade, but it posed several problems as well. The first of these was the continuous misalignment of the won exchange rate. The exchange rate neither correctly nor flexibly reflected the changes in the interest and inflation rate differentials and in the current account balance.

The fluctuations of other currencies vis-à-vis the US dollar in the international foreign exchange markets also posed a problem, for they could not be properly incorporated into the won–dollar exchange rate. Fluctuations in the value of the US dollar against other currencies in the international markets translated into corresponding changes in the value of the won against those same currencies. In other words, the Korean economy was at risk of excessive dependence on the US economy. The won, for example, tended to be overvalued relative to non-dollar currencies as the US dollar appreciated in the international market after the second oil shock. From January 1979 to February 1980, the US dollar appreciated by 19 per cent against the Japanese yen. Furthermore, as South Korea and the countries of Europe and East Asia became more interdependent in their trade and cross-border financial transactions, the relative importance of the exchange rate against those countries' currencies increased in equal measure. The South Korean economy had also suffered from four major and sudden devaluations of the won against the US dollar under the SCP system. It was therefore clear that the won was not being adjusted to changes in the current account balance or the inflation rate differential until enormous downward pressure had already accumulated. The big devaluations let the economy go through long and painful adjustment to the sudden shocks.

In order to resolve these problems, the government abandoned the SCP system and adopted the MCBP system. The exchange rate of the won per US dollar (E_t) under the MCBP system was determined according to the following equation:

$$E_t = \beta B_1 + (1 - \beta) B_2 + \alpha \qquad (5.1)$$

where B_1 and B_2 are won–dollar exchange rates which reflect changes in the special drawing rights (SDR) basket and the independent basket, respectively, and β and $(1 - \beta)$ are weights given to these two baskets. The variable, α, indicates the 'policy factor'.

The composition of the SDR basket was determined by the International Monetary Fund (IMF). While it was previously composed of sixteen currencies in 1981, the IMF excluded eleven currencies from the basket for which the foreign exchange markets were not well developed, leaving only five major currencies remaining: the US dollar, Deutsche Mark, Japanese yen, British pound and French franc. The IMF has since revised the relative weight of each currency in the SDR basket every five years. As of 1986, the weights of these currencies were 42 per cent, 19 per cent, 15 per cent, 12 per cent and 12 per cent, respectively.

The composition of the independent basket and relative weights between the two baskets were never disclosed to the public, however. The government was therefore heavily criticized, receiving many complaints that this non-disclosure generated unnecessary uncertainties about the future path of the exchange rate. The government countered by arguing that exchange rate policy would be less effective and would encourage destabilizing speculative transactions if the weights were unveiled. Many nevertheless conjectured that the independent basket might be composed of the currencies of Korea's major trading partners such as the USA, Japan, Germany and Canada with most weight being given to the US dollar and the Japanese yen, and that similar weights might be given to the SDR and independent baskets (Kim, 1992). Kim (1985) and Oum (1989) estimated the optimal weights of the currencies within the independent basket which minimize the variance of the won's real effective exchange rate. According to their results, the sum of the weights on the US dollar and the Japanese yen exceeded 90 per cent.

Very little was known about α in equation 5.1, the policy factor, except that it might reflect the interest and inflation rate differentials between home and abroad, the future prospects of the current account balance, and the supply of and demand for US dollars in the domestic market. The specific factors which were mainly considered in determining α and the degree to which α affected each day's exchange rate were never disclosed.

On the morning of each business day, the BOK announced the basic won–dollar exchange rate on the basis of equation 5.1. The basic rate applied to the central bank's transactions with commercial banks and foreign exchange banks' transactions with their customers. The allowable spreads for these transactions were restricted to a maximum of $+/-0.35$ per cent and $+/-0.4$ per cent of the basic rate, respectively. Since the interbank foreign exchange market was not yet well developed due to the strict enforcement of the foreign exchange concentration system, the basic rate announced by the BOK represented the actual exchange rate of the won vis-à-vis the US dollar. The won exchange rates against non-dollar currencies were determined by the cross-rates which assume the arbitrage relation. They too were announced on the morning of each business day.

As previously mentioned, the BOK neither publicized how it determined α nor gave any indications as to how important it was relative to the SDR and independent baskets. There is a great deal of speculation, however, that it was the most important factor in the monetary authorities' determination of the won–dollar exchange rate. According to empirical studies by Kwack and Kim (1990), the relative price, nominal effective exchange rate of the US dollar, and South Korea's net foreign debt were all important determinants of the exchange rate of the won with respect to the US dollar between 1981 and 1989. They, however, explain only a small part of the won's movement, which indicates that other factors such as α were in fact more important in determining the rate. Kwack (1989) calculated the exchange rate of the won to the dollar during the period 1980 to 1988 using equation 5.1 without α and found that it greatly and consistently deviated from the actual observed rates, sometimes even marking a reverse trend (he applied trade weights to the independent basket and assumed $\beta = 0.4$). This also implies that α might have been discretionary to a great degree.

South Korea's trade surplus with the USA had greatly expanded during the second half of the 1980s, but the won actually began to depreciate against the US dollar in the second half of 1988. While South Korea's trade surplus with the USA was recorded at $763 million in 1982, it increased to $4.3 billion in 1985, and then to $8.6 billion in 1988. This raised the ire of the US government: during 1988–9, it scathingly accused the BOK of manipulating the exchange rate by abusing or arbitrarily using α (US Department of Treasury 1989).

It would seem that α is the only factor in equation 5.1 which could be used for reflecting changes in the supply of and demand for US dollars resulting from international trade and cross-border financial transactions. However, they were not properly taken into account by α. In order to deflect pressure from the US government and to allow for more market-based determination of the exchange rate, a new system was needed. In March 1990, the Korean government finally abandoned the MCBP system and adopted the market average exchange rate (MAR) system, a variant of the managed floating rate system. Four consecutive years (1986–9) of current account surpluses had lessened the government's concerns that the shift to a more market-based system might lead to economic instability. The MAR system has since remained in effect to this day.

2.2 Market average exchange rate system (March 1990 – present)

With the introduction of the MAR system, the government relaxed the regulations on foreign exchange concentration in order to promote the development of the interbank foreign exchange market. Under the MAR system, the exchange rate of the won with respect to the US dollar is determined purely by the market forces in the interbank market, the Seoul Foreign Exchange Market. The BOK is merely one of the participants in the market, so it can only influence the exchange rate by trading with other participants. As of May 1997, there were 110 banking institutions in the market including the BOK as well as twenty-five domestic commercial banks, five specialized banks, three development banks, twenty-seven domestic merchant banks, and forty-nine branches of foreign banks. While the average daily turnover was only $0.2 billion in 1990, it increased tremendously to $2 billion in 1995.

Under this system, the intra-day fluctuation of the won–dollar spot exchange rate is restricted within a band which is moved every day. As of May 1997, the band is ±2.25 per cent of the basic rate which is announced in the morning of each trading day by the Fund Trading Center (FTC) of the

Korea Financial Telecommunications and Clearing Institute. The basic rate is the market average rate of the previous day which is determined by the weighted average of the market exchange rates. The weights are the volumes of each transaction. The band is imposed in order to prevent excessive volatility in the intra-day fluctuation of the exchange rate. The existence of the band may give rise to a disequilibrium in the foreign exchange market when the market exchange rate hits the lower or upper bound. When the MAR system was first introduced, the band was ±0.4 per cent of the basic rate, but the government widened it four times by December 1995 in an effort to improve the exchange rate price mechanism.[2]

However, the band has not actually acted as a constraint to the movement of the market exchange rate. The intra-day exchange rate of the won against the US dollar hit the band only a few times. It seems that the BOK has exercised window guidance in an effort to prevent large swings even within the band. The banks have by themselves refrained from quoting rates close to the upper or lower bounds of the band.

The exchange rates of the won with respect to non-dollar currencies have been determined by the cross-rates, as was the case under the MCBP system. The basic won exchange rates vis-à-vis the Japanese yen, British pound, Deutsche Mark, Swiss franc and Australian dollar are calculated using the exchange rates quoted in the Tokyo Foreign Exchange Market at 8.40 a.m. on the morning of each trading day, and the rates quoted in the New York Foreign Exchange Market at the close of the previous trading day are used to calculate the won exchange rates against the Canadian dollar, French franc, Italian lira, Singapore dollar and New Zealand dollar. Those basic rates are used by the commercial banks as reference rates for transactions with their customers. There are, however, no restrictions on the spreads.

The exchange rates of the won vis-à-vis non-dollar currencies have been exposed to shocks that these currencies have experienced against the US dollar in the international foreign exchange markets. For example, the exchange rate of the won with respect to the yen, which itself is one of the most important determinants of the competitiveness of South Korea's exports, has been more affected by changes in the yen–dollar exchange rate than in the won–dollar rate. From the end of June 1995 to the end of the same year, the yen depreciated by 18.1 per cent against the US dollar, forcing the won up 16.4 per cent against the yen. The current system of determining the won–yen rate, moreover, does not allow the domestic supply of and demand for the yen to affect the rate. To rectify this situation, the government established a won–yen foreign exchange market in October 1996, without restrictions on the degree of fluctuation. However, since the yen is thinly traded in the local market compared to other international foreign exchange markets, the exchange rate is determined largely by arbitrage. For this reason, the cross-rate is still used in determining the basic exchange rate of the won vis-à-vis the yen.

Unlike developed foreign exchange markets, no commercial foreign exchange brokerage firm has yet been allowed in the Seoul Foreign Exchange Market. Instead, most of the interbank transactions are mediated by the public brokerage houses, i.e. the FTC. Only 3.2 per cent of all interbank foreign exchange transactions were carried out through the over-the-counter (OTC) market in 1995. The current public foreign exchange brokerage system has helped the BOK closely monitor the foreign exchange market and has thereby allowed it to maintain the market's stability through implementation of effective supervision. Criticisms have nevertheless been voiced that this might be distorting the exchange rate of the won and hindering the development of the Korean foreign exchange market. Supervision of the market by the BOK could be excessive, thus discouraging active price quotation by the banks as market makers, and the FTC is not willing actively to develop new products and serve the market.

The market won–dollar exchange rate is mainly affected by the supply of and demand for the US dollar in relation to international trade or cross-border financial transactions. The volume of speculative trading or transactions by banks as market makers are relatively small. Table 5.1 shows indirect evidence of this. While the ratio of daily turnover to total volume of exports and imports in 1995 ranged anywhere from 8 to 93 per cent in countries which have well-developed foreign exchange markets, the corresponding figure in Korea was only 0.8 per cent.

South Korean banks have exhibited risk-averse behaviour in foreign exchange transactions, although there are some foreign exchange dealers

Table 5.1 Volume of daily turnover in foreign exchange markets (in US$ billion)

	Daily turnover (A)*	Exports + imports (B)**	(A/B) × 100
UK	463.8	500.0	92.8
USA	244.4	1,326.0	18.4
Japan	161.3	726.6	22.2
Singapore	105.4	235.5	44.8
Hong Kong	90.2	366.0	25.1
Switzerland	86.5	153.4	55.4
Germany	76.2	957.1	8.0
South Korea	2.0	251.0	0.8

Sources: Bank for International Settlements (1996) *Central Bank Survey of Foreign Exchange and Derivatives Market Activity 1995*, May; International Monetary Fund (1996) *International Financial Statistics*, September; Bank of Korea (1996) *Trends in the Foreign Exchange Market in Korea*, July (in Korean).

Notes
* Average daily turnover of foreign exchange transactions in April 1995, except for South Korea where the figure indicates that for all of 1995. Transactions include spot, forward and swaps.
** Total exports and imports in 1995.

who may take issue with this. It has only been a relatively short time since domestic banks first engaged in foreign exchange trading, so they still lack the expertise and experience which are necessary for success in it. They have also been reluctant to invest the resources needed to train employees in this business and develop trading skills, due to uncertainty over the returns to such investment. Hence, they have tried to minimize foreign exchange risks simply by maintaining square positions of foreign exchange holdings rather than exposing themselves to speculative positions.

Market participants' foreign exchange positions have also been limited by the Foreign Exchange Management Act. As of May 1997, for example, each bank's over-sold position in a spot transaction at the end of each trading day is allowed only up to the larger of 2 per cent of its paid-up capital or $3 million, and a bank's overall over-sold position should not exceed $20 million or 30 per cent of its average daily foreign exchange purchases in the previous month. In addition to the banks' risk-averse behaviour, this position restriction has served to discourage speculative trading in the market, by and large locking speculators out. It is one of the prudential requirements which applies equally to both domestic banks and branches of foreign banks participating in the Seoul Foreign Exchange Market. It has helped maintain the stability of the foreign exchange market and prevent the banks from becoming overexposed to foreign exchange risks. Despite the fact that some have criticized it, pointing out that it could hinder the development of the foreign exchange market in South Korea by discouraging aggressive trading, the government plans to relax the restrictions only gradually in order to ensure the market's continued stability and the soundness of the participating banks (Korea Institute of Finance, 1994).

2.3   Movement of the exchange rate

In Figure 5.1, we depict the daily fluctuation of the won–dollar exchange rates between 4 March 1980 and 30 September 1996, and in Table 5.2, we show the summary statistics of the rate of daily changes as measured by the log-difference. There have clearly been several large swings in the movement of the exchange rate during this period. The won rapidly depreciated against the US dollar between 1980 and 1985 and then rapidly appreciated between 1987 and 1989. Afterwards, it marked a depreciating trend, except during the period between early 1994 and July 1995 when the won slowly appreciated against the US dollar. On daily average, the won has depreciated by 0.007 per cent under the MCBP system and by 0.01 per cent under the MAR system.

The daily fluctuations in the exchange rate displayed interesting behaviour under the MCBP system. They had moved within a band which centred on zero even though the width of the band had varied. This implies that the exchange rate under the MCBP system had continuously moved up and

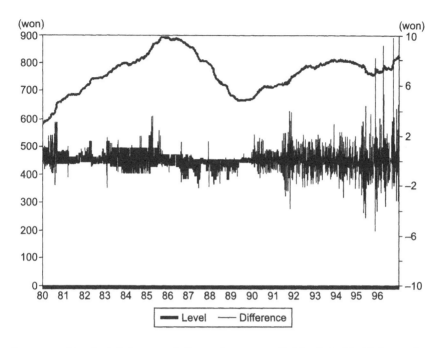

Figure 5.1 Trend of daily won–dollar exchange rate (3 March 1980–30 September 1996)

Table 5.2 Summary statistics of rate of changes in won–dollar exchange rate (%)

Variables	MCBP system (4 March 1980–28 February 1990)	MAR system (2 March 1990–28 September 1996)
Mean	0.0072	0.0107
Median	0.0000	0.0000
Maximum	0.4834	1.2207
Minimum	−0.3205	−0.7170
Standard deviation	0.0888	0.1372
Skewness	0.6120	1.3614
Kurtosis	6.0359	15.8781
Jarque-Bera	1 107.9 (0.000)	11 781.5 (0.000)
Number of observations	2 471	1 632

Notes
The rate of change is measured by log-difference.
The figures in parentheses indicate p-values.

down according to objectives of the monetary authorities even when the won showed a strong trend of depreciation or appreciation. This kind of behaviour cannot be detected at any time since the MAR system has been in effect.

As seen in Table 5.2, the distribution of the daily exchange rates of the won with respect to the US dollar during both periods is far from a normal distribution according to the Jarque–Bera statistics. The statistics for kurtosis, however, indicate that the distribution of the daily exchange rates has fatter tails under the MAR system. What is more, the standard deviation and the values of the maximum and minimum rates indicate that there might have been a discernible increase in exchange rate volatility after the MAR system was introduced. We can also expect that the foreign exchange market could be more volatile under the MAR system as the volume of speculative transactions increases. Furthermore, the movement of capital flows greatly increased in the 1990s due to the deregulation of capital movements including the opening up of the stock market. This, together with the deregulation of foreign exchange transactions, might have given rise to greater exchange rate volatility than during the period of the MCBP system.

In order to examine this more closely, we have estimated the GARCH (generalized autoregressive conditional heteroskedasticity) variance of the daily changes during the same period.[3] We have applied the GARCH (1,1) model as presented in equations 5.2–5.3:

$$\Delta S_t = c_0 + \sum_{i=1}^{m} \alpha_i \Delta S_{t-1} + u_t, \text{ with } u_t/\Omega_{t-1} \sim N(0, b_t) \tag{5.2}$$

$$b_t = c_1 + \beta_t u_{r-1}^2 + \beta_2 b_{t-1} + \beta_3 \, dummy \tag{5.3}$$

where S_t is log of the won–dollar spot exchange rate and Δ is difference operator; b_t is conditional variance of the error term (u_t). We include a regime dummy in equation 5.3 which takes zero under the MCBP system and 1 under the MAR system. In the actual estimation of equation 5.2, we have used three lags of the dependent variable on the basis of the Schwarz criterion. Also, we have estimated the model both with and without a regime dummy, and report the results in (I) and (II) in Table 5.3, respectively.

The GARCH variance of (I) can be seen in Figure 5.2. It shows that the degree of volatility has changed little despite the shift in exchange rate regimes. Compared to the MCBP system, no persistent increase in the volatility can be observed after the MAR system was adopted in March 1990, and this is statistically confirmed by (II). The coefficient of the regime dummy is statistically insignificant. This result could be explained as follows. The BOK has been effective in managing the exchange rate volatility by means of frequent intervention as well as sustaining the limit on the daily exchange rate fluctuation even though the limit was

Table 5.3 GARCH estimation of won–dollar exchange rate (sample period: 3 March 1980–30 September 1996)

Variables	(I)	(II)
c_0	$5.77 \times 10^{-5} (1.594)$	$6.03 \times 10^{-5} (1.674)$
ΔS_{t-1}	$0.291 (9.063)^{**}$	$0.291 (9.112)^{**}$
ΔS_{t-2}	$-0.038 \ (-1.257)$	$-0.038 \ (-1.263)$
ΔS_{t-3}	$0.042 \ (1.386)$	$0.042 \ (1.393)$
c_1	$1.15 \times 10^{-7} (0.979)$	$4.83 \times 10^{-7} (4.132)^{**}$
u_{t-1}^2	$0.150 \ (7.874)^{**}$	$0.150 \ (7.723)^{**}$
h_{t-1}	$0.600 \ (10.336)^{**}$	$0.600 \ (10.417)^{**}$
dummy	–	$-3.00 \times 10^{-8} (-0.606)$

Notes
(I): estimation without regime dummy; (II): estimation with regime dummy. The figures in parentheses indicate t-values.
* Significant at 5% level.
** Significant at 1% level.

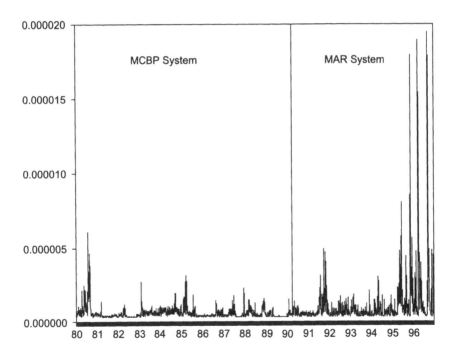

Figure 5.2 GARCH variance of daily won–dollar exchange rate (3 March 1980–30 September 1996)

gradually relaxed throughout the 1990s. There are those who may assert that the volatility of the economic fundamentals which ultimately determine the exchange rate has changed little, but this argument is not so convincing. The movement of the won–dollar exchange rate has become remarkably more volatile since early 1995 as the government has tended to refrain from intervention in the local foreign exchange market.

Efficient financial markets show signs of random walk in financial prices (Kim and Singal, 1994; Lo and MacKinlay, 1988). We have tested the random walk hypothesis of the daily won–dollar exchange rate by using the Dickey–Fuller model (Dickey and Fuller, 1979) as is described in equation 5.4 and report the results in Table 5.4.

$$\Delta S_t = c_0 + \alpha_1 S_{t-1} + u_t \tag{5.4}$$

The test for the whole period of the MCBP and MAR systems rejects the hypothesis that the daily won–dollar exchange rate followed a random walk pattern. The results are quite different, however, when the tests are done separately for each of the two different regimes. That is, the hypothesis is accepted for the MAR system while it is rejected for the MCBP system. This implies that, under the MAR system, information which arrives on any given day is more efficiently reflected in that day's exchange rate than under the MCBP system. In other words, the exchange rate became less predictable after the shift to a market-based system.

Table 5.4 Test of random walk hypothesis

Statistics	MCBP system (4 March 1980– 28 February 1990)	MAR system (2 March 1990– 30 September 1996)	Whole period (4 March 1980– 30 September 1996)
Test statistics	−6.515	−1.962	−5.566
Critical values:			
1%	−3.436	−3.437	−3.435
5%	−2.863	−2.864	−2.863
10%	−2.568	−2.568	−2.568

Notes
Dickey–Fuller tests are undertaken for testing the random walk hypothesis. Critical values are adopted from MacKinnon (1991).

3 Current account, capital flows and exchange rate

3.1 Current account and exchange rate

In general, the objective of each country's exchange rate policy is either economic growth or price stability or both. Even though a country which adopts a floating exchange rate system may not make the goals of its exchange rate policy known, it has been widely conjectured that developed countries generally place more weight on price stability whereas economic growth has been more important in developing countries. Some developing countries, however, have adopted a variant of the fixed exchange rate system to serve their specific goals. Argentina, for example, has maintained the Convertibility Law since April 1991 for the purpose of price stability by which the exchange rate of the Argentine peso is fixed to the US dollar at 1 peso per dollar. The law requires approval from the Congress for peso devaluation. Since the introduction of this law, the US dollar has been also used as a unit of account. Hong Kong has made use of a strictly managed US dollar-linked exchange rate system since 1982 with more emphasis on reducing the foreign exchange risk involved in cross-border capital flows.

Most of the industrial economies have adopted systems of independently floating exchange rates. In these countries, the goal of exchange rate policy must be accomplished through coordination with fiscal or monetary policy. Direct intervention by these countries' monetary authorities in the foreign exchange markets has become ever less effective due to the vast size of the foreign exchange markets relative to foreign reserve holdings. In the case of developing countries which adopt managed floating systems, on the other hand, direct intervention in the foreign exchange markets is still effective as their local markets are relatively small and their currencies are not yet very internationalized. Since the financial markets are not well developed and they are not well integrated into the world financial markets, developing countries can more easily realize the goals of the exchange rate policies by making use of managed floating systems rather than independently floating systems (Branson and Katseli-Papaefstratiou, 1981; Wickham, 1985).

The South Korean monetary authorities have never notified the public as to the objective of their exchange rate policy, but it is widely believed that the main objective has been to stabilize the current account balance. The export sector has been one of the main engines of economic growth in South Korea, and in order to promote exports during the early stages of economic development, the government implemented an export subsidy programme, granted exporting firms first preference in the allocation of financial resources, and encouraged investment in social infrastructure.[4]

Most importantly of all, the policy makers in South Korea have executed exchange rate policy with the purpose of maintaining the competitiveness of exports vis-à-vis international competitors. That is, the monetary authorities have gone to great efforts to stabilize the real effective exchange rates in response to changes in the price level at home and abroad, as well as the fluctuations in the exchange rates of non-dollar currencies vis-à-vis the US dollar. During periods of current account deficits, the government allowed the real effective exchange rate to depreciate, but permitted it to appreciate when the current account showed surpluses. This becomes readily evident in Figure 5.3.

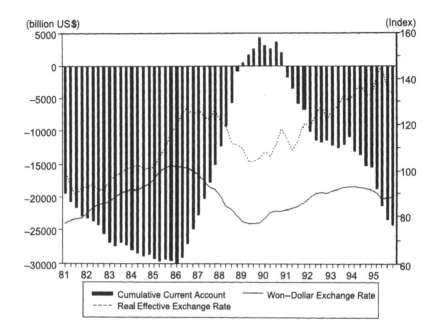

Figure 5.3 Exchange rates and cumulative current account balance in South Korea
(first quarter 1981–fourth quarter 1995)

Note 1 The cumulative current account indicates an accumulation since the first quarter of
1950.
2 Indexed won–dollar exchange rate is used (1985 = 100).
3 A rise in the real effective exchange rate indicates a real depreciation of the won
(1985 = 100).

Throughout the first half of the 1980s and the 1990s when the current
account was recording deficits, the real effective exchange rate continued to
depreciate. In contrast, during the second half of the 1980s when the current
account recorded huge surpluses, mainly due to the so-called 'three blessings'
or 'three lows' (low oil prices, low world interest rates and low values of the
US dollar against the yen), it tended to appreciate.

An asymmetric response by the real exchange rate to the development of
the current account could also be observed. That is, the real effective exchange rate seemed to adjust more slowly to the improvement in the current
account than it did to its deterioration. Although the current account
began to record surpluses in 1986, for example, and the surpluses grew
markedly during 1986–7, the real effective exchange rate showed little
change. It only started to appreciate in the first quarter of 1988. It then
began to depreciate early in the third quarter of 1989 even before the current
account began to record another deficit in 1990 as the size of the surplus
had shrunk compared to the previous year. In sharp contrast, the real effective

exchange rate displayed a continuous depreciation during the periods when current account deficits occurred, regardless of fluctuations in their size.

Given that the exchange rates of non-dollar currencies with respect to the US dollar are determined by external forces and the inflation rate gap between home and abroad had persisted, the changes in the nominal won–dollar exchange rate have been important in stabilizing the real value of the won. While the monetary authorities had at their disposal the policy factor in equation 5.1 under the MCBP system as a means of affecting the nominal won–dollar rate, they have had to intervene in the Seoul Foreign Exchange Market in order to bring about the same effect under the MAR system. As was noted on p. 73, it was widely conjectured that the monetary authorities had earlier used the policy factor in a discretionary way in order to realize the goals of exchange rate policy during the 1980s. And under the MAR system, intervention by the BOK was effective towards achieving its objectives because of the thinness of the local foreign exchange market. While the BOK held an average of $21.3 billion in foreign exchange reserves during 1991–5, the average daily market turnover of US dollars in the interbank foreign exchange market was only $1.2 billion during the same period. Maintaining the position restriction on foreign exchange holdings by banks as well as the band on daily fluctuations in the won–dollar exchange rate has also helped make intervention by the BOK more effective.

The monetary authorities duly take into account the movements of the yen against the dollar in the implementation of exchange rate policy. If the yen gets stronger (weaker) against the US dollar, it creates tremendous downward (upward) pressure on the real value of the won since the weight of the yen in calculating the real effective exchange rate is relatively high.

A stronger yen allows the South Korean monetary authorities more flexibility in their exchange rate policy. That is, they could more flexibly adjust the exchange rate policy according to the changes in the inflation rate, monetary aggregates and interest rates with less concern about the further deterioration of the current account balance. This was clearly the case between early 1994 and mid-1995. Despite the fact that the current account deficit was large at the time, the authorities allowed an appreciation of the won against the US dollar because the increased inflows of foreign capital were creating greater inflationary pressure. (See Figure 5.4.) It must be noted, though, that the authorities allowed the won to appreciate only slowly in order to maintain the international price competitiveness of South Korea's exports.

During those periods when the yen was weaker, on the other hand, it seems that the current account was the main concern with regard to exchange rate policy. Even though the current account was still recording a surplus in 1989, for example, the won began to depreciate because the yen had earlier begun to fall, threatening to reduce international export competitiveness.[5] Since mid-1995, the yen has been weak against the US dollar. Despite the fact that the inflation rate rose substantially this year mainly due to the expansion in

Figure 5.4 Trend of daily won–dollar and yen–dollar exchange rates (4 January 1988–30 September 1996)

aggregate demand, the monetary authorities have permitted the won to depreciate significantly.

In order to examine the effects of the movements of the yen–dollar rate on the won–dollar rate, we have done regression analyses. We used a simple autoregressive model as follows:

$$\Delta S_t = c_0 + \sum_{i=1}^{m} \alpha_i \Delta S_{t-i} + \sum_{j=0}^{n} \beta_j \Delta yen_{t-j} + u_t \qquad (5.5)$$

where yen_t indicates the spot yen–dollar rate. We have examined specific periods of yen appreciation and depreciation separately. In the 1990s, the yen generally appreciated from 11 June 1991 to 18 April 1995, and it generally depreciated during the period of 19 April 1995 to 30 September 1996. Of course, the yen did not necessarily appreciate or depreciate consistently against the dollar during these periods. There was obviously a great deal of fluctuation in the rate, but the general trends during these periods were appreciation or depreciation without any long swings. We have used the closing rates of the yen–dollar rate in the New York Foreign Exchange Market in the estimation, and we have adjusted the data according to the time difference. The estimation results are presented in Table 5.5.

Table 5.5 Effects of changes in yen–dollar rate on won–dollar rate

Variables	Period of yen appreciation (11 June 1991–18 April 1995)	Period of yen depreciation (19 April 1995–30 September 1995)
c_0	$5.74 \times 10^{-5}(1.471)$	$8.63 \times 10^{-5}(0.856)$
ΔS_{t-1}	0.259 (8.020)**	0.291 (5.334)**
Δ_{t-2}	$-0.181(-5.600)^{**}$	$-0.092(-1.703)$
Δyen_t	0.006 (0.985)	0.069 (5.133)**
Δyen_{t-1}	0.007 (1.166)	0.009 (0.636)
Δyen_{t-2}	$-0.003(-0.514)$	0.017 (1.243)
R^2	0.083	0.172
D.W.	1.998	2.006

Notes:
The figures in parentheses indicate t-values.
**Significant at 1% level.

The changes in the yen–dollar rate had significant contemporaneous effects on the won–dollar rate during the period of yen depreciation according to Table 5.5. A depreciation of 1 per cent in the yen with respect to the US dollar led to a 0.069 per cent depreciation of the won against the US dollar in the same day, although no lagged effects of changes in the yen on the won–dollar rate were found. During the yen appreciation period, no significant statistical relationship between the changes in the yen–dollar rate and the won–dollar rate could be ascertained.

These outcomes stem in part, though not necessarily, from the asymmetric responses of the South Korean monetary authorities' exchange rate policy to the development of the yen–dollar rate, as explained above. That is, since the monetary authorities did adjust the exchange rate policy depending on the changes in all the various economic fundamentals rather than focusing only on the current account when the yen was appreciating, no consistent relationship between the yen–dollar rate and the won–dollar rate could be found by our estimation. During the period of yen depreciation, however, the policy was mainly directed towards stabilizing the real effective exchange rate, letting the won depreciate against the US dollar in the local foreign exchange market.

The results, nevertheless, do not imply that the changes in the yen–dollar rate during the period of appreciation had no effects on the changes in the won–dollar rate. To the contrary, we argue that a significant relationship did in fact exist but that it could not be captured by our regression because an appreciation of the yen with respect to the US dollar has affected the won–dollar rate both ways. In order to examine this, we have estimated the effects of changes in the yen–dollar rate on the volatility of the won–dollar rate with using the same GARCH(1,1) model which was explained in equations 5.2–5.3, except that the absolute values of changes in the yen–dollar rate are included in the conditional variance equation as in equation 5.6. We report the estimation results in Table 5.6.

$$h_t = c_0 + \beta_1 u_{t-1}^2 + \beta_2 h_{t-1} + \sum_{j=0}^{n} \delta_j \left| \Delta yen_{t-j} \right| \tag{5.6}$$

The results show that the changes in the yen–dollar rate have significantly affected the volatility of the won–dollar rate during both the periods of depreciation and appreciation. The higher the rates of change in the yen–dollar rate, the greater the volatility in the won–dollar rate. This implies that the development of the yen–dollar rate also affected the won–dollar rate during the period of the appreciation even though a specific relationship could not be isolated.[6]

Table 5.6 Effects of changes in yen–dollar rate on the volatility of won–dollar rate

Variables	Period of yen appreciation (11 June 1991–18 April 1995)	Period of yen depreciation (19 April 1995–30 September 1996)
c_0	$3.37 \times 10^{-5}(1.412)$	$8.22 \times 10^{-5}(0.926)$
ΔS_{t-1}	0.256 (9.158)**	0.347 (5.614)**
ΔS_{t-2}	$-0.180(-6.369)^{**}$	$-0.089(-1.528)$
ΔS_{t-3}	$-0.013(-0.527)$	–
c_1	$1.38 \times 10^{-7}(3.998)^{**}$	$5.50 \times 10^{-7}(4.053)^{**}$
u_{t-1}^2	0.150 (11.642)**	0.151 (5.034)**
h_{t-1}	0.600 (22.328)**	0.600 (7.751)**
Δyen_t	$4.58 \times 10^{-5}(4.796)^{**}$	$0.01 \times 10^{-2}(5.775)^{**}$
Δyen_{t-1}	$-4.20 \times 10^{-5}(-6.130)^{**}$	$-8.94 \times 10^{-5}(-3.400)^{**}$
Δyen_{t-2}	$9.66 \times 10^{-6}(2.187)^{*}$	–

Notes
The figures in parentheses indicate t-values.
* Significant at 5% level.
** Significant at 1% level.

3.2 Capital flows and exchange rate

Compared to previous decades, the South Korean economy has experienced remarkably large inflows of foreign capital in the 1990s.[7] The large interest rate differential between domestic and foreign financial markets coupled with the favourable prospects of the economy has made South Korea one of the most attractive markets among emerging economies to foreign investors, and capital account deregulation has triggered a massive inflow. The total net inflow of capital during the 1990–5 period was $45.8 billion, more than three times the total for all of the 1970s and 1980s. The cumulative net inflow between 1990 and 1995 averaged 2.3 per cent of GDP. In the 1990s, capital has flowed into South Korea mainly in the form of portfolio investment, while foreign direct investment had been the main source of inflow in the second half of the 1980s. The cumulative net inflow of portfolio investment during 1990–5 was $35.7 billion, accounting for the lion's share, or about 82 per cent of the total foreign capital inflows during the period.[8] This enormous increase in portfolio investment was due primarily to the easing of restrictions on overseas issuances of securities by domestic firms and the opening of the South Korean stock market in 1992. The recession in the industrial economies at this time brought about a decline in world interest rates which naturally encouraged South Korean firms and banks to mobilize needed funds more cheaply in the international capital markets. At the same time, the low interest rates which prevailed in the industrial economies provided strong incentives for international investors to increase their holdings of securities in the emerging markets including South Korea.

Large inflows of foreign capital contribute to the economic growth of recipient countries if they are directed towards investment rather than financing consumption. It also can improve the efficiency of domestic financial markets by heightening competition and increasing liquidity as well as by making the markets deeper (Dornbusch and Park, 1995; IMF, 1995). Even though it has not yet been verified by rigorous empirical studies, the surge in the flow of foreign capital into South Korea in the 1990s has been considered a contributing factor towards its economic growth since the country has maintained high investment rates as well as high saving rates and the use of foreign capital has been directed almost entirely towards investment.[9] However, these capital flows do not seem to have brought about greater efficiency in the domestic financial markets as yet, partly because it is still too early to draw conclusions and also because strict restrictions on the markets remain in place.

Large inflows of foreign capital can also have adverse side-effects. They increase the upward pressure on the nominal and real exchange rates, thus possibly resulting in a deterioration in the current account. As the inflows of capital, mainly in the form of portfolio investment, have increased in the 1990s coupled with the introduction of the market-based MAR system, the current account became less important than it was in the 1980s in the determination of the won–dollar exchange rate (Kim, 1994; Oum and Cho, 1995). This does not imply, though, that the monetary authorities have since considered the current account less important in their foreign exchange rate policy. Between 1990 and 1993, foreign exchange rate policy was still geared towards maintaining a weak won regardless of whether the overall balance was recording a surplus or deficit. As a result, the South Korean won depreciated even in 1992 and 1993 when a large volume of capital inflows generated an overall account surplus (see Figure 5.5).

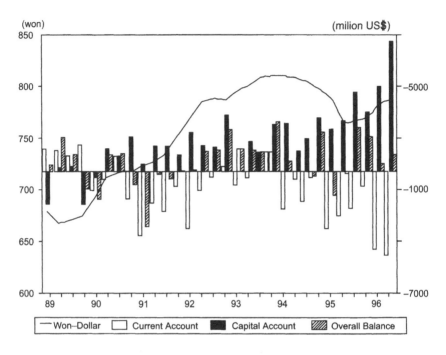

Figure 5.5 Exchange rate and balance of payments in South Korea (first quarter 1989–second quarter 1996)

The overall account recorded deficits in both 1990 and 1991 because of large current account deficits. This was accompanied by a depreciation of the won against the US dollar. Since 1992, the won has been experiencing strong upward pressures as a result of large overall surpluses. Both a large increase in foreign capital inflows and improvement in the current account have contributed to this. Despite the surpluses, the won continued to depreciate until the end of 1993, which suggests that the BOK actively intervened. Its foreign exchange reserves therefore increased by $8.6 billion between 1992 and 1993, while the total overall account recorded a surplus of $11.4 billion during the same two years.

The won reversed itself in 1994, showing a steady appreciation against the US dollar, and it continued rising until July 1995. Between the end of 1993 and the end of July 1995, it appreciated by 6.7 per cent. This appreciation partly reflected the government's confidence on the current account management: the current account showed a large amount of deficit reduction in 1992 and it recorded a small amount of surplus in 1993. It was also closely tied to the marked appreciation of the yen–dollar rate, which had led to a large depreciation in the real effective exchange rate of the won since 1992. Between the last quarter of 1993 and the first quarter of 1995, the real effective exchange rate of the won depreciated by 5.9 per cent, and this was entirely due to the yen's appreciation against the dollar. The large capital inflow and expansion in exports resulted in an overall account surplus of $2.8 billion in 1994 and $3 billion in 1995. Although the surplus was large, the BOK did not consider it necessary to intervene in the foreign exchange market as long as the yen remained strong. The central bank could let the won appreciate to some degree without risking erosion of the price competitiveness of South Korea's exports.

Entering 1996, the current account deficit increased markedly mainly due to the deterioration in the terms of trade, which itself occurred as a result of the rapid decline in the international prices for semiconductors, steel and petrochemical products. They have been major export goods in South Korea, accounting for 17.7 per cent, 8.3 per cent and 4.6 per cent of the total exports in 1995, respectively. The weak yen also contributed to this. Starting in mid-1995, the yen has weakened further against the US dollar, in turn causing the real effective exchange rate of the won to appreciate. During the first half of 1996, the current account deficit amounted to $9.4 billion, exceeding the deficit for all of 1995. Nevertheless, the overall account recorded a small surplus due to large inflows of foreign capital. Even so, the BOK let the won steadily depreciate until late May 1996.

As the deterioration in the current account accelerated and the inflow of foreign capital tended to decrease, a tremendous degree of excess demand for the US dollar arose in the local foreign exchange market, and it has continued. The BOK therefore let the won rapidly depreciate as dictated by market forces throughout June 1996 in an effort to prevent further deterioration in the current account balance. Over the month from 23 May to 22 June 1996 the won depreciated steeply by 3.9 per cent. Such rapid depreciation could cause domestic inflation to accelerate, however, and it indeed has risen unexpectedly fast in 1996.[10] The BOK has since been trying to stem the won's depreciation through intervention by selling dollars.

4   Foreign exchange market intervention

4.1   Mechanics of intervention

As we saw above, the South Korean monetary authorities have actively used exchange rate policy to achieve their objectives. Although it is believed that the BOK can still control the exchange rate, its direct intervention seems to become less effective as the foreign exchange market expands, the exchange rate system becomes more floating, and the financial markets grow more developed and integrated into the world financial market. This section examines how effective the BOK's intervention is under the current MAR system.

Foreign exchange market intervention is defined as an official sale or purchase of foreign assets against domestic assets in the foreign exchange market. In South Korea, the Ministry of Finance and Economy has the authority to intervene in the foreign exchange market as it deems necessary, but it is the BOK which is the executing agency and which undertakes all intervention using the exchange stabilization fund and its own account. The BOK prepares its monthly exchange rate execution plan while taking into account the latest trends in the current account, inflation and monetary policy. After consultations with the Ministry of Finance and Economy, the BOK undertakes exchange rate policy accordingly.

There are two types of foreign exchange market intervention: non-sterilized intervention which affects the money supply, and sterilized intervention which does not. When the central bank decides to intervene to lower the value of the domestic currency, for example, it will sell domestic currency in exchange for foreign currency, and the monetary base will expand as shown in equation 5.7:

$$\Delta NFA = \Delta MB \qquad (5.7)$$

where NFA and MB respectively denote net foreign assets and the monetary base. This sort of intervention operation where a change in the domestic monetary base is involved is called non-sterilized intervention.

The impact of intervention on the domestic money supply can be neutralized by an offsetting transaction in domestic assets which is equal in volume to the transaction in foreign assets. After the above purchase of foreign assets in the foreign exchange market, the central bank may carry out an open market sale of domestic assets in order to reduce its net domestic assets (NDA) and return the monetary base to its original level as in equation 5.8. This second transaction will leave the public with unchanged holdings of monetary assets but a larger stock of domestic assets. When foreign exchange market intervention is combined in this way with an open market operation, it is called sterilized intervention.

$$\Delta NFA + \Delta NDA = \Delta MB = 0 \qquad (5.8)$$

Most central banks use sterilized intervention to neutralize the expansionary effects on the money supply. There are several ways to undertake sterilized intervention operations. According to the first of these, the central bank can neutralize the impact through transaction of domestic assets in the open market as discussed above. Another way is to offset the increase in foreign assets through sales of domestic currency-denominated securities. This operation increases both the central bank's foreign assets and domestic liabilities, without affecting the monetary base. The third way is similar to the second except for the fact that it requires foreign rather than domestic currency-denominated securities.

The BOK has used the second means of sterilization. That is, it has depended on sales of monetary stabilization bonds (MSBs) for sterilization. After capital market opening, foreign exchange market intervention had been necessary to offset the upward pressure on the won due to the large inflows of foreign capital during the 1990s, and it caused the holdings of foreign assets by the central bank to increase, thereby increasing the money supply. To offset this increase, the monetary authorities required financial institutions to purchase MSBs. As a result, the balance of MSBs outstanding on average amounted to 101 per cent of the volume of monetary base during 1990–5.

4.2 Trends in intervention and sterilization

4.2.1 Intervention

To investigate the intervention operations of the BOK, we need daily intervention data to be made available to the public. These data are unfortunately not accessible, but there are two proxy variables which are available on a daily basis: the change in the BOK's foreign reserves and the change in its foreign exchange position.[11] It should be noted, though, that the foreign exchange reserve data may change simply due to transactions between the BOK and the depositary banks, which is captured in the monthly item of 'due from domestic banks in foreign currency' on the BOK's balance sheet. Since these transactions obviously do not pertain to foreign exchange market intervention, we cannot use these data. We therefore used the change in position of the central bank as the proxy for intervention. An increase in position implies that the BOK has purchased US dollars to devalue the Korean won.

Figure 5.6. shows the daily intervention as measured by the change in the BOK's net exchange position under the MAR system between 1990 and 1994.[12] Intervention was sporadic and the volumes of currency involved varied greatly. One notable episode of intervention is the period from the end of 1990 to the first half of 1991. Since the transition to the MAR system, the exchange rate had risen too fast, so beginning in late 1990, the central bank sold US dollars to prevent further rises. Another period of notable intervention is that since late 1992. Capital market opening attracted huge inflows of foreign capital and put tremendous appreciatory pressure on the South Korean won even though the current account continued to record deficits. The central bank therefore continued to maintain its US dollar purchasing position to accommodate the capital inflows, so the volume of foreign assets steadily increased. As a result, the BOK was a net purchaser of US dollars over the period of 1990 to 1994.

The BOK's intervention activities have also been on an enormous scale compared to those of other countries' central banks. For example, between 1982 and 1991, the largest intervention operation ever carried out by the Federal Reserve Bank in the USA in one day was $1.25 billion, and this accounted for less than 1 per cent of that day's trading in the foreign exchange market (Dominguez and Frankel, 1993). In Korea, the largest intervention operation occurred on 28 December 1993: the BOK purchased $1.883 billion, which itself was an enormous transaction, but what was more striking was

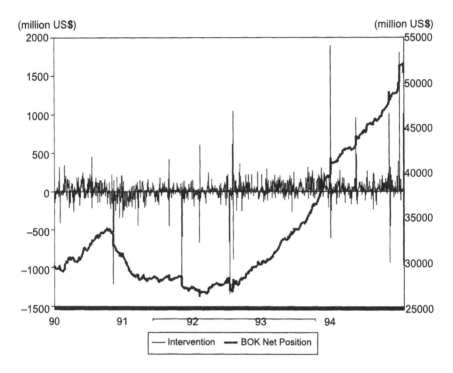

Figure 5.6 Daily intervention in the foreign exchange market by the Bank of Korea (2 March 1990–30 December 1994)

Table 5.7 Summary statistics of daily intervention (US$ million) (sample period: 2 March 1990–30 December 1994)

Mean	Variance	Skewness	Kurtosis	Minimum	Maximum	Number of observations
71.8	18 987.9	1.661	51.495	−1 338	1 883	1 233
				(10 August 1992)	(28 December 1993)	

that this accounted for more than 50 per cent of the won–dollar trading volume that day (see Table 5.7). Even when the BOK's interventions have not been so substantial, it has still accounted for large shares of total trading. The BOK is in fact known as the 'big brother' in the local foreign exchange market.

4.2.2 Sterilization

As the BOK's intervention activities change the monetary base, the BOK sterilizes its foreign exchange market operations through the issuance of

MSBs. Since the change in the monetary base is the sum of the change in net foreign assets and the change in net domestic assets, the extent of the BOK's sterilization can be estimated through the following reaction function of net domestic assets to increases in foreign assets.

$$\Delta NDA_t = \sum_{j=0}^{m} \gamma_j \Delta NFA_{t-j} + \sum_{j=1}^{n} \alpha_j \Delta NDA_{t-j} + u_t \qquad (5.9)$$

The extent of sterilization in the long run is indicated by the long-run sterilization coefficient:

$$\beta = \frac{\sum_{j=0}^{m} \gamma_j}{1 - \sum_{j=1}^{n} \alpha_j} \qquad (5.10)$$

$\beta = -1$ implies that intervention is fully sterilized, and $\beta = 0$ indicates that intervention is not sterilized at all. If β lies between -1 and 0, the intervention is partially sterilized. We have estimated β and present the results in Table 5.8.

Table 5.8 Degree of sterilization

Period	Long-run sterilization coefficient
March 1980–December 1994	−0.84
March 1990–December 1994	−0.85

It shows that the BOK sterilized 85 per cent of foreign exchange market operations between March 1990 and December 1994, which suggests that it may fully sterilize intervention in the short run, but not in the long run.[13] It would also seem to indicate that there is some expansionary pressure on the monetary base in the long run. The BOK purchases US dollars and issues MSBs to sterilize the effect of its intervention on the money supply. This practice may fully sterilize the intervention operation at the moment, but the bonds outstanding must be redeemed eventually, thus increasing the monetary base in the long run. Also, the interest payment to the bonds outstanding is burdensome and adds the expansionary pressure on the monetary base.

4.3   *Effectiveness of intervention*

4.3.1   *Model*

Those who assert that the sterilized intervention is effective emphasize two channels: the portfolio channel and the signalling channel channel.[14] In portfolio-balance models, investors diversify their holdings between domestic and foreign assets based on both expected returns and risk. As long as foreign and domestic assets are imperfect substitutes for each other in the investors' portfolios, an intervention that changes the relative outstanding supply of domestic assets will require a change in expected relative returns, which manifests itself as a change in the exchange rate.

Second, intervention operations affect the exchange rate through the signalling channel when they are used by the central bank as a means of conveying inside information about future policies. If market participants consider the central bank intervention signals to be credible, then interventions will change expectations of future fundamentals even though the interventions do not change today's fundamentals. When the market revises its expectations of future fundamentals, it also revises its expectations concerning the future spot exchange rate, which brings about a change in the current rate. As a variant of signalling channel, Huang (1995) introduces, there is the noise-trader channel. Since the exchange rate is determined by the marginal supply and demand in the short run, the central bank can conceivably manipulate the exchange rate by entering the market when it is relatively thin and uncertain. Once the exchange rate is moved by discreet intervention under such market conditions, noise traders may see this change in the exchange rate as an incipient signal of future movement in the same direction and jump into the market to help move the exchange rate further in the desired direction.

Although there is no universally used model by which we can examine the effectiveness of intervention, the literature on the effectiveness of intervention adopts the general view that the exchange rate is determined in the assets market. Following the literature, we use a simple ARCH (autoregressive conditional heteroschedasticity) model (5.11–5.12) to examine the effectiveness of the BOK's interventions.

$$\Delta S_t = c_0 + \alpha_1 I_t + \alpha_2(i_{t-1} - i^*_{t-1}) + \alpha_3 \Delta S_{t-1} + \\ \alpha_4 \Delta S_{t-2} + \alpha_5 \Delta S_{t-3} + u_t$$

with $U_t / \Omega_{t-1} \sim N(0, h_t)$ \hfill (5.11)

$$h_t = c_1 + \beta_1 u^2_{t-1}$$ \hfill (5.12)

In the mean equation (5.11), I_t is the amount of intervention, and $(i_{t-1} - i^*_{t-1})$ is the spread between domestic and foreign interest rates. The lagged terms are included to take into account the influence of other factors not shown in the model. If intervention is effective towards devaluing the exchange rate, the coefficient on the intervention in the mean equation, α_1, is expected to be significantly positive. The conditional variance equation (5.12) is introduced to take into account the ARCH effect.

When we examine the effectiveness of intervention, it is necessary to consider the motives of intervention simultaneously because intervention and exchange rates affect each other. The central bank is believed to intervene in the foreign exchange market to calm disorderly markets, to target the exchange rate, to achieve a macroeconomic policy objective, or to adjust a foreign exchange position as we mentioned in the previous section. Many studies attempt to assess the importance of competing motives by estimating the intervention reaction function of the central bank. We specify the model for intervention as follows:

$$I_t = c_2 + r_1 \Delta S_t + r_2(S_t - S_t^T) + r_3 I_{t-1} + r_4 I_{t-2} + v_t \qquad (5.13)$$

In the mean equation (5.13), S_t^T is the target exchange rate that may reflect the BOK's concern for international competitiveness of our products. The lagged intervention variables are included to serve as a proxy for other unobservable factors that influence intervention decisions. A significant negative coefficient on the log-difference of the won–dollar exchange rate (ΔS_t) indicates that the central bank leans against the wind. A significant negative coefficient on the deviation from the target exchange rate ($S_t - S_t^T$) indicates that the central bank targets the exchange rate.

The model specified for testing the effectiveness of intervention and the intervention reaction is a bi-variate ARCH which consists of equations 5.11–5.13. It can be estimated using the ML (maximum likelihood) procedure. Since the ML estimation, however, has shown unstable results, we have used an alternative method. In the first stage, we have estimated the mean equations using the three-stage least square method and estimated the conditional variance equations in the next stage using the residuals obtained from the estimation of mean equations.[15] We used daily deviations from monthly average data in the estimation to capture the possible short-run effects. The yield on three-year corporate bonds and the ninety-day Eurodollar LIBOR were used for the domestic and foreign interest rates, respectively. For the target exchange rate, we define it as the won–dollar exchange rate at which the real effective exchange rate of the won is constant because the BOK has never officially announced a target exchange rate.[16]

4.3.2   Empirical results

Table 5.9 shows the regression estimates from the model described by equations 5.11–5.13. The estimate of the reaction function suggests that, over the period of 1990 to 1994, the BOK had leaned against the wind (see (I) in Table 5.9). Contracy to expectation, there is little evidence that the BOK intervened when the won–dollar exchange rate wandered from the target rate. We suspect that it is because the targeting is reflected in the monthly change rather than the daily deviation from the monthly average. The lagged term also has a

Table 5.9 Intervention effectiveness and reaction (sample period: 2 March 1990–30 December 1994)

	(I)	*(II)*	*(III)*
		Effectiveness function	
c_0	$0.749 \times 10^{-6}(0.059)$	$0.134 \times 10^{-5}(0.089)$	$-0.171 \times 10^{-5}(-0.075)$
I_t	$0.067\ (2.094)^*$	$0.045\ (1.569)$	$0.091\ (1.914)$
$i_{t-1}-i^*_{t-1}$	$-0.431 \times 10^{-3}(-3.078)^{**}$	$-0.346 \times 10^{-3}(-2.720)^{**}$	$-0.216 \times 10^{-3}(-1.519)$
ΔS_{t-1}	$0.276\ (8.265)^{**}$	$0.195\ (4.672)^{**}$	$0.288\ (5.876)^{**}$
ΔS_{t-2}	$-0.255(-8.115)^{**}$	$-0.254(-6.550)^{**}$	$-0.251(-5.203)^{**}$
ΔS_{t-3}	$-0.049(1.533)$	$-0.044(1.073)$	$-0.058(1.207)$
c_1	$0.163 \times 10^{-6}(12.859)^{**}$	$0.154 \times 10^{-6}(12.376)^{**}$	$0.244 \times 10^{-6}(8.468)^{**}$
u^2_{t-1}	$0.182\ (6.375)^{**}$	$0.103\ (2.268)^{**}$	$0.119\ (2.653)^{**}$
		Reaction function	
c_2	$0.263 \times 10^{-5}(0.042)$	$0.247 \times 10^{-4}(0.163)$	$-0.104 \times 10^{-4}(0.111)$
ΔS_t	$-0.635(-2.034)^*$	$-0.883(-1.974)^*$	$-0.137(-0.302)$
$S_t - S^T_t$	$-0.156 \times 10^{-3}(-0.145)$	$-0.495 \times 10^{-3}(-0.222)$	$-0.386 \times 10^{-4}(-0.015)$
I_{t-1}	$-0.208(-6.386)^{**}$	$-0.257(-6.388)^{**}$	$-0.210(-3.989)^{**}$
I_{t-2}	$-0.037(-0.263)$	$-0.073(-1.946)$	$-0.067(-1.621)$

Notes
(I): whole period; (II): post-capital market opening period; (III): period of credible monetary policy. The figures in parentheses indicate t-values.
* Significant at 5 per cent level.
** Significant at 1 per cent level.

significant coefficient, which implies that the BOK was more likely to intervene if it had intervened in the previous day.

Such intervention has at least short-lived effects on the exchange rate. The coefficient on intervention has a significant positive sign. This indicates that, when the BOK purchases US dollars to devalue the domestic currency, the won depreciates against the US dollar. However, the effect quickly disappears: the impulse response function of Figure 5.7 shows that the effect lasts for only about one week. The short-lived effect of BOK's intervention can be confirmed by Rhee's (1997) study which used monthly data. We suspect that this outcome may be a reflection of monetary policy in South Korea. If intervention is to be effective, macroeconomic policies should be supported. In South Korea, however, the primary objective of the BOK has been to keep the annual M2 growth rate within the targeted range. The BOK intervention through the purchase of US dollars in the foreign exchange market may indeed be effective, causing the exchange rate to rise for a while. As we saw on p. 93, however, the intervention is not fully sterilized, so it ultimately gives rise to some pressure for the monetary base to expand. Market participants know that M2 targeting is the primary objective, and they expect that, unlike the signalling theory, a contractionary rather than expansionary monetary policy will follow the intervention in the future to remove the pressure on the monetary base. This perception of future contractionary policy would cancel out the effect of intervention and may actually result in an outcome which is contrary to the BOK's intentions to depreciate the won.

We also made estimations over the period of capital market opening and the period of credible monetary policy and report the results in (II) and (III) of Table 5.9, respectively. We considered the capital market opening period after 1992 in order to investigate whether foreign capital flows reduce the effectiveness of intervention. As was mentioned earlier, non-residents were first allowed to invest directly in the South Korean stock market in January 1992. The period of credible monetary policy was considered to investigate how the public's perception of the central bank's commitment to its stated objective influences the effectiveness of intervention. We identify the credible monetary policy period as the period when the BOK's credibility, which is defined as the mean of money supply growth rates divided by the standard deviation of money supply growth rates, is high. During the period 1990 to 1994, the BOK's credibility was high in 1991 and 1992 when it successfully achieved its announced M2 growth rate (see Table 5.10).

After the capital market was first opened, the BOK continued to intervene in the foreign exchange market, leaning against the wind, but it did not seem to consider the deviation from the target exchange rate to be of serious concern. The effectiveness of intervention does seem to have been somewhat compromised after the capital market was opened, even in the short run. We suspect that, as the won–dollar exchange market expanded and the volume of trading for financial purposes grew, it became increasingly difficult to affect market participants' behaviour through intervention. In the sub-period of credible monetary policy, the coefficient on the exchange rate change in the reaction function is not significantly negative. This indicates that the BOK was not seriously leaning against the wind but considered other factors which are reflected in the lagged intervention term. Intervention does not have a statistically significant effect on the exchange rate, and the impulse response of

Table 5.10 Bank of Korea's credibility

	Mean (A)	Standard deviation (B)	Credibility (A/B)
March 1990–December 1990	20.96	1.93	10.86
January 1991–December 1992	18.51	0.65	28.48
January 1993–December 1994	17.10	2.05	8.33

Source: Lee (1996).

Note
Mean and standard deviation are for M2 growth rates.

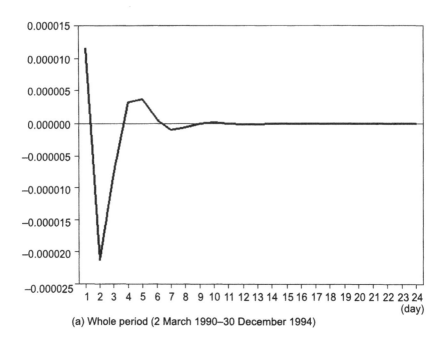

(a) Whole period (2 March 1990–30 December 1994)

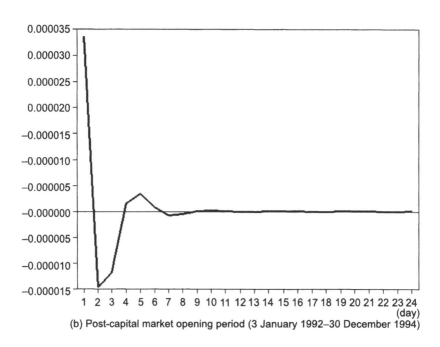

(b) Post-capital market opening period (3 January 1992–30 December 1994)

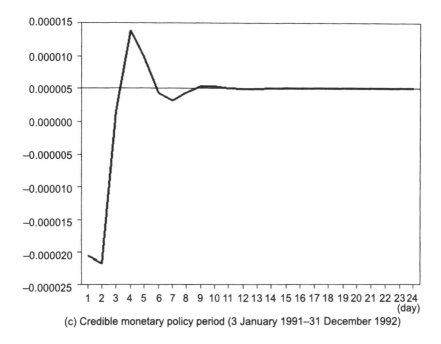

(c) Credible monetary policy period (3 January 1991–31 December 1992)

Figure 5.7 Responses of exchange rate to intervention

exchange rate to a shock of intervention which is also shown in Figure 5.7, is negative in the beginning. This may suggest that, when the central bank strongly commits to the M2 growth rate target, the perception of market participants for future policy may be reversed and intervention is more likely to result in an outcome which the BOK did not intend.

5 Concluding remarks

In this chapter, we have explained two exchange rate regimes which had been used in South Korea: the MCBP system in the 1980s and the MAR system in the 1990s, and we have examined the behaviour of the South Korean won exchange rate against the US dollar. We also examined the objectives of foreign exchange rate policy and how the South Korean monetary authorities have implemented its policies in response to the changes in the economic variables such as current account and capital flows. In addition, we empirically investigated the effectiveness of the BOK's intervention in the foreign exchange market.

It was found that the shift in the exchange rate regime from the MCBP system to the MAR system did not affect the volatility of the won–dollar exchange rate but that the foreign exchange market's efficiency has improved. We have argued in this chapter that the main objective of foreign exchange

99

rate policy in South Korea has been to stabilize the current account balance through the stabilization of the won's real effective exchange rate. It seems that the monetary authorities have been more or less successful towards this end. However, as massive volumes of foreign capital have flowed into the South Korean economy since 1990, the monetary authorities have experienced much more difficulty in achieving the objectives of exchange rate policy. In the face of this problem, they have maintained consistent macroeconomic policies including foreign exchange rate policy and have been able to maintain macroeconomic stability.

We also showed that the movements in the value of the Japanese yen vis-à-vis other currencies – especially the US dollar – have greatly influenced foreign exchange rate policy in South Korea. During the period of the yen appreciation, the country's monetary authorities had greater flexibility in implementing foreign exchange rate policy, while they focused mainly on the current account balance during the period of yen depreciation. We also found that the changes in the yen–dollar rate have significantly affected the volatility of the won–dollar exchange rate during the 1990s.

The investigation into the effectiveness of intervention indicates that the BOK has actively intervened in the foreign exchange market, leaning against the wind, and that it does have the capability to influence the exchange rate to move in the desired direction, though only for a short period of time. Since the BOK is known to be primarily concerned with M2 growth targeting, market participants expect that future monetary policy will not be consistent with the current intervention policy, and the effect of intervention quickly disappears. The empirical results also indicate that as the capital market is being more widely opened and the central bank firmly targets M2 growth rates, intervention is becoming increasingly less effective.

In South Korea, the policy makers have believed exchange rate policy to be effective towards improving the current account balance and have mainly used it for that purpose. However, as the foreign exchange market is becoming more integrated into the financial markets, exchange rate policy increasingly has ramifications for other economic factors in addition to the current account balance. Whereas it was not necessary before, the central bank must now take a comprehensive view, considering other objectives as well as the current account balance when it undertakes exchange rate policy. When exchange rate adjustment is required for a particular objective, corrective macroeconomic policies should be implemented in addition. If, however, exchange rate policy is subject to macroeconomic policies that are inconsistent, it will be likely to fail and result in an unsuccessful outcome, as we have seen in many developing countries.

Moreover, exchange rate policy cannot be easily implemented independent of other policies, particularly as the economy becomes increasingly interdependent with other economies and the economic structure becomes more complex. We suggest that it would be desirable to let the exchange rate move more freely as dictated by the foreign exchange market. The fact that the Korean government plans to widen the band further on daily fluctuations in the exchange rate in the near future and ultimately to adopt a free-floating exchange rate system is therefore welcome news. What is also necessary, though, is to allow some commercial brokerage firms to engage in foreign exchange transactions and to relax the restrictions on net foreign exchange position in order to encourage the development of the foreign exchange market.

As the foreign exchange market expands through capital market opening and financial liberalization, it will become more difficult for the BOK to control and stabilize exchange rates. In order for its intervention to be successful, it must be able to affect market participants' expectations and change their behaviour. The study therefore suggests that: first, intervention must be accompanied by corrective macroeconomic policies, as mentioned above; second, intervention would be more effective if made publicly known because, when it is announced, policy makers can more easily make the speculators work for them rather than against them; and third, the BOK must also be familiar with the reactions of market participants and be capable of taking timely action.

Notes

1   Since the foreign exchange concentration system was strictly enforced at that time, residents could not hold foreign currency. Instead, they could hold foreign exchange certificates issued by the BOK and trade them in the interbank market. This system was abolished in March 1980 when the exchange rate system was shifted to the MCBP System.

2   The band was first widened to ± 0.6 per cent in September 1991, and then to ± 1.0 per cent in October 1993, to ± 1.5 per cent in November 1994, and finally to ± 2.25 per cent in December 1995. The government widened the band only by a small increment each time in order to avoid a large increase in exchange rate volatility.

3   The theoretical and empirical issues pertaining to estimating the volatility of financial variables using the GARCH model are thoroughly surveyed in Bollerslev *et al.* (1992).

4   South Korea's export-oriented economic development is reflected in the high degree of economic openness ((exports + imports)/GDP) which was recorded at 59.8 per cent on average in the 1980s.

5   This explains why the real effective exchange rate started to depreciate in 1989 after the period of appreciation which was noted earlier.

6   Our findings are supported by Takagi (1996). He selected twelve episodes of yen appreciation or depreciation against the US dollar between 1982 and 1995, and examined the relationship between the monthly yen–dollar rate and the monthly exchange rate of six Asian countries' currencies against the US dollar including the won–dollar rate. He found that the won showed a depreciation against the US dollar three out of four occasions when the yen depreciated, whereas the won either depreciated or appreciated during the period of yen appreciation.

7 In fact, South Korea witnessed a net capital outflow in the second half of the 1980s mainly due to repayment of many of its foreign loans as helped by the large current account surplus.

8 The data of capital flows were obtained from the Bank of Korea (*Balance of Payment*, various issues).

9 For example, domestic firms have been permitted to issue overseas securities on the condition that the proceeds are used to finance capital goods imports.

10 Between December 1995 and October 1996, the inflation rate as measured by the consumer price index was recorded at 4.4 per cent, while it was 4.5 per cent for all 1995.

11 The foreign exchange position of the BOK is the net foreign assets in the balance sheet of the central bank. This includes the 'due from domestic banks in foreign currency' which is classified as a domestic asset in the accounts of the BOK.

12 The period covered is from March 1990 to December 1994 since we could obtain the daily position data only up to 1994.

13 $m = 3$ and $n = 2$ were used in the estimation.

14 See Edison (1993) for a thorough survey on the intervention literature and an explanation on the channels.

15 Compared to the ML estimation, this procedure incurs only a slight loss of efficiency. We thank Joon-Yong Park for this comment.

16 The target rates refer to monthly rates. January 1985 was used as a base period since the current account was very close to an equilibrium in 1985. For the detailed procedure to derive the target exchange rate applied in this chapter, see Kim (1995).

References

Bank for International Settlements (1996) *Central Bank Survey of Foreign Exchange and Derivatives Market Activity 1995*, May.

Bank of Korea, *Balance of Payment*, various issues.

—— *Monthly Bulletin*, various issues.

—— (1996) 'Trends in the Foreign Exchange Market in Korea', July (in Korean).

Bollerslev, Tim, Chou, Ray Y. and Kroner, Kenneth F. (1992) 'ARCH Modeling in Finance: Review of the Theory and Empirical Evidence', *Journal of Finance*, Vol. 52, pp. 5–59.

Branson, William H. and Katseli-Papaefstratiou, Louka T. (1981) 'Exchange Rate Policy in Developing Countries', in S. Grossman and E. Lunberg (eds) *The World Economic Order: Past and Prospects*, London, Macmillan.

Dickey, David A. and Fuller, Wayne A. (1979) 'Distribution of the Estimators for Autoregressive Time Series with a Unit Root', *Journal of the American Statistical Association*, Vol. 74, pp. 427–31.

Dominguez, Kathryn and Frankel, Jeffrey (1993) *Does Foreign Exchange Intervention Work?*, Washington, DC, Institute for International Economics.

Dornbusch, Rüdiger and Park, Yung Chul (1995) 'Financial Integration in a Second Best World: Are We Still Sure about Our Classical Prejudice?', in Rüdiger Dornbusch and Yung Chul Park (eds) *Financial Opening: Policy Lessons for Korea*, Seoul, Korea Institute of Finance and International Center for Economic Growth, pp. 112–53.

Edison, Hali J. (1993) *The Effectiveness of Central-Bank Intervention: A Survey of the Literature after 1982*, Special Papers in International Economics, No. 18, Princeton, NJ, Princeton University Press.

Huang, Juann H. (1995) *Intervention Strategies and Exchange Rate Volatility: A Noise Trading Perspective*, Research Paper, No. 9515, New York, Federal Reserve Bank of New York.

International Monetary Fund (1995) *International Capital Market: Developments, Prospects and Policy Issues, Washington, DC.*

——(1996) *International Financial Statistics*, Washington, DC, September.

Kim, E. Han and Singal, Vijay (1994) *Opening up of Stock Markets: Lessons from and for Emerging Economies*, Policy Research Series 94–06, Seoul, Korea Institute of Finance.

Kim, In-Chul (1985) *Foreign Exchange System in Developing Countries and Foreign Exchange Rate Policy in Korea*, Policy Research Series 85–04, Seoul, Korea Development Institute (in Korean).

Kim, In-Jun (1995) Cointegration Testing of Multi-Country Purchasing Power Parity: The Case of Korea, *Seoul Journal of Economics*, Vol. 8, No. 4, pp. 425–41.

Kim, Jin Chun (1992) *Korea's Recent Foreign Exchange Rate System: MCBP vs. MAR System*, Seoul, Korea Institute for International Economic Policy.

Kim, Joon-Kyung (1994) 'The Effects of the Stock Market Opening on the Value of the Won', *Korea Development Review*, Fall, pp. 69–96 (in Korean).

Korea Institute of Finance (1994) 'A Study on Foreign Exchange System Reform', Seoul (in Korean).

Kwack, Sung Y. and Kim, Seung Jin (1990) Determinants of the Won-Dollar Exchange Rate Under the Managed Floating Period, *Research on the Korean Economy*, No. 2, pp. 85–93.

Kwack, Tae Woon (1989) *Future Direction of the Korean Foreign Exchange System*, Research Paper Series, 89–05, Korea Economic Research Institute (in Korean).

Lee, Seungho (1996) *The Effects of Central Bank Intervention in Korea: By Exchange Rate System and Monetary Credibility*, Ph.D. Dissertation, American University.

Lo, Andrew and MacKinlay, A. Craig (1988) 'Stock Market Prices Do Not Follow Random Walks: Evidence from a Simple Specification Test', *Review of Financial Studies*, Vol. 1, pp. 41–66.

MacKinnon, James (1991) 'Critical Values for Cointegration Tests', in R.F. Engle and C.W.J. Granger (eds) *Long-Run Economic Relationships*, Oxford, Oxford University Press, pp. 267–76.

Oum, Bongsung (1989) *Evaluation of Foreign Exchange Rate Policy and Composition of the Currency Basket*, Policy Research Series 89–09, Seoul, Korea Development Institute (in Korean).

Oum, Bongsung and Cho, Dongchul (1995) 'Korea's Exchange Rate Movement in the 1990s: Evaluation and Policy Implications', paper presented at the KDI Symposium on Prospects for the Yen-Dollar Exchange Rates and Korea's Exchange Rate Policy, Korea Development Institute, Seoul, 12 December 1995.

Rhee, Yeongseop (1997) 'The Effects of Foreign Exchange Market Intervention in Korea: A Dynamic Analysis', *Korean Journal of Money and Finance*, Vol. 2, No. 1, pp. 35–60 (in Korean).

Takagi, Shinji (1996) *The Yen and its East Asian Neighbors, 1980–95: Cooperation or Competition?*, NBER Working Paper, 5720, Cambridge, Mass.

US Department of Treasury (1989) *Report to the Congress on International Economic and Exchange Rate Policy*, Washington, DC.

Wickham, Peter (1985) 'The Choice of Exchange Rate Regime in Developing Countries: A Survey of the Literature', *International Monetary Fund Staff Papers*, Vol. 32, pp. 248–88.

6

DISCUSSION

Agnès Bénassy-Quéré

Chapter 5 by Y. Rhee and C.-Y. Song presented a very rich analysis of the exchange rate policy in South Korea since 1980. But it is much more than a case study since it raises some general questions about the choice of a policy target and the effectiveness of official interventions in a country with a current account deficit and a global account surplus.

The chapter is divided into three sections. The first section describes the exchange rate regimes in South Korea and the evolution of the won since 1980. The second analyses the implicit exchange rate policy of the Bank of Korea during that period. The last section is concerned with the effectiveness of foreign exchange interventions.

The main findings of the chapter are the following:

1   The shift, in 1990, from a basket peg towards a more flexible regime did not basically modify the evolution of the won and the behaviour of the monetary authorities.
2   The aim of the foreign exchange rate policy has been to stabilize the current account. But this target was more important in periods when the yen depreciated against the US dollar than in periods when the yen appreciated.
3   Throughout the period, the Bank of Korea actively leaned against the wind on the foreign exchange market. Although interventions were not fully sterilized, they had only a short-run impact. The effectiveness of interventions declined after 1992 with the deregulation of the foreign exchange market and the subsequent inflow of foreign investments.

The results of the chapter first suggest a general question: how did the monetary authorities manage to stabilize the effective real exchange rate in recent years despite (i) the large inflow of foreign capital which exceeded the current account deficit, and (ii) the ineffectiveness of official interventions, at least in the long run? The authors advocate a global economic policy which would entail consistent exchange rates and monetary and fiscal policies. But the public authorities may have already undertaken such a policy in order to prevent the won from appreciating.

Now I turn to more specific comments.

In the first section, the multiple currency basket peg system, which ended by March 1980, is opposed to the market average exchange rate system, which replaced the basket peg in March 1980. But afterwards, the authors show that this institutional shift modified neither the volatility of the exchange rate nor the intervention policy.

Nevertheless, the random walk hypothesis is rejected under the basket peg regime but accepted under the moving average regime. The authors conclude that the exchange rate became less predictable after the regime shift. Alternatively, it can be said that the central bank did defend a target exchange rate under the former regime, while it did not under the latter regime.

In the next section, however, it is shown that under both regimes, the monetary authorities have followed not a nominal peg, but a real peg. According to the authors, the main target of the exchange rate policy has been to stabilize the current account through the stabilization of price competitiveness. But this does not perfectly fit the data which show a 45 per cent depreciation in the real effective exchange rate between 1981 and 1996 despite the fact that the net foreign asset position was about the same in 1981 and in 1996 (Figure 5.3). In Chapter 5, this apparent contradiction is explained as an asymmetric reaction to yen/dollar fluctuations: during periods when the yen appreciated, the monetary authorities in South Korea had more flexibility to target other macroeconomic variables; conversely, the current account target became more accurate when the yen depreciated. The won followed the yen only in the latter case, leading to a long-run depreciation.

In a recent NBER working paper, Takagi[1] concludes in a similar way. He finds that when the yen depreciated against the US dollar, the won depreciated too, while the reverse is not true: when the yen appreciated against the US dollar, the won either appreciated or depreciated.

In fact, yen fluctuations seem to have had a rather small impact on won fluctuations in any case, as shown in Table 5.5: even when the yen depreciated, a 1 per cent depreciation in the yen against the US dollar led to a depreciation in the won not exceeding 0.1 per cent in the short run as in the long run. The impact of yen/US dollar fluctuations appears more on the *volatility* of the won, but the way the yen varies does not matter.

Alternatively, the evolution of the won since 1980 is consistent with a broad peg to the US dollar, as shown in Figure 5.3, where the won/US dollar exchange rate appears stable in the long run, with middle-term fluctuations not exceeding 20 per cent. Of course, pegging to the US dollar was consistent with promoting exports since the US dollar depreciated against the yen in the long run.

The interesting point, made in Chapter 5, is that in recent years the won should have appreciated, given the surplus of the global account. But the monetary authorities targeted the current account (not the global account), which means that they accumulated external reserves. Figure 5.6 shows that they doubled their net external position between 1992 and 1995. Figures 5.4. and 5.6. together give the impression that foreign exchange interventions succeeded in preventing the won from appreciating. Yet this is not the conclusion of the final section which studies the effectiveness of interventions on the basis of daily data.

Looking at daily data is the best way of studying official intervention since the monthly aggregates are generally low compared to the sum of interventions in both directions during a month. Generally, daily interventions are not public information. Here, daily interventions are proxied by the daily change in the external position of the central bank. Although better than monthly data, this proxy raises the problem of valuation effects. More specifically, official reserves are revalued when the won depreciates, which gives the impression that central bank interventions magnify exchange rate fluctuations, which biases the results towards ineffective interventions.

The idea of the chapter is to estimate two equations jointly:

- an effectiveness function: the variations of the exchange rate as a function of interventions;
- a reaction function: the interventions as a function of the variations in the exchange rate.

The method makes for the simultaneity problem. Its results are in line with the estimates made by Weber[2] on G-3 interventions with a similar method: official interventions have no lasting effect on the exchange rate, although they efficiently stabilize the exchange rate in the short run within the Moving Average System.

Although in line with the existing literature, this result is surprising given that the won market is thinner and more regulated than other markets. In my view, the long-run impact of interventions might be caught by the inclusion of the lagged interest rate differential in the effectiveness function: if interventions are not fully sterilized, a possibility which is assessed in the chapter, the interest rate should fall after the BOK buys some foreign assets. The fall in the interest rate should make the exchange rate depreciate. Hence, although the intervention itself has no lasting effect on the exchange rate directly, it has one indirectly through the interest rate.

This interpretation would reconcile the econometric results with the stylized fact of a depreciating won with a global account surplus over 1990–5. It would also re-establish the rationality of leaning against the wind.

Notes

1 S. Takagi (1996) *The Yen and Its Asian Neighbors, 1980–95: Cooperation or Competition?*, NBER Working Paper 5720, Cambridge, Mass.
2 A. Weber (1995) 'Exchange Rates and the Effectiveness of Central Bank Intervention: New Evidence for the G-3 and the EMS', in *European Currency Crises and After*, Bordes C., Girardin E. and Meltz J. eds, Manchester University Press, Manchester.

7

FOREIGN EXCHANGE RATE FLUCTUATIONS AND MACROECONOMIC MANAGEMENT

The Case of Taiwan

Ray B. Dawn and Gang Shyy

1 Introduction

The volatilities of foreign exchange rates in international markets have increased noticeably since the breakdown of the Bretton Woods system in 1973. The Bretton Woods system emerged after the Second World War as an attempt to establish a monetary system that offered a high degree of foreign exchange rate stability without the perceived disadvantage of gold standard. Over time, however, structural weakness ultimately assured its demise. In short, governments tended to resist needed exchange rate adjustments and the dollar's position as the key international reserve currency was undermined. Moreover, speculative attacks on major currencies became more frequent. The Bretton Woods system of fixed exchange rates finally passed into history in 1973 when the Smithsonian Agreement of 1971 proved insufficient to repair its flaws.

The escalation in the volatility of foreign exchange rates may largely result from several causes. To begin with, the collapse of the fixed rate system and its replacement with the floating rate system undoubtedly increased the volatility in foreign exchange markets. In addition, economic integration and the liberalization in current as well as financial accounts contributed to the growing amounts of capital flow across borders and increased the likelihood of currency misalignment and hence speculation. Furthermore, sudden shifts in one country's comparative advantage due to internal or external fundamental factors can distort the delicate balance in foreign exchange markets and consequently initiate a dynamic adjustment process in the search for a new market equilibrium.

Generally speaking, foreign exchange rate fluctuations may create both short- and long-term effects. Short-term effects include, among others, changes in the relative prices among different countries and shifts in interest rate differentials. Long-term effects comprise changes in money supply and the positions of foreign reserves, the resulting swings in competition capability, the direction of foreign direct investment and so on. On the one hand, foreign exchange rate fluctuations can *internally* bring major impacts to an economy on a macro and a micro level. On the other hand, foreign exchange rate fluctuations can *externally* affect several countries simultaneously. Therefore, monetary authorities have been paying close attention to its movements and trying to eliminate the possible ill effects associated with its fluctuations.

As noted earlier, not only does a volatile foreign exchange rate cause concern to individual countries; it also receives due attention from several multilateral organizations such as the International Monetary Fund (IMF), the Asia Pacific Economic Cooperation (APEC), Pacific Economic Cooperation Council (PECC) and many others. The Mexico peso crisis of late 1994 triggered worldwide awareness that countries are vulnerable to foreign exchange rate fluctuations and that international cooperation either in terms of harmonized domestic macroeconomic policies or concerted intervention in international markets are necessary to mitigate the ill effects. As a result, the prevention of excess foreign exchange rate volatility and the cooperation of macroeconomic policies have been major issues of various G-7 meetings and APEC meetings.[1]

This chapter provides a case study of Taiwan's experience with respect to its foreign exchange rate fluctuations and macroeconomic management. The chapter is arranged as follows: Section 2 reviews the evolution of the foreign exchange rate system and the movement of the foreign exchange rate, with special emphasis upon the exchange rate between the New Taiwan dollar (NTD) and the US dollar (USD); Section 3 examines the real effective exchange rate movement of NTD since 1980; Section 4 analyses factors that affect the movement of NTD vis-à-vis USD; Section 5 discusses the consequences of NTD fluctuation; Section 6 focuses on the macroeconomic policies regarding exchange rate fluctuations; Section 7 investigates the intermarket relationship between foreign exchange and interest rates; and Section 8 concludes the chapter.

2 A review of Taiwan's exchange rate regime

Before examining foreign exchange rate fluctuations and macroeconomic management in Taiwan, one needs to know the evolution of its foreign exchange rate system. Similar to other major economies, Taiwan's foreign exchange rate system has been undergoing structural changes for the last four decades. To begin with, a system of *fixed* exchange rates had been adopted prior to 1969. The formal foreign exchange market was established and the *floating* exchange rate system was put to use in January 1979. However, *centre rate* and *daily movement restrictions* were implemented in Taiwan's foreign exchange market between February 1979 and May 1986. The revision of the Statute for the Administration of Foreign Exchange (SAFE) in May 1986 represented a significant step in the financial liberalization of Taiwan.

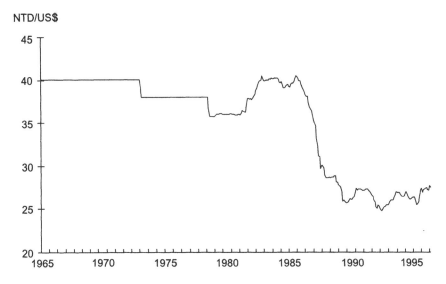

NTD/US$

Figure 7.1 The movement of the exchange rate of NTD vis-à-vis US$

The *dirty* floating system was abolished in April 1989. Since then, a *free* floating system has been employed in Taiwan's foreign exchange market.

Figure 7.1 illustrates the movements of the exchange rate of NTD vis-à-vis USD (NTD/USD hereafter) from 1965 to 1996. Prior to 1979, the exchange rate was practically constant apart from two exceptional instances of appreciation which occurred in February 1973 and July 1978. In contrast, from the early 1980s, the volatility of the exchange rate increased noticeably. A careful investigation into Taiwan's exchange rate regime finds that it has been undergoing several stages of structural change. Four phases are identified: (1) from 1949 to September 1963, a period of multiple exchange rates and heavy foreign exchange controls; (2) from October 1963 to February 1979, a period of fixed exchange rate; (3) from March 1979 to April 1989, a period of managed floating exchange rate; and (4) since May 1989, the period of financial liberalization. The characteristics and movements of NTD/USD in each period are discussed in the remainder of this section.

2.1   The period of multiple rates and heavy controls: 1949–September 1963

Immediately after the end of the Second World War and the Civil War, Taiwan suffered a serious shortage of merchandise and capital. High tariff rates and import quotas were therefore implemented in order to shield the domestic market from international competition. The *import substitution policy* led to a system of multiple exchange rates where export sectors were granted the highest selling rate. In contrast, imports of primary goods and necessities were subject to the lowest buying rate; the import of luxury goods was basically discouraged and hence the highest buying rate was applicable. During this period, as many as ten different exchange rates of NTD/USD were in practical use. Partly because this system severely hindered the price mechanism of the foreign exchange market and partly because the import substitution policy successfully established a number of competitive industries that were ready to march into the world market, the foreign exchange rate system needed to be revised. Therefore, the multiple rate system was first simplified into a twin rate system in 1958; then in September 1963, the single rate regime took over.

Although multiple rates were applicable during this period, exact data on the correspondence between transaction types and exchange rates were unavailable. The average exchange rate of NTD/USD is hence calculated by using the highest selling rate, granted to the export sector. As shown in Figure 7.2, the average exchange rate of NTD/USD was maintained at the level of 40.05:1. Moreover, since all the rates were held constant, the standard deviation is zero.

2.2   The period of the fixed rate: October 1963–February 1979

Prior to the establishment of Taiwan's foreign exchange market in February 1979, the exchange rate was in fact a fixed rate system. Several characteristics are worthy of mention. First, although the Bretton Woods fixed rate system collapsed in 1973, the exchange rate of NTD/USD was held constant from 1963 to 1979. Second, the Central Bank of Taiwan acted as the monopolist and the monoposonist in the foreign exchange market. In other words, all foreign exchange had to be sold to and bought from the central bank. Third, although transactions related to international trade in merchandise were not regulated, short-term capital flow was prohibited. Fourth, due to the implementation of an *export expansion policy*, which had successfully helped the economy to accumulate sizeable foreign reserves, NTD appreciated 5 per cent against USD in February 1973 and 5.26 per cent again in July 1978.

During this period, as shown in Figure 7.2, the average exchange rate of NTD/USD is 39.20:1, a result of NTD's slight appreciation against USD. As the result of two rounds of appreciation in 1973 and 1978, the standard deviation of NTD/USD increased from zero in the last period to 1.18 NTD in this period.

2.3   The period of the managed floating rate: March 1979–April 1989

During this period, the formal foreign exchange market was established and started its daily operation. In addition, deregulation in financial markets took place. For example, in contrast to previous periods where foreign reserve concentration policy was pursued, individuals were allowed to hold foreign currencies. Furthermore, the dominant role played by the central bank in

112

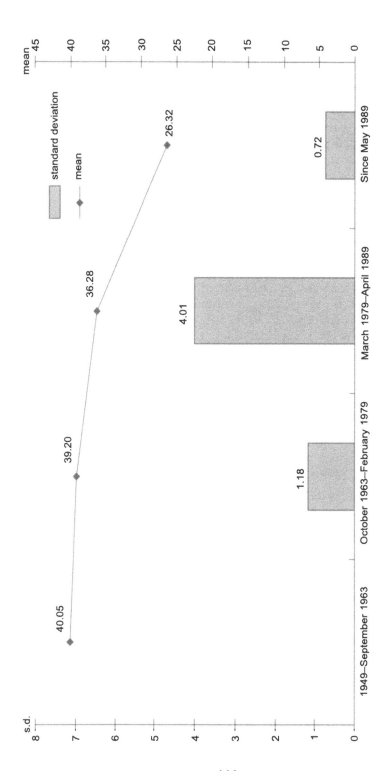

Figure 7.2 The means of standard deviations of NTD/US\$ in four sub-periods

the foreign exchange market was eased. However, a system of *centre rate* in the spot market had been in use from 1982 to 1989. In essence, this system included: the previous date's weighted average of spot rate was used as the centre rate for the very next transaction date; daily spot rate could not deviate from the centre rate beyond the margin of plus or minus 2.25 per cent; the exchange rate was free to float within the 4.5 per cent tunnel; and banks were allowed freely to set the exchange rates among NTD and other non-USD foreign currencies. Moreover, similar to the centre rate in spot market, a *reference rate* in the forward market was implemented in 1984 and 1987.

As Taiwan became more liberalized in both current and capital accounts, the exchange rate was inevitably subject to the volatility of external factors such as the variation in the balance of payments (BOP), the fluctuations in the prices of primary goods in the international market, and the movements of major currencies. During this period, as Figure 7.3. indicates, the movements of NTD/USD can be characterized as follows: (1) from 1979 to 1981, NTD slightly depreciated against USD due to the deterioration in Taiwan's BOP; (2) from 1982 to 1985, like the Japanese yen and German Deutsche Mark, NTD depreciated against USD because of the strong USD in the international market; (3) from 1986 to 1989, NTD went on a long and accelerated pace of appreciation against USD partly due to the weakening of the USD and largely due to the accumulation of huge foreign reserves. As indicated in Figure 7.2, the average exchange rate of NTD/USD is 36.28:1 while the standard deviation increased significantly from 1.18 NTD in the last period to 4.01 NTD in this period.

2.4 The period of financial liberalization: since May 1989

Since the abolition of the centre rate in April 1989, Taiwan's foreign exchange market has been regarded as a free floating market with occasional Central Bank intervention operations. During this period, financial liberalization, internationalization and institutionalization occurred on an accelerated pace that previous periods had never witnessed. For example, in July 1989, domestic interest rate was allowed to be set freely by individual deposit-taking institutions so as to inject more competition into financial markets. In addition, the establishment of sixteen new domestic commercial banks and the market opening to foreign banks in early 1990 together eroded the market share of the government-owned banks that once dominated Taiwan's banking industry. Furthermore, besides traditional deposit-taking and loan-granting business, the revised policy of *universal banking* allowed banks to conduct new types of business such as: billing financing, securities brokerage, underwriting and fund management. Due to a series of financial deregulation measures, the *informal* financial institutions finally legalized their operations and emerged as legitimate business entities.

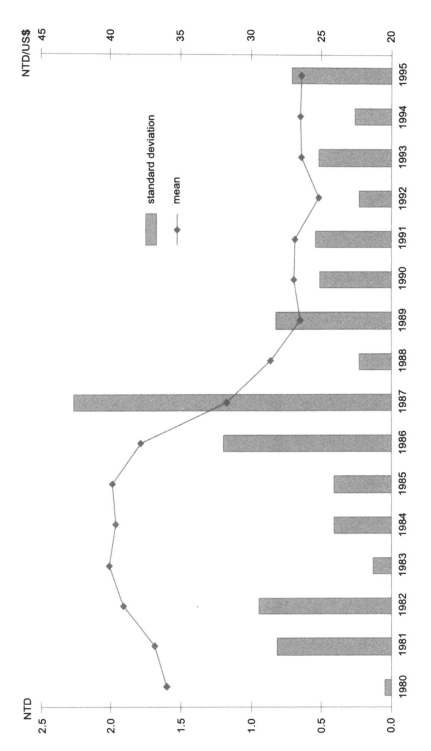

Figure 7.3 The annual means and standard deviations of NTD/US$ from 1980 to 1995

Compared with previous periods, the movement of NTD/USD during this period is unique in two ways. First, the fast pace of appreciation appeared to slow down and the exchange rate swung around 26.32:1. Second, as an indication of relatively stabilized NTD, the standard deviation is 0.72 NTD, significantly smaller than in the previous two periods.

3   The movement of REER index of NTD since 1980

Although nominal foreign exchange rate provides a useful tool in the examination of individual currencies' value, it has at least two flaws that inevitably call for modification. One drawback that nominal rate fails to solve is the net effect of relative price changes in different countries. In other words, purchasing power is not properly taken care of in the calculation of nominal exchange rate. Second, since nominal rate only reveals the relative value between two currencies, it is insufficient in the comparison of several currencies simultaneously. In order to tackle the flaws of nominal exchange rate, real effective exchange rate (REER) was established.

In the calculation of REER index, several major problems need to be solved. First, the composition of the basket of currencies determines the applicability of the index. Ideally, it would be better if the basket includes currencies of all of the countries with which the host country conducts business. This is, however, unrealistic; therefore, only *important* currencies are included in the basket. Second, to compare the changes in the purchasing power of interested currencies, price indices are needed. The consumer price index (CPI), wholesale price index (WPI), GDP deflator and unit labour cost index are possible candidates. Theoretically, the latter two indices may be more suitable than the former two, however, since the latter two are either difficult to obtain or unable to meet the timely demand, CPI and WPI are commonly adopted in the calculation of REER index. Other problems include whether to calculate REER index by using the method of geometric averaging or arithmetic averaging, how to choose the base period, how to decide the relative weights of different currencies in the basket, etc.

In this study, the REER index of NTD is calculated as: REER = EER index / PPP index.

$$\text{EER (effective exchange rate) index} = \prod_{j=1}^{n} \left(\frac{_tE_{ij}}{_oE_{ij}}\right)^{w_{ij}} \tag{7.1}$$

where i = host country; j = country j; n = number of currencies included in the basket; t = time of interest; o = base period; w_{ij} = weights calculated from share of bilateral trade; E_{ij} = nominal exchange rate per one unit of foreign currency.

$$\text{PPP (purchasing power parity) index} = \prod_{j=1}^{n}\left(\frac{{}_tP_j/{}_0P_j}{{}_tP_i/{}_0P_i}\right)^{w_{ij}} \qquad (7.2)$$

where P = consumer price index.

Several points are worth mentioning. First, the basket includes the currencies of Australia, Belgium, Canada, France, Germany, Hong Kong, Indonesia, Italy, Japan, South Korea, Malaysia, the Netherlands, New Zealand, the Philippines, Saudi Arabia, Singapore, Sweden, Switzerland, UK, the USA and Thailand. Second, on aggregate the bilateral trade of Taiwan with these twenty-one economies has accounted for 80–90 per cent of Taiwan's total trade between 1980 and 1996. Third, for comparison with the REER indices of USD, the Japanese yen and German DM, the base year of 1990 and consumer price index are chosen. The REER indices of DM, USD and yen are derived from various issues of the IMF's *International Financial Statistics*, while that of NTD is derived from research conducted by the Taiwan Institute of Economic Research.

As indicated by Figure 7.4, the REER index of NTD reached its peak of nearly 110 in late 1989. However, the REER index of NTD lay below 100 for most of the observation period except 1989–90 and 1991–2. A comparison of Figures 7.3 and 7.5 reveals the movement of REER index is similar to that of nominal exchange rate. According to nominal exchange rate, NTD depreciated in the early 1980s, appreciated in the late 1980s, and then stabilized in the early 1990s. Based on the REER index, NTD began its depreciation in 1981, then went into a process of appreciation starting from 1986 and peaking in 1989, and depreciated thereafter apart from a surge in 1992.

4 Factors that affect the fluctuations of NTD

Because of the importance attached to foreign exchange rates, the fluctuation of foreign exchange rate is one of the most studied economic phenomena in the literature. However, their determination remains unsatisfactorily settled. The forecasters with the most impressive records are frequently wrong by substantial margins. It seems that lack of understanding of exchange rate determination stems from complications caused partly by significant increases in the international mobility of capital due to improvements in telecommunications and partly by recent financial liberalization in the international community. Economic theory long regarded exchange rate determination as being dominated by flows of goods and services, but economists have been forced to revise their way of thinking and recognize that the foreign exchange market often behaves like a volatile stock market.

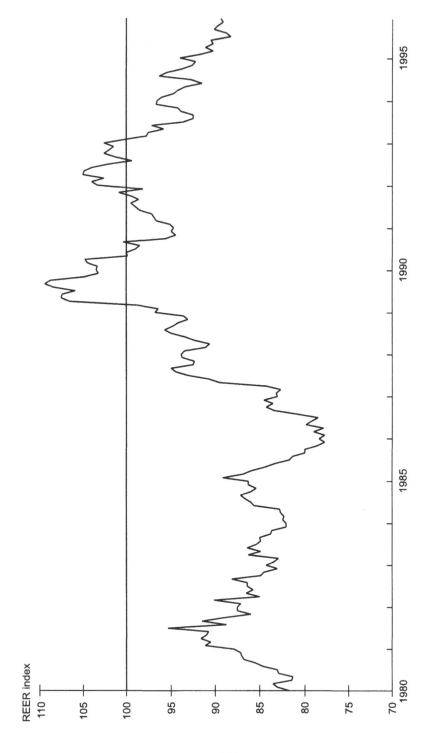

Figure 7.4 The movement of the REER index of NTD since 1980

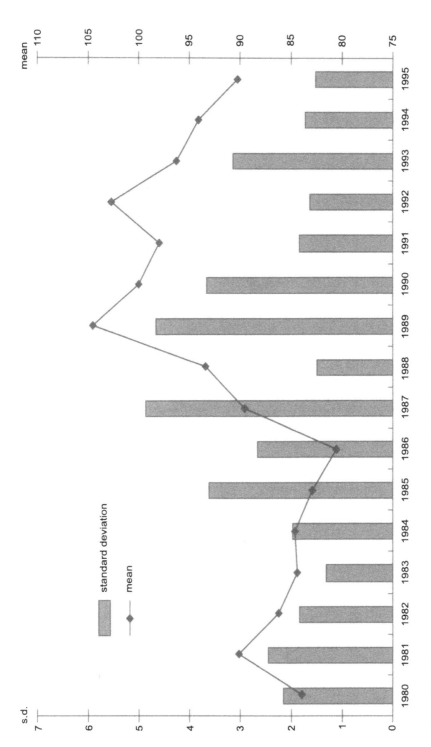

Figure 7.5 The annual means and standard deviations of REER index of NTD

119

Prior to 1970s, the Mundell–Flemming model seemed to dominate the literature. Since this line of thought was inadequate in that the stock-flow implications of interest rate differential changes were not worked out, several models have emerged recently. Taylor (1995) thoroughly surveyed exchange rate determination models that developed after the 1970s and found that they consisted of four major categories: (1) the flexible-price monetary model; (2) the sticky-price monetary model; (3) equilibrium models and liquidity models; and (4) the portfolio balance model. As for the empirical evidence that supported or rejected alternative models, Taylor also found: (1) neither the flexible-price nor the sticky-price monetary model was strongly supported beyond the late 1970s; (2) the very simplest equilibrium model was rejected, but it appeared difficult to draw any firm conclusions concerning the validity of the whole class of equilibrium or liquidity models; (3) inconclusive evidence was presented regarding the portfolio balance model; and (4) unexpected news about the fundamentals did cast significant effects on foreign exchange rate movements.

While there are differences among various theorems of exchange rate determination, there is a common core of analysis that appears in much of the theoretical and empirical work in this subject. This common core is built on four key relationships: (1) PPP, which links spot exchange rates to domestic and international price levels; (2) International Fisher Effect (IFE), which links exchange rates to domestic and international interest rate levels; (3) Interest Rate Parity (IRP), which links spot exchange rates, forward rates and nominal interest rates; and (4) the EER, which links exchange rate expectations to the forward rate. In this study, we implicitly follow the core analysis to identify the factors that affect foreign exchange rate fluctuations and estimate their sensitivity.

Identifying factors that might affect the nominal exchange rate of NTD is equivalent to finding out factors that influence the demand for and the supply of NTD in Taiwan's foreign exchange market.[2] There are several ways to achieve this goal. For example, as suggested in the general guidelines proposed by Professor A. Kohsaka,[3] one can focus on the internal/external factors, the nominal/real variables and the cyclical/structural factors. In this study, we examine money supply variables (M1A, M1B and M2), inflation rate (measured by the growth rates of CPI and WPI), nominal interest rate (the interest rate of 180-day commercial paper), trade surplus, real interest rate differential (measured by the differences between Taiwan and the USA, between Taiwan and Japan and between Taiwan and Germany), the exchange rates between the Japanese yen and USD (yen/USD) and the exchange rate between the German Deutsche Mark and USD (DM/USD).

Figures 7.6 to 7.10 illustrate the movements of the variables mentioned above. In addition, in order to determine which factors are most likely to affect the movements of NTD/USD, a series of correlation coefficients are hence calculated. The correlation coefficients matrix is tabulated in

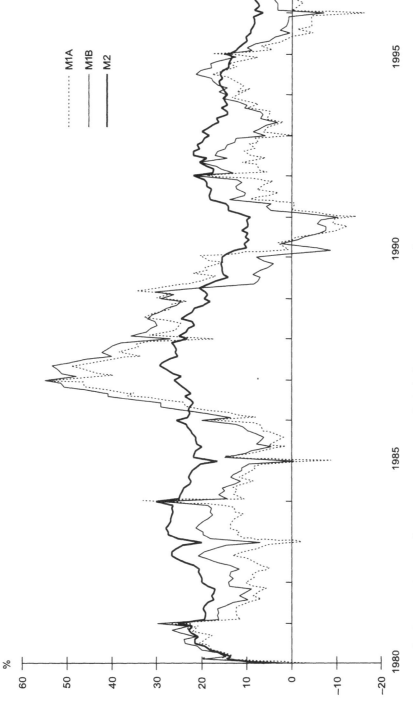

Figure 7.6 The growth rates of monetary aggregates of NTΔ from 1980 to June 1996

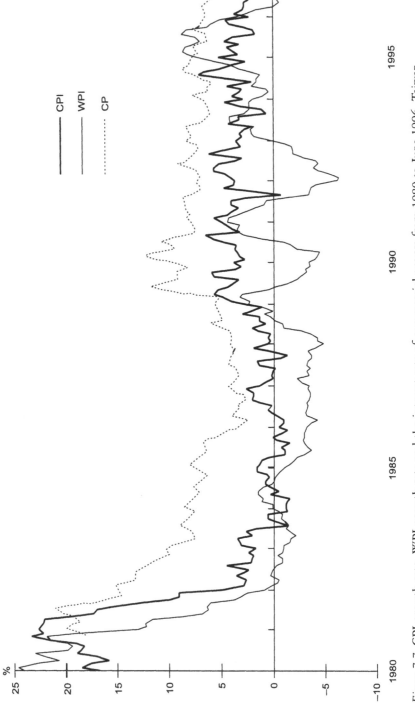

Figure 7.7 CPI growth rate, WPI growth rate and the interest rate of commercial papers from 1980 to June 1996, Taiwan

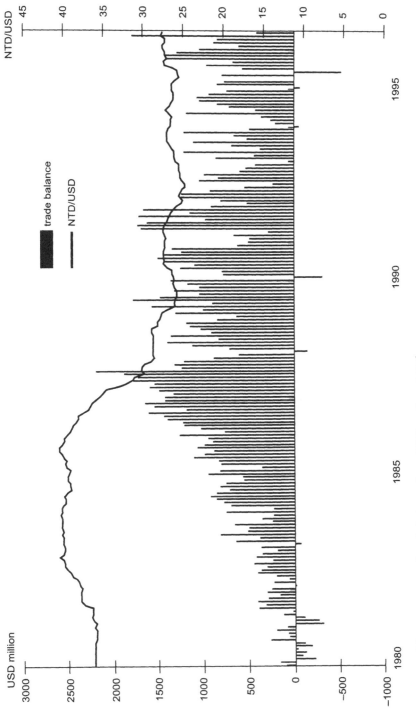

Figure 7.8 The movement of trade balance from 1980 to June 1996

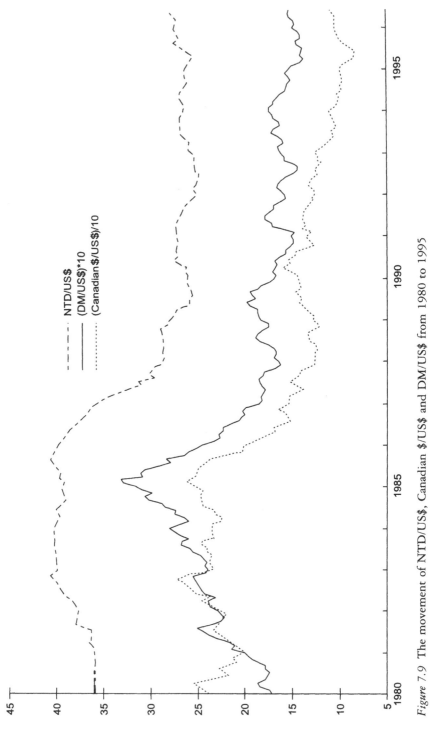

Figure 7.9 The movement of NTD/US$, Canadian $/US$ and DM/US$ from 1980 to 1995

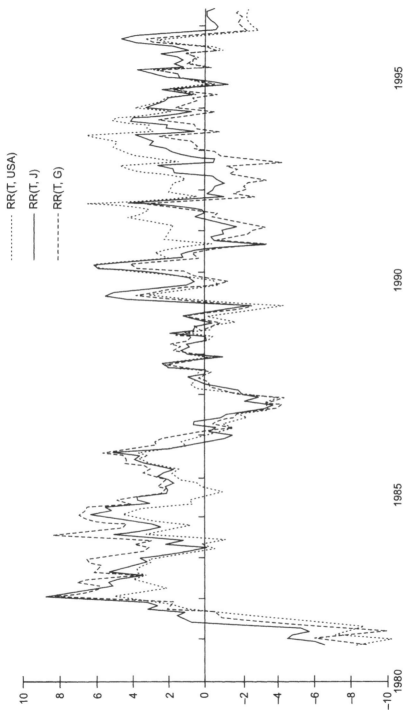

Figure 7.10 The real interest rate differentials from 1981 to June 1996

Table 7.1 The correlation coefficient matrix of the international and external factors that may influence NTD/USD

	NTD/USD	M1A	M1B	M2	CPI	WPI	CP	X-M	RR(T, USA)	RR(T, J)	RR(T, G)	Canadian D/USD	DM/USD
NTD/USD	1.00												
M1A	0.10	1.00											
M1B	0.20	0.93	1.00										
M2	0.60	0.61	0.70	1.00									
CPI	0.03	−0.05	−0.07	−0.22	1.00								
WPI	0.08	−0.13	−0.14	−0.32	0.81	1.00							
CP	0.17	−0.32	−0.36	−0.16	0.80	0.57	1.00						
X-M	0.00	0.37	0.34	0.24	−0.55	−0.56	−0.58	1.00					
RR (T, USA)	−0.20	−0.39	−0.38	−0.16	−0.56	−0.33	−0.15	−0.07	1.00				
RR(T, J)	0.17	−0.28	−0.33	−0.01	−0.40	−0.09	0.18	−0.22	0.71	1.00			
RR(T, G)	0.43	−0.18	−0.17	0.25	−0.58	−0.23	0.00	−0.08	0.62	0.88	1.00		
Canadian D/USD	0.91	−0.06	−0.01	0.48	0.18	0.15	0.39	−0.16	−0.07	0.29	0.49	1.00	
DM/USD	0.86	−0.02	0.01	0.53	−0.19	−0.18	0.15	0.09	−0.08	0.29	0.51	0.85	1.00

Note
T = Taiwan
J = Japan
G = Germany

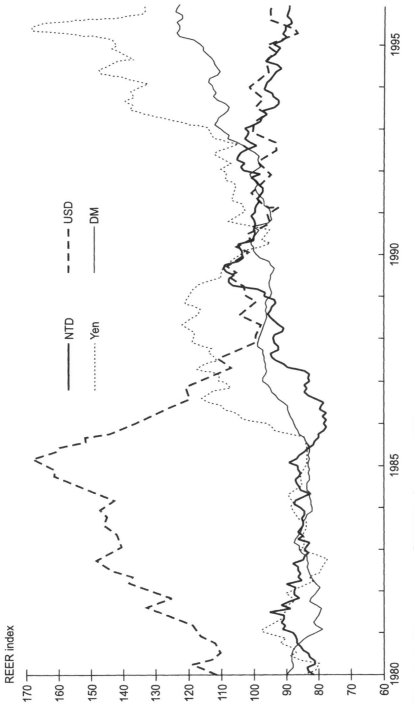

REER index

Figure 7.11 The movement of REER indices since 1980

Table 7.1. Although rigorous econometric tests are not provided in this study, it can be seen from Table 7.1 that some of the variables such as CPI and trade surplus are not highly correlated with NTD/USD. Judging from the high correlation coefficients between NTD/USD, yen/USD and DM/USD, it appears the long-term movements of NTD/USD are strongly influenced by yen/USD and DM/USD.

Figure 7.11 illustrates the movement of REER indices of the DM, NTD, USD and yen since 1980. As indicated, the REER index of USD soared in the early 1980s and declined sharply in the late 1980s. It then stabilized in the early 1990s. In contrast, the REER indices of the yen, the DM and NTD stayed relatively stable in the early 1980s and began to appreciate later. However, the REER index of the yen appears to be more volatile than those of the DM and NTD. In addition, the REER index of NTD since 1993 seemed to coincide with the trend of USD and be opposite to the yen and DM. During the whole observation period, as shown in Table 7.2, the correlation coefficients of REER indices of DM and USD, of yen and USD, and of NTD and USD are all negative.

Table 7.2 Correlation coefficients of REER indices

	NTD	*USD*	*Yen*	*DM*
NTD	1			
USD	−0.6468	1		
Yen	0.3681	−0.7546	1	
DM	0.4494	−0.7909	0.9008	1

5   Consequences of NTD fluctuations

As mentioned earlier, the long-term trend of NTD indicates that it depreciated slightly between 1980 and 1985, appreciated rapidly from 1986 to 1989, and has stabilized relatively since 1990. Although the fluctuations of NTD in the depreciation period and the stabilized period did cause some concern, the movement of NTD during the appreciation period produced the most significant consequences to the economy. In this section, we focus on the results of the fast appreciation in the late 1980s.

5.1   Fundamental changes in foreign direct investment

Inward and outward foreign direct investment (FDI) have been occurring since the early stage of Taiwan's economic development. Before 1987, Taiwan received more FDI than it gave to other economies. However, the whole picture changed once NTD started its rapid appreciation in 1986. The fast appreciation of NTD produced three fundamental changes to FDI. First, it practically drove Taiwan's labour-intensive industries such as textiles and sporting goods out of the world market. In order to solve the problem, these industries had to find overseas production bases where cheaper inputs were available. During late 1980s, outward FDI went to south-east Asian countries such as Malaysia, the Philippines and Thailand. In the early 1990s, China became Taiwan's favorite destination of outward investment. This phenomenon is usually referred as *the industry hollowing-out effect*.

Second, in addition to outward investment increasing significantly, inward FDI from developed countries was reduced at the same time. Therefore, as is shown in Figure 7.12, Taiwan suffered a remarkable degree of capital outflow in terms of FDI between 1988 and 1990. In other words, Taiwan has revised its status from capital importer to capital exporter since 1988 even if the remarkable amount of portfolio investment in the early 1990s is taken into account. Third, because the industries that drive Taiwan's economy have gradually shifted from labour-intensive to capital- and technology-intensive ones, not only is inward FDI focused in these *uprising* industries but outward FDI goes to developed countries, such as the USA and Japan, to secure their sources of technology.

5.2   The emergence and bursting of the bubble economy

Appreciation or even the expectation of appreciation of NTD undoubtedly induced *hot money* flows into Taiwan. Most of this hot money found its way to the stock market and real estate market, causing a bubble economy. As indicated in Figure 7.13, the stock market index soared from 945 in 1986 to 8,616 in 1989 and the annual transaction volume jumped from roughly 0.7 billion NTD in 1986 to 25 billion NTD in 1989. In addition to the bullish stock market, the real estate market also experienced a boom period. Although precise statistical data are not available, casual observation finds that the land prices of the Taipei metropolitan area almost quadrupled between 1986 and 1990. However, once NTD stabilized in the early 1990s, both the stock market and the real estate market became stale. Even seven years later, the stock market and real estate market have not recovered from the bursting of the bubble economy. Moreover, the money game atmosphere nurtured in the late 1980s has adversely affected the work ethic of the people on the island.

5.3   Stable price level

If no action were taken to offset its impact, the accumulation of foreign reserves eventually would either force the local currency to appreciate or put inflationary pressure on the local economy through the build-up of monetary aggregates. During the depreciation period, NTD significantly accumulated, and the consequence was the appreciation of NTD without

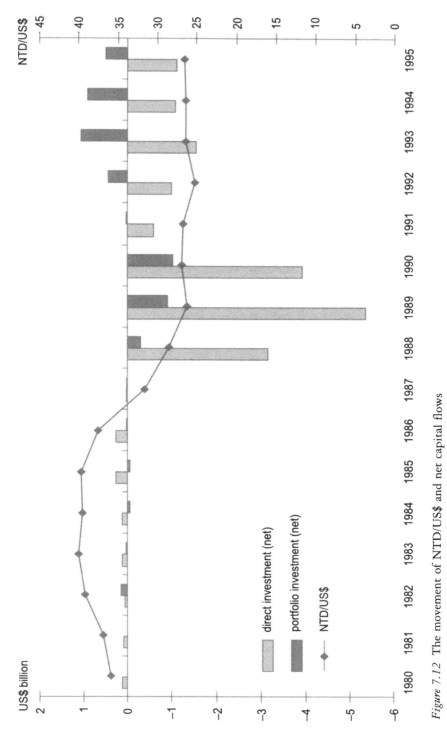

Figure 7.12 The movement of NTD/US$ and net capital flows

130

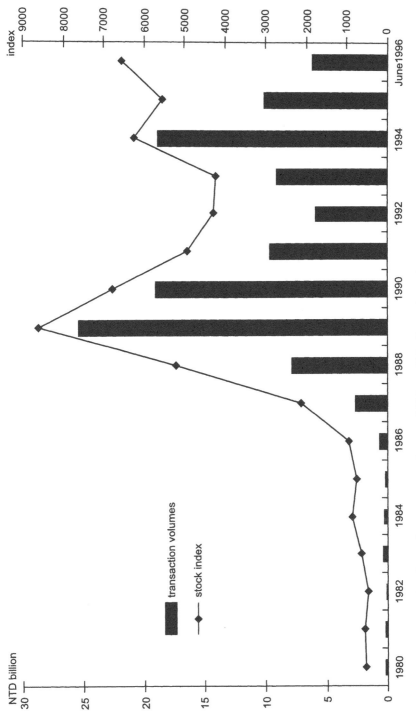

Figure 7.13 The annual index and transaction volumes of Chinese Taipei's stock market

the accompanying inflationary pressure. The central bank not only allowed NTD to appreciate, but also pursued a series of sterilization measures to mitigate inflationary pressure.[4] As indicated in Figure 7.7, the annual growth rate of CPI had never been higher than 5 per cent in the late 1980s, a remarkable decrease compared with that of the early 1980s. In addition, between 1985 and 1989, the annual growth rate of WPI had stayed below zero. In contrast, monetary aggregate in terms of M1B (net currency plus deposit money) reached an annual growth rate of as much as 55 per cent in 1987.

6 Macroeconomic policies regarding exchange rate fluctuations

A complete analysis of macroeconomic policy and practice regarding foreign exchange rate management requires investigation of both the policy and practice initiated by the domestic monetary authority and the cooperative actions taken by different monetary authorities from a group of countries with the common goal of intervening in foreign exchange markets. Since NTD is not a major currency traded in the international monetary markets and since the size of Taiwan's economy is small compared with the G-7 countries, the Central Bank of Taiwan is seldom involved in any cooperative actions. Hence this section focuses on domestic policy and practice.

Although macroeconomic policy includes monetary policy and fiscal policy, since the mid-1960s the government of Taiwan has been working very hard to maintain a balanced budget, especially in its current account. Therefore, from Taiwan's perspective, fiscal policy has little to do with macroeconomic management in the event of foreign exchange rate fluctuations. In this study, emphasis will be placed upon the monetary policy issues.

As is unambiguously stated in the Law of the Central Bank of Taiwan, it has to accomplish the following four goals: (1) provide a sound and stable financial environment; (2) supervise the banking industry; (3) maintain the internal as well as the external stability of NTD; and (4) promote economic development, provided the first three goals are fulfilled. In other words, similar to many other monetary authorities, the Central Bank of Taiwan is assigned the ultimate goals of price stability, economic growth and full employment, and balance of payments. To gain a better understanding of Taiwan's monetary policy and practice, Figures 7.14 to 7.16. summarize the instruments and goals, the transmission process and effectiveness, and the decision-making process of Taiwan's monetary policy.

In order to reach these ultimate goals, intermediate goals and operational goals are required. The tools at the central bank's disposal include textbook instruments (such as open market operations, rediscount rate, required reserve ratios, selective credit rationing) and transactions in the foreign exchange market. To ensure the effectiveness of monetary policy, the transmission process needs to take aggregate demand and supply, and domestic and international market fluctuations into account. So as to maintain the delicate

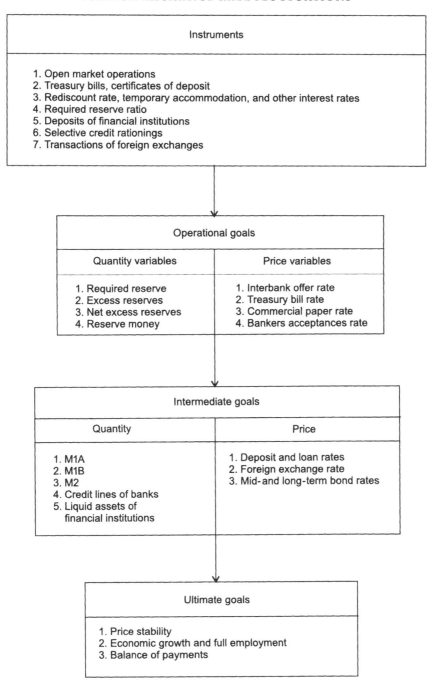

Figure 7.14 Instruments and goals of Chinese Taipei's monetary policy
Source: Shea (1995).

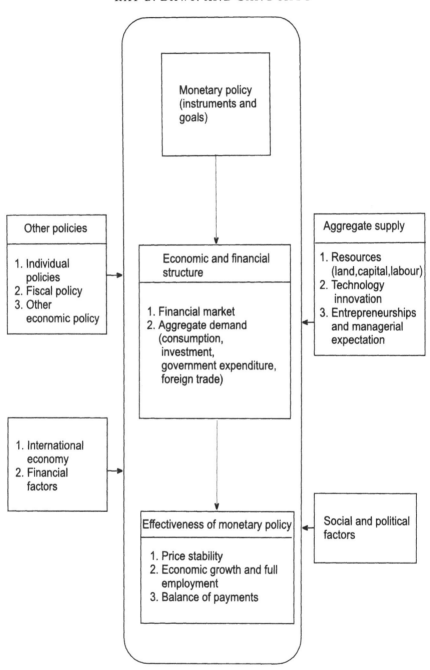

Figure 7.15 The transmission process and effectiveness of Chinese Taipei's monetary policy

Source: Shea (1995).

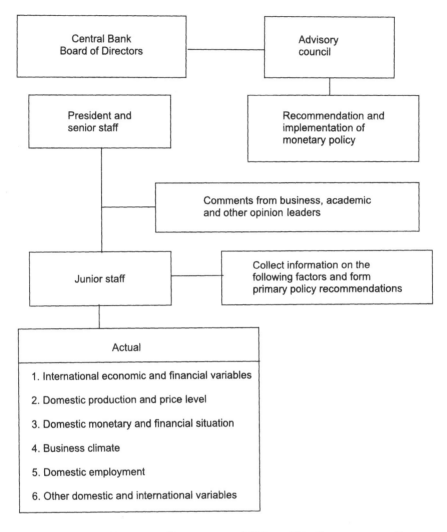

Figure 7.16 The decision-making process of Chinese Taipei's monetary policy
Source: Shea (1995).

balance between independence and transparency in monetary policy, the decision-making process of the central bank not only relies on its staff members closely monitoring contemporary changes in certain variables, but also is open to all comments from business and the academic sector as well as other opinion leaders. We will discuss the policies implemented by the Central Bank of Taiwan to mitigate the fluctuations of NTD in the following section.

6.1 Reserve requirement policy

The Central Bank of Taiwan has taken a cautious attitude to the adjustment of reserve requirement, due to its profound impacts on the economy. During the late 1980s, however, in order to cool down the overheated monetary aggregates, especially in M1A and M1B, the central bank adjusted the required reserve ratio upward in December 1988 and April 1989. As indicated in Figure 7.17, the required reserve ratio for checking account went up from 23 per cent in 1987 to 25 per cent in 1988 and then again to 29 per cent in 1989. Similarly, the required reserve ratio for time deposits went from 8 per cent to 9 per cent and then to 11 per cent during the same period. However, as NTD stabilized and the pace of Taiwan's economic growth slowed down, the required reserve ratios have been gradually adjusted downward.

6.2 Interest rate policy

Following the second oil shock in the late 1970s, the interest rate in Taiwan surged in the early 1980s. For example, the rediscount rate reached 13.25 per cent in January 1981. Due to the growing money supply fuelled by the current account surplus, the interest rate started to decline. The rediscount rate hit its trough of 4.5 per cent in October 1986 and stayed there for nearly thirty months. The rediscount rate was raised to 5.5 per cent in April 1989, for the central bank decided to implement a contractionary monetary policy. Since then, the rediscount rate has been adjusted up and down on the base of economic performance. One thing needs to be mentioned. Prior to July 1989, the bank interest rates were under the control of the central bank. In other words, the central bank was authorized to set rediscount rate and bank interest rate. In July 1989, however, the revised Banking Law abolished interest rate control, and hence the central bank can influence interest rate only through open market operations.

6.3 Open market operation

January 1979 marked the turning point for the development of Taiwan's money market because the central bank started its purchase of short-term bills. Since then, open market operations (OMO) have frequently been conducted. The TB-B (zero coupon treasury bills) is a commonly used instrument. In order to offset the inflationary pressure brought by the current account surplus in the early 1980s, the central bank started to issue certificates of deposits and savings bonds in 1985. Although TB-B can be purchased by financial institutions and the general public, certificates of deposits and savings bonds can only be purchased by financial institutions. The amounts offset by the issuance of the central bank's TB-B, certificates of deposits and savings bonds accounted for 49.6 per cent and 66.2 per cent of the foreign asset increments in 1986 and 1987 respectively.

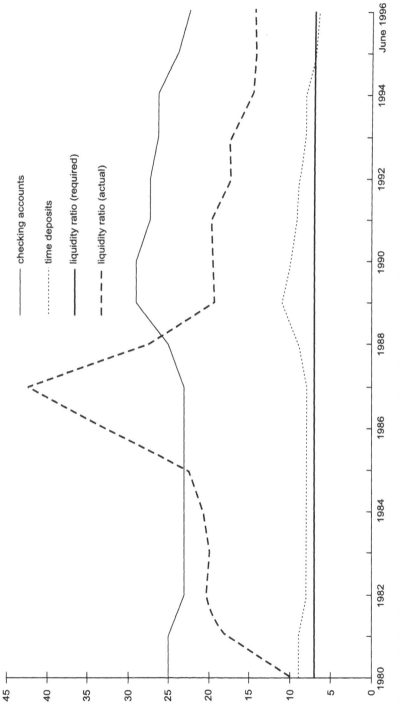

Figure 7.17 The changes in the required reserve ratios and liquidity ratios since 1980

6.4 Redeposit requirement on the Postal Savings System

Because of its widespread branch offices around the island and its convenient office hours, the Postal Savings System has been Taiwan's largest deposit-taking financial institution. From the beginning of its operation in the early 1960s, the savings deposits taken by the Postal Savings System were totally redeposited into the central bank for investing in infrastructure projects. Beginning in March 1982, a certain proportion of the new deposits were allowed to redeposit into four specialized banks for the purpose of increasing loanable funds in these banks. As the money supply kept building up because of current account surplus, in order to ease the inflationary pressure, in March 1986 the redeposit ratio was revised in such a way that 70 per cent of the new deposits were redeposited into the central bank and only 30 per cent was allowed to go to these four specialized banks. In addition to the Postal Savings System, community financial institutions such as credit unions and the credit departments of farmers' and fishermen's associations have also been under the supervision of the central bank.

6.5 Selective credit controls

According to the Banking Law and the Law Governing the Central Bank, the following selective credit controls, among others, are available to the central bank: (1) discretionary selection or collateral and mortgages used for collateral loans; (2) prescribing terms of repayment and maturities regarding housing procurement and construction loans and loans for the purchase of durable consumer goods undertaken by banks; and (3) stipulating the ceiling amount of lending for credit extension regarding specific financial institutions. During the heyday of the bubble economy, the central bank suspended bank loans for the purchase of idle land, established the ceiling amount of bank loans regarding the purchase of land for housing construction, and restricted the total amount of bank loans made to the investment companies so that they did not exceed the balance amount of the same loan at the end of February 1989. However, the central bank announced a significant relaxation of selective credit controls in October 1990. As the financial market became more and more liberalized over time, selective credit controls have been seldom used in recent days.

7   Intermarket relationship between foreign exchange rate and interest rate

One way to examine the effect of the policy changes in the foreign exchange market is to investigate the intermarket relationship between foreign exchange rate and interest rate during different subsample periods with different policy implications. In short, we separate the whole sample into three subsample periods: (1) 1980–4: traditional control period; (2) 1985–9: transitional periods with deregulation policy in progress and high volatility in the foreign exchange market; and (3) 1990–5: free market period with most marked deregulation policy in effect.

To investigate the intermarket relationship between the credit market and foreign exchange market, we conduct a cointegration and Granger Causality Test in this section. The first step in the empirical analysis is to examine the stationarity of the price series. The non-stationarity is tested using the Augmented Dickey–Fuller (ADF) test. Since one-month commercial paper is the most liquid short-term credit instrument, we use one-month commercial paper rate as a proxy for free market interest rate.

Not surprisingly, the ADF test based on Fuller (1976) for all last price series cannot reject the hypotheses of non-stationarity at the 0.01 level. On the other hand, all first-differenced series reject the non-stationary hypothesis at the 0.01 level. To conduct the cointegration test, we follow Engle and Granger (1987). If Y_t and X_t are cointegrated, then there exists a constant A, such that $e_t = Y_t - AX_t$ is stationary. As a result, we estimate:

$$Y_t = a + bX_t + \varepsilon_t \tag{7.3}$$

where Y_t is price series in foreign exchange rate and X_t is price series in commercial paper rate. The augmented Dickey-Fuller (ADF) test is used to test the significance of b in the following regression:

$$\Delta\varepsilon_t = \alpha + \beta\varepsilon_{t-1} + \sum_{i=1}^{n} \phi_i\Delta\varepsilon_{t-i} + v_t \tag{7.4}$$

where ε_t is the error term from the cointegration equation, v_t is a stationary random error term. Regressing foreign exchange rate price series against commercial paper rate price series, we have the following estimates.[5]

(1) Sample period: January 1985–December 1989

$$CPR_t = 32.95 - 8.37FX_t$$

$$(14.91) \qquad (-13.88)$$

$$R^2 = 0.7687$$

(2) Sample period: January 1985 – December 1989

$$CPR_t = 6.807 - 1.470FX_t$$

$$(6.94) \qquad (-5.13)$$

$$R^2 = 0.3127$$

(3) Sample period: January 1990 – December 1995

$$CPR_t = 7.19 + -1.605FX_t$$

$$(3.55) \quad (2.58)$$

$$R^2 = 0.1036$$

where FX_t and CPR_t are the NTD/USD foreign exchange rate and one-month commercial paper rate, respectively. Using the error terms from the previous equations, we find the t-statistics for b estimates for equation 7.4 are -0.98, -1.85 and -3.38 for subsample periods 1980–4, 1985–9 and 1990–5. The results show increasing cointegration between the foreign exchange market and credit market as deregulation policies in foreign exchange control are in progress.

After the cointegration test, we then conduct OLS regression for Granger causality test on foreign exchange rate and commercial paper rate. Parameters are estimated for lagged (5-period) independent variables (ΔX), lagged dependent variables (ΔY), and an error term from cointegration regression ($\hat{I}$).

$$\Delta Y_t = \alpha + \beta_y \Delta Y_{t-1} + \beta_x \Delta X_{t-1} + \gamma \varepsilon_{t-1} + e_t \tag{7.5}$$

A time series $\{X_t\}$ is said to Granger cause another time series $\{Y_t\}$ if present Y can be predicted better by using past values of X than by not doing so, other relevant information, including the past values of Y, being used in either case. An F test is conducted to test the causality between the credit market and foreign exchange market for each subsample period. We find that the significant level for CPR leading FX increases from 0.71 to 0.24 and for FX leading CPR increases from 0.75 to 0.32. In other words, the price transmission process from the foreign exchange market (credit market) to the credit market (foreign exchange market) has become much stronger as the deregulation process progresses.

8 Concluding remarks

In this case study of Taiwan's foreign exchange rate fluctuations and macroeconomic management, we first review the movements of nominal exchange rate of NTD vis-à-vis USD from 1963 to 1995, with special interest in the period from 1980 to 1995, and the associated changes in Taiwan's foreign exchange rate regime. In addition, the fluctuations of real effective exchange rate of NTD between 1980 and 1996 were also examined. We then propose a group of variables that possibly affect the movements of NTD/USD and find out that some of the listed variables appear to have high correlation coefficients with the fluctuation of NTD/USD. It seems that the long-term trend of NTD has been positively correlated with that of the yen and DM.

The volatile fluctuation of NTD in the observation period has produced several major consequences to the economy. For example, fundamental changes in FDI have occurred and Taiwan has shifted from being a capital importer to being a capital exporter, resulting in a so-called industry *hollowing-out effect*. In addition, the fluctuation of NTD contributed to the emergence and bursting of the bubble economy. However, the fluctuation of NTD did bring an environment of stable prices to the economy. Because of the NTD appreciation, CPI grew moderately and the growth rate of WPI stayed below zero in the late 1980s.

We also consider the goals, instruments and decision-making process of the Central Bank of Taiwan. In addition, monetary policy and practice related to the issues of exchange rate fluctuations are discussed. During the observation period, the central bank implemented monetary policies such as adjusting reserve requirements, monitoring interest rates, conducting open market operations, changing redeposit requirements on the Postal Savings System, and practising selective credit controls to mitigate the ill effects resulting from the fluctuation of NTD. From the relatively stable monetary environment of the late 1980s, it appears that the interventions made by the central bank produced satisfactory results. In addition, a cointegration test and Granger causality test between the credit market and foreign exchange market show that the co-movement between interest rate and foreign exchange rate has been increasing since the deregulation measures came into effect.

Notes

An earlier version of this chapter was presented at the Pacific Economic Cooperation Council (PECC) Pacific Economic Outlook (PEO)/Structure Specialists Meeting, Osaka, Japan, 27–28 September 1996.

The authors wish to thank Shu-Chuan Lee and Mei-Chen Feng for their research assistance.

1. For example, the G-7 Summit Meetings of 1995 and 1996 all recognized the imperativeness of a stable international monetary system and urged international cooperation in foreign exchange markets in the event of unwarranted disturbances. Furthermore, APEC Finance Ministerial Meetings of 1995 and 1996 have reached similar conclusions, that volatile exchange rates will slow down international trade and investment, and hence that cooperation among central banks must stabilize foreign exchange markets.
2. Although there may be a small amount of NTD in circulation in eastern Asia, NTD is seldom traded in the established exchanges outside Taiwan.
3. Professor Kohsaka's guidelines were given at the PECC PEO/Structure Specialist Meeting in Osaka, Japan, on 15–16 March 1996.

4. For a detailed discussion of the measures taken by the central bank, see Section 6 of this chapter.

5. All price series are measured in natural logarithms.

References

Almekinders, G.J. (1995) *Foreign Exchange Intervention: Theory and Evidence*, Edward Elgar, Aldershot.

Bureau of Monetary Affairs (1996) *The ROC Financial Market Integration*, Ministry of Finance, Taiwan.

Dominguez, Kathryn M. and Frankel, Jeffrey A. (1993) *Does Foreign Exchange Intervention Work?*, Institute of International Economics, Washington, DC.

Engle, R.F. and Granger, C.W.J. (1987) 'Co-integration and an error correction: representation, estimation and testing', *Econometrica* 55, 251–76.

Evans, John S. (1992) *International Finance: A Markets Approach*, Dryden Press; Florida.

Far, Ming-Shu and Jia, Jau-Nan (1995) 'Foreign exchange speculative attack and the volatility of exchange rate: a case study of Taiwanese foreign exchange market', *Quarterly Journal of the Bank of Taiwan* 46–1, 203–23.

Fuller, W.A. (1976) *Introduction to Statistical Time Series*, Wiley, New York.

IMF (1994) *Approaches to Exchange Rate Policy: Choices for Developing and Transition Economies*, edited by Barth, R.C. and Wong, C.H., Washington, DC.

——(1995) *Exchange Arrangements and Exchange Restrictions: Annual Report 1995*; Washington, DC.

Kawai, M. (1996) 'Capital flow liberalization and financial market opening in the PECC economies: an East Asian perspective', paper presented at the fourth meeting of PECC FMD Project.

Liang, Far-Jing (1995) 'Trade surplus and the monetary effect of exchange rate policy of Taiwan', *Quarterly Journal of the Bank of Taiwan* 46–3, 44–61.

Moreno, R. (1995) 'Macroeconomic behavior during periods of speculative pressure or realignment: evidence from Pacific Basin économies', *FRBSF Economic Review*, 3–16.

Semkow, Brian W. (1992) *Taiwan's Financial Markets and Institutions: The Legal and Financial Issues of Deregulation and Internationalization*, Quorum Books, Connecticut.

Shea, Sen-Chung (1995) 'Stability, growth, independence, but no isolation: a challenge to the dilemma of the monetary policy of the Central Bank', *Quarterly Journal of the Central Bank* 17–3, 17–52.

Spiegel, M.K. (1995) 'Sterilization of capital inflows through the banking sector: evidence from Asia', *FRBSF Economic Review*, 17–34.

Taylor, Mark P. (1995) 'The economics of exchange rates', *Journal of Economic Literature* 33–1, 13–47.

8

DISCUSSION

Martin Weale

Chapter 7 presents an account of the exchange rate policy since Taiwan was effectively separated from the mainland of China by the communist victory in 1949. Taiwan's experience provides a good example of the way in which a small industrializing economy has moved from a very controlled foreign exchange market to a free float.

From 1949 until 1979 the currency was fixed to the US dollar. But there was a change from a highly regulated system to a freer one. Until 1963 there were multiple exchange rates, with the rate of exchange depending on what it was that was being imported or exported. This effectively provided a system of tariffs and export taxes or subsidies; the profits which the central bank made on foreign exchange dealing presumably accrued to the government rather than being kept by the central bank. I suppose the logic of running a tariff system in this way is that, if the central bank is the sole supplier of foreign exchange, it can function as a tariff collection agency at the same time. There is no need to ask Customs and Excise to collect tariffs. At one time there were as many as ten exchange rates but by the end of this spell there were only two.

From 1963 onwards capital movements were still controlled. Other countries in a similar position (e.g. the UK) had only one official exchange rate, and a second market in investment currency. Investment currency could be bought by those who wished to invest abroad, in principle at least, only from those who wished to sell. Presumably there was little pressure on Taiwan to introduce such a system because there was not the long tradition of overseas investment found in the UK.

The final part of the fixed exchange rate period continued beyond the beginning of the US dollar float in 1972. Indeed, when general floating started in 1972–3 it affected only the major players (US dollar, sterling, DM, yen, Canadian dollar and some other European countries). Most countries remained pegged to one of these, and the majority of the pegged currencies chose to retain a US dollar peg. Taiwan did, however, allow the US dollar to depreciate twice, first in 1973 at the time of a general US dollar depreciation and again in 1978.

By 1979 the Central Bank of Taiwan felt that the market was broad enough to allow the exchange rate to float. It did not, however, allow free floating but instead defined a centre rate which was the closing rate of the day before, and then limited fluctuations within the day to 2.25 per cent on either side of this centre rate. Thus it aimed to stabilize very short-term movements. There is no indication that it steered the market in the longer term, but since foreign exchange reserves were built up there must have been some intervention of some sort. It would be interesting to know why. On the other hand exchange controls ended and in that sense the markets became free.

The perceived need to stabilize daily movements in this way is indicative of narrowness of the foreign exchange market of a small country. It would be difficult to imagine a major currency like the US dollar moving by as much as 2.25 per cent in one day except in the aftermath of a change in exchange rate regime. Since 1989 the Taiwan Central Bank has moved from this system of a centre rate to free floating; presumably the market has become broader both because of the greater size of Taiwan's economy and also because of greater liquidity in world markets generally. The standard deviation of the rate against the US dollar has declined. This may because the market is more liquid or it may be because the Taiwan dollar has in fact been more stable after the bubble overvaluation of the mid-1980s. Indeed one slightly disconcerting aspect of the chapter is that the US dollar exchange rate plainly dominates the authors' perception of the foreign exchanges. Perhaps the yen rate is more important by now, even if it was not in the 1970s.

Despite this perspective, an analysis of the exchange rate (presented in terms of correlations) and the real exchange rate (presented graphically) suggest that the New Taiwan dollar was decoupled from the US dollar once it started floating. We find strong correlations with the DM/US dollar and yen/US dollar rates, suggesting that it steered clear of the US dollar misalignment of the mid-1980s. It is suggested that the increase in the real exchange rate in the late 1980s, as the US dollar depreciated, was a factor leading to an outflow of foreign investment. To confirm this, it would be interesting to know whether the flow was to countries whose real exchange rates fell against the New Taiwan dollar.

Despite the movements in the exchange rate it seems that the domestic price level rose relatively modestly from the mid-1980s onward. Beyond being told that the money stock grew rapidly, we are left in the dark as to the factors behind this.

The authors also find it difficult to explain the causes of exchange rate changes in the floating period. They are unable to identify any (apart from the two cross-exchange rates mentioned above). While they are in good company, it is worth repeating that the question of intervention could have been studied.

From this account we move on to the central bank's policy goals. It is given four targets: (1) to provide a sound financial environment; (2) to supervise the banking industry; (3) to maintain internal and external stability of the currency; and (4) to promote economic development provided the other three goals are met.

Four targets need four instruments. Banking supervision we can regard as being different from macroeconomic management. (1) presumably means that interest and other policy instruments should not be varied too much. (2) is not directly connected with monetary policy although high interest rates might affect the functioning of banking supervision. (3) presumably means that inflationary policies should be avoided and (4) may imply that some direction of credit is undertaken.

Plainly the central bank has done more than just vary the interest rate. Reserve requirements exist and have been varied from time to time. The authors do not say whether or at what rate interest is paid on reserves, but the reserve requirement (with differential rates imposed on the post office savings bank) presumably functions as a tax on bank deposits; varying the tax rate independently of the interest rate gives extra room for manoeuvre. The authors describe open market operations as something independent of interest rate policies.

The mechanics of the system are not completely clear from this account, but one might conjecture that it functions like the British system before 1971. There is an interest rate set by the central bank which the joint-stock banks use as a reference for their borrowing and lending rates. There is a separate market in treasury bills, and the rate on these presumably influences interest rates paid by people who can borrow in the money markets. This means that open market operations can lead to small changes in the market rate without affecting the administered rates charged by the joint-stock bank. The British system was abandoned because it could not function with a competitive banking system. It would be interesting to know whether the Taiwan banking system avoids the 'vulgarity of competition'. Certainly the fact that credit controls are employed suggests that there cannot always have been free entry into the business of supplying credit.

The authors mention that, as markets have become liberalized, credit controls have been used less. It would be interested to know whether there is also a blurring between open market operations and interest rate policy.

The last part of the chapter is an attempt to relate the level of the foreign exchange rate (measured against the US dollar) to the interest rate in Taiwan. The authors find that both variables are I(1) but that both are cointegrated. I have no idea how to interpret the relationship which they identify. For example, I am unsure how it relates to the arbitrage condition relating interest rate differentials and expected changes in exchange rates. It also seems rather odd to relate the exchange rate only to the home interest rate and not the differential against the United States.

Chapter 7 is probably the first account of the exchange rate history pursued by Taiwan and it will be a useful source of information in this respect. On the other hand, it raises a number of important questions to which the outsider studying Taiwan would probably like to know the answers.

Part II

EXCHANGE RATES AND ECONOMIC DEVELOPMENT
Long-run views

9

INDUSTRIALIZATION AND THE OPTIMAL REAL EXCHANGE RATE POLICY FOR AN EMERGING ECONOMY*

Guillermo Larraín

1 Introduction

The achievement of high and sustained growth rates, like those in East Asia and particularly in South Korea, is a major objective of policy making in any emerging country. In such a context, we can analyse the role of exchange rate policies in a number of ways. For example, we could analyse which exchange rate policy can be used in such a way as to obtain a degree of monetary independence and so implement more successful stabilization policies. Alternatively, we could investigate which exchange rate system is the more suitable for dealing with different types of capital flows, or for responding to specific shocks. We could also study which exchange rate system is the best in the framework of growing interdependence among Asian countries.

Our concern is, however, quite different. We shall discuss which *real exchange rate* (*rer*) policy is the most suitable if sustained high growth is the objective. We shall *not* discuss how to achieve the *rer* movements the chapter proposes. We simply assume that, at any time, the government may choose the desired *rer* level. The central point is that a *rer* policy may affect growth through the *resource allocation* channel. In particular, we shall explore how a *rer* policy can induce *industrialization*.

Why does industrialization appear as a goal? One simple argument is that this has traditionally been the way countries have found to increase permanently their growth rates and living standards. Industrialization apparently creates a self-sustained growth process, unlike the growth periods led by export booms or agricultural productivity increases (Murphy *et al.*, 1989a). As a matter of fact, it is hard to find developed countries that seriously qualify as non-industrial (Rodrik, 1996b).

Beyond that casual empirical observation, we can provide at least three arguments in favour of industrialization. To start with, if we accept that

149

long-run growth has something to do with the nature of the goods produced, then industrial goods presumably provide higher potential productivity increases than natural resources. Hence, they are able to sustain a more permanent growth process. Probably the main source of productivity gains is the existence of externalities in industrial sectors. There is a significant body of empirical evidence that supports this view, for example World Bank (1993). This whole argument may be linked to Young's (1993) warning that trade liberalization may harm poor countries. Second, except in the particular case of a country that is very competitive and has some market power in natural resources, for example Arab countries in oil, growth based on natural resources will probably be based on international competition over wages in dollars. Industrialization, on the contrary, may deliver growth accompanied by higher wages. It is thus a source of competitiveness in the sense exposed by Dollar and Wolff (1994). Some people may argue that, as long as wages increase and profitability is squeezed in natural resource-based sectors, industrialization will take place naturally. This obvious comment, valid in the long run, dismisses the problems linked to the political economy surrounding *protectionist* decisions and how this may delay industrialization. In short, squeezing profits in the natural resources sector may start political pressures intended to increase protection. This point is developed in later sections. Finally, as industrial prices are less volatile than commodity prices, a wider industrial base could diminish the instability provided by unexpected terms of trade shocks. However, this is probably not the best policy to deal with terms of trade instability. We state that this is simply one important consequence of industrialization.

Why are we concerned with *rer* policy? Because under certain circumstances the government may be reluctant to apply first-best (and even second-best) policy options to resource allocation. It may prefer to use only policies that alter 'macroeconomic' prices, for instance the real exchange rate (*rer*). This choice could be explained by history: when a country has suffered from excess public intervention it may be unwilling (or unable due to political constraints) to use a more direct policy option. The same happens when the government is struggling to get rid of corruption. In fact, in many cases first-best policies are prone to rent-seeking activities, which may at last minimize its benefits. In that case, the government may prefer to induce resource allocation via a single and objective variable, common to all agents.

Certainly, this approach has not been the one undertaken in Asia. Exchange rate policies have not played a paramount role in the industrialization process. Several authors, including Rodrik (1996a), have shown that relative price incentives have not been crucial in explaining the extraordinary development of the region. In an environment of sane fundamentals, selective interventions (which often altered prices in ways that are difficult to estimate empirically) explain much better the Asian experience than exchange rate policies do. However, the lessons of East Asia can hardly be emulated by other countries. In Latin America, for instance, excessive past public intervention and corruption issues are some of the arguments against the use of discretionary policies. Hence, in these countries non-interventionist policies are put in place to alter resource allocation.

This chapter shows which is the simplest optimal *rer* policy, starting with a straightforward extension of the well-known model of Murphy *et al.* (1989b). The basic idea here is that a real devaluation increases profits in tradable sectors in such a way that firms can finance the required investment needed to industrialize.[1] We supply three amendments to that policy, linked respectively to the political support of the reform process, to the entrepreneurial effort required to industrialize and to the role of intermediate inputs. The first stage of the optimal strategy states that during an unknown period of time, a real *depreciation* must be achieved. In a second stage, a mild but sustained real *appreciation* is called for. As the first stage normally induces a period of relatively high growth (a period of catching up), the *rer* may display a trend of real appreciation. Hence the policy recommendation of the second stage is twofold: on the one hand, the real appreciation trend must be kept under control. In particular, it must be consistent with the movement of the equilibrium *rer*. Stabilization policies therefore become crucial. On the other side, the real appreciation as defined above must not be resisted.

A critical point for a successful non-interventionist policy is that the initial *depreciation* must be huge (or must be maintained for a long period).[2] In some cases, it is shown that this induces strong political opposition to the reform package and low entrepreneurial effort for economic transformation (defined as the passage towards an industrialized economy). The political costs of a devaluation may induce the government not to *depreciate* that much, but this will mean that the non-interventionist policy may not lead to industrialization. This implies there is a range for the *rer* realizations where the traditional big push arguments will probably remain valid. We show, however, that the higher the initial real devaluation, the less need to use 'big push' policies so as to take the economy away from the bad equilibrium.

This chapter is probably of limited interest for high-performing Asian economies (the World Bank's HPAEs), where industrialization is already a reality and where there is much expertise in *selective intervention*. However, it may be of interest for countries fulfilling the conditions suggested above: countries which are poor, where there may have been excessive public intervention in the past, and/or where corruption restrains first-best policy implementation. However, the interest they may have comes precisely for the opposite reasons they would have appealed in first instance.

In fact, this chapter highlights two aspects. First, for a given factor endowment including natural resources, a non-interventionist policy can deliver industrialization, but there are strong arguments to state that it may be delayed at best. Notably in Latin America, this suggests that together with economic liberalization, policy makers should not dismiss the use of more active, market-friendly policies. We compare two benchmark cases, South Korea and Chile, and we show that although some macro variables behave similarly after controlling for the time of implementation of the policies, Chile lags far behind in industrialization. This suggests that South Korean-style activist policies probably play a role in *accelerating* a process of resource reallocation that may *eventually* happen anyway without intervention. However, the fact that Chile is much richer in natural resources suggests that the optimal industrialization pattern in its case may indeed require more time. Second, this chapter suggests that keeping the *rer* permanently under-valued is not the way to bring about industrialization and that a sustained but mild real appreciation may create the necessary incentives. To some extent, the Chilean experience after 1988 illustrates this fact.

2 Two approaches to industrialization: active and interventionist (Asia) or passive and free-marketeer (Latin America)

In addition to the fact that for some authors like Balassa and Associates (1982) and Ranis (1981) and institutions like the World Bank (1993), the Asian case is the predictable result of freeing trade and removing discrimination against exports, there is increasing evidence that the role played by the state has been crucial. As Chenery *et al.* (1986) put it, these experiences are known more for their outstanding productivity (Japan) or, as emphasized by Young (1994), their capacity to save and invest (the Dragons), than for their openness to trade and non-interventionist policies.

This point was stressed long ago by Diaz-Alejandro (1975) and Streeten (1982) and more recently by Amsden (1986), Bradford (1990), Gereffi (1990), Helleiner (1992), Wade (1991), Rodrik (1995, 1996a) and Mes-quita-Moreira (1994) among others. In general this branch of the literature does not neglect the role of a freer trade environment (especially concerning exports) and the discrimination issue mentioned above, but stresses that all this was crucially supported, coordinated and accelerated by an ex-post quite successful public policy. In particular, this included resource allocation policy through credit subsidies, coordination of big conglomerates, tax incentives, etc. Whereas this policy has led to overinvestment in some sectors, it has been highly successful in developing a widely diversified, sophisticated and competitive industry.

In particular in South Korea and Taiwan, the export boom has not been induced by a dramatic increase in the profitability of exports relative to pro-ducing for the home market. Resource allocation has had more to do with state intervention than with price incentives. From this respect, in Latin America and particularly in Chile, the export boom seems much more correl-ated with price incentives. Rodrik (1996b) provides a useful graph showing this fact, which we reproduce here as Figure 9.1.

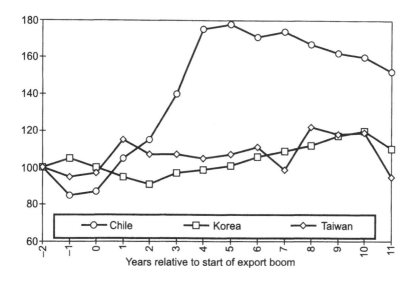

Figure 9.1 Relative prices of exports in selected countries experiencing export booms
Source: Figure 3 in Rodrik (1996b).

Concerning the free market approach we may state as a good approximation that this is the way industrialization is conceived today in Latin America.
This approach states that once resource allocation is improved by the elimina-
tion of distortions and due to the normal operation of the price mechanism,
industrialization will take place naturally as the result of market forces. Price
flexibility, including wages, is accompanied by two major policies: trade liberalization and shrinking government expenditures (the latter normally inducing fiscal savings). Other benefits such as low inflation, low unemployment
and stability in capital flows would naturally emerge from the main policies.
This approach to development, and therefore to industrialization, is mainly
characterized by a massive retreat of the state from all productive functions[3]
and away from any form of microeconomic intervention.[4]

The reasons behind the relative lag of Latin America have been classified as
twofold. One is the excessive and often irrational public sector intervention.
The second is the anti-export bias implicit in the import substitution
model. With differences in emphasis depending on the country and the
epoch, both elements led to an overextended public sector, lack of internal
and external competition, less than optimal exploitation of economies of
scale, rent-seeking activities in preference to productive effort, and a corpor-
atism that stopped any possible reform to the system (Larraín and Winograd,
1996). As that development model exhausted its natural possibilities, the
pendulum moved towards an ultra neo-conservatism in which all state
intervention is seen with (great) suspicion. This political constraint limits

the possibilities of policy implementation. In particular, it makes irrelevant most of the suggestions of the 'big push' literature, even though those policies represent in many cases the first-best policy option.

3 The pitfalls of optimal industrialization policies

It is one thing to say that industrialization is a desirable goal, but another to justify policy measures directed to achieving it. The reasons for a policy of intervention must be found in market failures or externalities. As emphasized by Rodrik (1992), most of the arguments raised from that perspective have problems. First, many of the distortions are unobservable and hard to measure quantitatively. This means that they cannot be implemented and are probably subject to (inadequate) discretionary policies. Second, some distortions also apply to sectors other than industry. Third, first-best policies, namely those based on the *targeting principle* expressed by Bhagwati and Johnson,[5] present further implementation problems, including pressures on the budget (when a subsidy is due), strong requirements concerning public sector flexibility in policy implementation (when economic conditions change and call for a sudden change in policy, for example in taxes), vast information needs (when moral hazard problems arise) and policy commitments that are not always credible (typically in protectionist policies).

On the other hand, second-best policies, while lacking the power of first-best policies, are often the ones that are available for policy making. For example, Rodrik (1992) and Venables (1996) discuss the role of trade policy whereas Murphy *et al.* (1989b) discuss the role of public investment. Trade policy may imply export promotion or import protection. At this point Rodrik and Venables diverge. Rodrik states that import protection may be useful because it is achievable in the real world and it generates government revenue, while export promotion may put too much pressure on the budget. The optimal protection, while claimed to have a ceiling depending upon each country's characteristics, should disappear in the long run. However, inter-temporal considerations suggest that this may not be the result if the government is weak or its policy is inconsistent (Tornell, 1990). Venables, on the contrary, suggests that trade liberalization may induce industrialization if it enables the import of cheaper key inputs. As suggested by Rodrik, this seem to indicate that a mixture of selective protection and export promotion are the more suitable policies.

Non-interventionist policies, like the one discussed in this chapter, belong to a *third-best* class of policies. This is due to two considerations. First, following the Dixit criteria quoted in Note 5, the 'degree of targeting' this policy provides is one step lower than trade policy or public investment. Indeed, as an undervalued *rer* increases profits all over the tradable sector, it encourages exports homogeneously. Which sectors will finally export depends on the specific characteristics of each. A country rich in natural resources will probably face relatively lower costs in activities that exploit them, so exports will arise in those sectors. This may of course be an optimal situation. However, if industrialization is the goal, other policies are much more closely related to its achievement than the *rer* policy. The second reason why a *rer* policy is a third-best one is related to the fact that the degree of control over the policy instrument, the *rer*, is much more limited than in the cases of taxes, subsidies, tariffs or public investment. For all practical matters, these policy instruments are exogenously determined by the government while the *rer* is an endogenous variable in the economic system. Additionally, experience shows that the *rer* is often subject to shocks of significant size and unpredictable frequency.[6].

A question therefore arises concerning the relevance of discussing a third-best policy. Two arguments may be raised at this point. The first is linked to its real implementation possibilities. For example, the government's average manpower requirements for the first-best and second-best policies are probably higher than for the simpler *rer* rule. In the former, a skilled group of public functionaries working at the microeconomic level must periodically verify the suitability of the implemented policies and react adequately to changing economic conditions. On the other hand, the *rer* policy needs macroeconomic management which, on *average*, requires less skilled public servants. Hence, the less educated the country is, the more attractive the use of *rer* policies. The second argument is linked to current political support for non-interventionist policies. Additionally, various international accords, notably the World Trade Organization, significantly limit the use of alternative tools like tariffs. Therefore, there is increasing (institutional) pressure to use exchange rates instead of tariffs as a trade policy device.

We now present the logic of *rer* policy and industrialization. We continue to analyse three arguments complementary to the basic policy. We finish by making a comparison between the experiences of Chile and South Korea.

4   The logic of price incentives and industrialization: a model

The model is a straightforward extension of the industrialization model in Murphy *et al.* (1989b). It assumes a representative consumer who has a Cobb–Douglas utility function $\int_0^1 \ln(q)dq$ defined over a unit interval of goods indexed by q. All expenditure shares are the same. When his income is y it can be thought that the consumer spends y in each good $x(q)$. Labour supply is inelastic at L. All profits accrue to the consumer. Each firm produces a *tradable* good whose price is given by the law of one price and we normalize foreign prices to 1. There is a government which makes no spending and levies no taxes: it simply chooses the level of the real exchange rate defined as:

$$\lambda = \frac{e}{\omega} \qquad\qquad\qquad (9.1)$$

where e is the nominal exchange rate and ω the nominal wage. Our concern is with the real exchange rate *as a relative price* among sectors, not as an asset price. The model occurs in one period. At the beginning of the period, each entrepreneur decides whether to industrialize. In the middle of the period, the government announces the level of the real exchange rate and at the end of the period, agents realize the earnings and losses.

Following the *'big push'* literature, we assume an economy capable of running two technologies. In the low technology case, firms' production functions present constant returns to scale. We assume that each enterprise i uses the following technology which is the same for all firms in the sector, $y_i = L_i$. As all firms use the same technology and face the same demand, they will all produce the same amount and demand the same quantity of labour. For simplicity in the notation we drop indexes hereafter.

Nominal profits by the single firm are $\pi = ey - \omega L$. As in this sector there is competition, $\pi = 0$ in equilibrium. Real profits, in terms of units of labour, can be written $\tilde{\pi} = \lambda y - L$. To some extent, these profits can be considered to be *ex ante*. In order to simplify the exposition, we omit any explicit reference to the a priori distribution of λ. However, one way to handle this would be to think of λ as an expected value. We assume that the economy spent all its past existence in equilibrium. In this equilibrium there are n_1 firms that use CRS. Aggregate profits can be written $\tilde{\Pi}(n_1) = n_1(\lambda - 1)y$.

We therefore define the *equilibrium real exchange rate* as the one consistent with the equilibrium prevailing until now, that is, with a situation characterized by the fact that aggregate profits are nil in the CRS sectors, i.e. $\lambda = 1$. That is, we assume that so far the expected value and the realisation of λ have coincided. However, agents are rational and may forecast for tomorrow a different λ.

Aggregate national income, expressed in terms of labour, is $y(n_1) = \tilde{\Pi}(n_1) + L$. If there were only CRS firms, $n_1 = 1$ and we can see that national income is $y = L/(2 - \lambda)$. This says that when the *rer* is in equilibrium, $\lambda = 1$, national income is just the wage bill because there are no profits. It is apparent that a real depreciation, $\Delta^+\lambda$, increases national income (in terms of non-tradable goods, i.e. labour) because it creates profits in the private sector. However, if there are no installation costs, then when these profits appear, new firms will enter into the market forcing profits down until they are nil again.

We pass now to the high technology case, where this term designates a technology able to generate increasing returns to scale. If a single enterprise adopts this technology it would become the only producer in the economy as its average costs would always be decreasing. In that case, the whole workforce available would be used in it. This does not mean that this producer will become monopolist since there is free competition with foreign firms that fix the foreign nominal price (assumed to be 1). In the case where n_2 enterprises decide to industrialize, as all have access to the same technology, they will all survive and its maximum production will be limited by L/n_2.

For simplicity and following Murphy *et al.* (1989b), we adopt the following specification of the production function in the IRS sector: $y_j = (1 + \alpha)L_j$.

Hence, if a firm j adopts this technology, with the same amount of inputs it is able to produce α per cent more output. This productivity gain is the one that will eventually induce entrepreneurs to change technology. However, in order to make such a change, firms must engage in irreversible investments. We assume they may take two forms: labour, F, or foreign goods, X. We also assume that neither F nor X is sector-dependent. As there are no differences across firms concerning the parameters in the production functions, both output and labour demand will be the same for all enterprises using IRS. Therefore, we may also drop hereafter index j.

Real profits are now written:

$$\tilde{\pi} = \lambda y - L - F - \lambda X \tag{9.2}$$

If n_2 firms implement this technology, calculating real profits and replacing them we obtain, as before, an expression for the budget constraint that is a function of n_2.

We must now introduce the externalities. For simplicity, we follow Murphy *et al.* and assume *demand externalities*. These can arise in a framework with demand linkages in upstream and downstream industries, as in Venables (1996). Our demand externalities are simpler than those. We simply model them assuming that if a firm makes profits, it increases national income (the income of all the other firms) and then makes industrialization possible. If, on the other hand, the firm incurs losses, then it reduces the others' income and therefore industrialization is not attained. This setting simply replicates the main ideas of the more complex case with upstream and downstream industries.

Therefore, by examining the effect of the marginal investing firm on national income, we can deduce which exchange rate policy is compatible with industrialization. We find that

$$\frac{dy}{dn_2} > 0 \Leftrightarrow \lambda > \lambda^* \equiv \left(\frac{1}{1+\alpha} + \frac{F}{L} \right) \frac{L}{L - X} \tag{9.3}$$

when $L \neq X$. If the *rer* is depreciated enough, it may induce industrialization. The reason is that in this case marginal firms would make some profits, so would have an incentive. The needed depreciation depends on three factors. First, on the improvement of labour productivity after the technology change, α. The higher this improvement, the lower the depreciation needed. Second, if L > X, the required depreciation depends positively on the amount of the required investment in domestic goods as a share of the labour (F/L). The lower the fixed cost in domestic currency terms, the lower λ^*. The contrary happens if X is big (greater than L). Third, it depends positively on the investment denominated in foreign currency, X. A smaller X needs a less depreciated *rer* to generate enough profits to pay the investment in foreign currency. Adding up, λ^* depends positively on any fixed costs needed to industrialize and negatively on the productivity gains.

4.1 The scope for multiple equilibria

In this model there may be multiple equilibria. In order to show this denote $\pi(n_2)$ the profits obtained by a firm in the IRS sector. It depends on n_2 because of the externalities we have discussed before. We must look for the conditions under which the marginal enterprise in the IRS sector loses money if no other firms invest $(\pi(n_2 = 0) < 0)$ in which case no investment is in equilibrium. On the other side, we need to look for the conditions under which investment is in equilibrium given that the others have invested $(\pi(n_2 = 1) > 0)$.

We can show that there will be multiple equilibria if both conditions are met, that is if:

$$\frac{1}{1+\alpha} + 1 < \lambda < \left(\frac{1}{1+\alpha} + \frac{F}{L}\right)\frac{L}{L - X} \qquad (9.4)$$

First, note that if agents expect the equilibrium real exchange rate $\lambda = 1$, then this does not lead to multiple equilibria. If the government sets $\lambda = 1$, then there is only one equilibrium with CRS. Second, examining equation 9.4 clearly multiple equilibria require $L < F + (1 + 1/1 + \alpha)X$. This implies huge fixed investments. Traditional '*big push*' literature suggests that huge investments such as railroads may lead to multiple equilibria. See section VI in Murphy *et al.* (1989b).

Third, following the right-hand side of equation 9.4, if $\lambda > \lambda^*$ multiple equilibria disappear: only the IRS equilibrium remains valid. Therefore, all the equations in this section are characterized by: (a) one equilibrium where all firms use a CRS technology if $\lambda < 1 + (1 + \alpha)^{-1}$; (b) one equilibrium where all firms use an IRS technology if $\lambda > \lambda^*$, defined by the right-hand side of equation 9.4; and (c) a multiplicity of equilibria if $\lambda \in [1 + (1 + \alpha)^{-1}, \lambda^*]$. This suggests that industrialization may reliably be achieved using only the real exchange rate as an instrument if $\lambda > \lambda^*$. Additionally, if equation 9.4 holds, and consequently there is a multiplicity of equilibria due to coordination problems, then there is room for the kind of fiscal policies suggested by the '*big push*' literature. It can be shown that when there is a multiplicity of equilibria, the more depreciated the real exchange rate, the less difficult becomes the coordination problem, making it possible to advance towards the industrialized equilibrium. In other words, the level of the *rer* and the strength of the coordination problem that impedes industrialization are inversely correlated: the more depreciated the *rer*, the less important the coordination problem and therefore the smaller the need to implement '*big push*' style policies.

5 Three complementary arguments to the optimal policy

The model suggests that the optimal policy includes a real devaluation. We now give three arguments that support the idea that this is only the first stage of the overall optimal policy. This section draws heavily on Larraín (1996a).

5.1 Political support for the reform package

So far, it seems as if industrialization is just a matter of depreciating the *rer* sufficiently. The question is therefore: why don't governments simply devalue? The answer is that a real depreciation has side-effects which are not negligible. By the definition of λ, it is apparent that, given e, a higher λ implies a lower ω. Hence, as in Kuznets's stylized facts, the proposed strategy involves a deterioration of income distribution and, therefore, political economy arguments put a counterweight to the desired depreciation. However, in Larraín (1996a) we show that if electors are rational in the sense that they maximize over long horizon periods, the government may play the role of referee and induce industrialization using the *rer*. In the framework of a Nash bargain, that paper proves that workers, who are the majority of voters, may be disposed to accept a lower wage for themselves and higher profits for the entrepreneur today in exchange for higher wages after industrialization is completed. We show there that the condition for industrialization is $\lambda_2/\lambda_1 = \sqrt{\varepsilon/\zeta}$ where $\lambda_1(\lambda_2)$ is the real exchange rate in period 1 (2), ε is the entrepreneurs' discount factor and ζ is the consumers' one. The second-period *rer* policy depends upon the ratio of discount factors. In particular, if $\zeta > \varepsilon$, i.e. if workers are more impatient than entrepreneurs, there must be a second-period real appreciation. In fact this must be the case for workers' consumption to increase over the alternative case of no policy adoption.

5.2 Entrepreneurial effort in the tradable sector

A *potential* obstacle to the success of a non-interventionist policy relates to entrepreneurial effort *in the tradable sector*.[7]. In fact if the investment shown in equation 9.2 includes some form of further requirement over the entrepreneurial effort it can be shown that there may be a negative link between the level of the *rer* and entrepreneurial effort. Let us first consider effort supply. When the *rer* is the marginal reward to entrepreneurial capacity, from the entrepreneur's point of view, a real devaluation has an income effect (the increase in profits, which calls for more consumption of leisure) and a substitution effect (leisure becomes more expensive). *Effort supply* may increase or fall depending on the relative strengths of each effect. If the substitution effect dominates, then the entrepreneurial effort issue is unimportant. If the income effect is stronger, then a higher *rer* conveys less effort. If the model is extended to include a non-tradable sector, then the effect of the real devaluation on *aggregate* entrepreneurial effort is not clear.

On the demand side, the link between effort and *rer* is also ambiguous. On the one hand a real depreciation increases profits, and so it does with factor demand. On the other hand, it increases the marginal reward to entrepreneurial capacity. The result will therefore depend on the elasticity of substitution between entrepreneurial capacity and other factors. In the benchmark case of Cobb–Douglas technology, we can show that a real devaluation increases effort demand. The same happens with elasticities smaller than 1. With substitution elasticities bigger than 1, the result depends crucially on the *initial level* of the *rer*: if it is already high (a threshold undervaluation), then for all elasticities of substitution bigger than 1 the converse relationship holds. Adding up supply and demand effects, several cases may arise. Assuming Cobb–Douglas technology, there will generally be a negative relationship between *actual effort* and *rer*. This is the first relationship between effort and *rer*. We call it λ^{actual}.[8]

A second one can be found by exploring the conditions under which industrialization arises. Using the same methodology as the one used to derive equation 9.3, we may show that industrialization occurs when the following condition holds:

$$\lambda > \lambda^{**} \equiv \frac{1}{(1+\mu)E} + \frac{F}{L}$$

where μ is now the productivity gain associated with industrialization. The depreciation needed is a positive function of the fixed investment per worker and *decreasing* on the entrepreneurial effort. The higher actual effort is, the lower the required real depreciation, λ^{**}. We call this second relationship λ^{Ind}.

We have therefore two curves, both negatively sloped. Multiple cases may arise again. Let us consider the two simplest cases.

Panel I in Figure 9.2 illustrates the simplest possible case where a real devaluation may induce industrialization but at the expense of entrepreneurial effort. As the devaluation changes the input mix, it also changes the nature

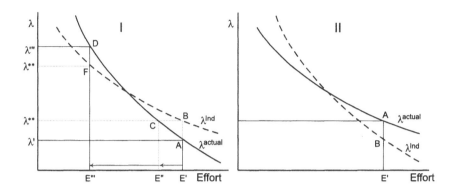

Figure 9.2 Entrepreneurial effort in the tradable sector and real exchange rate

of the goods produced. Imagine we are initially at point A, with high effort. The corresponding λ^{**} is just above at point B. If the government implements λ^{**}, the result will not be industrialization because the real devaluation will induce a fall in actual effort. The economy will then go to point C, where we still have $\lambda < \lambda^{**}$. However, a big depreciation, for instance one like λ''', is able to do it, because the fall in entrepreneurial effort is more than matched by the increase in λ and the consequent factor substitution. However, the produced good will be more intensive in factors other than entrepreneurial capacity. As the real depreciation reduces real wages, it is likely that industrialization will be labour- and/or natural resource-intensive. Panel II is different in that now the λ^{actual} curve lies above the λ^{Ind} curve. Hence, if the economy starts in point A in Panel II it will get industrialized immediately as the threshold level for λ is below it. This panel is therefore less exigent on the required level for λ. In fact, for huge real depreciation it states that effort falls so much that industrialization never arises.

5.3 Optimal rer policy in a second stage of industrialization

Assume that the *rer* has been depreciated, some IRS sectors have developed and, consequently, there is growth. As far as the *rer* is concerned, starting from this undervalued level, its long-run trend will most likely be towards an appreciation.[9] The main reason lies in the Ricardo–Balassa effect. Should the government let this happen? Can the appreciation induce *deindustrialization* as the Dutch disease problem suggests? This section will show that, on the contrary, letting the *rer* appreciate in the second stage of industrialization is in many cases the appropriate way to put incentives on the right track.

To analyse this problem let us assume that along with the sectoral differences among the F_i there are two other differences among subsectors *within the tradable sector*. First, we assume that they differ in their imported input intensities. Table 9.1 shows some data that back the choices they follow.

Table 9.1 Share of imported inputs by sector in selected countries

	Chile	Argentina	Brazil	China	India	Europe	Asia
Agriculture	2.2%	0.6%	0.8%	0.6%	0.6%	4.3%	8.4%
Minerals	4.4%	8.6%	11.2%	1.8%	43.5%	37.9%	25.3%
Energy	5.8%	0.7%	2.7%	1.8%	4.6%	5.1%	11.0%
Food processing	2.1%	0.2%	0.9%	0.5%	1.5%	3.7%	3.8%
Textiles	6.7%	0.4%	0.6%	1.5%	0.8%	5.8%	4.1%
Average	4.2%	2.1%	3.2%	1.2%	10.2%	11.4%	10.5%
Motors and machinery	37.0%	14.8%	8.4%	2.5%	10.5%	10.0%	4.5%
Instruments, electronics & machinery	33.3%	11.9%	7.9%	3.7%	16.2%	13.2%	11.5%
Vehicle parts	5.0%	1.1%	2.3%	1.1%	9.5%	5.4%	0.9%
Vehicles	13.2%	13.9%	1.1%	2.3%	1.9%	7.1%	14.9%
Other transport	38.0%	20.6%	59.3%	4.7%	10.1%	11.0%	7.1%
Other manufacturing	19.5%	5.0%	2.6%	17.1%	21.9%	29.7%	10.4%
Average	24.3%	11.2%	13.6%	5.2%	11.7%	12.7%	8.2%
Ratio manufactured/ natural resources	5.7	5.3	4.2	4.3	1.1	1.1	0.8

Source: OECD Development Centre, Social Accounting Matrices [***1].

In fact, in Latin America it appears that industrial (I) sectors use more intensively imported inputs than natural resource-based sectors (NR). This also appears the case in China. In India, as there is strong import substitution, there is no significant sectoral differentiation in imported input intensities. As we do not have data for specific European or Asian countries all trade among countries within the region is taken into account in the social accounting matrices (SAMs).

The second difference concerns productivity gains. We make here a strong assumption which needs some explanation. Let the production function be

$$y_i = A_i L\alpha_i M\beta_i \tag{9.5}$$

where A_i is a total factor productivity (TFP) function and M is an imported input. There is no capital. We assume that the TFP behaves differently depending on each sector. One reason which we do not consider could be that some sectors use human capital more intensively so the TFP can be

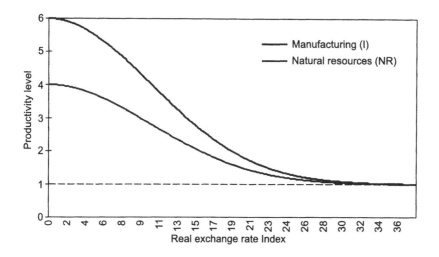

Figure 9.3 Productivity and real exchange rate level in the tradable sector

higher in those sectors. As in Young (1993), our specific assumption is that the potential productivity gains that a producer can make are sector-dependent. However, we depart from Young's approach by explicitly assuming what drives productivity increases. We state that:

$$A_i = A_i(\lambda), \quad A_{i'} < 0, A_{i'}(0) = A_{i'}(\infty) = 0, i = NR, I \tag{9.6}$$

Equation 9.6 suggests that a real appreciation induces productivity gains in tradable sectors. Intuitively the reason is clear: a real appreciation generates a profit squeeze in the tradable sector which induces management to improve efficiency and therefore to get productivity gains. The causality here is precisely the opposite from in the Balassa–Samuelson case and in fact it reinforces it. Indeed, assume that productivity is already higher in tradable than in nontradable sectors, so there is a real appreciation trend. As the latter increases productivity in the tradable sector, it reinforces the sectoral productivity differential, making the trend stronger. For this not to become an explosive path, equation 9.6 must look as shown in Figure 9.3.

Figure 9.3 assumes that the impact of the real appreciation on productivity is stronger in manufacturing than in natural resources. In what follows we will of course sensibilize the model to this variable.

Assuming this specification for productivity, we may now proceed to solve the model for profits defined as $\pi_i = \lambda y - L - \lambda M - F - \lambda X$. The profit function is therefore obtained from the maximization of this function under L and M. From the first-order conditions we may calculate factor demand functions, which using the production function determine the supply function. Finally, the latter and the definition of profits determine the profit

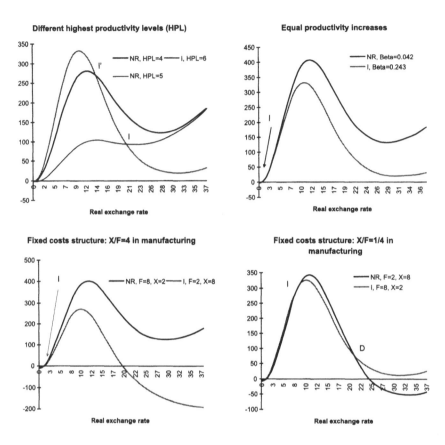

Figure 9.4 Stimulations of the profit function

function $\pi_i = \pi(\alpha_i, \beta_i, \lambda)$. Hence, this function depends exclusively on the real exchange rate and the technical parameters.

Figure 9.4 displays the profit function. We sensibilize it assuming various different parameter configurations. The upper-left panel is the key one. It illustrates the paramount role of the link between productivity level and real exchange rate. As in Figure 9.3, if for each *rer* the productivity level is bigger in manufacturing (a highest productivity level (HPL) of 6 in manufacturing versus 4 in natural resources), then profits are greater in *natural resources* for very depreciated *rer*s while they are higher in manufacturing if λ is low enough. The point at which profit functions cross each other (signalled with an I) depends on the different relationships between productivity and real exchange rate. One crossing point is I (with the HPL in natural resources equal to 4) or I' (with HPL in natural resources equal to 5). A consistent result of the simulations is that the crossing points occur with positive profits as long as HPL in manufacturing exceeds HPL in natural resources.

The upper-right panel shows a situation where both HPLs are equal to 6 (the HPL for manufacturing in Figure 9.4), the difference arising from the βs, the imported input intensity. We used as values the parameters we found for Chile in Table 9.1. As manufacturing uses imported inputs much more intensively, then profits are lower except for very appreciated *rer*, but at negative profits. Crossing of the profit functions also happens at negative profits when we assume different fixed cost structure, as in the bottom-left panel. An interesting situation occurs in the bottom-right panel where we also deal with the fixed cost structure. Here we assume that manufacturing uses intensively domestic factors as fixed investment. A very depreciated *rer* therefore reduces the fixed cost and generates profits. For more appreciated *rer*s, the curves cross each other and a second crossing obtains for very low λs at negative profits.

Let us now introduce the real appreciation trend. We take the *trajectory of* λ *as given*. One way of understanding this is to assume that productivity in tradable sectors is initially higher than in non-tradable sectors. We do not model the latter explicitly. We consider explicitly only the upper-left panel in Figure 9.4 because profit functions cross at positive profit levels and, contrary to the bottom-right panel, a very undervalued *rer* does not immediately induce industrialization (this seems more in accordance with reality). Finally, this case seems the crucial one as the different evolutions of productivity were the main determinants of functions' crossings.

On the right-hand side of Figure 9.5 we display the *rer* trend appreciation described above. In the left-hand side panel we show the profit functions described previously. The economy starts at a time near the origin. Following the discussion in Section 1, we assume that the government has already devalued the currency, so λ is big. The left-hand panel tells us that for a

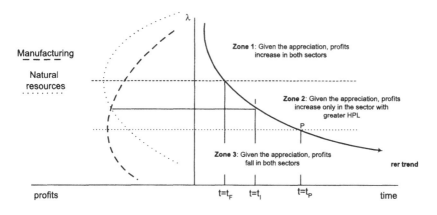

Figure 9.5 Impact of the Balassa–Samuelson effect on profits (based on upper-left panel, Figure 9.4)

sufficiently undervalued *rer*, profits in natural resources will exceed those in manufacturing. As the country is specialized, its tradable sector consists only of that sector. We assume that productivity in this sector is already higher than that of the underlying non-tradable sector. Following the Balassa–Samuelson effect, this will induce a real appreciation trend. As assumed in equation 9.6 and shown in Figure 9.5, the appreciation will induce productivity gains in the tradable sector which will further increase the productivity differential. In the process of appreciation, profits in the natural resource sector start falling at a more depreciated real exchange rate. However, during time $t < t_I$, they are bigger than profits in manufacturing. But starting at $t = t_F$ profits in natural resources fall. We shall see what this may mean in a political economy framework.

The real appreciation due to the Balassa–Samuelson effect may be a source of industrialization, unlike the Dutch disease. In fact, since $t = t_I$, profits are higher in the manufacturing sector, so resources should naturally flow towards it, as stated in Rodrik (1992). The sustained real appreciation induces industrialization because rational entrepreneurs foresee that using a technology whose potential productivity gains are relatively small and which is too dependent on domestic factors increases their vulnerability to *rer* fluctuations. In this sense, the steady state real *appreciation* that the country is suffering is a *source of industrialization*, not the reverse.

One caveat must be raised at this point. It concerns the political economy accompanying this framework. One aspect is that $t = t_I$ may be so far in the future that entrepreneurs may find it profitable to face the trend appreciation by lobbying for an earlier depreciation. This reaction may be due to short investment horizons or low entrepreneurial effort. Alternatively, assume that entrepreneurs want to have a rate of return on their capital equal to r (which may be given by the international financial market). Given this and the capital already invested, it can be seen in Figure 9.6 that there exists some 'desired' level of profits, π_d, which determines the 'start' of political pressures.

In fact when the economy arrives at point L (from above as time moves unidirectionally), entrepreneurs in the natural resource sectors will see that their profitability will fall below their reservation level. At the same time, profitability in the manufacturing sector is low, so that sector may even not exist. Therefore at $t = t_{lobby}$ political pressures will clearly be towards a depreciation. The depreciation makes the trend curve move upwards. The *rer* jumps from point L to point D. On the profit side, this implies that profits increase in the natural resource sector, D^R, while they fall in the manufacturing sector.

The interesting question is what will happen when the economy suffers another real appreciation and finds itself at point L'. The answer is a function of how the government reacted at point L. In this simple setting, there is no reason to doubt that the government will again devalue the currency. In that case the previous cycle can be repeated *ad infinitum*.

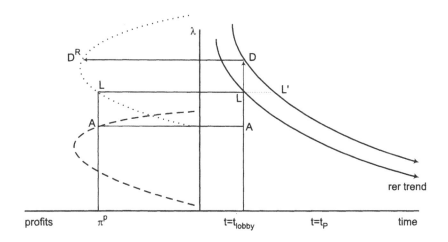

Figure 9.6 A non-industrialization trap due to protectionism

The alternative policy when first arriving at point L is to appreciate the currency. This would mean passing from points such as L to points such as A. This extreme and simplistic case, which neglects all sorts of installation costs, indicates that the appreciation would make the natural resource sector disappear whereas a manufacturing sector would emerge instantaneously. To some extent industrialization appears as *self-fulfilling*:[10] if entrepreneurs believe that at points like L or L' the government will depreciate the currency to protect a sector not ready to accommodate the appreciation, firms will not invest and the sector will never be ready to accommodate it. If, on the contrary, they expect the government to let the currency appreciate they are obliged to choose between alternatives: make the investment effort while the natural resource sector is profitable and raise future profits in a different sector or no effort but cessation. Therefore the Balassa–Samuelson effect may induce industrialization or, alternatively, it may delay it depending on the lobbies' strength.

It must be clear that a real appreciation will not necessarily be able to induce that. If the appreciation is too strong, firms will fail to adjust and lobbying will become a highly attractive alternative. A mild real appreciation, which some preliminary back-of-the-envelope estimates put at around 2 per cent a year, gives time for firms to explore market opportunities, choose technologies and eventual partners, seek international linkages, including distribution channels, etc.

6 A view of two benchmark cases: Chile and South Korea

Chile represents the best example of the free market strategy in Latin America. In fact, the Chilean government started to reform the economy in 1975.

Since then, with ups and downs and minor exceptions, it has privatized most public enterprises and given access to competition to those that still remain under public control, it has freed all prices in the economy, liberalized the labour market, privatized and funded social security, diminished the progressiveness of the tax system using a uniform and universal VAT as a main source of tax collection, unilaterally opened the economy to international trade, homogenizing tariffs and eliminating all quota restrictions, freed all capital movements almost completely (with recent exceptions for very short-run speculative capital movements) and renounced any sort of industrial policy. It is the most interesting case to use as a benchmark as it has already two decades of existence.[11] The reforms have been different in other Latin American countries but they share at least one common important feature, namely their (increasing) reliance on price signals to induce resource allocation. This is strictly the case in Chile, and to a lesser extent in other cases like Argentina or Mexico. Brazil still uses active industrial policies but the MERCOSUR trade agreement and the promised free trade area of the Americas will probably lead Brazil and its partners to rely more and more on price incentives. Finally, many of the reforms actually under implementation in Latin American countries follow the Chilean pattern.[12]

On the other hand, South Korea (like Taiwan) is probably the best example of the activist approach to industrialization. Starting in the 1960s, South Korea implemented a controlled external liberalization and managed to have sound fundamentals. A battery of *selective interventions* has been used to try to change resource allocation. a wide range of policies have been implemented to intervene in markets, from direct cash subsidies, credit preferences and preferential electricity and railroad rates to the Heavy and Chemical Industries Drive (1973–9). There is a growing consensus that they have played a paramount role in the development of South Korea, although the strength of their impact is obviously a subject of much discussion (see for instance Rodrik, 1995; Amsden, 1986; World Bank, 1993). As a result, for three decades, growth rates have been very high except for specific years linked to the oil and debt crises. South Korea also displayed enormous flexibility, adapting to changing economic conditions when those shocks took place (Corbo and Suh, 1992).

We assume that the start of economic reform, year 0, is 1960 for South Korea and 1976 for Chile (Sachs and Warner, 1994). This may induce some errors because, as policies have changed in both countries since then, the selection of year 0 must be somewhat arbitrary. For instance, in Chile the use of the *rer* as a resource allocation device to promote the development of the tradable sector really started in 1983–4 after the debt crisis. On the other hand, South Korea started actively to promote exports in 1963, abandoning its import substitution strategy (Lee, 1996). However, in the case of Chile this choice may induce a stronger bias as in 1982 there was the most severe crisis since the 1930s. As a way of dealing with this we present in all

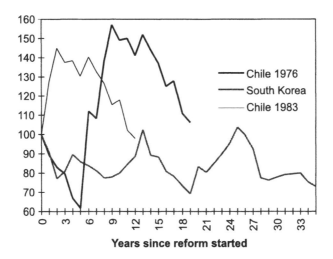

Figure 9.7 Real exchange rate indices

Source: Chile: author's calculations; refers to *rer* relative to the USA only and deflated by CPI. South Korea: until 1975 real exchange rate for exports taken from Westphal and Kim (1982), which correct for price distortions; since then, identical methodology as for Chile.

Note: Latin American definition, year 0 = 100.

the figures that follow two starting points for Chile, 1976 and 1983 (which by the way creates the opposite bias). The latter date is chosen so as to extend the series for comparability reasons. Figure 9.7 shows the evolution of the real exchange rate in Chile and South Korea.

Figure 9.7 illustrates quite well the relative importance of the real exchange rate in each country's economic record. In Chile, the first appreciation period reflects the policy in which the exchange rate was used as a stabilization tool. The poor macroeconomic management that accompanied it led to the big crisis in 1982, year 5. The huge devaluation that followed (less exaggerated if one considers other commercial partners) illustrates not only the policy reaction due to the huge external crisis but also the desire to induce a massive resource reallocation towards tradable sectors.

This does not mean that South Korea did not use price incentives. Indeed the *rer* shown in Figure 9.7 takes those distortions into account (it assumes that from 1976 those distortions have been negligible). The point is that the sorts of price incentives used in each country are totally different in nature. In South Korea there have been significant distortions at the *micro*economic level, *within the tradable sector*. For example, all such distortions implied that the *rer* for imports and exports differed quite considerably, as Table 9.2 shows. In discussing the role of government policies in the case of South Korea, Lee (1996) finds econometric support for the positive role

Table 9.2 Ratio of effective exchange rates for exports relative
          to imports in South Korea

1962	1.03	1969	1.18
1963	1.28	1970	1.18
1964	1.14	1971	1.22
1965	1.04	1972	1.20
1966	1.09	1973	1.19
1967	1.13	1974	1.17
1968	1.17	1975	1.12

Source: World Bank (1993: p. 128).

played by *tax incentives* in promoting labour productivity and capital accumulation, but not total factor productivity. He also finds that *trade* policies had a
negative impact on productivity.

The wedge between the effective exchange rate for exports and imports was
maintained at around 20 per cent from 1968 to 1974. It was rarely smaller
than 10 per cent. For all practical purposes, this sort of intersectoral
discrimination has not existed in Chile. The only 'distortion' implemented
in Chile concerns the relative price of tradable goods, for which a reasonable
approximation is the *rer* in Figure 9.7.

6.1 The similarities

We start the comparison by noting that, during the first sixteen years of
reform implementation, per capita GDP growth in South Korea significantly
exceeded the Chilean rate (6.7 per cent versus 3.2 per cent). It was also more
stable. Both reform programmes led to an increase in the growth rates from
previous periods.

The most striking similarity between the Chilean and South Korean
experiences concerns investment, which is shown in Figure 9.9.

Starting from very low investment levels (7 per cent of GDP in South Korea
and 15 per cent in Chile), both countries were able to increase their respective
investment ratios to more than 25 per cent of GDP by year 16. This feature has
also been present in other Asian countries but in a less spectacular fashion.

The increase in investment in South Korea was also accompanied by a fall
in consumption, both private and public, measured as a share of GDP. In the
case of private consumption this fall is normal because the initial income level
in South Korea was very low. After thirty years, private consumption seems to
be stabilizing at around 60 per cent of GDP, a similar figure to Chile's today.
Private consumption in Chile has been much more volatile. The huge increase
during the first five years reflects the boom at the end of the 1970s. This,
coupled with the increase in investment, led to a major crisis in 1982.
Since then, private consumption seems to have stabilized at slightly below

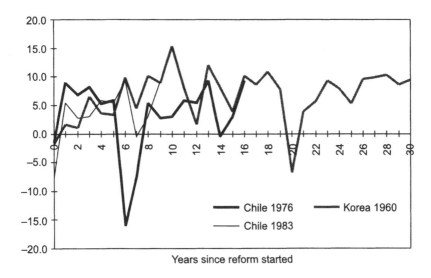

Figure 9.8 Per capita growth since reform started (%)

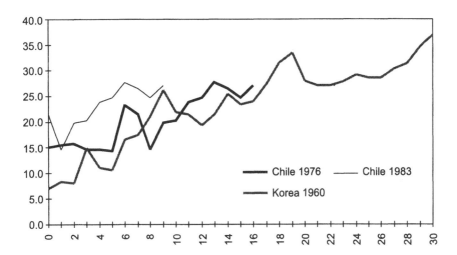

Figure 9.9 Investment (% GDP)

60 per cent of GDP. Government consumption in Chile is bigger than in South Korea. It has also represented a very important part of the adjustment: sixteen years after the reform started, it has been reduced to nearly half what it was at the beginning (see Figure 9.10).

The adjustment in total consumption led to an increase in the savings ratio in both countries. In South Korea they passed from almost nil at the time the

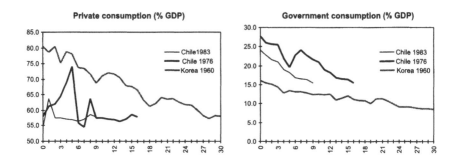

Figure 9.10 Private and government consumption

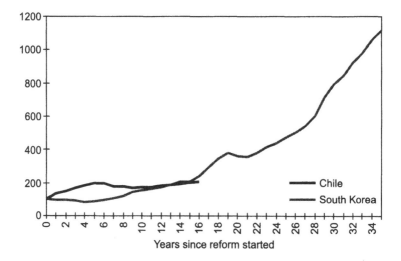

Figure 9.11 Real wages (index, reform year = 100)
Source: IMF, *International Financial Statistics*, CD-ROM.

reforms started to a figure of about 35 per cent today. In Chile they represented approximately 15 per cent of GDP at the beginning of the reforms
and today they have reached almost 27 per cent of GDP (Morandé, 1996).

Real wages have behaved similarly (see Figure 9.11): since the reforms
started, both countries have seen their real wages increase to a comparable
extent by year 16. The evolution, however, differed during the first five
years. This difference is not attributable to the 'model' itself, but, in the Chilean case, to the macroeconomic management that led to the 1982 crisis.

One final similarity is provided by the behaviour of R&D. In Table 9.3 we
present R&D expenditures for different countries at the beginning of the
1970s and around 1990.

Table 9.3 R&D and its sources

		R&D	Public funds	Firms	Foreign funds	Other		R&D	Public funds	Firms	Foreign funds	Other
		(% GDP)	(% R&D)					(% GDP)	(% R&D)			
Argentina	1974	0.3	87.0	7.2	3.0	2.8	1992	0.3	85.0	8.0	2.0	5.0
Brazil	1974	0.3	89.7	n.d.	4.8	5.5	1982	0.6	66.9	19.8	5.3	8.1
Mexico	1973	0.1	62.2	17.0	1.6	19.3	1989	0.2	95.0	5.0	0.0	0.0
Chile	n.d.	n.d.	n.d.	n.d.	n.d.		1988	0.4	70.4	18.2	3.3	8.1
South Korea	1974	0.3	71.9	8.7	3.1	16.3	1992	2.1	17.2	82.4	0.4	0.0
USA	1974	2.2	52.3	44.1	n.d.	3.6	1988	2.8	45.9	50.2	0.0	3.9
France	1974	1.8	55.3	40.1	3.9	0.8	1991	2.5	48.8	42.5	8.0	0.7
Germany	1973	2.1	49.8	48.6	1.1	0.4	1989	2.9	34.1	63.3	2.1	0.5
UK	1972	2.0	48.9	44.6	5.5	1.0	1991	2.1	34.2	50.2	11.7	3.8

Sources: UNESCO, Statistical Yearbook, 1976 (Table 8.4, p. 702), 1995 (Table 5.7, pp. 5–40); IMF for GDP figures.

In 1973, year 13 following our notation, South Korea spent 0.3 per cent of GDP on R&D. Chile, in year 12, 1988, spent 0.4 per cent of GDP. Moreover, the funding sources were similar: in South Korea, the government funded 71.9 per cent of all R&D whereas the Chilean government funded 70.4 per cent. If one adds firms and others in South Korea, one arrives at similar figures to those for firms in Chile. However, it remains to be seen whether Chile will be able to increase its expenditures on R&D from its low present level to developed-country levels, as South Korea did. This implies a huge effort for firms.

6.2 One unsettled aspect: income distribution dynamics

In the two countries under consideration income distribution is normally regarded as a difference rather than a similarity; and certainly this is the case for income levels. To be sure, income is much more equally distributed in South Korea than in Chile. However, the dynamics of income distribution show some similarities. The non-interventionist approach led to a worsening income distribution in the first phase, just as Kusnetz showed. Indeed income distribution has worsened in Chile: the Gini coefficient passed from 0.49 in the period 1969–71, to 0.52 in 1979–81 and then to 0.54 in 1982–4 (Meller, 1992). But surprisingly, this also happened in South Korea but at a lower level. In fact, South Korea's income distribution first worsened from 0.33 in the period 1965–70 to 0.39 in 1971–80 (World Bank, 1993). However, during the 1980s it improved, returning to a figure similar to the initial one. To decide whether the income distribution issue is a similarity or a difference we need to see what will happen in Chile in future years. One positive but partial signal concerns the evolution of poverty: from 44.6 per cent of the whole population in 1987 it decreased to 26 per cent in 1995 (Ffrench-Davis, 1996).

6.3 A look at the differences

Despite the similarities displayed at the aggregate level, there are significant differences in outcome in each case. We illustrate a few of them.

An apparent similarity between South Korea and Chile concerns total exports. This can be seen in Figure 9.12.

By year 19, the export share in both countries looks similar. However, the starting point differs considerably: in year 0, 1960, South Korea exported only 3.4 per cent of its GDP, whereas Chile's figure was 25.1 per cent. From this point of view, the experiences look very different.

Also, the similar behaviour of aggregate investment in Chile and South Korea hides profound differences in composition. This is shown in Figure 9.13. Apparently, from the beginning, most investment in South Korea went into *business construction*. In some years this represented 60 per cent of

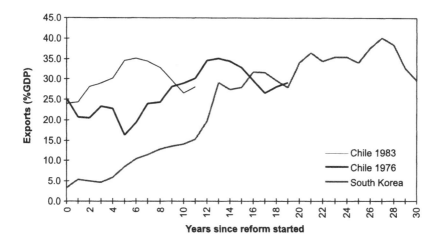

Figure 9.12 Exports (% GDP)
Source: IMF, *International Financial Statistics*, CD-ROM.

total investment. Residential construction was initially high in South Korea but fell abruptly from the second year.

In Chile the two main components of total investment have been *residential construction* and *transport equipment*. Business construction remained low during the first decade of implementation of reforms and since then it has increased more than twofold. *Investment in machinery* has been relatively low *and* decreasing. In South Korea, the level is similar, but the trend is the opposite (preliminary figures shown on the dotted line seem to indicate that this situation is reversing).

Two pieces of evidence suggest that all this implies that Chile is late with respect to industrialisation. First, as shown in Figure 9.14, manufacturing value added, as a share of GDP, moved in exactly opposite directions in the two countries.

Unfortunately, the data for South Korea began in 1970, ten years after the reforms started. However, it is very likely that by year 0 manufacturing value added was lower there than in Chile. By year 10 both ratios were similar, but South Korea continued to grow at a very high pace, whereas in Chile the manufacturing sector has been contracting.

A second piece of evidence is the case of manufacturing exports. They are shown in Figure 9.15 (as a share of total exports and compared with income in the USA in PPP terms). It can be seen that in the last twenty years, the share of manufacturing exports in Chile has remained remarkably stable whereas in Asia it has increased steadily.

Figure 9.15 suggests that as far as manufacturing exports are concerned, and consequently industrialization, the Asian countries look much more

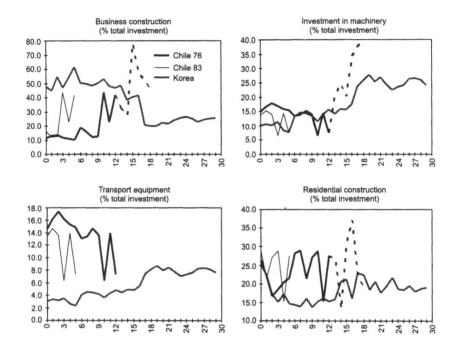

Figure 9.13 Sectoral composition of investment

Source: Penn World Table, investment data. Chilean data have been updated using the *Boletín Mensual*, Banco Central de Chile, various issues. For residential construction and business construction we used data for construction started in the entire country. The evolution of machinery was proxied using data from national accounts.

successful than Chile.[13] Certainly, in the latter case there has been industrialization in terms of basic processing of raw materials but not, in a significant way, in more sophisticated goods.

A note of caution is worth signalling here. Chile differs in a very significant way from South Korea, namely in its wealthier natural resource base. This suggests that the lag registered in Chilean industrialization relative to South Korea may simply reflect the stronger comparative advantage in producing these goods and not be an outcome of actual policies. On other hand, if we take the cases of Thailand and, especially, Malaysia, which are somewhat more similar to Chile as regards natural resources, Chile's industrialization probably still lags behind and one cannot avoid considering that this may have something to do with policy.

7 Conclusions

The real exchange rate is the key relative price which a non-interventionist approach to development should first consider. From a theoretical point of

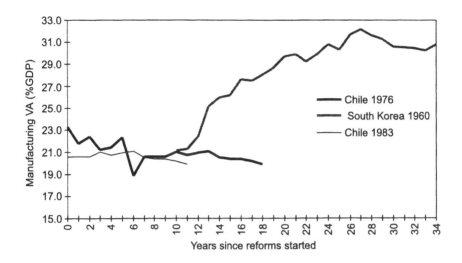

Figure 9.14 Manufacturing value added

Source: 1970–90: World Bank Stars database. Chile since 1986: IDB (1995), South Korea since 1990: ADB (1996).

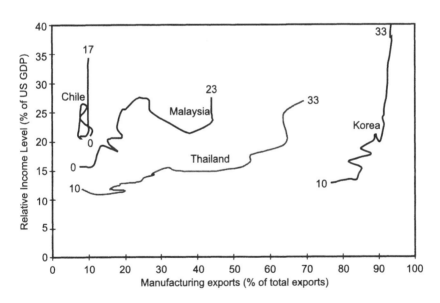

Figure 9.15 Manufacturing exports and income level in selected countries

Source: Income level, Penn World Table; manufacturing exports, World Bank.

Note

Data start in 1970.

view, industrialization may be achieved through real exchange rate management because an undervalued currency creates profits *all over* the tradable sector which can be reinvested in industrialization. However, we have seen that as a result of this approach, industrialization may be delayed. Three reasons have been presented. First, a policy of undervalued currency involves a worsening in income distribution. This implies that the strong initial real devaluation may probably not be undertaken. As a consequence, industrialization is delayed. However, *if* the government is able to enforce a contract ensuring a future real appreciation (that is, a further improvement in income distribution), rational workers should be willing to accept lower wages in early periods. However, this is most likely in countries with good initial income distribution.

Second, we have also seen that, under certain circumstances, the real devaluation may reduce entrepreneurial effort. This may also delay industrialization or at least change its characteristics, making it more intensive in factors other than entrepreneurial capacity, i.e. raw labour or natural resources. The third explanation is that after the initial real devaluation, a policy of real appreciation is optimal (moreover, if the initial phase starts a period of strong growth, this is *unavoidable*). One reason is that entrepreneurs will then have incentives to shift production towards products that can better resist real exchange rate movements. Manufacturing goods provide this because, on average, the imported component of their inputs is more important. Another reason is that manufacturing goods may provide higher potential productivity gains enabling firms to afford the long-term real appreciation. This would mean that in the long run it is better for the country to shift to these goods as growth will then be higher. However, if the entrepreneurs' lobby is strong enough, it may bring pressure for further real devaluation once profits arrive at some threshold level. In that case, the shift towards industrialization is delayed.

The model in the first section shows that only a huge real depreciation is able to induce industrialization. As this is probably not feasible, the economy will probably remain in a situation of indeterminate equilibrium. The range of indeterminacy depends on the investments needed to industrialize. The model thus suggests that, within the indeterminacy range, the traditional 'big push' arguments remain valid. In other words, if industrialization is not feasible or is likely to be delayed, then a more activist policy may make it a real possibility (if it was not) or accelerate it (if it was already under way).

We have briefly examined two benchmark cases, Chile (non-interventionist or passive) and South Korea (activist or interventionist). Since reforms started, in 1960 in South Korea and in 1976 in Chile, some macroeconomic variables have behaved similarly: GDP growth has been high in both countries (though much higher and less volatile in South Korea), whereas consumption, both private and public, has fallen. On the other hand, savings and investment have risen impressively. However, this picture is misleading if one analyses the details. Even though total exports have reached similar levels after sixteen years of implementation, Chile started from a much higher level. Hence, the Chilean strategy appears to be less successful than the South Korean one if one compares total exports. A look at the composition of exports shows that manufacturing exports, as a share of total exports, has remained remarkably stable in Chile. In the case of South Korea they have increased very significantly. In part, this reflects the structure of production in each country: while value added in South Korea's manufacturing sectors has been increasing steadily, in Chile, on the contrary, it has been falling (as a share of total output). The composition of investment also suggests that there are strong differences. Only very recently has Chilean investment in machinery and business construction started increasing. Before, residential construction and transport equipment absorbed most capital formation in Chile; exactly the opposite occurred in South Korea.

One is tempted, then, to conclude that relative to the starting dates and as far as industrialization is concerned, Chile lags behind South Korea. At least three elements suggest that the recent policy measures adopted by the Chilean government, notably a major educational reform and a vast public works programme, are a step in the right direction. One element is that, as the real exchange rate has been appreciating since 1990, traditional export sectors are now suffering a profit squeeze. As at least part of that appreciation is undoubtedly permanent, these sectors should think about shifting efforts towards products with higher value added. Indeed, this is creating an interesting dynamic where firms are actively looking for new investment opportunities. Better infrastructure and a more qualified labour force may certainly help in this process. Furthermore, Chile's recent membership of MERCOSUR should encourage firms in manufacturing sectors looking for investment opportunities in that vast market. Moreover, the worsening income distribution is starting to become a serious threat to stability. This implies that there will be increasing pressures directed to reduce the already very high fiscal savings ratio. Once again, infrastructure and education are socially profitable public expenditures that strike at both problems: they increase wages, reduce unemployment and create better prospects for poor people, while favouring industrial restructuring. However, as this may induce a further real appreciation, efforts must be made to reallocate actual public expenditures. This does not prevent the government from implementing policies that are better focused on the objective.

It remains to be seen whether income distribution improves in Chile after its continuous deterioration since the 1970s, as it did in South Korea during the last decade and a half. In the case of Chile, this issue constitutes a major policy concern. To be sure, some crucial progress has been made: poverty has decreased from 45 per cent of families in 1985–8 to around 26 per cent in 1994. However, the increasing opulence of the richer part of the population is incompatible with any reduction in the misery of the poor, at least for any length of time. The improvement in income distribution is a key element for the long-run political sustainability of the Chilean approach to development.

Notes

* This paper was prepared for the conference 'Exchange rate policies in the emerging Asian countries: Domestic and international issues' held in Seoul, South Korea the 15 and 16 November 1996. The conference was organized by the Association of the Monetary Union of Europe, the Centre d'études prospectives et d'informations internationales (CEPII), both in Paris, and the Korean Institute of Finance in Seoul. It was presented in the session 'What is the optimal exchange rate policy for an emerging economy?'. I acknowledge the discussions held with, and the comments made to, previous versions by F. Bourguignon, M. Bussolo, S. Collignon, J. de Gregorio, G. de Ménil, S. Dessus, P. Petri, J. Pisany-Ferry, G. Saint Paul, J. von Maltzan, C. Winograd and Ch. Wyplosz. I am especially indebted to J. Williamson for his detailed comments. I also thank P. Owoaje for her corrections to the English version. Any remaining errors are my responsibility. The opinions expressed here do not necessarily represent the OECD. Address: OECD Development Centre, 94 rue Chardon Lagache, 75016 Paris, France, Tel. (331) 45-24-78-27, Fax: (331) 45-24-79-43. Since February 1997: Ministry of Finance, Teatinos 120 Piso 12, Santiago, Chile, Fax: (562) 696-47-98.

1 For this to be true, we need to assume as a background the absence of perfect capital markets. Should they exist, then any firm wishing to industrialize could obtain the required funds in the capital market. However, typically industrialization may need a critical mass of firms investing. In that case, even a perfect financial system may fail to finance the investments if there is no coordination among firms. Each isolated firm could not get the financing, whereas a threshold number of them could.

2 The practical implementation of a real devaluation often contemplates the use of PPP rules. As many authors have argued, these rules normally convey a higher inflation rate as a by-product. See Adams and Gros (1986), Lizondo (1991) and Calvo *et al.* (1995).

3 Privatization has been the most massive outside Eastern Europe. See Larraín and Winograd (1996) for the cases of Argentina and Chile.

4 To understand why this is so, we should analyse the causes and consequences of the import substitution model that prevailed over almost all Latin America during the post-war period. For the purposes of this chapter, let's accept that the above statements apply.

5 This principle states that

a distortion is best countered, or conversely, deliberately introduced if desired as a non-economic objective, by a tax instrument that acts directly on the relevant margin. Thus the first-best policy response to an external economy in production is an appropriate Pigovian subsidy; it is only if this is impossible that the indirect effect of a tariff to stimulate domestic production can be useful as a second-best (or worse) policy.

(Dixit, 1985: 314)

Therefore, in order to maximize welfare, policy instruments must be targeted as closely as possible to the source of the market failure.

6 A successful policy as defined in this chapter therefore relies to a large extent on the ability to implement adequate stabilization policies. For example, this requires the existence of a quite sophisticated and deep financial market and satisfactory insertion in world capital markets.

7 The term 'effort' does not primarily imply working hours. We are thinking more in terms of the decisions of structural transformation that characterizes industrialization. For instance, some of them are uncomfortable, like firing workers whose abilities have no place in the new structure, others are risky, like deciding what to produce, which partly depends on what other firms are doing, or how to finance new investments, while other decisions involve huge efforts of coordination with unknown suppliers and distributors.

One way to understand this section is to put it in the perspective of the broader literature concerning *competition* and *effort*. In so doing, we must accept that an undervalued currency is like a protectionist policy, which by reducing competition with foreign firms in product markets may affect effort supply. The traditional view, consistent with the view taken in this section, is that more competition (i.e. a less undervalued currency) induces an increase in effort supply. In trade theory this point of view has appeared in the discussion of X-inefficiency (for example, Balassa, 1975). Horn *et al.* (1992) arrive at a similar conclusion but in the context of contract theory. On the contrary, our argument is linked to the diverging effects of income and substitution effects on entrepreneurial effort in the tradable sector derived from a real devaluation.

8 As a motivation to this point, let me mention that part of the huge productivity increases experienced in Argentina at the same time as the privatization of public enterprises, the opening of the economy and the increased degree of competition can be attributed, especially in recent years, to the real appreciation of the Argentine peso. Something similar has seemingly happened also in France since the franc has been pegged to the Deutsche Mark, i.e. the *franc fort* policy.

9 This assumption may appear strong. In fact, for developed countries the *rer* seems to converge over very long periods of time to its PPP value. For shorter periods (half a century), the evidence favours the random walk hypothesis more than a decreasing trend (Rogoff, 1996). We are thinking more of developing economies that are catching up. Some evidence for this may be found in De Gregorio and Wolf (1994) and De Gregorio *et al.* (1994). The empirical evidence for the thesis also supports this hypothesis.

10 Industrialization (or the 'good' equilibrium) appears as being self-fulfilling in a number of other papers. The common feature of those models is the presence of returns to scale or externalities of different types. The list includes pecuniary externalities in Murphy *et al.* (1989a, 1989b), increasing social returns to scale in human capital accumulation in Azariadis and Drazen (1990), external economies plus adjustment costs in Krugman (1991), increasing returns in manufacturing in Matsuyama (1991), coordination problems in Rodrik (1996a) and Rodriguez-Clare (1996), and increasing returns and pecuniary externalities in Ciconne and Matsuyama (1996) among others.

11 On industrialization in Chile see Ffrench-Davis (1985), Centro de Estudios del Desarrollo (1986) and Gatica (1989) among others. Argentina and Peru initiated their reforms in 1991 and Mexico in 1986.

12 For example, privatization has been implemented in Argentina, Peru and Mexico and social security reform (closely following the Chilean model) has also been adopted in Argentina and Peru. More recently, the Chilean approach to speculative capital movements has also gained much attention in the continent.

13 There is some evidence that in Chile some (endogenous) import substitution is under way. This seems to be a stylized fact on industrialization, but in the Chilean case this is still a minor point. However, it may suggest that the process is at a very early stage.

References

Adams, C. and, Gros D. (1986) 'The consequences of real exchange rate rules for inflation: some illustrative examples', *IMF Staff Papers*, 33.

Amsden, A. (1986), *Asia's Next Giant: South Korea and Late Industrialisation*, Oxford University Press, Oxford.

Asian Development Bank (ADB) (1996) *Asian Development Outlook*.

Azariadis, C. and Drazen A. (1993) 'Threshold externalities in economic development', *Quarterly Journal of Economics*, 105(2), May, 501–74.

Balassa, B. (1975) 'Trade, protection and domestic production: a comment', in B. Kenen (ed.) *International Trade and Finance: Frontiers of Research*, Cambridge University Press, Cambridge.

Balassa, B. and Associates (1982) *Development Strategies in Semi-industrial Economies*, The Johns Hopkins University Press, Baltimore, Md., and London

Bradford C.I. (1990) 'Policy interventions and markets: development strategy typologies and policy options', in G. Gereffi and D. Wyman (eds) *Manufacturing Miracles: Paths of Industrialization in Latin America and East Asia*, Princeton Books, Princeton, NJ.

Calvo, G., Reinhart, C. and Végh, C. (1995) 'Targeting the real exchange rate: theory and evidence', *Journal of Development Economics*, 47.

Centro de Estudios del Desarrollo (1986) *La industria Chilena: Cuatro visiones sectoriales*, CED, Santiago.

Chenery, H., Robinson, S. and Syrquin, M. (1986) *Industrialisation and Growth. A Comparative Study*, Oxford University Press for the World Bank, New York

Ciccone, A. and Matsuyama, K. (1996) 'Start-up costs and pecuniary externalities as barriers to economic development', *Journal of Development Economics*, 49, 33–59.

Corbo, V. and Suh, S. (1992) *Structural Adjustment in a Newly Industrialized Country: The Korean Experience*, The Johns Hopkins University Press, Baltimore, Md.

de Gregorio, J. and Wolf, H. (1994) *Terms of Trade, Productivity, and the Real Exchange Rate*, NBER 4807, Cambridge, Mass.

de Gregorio, J. Giovannini, A. and Wolf, H. (1994) 'International Evidence on Tradables and Nontradables Inflation', *European Economic Review*, June.

Diaz-Alejandro, C. (1975) 'Trade policies and economic development', in P.B. Kenen (ed.) *International Trade and Finance*, Cambridge University Press, Cambridge.

Dixit, A. (1985) 'Tax policy in open economies', in A. Auerbach and M. Feldstein (eds) *Handbook of Public Economics*, Vol. I, North-Holland, Amsterdam.

Dollar, D. and Wolff, E. (1994) *Competitiveness, Convergence and International Specialization*, The MIT Press, Boston, Mass.

Ffrench-Davis, R. (1985) 'Deuda externa, industrialización y ahorro en América Latina', *Colección Estudios CIEPLAN* No. 17, September.

——(1996) 'Distribución y pobreza', mimeo, Instituto chileno de estudios humanísticos, ICHEH, Santiago.

Gatica, J. (1986) *Deindustrialization in Chile*, Westview Press, Boulder, Colo.

Gereffi, G. (1990) 'Big business and the state', G. Gereffi and D. Wyman (eds) *Manufacturing Miracles: Paths of Industrialization in Latin America and East Asia*, Princeton Press, Princeton, NJ.

Helleiner, G.K. (1992) *Trade Policy, Industrialisation and Development*, Clarendon Press, Oxford.

Horn, H., Lang, H. and Lundgren, S. (1992) 'Managerial effort incentives, X-inefficiency and international trade', Seminar Paper No. 507, Institute for International Economic Studies, Stockholm University.

Inter-American Development Bank (IDB) (1995) *Overcoming Volatility, Economic and Social Progress in Latin America*, Washington DC.

Krugman, P. (1991) 'History versus expectations', *Quarterly Journal of Economics*, 106(2), May, 651–67.

Larraín, G. (1996a) 'Relative price incentives and industrialisation', mimeo DELTA, Paris.

——(1996b) 'Public investment and the real exchange rate', paper presented at the XIV Latin American Meeting of the Econometric Society, Rio de Janeiro.

——(1996c) 'Politiques budgétaires et taux de change réel: une revue sélective de la littérature', mimeo DELTA, Paris.

Larraín, G. and Winograd, C. (1996) 'Privatisations massives et finances publiques et macro-économie: le cas de l'Argentine et le Chili', *Revue Économique*, November.

Lee, J.W. (1996) 'Government interventions and productivity growth', *Journal of Economic Growth*, Vol. 1, No. 3, September.

Lizondo, J.S. (1991) 'Real exchange rate targets, nominal exchange rate policies and inflation', *Revista de Análisis Económico*, 6.

Matsuyama, K. (1991) 'Increasing returns, industrialisation and indeterminacy of equilibrium', *Quarterly Journal of Economics*, 106, 617–50.

Meller, P. (1992) *Adjustment and Equity in Chile*, Adjustment and Equity in Developing Countries Series, OECD Development Centre Studies, Paris.

Mesquita-Moreira, M. (1994) *Co-ordination Failures and Government Intervention: Brazil and South Korea Compared*, Macmillan, London.

Morandé, F. (1996) *Savings in Chile: What Went Right?*, IDB Working Paper Series 322, Washington, DC.

Murphy K., Shleifer A. and Vishny R. (1989a) 'Income distribution, market size and industrialisation', *Quarterly Journal of Economics*, 114(3), August, 537–619.

——(1989b) 'Industrialisation and the big push', *Journal of Political Economy*, 97(5), October, 1003–59.

Ranis (1981) 'Challenges and opportunities posed by Asia's superexporters: implications for manufactured export from Latin America', in W. Baer and M. Gillis (eds) *Export Diversification and the New Protectionism*, University of Illinois Bureau of Economic and Business Research, Urbana.

Rodriguez-Clare, A. (1996) 'The division of labor and economic development', *Journal of Development Economics*, 49, 3–32.

Rodrik, D. (1992) 'Conceptual issues in the design of trade policy for industrialization', *World Development*, 20, 3, 309–20.

Rodrik, D. (1996a) 'Coordination failures and government policy: a model with applications to East Asia and Eastern Europe, *Journal of International Economics*, 40, 1–22.

—— (1996b) 'The "paradoxes" of the successful state', paper presented at the Alfred Marshall Lecture, European Economic Association Meeting, Istanbul.

Rogoff, K. (1996) 'The purchasing power parity puzzle', *Journal of Economic Literature*.

Sachs, J. and Warner, A. (1995) *Natural Resource Abundance and Economic Growth*', NBER 5398, Cambridge, Mass.

Streeten (1982) 'A cool look at outward-looking strategies for development', *World Economy*, 5, September, 159–69.

Tornell, A. (1990) 'The inconsistency of protectionist programs', *Quarterly Journal of Economics*.

Venables, A. (1996) 'Trade policy, cumulative causation and industrial development', *Journal of Development Economics*, 49, 179–97.

Wade, R. (1991) *Governing the Market: Economic Theory and the Role of Government in East Asian Industrialisation*, Princeton University Press, Princeton, NJ.

Westphal, L. and Kim, K. (1982) *Korea*, in B. Balassa and Associates, *Development Strategies in Semi-Industrial Economies*, The Johns Hopkins University Press, Baltimore, Md., and London.

World Bank (1993) *The East Asian Miracle*, Washington DC.

Young, A. (1993) 'Learning by doing and the dynamic effects of international trade', *Quarterly Journal of Economics*, 106(2), May, 369–405.

—— (1994) 'The Tyranny of Numbers', *European Economic Review*.

10

DISCUSSION

John Williamson

Chapter 9 makes a number of important points that have not been brought together systematically in the literature. It argues that a large real depreciation is a natural first step in inducing industrialization, which is the key to development (at least in all except very small economies) because a country that wants to start to export industrial goods has no advantage that it can deploy other than hyper-competitive labor costs. A corollary is that Dutch disease is dangerous, because it threatens to halt industrialization, rather than the rational exploitation of good fortune as portrayed in the neoclassical literature. The chapter recognizes the existence of potential constraints on the feasible real depreciation. And it accepts that real appreciation is a natural and healthy accompaniment of successful industrialization, as argued by Balassa and Samuelson. I know of no other work that has discussed the desirable behavior of the real exchange rate in the course of development in this way, and that has got the answer basically right.

I cannot say, however, that I found the formal model used to justify the need for a large initial depreciation to be particularly convincing. I worry about the arbitrariness of imposing an assumption that all firms will have identical output with an increasing returns to scale technology, where we know that any firm that expands more will have a progressively larger advantage over its peers. For this reason I find the formalization of Paul Krugman (1987) that the benefits of industrialization come from cumulative learning by doing, far more convincing than that of Larraín. This also allows a more natural role for positive spillovers from one firm to another than in Larraín's model, where the fact that the firms are competing for a fixed supply of labor suggests that externalities should be negative rather than positive. Furthermore, I certainly do not find myself convinced that the formal model provides any basis for Larraín's repeated assertion that the initial real depreciation must be 'huge'.

Larraín posits two constraints to successful initial real depreciation. The first is unproblematic: real depreciation reduces the real wage, at least in the short run, which may be resisted by organized labor unless its discount rate is sufficiently low. The second I find less convincing: the postulate that

185

entrepreneurs in the tradable sector may choose to enjoy the increased real income from real depreciation in enjoying a quiet life rather than undertaking the effort needed to launch industrialization. This would be convincing enough if the entrepreneurial class were a closed one, but today even least developed countries are sending abroad a stream of young men who acquire MBAs and another stream of emigrants who acquire some entrepreneurial experience abroad and are constantly on the lookout for opportunities to return to their home country. Thus I see little danger that the profits from real depreciation will in the long run be dissipated in lethargy.

Larraín's optimality ranking strikes me as quixotic. He argues that the first-best policy to induce industrialization is selective targeting of (subsidies to) particular export industries, and the second-best policy consists of selective protection and export promotion, while a 'noninterventionist' use of exchange rate policy as analyzed in the bulk of the chapter is only third best. He justifies his preference for selective policies by appealing to the Bhagwati–Johnson theory of optimal intervention, which states that the most efficient way of achieving any well-defined goal is to subsidize the activity itself rather than other, loosely related, activities (see Bhagwati and Ramaswami, 1963; Johnson, 1965). In the present context, I interpret that as saying that if the government wants exports to consist of cotton shirts, silk blouses, and wigs of human hair, then it should subsidize those particular exports rather than depreciate the currency. But in the absence of externalities the government will maximize welfare as economists normally understand the term only if those are the exports that would be chosen by the market, so surely the first-best policy is to let the market do the choosing except to the extent that one can identify particular externalities that need to be offset. One such externality that may well often be important in the present context is the diversion of savings from the industrial sector that may result from exporters of traditional products reaping windfall gains from a real depreciation, which suggests that an optimal policy may well be to accompany the initial real depreciation with a tax on traditional exports. Beyond that, neutrality (nonintervention) would seem first best. (That is not to say that strict neutrality is necessarily particularly important, and the evidence that it was absent in the East Asian countries suggests that it is not.)

Dani Rodrik (1995) has shown that the initial impetus to South Korea's industrial exports came not from a real depreciation but from an increase in the profitability of investing, but he does not deny that a necessary condition for much of the investment to be directed to the production of tradables was that the real exchange rate was (already) highly competitive, and that, without that, the process of industrial growth would have been halted by import strangulation as it was in so many of the countries that set out on the import substitution strategy. This casts doubt on Larraín's repeated but essentially arbitrary assertion that an exchange rate policy supportive of industrialization has to start with a 'huge' devaluation. What a country does need to start the process off is an exchange rate that is sufficiently competitive to make it an attractive platform from which to export manufactures. That is the fundamental truth that I hope readers of Chapter 9 will absorb.

References

Bhagwati, J.N. and Ramaswami, V.K. (1963) 'Domestic distortions, tariffs, and the theory of the optimal subsidy', *Journal of Political Economy*, 1, 44–50.

Johnson, H.G. (1965) 'Optimal trade interventions in the presence of domestic distortions', in *Trade, Growth, and the Balance of Payments: Essays in Honour of Gottfried Haberler*, New York, Rand McNally.

Krugman, Paul (1987) 'Narrow moving band, the Dutch disease, and the competitive consequences of Mrs. Thatcher; Notes on trade in the presence of dynamic scale economies', *Journal of Development Economies*, 27, 41–55.

Rodrik, Dani (1995) *Trade Strategy, Investment and Exports: Another Look at East Asia*, NBER 5339, Cambridge, Mass.

11

ASIAN CURRENCIES IN THE CONTEXT OF EXPORT-ORIENTED INDUSTRIAL DEVELOPMENT

Lam Keong Yeoh and Ai Ning Wee

1 Introduction

This chapter attempts to situate Asian currency experience and prospects in the context of a 'life cycle' model of East Asian currency behaviour rooted in the different stages of industrial development. It is our thesis that the different stages of export-oriented industrialization produce systematic improvements in the structural balance of payments and hence increasing long-term currency stability. This has several interesting implications.

First, for the long-term investor, hedging currency exposure of direct or portfolio investments exposure is still impractical in many emerging markets. The ability to assess devaluation risk more accurately will thus be useful to the long-term investor and potentially helpful in stimulating such beneficial inflows. It is with this motivation, in fact, that we embarked on this study.

Second, for the policy maker in a developing country, it provides a broad framework for assessing the appropriateness of various foreign exchange policy regimes. An increasingly stable to strong currency environment would imply that an economy can afford correspondingly flexible, less managed currency regimes that allow more effective control of monetary policy and inflation and greater financial sector liberalization. The framework thus explores and argues for more systematic theoretical and empirical links between industrial maturity and exchange rate policy. For example, countries in the early stages of stabilization and industrialization programmes may benefit from narrow or even fixed exchange rate bands with a downward crawl.[1] Intermediate levels of industrialization could benefit from a broader band and a neutral or even mild upward crawl to stimulate capital deepening.

Finally, our framework argues that even short-term capital inflows need not be the enemy of policy makers. The substantive thesis of this chapter is that currencies experience increasing fundamental stability and strength as industrial development, spurred by the right policies, proceeds. If this argument is broadly correct, then policy makers in economies that have made sufficient progress in structural reform and industrialization would be better able to defend their currencies from speculative attack owing to underlying support from long-term capital flows. It thus pays 'smart money' that understands these fundamentals to buy these currencies together with central banks, when they are cheaper in the face of speculative attack. Short-term capital inflows could then tend automatically to exert a stabilizing effect on capital flight, rewarding authorities for taking the right policy directions that promote successful export-oriented industrialization. The interests of the capital market and policy makers will then be to some extent realigned, allowing further pursuit of exchange rate and capital market liberalization and increasing monetary autonomy.

2 Typical stages of Asian industrial development

Section 2 sets out an ideal-type schema of the typical process of industrial development experienced in emerging economies in general and Asia in particular. Section 3 will then relate the fundamental characteristics of these stages to currency theory to construct a 'life cycle' model for Asian currency behaviour.

The typical stages of Asian industrial development are those experienced by a relatively small economy in the context of increasingly large and free goods and capital mobility. They can be characterized as moving from an initial balance of payments crisis via a programme of deregulation and structural adjustment to a sustainable process of export-oriented, foreign investment-intensive industrialization (EOI)[2] accompanied increasingly by long-term balance of payments surplus and currency strength. Four stages can be outlined as follows.

2.1 Stage 1: balance of payments crisis

Characteristics of this stage would include a failed attempt at commodity-driven or import-substituting growth resulting in large trade and current account and balance of payments deficits, anaemic export growth, a large budget deficit, an exploding government and/or external debt burden and very high inflation. Effective deregulation and structural adjustment have to focus on neutralizing the effective rate of protection, liberalization of long-term capital inflows and fiscal and monetary consolidation. Typical measures would include correcting overvalued real effective exchange rates, reducing the effective tariff rate to allow intermediate inputs to be sourced at cheapest cost and liberalizing/incentivizing foreign direct investment.[3]

2.2 Stage 2: labour-intensive export-oriented industrialization (EOI)

Once cheap domestic labour can be combined with cheap intermediate inputs financed freely by both local and foreign equity capital, the country typically enjoys a sustained boom of labour-intensive exports. The external deficit may initially improve. Inflation stabilizes with structural improvements in productivity growth and budget deficits and government/external debt ratios subside. The key assessment here is how self-sustaining and entrenched labour-intensive export-oriented industrialization becomes.[4] As the return on capital rises sharply with the firm establishment of this process, it becomes the source of sustained, high growth, pulling up investment and savings rates through virtuous-cycle effects on capital accumulation and higher incomes. A mature Stage 2 is usually also accompanied by a rapid growth of labour-intensive electronic assembly.

2.3 Stage 3: rising value-added-per-worker (EOI)

This stage occurs when shortages of semi-skilled and then increasingly even unskilled workers begin to appear. The skew of comparative and competitive advantage then shifts to low but rising value-added-per-worker manufactures. Various rudimentary, then increasingly capital-intensive mechanizations of the production process take place. The electronics, electrical machinery and metal products industries typically grow rapidly in importance as they encompass a wide range of incrementally higher value-added production processes like automated machining or assembly, testing or even simple design.[5]

Where Stage 2 industrial growth was based on an Arthur Lewis-style utilization of infinite supplies of relatively unskilled labour, Stage 3 industrial growth mines the wide array of existing techniques previously established by the industrial countries. As the costs of innovation are low, particularly for older, less technology-intensive techniques, rapid productivity growth can be sustained for a decade or two. Productivity rather than labour supply growth, then, tends to account for the maintenance of high growth rates in Stage 3. Investment and savings rates may rise yet further as production becomes more capital intensive and real wages begin to rise secularly in line with strong productivity growth.[6]

It is at this stage that a current account deficit could rise sharply again but with several key differences compared to Stage 1. While Stage 1 external deficits are dominated by consumption imports and low export growth, Stage 3 deficits (which could be even higher as a ratio to GDP!) tend to be caused by high capital and intermediate goods imports, and intrinsically accompany strong export growth.[7] There is also rapid growth of lumpy one-time infrastructure imports. If capital markets are sufficiently open, a basic balance surplus may even accompany the external deficit, which is financed by strong foreign direct investment and equity inflows. Debt ratios thus fall sharply as income aggregates rise strongly but debt accumulation stagnates. This stage could last two to three decades. The transition from late Stage 2 (widespread labour-intensive EOI) to early Stage 3 (initial rising value-added-per worker EOI) clearly defines the process of industrial take-off.

2.4   Stage 4: high value-added-per-worker (EOI)

This stage marks the coming of industrial maturity as production techniques and absolute productivity levels in manufacturing approach those of the developed economies. Investment and savings rates, while high, begin to stabilize or moderate as does productivity growth. Real wages continue to rise strongly, driven by both productivity gains and tight labour markets.[8]

Around this stage the external deficit typically falls sharply, often turning into surplus. Countries may eventually shift from net debtor to creditor status. The need for imports linked to large, one-time infrastructure investments are past. Skills and technology intensity begin to account for an increasing share of productivity growth. Growth of machinery and intermediate input imports thus also decelerate. With the persistence of full employment, the focus of the central bank and monetary policy typically shifts further in favour of inflation control as opposed to sustaining growth. For small open economies, this also involves the recognition of the need to use the real exchange rate effectively as a tool of monetary policy and to shift to increasingly flexible exchange rate regimes.[9]

Stage 4 ends with full graduation to developed country status when manufacturing productivity levels approach those in the OECD. Thereafter productivity growth rates fall, converging with those in the OECD as the benefit of cheap innovation from an international technology gap has been exhausted. Potential GDP growth rates typically decelerate to 2–4 per cent by the end of Stage 4 and to 4–6 per cent from 6–10 per cent between Stages 3 and 4.

3   Stages of industrial development, currency theory and behaviour: a life cycle model of Asian currencies

To make the transition between the observed stages of industrial development outlined above and currency behaviour, we had first to do some theoretical and empirical spade-work. The first task was to examine more carefully the theoretical basis for a life cycle for currencies that parallels the above stages of industrial development. We thus attempted to relate exchange rate theory to the various stages of industrial development and identify measurable variables that could both assess which stage of the life cycle the currencies examined were in as well as explain currency behaviour. The variables had then to be tested against the experience of Asian economies to see if the expected life cycle currency patterns would emerge.

We think that a currency life cycle hypothesis related to the different stages of industrial development encompasses three fundamental approaches to exchange rate evaluation. First, the classical purchasing power parity (PPP) approach: basically, PPP states that if domestic and foreign prices diverge chronically, trade imbalances would result, necessitating that the nominal exchange rate adjusts to restore real exchange rate equilibrium in the long run. In order to assess currency fundamentals based on PPP, the economic variables typically examined are various inflation measures – GDP deflator, CPI, WPI and export price indices, as well as relative wage and productivity growth rates which measure export competitiveness, and finally trade and current account balances.

The second fundamental approach to exchange rate evaluation is the macroeconomic balance and fundamental equilibrium exchange rate (FEER) approach. This approach was first developed by Swan in 1963 and expanded by Williamson in his now famous work on FEER (1985). It states that a real exchange rate is in equilibrium when an economy is in both internal and external balance. Internal balance is normally defined as achieving a full employment level of output, while external balance is defined as long-term basic balance, i.e. when any long-term or structural current account imbalances are offset by net long-term capital inflows.[10]

The macroeconomic balance–FEER approach is more comprehensive than PPP as it allows for cyclical exchange rate adjustments. More importantly, it focuses on the long-term balance of payments and its determinants rather than narrowly on competitiveness and the trade balance. This gets closer to long-term supply and demand of a currency which in the final analysis determine the nominal exchange rate. A number of other economic variables in addition to the competitiveness indicators of the PPP are needed to assess a currency's strength based on the macroeconomic balance–FEER approach – the economy's private savings and investment balance, the government's fiscal position, the current account balance. This approach would focus on the basic balance, which includes net foreign direct investment, net portfolio and other long-term capital balance.

Finally, the portfolio balance approach provides some explanations which are useful in explaining emerging Asian currency behaviour. This approach was pioneered by Dornbusch, who posited that exchange rates are determined by the interaction of supply and demand for financial assets. Applying it to long-term currency demand, we posit that investors will invest in a foreign asset, either through long-term foreign direct investment or portfolio investment, if they believe that the risk-adjusted long-term rates of return exceed what they can get by investing domestically.

Relative returns on capital and investment risk are thus the key determinants of currency performance by the portfolio balance approach. The portfolio balance approach focuses on economic variables that are proxy for the high rates of return characteristic of successful industrial development, such as strong productivity growth, strong foreign direct and long-term portfolio investments as well as rising investment and savings rates. It also focuses on variables which measure the risk to long-term investments, namely external or government debt and deficits.

The PPP, macroeconomic–FEER and portfolio balance approaches taken together jointly explain long-term currency behaviour experienced by developing Asian economies.[11] Successful industrial development first leads to high rates of return on domestic, foreign direct and long-term portfolio investments. This implies strong currency demand by the criteria of the portfolio balance approach. The nominal exchange rate should thus begin to experience long-term stability. High rates of return also attract more long-term foreign capital inflows generating a strengthening basic balance and strong employment growth, leading to positive fundamentals on the FEER basis as well.

Over time, strong income growth combined with strong equity capital inflows slow debt accumulation, leading to a decline in debt ratios. Investment risks are then rerated leading to a fall in currency risk-premiums. Overall, currency fundamentals would then improve significantly and long-term nominal currency strength begins to emerge. Eventually, as central banks mature and current account deficits turn into surpluses, PPP fundamentals would improve as well. Long-term currency fundamentals turn positive by the criteria of all three approaches. As a result, this typically develops into the strongest phase of a currency's life cycle in the industrialization process.

The complete life cycle framework thus uses the economic variables used by all three approaches in order to assess a currency's fundamentals at different stages of industrial development. It explains, for example, why the Singapore dollar appreciated in the late 1970s and early 1980s amid rapid economic development and in spite of current account deficits over 15 per cent of GDP, as investors were attracted to Singapore assets owing to high long-term returns. Foreign direct investment and long-term portfolio flows were attracted to export sectors which promised high profit margins due to high productivity and low unit labour cost growth. This is in accordance with the portfolio balance approach. Strong FDI and long-term capital inflows in turn resulted in a strong basic balance and overall balance of payments surplus. Full employment was achieved by the mid-1970s. This resulted in strong currency fundamentals in line with the FEER approach. The Monetary Authority of Singapore's strong exchange rate policy in pursuit of low inflation and eventual large current account surpluses in the late 1980s and 1990s strengthened currency fundamentals defined by the PPP approach. The SGD is thus currently in the strongest phase of its life cycle.

4   Empirical methodology and results

To test the life cycle approach to long-term currency assessment empirically, we first examined the major Asian currencies which have gone through at least two phases in the industrialization process. These include Japan and the young Asian currencies of Singapore, Taiwan, South Korea, Malaysia, Thailand, Indonesia and the Philippines.[12]

The statistical methodology is as follows. Sample size was enlarged by using both time series and panel data from the G-4 and the seven Asian economies listed above divided into five-year time periods (1975–80, 1980–5, 1985–90, 1990–5). G-4 currencies were included in the sample to ensure that the long-term fundamental drivers of currency strength also worked with the major liquid, heavily traded currencies. First, economic variables (five-year averages for the above periods) typical of the PPP, FEER and portfolio approaches were regressed singly and together against currency performance. The variables finally selected were inflation, external debt/GDP, current account/GDP, productivity growth, the ratio of each country's per capita GDP to the US equivalent, savings rate, fiscal balance, basic balance and foreign direct investment/GDP. Variables chosen were those that had both strong theoretical links with exchange rate behaviour at different stages of industrial development as well as reasonable empirical links measured by sufficiently high R-squares and t-statistics either using OLS or LOGIT regression.[13]

Next, a composite indicator using the economic variables selected weighted by their correlation coefficients was constructed. The methodology used here was similar to the type used for constructing multiple variable leading or coincident indicators of economic activity.[14] Currency behaviour in each period was then divided into different zones – (1) weak; (2) stable to weak; (3) stable; (4) stable to strong; and (5) strong – according to the composite indicator readings which were scaled on an index 0–100. Finally, Mexico's scores were calculated using fundamental variables to see if their actual currency behaviour conformed to their respective zones as indicated by their composite indicator scores. This was used as an additional 'out-of-sample test' to see if our indicator approach would have provided warning of the recent Mexican peso devaluation.

The variables used and their weights are shown in Appendix 1(a). Inflation and external debt variables have the greatest weight. Current account, productivity growth, per capita GDP ratio,[15] savings rate and fiscal balance variables have all roughly the same weight. Foreign direct investment has the smallest weight. The theoretical role of these variables is important in understanding the life cycle model of currency behaviour. Countries progressing from Stage 1 to Stage 4 would typically first show improvements in inflation and fiscal and external balance variables as part of a macroeconomic stabilization package. As industrialization proceeds, productivity growth, savings rates, foreign direct investment and basic balances rise as the return on capital rises and capital deepening occurs, albeit with worsening of the current account deficit in early to mid-Stage 3. Stage 4 would in addition see sharp improvements in current account balances and inflation. External debt ratios would also stabilize in Stage 2, falling secularly thereafter.

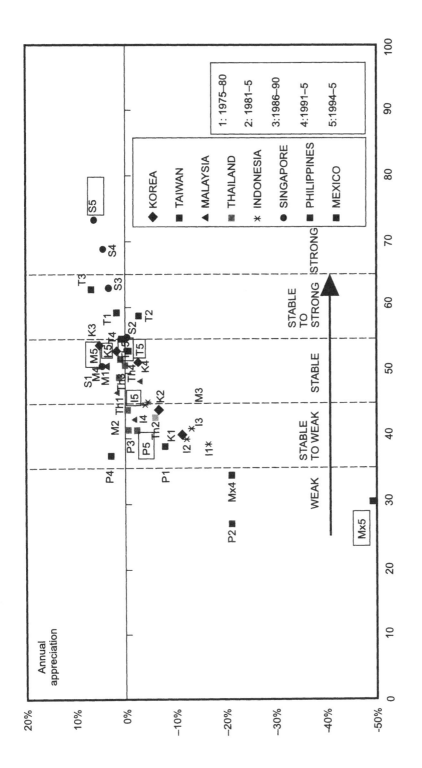

Figure 11.1 Asian currencies and the Mexican peso

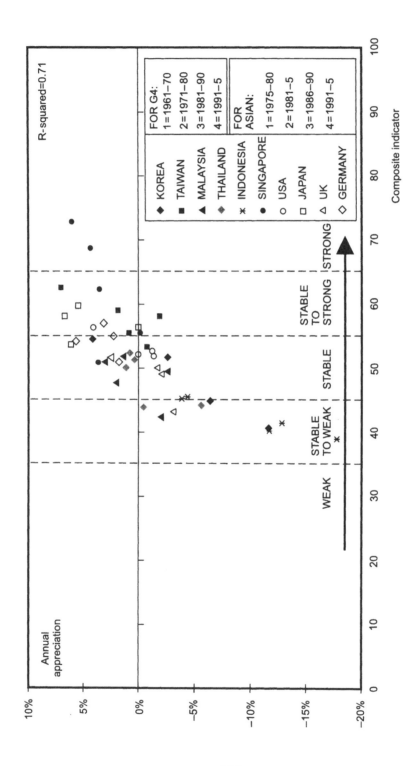

Figure 11.2 G-4 and Asia – currency versus economic performance

Fairly distinct life cycle characteristics are seen both in single countries over time (time series data) and across countries at any point in time (cross-section or panel data). For the overall sample, the composite indicator had a correlation coefficient of 0.84 (R-square of 0.71) to five-year bilateral nominal currency changes against the US dollar. Figure 11.1 shows the broad visual relationship between long term currency fundamentals and currency behaviour for the Asian currencies. Interestingly, Mexico fell into the weak currency zone on the composite indicator score and also experienced significant devaluation in the 1990–5 period.[16]

Furthermore, the variables used showed consistent relationships to long-term currency performance for both G-4 and Asian currencies blocs (Figure 11.2). Together, this provides initial empirical evidence that our industrialization life cycle approach is a useful framework with which to evaluate an Asian or developing country's long-term currency prospects.

5   The life cycle model and selected Asian currencies

This section tries to illustrate more clearly the basic links between the stages of industrial development, composite indicator scores and long-run currency strength. To do this, it looks at the actual development and macroeconomic experience of five economies that over the last 20–35 years have spanned all four stages of industrial development – Japan, Singapore, South Korea, Thailand and Indonesia – and traces out these links over their actual economic development and currency history.

Japan has consistently shown high composite scores (see Figure 11.3). Japan made the transition from Stage 3 (rising value added per worker EOI) to Stage 4 (high value added per worker EOI) during the first half of the 1970s (Period J2) and moved to the end of Stage 4 to fully developed status by 1990 (J3). It has thus been in the stable-to-strong zone over the last thirty-five years. The composite score strengthened further in the 1980s and early 1990s (J3 and J4) with a typical Stage 4 move to current account surplus and a sharp fall in long-term inflation. These accounted for the endaka of 1985–95, a structural appreciation characteristic of the strongest stage in the currency life cycle of a maturing industrial economy.[17]

Singapore's currency fundamentals have improved steadily over the last twenty years (see Figure 11.4). During this period Singapore has moved from a late Stage 2 (labour-intensive EOI) in 1975–80 (period S1) and moved steadily through Stage 3, arriving by 1995 probably on the cusp of Stage 4 (periods S2 to S5). In Singapore's case, this has pushed the composite score from the stable through the stable-to-strong and firmly into the strong zone. Over this period, Singapore experienced the typical rises in the productivity growth, savings rate and foreign direct investment rates of a maturing Stage 3 economy. It also saw the characteristic move from high current account deficits in early Stage 3 through to large current account surplus

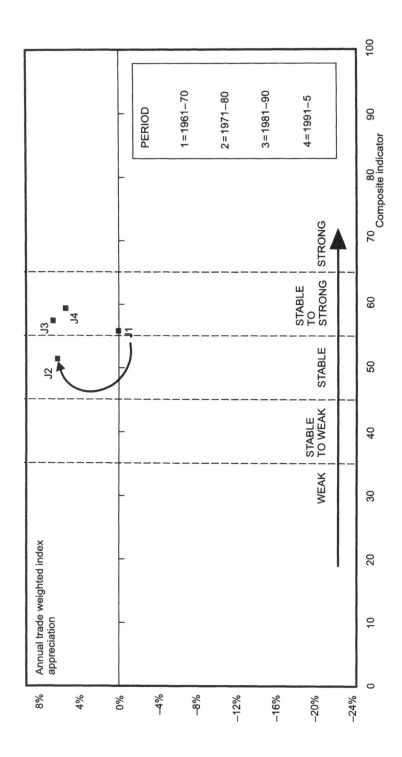

Figure 11.3 Japanese yen life cycle, 1961–95

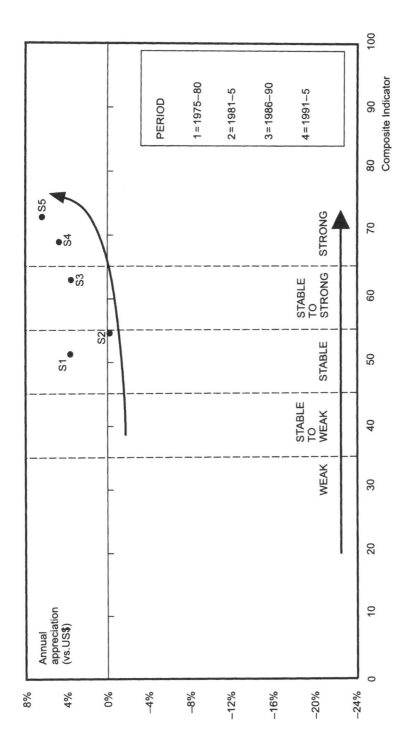

Figure 11.4 Singapore dollar life cycle, 1975–95

by late Stage 3–early Stage 4 and a concomitant improvement in the basic balance. This has resulted in secular Singapore dollar strength over the last two decades.[18]

Another Asian currency which has exhibited an interesting variant of typical life cycle characteristics is the Korean won (see Figure 11.5). Over the last twenty years, South Korea has progressed through most of the same stages as Singapore (i.e. the whole of Stage 3 to early Stage 4). However, there have been two key institutional policy differences. First, long-term capital inflows were highly restricted in South Korea whereas they were largely open in Singapore. Second, the Bank of Korea had a much higher inflation tolerance than the MAS. As a result, the won underwent significant devaluation in the 1975–85 period (early to mid Stage 3). This was because South Korea experienced huge basic balance deficits as the current account worsened sharply with the need for capital imports on the one hand and the prohibition foreign direct or equity investment to finance these external deficits on the other. The result was a continued escalation of debt ratios despite the relatively advanced stage of industrial development. Inflation, too, remained high.

The won thus retained many of the balance of payments characteristics of a weak currency in the macroeconomic crisis stage. Only as liberalization of long-term capital flows and an improvement in the current account, basic balance and inflation occurred as South Korea approached Stage 4 during the 1985–95 period (Periods K3 to K5) did currency fundamentals shift steadily to underlying stability and strength.

The Indonesian rupiah (see Figure 11.6) composite scores and fundamental variables trace out a classic pattern of early industrial development, i.e. a classic successful transition from Stage 1 (macroeconomic crisis) to mid Stage 2 (well-established labour-intensive EOI). In the late 1970s to early 1980s (Periods I1 and I2) policy makers still pursued an import-substitution-oriented industrialization programme funded from oil revenues. Industrial entry was controlled, local content requirements enforced, foreign investment was discouraged. Massive capital-intensive forays into steel, plastics and petrochemicals subsidized by official credit and trade protection eventually failed. This resulted in low savings rates and worsening fiscal, current account and basic balances combined with high inflation. Between 1985 and 1988, the government changed course. It reduced its share in the industrial sector from 43 to 23 per cent, bringing fiscal deficits to balance by 1990. Trade was dramatically liberalized and foreign investment encouraged. By 1995 export-oriented industrialization was fairly well established. Non-oil manufactured exports boomed and productivity growth accelerated sharply, combined with significant improvements in the basic balance, foreign direct investment and a sharp fall in external debt ratios.[19] As a result the rupiah has left the era of big devaluation and has been sufficiently stable (Periods I4, I5) to allow the Indonesian authorities to widen the exchange rate band vs. the US dollar from

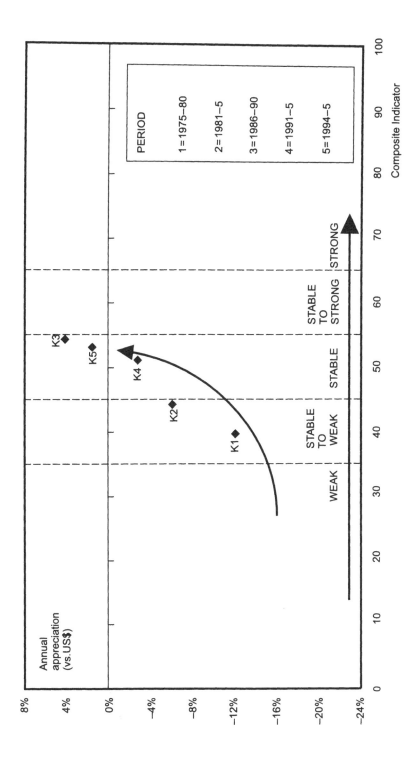

Figure 11.5 Korean won life cycle, 1975–95

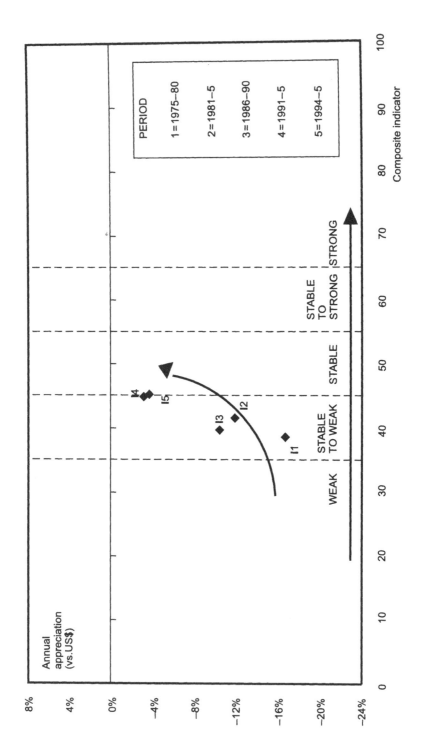

Figure 11.6 Indonesian rupiah life cycle, 1975–95

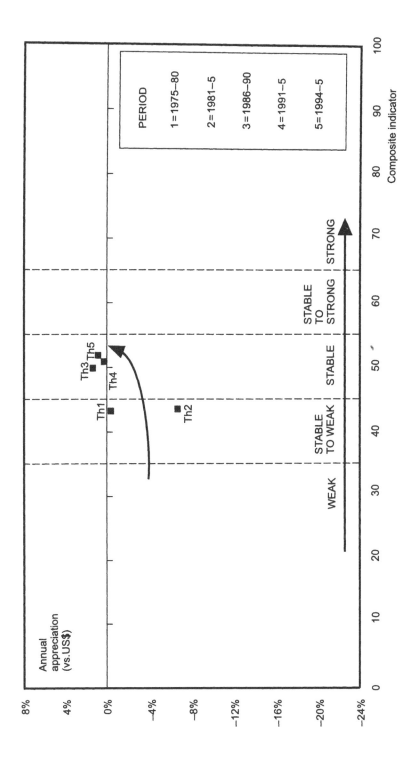

Figure 11.7 Thai baht life cycle, 1975–95

1 per cent in 1994 to 8 per cent in 1996. Further band widening to 15 per cent is likely in 1997.

The Thai baht is another more successful variation of the same story (see Figure 11.7). Thailand has moved much more rapidly from crisis and long-term currency weakness through Stage 2 to early Stage 3 and long-term currency stability. State-funded capital-intensive import-substitution policies in the 1970s were reversed in the early 1980s to export development and import liberalization. Effective protection rates came down sharply by the mid-1980s. The result was a boom in manufactured exports and a sharp acceleration in productivity growth and the savings rate, and a sharp fall in fiscal deficits and external deficits as well as debt ratios by the early 1990s. However, as Thailand moved into early Stage 3 in the 1990–5 period (Periods Th4 and Th5), the external deficit worsened as capital imports surged even as the basic balance and foreign direct investment rates continued to improve.

6   The current life cycle stages of Asian currencies looking at recent cross-section data

Figure 11.8 shows the scores of Asian and G-4 currencies at this point in time, i.e. in the three years up to 1996. It places the currencies quite clearly in different phases of the currency life cycle. Singapore's performance is in the unambiguously strong category. Japan, followed by South Korea and Taiwan, are in the stable-to-strong category. Thailand and Malaysia have similar composite scores as they are on the borderline between the stable-to-strong and stable-to-weak categories. The Philippines remains in the weak category. The USA, UK and Germany are obviously well beyond Stage 4 in terms of industrial development. Their scores are used here to indicate broadly their balance of payments fundamentals in the context of the PPP, FEER and portfolio balance approaches to currency determination rather than to place them in the light of the same dynamics that drive long-term Asian currency strengths.

7   Medium-term outlook for Asian currencies based on life cycle hypothesis: North-East Asia and ASEAN

The next section uses our industrialization life cycle model of currency fundamentals to examine Asian currency prospects over the next five years. While this may seem a bold prognosis at best (foolhardy at worst), we believe that our theoretical model allows a reasonably robust, educated guess in this direction. The indicators of industrial development in the model are fairly predictable and slow changing. We believe that the dynamics of this process, driven by high returns on capital, technological diffusion and comparative advantage, are not easily halted. The basic methodology was to obtain five-year forecasts of the variables making up the composite indicator. The main changes

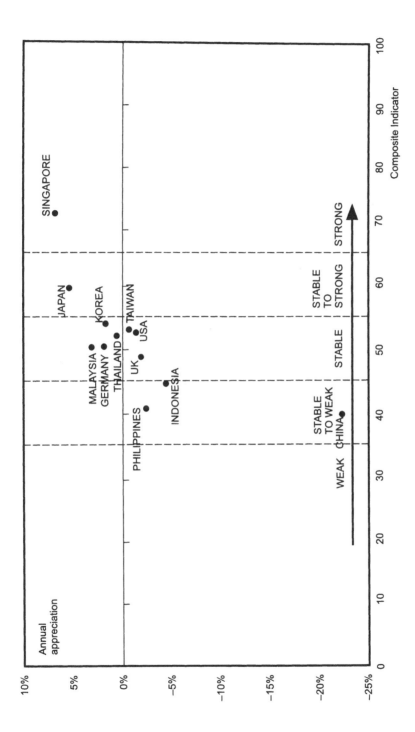

Figure 11.8 G-4 and Asian currencies life cycle behaviour, November 1996

assumed to the variables were further rises in the savings rate with positive demographics and strong income growth, and falls in external debt ratios as income growth continues to outpace debt accumulation, given high foreign direct investment rates and neutral basic balances.

Singapore's positive economic fundamentals should continue to underpin the Singapore dollar (S$) as a strong currency over the next five years. As a late Stage 3 to early Stage 4 economy, its currency fundamentals should still maintain their unusually strong momentum for at least another decade in the same way that the Japanese yen's did between 1985 and 1995.

What about Singapore's NIE counterparts, Taiwan and South Korea (see Figure 11.9)? Broadly speaking, they should also be stable to strong in line with their fundamentals as late Stage 3 to early Stage 4 economies. Taiwan's current account surplus and strength in FX reserves are well known, although chronic foreign direct investment outflows have somewhat weakened its basic balance position. Inflation is low. Productivity and capital investment growth are healthy, suggesting continued high returns on investment. External debt is practically non-existent. In the next three to five years, Taiwan's positive currency fundamentals should remain intact. According to the life cycle hypothesis the New Taiwan dollar (NTD) should thus be stable to strong in line with Taiwan's steady expected improvement in its composite indicator score.

South Korea's currency fundamentals are also stable to strong, albeit somewhat less favourable than Taiwan's and Singapore's. Its composite score is not expected to improve as much as Taiwan's in the next few years. Inflation has been a chronic problem, the domestic savings rate is lower, the current account has been in mild deficit and as a result external debt is high. The currency-positive developments for South Korea in the next few years would be a secular decline in inflation, a rise in the savings rate and greater fiscal discipline by the government.

Thailand and Malaysia are roughly in the same phase of industrial development (early and mid Stage 3 respectively) (see Figure 11.10). Their continued movement to mid to late Stage 3 over the next five years has strong momentum. Both Malaysia and Thailand enjoy high returns to capital and productivity growth rates which will continue to attract strong foreign direct investment inflows. Although both economies are currently experiencing significant rises in current account deficits, both Malaysia and Thailand have managed broadly to achieve a neutral basic balance as foreign direct and long-term capital investments have roughly funded external deficits. In terms of monetary management, both Bank Negara and the Bank of Thailand have reasonable inflation-fighting credibility and commitment to maintaining stable currencies. Looking five years ahead, both economies and currencies are likely to progress further to mid to late Stage 3, i.e. towards the stable-to-strong currency zone. Based on longer-term demographic and income growth projections, both economies should see a further significant rise in domestic

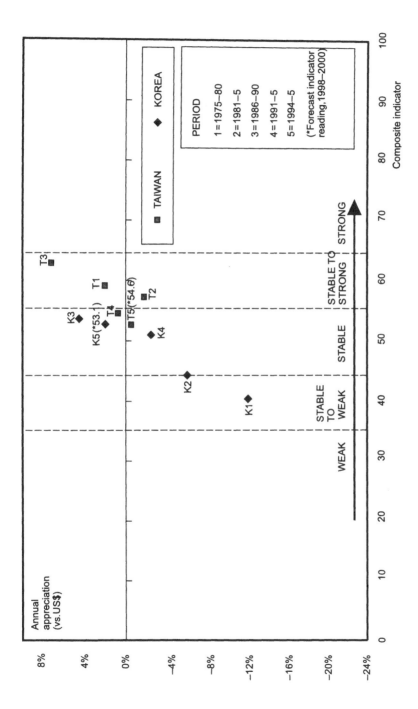

Figure 11.9 Taiwan dollar and Korean won life cycle and forecast

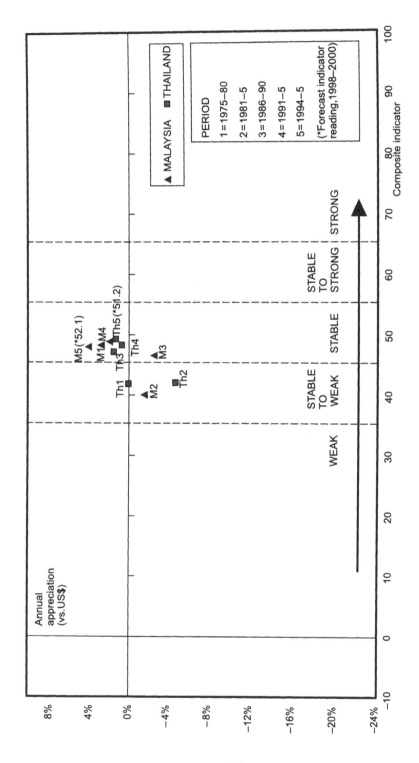

Figure 11.10 Malaysian ringgit and Thai baht life cycle and forecast

savings rates. Thailand has already achieved a fiscal surplus while Malaysia's fiscal balance is likely to improve a little further. Their currencies should thus experience increasing long-term firmness.[20]

The Philippines and Indonesia are currently in early and mid Stage 2 respectively (see Figure 11.11). The Indonesian rupiah is thus now ranked in the early part of the stable currency zone while the Philippine peso is at the beginning of the stable-to-weak zone. Both the Indonesian and Philippine economies still have relatively high inflation rates. Both suffer from fiscal and current account deficits as well as high external debt ratios. However, both have seen significant improvements in economic management over the last few years. The Indonesian government has achieved a fiscal surplus for FY1994/5, the first time in the last twenty years. It has used proceeds from state enterprise privatizations to prepay some of its external debt, thus reducing the external debt ratio. Bank Indonesia has pursued a tight monetary policy in a strong growth environment in 1995–6. As a result, inflation has declined. Investing in Indonesia has become more profitable with strong productivity growth over the last five years. The evident improvement in export competitiveness has attracted strong foreign direct investments indicating that export-oriented industrialization is becoming firmly entrenched.

By the year 2000, Indonesia's currency fundamentals could be as good as those of Thailand or Malaysia in the late 1980s, i.e. the rupiah should graduate decisively into the stable zone (mid to late Stage 2). There would then be no necessity for Bank Indonesia to pursue the crawling peg policy, under which the Indonesian rupiah follows an automatic depreciation of about 5 per cent per year. Already the authorities have widened rupiah fluctuation bands from 1 per cent around the US dollar in 1995 to 8 per cent currently. Observers expect that the bands are likely to be widened in future to 15–20 per cent over the next 1–2 years.[21]

The Philippines has also seen significant improvements in currency fundamentals. Inflation has declined, attesting to the policy commitment of the Bangko Sentral ng Pilipinas. Fiscal consolidation has changed the fiscal deficit to a surplus. The basic balance has been in surplus as foreign direct and long-term capital investments have more than adequately funded the Philippines' current account deficit. As a result, the central bank's FX reserves have been rising. However, the industrial development process in the Philippines is still in its infancy (i.e. early Stage 2). Productivity growth and savings rates are still low and export-oriented manufacturing has only been booming for 3–5 years. On the longer time scale of export-oriented industrial development, the trajectory of the Philippine peso's fundamentals, albeit improving rapidly, still places it in the stable-to-weak currency zone over the next three years. Like Mexico, therefore, it could be particularly vulnerable to reversals of short-term capital inflows, especially if the currency is allowed to appreciate too strongly.[22] Beyond the next five years, however, Philippine peso fundamentals should become more durable as its rating continues to improve to

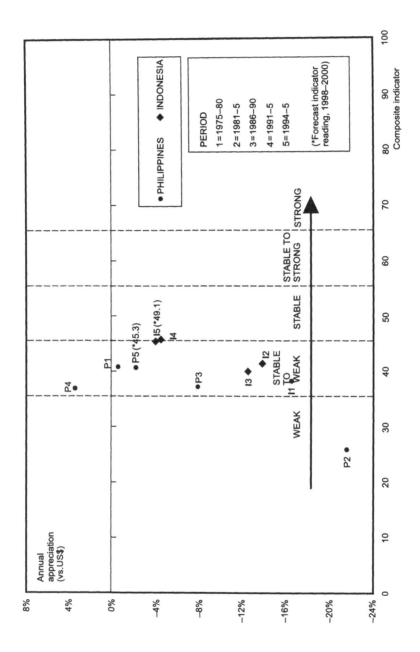

Figure 11.11 Indonesian rupiah and Philippine peso life cycle and forecast

the weak-to-stable zone (where the rupiah is today), and labour-intensive export manufacturing becomes firmly established.

8 Conclusion and implications of an Asian currency life cycle model

The 'life cycle' model outlined above thus provides preliminary theoretical and empirical underpinning for assessing the long-term currency prospects of a developing Asian economy. The life cycle model is essentially rooted in the various stages of industrial development and their implications for the balance of payments. It gives both long-term investors and policy makers key macroeconomic benchmarks for charting the successful progress of industrial development and its concomitant pressures on exchange rate regimes and monetary policy. Besides its utility as an investment tool, it could thus also be used to gauge when an economy is sufficiently mature to evolve from narrower to broader exchange rate bands and from more managed to cleaner floats. In this regard, it could indicate when large currency devaluations are no longer likely or necessary. This would then give scope for an increasing autonomy of monetary policy.

For currency investors, it is interesting to note that over the last two years, the ASEAN currencies (ringgit, baht and rupiah) have consistently provided total returns which exceed those of the major G-4 and even NIE currencies. Total return refers to the sum of spot currency return and the interest differential earned from funding an ASEAN currency investment with US dollars. Table 11.1. shows that while spot currency returns are very closely in line with the life cycle composite readings, total returns are not. In 1994–6, for example, the total returns on the ASEAN currencies vs. the US dollar range from 4 to 6 per cent, significantly exceeding those of the NIEs' 1–3 per cent, although their composite indicators remain lower than those of the NIEs.

Table 11.1 Ranking of Asian currencies by total returns, spot returns and composite indicator readings, 1994–5

Currency	Total returns (%)	Currency	Spot returns (%)	Country	Composite indicator
1 Rupiah	5.8	1 Singapore dollar	6.1	1 Singapore	88.3
2 Baht	4.7	2 Ringgit	3.0	2 South Korea	37.0
3 Ringgit	4.5	3 Won	1.8	3 Taiwan	32.8
4 Singapore dollar	3.2	4 Baht	0.7	4 Thailand	32.6
5 Won	0.8	5 NT dollar	−0.7	5 Malaysia	29.8
6 NT dollar	0.0	6 Rupiah	−4.2	6 Indonesia	17.3

In particular, the Thai baht and Indonesian rupiah's high interest differentials against the US dollar constituted the main components of their total returns.

This finding suggests that the risk premia paid for holding the ASEAN currencies significantly exceed their actual long-term investment risks. Provided fundamentals continue to improve, strategic currency investors should thus take the opportunity to accumulate these currencies whenever their interest differentials against the US dollar rise. It also implies that they should have a long-term strategy for investing in the ASEAN currencies by investing in their longer duration fixed income securities. In this way, they would achieve the greatest returns from both high coupon payments and a decline in yields from potential falls in risk premia as a result of eventual reratings of their investment risk status.

The above investment implications, if correct, bring about a significant realignment of interest between providers of shorter-term capital inflows and policy makers. As policy makers undertake measures that entrench and stimulate export- and investment-led industrialization, even short-term capital flows could become more stabilizing as it becomes better recognized that devaluation risk has diminished sharply and either spot or forward currency appreciation has become a secular trend. 'Smart money' would then increasingly find itself on the same side as central banks' currency stabilization operations in the event of temporary balance of payments crises. Successful developing countries like Malaysia, Thailand and Indonesia would then need to be less mistrustful of speculative capital inflows as a hindrance to capital market liberalization, and this would increase monetary policy autonomy and financial sector development. Short-term capital market liberalization could then become a more unambiguous ally of both long-term economic development and greater macroeconomic stability and control.

APPENDIX 1(a)

We used the ordinary least squares (OLS) estimation method to test if the economic variables we included in the construction of the composite indicator would be jointly significant in explaining: (1) bilateral local currency/US dollar movement; (2) nominal effective exchange rate movement; (3) real effective exchange rate movement. The results are shown in equations 11.1–11.3.

For all three equations, the explanatory variables are expressed as a percentage of GDP (basic balance BAS, current account balance CA, debt DEB, share of manufacturing and finance MFG), or as yearly changes (inflation INF, productivity PROD), or as a ratio (country productivity level to US productivity level PRODDIFF). As the intention of performing the OLS regression was primarily to test the validity of each variable rather than for forecasting, we made the a-priori assumption that all sample observations were normal variables. Identical transformations were performed for all sample observations (endogenous and explanatory), they were all normalized as

N(0,1). The New Taiwan dollar was not included in the estimation sample because its nominal and real effective exchange rates were not available.

Q-statistics and residual correlograms show no significant serial correlation.

Equation 11.1
LS // Dependent Variable is FX.
Date: 16 January 1997; time: 14.07
Sample: 1 96
Included observations: 96

Variable	Coefficient	Std. error	t-Statistic	Prob.
BAS	0.187214	0.078858	2.374068	0.0197
CA	0.070307	0.071991	0.976615	0.3314
DEB	−0.057727	0.073175	−0.788897	0.4322
INF	−0.157559	0.063603	−2.477236	0.0151
MFG	0.042339	0.065307	0.648305	0.5184
PROD	0.429202	0.081732	5.251350	0.0000

R-squared	0.574469	Mean dependent var	−0.035110
Adjusted R-squared	0.550829	S.D. dependent var	0.737225
S.E. of regression	0.494090	Akaike info criterion	−1.349614
Sum squared resid	21.97124	Schwarz criterion	−1.189342
Log likelihood	−65.43664	F-statistic	24.30010
Durbin–Watson stat	0.802631	Prob(F-statistic)	0.000000

Equation 11.2
LS // Dependent Variable is SDR.
Date: 18 January 1997; time: 13.42
Sample: 1 96
Included observations: 96

Variable	Coefficient	Std. error	t-Statistic	Prob.
BAS	0.097159	0.066543	1.460100	0.1477
DEB	−0.247059	0.072758	−3.395629	0.0010
PROD	0.346505	0.081574	4.247725	0.0001
PRODDIFF	0.175061	0.377296	0.463990	0.6438

R-squared	0.463147	Mean dependent var	−0.001871
Adjusted R-squared	0.445641	S.D. dependent var	0.711845
S.E. of regression	0.530006	Akaike info criterion	−1.228960
Sum squared resid	25.84340	Schwarz criterion	−1.122112
Log likelihood	−73.22804	F-statistic	26.45634
Durbin–Watson stat	0.603705	Prob(F-statistic)	0.000000

Equation 11.3
LS // Dependent Variable is REER.
Date: 18 January 1997; time: 13.45

Sample: 1 96
Included observations: 96

Variable	Coefficient	Std. error	t-Statistic	Prob.
DEB	−0.200390	0.093324	−2.147258	0.0344
MFG	0.069819	0.089499	0.780112	0.4373
PRODDIFF	0.446783	0.507070	0.881107	0.3805

R-squared	0.117802	Mean dependent var	0.003053
Adjusted R-squared	0.098830	S.D. dependent var	0.743122
S.E. of regression	0.705446	Akaike info criterion	−0.667099
Sum squared resid	46.28183	Schwarz criterion	−0.586963
Log likelihood	−101.1974	F-statistic	6.209236
Durbin–Watson stat	1.132139	Prob(F-statistic)	0.002943

APPENDIX 1(b)

The probit/logit estimation method was tried because it was noted that over the 1970s and 1980s most Asian currencies which were pegged to the US dollar experienced sharp and discrete adjustments. This was especially so when there were regime changes, e.g. a switch from fixed exchange rate to basket peg as for the Thai baht (a depreciation of 17 per cent accompanied the regime change). We thought it would be interesting to test if the variables used to construct the composite indicator could contribute to estimating the change in cumulative probability of a sharp exchange rate depreciation.

In the logit model we used: 1 = a depreciation of the local currency/US dollar exchange rate of more than 5 per cent, 0 = otherwise. As shown by the results of the logit estimation, our hypothesis that a worsening of certain economic fundamentals increases the probability of a significant currency depreciation (more than 5 per cent) seems sound. The variables found to be significant were foreign direct investment (FDI), basic balance (BAS), fiscal balance (FIS), debt (DEB), all expressed as percentages of GDP, and yearly inflation rate (INF). As we would expect, FDI, BAS and FIS have negative coefficients as an improvement in these variable readings would reduce the cumulative probability of an exchange rate depreciation. DEB and INF have positive coefficients as an increase in these two variable readings would increase the cumulative probability of an exchange rate depreciation.

Equation 11.4
LOGIT // Dependent Variable is FX.
Date: 15 January 1997; time: 18.36
Sample: 1 133
Included observations: 133
Convergence achieved after 6 iterations

214

Variable	Coefficient	Std. error	t-Statistic	Prob.
C	−2.452972	0.562391	−4.361688	0.0000
FDI	−2.524437	0.775070	−3.257042	0.0014
BAS	−0.632060	0.355374	−1.778576	0.0777
FIS	−1.459420	0.467843	−3.119463	0.0022
DEB	0.925911	0.276313	3.350947	0.0011
INF	0.272621	0.266600	1.022584	0.3084

Log likelihood	−53.25601
Obs with Dep = 1	39
Obs with Dep = 0	94

Variable	Mean all	Mean D = 1	Mean D = 0
C	1.000000	1.000000	1.000000
FDI	8.01E-17	−0.442996	0.183796
BAS	1.74E-16	−0.359724	0.149247
FIS	−1.60E-16	−0.427504	0.177369
DEB	1.36E-15	0.667505	−0.276944
INF	1.34E-16	0.454267	−0.188472

Notes

The research for this chapter came from Government of Singapore Investment Company's own investment policy research. The authors wish to thank Ng Kok Song of GIC for initiating the research project and crystallizing the idea of a life cycle for currency behaviour. Our thanks also go to Freddy Orchard from GIC for his comments on using Singapore's experience as a template for examining a developing country's currency life cycle. We have also benefited from detailed comments from Virginie Coudert from CEPII, Shandi Mohdi, Alan Ruskin and Mike Gallagher from IDEA and Brian Reading from Lombard Street Research. We would also like to especially thank Rüdiger Dornbusch, John Williamson and Yung Chul Park for their comments and encouragement at the Seoul conference. The final opinions here are the authors' own and do not necessarily represent those of GIC.

1 For an excellent recent discussion of target zone arrangements embodied in a 'band-basket-crawl' as the most flexible regime for emerging economies, see Dornbusch and Park (1998).

2 See e.g. Balassa and Corden (1988) for an overview of such policies.

3 There is a considerable neo-classical literature and significant empirical evidence to argue that openness to international trade in general combined with macro-economic stability are the critical factors behind Asian industrial take-off (Petri, 1993). Counter-arguments to open trade centre on the inherently static theoretical framework of trade theory and the apparent success of export promotion in less open trade regimes like South Korea or Taiwan. Theoretically, a more satisfying framework to explain export-oriented industrialization is provided by post-Keynesian writers like Cornwall (1977). Petri (1993: 8–14) also provides some evidence that Taiwan and South Korea are still largely open compared to Latin American countries where industrial take-off has been much slower.

4 See discussion in Little (1981).

5 See a description of the importance of the electronics industry in Asian industrialization and innovation in Hobday (1995).

6 For an excellent theoretical discussion of the international technology gap and its effect on productivity growth see Cornwall (1977: Ch. 6). For a clear exposition of a post-Keynesian 'virtuous circle' model of export-led industrial growth see Cornwall (1977: Chs 9–10).

7 In Singapore in the late 1970s current account deficits often exceeded 10 per cent of GDP together with BOP surpluses. This is the situation in Malaysia and Thailand currently.

8 For example Japan between 1975 and 1990, or arguably Hongkong and Singapore beginning in the mid to late 1990s.

9 See Eichengreen and Bayoumi (1998).

10 For theoretical discussion and empirical work on the FEER concept see Williamson (1985) and (1994).

11 See a good exposition of the relative strengths and weaknesses of the PPP, FEER and portfolio balance approaches for currency forecasting in Rosenberg (1996).

12 A discussion of how export- and investment-led industrialization in Asia beginning in Japan would lead to various Asian economies going through different stages of industrial development was originally envisioned by Akamatsu (1956) in his seminal article on the 'wild geese flying pattern' of industrial development. A more trade-driven model has recently been adapted by Rana (1990).

13 See Appendix 1(a) for details of regression results, indicator weights and a breakdown of the raw variable readings for each country in each period. LOGIT analysis was relevant as many Asian exchange rates operate on dirty floats or restricted bands vs. the US dollar. Devaluations therefore represent discontinuous changes usually forced on central banks by capital markets or economic crises.

14 For example, those used by the Centre for International Business Cycle Research. A composite indicator was preferred to multivariate regression, given the theoretical significance of all eight variables.

15 As pointed out to us by Virginie Coudert from CEPII, the Asian–US productivity differential was theoretically particularly interesting to use as an indicator both of economic development and currency stability. This is because of the Balassa–Samuelson effect which predicts that low income per capita countries would have systematically larger undervaluations relative to PPP due to a greater technological differential in the traded vs. non-traded sectors (see Benaroya and Jenci, 1998). This implies that as industrialization proceeds and this differential narrows, undervaluation relative to PPP tends to diminish, causing greater nominal exchange rate strength over the long term.

16 China would be another interesting case for a similar out-of-sample test. However, reliable fiscal balance data are not available. Using our framework, China appears to be in a fairly advanced Stage 2 industrially. Yuan weakness is probably mainly due to institutional fiscal and monetary underdevelopment which, together with high state enterprise debt, provides significant risk of debt monetization leading to hyperinflation. However, this implies that once Chinese inflation is decisively controlled, the yuan could quickly become fairly stable.

17 This raises the interesting question of typical exchange rate fundamentals for a 'newly developed' economy like Japan. Given probable fairly sharp falls in productivity growth, the savings rate, fiscal, current account and basic balances as a country approaches industrial maturity, it would suggest that a regression towards medium-term stability from long-term strength would be the typical fate of a newly developed economy's currency as its fundamentals correspondingly lose vitality.

18 It should be pointed out that Singapore, as a city state, has artificially strong currency fundamentals. First, its current account surplus would be large as cities are large service providers to their regional hinterlands. By similar argument, the rate of foreign direct investment would tend to be higher for a capital city compared to a country as a whole. There are also institutional advantages. The mandatory savings scheme of the Central Provident Fund (CPF) requires an average worker to save 40 per cent of monthly income. The Monetary Authority of Singapore (MAS) is also an unusually conservative central bank.

19 For a concise account of the policy and development experiences of East Asia, see Leipziger and Thomas (1993).

20 Bank Negara has already stated that modest nominal appreciation of the ringgit would be desirable to stimulate industrial upgrading. It is likely that the Bank of Thailand will widen baht/US$ exchange rate bands from the current ±2 satangs (0.16 per cent) over the medium term.

21 Interestingly, the Indonesian rupiah has consistently traded to the strong end of its band throughout the recent band widening exercise.

22 The Philippines peso has appreciated some 25 per cent in real effective terms since end 1993, a rate similar to the Mexican peso appreciation 3–4 years prior to devaluation in 1994.

References

Akamatsu, K. (1956) 'A Wild Geese Flying Pattern of Japanese Industrial Development: Machine and Tool Industries', *Hitosubashi Review*, Vol. 6, No. 5.

Balassa, Bela and Corden, W. Max (1988) 'The Lessons of East Asian Development: An Overview', *Economic Development and Cultural Change*, Vol. 36, No. 3.

Benaroya, François and Janci, Didier (1998) 'Measuring Exchange Rate Misalignments in Emerging Asia with Purchasing Power Parity Estimates this volume, pp. 224–44.

Cornwall, John (1977) *Modern Capitalism: its growth and transformation*, Martin Robertson, London.

Dornbusch Rüdiger (1980) *Exchange Rate Economics: Where Do We Stand?* Brookings Papers on Economic Activity, Washington, DC, pp. 143–94.

Dornbusch, Rüdiger and Park, Yung Chul (1998) 'Flexibility or Nominal Anchors?', this volume, pp. 3–34.

Eichengreen, Barry and Bayoumi, Tamim (1998) 'Is Asia an Optimum Currency Area? Can it Become One? Regional, Global, and Historical Perspectives on Asian Monetary Relations', this volume, pp. 348–67.

Hobday, Michael (1995) *Innovation in East Asia*, Edward Elgar, Aldershot.

Krueger, A. (1984) 'Comparative Advantage and Development Policy: 20 years Later', in Syrquin, M., Taylor, L. and Westphal, L.E. (eds) *Economic Structure and Performance*, Orlando, Fla.

Leipziger, Danny M. and Thomas, Vinod (1993) *The Lessons of East Asia, An Overview of Country Experience*, World Bank, Washington, DC.

Little, I.M.D. (1981) 'The Experience and Causes of Rapid Labour-Intensive Development in Korea, Taiwan Province, Hongkong and Singapore', in Lee, E. (ed.) *Export Led Industrialization and Development*, ILO Asian Employment Programme, Singapore.

Petri, Peter (1993) *The Lessons of East Asia – Common Foundations of East Asian Success*, World Bank, Washington, DC.

Rana, P.B. (1990) 'Shifting Comparative Advantage Among Asian and Pacific Countries', *The International Trade Journal*, No. 3, Spring, pp. 243–58.

Rosenberg, Michael (1996) *Currency Forecasting: A Guide to Fundamental and Technical Models of Exchange Rate Determination* Irwin Professional Publishing, Chicago.

Williamson, John (1985) *The Exchange Rate System*, Policy Analyses in International Economics, rev. edn, Institute for International Economics, Washington, DC.

——(ed.) (1994), *Estimating Equilibrium Exchange Rates*, Institute for International Economics, Washington, DC.

12

DISCUSSION

Virginie Coudert

Lam Keong Yeoh and Ai Ning Wee have provided us with a very stimulating argument, for they propose an original approach to the evolution of the exchange rates in the long run. The scope of Chapter 11 is very broad, since it covers the major Asian countries and includes long-term historical data as well as long-run forecasts.

The bulk of the chapter is organized around the link between the 'fundamentals' and exchange rates. This seems relevant, as in the long run, the role of the 'fundamentals' is certainly the most important and the role of speculative factors tends to be weak. Recent economic literature has furnished a great deal of new evidence that fundamental factors do play an important part in the determination of the long-run exchange rate.

The idea of their chapter is that there is a 'life cycle hypothesis' of a currency, related to the different stages of international development. In the 'life cycle hypothesis' of the currency mentioned by Ai Ning Wee and Lam Keong Yeoh, the first stage of development is characterized by a continuous depreciation of the currency as export capacity is weak and inflation is high; in the second stage, there is an improvement in the trade deficit and a reduction of inflation as productivity increases; this leads to a reduction in the depreciation of the currency, and then to an appreciation of the currency. As these improvements in growth and price stability go on, the currency stabilizes in the third stage and finally appreciates in the fourth one.

In this 'life cycle' of the currency, growth leads to a trend of, first, smaller depreciation and then to an appreciation of the currency. Therefore, the evolution is continuous towards appreciation.

At first sight, this life cycle hypothesis of the currency could be linked to the life cycle of the current account. In the life cycle hypothesis of the balance of payments, a given country has first to face a deficit, due to borrowing requirements because of investment needs, which makes the real exchange rate depreciate. Then, the deficit is progressively absorbed and replaced by a surplus. In a final stage, when the country has accumulated large foreign assets, a trade deficit is then consistent with a current surplus, but growing trade deficits will eventually lead to current surplus deficit. This last stage is omitted here: there is no final stage where the appreciation trend is reversed. This may be because it is not really relevant for Asian countries.

Although the life cycle of the exchange rate proposed here is clearly related to the life cycle of the balance of payments, the matching is not complete, for the authors analyse the nominal, not the real, exchange rates.

This life cycle hypothesis of the exchange rate is said to be based on three theoretical approaches: the purchasing power parity, the FEER approach and the portfolio approach. These approaches seem relevant to provide a good estimation of equilibrium exchange rates in the long run. However, it is not at all clear how these three approaches are combined here to get the 'life cycle approach'. The main point is that the key variables identified in the three approaches as explaining the evolution of the exchange rates are put together in a regression. Therefore, the approach proposed by Lam Keong Yeoh and Ai Ning Wee is mainly empirical. The authors identify some key variables that may explain the evolution of the exchange rates, and then run a regression to select the relevant variables. Afterwards, all these identified variables are aggregated into a single one, called the 'score index', which appears to be a good proxy as a measure of the 'stage' of development. One caveat is that the study does not provide us with the exact make-up of this composite index, and the weight of the variables that enter in it.

The idea of the authors about this 'life cycle approach' seems intuitive but unfortunately remains intuitive, for there is no attempt to model precisely the path of the exchange rates. It could be criticized on these grounds. However, its great advantage is that it 'works', for it really seems to fit the data of the Asian exchange rates. Let us try to understand better why.

What 'the life cycle of the exchange rate' says is roughly that industrial development generates a tendency for a currency to appreciate. This phenomenon is well known for the real exchange rate, as the 'Balassa effect', which links the level of prices in one country to its level of GDP. As the productivity in the non-traded sector always lags behind the productivity of the industrial sector, the level of prices in a country generally rises with the GDP, as wage pressures make wages rise in the manufacturing sector as far as productivity. Then the increase of wages spreads to all the economic sectors, even if the increase in productivity is much weaker in the non-traded goods.

So this effect by itself could explain a strengthening of the real exchange rate of the Asian countries, as their relative growth is certainly high, compared to the rest of the world. However, this approach is only in real terms. And the exchange rates used here are nominal.

In fact, it seems to me that the real exchange rate behaves according to the 'Balassa effect' and the movement of inflation strengthens the process. Growth provides countries with a real appreciation of their currency, but also typically makes inflation decrease, as is described in Chapter 11. The decrease in inflation reduces the nominal depreciation, as the PPP roughly applies in the medium run. So these two effects – Balassa effect and PPP – in a context of decreasing inflation certainly explain most of the results. The balance of payments variables explain the remainder.

Using nominal instead of real exchange rates seems strange in a long-run approach. Using real exchange rates would have been clearer in assessing competitiveness. Also, it would have spared the additional uncertainty, which is linked to inflation forecasts. A great part of the variance of nominal exchange rates is certainly due to relative price movements. However, the results may not be so striking in real terms if the appreciation in the nominal exchange rate is due only to the reduction in inflation.

13

MEASURING EXCHANGE RATE MISALIGNMENTS WITH PURCHASING POWER PARITY ESTIMATES

François Benaroya and Didier Janci

Since the mid-1980s, exchange rate levels of emerging Asian countries have received considerable interest in France among both economists and policy makers. In the controversy on the relocation of industrial activities in several emerging economies (the so-called *délocalisations*) and on the consequences of trade competition with these countries, it has often been argued that currencies of emerging Asian countries were severely undervalued *on purpose* and that this undervaluation was exacerbating current unemployment issues in developed economies.

Concerns about the social impact of the emerging Asian countries' competitiveness are widespread among old industrialized economies (see the *hollowing out* debate in Japan, the *standort* issue in Germany, and in the United States, a controversy on the respective roles of trade and biased technological progress in the recent increase in income inequalities).[1] But the emphasis laid on exchange rate issues and, in particular, on the exchange rate policies followed by the emerging countries seems peculiar to the French debate.

In this national debate, the most serious arguments supporting the existence of such an undervaluation have been based on purchasing power parity (PPP). Given differences of productivity in tradables and non-tradables sectors (the Balassa–Samuelson effect), exchange rate levels of developing economies should be undervalued relative to the (absolute) PPP. However, several authors (for instance Allais, 1994; Lafay, 1994) argue that *the observed undervaluation cannot be fully explained by the Balassa–Samuelson effect*. Exchange rate policies, and in particular opportunist dollar pegs, have therefore been suspected of generating an additional and harmful misalignment.

The use of PPP and the Balassa–Samuelson effect to derive equilibrium exchange rate levels can be questioned on several grounds: in particular, empirical evidence hardly supports PPP except over long periods and, contrary to the fundamental equilibrium exchange rates (FEERs) approaches, the

222

Balassa–Samuelson theory ignores the macroeconomic disequilibria that *de facto* drive the exchange rate.

We have still decided to derive equilibrium exchange rates in emerging Asia countries from PPP estimates and the Balassa–Samuelson effect, rather than from what could be a more satisfactory framework (see Barrell *et al.*, 1998, for an estimate of FEERs for the NIEs), because the Balassa–Samuelson model, when improved, shows a good predictive power, and provides an adapted explanation in the policy debate.

Our results are threefold:

- We improve the basic Balassa–Samuelson framework used in cross-section estimates, by relaxing some extreme assumptions.
- We show that, with these complements, the statistical significance of the Balassa–Samuelson model is strengthened, implying that PPP estimates can be a useful tool for studying exchange rate levels in the long run.
- We compute estimates of exchange rate deviations from PPP in 1993. They appear to be largely explained by our framework. Once the undervaluation of the US dollar is taken into account, only a limited undervaluation can be observed in 1993 for a small set of Asian countries.[1] For some of these countries, questions remain open, however.

This chapter is organized as follows. Section 1 reviews the evidence of the Balassa–Samuelson effect and its application to measure exchange rate misalignments in emerging Asian countries. Section 2 describes the basic Balassa–Samuelson model, generally used to explain these misalignments, and proposes an extended model, in which several assumptions are relaxed. Estimates of this model are developed in Section 3. Section 4 describes the results found for emerging Asian countries. Section 5 concludes.

1 The Balassa–Samuelson effect and its application to measure exchange rate misalignments: a brief review

In two seminal papers, Balassa (1964) and Samuelson (1964) argued independently that productivity differentials between tradable and non-tradable sectors lead to divergence in real exchange rate levels among countries. The technological advantage of a high-income country over a low-income country is greater in the tradable sector than in the non-tradable sector. By the law of one price, the price of the tradable goods is supposed to be the same across countries, but this is not the case for the non-tradables. Increased productivity in the tradable sector increases real wages and as a result leads to an increase in the price of non-tradables. Long-run productivity differentials thus lead to deviations from PPP: the greater are productivity differentials in the production of tradable goods, the larger is the gap between PPP and the equilibrium exchange rate.

The Balassa–Samuelson model provides a useful framework to undertake inter-country comparisons. Balassa showed that if international productivity differences are greater in the production of tradables than in the production of non-tradables, the currency of the country with the lower productivity will appear to be undervalued in terms of PPP. As productivity and per capita income are closely related, the ratio of PPP to exchange rate will then be a decreasing function of income.[2]

Several different predictions of the Balassa–Samuelson model have been tested in the literature, with the evidence being somewhat mixed, in particular for OECD countries samples (see Froot and Rogoff, 1996, for a recent survey). Some studies examine the relevance of productivity differentials in determining the relative price of non-tradables (e.g. Asea and Mendoza, 1994; de Gregorio *et al.*, 1993).[3] Others consider sectoral inflation or productivity differentials to explain differences in real exchange rate (Hsieh, 1982; Froot and Rogoff, 1991). Finally, some authors (Balassa, 1964; Summers and Heston, 1991; Goldfajn, 1996), as we do, focus on the inter-country relationship between the level of real exchange rate and the level of income per capita.

According to the latter group, the Balassa–Samuelson model is consistent with the evidence showed by the broad international comparison programme of the United Nations: as non-tradable prices tend to be lower in developing countries, most developing countries–and in particular Asian ones–are undervalued in terms of PPP relative to the United States, and the expected decreasing function of income can be observed (see Figure 13.1).

If one admits that the Balassa–Samuelson framework provides a reasonable explanation to the long-run exchange rate deviations from PPP, the next step

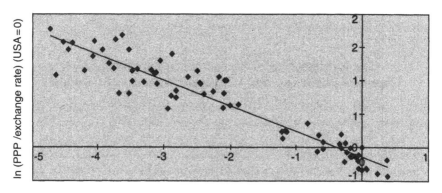

Figure 13.1 Price level and income for selected countries in 1993
Source: World Bank data.

Note
See Section 3 of this chapter.

is to examine the remaining deviations, which are *not* explained by the Balassa–Samuelson model. The idea is quite simple: after regressing the ratio of PPP over the exchange rate on income per capita levels (or productivity levels, and possibly other variables that can be included in the model), residuals provide a useful information about other effects which are not captured in the basic framework. Balassa (1964) himself suggested that 'the observed relation between PPP and exchange rates may provide some clues as to the overvaluation or undervaluation of a currency', and on such grounds, posited for instance that the French franc was overvalued prior to 1957. Countries above the line in Figure 13.1 have, then, an undervalued currency.

A surprisingly low number of studies have focused on these exchange rate deviations from the Balassa–Samuelson model. Dollar (1992) has computed these deviations for ninety-five countries over the 1979–85 period but his aim was to derive a measure of a country's openness and then to demonstrate that open economies grow faster. Consistent with the special focus mentioned in the introduction, recent studies considering residuals of the standard Balassa regression as measures of over or undervaluation of exchange rates are mainly to be found among French academics (Busson and Villa, 1996; Lafay, 1996; Mathieu and Sterdyniak, 1994).

Using the standard Balassa–Samuelson framework to measure exchange rate misalignments presents several weaknesses:

1 The Balassa–Samuelson model is not necessarily the main theoretical explanation of the observed deviations from PPP: Bhagwati argued for instance that the adoption of more capital-intensive manufacturing as a country develops, rather than exogenous technical progress, can explain the changing relative price of non-tradables.

2 PPP estimates tend to diverge significantly: recent estimates of Japanese PPP exchange rate vary for instance in a 50 per cent range. Estimates for China are also controversial. Among other methodological issues, it is quite difficult to disentangle in practice between tradable and non-tradable sectors, even with fairly disaggregated data (Heston *et al.*, 1994).

3 Some doubt has been cast on the statistical significance of the observed relationship between purchasing parities, exchange rate and income level in Figure 13.1: there seem to be striking differences between low-income countries and rich ones, and, once divided into two groups, the within-group correlations between income and price level are much less apparent (the existence of a break in the sample and of some heteroskedasticity is pointed out by Summers and Heston, 1991, with their 1980 data, and underlined by Froot and Rogoff, 1996; Goldfajn, 1996, dividing a 1990 sample in four quartiles, also shows the absence of correlation within subgroups).

4 The standard regression hinges on a questionable assumption: identical relative size of the tradable sectors across all economies. Summers and

Table 13.1 Changes in the manufacturing sector relative to the overall economy for selected Asian countries

	Japan	South Korea	Singapore	Philippines	Indonesia	Thailand	Taiwan	China
	Relative size of the manufacturing sector							
1973	28.1%	15.9%	32.9%	31.0%	6.5%	22.4%	31.9%	24.1%
1993	33.1%	35.1%	31.8%	26.9%	20.8%	34.3%	31.1%	44.0%
Annual change	0.9%	4.2%	−0.2%	−0.7%	5.9%	2.1%	−0.1%	3.0%
	Relative price index (1987 = 100)							
1973	133.3	168.6	79.4	93.1	164.3	95.7	115.4	128.8
1993	90.2	88.4	94.7	97.2	107.2	94.4	98.0	85.7
Annual change	−2.1%	−3.4%	0.9%	0.2%	−2.1%	−0.1%	−0.8%	−2.0%

Source: World Bank.

Heston (1991) found some support for this assumption, but their analysis relies on a crude definition of the non-tradable sector (all services plus construction), which does not fit with the increasing tradability of services (see World Bank, 1995a), the international competition in large infrastructure construction, or, for example, the fact that a rice crop is less internationally tradable in a remote Chinese province than in the United States. Intuitively, the size of the tradable sector is quite different across countries, and increasingly over time, as countries are gradually getting more open. The changing economic structures may then have a larger effect than the change in relative prices, which is the only one considered in the basic Balassa–Samuelson framework, in particular for the Asian fast-developing countries. Though the manufacturing sector cannot be equated with the tradable one, these changes are apparent in Table 13.1.

5   Finally, the Balassa–Samuelson model relies on the law of one price (LOP) in the tradable sector: this law seems, however, not to be observed. More generally, and contrary to the FEERs approach to the equilibrium exchange rate, the Balassa–Samuelson framework does not consider the macro disequilibria which in fact drive the exchange rate: it seems for instance natural to consider that the equilibrium exchange rate of the United States, or of Mexico in 1994, is influenced by the size of the current account deficit.

We have nevertheless decided to base our contribution on the Balassa–Samuelson model, for at least two reasons.

First, as far as the political debate is concerned, it was important to contradict some protectionist-oriented papers using the same theory. The Balassa–

Samuelson framework, when proved relevant, provides a straightforward explanation of the deviations from PPP, which is the base of common under-valuation beliefs.

Second, we have adopted an extended version of the Balassa–Samuelson model to try to get around most of the theoretical weaknesses that we have mentioned. The identical relative size of the tradable sectors and the LOP (law of one price) assumptions have been somewhat relaxed, and the results of the new model strengthen the statistical significance of the observed inter-country relationship between purchasing power parities and income level. This model is described in Section 2.

2   An extended Balassa–Samuelson model

We first recall the original Balassa–Samuelson model before relaxing some restrictive assumptions.

2.1   Model 1: the original model

Consider a small open economy that produces tradable goods (T), priced in the world market, and non-tradable goods (NT), priced in the domestic market, with one factor (labour) mobile between sectors but not internationally.[4] World variables are denoted with an asterisk (*).

The tradable sector determines the wage in the small economy

The price of the tradable good in the world market p_T^* is equal to a producer margin (assumed constant across sectors) multiplied by the unit labour cost, measured by the ratio of the world nominal wages (ω^*) to the world productivity (π_T^*), that is, in logarithms:

$$p_T^* = \omega^* - \pi_T^* \tag{13.1}$$

The law of one price is supposed to hold in the tradable sector. The domestic price of the tradables equals the international one, with e, exchange rate, defined as the number of foreign currency units equivalent to one domestic unit:

$$p_T + e = p_T^* \tag{13.2}$$

With π_T local productivity in the tradable sector, the wage in the small economy ω is therefore determined by:

$$\omega = p_T + \pi_T \tag{13.3}$$

The price in the non-tradable sector is given by the wage rate

The labour is mobile within each country. Hence the non-tradable price is determined by the unit labour cost, in the small economy and in the world:

$$p_{NT} = \omega - \pi_{NT} \tag{13.4}$$

$$p_{NT}^* = \omega^* - \pi_{NT}^* \tag{13.5}$$

Using equations 13.3 and 13.4 implies:

$$(p_{NT} - p_T) = (\pi_T - \pi_{NT}) \tag{13.6}$$

Price levels and exchange rates follow by aggregating

The aggregate price level (GDP deflator),[5] p, is a weighted mean of the prices p_{NT} and p_T

$$p = \alpha p_{NT} + (1 - \alpha)p_T \tag{13.7}$$

α being the relative size of the non-tradable sector.

An identical relation holds in the rest of the world:

$$p^* = \alpha^* p_{NT}^* + (1 - \alpha^*)p_T^* \tag{13.8}$$

The exchange rate compatible with the PPP is given by:

$$e_{PPP} = p^* - p \tag{13.9}$$

From equations 13.7 to 13.9 can be derived the difference between the PPP exchange rate and the current exchange rate:

$$e_{PPP} - e = p^* - p - e = (p_T^* - p_T - e) - \alpha(\pi_T - \pi_{NT}) + \alpha^*(\pi_T^* - \pi_{NT}^*) \tag{13.10}$$

$e + p_T - p_T^*$ equals 0 according to equation 13.2 (LOP). The overall productivity in the small economy can be defined as: $\pi = (\alpha\pi_{NT} + (1 - \alpha)\pi_T)$. We define analogously π^*. If we assume that the overall productivity growth is concentrated in the tradable sector and positively correlated with the national differential between productivity growth in tradables and non-tradables (there exist constants k, positive, and C, such that $(\pi_T - \pi_{NT} = k\pi + C)$,[6] we get:

$$e_{PPP} - e = [k\alpha^*](\pi^* - \pi) - k(\alpha - \alpha^*)\pi - C(\alpha - \alpha^*) \tag{13.11}$$

The basic Balassa–Samuelson model further assumes that the relative share of the non-tradable sector is identical across countries, i.e. $\alpha = \alpha^*$:

$$e_{PPP} - e = [k\alpha^*](\pi^* - \pi) \tag{13.12}$$

This provides a simple (log)linear relation, and, taking GNP per capita as a proxy for a country's productivity,[7] a rationale for the curve observed in Figure 13.1: for a low-income country, π is smaller than π^*, implying that $e_{PPP} > e$.

2.2   Model 2: relaxing $\alpha = \alpha^*$

As argued in Section 1, if α^* (the relative size of the non-tradable sector in the rest of the world) can be seen as roughly constant, considering that the relative size α of the non-tradable sector is identical across countries is a far-fetched assumption. Beyond relative price heterogeneity, one cannot ignore the structural differences across countries: the parameter α must be shaped by geographic (country size, transport bottlenecks, etc.), cultural (preference for non-tradable goods etc.), political (trade barriers etc.) and economic (income level) factors.

Relaxing this assumption leads to equation 13.11. Two countries with the same GNP per capita may have different tradable sector size, and thus different equilibrium exchange rates. In particular, as k is positive, the first additional term implies that, other things being equal, the bigger the relative size of the non-tradable sector in a given economy, the larger the weight of this relatively low productivity sector in the price index, the more overvalued the exchange rate relative to the PPP. Estimation of this equation is not feasible unless some kind of direct measure of α is used. There is, however, no fully satisfactory measure of the non-tradable sector size.

2.3   Model 3: relaxing $\alpha = \alpha^*$ and partly relaxing the LOP

The LOP is, at least in the short run, not observed, even in the tradable sector (Obstfeld, 1995). Divergent tradable prices can therefore affect the Balassa–Samuelson analysis.

Relaxing the LOP leads to equation 13.10, or alternatively, to add $(p_T^* - p_T - e)$ to equation 13.11. If national tradable goods are more expensive than foreign ones, the Balassa–Samuelson inter-sectoral price effect could seem larger than it is in reality.

Divergent tradable prices can derive for instance from transport costs, restrictive trade policies or different market structure. $(p_T^* - p_T - e)$ is not exactly equal to the terms of trade, as all national tradable goods are not exported, and all foreign tradable goods are not imported. This factor can, however, be connected with both the external balance (relatively cheap national tradable goods help increase, in the long run, the trade balance) and the internal balance (cheap national tradable goods may foster growth and, possibly, inflation). In this respect, relaxing the LOP may help bridge the gap between the Balassa–Samuelson model and macroeconomic approaches to the equilibrium exchange rates, such as Williamson's (1985: 94).[8]

We have therefore tested whether macroeconomic disequilibria were influencing, through deviations from the LOP, the Balassa–Samuelson effect. We have simply added to the regression a variable representative of the external balance (deviations from a current account target) and a variable representative of the internal balance (deviations from a non-inflationary rate of growth).

3 Data and econometric estimates

For each of the three models described, a regression has been run on data for 1993. Econometric results are presented in Table 13.2.

Data are from the World Bank. In particular, PPP exchange rate estimates have been taken from the World Bank Atlas (1995) by dividing GNP per capita at PPP estimates by GNP per capita figures. Other sources (the PENN tables, for instance) have been rejected because they do not provide recent data. Countries for which the PPP estimate is itself the result of an adjustment (Balassa–Samuelson style) on other countries have been removed from the sample for the econometric estimation: this is for instance the case of Singapore. A few economies for which additional variables were missing have also been removed. Among the remaining sixty-one countries, eleven are from Africa, ten from Asia, fourteen from Latin America, eighteen from Western Europe. All countries have the same weight in the regressions.

3.1 Testing model 1, the original Balassa–Samuelson model

(R1): ln (PPP/exchange rate) = A ln GNP per capita + B

As shown in Table 13.2 (and as could be inferred from Figure 13.1), the Balassa–Samuelson model provides a fairly good explanation of the deviations from PPP. The sign for A is as expected. GNP per capita is, in all estimations, the most significant explanatory variable.

However, two serious problems, already mentioned in Summers and Heston (1991), can be raised.

1 There is a clear break in the sample between developing and industrialized countries. Once divided in two subsamples (countries with a GNP per capita below or over US$6,000 approximately), estimates are (contrary to Summers and Heston's findings) still significant, but they differ

Table 13.2 Regressing e_{PPP-e} (logarithm of the exchange rate at PPP over the actual exchange rate) (t-statistics in parentheses)

Explaining variables	(R1)	(R1) + break	(R2)	(R2) + break	(R3)[a]	(R3)[b]	(R3)[c]	(R3)[d]
Constant	3.85	3.25	3.93	3.64	4.05	3.82	3.78	3.90
	(33.7)	(14.6)	(37.6)	(14.6)	(39.5)	(44.5)	(41.0)	(39.6)
ln GNP per capita π	−0.399		−0.41		−0.424	−0.408	−0.404	−0.422
	(−28.8)		(−32.2)		(−33.8)	(−40.1)	(−37.1)	(−33.6)
ln GNP per capita > US$ 6000		−0.342		−0.381				
		(−14.9)		(−14.8)				
ln GNP per capita < US$ 6000		−0.310		−0.367				
		(−9.67)		(−10.2)				
Relative non-tradables share × ln GNP per capita: $(\alpha - \alpha^*)\pi$			−0.695	−0.558	−0.586	−0.505	−0.474	−0.495
			(−3.39)	(−2.42)	(−3.06)	(−3.02)	(−2.80)	(−2.45)
Relative non-tradables share $(\alpha - \alpha^*)$			7.08	5.71	6.30	5.65	5.27	5.12
			(3.61)	(2.57)	(3.46)	(3.56)	(3.52)	(2.6)
Current account deficit minus sustainable current account deficit					1.19			
					(3.32)			
Sustainable current account deficit (as a % of GNP)						3.22	2.65	
						(5.73)	(3.52)	
Average growth rate							0.846	
							(1.11)	
National savings/GNP								0.814
								(3.02)
R^2	0.934	0.943	0.949	0.951	0.957	0.968	0.968	0.956
Standard error	0.169	0.159	0.151	0.150	0.139	0.121	0.121	0.141
Sum square residuals	1.70	1.47	1.30	1.26	1.08	0.817	0.800	1.11

231

markedly (see Table 13.2; the Fisher test clearly rejects the identical coefficients hypothesis).

2 Some heteroskedasticity can be observed: the square of the residuals is significantly correlated with the ln GNP per capita variable.

3.2 Testing model 2

Two terms capturing the effect of the variation in the non-tradable sector's relative size $(\alpha - \alpha^*)$ are added to the regression.

$$\text{(R2): } \ln (\text{PPP}/\text{exchange rate}) = A \ln \text{GNP per capita}$$
$$+ B(\alpha - \alpha^*) \ln \text{GNP per capita} + C(\alpha - \alpha^*) + D$$

There is no fully satisfactory evaluation of the non-tradable sector relative size α. Measures used in the literature, based on purely theoretical considerations of sectoral tradability, are not convincing, as argued in Section 1. The estimation for 1980 by Summers and Heston (1991) concludes, quite surprisingly, that this (real) share is flat across country income groups. Unfortunately, no country data are given to examine potential disparities within country groups.

We have therefore constructed a proxy for $(\alpha - \alpha^*)$, derived from the ratio of importations of goods and non-factor services over GNP at PPP. This ratio captures several factors (country size, trade restrictions, transport costs, etc.) that are supposed to influence the tradability of goods and services. The more open a country, the larger can be its tradable sector. One shortcoming is that this ratio could be theoretically larger than one. But this ratio appears smaller than one for all countries in the sample.[9] To eliminate any price effect (the ratio is increasing with income, because of its denominator), the result has been regressed on the GNP per capita. $(\alpha - \alpha^*)$ has then been identified to the residual of this intermediary regression, after changing in sign.[10] By construction, α on average does not depend on income level, thus fulfilling the condition found by Heston and Summers.

As shown in Table 13.2, the (two) structural terms are significant and improve the quality of the model estimate. The first term is of the expected sign. Furthermore, the structural break in the sample disappears (according to a Fisher test) and the observed heteroskedasticity is reduced (in the regression of the residual on the GNP per capita, t-test falls from 2.2 to 1.8).

3.3 Testing model 3

Ideally, the remaining residual of the regression could be explained by the disequilibria of both the internal and external balance, namely, the difference between the actual rate of growth and the long-term rate, and the difference between the current account balance and a sustainable current account target. For instance, relatively low growth and a large current account deficit in Mexico in 1994 may imply that the exchange rate of this country is significatively more overvalued than it appears in a standard Balassa analysis.

Hence, four new terms have been considered for the regression:

- the growth rate in 1993;
- the average growth rate in 1989–93, as a proxy for the long-term growth rate;
- the current account balance in 1993, divided by the GNP;
- a sustainable current account deficit target, as a percentage of GNP: it is defined, following Dadush and Brahmatt (1995), by the average growth rate of exports (over 1989–93) multiplied by 2, times the ratio of exports over GNP.[11]

We have first tested their difference (difference between the actual rate of growth and the long-term rate, and difference between the current account balance and a sustainable current account target). While difference in growth is not significant, deviation from the sustainable current account as a percentage of GNP seems to improve the regression.

However, as shown in Table 13.2, including only the sustainable current account variable improves the regression even more. The average growth rate and the sustainable current account deficit (in fact, the average export growth rate) are more significant than the differences. The best adjustment is made with the sustainable current account deficit only: (R3)[b].

This regression is very significant and eliminates any visible heteroskedasticity (t-statistic at 0.85 for the regression of the residual).

Three conclusions can be derived from the empirical analysis of model 3.

1   Confirming previous correlation tests between current account imbalances and deviations to the PPP Big Mac index (Pakko and Pollard, 1996), it appears that current account balance cannot be correlated with deviations from the Balassa–Samuelson model. Indeed, there is no clear link: a current account deficit can explain why a currency is undervalued relative to the PPP or the Balassa–Samuelson model, while some undervaluation may help a current account to stay in surplus.

2   The most significant regressions bring a serious theoretical challenge: instead of a bridge between the Balassa–Samuelson and Williamson approaches, we simply find that, other things being equal, countries whose exchange rate is undervalued relative to the (extended) Balassa–Samuelson rule, grow on average relatively faster or, more exactly, have a higher export growth. This is consistent with the evidence in Dollar (1992): he found that exchange rate undervaluation relative to the Balassa–Samuelson rule had a positive effect on average growth. But his

interpretation, identifying exchange rate undervaluation as a proxy for outward-oriented strategies,[12] can be criticized and provide an argument for those who judge that the real exchange rates of emerging Asian countries are undervalued on purpose (through restrictive financial policies) and may harm European economies.

3 More generally, there is a striking correlation between the deviations from the Balassa–Samuelson model and a set of variables related to economic growth: the savings ratio appears also, for instance, as a significant additional variable (see regression R3^d). Further research could therefore be fruitful.

4 Implications for exchange rate levels in emerging Asia

Deviations from the Balassa–Samuelson model and from the (theoretically grounded) extended model (R2) are shown in Table 13.3–for selected emerging Asian and developed countries in 1993, and in Figures 13.2 and 13.3 for a larger number of countries.

As we are basically interpreting residuals from a worldwide regression, country results are not always reliable. Specific country characteristics and a

Table 13.3 Deviations from the standard and extended Balassa–Samuelson model, 1993

	PPP exchange rate/current exchange rate	Difference explained (model 2)	Residual (%)*	Difference explained (model 1) (Balassa)	Residual (in %)*
China	4.33	4.26	−1.5	3.95	−8.7
Indonesia	4.30	3.65	−15.1	3.37	−21.7
Philippines	3.20	3.05	−5.0	3.20	−0.1
Thailand	3.13	2.33	−25.6	2.24	−28.6
Malaysia	2.73	1.56	−42.7	1.88	−31.3
Korea	1.28	1.33	4.3	1.32	3.0
Taiwan**	1.43	1.12	−21.8	1.15	−19.9
Hong Kong**	1.21	0.87	−28.6	0.94	−22.5
Singapore**	1.06	0.74	−30.5	0.91	−14.0
France	0.87	0.85	−2.1	0.86	−1.1
USA	1,00	0.82	−18.4	0.83	−17.4
Japan	0.67	0.71	6.3	0.75	11.9

Source: World Bank, Hong Kong Census and Statistics Department, and authors' calculations.
Notes
* A minus sign implies an undervaluation of the exchange rate.
** These countries were not used in the regression. Results of model 2 are with retained imports only.

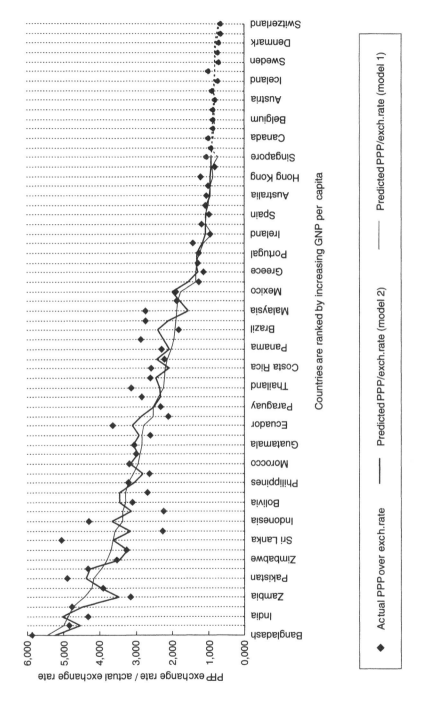

Figure 13.2 PPP over exchange rate, actual and predicted

235

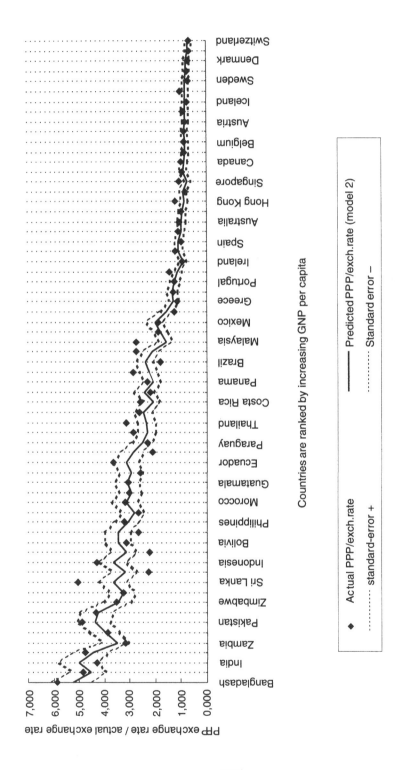

Figure 13.3 PPP over exchange rate, actual and predicted (model 2)

236

10 per cent uncertainty over the PPP estimates must be taken into account. Several regional conclusions can still be drawn:

- African countries whose currency is pegged to the French franc were over-valued in 1993: this is quite a satisfactory result. Magnitudes of overvaluation are similar to results found with other methods (relative PPP or statistical estimates, see Devarajan, 1996).
- The US dollar is significantly undervalued. But the small country hypothesis is of course, in this case, questionable.
- Most Asian countries' exchange rates also appear undervalued, but much less than in previous studies like Lafay (1996). This is particularly the case for Taiwan, Thailand, Hong Kong and (up to around 40 per cent) Malaysia.[13] Exceptions are the Philippines and South Korea. The results are close to those of Barrell et al. (1998) for the four countries they have studied. If one considers that Asian currencies are informally pegged to the dollar (see Bénassy, 1996), their 'own' undervaluation should be measured relative to the US dollar and is, in general, less than 20 per cent.
- The extended model does not fundamentally diverge from the Balassa–Samuelson model in its results: differences are typically of less than 10 per cent (more open countries appearing more undervalued). But some support is given by the Mexican case: according to the standard model, the Mexican peso was undervalued by 7 per cent in 1993 (larger undervaluation figures were even found in previous studies using this model); with the extended model, it appears overvalued by 6 per cent. This seems of course more realistic.

These conclusions are rather robust, though two remarks must be made.

- The reference for under (over) valuation may be biased by the absence of country weights: it may seem strange to assert that all Asian countries (except Japan), the United States and (though not significantly) France and Germany, all have an undervalued currency; if countries were to be weighted by their GNP, the reference could be lower, and make European countries overvalued and Asian countries a bit less undervalued.
- Even if there is no selection bias in our sample, inclusion of several African countries, whose currency was severely overvalued in 1993, may distort the regression (see also Dollar, 1992). A sensitivity analysis, performed by adding a dummy variable for African countries, shows that the regression is only slightly modified, and that undervaluation of Asian countries is simply reduced by a few percentage points.

Our approach can, however, be criticized because it applies a long-term analysis (the Balassa–Samuelson effect) to a given year (1993). Deviations from relative PPP have a half life of approximately four years, according to recent panel data estimates (Frankel and Rose, 1996). Country results must therefore be carefully interpreted, and take longer evolutions into account.

To illustrate this point, we have computed, using the same regressions, values of undervaluations with 1998 data from the World Bank Atlas 6 (see Table 13.4). This is legitimate, as other studies have proved the relative stability of the Balassa–Samuelson regression coefficients (Busson and Villa, 1996).[14] Results are:

- Undervaluation has decreased relative to 1993 in the case of Hong Kong and Singapore.[15] These countries show, from the beginning of the 1990s, a significant real exchange rate appreciation which is compatible with the Balassa–Samuelson theory: as countries get richer, their real exchange rate must get closer to the PPP.
- China appears more undervalued, following the devaluation of the renminbi as of 1 January 1994. This is consistent with the large trade surplus registered thereafter.
- Last but not least, the undervaluation of the Indonesian Rupiah has disappeared and the Thai Baht was much less under valued than in 1993. Once taken into the sharp appreciation of ths US dollar in 1997 vis-à-vis the other main international currencies (particularly the yen), most of the Asian currencies which were since attached appear to be overvaluated just before the exchange rule crises.

Table 13.4 Deviations from the standard and extended Balassa–Samuelson model, 1996

	PPP exchange rate / current exchange rate	Difference explained (model 2)	Residual (in %)*	Difference explained (model 1) (Balassa)	Residual (in %)*
China	4.44	3.56	−19.8	3.33	−24.9
Indonesia	3.06	3.09	0.7	2.88	−6.0
Philippines	3.06	2.67	−12.7	2.80	−8.5
Thailand	2.26	1.99	−12.0	1.93	−14.9
Malaysia	2.38	1.41	−40.7	1.65	−30.6
Korea	1.23	1.16	−5.8	1.16	−6.1
Taiwan	1.48	1.05	−28.9	1.08	−27.1
Hong Kong**	1.00	0.80	−19.6	0.83	−16.7
Singapore**	0.88	0.81	−8.0	0.76	−13.8
France	0.82	0.79	−3.6	0.81	−1.5
USA	1.00	0.76	−23.8	0.79	−21.4
Japan	0.57	0.61	7.3	0.68	18.1

Source: World Bank, Hong Kong Census Statistics Department, and authors' calculations.

Notes

* A minus sign implies an undervaluation of the exchange rate.
** These countries were not used in the regression.

5 Conclusion

Using PPP figures, in an improved Balassa–Samuelson framework, can be useful to determine appropriate exchange rate levels in the long run. While the general relation is statistically significant, results for emerging Asian countries are broadly in line with other kinds of estimates. Once taken into account the undervaluation of the US dollar, a picture of small, albeit gradually reducing, undervaluation generally emerges for these countries.

The approach developed in this chapter should be complemented, however, in at least three dimensions, in order to understand fully the exchange rate levels in emerging Asian countries.

1 The analysis should be performed not only for a sole year, but over longer periods, in order to examine the persistence of the observed undervaluations and to test the expected convergence of the exchange rate levels to the PPP (see the real exchange rate long-term evolutions in Benaroya and Janci, 1996, the long-run test of the standard Balassa framework in Busson and Villa, 1996, or Barrell et al., 1998, with another methodology).

2 As far as the policy debate is concerned, the explanation of the causes of any observed undervaluation is at least as important as its measure: one should not blame the emerging Asian countries for having a slightly undervalued currency, if this undervaluation is the result of external factors, either directly (the volatile yen–dollar exchange rate) or indirectly: restrictive financial measures, preventing the exchange rate appreciation, are for instance justified in several developing Asian countries, by the potential destabilizing effect of capital inflows (see the descriptive analysis in Benaroya and Janci, 1996).

3 Finally, further theoretical and empirical analysis is needed to reconcile the Balassa–Samuelson and macroeconomic approaches to the equilibrium exchange rate. Controlling for other variables that may influence growth, such as savings or investment, and improving the measures of long-run internal and external balance targets is probably necessary. More satisfactory measures of the non-tradable sector size effect could be explored as well.

Notes

This contribution is partly based on Benaroya and Janci (1996). They are grateful to Agnès Bénassy-Quéré, Jean Pisani-Ferry, Rüdiger Dornbusch and other participants at the CEPII/AMUE/KIF conference for their comments on earlier versions of this chapter. It, however, only reflects the views of the authors, who take full responsibility for all remaining errors.

1 Recent valuable studies on these topics include, respectively, Kwan (1996), Ochel and Sherman (1996), P. Krugman (1995).

239

2 With the exchange rate defined as the number of foreign currency units equivalent to one domestic unit.

3 These authors also consider the role of demand factors.

4 Balassa used this Ricardian model. It can be extended to several factors, with no substantial differences (see Asea and Corden, 1994).

5 The consumer price is a weighted mean of the non-tradable sector price, of the local price of the tradable goods produced within the country, and of the imported goods in the tradable sector. Respective to the GDP deflator, the consumer price is therefore distorted by the imported goods price and by the local producer pricing behaviour.

6 This assumption is used for instance in Obstfeld (1995). It can be challenged, however, for countries like Singapore, with a fast productivity growth in services (see Young, 1992).

7 Recent productivity figures are not available for large samples including LDCs.

8 This idea was suggested to us by Agnès Bénassy-Quéré.

9 Singapore, which is not in the sample for the estimation, has a ratio larger than one, even once re-exports are subtracted from total imports.

10 The sign must be changed, otherwise we get a proxy for the variation in the tradable sector size. We have constructed similarly a variable, which may seem more natural, derived from the (nominal) share of services in the GDP. But this variable is not significant, thus implying that the share of services may not be a good proxy.

11 This definition means that the sustainable current account deficit is such that the ratio of debt over exports equals 2 on the long run.

12 This interpretation is also to be found in World Bank (1993).

13 The World Bank PPP figure for Singapore in 1993, which has been, as said previously, estimated by a regression, seems, however, rather odd (it has been substantially modified in the World Bank Atlas of 1996). Undervaluation should be probably smaller. Results for Singapore in model 2 must also be considered carefully (see Note 9).

14 Devaluation by CFA franc countries may have modified the regression and reduced slightly the observed Asian countries' undervaluation.

15 See Note 13: for Singapore, it is also the consequence of the PPP re-estimation by the World Bank.

References

Allais, M. (1994) 'La concurrence des pays à bas salaires', *Le Figaro*, 20 December.

Asea, P. and Corden, W. (1994) 'The Balassa–Samuelson model: an overview, *Review of International Economics*, October, pp. 191–200.

Asea, P. and Mendoza, E. (1994) 'The Balassa–Samuelson model: a general equilibrium appraisal', *Review of International Economics*, October.

Balassa, B. (1964) 'The Purchasing Power Parity doctrine: a reappraisal', *Journal of Political Economy*, December, pp. 584–96.

Barrell, R., Anderton, B., Lansbury, M. and Sefton, J. (1998) 'FEERS for the NICs: exchange rate policies and development strategies in Taiwan, South Korea, Singapore and Thailand', this volume, pp. 247–81.

Benaroya, F. and Janci, D. (1996) 'La sous-évaluation des monnaies asiatiques', Éco-nomie Internationale, 66.

Bénassy, A. (1996) 'Régimes et politiques de change en Asie', Économie Internationale, 66.

Busson, F. and Villa, P. (1966) 'L'effet Balassa: un effet robuste et de longue période', Économic Internationale, 66.

Clark, P., Bartolini, L., Bayoumi, T. and Symansky, S. (1994) Exchange Rates and Eco-nomic Fundamentals, a Framework for Analysis, IMF Occasional Paper No. 115, Washington, DC.

Dadush, U. and Brahmatt, M. (1995) 'Prévoir les renversements de flux de capitaux', Finances et Développement, IMF, December.

de Gregorio, J., Giovannini, A. and Krueger, T.H. (1993) 'The behavior of nontrad-able goods prices in Europe: evidence and interpretation', IMF Working Paper WP/93/45, Washington, DC.

Devarajan, S. (1996) 'La sous-évaluation du taux de change réel dans la zone CFA', mimeo, World Bank, Washington, DC.

Dollar, D. (1992) 'Outward-oriented developing economies really do grow more rapidly', Economic Development and Cultural Change, April.

Dornbusch, R. and Werner, A. (1994) Mexico: Stabilization, Reform, and No Growth, Brookings Papers on Economic Activity, Washington, DC.

Frankel, J. and Rose, A. (1996) 'A panel project on purchasing power parity: mean reversion within and between countries', Journal of International Economics, February.

Froot, K. and Rogoff, K. (1991) 'Government consumption and the real exchange rate', mimeo, Harvard Business School, Cambridge, Mass.

—— (1996) 'Perspectives on PPP and long-run real exchange rates', Handbook in International Economics, vol. 3, North-Holland, Amsterdam.

Goldfajn, I. (1996) 'The long-run appreciation process', Brandeis University, Work-ing Paper 344.

Heston, A., Nuxoll, D. and Summers, R. (1994) 'The differential productivity hypothesis and purchasing power parities: some new evidence', Review of Interna-tional Economics, Vol. 2, Issue 3, October, pp. 227–43.

Hsieh, D. (1982) 'The determinants of the real exchange rate: the productivity approach', Journal of International Economics 12, pp. 355–62.

Krugman, P. (1995) Growing World Trade: Causes and Consequences, Brookings Papers on Economic Activity, No. 1, Washington, DC.

Kwan, C. (1996) 'The rise of Asia and Japan hollowing out problem', mimeo, Nomura Research Institute.

Lafay, G. (1994) 'Concurrence internationale: des enjeux occultés', Le Figaro, 15 December.

—— (1996) 'L'origine internationale du chômage européen', Revue d'Économie Poli-tique, December.

Mathieu, C. and Sterdyniak, H. (1994) 'L'émergence de l'Asie menace-t-elle l'em-ploi?', Revue de l'OFCE, January.

Obstfeld, M. (1995) International Currency Experience: New Lessons and Lessons Relearned, Brookings Papers on Economic Activity, No. 1.

Ochel, W. and Sherman, H. (1996) 'Rebuilding the international competitiveness of German industry', mimeo, Ifo Institute.

Pakko, M. and Pollard, P. (1996) 'For here or to go? Purchasing power parity and the Big Mac', *Federal Reserve Bank of Saint Louis Economic Review*, January.

Samuelson, Paul A. (1964) 'Theoretical Notes on Trade Problems', *Review of Economics and Statistics* 23.

Summers, R. and Heston, A. (1991) 'The Penn world table (mark 5): an expanded set of international comparisons 1950–1988', The *Quarterly Journal of Economics*, May.

Williamson, J. (1985) *The Exchange Rate System*, Institute for International Economics, Washington, DC.

——(1994) *Estimating Equilibrium Exchange Rates*, Institute for International Economics, Washington, DC.

World Bank (1993) *The East Asian Miracle: Economic Growth and Public Policy*, Washington, DC.

——(1995a) *Global Economic Prospects and the Developing Countries*, Washington, DC, p. 51.

——(1995b), Atlas, Washington, DC.

Young, A. (1992) 'A tale of two cities: factor accumulation and technical change in Hong Kong and Singapore', in NBER, *Macroeconomics Annual*, Cambridge, Mass., pp. 13–54.

Note

1 This paper was written in 1996. The appreciation of the US Dollar since mid-1995 considerably reduced, and in some cases reversed, the undervaluation of the Asian currencies observed in this chapter (see Table 13.4, p. 238). The recent currency crisis in Asia is not, henceforth, in contradiction with these findings.

14

DISCUSSION

Gang Shyy

Chapter 13 tries to achieve three goals: (1) to improve the basic Balassa–Samuelson framework used in cross-section estimates, by relaxing some extreme assumptions; (2) to use the model further and estimate the overvaluation and undervaluation of currencies of specific countries; and (3) to engage in a debate on the linkage between high unemployment in Europe and undervaluation in Asian emerging countries. In my opinion, I think the authors fulfil the first goal quite well but fail to achieve the second and the third goal of the chapter.

As far as the first goal is concerned, the authors seem to prove quite forcefully that models 2 and 3 have better explanatory power than the tradition Balassa–Samuelson model as specified in model 1.

However, the method that the authors employ to analyse the second issue on over/undervaluation of the foreign exchange rate for Asian emerging economies is fairly questionable. In Section 4 on implications for exchange rate levels in emerging Asia, the authors define the residual term from each country's estimate in 1993 by the model as overvaluation (if the residual is positive) and undervaluation (if the residual is negative). In view of the Balassa–Samuelson approach being a long-term equilibrium model, this kind of definition is hard to accept. In a sense, the condition for the definition to be correct is that the model has a 100 per cent explanatory power, a level no econometric model can achieve. (That is why we call the residual an 'error' term in statistics.) The fact that PPP exchange rate/current exchange rate ratios for Asian emerging economies are deviating from the long-term equilibrium might be due short-term disequilibrium in Asian economies rather than a deliberate policy to undervalue their currency.

I summarize as follows the short-term events which have had huge impacts on the long-term equilibrium discussed in the chapter.

First, the emerging Chinese economy in the early 1980s: China's open door policy since 1978 has had a huge impact on world trade equilibrium and intra-regional trade in Asia. For example, Hong Kong, Taiwan, Japan and Korea have increasing SDI into China since the 1980s and the trade patterns among these countries (and the USA) have since changed dramatically. The effect of the Chinese economy on Asian emerging countries could be clearly sensed during the recession period of the early 1990s: Hong Kong and Taiwan maintained high growth due to the increasing demand for imports by China during this period. This 'China connection' has obviously not been taken into account in the equilibrium calculation described by the Balassa–Samuelson model in the chapter.

Second, deregulation of the Asian financial industry in the early 1990s: it is very important to note that the deregulation of the financial industry in Asian emerging economies has had a huge impact in terms of the capital flow of global investment portfolio. Before the deregulation, most Asian countries had strict regulations prohibiting foreign institutions from investing in the financial market in their countries. As a result, the huge inflow of foreign investment into Asian's emerging market, along with the process of deregulation, is certainly a major factor affecting the long-term equilibrium of currency level in these Asian countries.

Third, self-adjustment and the technology shift after 1986: for most of the Asian emerging economies, the dramatic appreciation from 1985 to 1989 caused a permanent shift in industry structure and technology level. For example, Taiwan has shifted most of its labour-intensive industry (e.g. shoes, umbrellas, low-end textile industry) to China and South-East Asia and has moved into the information and computer industry successfully. It seems that the model proposed by the authors cannot effectively include these dynamic factors into the Balassa–Samuelson model.

In sum, I am not convinced that the short-term currency level (in 1993 as specified in the chapter) can be explained perfectly by the model proposed by the authors due to short-term disequilibrium created by these dynamic factors mentioned above.

15

FEERs FOR THE NICs

Exchange rate policies and development strategies
in Taiwan, South Korea, Singapore and Thailand

Ray Barrell, Bob Anderton, Melanie Lansbury and James Sefton

This research was funded as part of a wider project by the Association for
Monetary Union in Europe. The results reflect the views of the authors, and
the first author takes responsibility for all errors. We would like to thank participants at a conference at Bordeaux University in July 1996 for their comments, and we have received useful advice from John Williamson.

1 The Growth Experience of South Korea, Singapore, Taiwan and Thailand

The economic performance of East Asia since the 1950s has been remarkable.
However, this region's high growth can be primarily attributed to just eight
economies: Japan, whose growth began during the 1950s; Hong Kong, Taiwan, Singapore and South Korea – the so-called Asian Tigers whose rapid
growth was initiated in the late 1960s; and Thailand, Malaysia and Indonesia,
the second-tier Asian NICs whose growth began a decade later. Together,
these countries have experienced average annual growth of GNP per capita
of around 5.5 per cent between 1965 and 1990 as opposed to nearly 2.5 per
cent for the OECD economies.

These economies all share some similar characteristics that have set them
apart from other developing countries. All have invested in increasing their
human and physical capital and in reducing income inequality within the
countries. These high levels of investment have been sustained over long periods of time as the Asian NICs have all enacted policies to encourage high
rates of domestic saving and maintained a stable macroeconomic performance
through sound economic policy. Comparing the savings ratios of these countries with the OECD shows that on the whole this ratio has been rising in the
Asian NICs over the past twenty years whilst in the OECD it has remained at
around 20 per cent (Figure 15.1). Of the four countries in this study, Singapore has a savings ratio of around 45 per cent, up 15 percentage points over

the mid-1970s. South Korea and Thailand have also experienced increases in their savings ratios which are now around 35 per cent. Only Taiwan has seen a drop in the ratio since the late 1980s.

Although high growth has been largely driven by high levels of investment, the promotion of exports has also been a key factor in these economies' development and the governments of the NICs have, at various times, intervened in order to help follow this economic strategy. The success of this

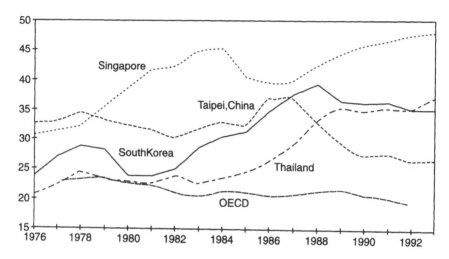

Figure 15.1 Domestic saving ratios (% GDP)
Source: Asian Development Bank and IFS.

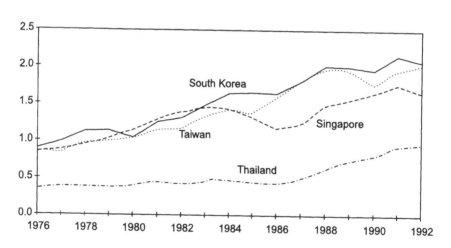

Figure 15.2 Share of world exports of manufactures (%)
Source: Asian Development Bank and IFS.

246

policy to promote exports is shown in Figure 15.2. The three first-tier NICs (South Korea, Singapore and Taiwan) all produced less than 1 per cent of world manufactured exports in the mid-1970s. During the latter half of this decade and into the 1980s this share grew, and by the 1990s these countries' share of world manufactured exports had risen to around 2 per cent each. Thailand's manufactured exports did not take off until the mid-1980s. Their share is now around 1 per cent.

Despite the increasing share of world manufactured exports the importance of manufacturing in domestic output has not increased substantially over the long run (Figure 15.3). In Singapore the share of manufacturing in output has remained around 25 per cent since the mid-1970s and in South Korea the share has increased by just 5 percentage points over this period. In Taiwan the manufacturing share increased from 30 per cent to 40 per cent between the mid-1970s and mid-1980s but has now fallen back down to just above its mid-1970s level. In view of the increasing exports of manufactured products, this suggests that in these first-tier NICs manufacturing has over the past ten years become increasingly export oriented. In Thailand, where development is a stage behind these other countries, the share of manufacturing in output has been rising from the mid-1980s. Manufacturing here currently accounts for over 25 per cent of GDP.

There is much debate about the role of economic policy in the development process in these countries. Some argue that it underlies the superior economic performance of the Asian Tigers. Countries may gain in their share of world trade either because they are more competitive than their rivals, or because they innovate and produce new and more superior goods that replace older

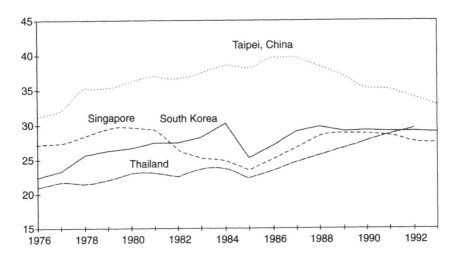

Figure 15.3 Share of manufacturing in output (%)
Source: Asian Development Bank and IFS.

substitutes. In broad terms, two schools of thought may be discerned in the literature: a school which argues that these countries did not essentially impede the free workings of markets or cause gross distortions of relative prices; and a school which suggests that, to the contrary, markets were tampered with in a deliberate attempt to overcome important market failures which would have prevented rapid growth.

Getting the fundamentals of economic policy right, such as ensuring macroeconomic stability and encouraging high savings, was as much a reason for economic success as were openness to the international economy and realistic prices, according to Rodrik (1995). Rodrik claims that although exports did contribute something to high GDP growth, the relatively small size of the export sector in the 1960s (between 10 and 20 per cent of GDP) means that export performance could not have contributed markedly to output growth until at least the mid-1970s; furthermore, there is little empirical evidence that the growth in exports led to productivity spillovers to the rest of the economy. He also points out that there was a lag of several years between the putting in place of the major export incentives and sharp export growth, suggesting the former was a necessary but not sufficient condition for high export growth. Thus, the evidence does not support the hypothesis that export growth, and in turn productivity growth, were the chief causes of exceptionally high GDP growth. In the view of Rodrik, a more plausible explanation of the East Asian miracle is the boom in investments which took place in the early 1960s under conditions of high levels of social infrastructure but low levels of physical infrastructure. This combination alone meant that the return to investment was relatively high. In addition a high level of intervention in many of these countries served to encourage investment. This in turn rendered these economies more open to trade.

According to the second school of thought, a policy of export-led growth adopted by these economies lay behind the so-called East Asian miracle over the past quarter of a century (Amsden, 1989; Wade, 1990). Before this, during the 1950s, the first-tier NICs pursued import-substitution policies often with high levels of protection, multiple exchange rates and restricted financial markets. However, from the 1960s these countries changed their trade strategies and adopted export-oriented policies which encouraged a rapid expansion of exports. These policies included the devaluation of exchange rates, some liberalization of trade, higher interest rates and duty-free access for exporters to imported goods.

In the following sections we focus on three of the first-tier NICs – South Korea, Singapore, Taiwan – and just one from the second tier – Thailand. The role of the real exchange rate, the main subject of this chapter, is investigated below. We first discuss the concept of the equilibrium real exchange rate, or FEER. We then calculate FEERs for different sets of assumptions. We assess the concept of the equilibrium real exchange rate. In order to evaluate exchange rate policies using the FEER we have to discuss econometric models of these countries. After we have done this we analyse whether the rapid growth of the Asian NICs was a result of export-led growth policies adopted by the countries.

2 Exchange rate policies – the concept of equilibrium

There is much debate as to whether the currencies of these Asian NICs have been competitively undervalued to promote exports. Experience in these and other countries has shown that there is a close link between export growth and the level of the real exchange rate. It is certainly true that the East Asian NICs and the ASEAN countries avoided the sustained real overvaluation of their exchange rates which afflicted many countries in Africa and Latin America from the 1960s. They managed this by both maintaining macroeconomic stability and not committing themselves to a fixed nominal exchange rate. In the 1970s and much of the 1980s they tied their currencies to movements in the US dollar, the United States being the major export market of countries in the region. By pegging their currencies to the dollar their competitiveness vis-à-vis a basket of trade partners' currencies would have worsened when the dollar appreciated sharply from 1980 to 1984, while it must have improved with the fall in the dollar after 1984. But it also appears that South Korea and Taiwan, and to a lesser extent Thailand, slightly undervalued their exchange rates vis-à-vis the dollar as a tool of commercial policy:

> several HPAE (high performing Asian economies) governments used exchange rate policies to offset the adverse impact of trade liberalisations on producers of import substitutes. A few went beyond this objective, however, and used deliberately undervalued exchange rates to assist exporters. In these instances, exchange rate policy and the fiscal and monetary tools to carry it out became a part of an overall export-push strategy. Taiwan, China, is the most notable example of this, but Korea and Indonesia also deliberately undervalued their currencies to boost exports.
>
> (World Bank, 1993: 125)

In order to evaluate the role of exchange rate policy on the economy we first have to ask whether it is possible to change the real exchange rate, and second we have to evaluate what real alternative real exchange rate trajectories would have been sustainable. In Barrell and Wren-Lewis (1989) and Barrell and Veld (1991) we used a large econometric model of the advanced economies to evaluate the trajectory for the fundamental equilibrium exchange rate (FEER, or in IMF parlance, the DEER). These analyses were designed for a series of exercises undertaken for Williamson (1994).

There is frequent misunderstanding of the concept of the FEER and our use of it, in part because the initial discussion of it in relation to target zones gave it a normative element that suggested it was a subjective concept. The concept of the equilibrium real exchange rate used here is not inconsistent with a rational expectations view of exchange markets. The market determines the nominal exchange rate, and governments have a hand in this because they are large players. However, the current nominal rate may be some distance away from the equilibrium that would be associated with current relative prices. As with all equilibrium concepts, we can distinguish both long-run and short-run concepts. The market determines the short-run nominal equilibrium based on the assumption that there are equilibrating forces at work, pulling the real exchange rate to its long-run equilibrium. However, the trajectory to that equilibrium depends on market expectations of government monetary and fiscal policy both at home and abroad as well as on the conceptual model of the economy used by the representative market participant.

We do not use the concept of purchasing power parity (PPP) for several reasons, although it is not necessarily inconsistent with the concept of the FEER. If supply and demand elasticities in international trade are (in the long run) sufficiently large, then the economy will be attracted to a relative price level that is justified by PPP. However, the long run may be rather longer than we feel is useful for policy analysis, because it may have to involve the relocation of economic activity. There is evidence from studies such as Gan (1994) that even the economies considered here have exchange rates that display some long-run properties that can be uncovered by cointegration analysis. The literature in this area is surveyed by Breuer (1994), and the common approach is to demonstrate that prices and the exchange rate cointegrate. This should not be interpreted as evidence in favour of PPP. The existence of an equilibrium real exchange rate should not be doubted, but all we may conclude from cointegration results is that it may be above or below PPP. Careful analysis of the relative prices of similar goods is necessary.

Empirical work on trade volumes and prices tends to find that competitiveness elasticities are not great. Whitley (1991), for instance, looks at trade elasticities for goods in Europe and finds them to be small. PPP may be brought about by the relocation of economic activity. Barrell and Pain (1996a, 1996b) do find some evidence that relative costs affect foreign direct investment (FDI) flows, although such effects are small and slow acting. However, the economies studied here may be different from those in Europe for numbers of reasons; in particular, they may have no market power since they are price takers in the markets in which they operate. We regard this as an empirical question and we address it below. It is clear that many countries can affect their current real exchange rate for some periods of time, even if there are strong forces driving the real exchange rate back to equilibrium. The manipulation of the real exchange rate can be, and has been, used as a tool for increasing exports and accumulation.

In order to evaluate the FEER we require a set of empirical relationships determining internal balance, external balance and asset accumulation The external balance relationship is the most important, and we require volume and price equations that determine the current account given the real exchange rate:

XVOL $=$ f(World Demand, Relative Prices)
MVOL $=$ g(Domestic Demand, Relative Prices)
PX $\quad=$ h(Domestic Prices, World Prices, Capacity Utilization)
PM $\quad=$ k(Domestic Prices, World Prices)

where XVOL and MVOL are exports and imports of goods and non-factor services, and PX and PM are export and import prices for goods and services.[1] For given levels of world and domestic demand, the real exchange rate, as described by relative prices, will deliver a current account balance. The factors involved in the internal balance relationship will vary depending on the structure of the economy and the factors involved in the wage bargaining relationship. We require wage, price and demand relationships:

PD $\ = f_1$ (Domestic Costs, Capacity Utilization)
WC $= g_1$ (Domestic Prices, Real Exchange Rate, Unemployment)
DD $= h_1$ (Domestic Incomes, Asset Stocks)

where PD is domestic prices, WC domestic wage costs, and DD is domestic demand. In early analyses of FEERs it was assumed that the wage bargain displayed a real exchange rate wedge, and hence internal balance was a function of the real exchange rate. However, as Barrell (1993) argues, the empirical and theoretical support for this proposition is weak. The level of domestic capacity affects wages through unemployment, and prices through capacity utilization. If capacity increases, then domestic wages and prices would have to be lower than they would otherwise have been. However, if the economy is operating at full capacity then there may be no domestic forces putting pressure on the real exchange rate.

If the economy is in internal and external balance at a point in time, then full equilibrium requires that the economy is at an asset equilibrium. This will depend, *inter alia*, on the size of the government debt stock, and the level of overseas assets. As Barrell and Sefton (1997) show, the equilibrium level of overseas assets depends in part on the size of the government debt stock. It will also depend on the time profile of domestic income and spending, with countries having long-term accumulation needs running balance of payments surpluses. Unless trade elasticities are extremely large, this requires that the real exchange rate accommodates the need for accumulation to achieve asset equilibrium.

In order to calculate an estimate of the FEER we require a model of the economy that encapsulates the above, and we need an idea of the private sector equilibrium asset accumulation. As the concept of the FEER is a medium-term one, we can abstract from the effects of short-run dynamics. Hence, in solving the system above we can find the long-run structure of our model and invert it to solve for the real exchange rate consistent with the trajectory for the current account given by asset equilibrium. We discuss our models of the four countries in question below, and we utilize the method described here to evaluate exchange rate policies in the 1980s and 1990s. We stress relative import prices as the best real exchange rate measure available for these countries, as some of them may be seen as price takers in their export markets.

3 Econometric models of Singapore, Thailand, South Korea and Taiwan

In this section we describe the econometric models which we use to calculate the FEERs of the four countries. We begin by explaining the theoretical models underlying the individual equations and then describe the long-run parameters of the specifications. Full details of the estimated equations, along with definitions of the variables and data sources, are given in an Appendix. In constructing models of these economies we have to remember that they have been undergoing continual structural change, and hence we have not attempted to construct models that describe their behaviour over long periods of time. We have concentrated on constructing models that we think adequately describe them during the 1980s and 1990s, and we have concentrated on the trade sector.

Trade relationships form a major part of the econometric model and include estimated equations for export and import volumes of goods; export prices of goods; and imports and exports of services. The relative price elasticities of the trade volume equations confirm that the Marshall–Lerner conditions are satisfied for all of the countries. The export volume elasticities are usually large and reflect the increasing share of world trade accounted for by these countries (e.g. a 1 per cent rise in world import volumes results in more than a 2 per cent increase in export volumes for the NICs). With the exception of Thailand, export prices rise in line with world prices, suggesting that these countries are price takers with no monopoly power. As a consequence, fluctuations in the exchange rate do not influence export demand for the majority of the NICs. The behaviour of the domestic economy is captured by equations explaining the determination of domestic demand and domestic prices.

3.1 *Goods trade volumes*

Export volumes of goods equations are based on the traditional specifications described in Anderton and Dunnett (1987) and depend on competitiveness (i.e. relative prices) and world demand (proxied by world import volumes of goods). Import volumes are determined by relative prices and domestic demand (proxied by real GDP).

$$XGI = f(PX/WPX, WMVOL, TREND)$$
$$MGI = f(PM/PD\$, GDP, TREND)$$

where: XGI = export volumes of goods; MGI = import volumes of goods; PX = export price in dollars; WPX = world export price in dollars; WMVOL = world import volumes of goods; PM = import price in dollars; PD\$ = domestic price in dollars; GDP = gross domestic product in constant 1990 prices (domestic currency); TREND = time trend.

The long-run parameters are as follows (ln denotes that the variable is in logarithms).

Export volumes of goods

$$\ln SGXGI = -0.6 \ln (SGPX/WPX) + \ln WMVOL + 0.06 \, TREND$$
$$\ln THXGI = -0.44 \ln (THPX/WPX) + 2.5 \ln WMVOL$$
$$\ln KOXGI = -2.2 \ln (KOPX/WPX) + 2.0 \ln WMVOL$$
$$\ln TWXGI = -0.9 \ln (TWPX/WPX) + 2.2 \ln WMVOL$$

Import volumes of goods

$$\ln SGMGI = -0.31 \ln (SGPM/SGPD\$) + 1.2 \ln SGGDP$$
$$\ln THMGI = -1.1 \ln (THPM/THPDS\$) + 1.60 \ln THGDP$$
$$\ln KOMGI = -1.2 \ln (KOPM/KOPD\$) + 1.2 \ln KOGDP$$
$$\ln TWMGI = -1.8 \ln (TWPM/TWPD\$) + 1.2 \ln TWGDP$$

SG = Singapore; TH = Thailand; KO = South Korea; TW = Taiwan.

We have measured export prices relative to world export prices. This gave better econometric results than the alternative of using world destination weights. The activity measure is overall world trade. Again, this proved better than measures related specifically to activity in destination countries. Our estimates for export relative price elasticities fall in the usual range of estimated coefficients for developed or developing countries (i.e. between 0.5 and 1 as summarized in Goldstein and Khan, 1985). South Korea stands out as having the highest relative price elasticity (a result that is also obtained by Yoo (1994)). However, some studies which take into account supply-side factors –

such as Riedel (1988) and Athukorala and Riedel (1992) – claim that price elasticities for the NICs are actually much higher, and demand elasticities are much lower, than our estimates and similar studies suggest. More recent studies, which also include supply effects, or are based on disaggregated data, also find higher price elasticities of around 1.5 to 2.0 (see Muscatelli *et al.*, 1995; Marquez and McNeilly, 1988). However, it should be noted that our equations are for total goods whereas most of the others are for manufactured goods. Our estimates show that price elasticities for import volumes tend to be higher than those for exports, perhaps reflecting the different commodity composition of imports and exports.

3.2 Trade prices

The export price specification follows that of Deppler and Ripley (1978) and can be derived from the assumption of profit maximization in an imperfectly competitive market where exporters attempt to maintain profit margins and simultaneously maintain competitiveness against other export competitors (i.e. export prices are determined by a weighted combination of domestic costs and competitors' export prices, with the weights summing to unity). Deppler and Ripley show that the weight given to competitors' prices rises in line with the price elasticity of demand (i.e. the weight will tend to decline in line with the degree of monopoly power). In the limiting case of perfect competition, which may be an appropriate assumption for many of the goods exported by the NICs for most of the sample period, the parameter for competitors' prices tends to unity, and the parameter for domestic costs tends to zero. In general, competitor prices tend to have a greater weight for smaller countries, whereas for larger exporters such as the USA – where exports represent a relatively small fraction of domestic production but a large fraction of the international market – export prices tend to be dominated by domestic cost considerations, with competitor prices being of secondary importance. The general form of the equations is as follows:

$$\ln PX = \beta \ln PD\$ + (1 - \beta) \ln WPX$$

Our estimates of export price determination correspond with the above analysis. Three of the countries have export prices which simply grow in line with the world price (and zero effect from domestic prices – which are used to proxy domestic costs). Hence they are price takers in their markets, and in the long run if the real exchange rate is held above the equilibrium, then all goods trade will disappear. However, such adjustment will take some time, and in particular the real exchange rate could be held below its equilibrium for an extended period while there were gains in market share. In the calculation of the FEER we take elasticities for both goods and services, and hence in our medium-term analysis here the weight on the world price is the average of that in the goods price equation and the services price equation, and hence it is below one in all cases, making it possible to calculate FEERs sensibly.

In contrast to the other NICs, export prices for Thailand – the largest country among our sample of NICs when the domestic market is measured by population size – are determined by both competitor prices and domestic costs (i.e. a weight of two-thirds on domestic costs and one-third on world prices).

3.3   Exports and imports of services

Both exports and imports of services are specified as depending on relative prices (proxied by the real exchange rate defined in terms of consumer prices, which is particularly relevant when much of services trade is in domestically produced tourism) and an activity term (i.e. the volume of world imports for the exports equations; real GDP for the imports of services equations). The general form of the equation is as follows:

$$\text{VXSER} = f(\text{REX}, \text{WMVOL})$$
$$\text{VMSER} = f(\text{REX}, \text{GDP})$$

where: VXSER = export volume of services; VMSER = import volume of services; REX = real exchange rate = CED\$/WDCED\$; CED\$ = consumers' expenditure deflator in US dollars; WDCED\$ = world consumers' expenditure deflator in US dollars; XSER = value of exports of services in US dollars; MSER = value of imports of services in US dollars.
The long-run parameters are as follows.

Export volumes of services

$$\ln \text{SGVXSER} = -2.25 \ln \text{SGREX} + \ln \text{WMVOL}$$
$$\ln \text{THVXSER} = -3.39 \ln \text{THREX} + \ln \text{WMVOL}$$
$$\ln \text{KOVXSER} = -2.40 \ln \text{KOREX} + \ln \text{WMVOL}$$
$$\ln \text{TWVXSER} = -4.90 \ln \text{TWREX} + \ln \text{WMVOL}$$

Import volumes of services

$$\ln \text{SGVMSER} = 0.30 \ln \text{SGREX} + 0.71 \ln \text{SGGDP}$$
$$\ln \text{THVMSER} = 2.32 \ln \text{THGDP}$$
$$\ln \text{KOVMSER} = 0.5 \ln \text{KOREX} + 0.72 \ln \text{KOGDP}$$
$$\ln \text{TWVMSER} = 0.41 \ln \text{TWREX} + 1.19 \ln \text{TWGDP}$$

Although the demand elasticities for both exports and imports are approximately unity, the relative price elasticities are quite different. Exports of services seem very responsive to changes in price competitiveness (with elasticities ranging from just over 2 to around 5), but the price elasticity for imports is usually below 0.5. The different price responses probably reflect differences in the composition of services exports and imports (i.e. in general, the NICs export price-sensitive services such as tourism and import price-inelastic services such as insurance and shipping).

3.4 *Domestic prices*

In the long run, domestic prices are assumed to be determined by a combination of import prices and unit labour costs. Changes in the mark-up are captured by cyclical activity effects proxied by a capacity utilization term (the latter is proxied by movements in GDP relative to trend). Although the long-run parameters are determined by the data, homogeneity is maintained by constraining the sum of parameters for import prices and unit labour costs to sum to unity. The form of the equations is as follows:

$$\ln PD = \beta \ln ULC + (1 - \beta) \ln PMC + \alpha CU$$

where: ULC = unit labour costs; CU = capacity utilization; PD = domestic prices in domestic currency; PMC = import prices in domestic currency.
  The long-run parameters are as follows:

$$\ln SGPD = 1.0 \ln SGPMC$$

$$\ln THPD = 0.72 \ln THPMC + 0.23 THCU$$

$$\ln KOPD = 0.5 \ln KOPMC + 0.5 \ln KOULC + 0.19 KOCU$$
$$- 0.003 TREND$$

$$\ln TWPD = +1.0 \ln TWULC + 4.0 \ln TWCU$$

3.5 *Private sector demand*

We incorporate a very simple IS curve into our models by specifying that real domestic demand is determined by export volumes and long-term interest rates.

$$DD = f (XVOLC, LR)$$

where: DD = domestic demand = GDP + MVOLC − XVOLC; MVOLC = import of goods and services in constant 1990 prices (domestic currency); XVOLC = export of goods and services in constant 1990 prices (domestic currency); LR = long-term interest rates.

The long-run parameters are as follows:

$\ln \text{SGDD} = 0.52 \ln \text{SGXVOLC}$

$\ln \text{THDD} = 0.63 \ln \text{THXVOLC} - 0.08 \text{ THLR}$

$\ln \text{KODD} = 0.64 \ln \text{KOXVOLC} - 0.014 \text{ KOLR}$

$\ln \text{TWDD} = 0.8 \ln \text{TWXVOLC}$

4   Exchange rates and development policies in East Asia

We assess the equilibrium exchange rates for our four economies in the light of policy developments, because it is only in terms of such a narrative that it is possible to evaluate the objectives of policy. It is clear in all cases that policy had multiple objectives, for instance the avoidance of exchange crises, and they change over time in their relative importance. As it is difficult to justify continuous surpluses in these rapidly growing economies, we present estimates of FEERs based on a zero current balance. However, the need to accumulate foreign assets may not be easily captured by simple econometric descriptions of the macro economy. Hence we also present FEER estimates based on a current account similar to the historical average. As a result we are able to present a range of estimates, and also indicate the sensitivity of the current account to changes in the real exchange rate.

4.1   South Korea

South Korea has been one of the most successful of the developing countries. In the 1960s it was one of the world's poorest countries, largely dependent on agriculture. However, since 1962 GDP has grown thirty times while GDP per capita has increased fifteen times. Underlying much of this growth has been a massive growth in exports, in real terms of around 20 per cent annually. It is now the world's eleventh largest trading nation. In addition, it has made large social improvements with increases in life expectancy and literacy (which among adults is now practically universal), and reductions in inequality.

The real effective exchange rate of the Korean won, like that of many other currencies of the Asian NICs, showed dramatic movements between the mid-1970s and late 1980s. The Korean won, in nominal terms, depreciated significantly over the latter half of the 1970s although high inflation relative to its trading partners meant that in real terms the exchange rate appreciated. During the first half of the 1980s this situation was reversed with a depreciating real effective exchange rate until the middle of the decade. This was the result of both a substantial devaluation of the currency in 1980 and a 59 per cent depreciation of the won against the Japanese yen between 1985 and April 1987. By 1987 South Korea was running a huge current account surplus amounting to nearly $10 billion. Around this time it was estimated that a 10 per cent appreciation would reduce the current account by only $1 billion (Yoo, 1986) although others predicted a larger effect. Lee (1986) estimated that this appreciation would cause a $1.3 billion reduction. Our own estimates, discussed below, suggest that the effects would have been significantly larger. What was agreed on was the need for a substantial appreciation. In 1987–8 adjustment measures were adopted and the won appreciated, both in nominal and in real terms, partly offsetting the depreciation of the previous two years. However, since adjustment the won has steadily depreciated back to its 1986 level and has stabilised through the 1990s.

South Korea saw falling relative unit labour costs during the first part of its period of industrialization. Wage increases were offset by exchange rate movements. During the latter half of the 1980s inflationary pressures in South Korea led to the implementation of adjustment measures and an appreciation of the won. This, coupled with general wage increases, led to a rapid increase in South Korea's relative unit labour costs. Its unit labour costs have continued to rise into the 1990s although these have been offset by a depreciating nominal exchange rate and thus relative unit labour costs have fallen.

During the 1960s and 1970s South Korea borrowed heavily from abroad in order to finance development. This resulted in huge debts being accumulated and consequently a fear that the country had over-borrowed. By 1980 its debt–export ratio had risen to 1.8. The subsequent adjustment programme that was implemented in 1980–1 succeeded in restoring growth, lowering inflation and reducing the current account deficit through a rapid expansion of exports. Significant moves were made towards liberalizing trade although there were exceptions, for example imports of agricultural goods and services. However, restrictions on these products have started to be reduced since 1990. By 1986 the current account showed a surplus of nearly $5 billion largely due to a $5.5 billion rise in exports, but also partly due to a fall in oil prices and a decline in world market interest rates. In 1986 exports accounted for nearly 40 per cent of GDP as opposed to 34 per cent in 1980. This surplus was to a large extent used to pay back South Korea's debts rapidly. However, over the 1980s a number of commentators expressed doubt about the sustainability of Korea's macroeconomic performance and since the late 1980s growth in GDP has fallen and increasing domestic demand has increased inflationary pressures and reversed the current account position of the mid-1980s.

Much of this change in South Korea's economic performance has been a result of large wage rises secured by the militant trade unions rather than the government responding to the need for adjustment. In 1989 total wage costs rose by 20 per cent. Although partly offset by high growth in productivity, this has led to increasing inflationary pressures. Higher wage costs coupled with rising oil prices as a result of the Gulf war pushed the inflation rate to 9 per cent in the early 1990s. In addition, appreciation of the Korean won also contributed to eroding the country's competitive advantages.

At the end of 1991 a stabilization programme of tighter monetary policy and restrictions on the construction sector helped slow the pace of growth. GDP growth in 1992 was just 5 per cent, the slowest since 1980. The stabilization policy also succeeded in nearly halving inflation. The government's New Five-Year Economic Plan of 1993–7 has effectively reversed the stabilization policies of 1991. This plan aims to establish South Korea as a true industrial economy by the turn of the century and sets out detailed plans to liberalize the financial sector as well as reducing income inequality. This change in economic policy has resulted in the growth of investment in machinery and equipment, as well as in construction which has further benefited from an expansion of government projects aimed at improving South Korea's infrastructure. Private consumption has also risen, spurred by the boom in sales of consumer durables such as personal computers and mobile phones.

Korean exchange rate policy is often described by the authorities as one which pegs the won to a basket of five currencies with weights reflecting their relative importance to South Korea. However, in view of the movement of the won over the 1980s, Balassa and Williamson (1990) claim that this is mathematically impossible unless one of these currencies had a negative weight.[2] This suggests that it may be that there was a deliberate policy to undervalue the currency. Furthermore, a World Bank study argues that the large current account surplus in the years 1986–9 was due to exchange rate management, although the apparent motive was not only to boost exports but also to target a large current account surplus to accumulate assets and thus reduce the risk of another balance of payments crisis.

The size of the undervaluation can be judged from our chart of the FEER and the actual exchange rate (Figure 15.4). Our FEER has been calculated for a zero current balance target and also for a 6 per cent of GDP target, and the higher surplus requires an exchange rate that is around 10 per cent lower. The large increase in the surplus for such a small change in the exchange rate reflects the high levels of the competitiveness elasticities in our model. Figure 15.5 plots the Korean current balance as a percentage of GDP. After large deficits in the early 1990s the balance was around zero in 1993.

However, Intal (1992) claims that the devaluation of the won was more or less forced onto South Korea rather than being a deliberate policy action. He classifies South Korea as a reluctant adjuster which allowed its balance of payments situation to deteriorate to almost a state of crisis before adopting major exchange rate adjustments. Thus South Korea allowed its real exchange rate to appreciate throughout the latter 1970s. Much of this was a result of a boom in private investment which, as a proportion of GDP, increased from 26 per cent to 37 per cent between 1976 and 1979. Coupled with the second oil price shock, by 1980 South Korea's balance of payments was at a point of crisis and the authorities were forced to adopt adjustment measures which included a devaluation of the won, a reduction in the investment rate and

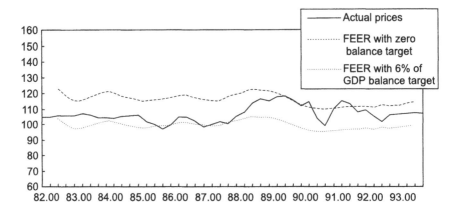

Figure 15.4 South Korea: FEER based on import prices

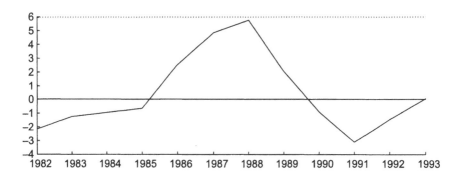

Figure 15.5 South Korea: current balance as a percentage of GDP

a tightening of the money supply. Hence we would say that there were periods when South Korea held its exchange rate below its sustainable level, and hence gained market share, but that this policy was interspersed with other periods when exchange rate objectives were not related to long-term growth.

4.2 Singapore

Since independence in 1959 Singapore has achieved an impressive rate of growth. Over the past thirty years the average annual growth rate of real GDP per capita has been 7.25 per cent. Much of this rapid growth can be attributed to government policies such as liberal foreign trade and investment policies. These have helped maintain macroeconomic stability and helped limit large distortions in relative prices, thus providing the ideal environment for export- and investment-led growth. In addition, the government invested heavily in improving the country's physical and human capital. These policies have moved the economy away from a low wage producer of labour-intensive products towards a high-wage industrialized economy.

When Singapore gained self-rule in 1959 unemployment was around 10 per cent of the labour force, the traditional industrial activities (largely processing and distribution industries) were in decline and levels of human capital were low due to a poor and badly educated population. In view of the high levels of unemployment, the government adopted a strategy of import substitution which involved rapid industrialization. This was achieved partly through political and economic union with Malaya in 1963, which almost doubled the size of Singapore's market in terms of GDP, and partly through some protective measures. In addition, fiscal incentives were offered to domestic manufacturers. These policies succeeded in achieving economic growth with average real GDP growth at 5.75 per cent per annum between 1960 and 1965, when the federation with Malaya broke up. Furthermore, the manufacturing sector expanded with its share in GDP increasing by 2 percentage points to 19 per cent over this period. However, the creation of new jobs was poor and unemployment remained constant. Alongside these policies, the government also introduced a very successful five-year plan in 1960 aimed at improving the educational standards of the population.

In the mid-1960s Singapore changed its strategy to one of export orientation. At the time this was an unusual move for a developing country to take but the previous strategy had fail to solve the unemployment problem. This was largely due to the fact that even with the inclusion of the Malaysian market domestic production was insufficient to create large numbers of jobs. The policy measures introduced involved the removal of quotas and the reduction of tariffs, and a number of industry-specific incentives. These led to export growth, an improvement in the balance of payments and the reduction in the unemployment of both labour and capital. In addition, the change in policy, along with other characteristics such as low labour costs, improving human capital and its geographic position, made Singapore an ideal host country for foreign investors. These policies were exceedingly successful not only in producing rapid growth in exports and investment, but also in achieving full employment – by the early 1970s the country was actually experiencing labour shortages.

During the mid-1970s, after a period of export-oriented policies, Singapore once again changed its strategy, this time to one of industrial restructuring and technological up-grading. Having achieved full employment, the government now aimed to encourage investments in high-technology sectors as opposed to labour-intensive ones. Foreign investors in high-technology industries were offered incentives such as tax holidays, and those enterprises already operating in Singapore were offered incentives to invest in up-grading both their human and their physical capital. In addition, the government in cooperation with multinational corporations set up joint industrial training centres in order to help service the growing demand for skilled workers. Although successful in restructuring the country's industrial sector, this policy led to excess demand in the labour market and increasing upward pressure on real wages. This loss in competitiveness, coupled with savings rates of over 40 per cent, led to recession in 1985–6. During this period GDP declined, by 1.6 per cent in 1985 and again by 1.8 per cent in 1986.

Until 1973 the Singapore dollar was pegged first to the UK pound and then to the US dollar. After 1973 and until 1981 the currency was floated. Following the first oil shock the real effective exchange rate appreciated as monetary policy was tightened to dampen inflationary pressures. From the mid-1970s, as this policy was relaxed, the real exchange rate depreciated only to reappreciate following the second oil shock. In 1981 exchange rate policy shifted towards pegging the dollar to a trade-weighted basket of currencies within a target band in an attempt to use the exchange rate as a tool for achieving non-inflationary growth. Since this change the nominal effective exchange rate has more or less continuously appreciated, by a cumulative 25 per cent. However, Singapore's real exchange rate depreciated sharply during the mid-1980s due to a dramatic drop in domestic inflation and falling oil prices. After 1987 the real effective exchange rate appreciated slightly, due to increasing wage rates and higher savings rates. However, through the 1990s the currency has continued to appreciate, albeit at a slower rate.

The National Wages Council, which was established in 1972, provides a framework for wage settlements in view of the government's economic objectives. During the 1970s the NWC recommended wage restraint to dampen inflationary pressures caused by a tight labour market. However, such policy was both unsustainable and incompatible with the industrial restructuring policy introduced in the mid-1970s since it encouraged low-skilled and low-technology industries. In the early 1980s the NWC recommended a series of general wage increases.[3] In addition, labour costs were further raised by increases in employer Central Provident Fund (CPF) contributions, from 16.5 per cent of the wage bill in 1979 to 25 per cent in 1984, and the introduction of a levy for the Skills Development Fund.[4] The rationale behind this growth in manufacturing unit labour costs was that employers would be encouraged to restructure and up-grade their labour skills, thus increasing productivity. However, wages continued to rise even after 1981 resulting in real wage growth far in excess of productivity. In view of this substantial decline in competitiveness and the resulting recession, the NWC recommended wage-restraining measures in 1986 in order to achieve a freeze in the general wage level. Furthermore, a 'flexi-wage' system was introduced to increase wage flexibility. This remains in operation and relative unit costs have stabilized recently.

By the mid-1980s growth in manufacturing had slowed and efforts were made to encourage production in new, potential high-growth sectors such as biotechnology, computer peripherals and aerospace. In addition, diversification outside manufacturing and into business and financial services was also promoted. This policy succeeded in restoring growth: by 1988 GDP growth had risen to 11 per cent.

Since the late 1980s output growth has slowed in response to a reduction of export growth. By 1995 GDP growth had fallen to a rate of 8.5 per cent. This decline is expected to continue into 1996 when GDP growth of 7.8 per cent is forecast. Singapore has also succeeded in restraining inflationary pressures despite labour shortages that have resulted in unemployment rates of less than 2 per cent in 1991. Inflation over recent years has been the lowest among the Asian NICs, at around 2 per cent, although as in the other Asian NICs, which are also large oil importers, increasing oil prices as a result of the Gulf war caused inflation to rise slightly in the early 1990s. Low inflation at around 2.5 per cent continued into 1996 due to slower growth of the economy and the effects of an appreciating Singapore dollar stabilizing import prices. Current account surpluses rose to record levels as a percentage of GDP, in part because of slow growth in domestic demand.

The ultimate objective of exchange rate policy has been price stability and the target bands are set in view of current and expected inflation. The authorities in Singapore aim to keep inflation 'low and stable' (*Monetary Authority of Singapore Annual Report*, 1991–2); this generally means less than 3 per cent. Thus, although exchange rate policy in Singapore does involve government intervention, the objective has been one of price stability rather than the increased competitiveness sought by some other Asian NICs. This can be seen from our chart of the FEER and the actual real exchange rate (Figure 15.6). We plot a 6 per cent of GDP target and zero target, and they differ

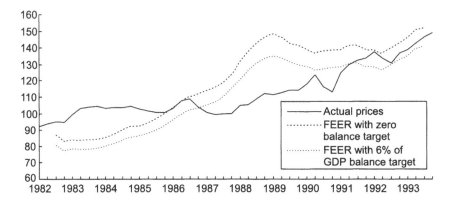

Figure 15.6 Singapore: FEER based on relative import prices

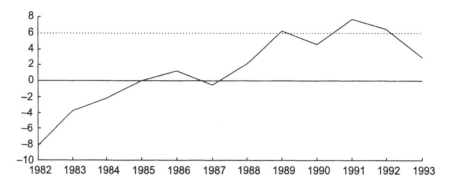

Figure 15.7 Singapore: current balance as a percentage of GDP

by only 7 per cent, indicating the very open nature of the Singapore economy. In the early 1980s the exchange rate displayed both overvaluations and under-valuations compared to either target for the current balance, while in the late 1980s and early 1990s it has been around the level that would give, in equilibrium, a current account between our two targets. Surpluses have more recently exceeded these levels because growth has been below capacity.

It would appear that the export success of the Singapore economy has been the result of a very open market with a great deal of generally successful support and guidance from the government. There are lessons to be learnt from this experience, but it is clear that real exchange rate management is not necessary for a newly industrializing economy to gain market share. Positive and flexible industrial policies, along with a strong commitment to education, have been important. Commitment to regional integration through government-supported direct investment programmes has also helped raise exports, and has integrated the Singapore economy into a wider network in South-East Asia where intra-industry trade and specialization within industries by country have become increasingly important.

4.3 *Taiwan*

Before the significant reforms undertaken at the end of the 1950s, Taiwan's economic performance was anything but impressive. Like many other developing countries at the time, the economy was inward-oriented with considerable emphasis on import-substituting production. However, domestic production was hampered by fiscal mismanagement which meant that funds were not invested in productive areas such as infrastructure. Inflation was also a serious problem. Rising inflation caused exports to become increasingly unprofitable while imports grew cheaper. From 1952 to 1961 commodity exports were on average only 60 per cent of the level of commodity imports, so that during this time the average annual trade deficit was 6.5

per cent of GNP. Over the same period the export-to-GDP and investment-to-GDP ratios remained constant at levels of just over 10 per cent, and growth of GDP per capita declined from 6 to below 3 per cent per annum.

In 1958 and the succeeding three years a change in development strategy occurred. Taiwan opened up its economy and began to pursue a more out-ward-oriented strategy. In 1958 the multiple exchange rates were unified into a single rate which involved something of a depreciation against the US dollar, and this was followed by a further devaluation in 1961, bringing the exchange rate to NT$40 to US$1. This allowed import and foreign exchange controls to be eased. In order to boost domestic production the government introduced a wide array of subsidies and incentives as part of its industrial policy despite the retention of extensive regulations and protection.

In the early 1960s the economy of Taiwan began its 'take-off'. Per capita GDP growth steadily rose until it reached rates of between 6 and 9 per cent throughout the 1970s, one of the highest in the world. The export sector, in particular, experienced rapid growth with the export–GDP ratio increasing from a base of 11 per cent to a sustained plateau of just under 50 per cent in the late 1970s. The average annual growth rates of exports was 18 per cent over 1960–70, falling to 14 per cent over 1970–80. High savings rates were in part a response to government policy. Both the savings and investment ratios steadily climbed to between 30 and 35 per cent in the mid-1970s.

A major turning point in the economic strategy of Taiwan occurred in the mid-1980s after a quarter-century of little change. The most salient economic problem at this time was the series of huge current account surpluses built up with the help of an outward-oriented government policy which involved a competitive exchange rate and strong incentives to save. The external balance, in deficit in the 1960s, had been continuously positive since 1971 except during the disruptions caused by the oil price. From 1985 to 1987 the current account expressed as a percentage of GDP exceeded 14 per cent, with a peak of 20 per cent in 1985. Towards the end of the decade the Taiwanese authorities acknowledged the problems of maintaining such a large current account surplus. Not only did this reflect a misallocation of the country's resources but fears of a build-up of inflationary pressures along with the threat of possible foreign retaliation led to a change in policy. The adjustment measures introduced included a relaxation of controls on outward capital flows, fiscal expansion, reductions of import tariffs, an expansion of credit and a revaluation of the exchange rate. The change in policy in the late 1980s succeeded in limiting inflation but has also led to a decline in output growth. In 1987 the GDP growth rate was 12.4 per cent; this then fell to 7.3 per cent in 1988 and further to 4.9 per cent in 1990. However, as a result, private investment fell. In response to this and in view of low and stable inflation, the Taiwanese Central Bank cut the rediscount rate several times in 1991 which succeeded in sparking off an investment boom. GDP growth in 1991 rose to over 7 per cent, and then gradually fell to around 6 per cent in 1995, while inflation stabilized at around 4 per cent. Continuing worries about relations with mainland China have kept growth relatively modest and have put downward pressure on the exchange rate.

Since the late 1980s the current account surplus in Taiwan has declined. The main exception to this was in 1989 which to some extent was a result of the cessation of gold imports which were more than US$2.5 billion in 1988. The continuing fall in the current account balance over the 1990s has to a large extent been a result of a declining service balance. The trade balance, on the other hand, remained roughly level until 1991 when Taiwan exports were hit by the world-wide recession and a slowing in the Chinese economy. As the Chinese economy recovered, so did the Taiwanese trade balance, and it ran at around $13 billion per annum in 1995 and 1996. The main explanation for the sustainability of the trade surplus despite an appreciating currency is the continuing shift in the composition of exports away from the less competitive traditional products and towards more sophisticated goods. In addition, increasing trade with China has also helped maintain a fairly high level of exports, with many of these being directed through Hong Kong.

The Taiwanese dollar was pegged to the US dollar since the USA was the main export market. It remained pegged at NT$40 to US$1 until 1973, when it was revalued to NT$38 to US$1. A further revaluation in 1978 was undone in the early 1980s when the currency was floated and its rate depreciated to its former level of NT$40 to US$1. More importantly, the real effective exchange rate was broadly constant from 1970 to 1985. This was in spite of increasingly large trade surpluses over the period, so that had market forces been allowed to restore the current account balance the nominal effective exchange rate would have appreciated somewhat in the late 1970s and the first half of the 1980s. But the nominal effective exchange

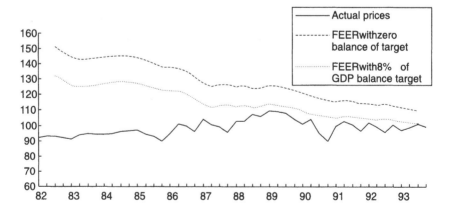

Figure 15.8 Taiwan: FEER based on relative import prices

266

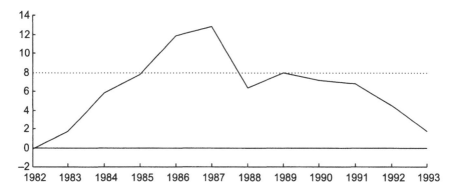

Figure 15.9 Taiwan: current balance as a percentage of GDP

rate slightly *depreciated* over this period, reinforcing the view that the value of the New Taiwan dollar was deliberately kept undervalued. Depreciation continued in the mid-1990s, with fears of changing relations with mainland China causing a significant depreciation in the middle of 1995. The extent of the potential real undervaluation in the early 1980s can be seen from our chart of the FEER (Figure 15.8), which plots the real exchange rate associated with a zero current account target and an 8 per cent of GDP target (the average over the period). The current account over this period is plotted in Figure 15.9. The combination of fears over relations with China, and the related desire on the part of much of the population to accumulate overseas assets, has probably had more influence on the real exchange rate than have positive policies to induce an undervaluation that would lead to gains in market shares.

4.4 *Thailand*

The Thai economy has experienced sustained high GDP growth rates and made the transition from an essentially agrarian economy to one based heavily on services and manufacturing. Manufactured exports now account for four-fifths of total exports. As a second-tier newly industrializing economy, Thailand's rapid industrialization started later than the NICs' and the economic and social indicators are today still some way behind those of the NICs. However, in recent years the expansion of GDP and exports has continued at very high rates. In the 1950s real GDP growth was only 5.2 per cent per annum, which was not significantly better than OECD growth at that time. This reflects the attempt to expand manufacturing production through the use of state enterprises which had a poor record of economic performance due to inefficiency and corruption. Thus, although the Thai economy had always been traditionally open (except for extensive restrictions on outward capital movements), exports by the early 1960s were still concentrated heavily in agriculture, with rice exports providing two-thirds of total export receipts. Manufactured exports were a mere 2.4 per cent of total exports, while manufacturing output was less than 15 per cent of GDP.

From 1959 onwards the government changed its industrialization strategy. It promoted the role of the private sector by the provision of investment incentives, while it limited its role to improving public infrastructure. Macroeconomic stability was secured by disciplined financial policies which kept money growth to between 10 and 15 per cent, and the budget deficit to below 2 per cent of GDP. As a result, many industries which produced goods that replaced imports were successfully started, while substantial improvements were made in agriculture and in important services such as commercial banking and construction. Domestic savings and investment as a fraction of GDP boomed from 15 per cent to between 23 and 26 per cent over the decade. Average annual real growth for the 1960s rose to just over 8 per cent per annum.

By the end of the 1960s Thailand was confronted with the need for adjustment in the face of a deteriorating current account. The current account balance was in deficit in the second half of the 1960s, reaching a peak of 3 per cent of GDP in 1970. This was expected to worsen as the industries producing for the domestic market imported a high proportion of their inputs in the form of raw materials and capital. Together with the faltering growth of certain of these enterprises, the rapid export growth of the East Asian NICs during the 1960s, and the desire to relieve the industrial congestion around Bangkok, these factors explain the decided shift in incentives towards promoting export production in the early 1970s. Although relatively high tariffs persisted, a change in the investment incentives made exports increasingly profitable. This was helped by the pegging of the baht to the US dollar from 1963, providing exchange rate stability, and with the depreciation of the US dollar over the 1970s increasing profitability. The shift in industrial strategy towards export promotion rapidly bore fruit as the share in merchandise exports of manufactured exports rose from 10 per cent in 1971 to 36 per cent in 1981.

A severe fall in the terms of trade at the time of the first oil price shock in 1973 created economic difficulties. However, this was managed by expanding the economy through higher fiscal spending. Adjustment problems became worse after the second oil price shock in 1979, which brought about a significant slowdown in GDP growth. The growth of the economy, which had averaged 7.9 per cent per annum in the 1970s, declined to a little over half that rate. At the same time, the current account reached its highest deficit ever, at 7 per cent of GDP in 1980. Consequently, Thailand had recourse to the IMF and the World Bank, implementing three stabilization and two structural adjustment programmes in the first half of the 1980s. These were concerned with restoring internal and external balance, reducing distortions in relative prices and liberalizing what was still a restrictive trade regime.

In the short term, slower growth continued as fiscal and monetary austerity measures were taken and the baht appreciated along with the dollar, in spite of two devaluations in 1981. Although real growth was only 3.5 and 4.2 per cent in 1985 and 1986 respectively, the policies were achieving their other objectives: inflation dropped to around 5 per cent in the mid-1980s from 19 per cent in 1979, and the current account deficit started to diminish in 1983. By 1986 the current account was in balance. A strong recovery followed as the growth of the economy picked up to 8.4 per cent in 1987 and to 11 per cent in 1988.

The boom lasted until the end of the decade with high GDP growth from 1988 to 1990. This reflected a rise in the total (public and private) investment ratio from 27.5 per cent over 1980–6 to 40 per cent by 1990; over the same period, exports as a fraction of GDP increased dramatically from 23 per cent to 35 per cent. In particular, the share of manufactured exports in the total nearly doubled to two-thirds in the late 1980s. A number of causes lie behind the recent boom. First, in 1984 the baht was devalued by 14 per cent against the US dollar. In this year also the baht was pegged to a basket of currencies reflecting trade weights, so that as these currencies appreciated vis-à-vis the baht over the next four years, the real effective depreciation of the baht from 1984 to 1988 was of the order of 30 per cent. Second, Thailand benefited from substantial inflows of foreign direct investment. By 1990 the stock of foreign direct investment in Thailand was seven times its level in 1986. Most of this new FDI originated from Japan and the four NICs. Low labour costs and a depreciated baht relative to the investing countries both explain much of the FDI inflows. Third, major improvements in public finance in the mid-1980s and a reduction in export taxes also played a role.

Growth in output slowed during the early 1990s. Following the military coup in 1991, monetary tightening, political uncertainty and communication and transport problems meant that the growth rate of GDP dropped sharply, by 3.5 percentage points. However, the slight fall in inflation over this period led the authorities to ease monetary policy in order to prevent further slowing of the economy. Output has begun to pick up over the past few years as a result of two interest rate cuts in 1993 and a badly needed increase in public infrastructure investment.

Thailand has actively used the exchange rate as a policy tool in order to increase competitiveness (Intal, 1992). In 1981 and 1984 the Thai authorities devalued the baht. This was not a move to combat real exchange rate appreciation but rather was a deliberate policy move to prevent future balance of payments problems in view of the deteriorating economic situation during this period. Our estimates of the FEER based on a zero current balance, plotted in Figure 15.10, along with a FEER for a 3 per cent of GDP current account deficit, suggest that the authorities held the currency at a high level in the early 1980s as part of an anti-inflation strategy, but the depreciations in the mid-1980s took the exchange rate back to around its equilibrium, where

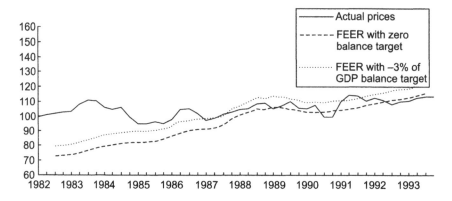

Figure 15.10 Thailand: FEER based on relative import prices

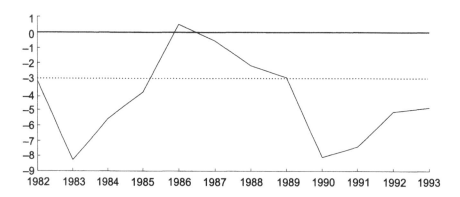

Figure 15.11 Thailand: current balance as a percentage of GDP

it has stayed for some time. From 1984 to 1987 the more competitive exchange rate led to significantly higher exports. This proved to be a successful move and helped Thailand's competitiveness improve. However, since the late 1980s openness and structural reforms appear to have played a much more important role in increasing exports than have positive exchange rate policies. The increasing integration of the South Asian region, along with increasing direct investment flows especially from Singapore, have also helped in the process, generating rapid economic growth.

5 Conclusions

The main conclusion to be drawn from this study is that, in terms both of trade and exchange rate policy and in terms of the role of foreign investment, the four countries have had very different experiences. On the one hand, Singapore has relied on monetary policy as a tool for controlling inflation, rather than as a means of depreciating the exchange rate as a tool for promoting export-led growth. Rapid economic growth has been driven largely by high levels of saving, and export performance has been good because of well-designed and flexible government-driven industrial policies. Korea experienced a rising real exchange rate in the 1970s, leading to a balance of payments crisis associated with the second oil shock in 1980. Since then the exchange rate may have been undervalued, but it should be remembered that rapid growth was associated with periods of both under and overvaluation. Exchange crises have also played a significant role in exchange rate policy. However, there is evidence for South Korea, and only for South Korea, that the exchange rate has been used as a tool for increasing the rate of growth of exports and gaining market share.

Thailand and Taiwan have at times pursued more active exchange rate policies. These have not always been aimed at gaining market share. Thailand used its exchange rate to put downward pressure on inflation for some years, and this will have also limited its market share gain, as would the sharp rise in the US dollar in the 1980s, because its currency was pegged to the dollar at this time. In Taiwan's case between 1984 and 1987 a depreciated exchange rate clearly led to rapid growth and a large balance of payments surplus. Even in this case, other factors to do with relations with mainland China may have been at work. Individuals and the government may have felt the need to protect their wealth by accumulating overseas assets, and this can only be done when running a current account surplus. The market share gain may have been incidental to this process. Recent currency turmoil has also led to depreciations, but in the mid-1990s this has led to higher inflation rather than greater competitiveness.

APPENDIX: THE ECONOMETRIC MODELS IN DETAIL

All variable mnemonics are defined in main text above and t-statistics are given in parentheses.

Export volumes of goods

$$\Delta \ln \text{SGXVOL}_t = -0.151 - 0.266 \, (\ln \text{SGXVOL} - \ln \text{WMVOL})_{t-1}$$
$$\phantom{\Delta \ln \text{SGXVOL}_t = } (2.23) \quad (3.38)$$

$$+ \, 0.0039 \, \text{TIME} - 0.0152 \ln \, (\text{SGPX/WPX})_{t-1}$$
$$ (3.11) \qquad\quad (3.32)$$

$$+ 0.24 \ln (\text{SGPX}/\text{WPX})_{t-2} + 0.23 \, \Delta \ln (\text{SGPX}/\text{WPX})$$
$$\quad\;\, (1.71) \qquad\qquad\qquad\qquad (1.69)$$

+ seasonals

OLS: 1974Q4–1994Q2
$\bar{R}^2 = 0.5846$ SEE $= 0.037$ RESET$(1) = 2.02$
LM$(4) = 1.84$ NORM$(2) = 1.08$ HET$(1) = 0.477$

$$\Delta \ln \text{THXVOL} = 0.0989 - 0.384 \ln \text{THXVOL}_{-1} - 0.977 \ln \text{WMVOL}_{t-1}$$
$$\qquad\qquad (4.46) \quad (4.35) \qquad\qquad\qquad (4.59)$$
$$-0.172 \ln (\text{THPX}/\text{WPX})_{t-1} - 0.43 \, \Delta \ln \text{THXVOL}_{t-2}$$
$$(1.86) \qquad\qquad\qquad (5.08)$$
$$+0.70 \, \Delta \ln \text{WMVOL}_{t-1} - 0.439 \, \Delta \ln (\text{THPX}/\text{WPX})_{t-2}$$
$$(1.66) \qquad\qquad\qquad (2.29)$$
$$+ \text{seasonals}$$

OLS: 1972Q4–1994Q3
$\bar{R}^2 = 0.56147$ SEE $= 0.069$ RESET$(1) = 4.56$
LM$(4) = 5.81$ NORM$(2) = 0.144$ HET$(1) = 0.0789$

$$\Delta \ln \text{KOXVOL}_t = -0.145 - 0.103 \ln \text{KOXVOL}_{t-1} - 0.229 \ln (\text{KOPX}/\text{WPX})$$
$$(5.53) \quad (3.13) \qquad\qquad\qquad (2.01)$$
$$+0.204 \ln \text{WMVOL}_{t-1} - 0.23 \, \Delta \ln \text{KOXVOL}_{t-1}$$
$$(2.57) \qquad\qquad\qquad (3.07)$$
$$-0.48 \, \Delta \ln \text{WMVOL}_{t-4} + \text{seasonal dummies}$$
$$(1.41)$$

OLS: 1973Q2–1995Q2
$\bar{R}^2 = 0.825$ SEE $= 0.0615$ RESET$(1) = 0.43$
LM$(4) = 3.71$ NORM$(2) = 0.225$ HET$(1) = 3.04$

Long-run equation
$$\ln \text{TWXVOL} = -14.496 - 0.891 \ln (\text{TWPX}/\text{WPX}) + 2.18 \ln \text{WMVOL}$$
$$(8.25) \quad (2.64) \qquad\qquad\qquad (31.52)$$
where RES = Residual from long-run equation
OLS: 1976Q2–1994Q1
$\bar{R}^2 = 0.7504$ SEE $= 0.05188$ RESET$(1) = 1.73$
LM$(4) = 4.14$ NORM$(2) = 7.48$ HET$(1) = 3.85$

Dynamic equation
$$\Delta \ln \text{TWXVOL} = -0.003 - 0.053 \, \text{RES}_{-1} - 0.36 \, \Delta \ln (\text{TWPX} / \text{WPX})_{t-4}$$
$$(0.26) \quad (0.99) \qquad\quad (2.36)$$
$$-0.765 \, \Delta \ln \text{WMVOL}_{t-4} + \text{seasonal dummies}$$
$$(1.92)$$

Import volumes

Long-run equation
$$\ln \text{SGMVOL} = 10.98 - 0.31 \ln (\text{SGPM}/\text{SGPD\$}) + 1.19 \ln \text{SGGDP}$$
$$(62.75) \quad (7.01) \qquad\qquad\qquad (63.94)$$

OLS: 1972Q1–1994Q4
$\bar{R}^2 = 0.98636$ SEE $= 0.0719$

$$\Delta \ln \text{THMVOL} = -2.51 - 0.245 \ln \text{THMVOL}_{-1} - 0.227 \ln (\text{THPM/THPD\$})_{-1}$$
$$(4.54)\,(4.56) \qquad\qquad (2.77)$$
$$+ 0.39 \ln \text{THGDP}_{-1} + 2.27 \, \Delta \ln \text{THGDP}_{-3}$$
$$(4.52) \qquad\qquad (3.41)$$

OLS: 1973Q1–1994Q3
$\bar{R}^2 = 0.452$ SEE $= 0.0496$ LM$(4) = 2.86$
RESET$(1) = 0.241$ NORM$(2) = 3.24$ HET$(1) = 1.62$

$$\Delta \ln \text{KOMVOL} = -4.09 - 0.331 \ln \text{KOMVOL}_{-1} - 0.390 \ln (\text{KOPM/KOPD\$})_{-1}$$
$$(3.74)\,(3.97) \qquad\qquad (2.78)$$
$$+ 0.394 \ln \text{KOGDP}_{-1} - 0.304 \, \Delta \ln \text{KOMVOL}_{-4}$$
$$(3.85) \qquad\qquad (3.19)$$
$$- 0.473 \, \Delta \ln \text{KOGDP}_{-1} + \text{seasonal dummies}$$
$$(4.82)$$

OLS: 1975Q4–1995Q1
$\bar{R}^2 = 0.5924$ SEE $= 0.05936$ LM$(4) = 0.06$
RESET$(1) = 0.66$ NORM$(2) = 2.34$ HET$(1) = 2.43$

$$\Delta \ln \text{TWMVOL} = -4.29 - 0.174 \ln \text{TMWVOL}_{-1} - 3.03 \ln (\text{TWPM/TWPD\$})_{-1}$$
$$(2.95)\,(2.56) \qquad\qquad (2.39)$$
$$+ 0.203 \ln \text{TWGDP}_{-1} - 0.332 \, \Delta \ln \text{TWMVOL}_{-1}$$
$$(2.53) \qquad\qquad (3.13)$$
$$+ 1.38 \, \Delta \ln \text{TWGDP}_{-1} - 0.98 \, \Delta \ln \text{TWGDP}_{-2}$$
$$(4.18) \qquad\qquad (2.84)$$
$$+ \text{seasonal dummies}$$

OLS: 1972Q4–1994Q4
$R^2 = 0.486$ SEE $= 0.056$ LM$(4) = 6.74$
RESET$(1) = 0.458$ NORM$(1) = 0.889$ HET$(1) = 0.759$

Domestic prices

$$\ln \text{SGPD} = -0.134 + 1.515 \, (\ln \text{SGPMC} - \ln \text{SGPMC})_{-1}$$
$$(7.87)\,(7.07)$$
$$- 0.796 \, (\ln \text{SGPD} - \ln \text{SGPMC})$$
$$(3.38)$$

OLS: 1973Q4–1994Q4
$\bar{R}^2 = 0.745$ SEE $= 0.0964$ LM$(4) = 5.35$
RESET$(1) = 1.38$ NORM$(2) = 6.39$ HET$(1) = 1.66$

$$\Delta \ln \text{THPD} = 0.265 - 0.239 \ln \text{THPD}_{-1} + 0.171 \ln \text{THPMC}_{-1} + 0.056 \, \text{THCU}_{-1}$$
$$(3.98)\,(3.92) \qquad\qquad (3.67) \qquad\qquad (2.01)$$
$$+ 0.481 \, \Delta \ln \text{THPD}_{-1} + 0.261 \, \Delta \ln \text{THDP}_{-3}$$
$$(2.57)$$
$$- 0.082 \, \Delta \ln \text{THPM}_{-2} - 0.061 \, \Delta \ln \text{THPMC}_{-3}$$
$$(1.23) \qquad\qquad (0.96)$$

$$-0.106 \, \Delta \ln \text{THPMC}_{-4}$$
$$(1.82)$$

OLS: 1975Q1–1994Q4

$\bar{R}^2 = 0.555$ SEE = 0.0121 LM(4) = 3.23

RESET(1) = 0.0925 NORM(2) = 0.712 HET(1) = 0.779

$$\Delta \ln \text{THPD} = 0.004 - 0.049 \, (\ln \text{THPD} - \ln \text{THPMC})_{-1} + 0.040 \, \text{THCU}_{-1}$$
$$(0.152)(1.22) \qquad\qquad\qquad\qquad (1.21)$$
$$-0.00026 \, \text{TREND}$$
$$(1.62)$$

$\bar{R}^2 = 0.407$ SEE = 0.0137 LM(4) = 3.15

RESET(1) = 0.069 NORM(2) = 4.93 HET(1) = 0.659

OLS: 1975Q1–1994Q4

$$\Delta \ln \text{KOPD} = 0.948 - 0.0867 \, (\ln \text{KOPD} - \ln \text{KOPMC})_{-1}$$
$$(2.73) \quad (2.13)$$
$$-0.084 \, (\ln \text{KOPD} - \ln \text{KOULC})_{-1} + 0.032 \, \text{KOCU}_{-1}$$
$$(2.81) \qquad\qquad\qquad\qquad (2.26)$$
$$-0.00058 \, \text{TREND} + 0.366 \, \Delta \ln \text{KOPD}_{-1}$$
$$(2.68) \qquad\qquad (5.84)$$
$$+0.262 \, \Delta \ln \text{KOPD}_{-3}$$
$$(4.20)$$

OLS: 1976Q1–1994Q4

$\bar{R}^2 = 0.870$ SEE = 0.0090557 LM(4) = 1.56

RESET(1) = 11.98 NORM(2) = 0.414 HET(1) = 0.0347

$$\Delta \ln \text{TWPD} = 0.619 - 0.028 \, (\ln \text{TWPD} - \ln \text{TWPMC})_{-1}$$
$$(2.92) \quad (1.02)$$
$$-0.0398 \, (\ln \text{TWPD} - \ln \text{TWULC})_{-1} + 0.147 \, \text{TWCU}_{-1}$$
$$(3.79) \qquad\qquad\qquad\qquad (3.78)$$

OLS: 1976Q2–1993Q4

$\bar{R}^2 = 0.756$ SEE = 0.0094 LM(4) = 6.99

RESET(1) = 0.955 NORM(1) = 1.89 HET(1) = 0.015

Export of services

$$\Delta \ln \text{SGXSER} = 3.99 - 0.403 \, (\ln \text{SGXSER} - \ln \text{WMVOL})_{-1}$$
$$(3.02)(2.85)$$
$$-0.501 \, \ln \, (\text{SGCED\$/WDCED\$})_{-1}$$
$$(2.85)$$
$$+0.715 \Delta \ln \, (\text{SGCED\$/WDCED\$})_{-1}$$

$\bar{R}^2 = 0.522$ SEE = 0.107 LM(4) = 0.711

RESET(1) = 1.066 NORM(2) = 0.429 HET(1) = 0.690

$$\Delta \ln \text{THXSER} = 0.9798 - 0.112 \, (\ln \text{THXSER} - \ln \text{WMVOL})_{-1}$$
$$(5.26) \quad (4.46)$$
$$-0.268 \, \ln \, (\text{THCED\$/WDCED\$})_{-1} + \text{seasonal dummies}$$
$$(4.31)$$

($\bar{R}^2 = 0.755$ SEE = 0.069 LM(4) = 5.49

RESET(1) = 0.009 NORM(2) = 3.79 HET(1) = 8.73

$$\Delta \ln \text{KOXSER} = 1.073 - 0.122 \, (\ln \text{KOXSER} - \ln \text{WMVOL})_{-1}$$
$$(5.29) \quad (4.89)$$
$$-0.165 \ln (\text{KOCED\$/WDCED\$})_{-1} - 0.072 \, \Delta \ln \text{KOXSER}_{-1}$$
$$(2.92) \hspace{4cm} (2.29)$$
$$-0.088 \, \Delta \ln \text{KOXSER}_{-2} + \text{seasonal dummies}$$
$$(2.78)$$

$\bar{R}^2 = 0.751$ \quad SEE = 0.06175 \quad LM(4) = 5.51
RESET(1) = 1.33 \quad NORM(2) = 1.91 \quad HET(1) = 0.212

$$\Delta \ln \text{TWXSER} = 0.046 - 0.054 \, (\ln \text{TWXSER} - \ln \text{WMVOL})_{-1}$$
$$(2.48) \quad (1.96)$$
$$-0.212 \ln (\text{TWCED\$/WDCED\$})_{-1} - 0.184 \, \Delta \text{TWXSER}_{-1}$$
$$(2.35) \hspace{4cm} (1.81)$$
$$+ \text{seasonal dummies}$$

$\bar{R}^2 = 0.345$ \quad SEE = 0.074 \quad LM(4) = 10.32
RESET(1) = 2.13 \quad NORM(2) = 0.335 \quad HET(1) = 0.286

Imports of services

$$\Delta (\ln \text{SGMSER} - \ln \text{SGCED\$}) = 0.518 - 0.364 \, (\ln \text{SGMSER} - \ln \text{SGCED\$})_{-1}$$
$$(0.608) \quad (1.81)$$
$$-0.257 \ln (\text{SGCED\$/WDCED\$})_{-1}$$
$$(2.11)$$
$$+0.253 \ln \text{SGGDP}_{-1}$$
$$(1.13)$$

$\bar{R}^2 = 0.307$ \quad SEE = 0.064 \quad LM(4) = 0.0929
RESET(1) = 4.25 \quad NORM(2) = 0.586 \quad HET(1) = 2.35

$$\Delta (\ln \text{THMSER} - \ln \text{THCED\$}) = 0.337 - 0.047 \, (\ln \text{THMSER} - \ln \text{THCED\$})_{-1}$$
$$(2.03) \quad (1.19)$$
$$-0.109 \ln \text{THGDP}_{-1} + 2.25 \ln \text{THGDP}_{-3}$$
$$(1.57) \hspace{3cm} (2.63)$$

$\bar{R}^2 = 0.641$ \quad SEE = 0.0525 \quad LM(4) = 4.16
RESET(1) = 3.40 \quad NORM(2) = 2.19 \quad HET(1) = 0.196

$$\Delta (\ln \text{KOMSER} - \ln \text{KOCED\$}) = 0.181 - 0.152 \, (\ln \text{KOMSER} - \ln \text{KOCED\$})_{-1}$$
$$(0.56) \quad (2.93)$$
$$-0.072 \, (\ln \text{KOCED\$/WDCED\$})_{-1}$$
$$(0.74)$$
$$+0.109 \ln \text{KOGDP}_{-1}$$
$$(1.82)$$
$$-0.326 \Delta (\ln \text{KOMSER} - \ln \text{KOCED\$})_{-1}$$
$$(3.12)$$
$$+0.244 \Delta \, (\ln \text{KOMSER} - \ln \text{KOCED\$})_{-3}$$
$$2.53$$
$$-0.459 \Delta \ln \text{KOGDP}_{-1}$$

$\bar{R}^2 = 0.576$ \quad SEE = 0.0762 \quad LM(4) = 2.04
RESET(1) = 0.158 \quad NORM(2) = 5.40 \quad HET(1) = 2.66

$$\Delta\,(\ln\text{TWMSER}-\ln\text{TWCED\$})=3.28-0.195\,(\ln\text{TWMSER}-\ln\text{TWCED\$})_{-1}$$
$$(2.26)\,(2.93)$$
$$+0.231\,\ln\text{TWGDP}_{-1}$$
$$(2.22)$$
$$-0.12\,\ln\,(\text{TWCED\$}/\text{WDCED\$})_{-1}$$
$$(1.21)$$
$$-0.235\,\Delta\,(\ln\text{TWMSER}-\ln\text{TWCED\$})_{-4}$$
$$(2.59)$$

$\bar{R}^2 = 0.6902$ SEE $= 0.0749$ LM$(4) = 9.98$
RESET$(1) = 0.91$ NORM$(2) = 3.13$ HET$(1) = 0.041$

Exports prices

$$\Delta\ln\text{SGPX}=0.016-0.059\,(\ln\text{SGPX}-\ln\text{WPX})_{-1}-0.474\,\Delta\ln\text{SGRX}_{-1}$$
$$(2.99)\quad(2.09)\qquad\qquad\qquad(2.57)$$
$$-0.189\,\Delta\ln\text{SGPX}_{-2}+0.234\,\Delta\ln\text{SGPX}_{-3}$$
$$(2.46)\qquad\qquad(2.59)$$
$$+0.561\,\Delta\ln\text{WPX}_{-1}-0.314\,\Delta\ln\text{SGPD\$}_{3}$$
$$(4.62)\qquad\qquad(2.02)$$

$\bar{R}^2 = 0.581$ SEE $= 0.0302$ LM$(1) = 1055$
RESET$(1) = 0.005$ NORM$(2) = 2.15$ HET $= 1$

$$\Delta\ln\text{THPX}=0.677-0.144\,(\ln\text{THPX}-\ln\text{THPD\$})_{-1}$$
$$(2.66)\quad(2.62)$$
$$-0.073\,(\ln\text{THPX}-\ln\text{WPX})_{-1}+0.477\,\Delta\ln\text{THPX}_{-1}$$
$$(1.79)\qquad\qquad\qquad(5.48)$$
$$+0.379\,\Delta\ln\text{THPX}_{-3}$$
$$(3.88)$$

$\bar{R}^2 = 0.606$ SEE $= 0.0203$ LM$(4) = 1.765$
RESET$(1) = 1.69$ NORM$(2) = 1.44$ HET $= 0.44$

$$\Delta\ln\text{KOPX}=0.0018-0.102\,(\ln\text{KOPX}-\ln\text{WPX})_{-1}+0.574\,\Delta\ln\text{KOPX}_{-1}$$
$$(0.81)\quad(3.34)\qquad\qquad\qquad(6.63)$$
$$-0.332\,\Delta\ln\text{KOPX}+0.283\,\Delta\ln\text{KOPD\$}_{-1}-0.269\,\Delta\ln\text{KOPD\$}_{-2}$$
$$(4.52)\qquad\qquad(3.81)\qquad\qquad(3.35)$$
$$+0.269\,\Delta\ln\text{KOPD}_{-3}+0.370\,\Delta\ln\text{KORX}_{-2}+0.235\,\Delta\ln\text{KORX}_{-3}$$
$$(3.66)\qquad\qquad(5.28)\qquad\qquad(3.0)$$
$$+0.161\,\Delta\ln\text{KORX}_{-4}+\text{seasonal dummies}$$
$$(2.48)$$

$\bar{R}^2 = 0.701$ SEE $= 0.0126$ LM$(4) = 10.61$
RESET$(1) = 0.587$ NORM$(1) = 0.481$ HET $= 5.42$

$$\Delta\ln\text{TWPX}=0.867-0.187\,(\ln\text{TWPX}-\ln\text{WPX})_{-1}+0.79\,\Delta\ln\text{TWPX}_{-4}$$
$$(2.03)\quad(2.04)\qquad\qquad\qquad(5.09)$$
$$-0.454\,\Delta\ln\text{WPX}_{-1}+0.41\,\Delta\ln\text{TWPD\$}_{-3}-0.556\,\Delta\ln\text{TWPD}_{-4}$$
$$(4.52)\qquad\qquad(3.51)\qquad\qquad(3.15)$$

$\bar{R}^2 = 0.4357$ SEE $= 0.0362$ LM$(4) = 3.06$
RESET$(1) = 0.228$ NORM$(2) = 2.98$ HET $= 0.32$

Domestic demand

$$\Delta \ln SGDD = 0.398 - 0.084 \ln SGDD_{-1} + 0.0439 \ln SGXVOL_{-1}$$
$$(2.12) \quad (2.19) \qquad\qquad (2.14)$$
$$+0.269 \, \Delta \ln SGDD_{-3} + 0.133 \, \Delta \ln SGXVOL$$
$$(2.33) \qquad\qquad (1.63)$$

$\bar{R}^2 = 0.253$ $\qquad$ SEE $= 0.0363$ $\qquad$ LM$(4) = 16.83$
RESET$(1) = 0.348$ NORM$(2) = 0.987$ HET $= 0.132$

$$\Delta \ln THDD = 0.659 - 0.085 \ln THDD_{-1} + 0.053 \ln TXVOL_{-1}$$
$$(1.87) \quad (1.66) \qquad\qquad (1.76)$$
$$-0.0067 \, THILR_{-1} + \text{seasonal dummies}$$
$$(3.45)$$

$\bar{R}^2 = 0.284$ $\qquad$ SEE $= 0.0302$ $\qquad$ LM$(4) = 1.40$
RESET$(1) = 1.76$ NORM$(2) = 0.945$ HET $= 0.0022$

$$\Delta \ln KODD = 0.657 - 0.119 \ln KODD_{-1} + 0.0764 \ln KOXVOL_{-1}$$
$$(3.11) \quad (2.69) \qquad\qquad (2.27)$$
$$-0.00169 \, KOILR_{-1} - 0.207 \, \Delta \ln KODD_{-1}$$
$$(1.09) \qquad\qquad (2.78)$$
$$+0.588 \, \Delta \ln KODD_{-4}$$
$$(8.27)$$

$\bar{R}^2 = 0.9521$ $\qquad$ SEE $= 0.04952$ $\qquad$ LM$(4) = 10.89$
RESET$(1) = 0.211$ NORM$(2) = 1.25$ HET $= 5.22$

$$\Delta \ln TWDD = 0.338 - 0.094 \ln TWDD_{-1} + 0.075 \ln TWXVOL_{-1}$$
$$(2.82) \quad (3.56) \qquad\qquad (3.64)$$
$$-0.303 \, \Delta \ln TWDD_{-1} + 0.293 \ln TWDD_{-4}$$
$$(3.13) \qquad\qquad (3.01)$$
$$+0.052 \, \Delta \, TWXVOL_{-4}$$
$$(1.84)$$

$\bar{R}^2 = 0.289$ $\qquad$ SEE $= 0.023$ $\qquad$ LM$(4) = 6.36$
RESET$(1) = 0.123$ $\quad$ NORM$(2) = 0.50$ $\quad$ HET $= 1.19$

Data sources

Source: International Monetary Fund, International Financial Statistics:
For SG, TH, KO: XVOL, MVOL, XVOLC, MVOLC, WMVOL, PM, PX: derived from Tables 70d (Export values), 71d (Import values), 74d (Export unit values), and 75d (Import unit values). For WPX, PD, XSER, MSER, CED, WDCED, RX, LR: taken from individual country tables in IMF, *International Financial Statistics*. For all variables for Taiwan: Taiwan National Accounts (Datastream). Various data. Asian Development Bank.

Estimation periods: ln SGXSER: annual data, 1977–94; ln THXSER: 1976Q3–1995Q1; ln KOXSER: 1975Q2–1994Q4; ln TWXSER: 1977Q4–1994Q4; ln SGMSER – ln SGCED$: annual data, 1978–94; ln THMSER – ln THCED$: 1977Q2–1995Q1; ln KOMSER – ln KOCED$: 1976Q1–1994Q4; ln TWMSER – ln TWCED$: 1977Q2–1995Q3; ln SGPX: 1973Q4–1994Q3; ln THPX:

1977Q4–1994Q3; ln KOPX: 1974Q2–1994Q1; ln TWPX: 1977Q2–1994Q1; ln SGDD: 1973Q1–1994Q4; ln THDD: 1976Q2–1994Q3; ln KODD: 1974Q2–1994Q4; ln TWDD: 1976Q2–1995Q3.

Notes

1   We aggregate goods and services for ease of exposition here. As market conditions differ significantly for these categories we separate them in our empirical work.
2   Between 1984 and April 1987 the won depreciated by 5 per cent against the US dollar, 79 per cent against the yen, 64 per cent against the Deutsche Mark, 51 per cent against the French franc and 27 per cent against the UK pound.
3   In June 1979 the NWC recommended a general wage increase of around 12 per cent of average wages. This was followed by two further recommended increases of 15 per cent in 1980 and 12–16 per cent in 1981.
4   The Skills Development Fund was introduced in 1979 to finance adult education and training programmes.

References

Amsden, A.H. (1989) *Asia's Next Giant: South Korea and Late Industrialisation*, Oxford University Press, New York.
Anderton, R. and Dunnett, A. (1987) 'Modelling the behaviour of export volumes of manufactures: an evaluation of the performance of different measures of international competitiveness', *National Institute Economic Review*, No. 121, August.
Asian Development Bank (1994) *Key Indicators of Developing Asian and Pacific Countries*, Economics and Development Resource Center, Metro Manila.
Athukorala, P. and Riedel, J. (1990) 'How valid is the small country assumption?', mimeo, Johns Hopkins University, Baltiore, Md.
Balassa, B. and Williamson, J. (1990) 'Adjusting to success: balance of payments policy in the East Asian NICs', *Policy Analysis in International Economics*, 17.
Barrell, R. (1993) 'Internal and external balance', *Journal of Economic Studies*, 20, pp. 73–86.
Barrell, R. and Pain, N. (1996a) 'Trade restraints and Japanese direct investment flows', *European Economic Review*, 1998.
——(1996b) 'An econometric analysis of US foreign direct investment', *Review of Economics and Statistics*, March.
Barrell, R. and Sefton, J. (1997) 'Fiscal policy and the Maastricht solvency criteria', *Manchester School*, June.
Barrell, R. and Veld, J. (1991) 'FEERs and the path to EMU', *National Institute Economic Review*, No. 137, pp. 51–7.
Barrell, R. and Wren-Lewis, S. (1989) *Equilibrium Exchange Rates for the G7*, Discussion Paper No. 323, Centre for Economic Policy Research, London.
Bercuson, K. (ed.) (1995) *Singapore: A Case in Rapid Development*, IMF Occasional Paper, Washington, DC.
Breuer, J.B. (1994) 'An assessment of the evidence on purchasing power parity', in Williamson, J. (ed.) *Estimating Equilibrium Exchange Rates*, Longman, London.
Deppler, M. and Ripley, D. (1978) 'The world trade model: merchandise trade', *IMF Staff Papers*, Vol. 25, No. 1, pp. 147–206.

Gan, W.-B. (1994) 'Characterising real exchange rate behaviour of selected Eeast Asian economies', *Journal of Economic Development*, Vol. 19, No. 2, pp. 67–92.

Goldman Sachs (1995) *Asia Economic Quarterly*, December.

Goldstein, M. and Khan, M. (1985) 'Income and price effects in international trade', in Jones, R. and Kenen, P. (eds), *Handbook of International Economics*, Elsevier, Amsterdam.

Intal, P.S. (1992) 'Real exchange rates, price competitiveness and structural adjustment in Asian and Pacific economies', *Asian Development Review*, Vol. 10, No. 2, pp. 86–123.

Jansen, K. (1995) 'The macroeconomic effects of direct foreign investment: the case of Thailand', *World Development*, Vol. 23, No. 2, pp. 193–210.

Lee, J.-W. (1986) 'Trends in exchange rates show stronger won, dollar', *Korea Business World*, December, pp. 29–30.

Marquez, J. and McNeilly, C. (1988) 'Income and price elasticities for exports of developing countries', *Review of Economic Studies*, Vol. 70, No. 2, May, pp. 306–14.

Muscatelli, V., Stevenson, A. and Montagna, C. (1995) 'Modeling aggregate manufacturing exports for some Asian newly industrialized economies', *Review of Economic Studies*, Vol. 77, No. 1, February, pp. 147–55.

Nomura Research Institute and Institute of Southeast Asia Studies (1995) *The New Wave of Foreign Direct Investment*, Tokyo.

OECD (1994) *Economic Survey – Korea*, Paris.

Riedel, J. (1988) 'The demand for LDC exports of manufactures: estimates from Hong Kong', *The Economic Journal*, Vol. 98, No. 389, March.

Rodrik, D. (1995) 'Getting interventions right: how South Korea and Taiwan grew rich', *Economic Policy*, 20.

UN (1994) *World Investment Report: Transnational Corporations, Employment and the Workplace*, New York.

——(1995) *Economic and Social Survey of Asia and the Pacific*, New York.

UNCTAD (1994) *Trade and Development Report*, New York.

——(1995) *Trade and Development Report*, New York.

Wade, R. (1990) *The East Asian Miracle: Economic Growth and Public Policy*, Oxford University Press for the World Bank, Washington, DC.

Whitley, J. (1991) *Multinational Macroeconmic Model Comparisons: Trade Equations*, Deutsches Institut für Wirtschaftsforchung, Vierteljahresheft (3/4), Berlin.

Williamson, J. (1994) 'Estimates of FEERs', in Williamson, J. (ed.) *Estimating Equilibrium Exchange Rates*, Longman, London.

World Bank (1993) *The East Asian Miracle: Economic Growth and Public Policy*, Washington, DC.

Yoo, J. (1986) 'Should Korea revalue the won', *Korea Business World*, November, pp. 9–11.

——(1994) 'A quarterly econometric model of the Korean economy', in Ichimura, S. and Matsumoto, Y. (eds), *Econometric Models of Asian Pacific Countries*, Springer-Verlag, London.

Young, A. (1994) 'Lessons from the East Asian NICs: a contrarian view', *European Economic Review*, Vol. 38, No. 3/4, pp. 964–73.

16

DISCUSSION

Benoît Coeuré

Rüdiger Dornbusch and Yung Chul Park have made a convincing case for the band-basket-crawl solution for exchange rate regimes in East Asia (see Chapter 1). At the heart of the 'BBC' approach, the level of the exchange rate has something to do with the notion of equilibrium real exchange rate, for which a natural candidate is John Williamson's (1994) FEER. Once the need for FEERs in Asian countries has been made clear, a vast and yet largely unexplored territory opens to empirical researchers in the field. Given its past research with John Williamson (Barrell and Wren-Lewis, 1989), the National Institute of Economic and Social Research (NIESR) was best qualified to undertake such an exercise, and the result is quite convincing. Chapter 15 is pioneering and delivers already clear-cut results (such as the presumption of undervaluation in Taiwan and Thailand but not in Singapore and South Korea). It paves the way for future researchers, who are likely to be numerous.

It would be easy to question particular estimation results and to stress the implications of even small changes for the resulting paths for FEERs. For instance, I am not at ease with the choice of including a time trend in the export volume equation, a choice which has been made for Singapore only: since this dramatically changes the pattern of the equilibrium exchange rate, thus the final 'no undervaluation' message, I wonder how the decision was taken and whether it can be left to the sole Student coefficient of the corresponding estimate. But I am confident that the authors had a hard time making their results as robust as possible. Rather, I shall concentrate on two issues raised by the method itself, having in mind that the difficulties encountered when computing FEERs may help uncover some tricky aspects of the theory.

1 Defining the external balance: the case of NIEs

The FEER approach is attractive because it is flexible, and this is partly due to the fact that current account targets are allowed to vary over time. Indeed, many authors, beginning with John Williamson, have emphasized the underlying theoretical difficulties and the normative content of the idea of a current

280

account target. But the choice of a constant target of zero or 6 per cent for the current account-to-GDP ratio, irrespective of the country, is somewhat disappointing. At best, the result can be thought of as a two-sided benchmark or a 'target zone' for the FEER, providing a broad diagnosis on the undervaluation of the currency. This is how the authors honestly take it. But in this respect, it would still be preferable to conduct a sensitivity analysis and produce proper confidence intervals around the estimated FEERs, for instance using Monte Carlo simulations.

Anyway, I wonder whether an Asian policy maker, once he has been convinced by Dornbusch and Park of the necessity of FEERs, would be happy with such broad conclusions. But is it possible to do better? To define more precisely the current account target, fundamental choices have to be made. Some of them are nicely discussed in Chapter 15, although they are not much taken into account in practice. I will make two more points.

First, as it has often been pointed out, when deciding on a current account target, one can be guided by average past performances as well as all the future needs of the economy, including unfounded liabilities on retirement pensions. This is appropriate for a G-7 country but it may prove quite difficult in rapidly changing economies such as the NIEs. An opposite approach would be to start from the bottom of the balance of payments sheet and decide on a sustainable target for the financial account, that is, on the amount of capital inflows and outflows needed by the economy. Obviously, the former method is coherent with the presumption that excess capital inflows are not relevant, being merely 'hot money', which may be the dominant feeling today in the NIEs. But the latter could be appropriate for other Asian countries, which rely so much on FDI and foreign capital in their development process. At any rate, the definition of the current account target deserves a careful, case-by-case discussion.

Second, the model relies entirely on flows and gives no role to existing assets and liabilities with respect to the rest of the world. Indeed, factor payments play a role in determining the current account: as an example, the deficit on investment income amounted to $2.4 billion in 1995 in South Korea, to be compared to the $6.6 billion deficit on trade and services. For a given current account target, the accumulation of external debt increases the trade balance target, thus lowering the equilibrium level of the exchange rate for the NIEs, particularly in their bilateral relation with Japan and with South-East Asia.

Besides, from an internal point of view, investment is always central to growth, even in the export-led Asian economies, as has been convincingly argued by Dani Rodrik (e.g. in Rodrik, 1995). It can be argued that accumulating capital reduces the need for an undervalued currency, raising the FEER as time goes by — arguments along this line can be found in the nice model presented by Guillermo Larraín. The role of investment may be relevant in practice, and it has probably been overlooked in the FEER theory.

2 The role of the US dollar and the need for a global approach

As has been stressed by the NIESR, the traditional approach to computing FEER is basically a partial equilibrium one, relying usually on the estimation of separate small country models. This raises the question of the *consistency* of the resulting FEER estimates for various currencies. This question matters particularly from an outsider's point of view: indeed, when questioning the global under/overvaluation of Asian currencies, it seems natural to ask for the role of the dollar as an exchange rate peg and of its possible misalignment with respect to European currencies. But maybe this is a typical European, not to say French, bias? It turns out that the NIESR approach could help in answering the question. It uses tailor-made country blocs, but within the framework of an integrated multi-country model, NiGEM, which could very well be used to produce FEERs for the dollar, the yen and the Deutsche Mark along with Asian currencies. Indeed NiGEM has already been used for such a purpose in a previous version (see Barrell and Wren-Lewis, 1989). It would help us in disentangling the role of the dollar and the yen on the one hand, and of local policies on the other hand, in the misalignment of Asian currencies. This would tell us a little more on the global consequences of these countries exchange rate policies.

Note

The views expressed here are personal and do not necessarily correspond to the position of the Ministry of Finance.

References

Artis, Michael and Taylor, Mark (1993) *DEER Hunting: Misalignment, Debt Accumulation and Desired Equilibrium Exchange Rates*, IMF Working Paper No. 93/48, Washington, DC.

Barrel, Ray and Wren-Lewis, Simon (1989) *FEERs for the G7*, Discussion Paper No. 323, Centre for Economic Policy Research, London.

Rodrik, Dani (1995) 'Getting interventions right: how South Korea and Taiwan grew rich', *Economic Policy* No. 20.

Williamson, John (1994) 'Estimates of FEERs', in John Williamson (ed.) *Estimating Equilibrium Exchange Rates*, Longman, London.

Part III

REGIONAL MONETARY COOPERATION
Rationale and effects

17

BLOC FLOATING AND EXCHANGE RATE VOLATILITY

The causes and consequences of currency blocs

Stefan Collignon

1 Introduction

The world economy is increasingly characterized not only by the variety of preferential trading arrangements between regions, but also by the emergence of currency blocs. This chapter tries to explain why currency blocs have replaced free-floating exchange rate regimes and what consequences for international monetary relations will follow. Will the emergence of Europe's single currency and the increasing integration of high-performing Asian economies into the world economy affect the trends of recent years?

It is well known that since the end of the Bretton Woods system in the early 1970s, exchange rates have not always behaved as expected by the protagonists of greater flexibility. Friedman (1953) had argued that flexible exchange rates would help to correct imbalances caused by fundamental factors such as fiscal and monetary policies, but ultimately exchange rates were supposed to be as stable as macroeconomic fundamentals. Speculation was thought to be stabilizing and it was assumed that in the long run purchasing power parity (PPP) would hold. In reality exchange rates have shown excessive volatility, quite unrelated to macroeconomic fundamentals, thereby increasing risk and uncertainty. While under fixed exchange rates, policy errors have led to currency overvaluations, under flexible exchange rates market errors have produced similar effects (Bergsten and Henning, 1996). Because goods prices are more rigid than prices for foreign currency, nominal exchange rate movements cause real exchange rate movements and not the opposite. Current account and trade imbalances were not 'automatically' equilibrated, but financed by borrowing from abroad on an unprecedented scale. There is little evidence of stabilizing speculation, and exchange rates seem to follow a random walk. Furthermore, while purchasing power parity may hold in the 'ultra-long run', not only does it fail in the short run but real exchange rate fluctuations can still be long-lasting, sizeable and even permanent (Breuer, 1994).

This raises theoretical questions about the nature of the equilibrium exchange rate and practical issues of choosing the best exchange rate regime. For the East Asian economies the choice must be about sustaining their high performance. Existing models of exchange rate determination provide little help. In the Dornbusch (1976) overshooting model, equilibrium is given by the long run to which the economy will eventually converge and the expected movement of the exchange rate is proportional to the discrepancy between the long-run equilibrium and the current spot rate. The former depends on economic fundamentals and the dynamics of the model require market participants to know the equilibrium rate. Early PPP theories assumed the spot rate to adjust instantaneously. Dornbusch's overshooting theory was more realistic in assuming adjustment in goods markets to be less flexible, although at times it seems that the exchange rate even 'overshoots the overshooting equilibrium' (Frankel, 1995). Subsequent studies have confirmed the slow adjustment by estimating the speed of adjustment to PPP to be 9 to 15 per cent a year of the gap. Others estimate a seventy-year time frame to confirm real exchange rate stationarity (Breuer, 1994). Thus, models based on economic fundamentals have some difficulty in explaining the shorter-term dynamics. The same applies to monetarist models where the exchange rate should react to news about monetary policy in big jumps, while in reality adjustment is gradual. Attempts to explain these contradictions have taken several directions. Most abandon the view that exchange rates move with economic fundamentals. First, there is the theory of rational speculative bubbles. Second, only a weak form of rational expectations may apply. If exchange rates follow a random walk and foreign exchange traders have a very short time horizon, they would ignore fundamentals and form expectations conditional on past information using technical analysis instead (Dornbusch and Frankel, 1988). As a consequence, the spot rate may drift away from the equilibrium rate. Finally, one may abandon the rational expectations hypothesis if markets systematically mispredict the direction of policy.

These different models lead to different theories about exchange rate variability and how to deal with it. According to the fundamentalist school, exchange rates reflect variability in the fundamentals. Stabilizing exchange rates requires stabilizing fundamentals, essentially by converging policies. Currency blocs emerge because countries form 'optimum currency areas' (OCA). However, the empirical evidence, especially from East Asia, throws some doubt on this explanation. The alternative view observes that exchange rate movements are quite often not a result of exogenous shocks in fundamentals. They result from uncertainty when economic agents are unable to detect how the exchange rate is influenced by fundamentals. As a consequence exchange rate volatility is disconnected from the variability of the underlying fundamentals (de Grauwe, 1989). Such limited rationality models are based on small 'menu costs' which create ranges for exchange rate movements where it will not be worth while for economic agents to change their portfolio. Consequently, exchange rates remain fairly stable within that range, even if they do not reflect equilibrium. The misalignment shows up in other variables, such as the current account or unemployment. In an uncertain world, economic agents find it difficult to interpret whether a current change in the exchange rate is a move towards equilibrium. Only when the gap between spot and equilibrium rate has become sufficiently important will the process of adjustment be put in motion. Therefore in limited rationality models, exchange rates exhibit inertia, and the importance of this phenomenon is the greater, the larger is the uncertainty. The creation of currency blocs is, then, an attempt to reduce uncertainty by pegging to an anchor and adjusting fundamentals accordingly.

Most models take the equilibrium rate as relatively stable and try to explain why the spot rate has drifted away from it. In this chapter, the stability of the attractor itself is put into question as a result of currency bloc formation. If the equilibrium exchange rate is volatile, then the adjustment process becomes much more uncertain. Market participants would act rationally if they based their expectations on a rather vaguely defined range of equilibria as well as on past spot rates.

The question, of course, is: why should the equilibrium rate be volatile? We have to define *changes* in the structural relationship of the fundamentals which are supposed to define an otherwise invariant equilibrium exchange rate. The most extreme approach of this kind is represented by general equilibrium exchange rate models where any rate reflects an equilibrium and changes are a consequence of changes in technology, factor endowment or taste and preferences for consumption, saving and investment (Stockman, 1987). This chapter takes a different line. It shows 'bloc floating' as the structural variable which makes the fundamental equilibrium exchange rate more volatile.

The concept of 'bloc floating' describes the present world system where key or anchor currencies are floating with respect to each other, while regional currencies peg themselves to those anchors in some way. As a result, intra-regional volatility is reduced at the expense of inter-regional stability between key currencies.

Bloc floating is, of course, a practical answer to the problem of volatile exchange rates after the demise of Bretton Woods. Given the uncertainty of economists about exchange rate movements, it should be no surprise that business people and policy makers require concrete measures to reduce risk. The objective of bloc floating is to stabilize macroeconomic financial variables and microeconomic competitiveness in increasingly integrated markets by managed floating regimes that avoid severe exchange rate appreciations. By focusing on volatility, bloc floating is perfectly compatible with crawling pegs and long-run stable real exchange rates within the zone. It therefore transcends the traditional dichotomy of fixed versus flexible exchange rates and can be achieved under a variety of different 'official' (IMF) currency regimes.[1]

Evidence for the emergence of monetary blocs has been provided by Frankel and Wei (1993) and Bénassy-Quéré (1998 and unpublished work). These studies take relative volatility with respect to key currencies as an indicator for *de facto* exchange rate pegging. A currency bloc is defined by a tendency for exchange rate variability to be lower within groups of countries than across groups. The size of the currency bloc can be measured by the share of foreign trade between countries belonging to the bloc compared to total world trade. The emergence of currency blocs is then documented by the parts of world trade which are linked by more stable exchange rates. Interestingly, it appears that the dominant characteristic of the last twenty years was the emergence of the DM bloc, while Asia with the exception of Japan belongs to the dollar zone. Bénassy-Quéré has observed that the world trade share of currencies without an exchange rate anchor has fallen from 27 per cent in 1978 to 6 per cent in 1992 (see Figure 17.1). Over the same time, the DM zone has continuously expanded. While it covered only Germany,

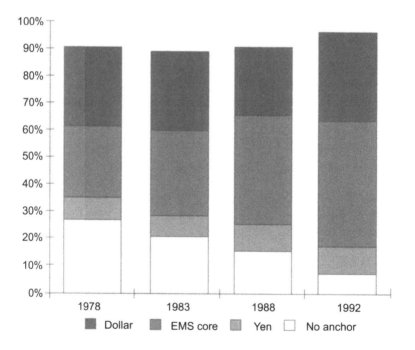

Figure 17.1 Share of currency zones in world exports

Source: Bénassy-Quéré, A. (1995): Ni change fixe, ni change flexible in: La lettre du CEPII N°133, Mars

Benelux and Denmark in the 1970s, it has nearly doubled in weight, progressing from 26 per cent to 47 per cent in world trade and linking most of (Western) Europe. This growth is primarily due to the growth of Europe's single market after the creation of the European Monetary System: intra-European trade as a share of total exports has increased from 39 to 71 per cent from 1978 to 1992. The dollar zone, on the other hand, has roughly remained stable over time – at about 30 per cent of world trade, although it shrank slightly in the late 1980s (caused by the dollar depreciation) and picked up again in the 1990s. The dollar has lost ground in Africa and the Middle East, but increased in Asia, where it now covers nearly all countries with the exception of Japan. The Japanese yen, however, does not serve as an anchor for any currency. Clearly, non-Japanese Asia's integration into the world economy has been achieved by reference to the US dollar. In 1988, East Asian exports to North America amounted to 29.5 per cent of their total, to Europe only 18.6 per cent; 38 per cent of exports went to other Asian countries, of which only one-third was directed to Japan and about 45 per cent to dollar-pegged NICs or ASEAN countries (Riedel, 1996). Thus, given that many countries in the rest of the world are also dollar dominated, the US dollar zone covers between one-half and two-thirds of Asia's exports.

This emergence of currency blocs demands an explanation. As Agnès Bénassy-Quéré points out, neither the optimum currency area literature nor nominal anchor theories provide a satisfying answer.[2] In Section 2 I will explain bloc floating as a consequence of interacting micro and macro objectives by market agents and public authorities in an environment of limited rationality. Section 3 develops the consequences of bloc floating for exchange rate volatility between international currencies. Section 4 looks at the effects of bloc floating on key currencies.

2 Investment and exchange risk reduction: why currency blocs emerge

The accumulation of productive assets is the foundation of economic growth. East Asia's economic success, similar to Europe's after the war, is based on unusually high rates of private investment (7 percentage points of GDP higher than other low-or middle-income countries) and savings coupled with rapid export growth.[3] A wide variety of macro and micro policies was used to ignite and keep running these two engines of growth.[4] Most successful East Asian governments concentrated on creating an environment with profitable investment opportunities and on lowering uncertainty associated with real investment (World Bank, 1993). With respect to exchange rate policies this implied both maintaining a competitive exchange rate[5] and reducing its volatility.

The underlying logic is most easily described by a simple mean-variance portfolio model linked to a standard investment demand function in a three-country world. Private investors are assumed to be risk-averse, maximizing their expected utility subject to their portfolio wealth constraint. Public authorities are to maximize the aggregate capital stock subject to private investor behaviour. Thus, firms invest as long as the net present value of new investment opportunities is greater than zero, i.e. as long as marginal income of the investment exceeds the 'user cost' of capital. However, if capital expenditure is postponable and entails substantial fixed cost, then, given the uncertain character of future returns, user cost must include a premium for risk.[6] Therefore, the required expected return is higher than the risk-free discount rate. For the purpose of this chapter, we will focus on exchange risk and treat real returns as deterministic while only exchange rates are stochastic.[7] Thus, among all investments with a given expected rate of return, the one with the lowest exchange rate risk is the most desirable. In an open economy with increasing capital mobility, expected returns may converge, but exchange rate volatility would rise, thereby adding a risk premium and pushing required returns up.

The impact of exchange risk on aggregate investment can be modelled by an additive separable investment demand function with each currency area as a separate argument. We will consider real investment, i.e. capital expenditure and will assume that selling in different markets requires separate amounts of previously installed capital. Thus, in a three-country world we may divide total output in A (Y_A) into non-tradables (N) and tradables related to B and C, requiring different amounts of capital (K) and labour (L):

$$Y_i = F(K_i, L_i), \qquad\qquad i = N, B, C$$
$$F_{K_i}, L_{L_i} > 0, F_{KK}, F_{LL} < 0 \tag{17.1}$$

This gives the investment demand function for each market:

$$\frac{dK_i}{dt} = I_i = I_i(F_{K_i} - E[R_i]) \tag{17.2}$$

where $E[R_i]$ is the expected return on investment related to the domestic or foreign market which is required to make undertaking the project worth while. This equation is assumed to reflect an individual firm's capital expenditure functions of the same form. We obtain aggregate investment demand in country A as:

$$I_A = I_N(F_{K_N} - E[R_N]) + I_B(F_{K_B} - E[R_B]) + I_C(F_{K_C} - E[R_C]) \tag{17.3}$$

with $\partial I_i / \partial F_{K_i} > 0, \quad \partial I_i / \partial E[R_i] < 0$; r_A is the safe return on domestic investment or the discount factor for calculating the net present value of domestic investment. The realized (ex post) return on investment related to country B and C would yield the local returns r_B and r_C in foreign currencies plus the respective rates of (real) appreciation of the foreign currencies depreciation of the domestic currency after converting the return into domestic currency.[8] Thus: $R_N = r_A; R_B = r_B + dp_1; R_C = r_c + dp_2$.

Assuming all local returns (r_A, r_B, r_C) to be deterministically given, the realised (ex post) returns for an entrepreneur in A engaged in foreign trade are random due to the change in the real exchange rate dp_i, but not for domestic investment projects (R_N). Given this uncertainty, risk-averse investors will require a risk premium u as a compensation for undertaking the activity. Otherwise they will abstain.[9] The expected return on the foreign investment[10]

$$E[R_N] = r_A$$
$$E[R_B] = r_B + E[dp_1] \quad ; \quad var(R_B) = var(dp_1) = \sigma_1^2$$
$$E[R_C] = r_C + E[dp_2] \quad ; \quad var(R_c) = var(dp_2) = \sigma_2^2$$

The ex post excess return earned on investing in tradables is

$$R_i - r_A = r_i - r_A + dp_1 = u_i \qquad (17.4)$$

with the means and variances μ_i and σ_i^2. The required risk premium (ex ante) is

$$E[R_i] - r_A = r_i - r_A + E(dp_i) = E(u_i) = \mu_i \qquad (17.14a)$$

The forecast error is the difference between the realized excess return and the required risk premium:

$$R_i - E(R_i) = u_i - \mu_i = \varepsilon_i \qquad (17.4b)$$

which in efficient markets would be unforeseeable with $E(\varepsilon) = 0$ and $var(\varepsilon_i) = h_{it} = \sigma_i^2$. It is clear from equation 17.3 that investment in tradables related to B or C will be lower, the higher the required excess return. Public authorities maximize capital accumulation by increasing the marginal product of capital (F_{K_i}[11] or by reducing the risk premium required to compensate for exchange risk.[12] Empirical work by Montiel (1994) shows that the financial risk premia for developing countries over the relevant US interest rate are sometimes substantial.

The figures for high-performing East Asian countries are shown in Table 17.1. Column 2 shows the nominal interest rate used in the relevant country which is compared with the equivalent US rate. The mean financial excess return corresponds to our equation 17.4. The last three columns show the absolute excess return as a ratio to the mean of the exchange rate-corrected foreign interest rate. Because the 'mean excess return' in Table 17.1 refers to financial assets and not to real assets as in our model, the signs are inverted:

Table 17.1 Financial risk premia in Asian countries 1985–90

	Interest rate*	Mean excess return i − (i_US + Δe) 1985–90	Standard error	Ratio: excess return to exchange rate corrected foreign interest rate [i − (i_US + Δe)]/(i_US + Δe)		
				1985–90	1985–June 1987	July 1987– 1990
Indonesia	Deposit rate	−6.10	4.16	1.00	0.95	1.04
South Korea	Deposit rate	0.76	2.22	1.00	0.91	1.09
Malaysia	Deposit rate	−4.29**	1.09	0.79	0.81	0.77
Philippines	Treasury bill rate	3.55**	1.37	0.59	0.71	0.48
Singapore	Deposit rate	−0.20	1.06	1.83	1.69	1.97
Thailand	Deposit rate	4.14**	0.70	0.94	1.11	0.77

Notes:
* The foreign interest rate refers to the relevant US rate.
** Different from zero at a 5% level.

a negative financial excess return of −6.10 implies that an Indonesian company would require a profit rate for exports or imports to the USA 6 percentage points higher or twice as much as on domestic sales. In Thailand, by contrast, exporters or importers to the dollar bloc would have made an extra profit of 4.14 percentage points or double the rate on non-tradables. These excess returns are not insignificant. Clearly, policy strategies for reducing the risk premia must play a significant role in the development process.[13]

Individual investors on the other hand maximize their (given) wealth by optimally diversifying their asset holdings in terms of expected returns and risk. Exchange risk is measured as the variance of the rate of depreciation and risk-averse investors will require a premium in order to hold assets related to B or C. If the exchange rate volatility for P_2 exceeds P_1 ($\sigma_2 > \sigma_1$), then the required expected return $E[R_C]$ must be higher than $E[R_B]$ and both are higher than r_A.[14] Consequently, aggregate investment related to C (tradables) will be lower than under certainty. The typical investor therefore allocates his assets between the three regions by maximizing the utility of his real wealth at the end of the investment period. $E[U(W)] = U(W, \sigma_W^2) \, |U' > 0; U'' < 0$ with respect to m_B and m_C and subject to:

$$W = [m_B R_B + m_C R_C + (1 - m_B - m_c)r_A]W_0 \qquad (17.5)$$

Here W is a real wealth index with W_0 as base; m_B and m_C are the shares of real assets related to the respective countries B and C in the portfolio of investors in A. In order to simplify our analysis, we will assume they are identical to trade shares α_i.

It can be shown (e.g. Minford, 1992) that the solution of this maximization yields the following equations:

$$E[R_B] = r_A + \vartheta(m_B\sigma_1^2 + m_C\sigma_{1,2}) = r_A + \vartheta m(\alpha_1[\sigma_1^2 - \sigma_{1,2} + \sigma_{1,2})$$

$$(17.5a)$$

$$E[R_C] = r_A + \vartheta(m_C\sigma_2^2 + m_B\sigma_{1,2}) = r_A + \vartheta m(\alpha_2[\sigma_2^2 - \sigma_{1,2}] + \sigma_{1,2})$$

$$(17.5b)$$

The expected return required in country A to hold real assets related to country B is $E_t[R_B]$ which is equal to the safe domestic return r_A plus the risk premium which depends on the degree of risk aversion $\vartheta = -U''/U' > 0$, the variances (σ_1^2, σ_2^2) and covariance $(\sigma_{1,2})$ of the two returns.[15] $m = m_B + m_C$ is the degree of openness of the economy and α_1 and α_2 are the regional trade shares, assumed to be equal to shares of investment related to country A and B or C, whereby $\alpha_1 + \alpha_2 = 1$ and $m\alpha_1 = m_B$. Thus, the larger the degree of openness, the larger is the required degree of risk premium on top of the domestic discount rate (*ceteris paribus*). Hence, it is clear that at a given degree of risk aversion small countries must reduce the variance of foreign returns, i.e. exchange rate volatility, if they wish to lower the required expected return and to improve their rate of capital accumulation.[16]

The expected return on the total wealth in country A is, because of 17.5,

$$E[R_A] = m_B E[R_B] + m_C E[R_C] + (1 - m)r_A \qquad (17.6a)$$

with the variance

$$\sigma_{r_A}^2 = m^2[\alpha_1^2\sigma_1^2 + \alpha_2^2\sigma_2 + 2\alpha_1\alpha_2\sigma_{1,2}] = m^2\sigma_A^2 \qquad (17.6b)$$

The term in brackets is an expression for the variance σ_A^2 of the (log of the) real effective exchange rate index.[17]

If authorities in A wish to maximize investment by reducing the required excess return, they have three options.

- They may reduce the degree of openness m. Import-substituting strategies implicitly follow such strategies. In the development literature this has been favoured by the Dependency School. However, for individual national states such 'delinking' would reduce the scope of investment opportunities in equation 17.3. Furthermore, protectionist measures may create distortions, which actually increase the excess return and lead to financial repression. For this reason, delinking policies have been abandoned for export promotion which raises the degree of openness. However, as we will see below, the redistribution of international trade shares, for example by the creation of the European Monetary Union, is a different way of reducing m and could have more beneficial effects on international risk premia.

- They may peg their currency to an anchor and reduce the volatility of one particular exchange rate (say P_1), while the other remains freely floating. This is what I call bloc floating.[18] For the sake of simplicity we will assume a perfect peg where $\sigma_1 = 0$ and therefore also $\sigma_{1,2} = 0$. In reality, as Bénassy-Quéré has demonstrated, it is sufficient to postulate that σ_1 is significantly lower than σ_2.[19]
- they may peg to a basket of currencies and aim to stabilise the real effective exchange rate. This is the essence of the BBC proposal by Williamson and Park/Dornbusch.[20]

Based on equations 17.6b and 17.5b we can now assess the implications of bloc floating versus a basket peg. Table 17.2 shows the structural differences between the two regimes. By applying Table 17.2 to equations 17.5a and 17.5b and substituting into equation 17.3 we obtain aggregate investment under bloc floating:

$$I_A^{BF} = I_A(F_{K_N} - r_A) + I_B(F_{K_B} - r_A) + F_C(F_{K_C} - [r_A + \vartheta m \alpha_2^2]) \text{ for m } \alpha_2 \neq 0 \quad (17.7)$$

Table 17.2 Volatility under bloc floating and basket pegs

Variances	Bloc floating	Basket peg
σ_1^2	0 by definition	$\left(\frac{\alpha_2}{\alpha_1}\right)^2 \sigma_2^2 = \alpha_2^2 \sigma_3^2$
σ_2^2	$\frac{1}{\alpha_2}\sigma_A^2 = \sigma_3^2$	$\left(\frac{\alpha_1}{\alpha_2}\right)^2 \sigma_1^2 = \alpha_1^2 \sigma_3^2$
σ_A^2	$\alpha_2^2 \sigma_2^2 = \alpha_2^2 \sigma_3^2$	0 by definition
Covariances		
$\sigma_{1,2}^2$	0 by definition	$-[\frac{\alpha_1^2}{2\alpha_1\alpha_2}\sigma_1^2 + \frac{\alpha_2^2}{2\alpha_1\alpha_2}\sigma_2^2] < 0$
$\sigma_{A,1}^2$	0 by definition	0 by definition
$\sigma_{A,2}^2$	$-[\frac{1}{2\alpha_2^2}\sigma_A^2 + \frac{1}{2}\sigma_2^2] < 0$	0 by definition
$\sigma_{A,3}^2$	$-\sigma_{A,2}^2 > 0$	0 by definition

Under a perfect bilateral peg between currencies A and B, exchange risk in p_1 is eliminated. However, the exchange rate p_2 with C remains volatile and, given a three-country world, the variance in p_2 is equivalent to the volatility in p_3, i.e. between the currencies of B and C over which A has no control. Therefore, unless A can exert some control over p_2, it is completely at the mercy of exchange policies between B and C (small country case). Thus, a small country A has a strong incentive to diversify into AB economic relations, investing in import and export activities, thereby extending the α_1 share (reducing the α_2) in its portfolio. This will increase overall investment (because of I_B) and simultaneously reduce volatility in the real effective exchange rate (lower σ_A^2), while the volatility with respect to $C(\sigma_2^2)$ rises relative to the real effective exchange rate.[21]

What this analysis shows is that the emergence of currency blocs is the natural outcome when authorities aim at maximizing growth and risk-averse private investors maximize profits. Clearly, this logic must have been underlying the emergence of the EMS/DM zone or the choice of a dollar peg for non-Japanese Asian countries. But while Asia represents the case of small countries pegging to a large country, Europe reflects a strategy of jointly pegging a small currency (the DM) or a basket (the Ecu) in order to gain protection from third currency variations. Obviously, the choice of an anchor currency would depend on its initial weight (α_1) as well as on the elasticity of the investment function ($\partial I_B / \partial E[R_B]$).

Let us now consider the alternative option of a basket peg. Under what conditions is it preferable over an anchor currency peg? Pegging a basket implies stability in the effective exchange rate, i.e. $\sigma_A^2 = 0$. The bilateral volatilities are independently given. In our three-country model this implies that the exchange rates p_1 and p_2 are negatively correlated (see Table 17.2). Consequently, at least part of the risk premium can be diversified away and basket pegging would appear superior to bilateral pegging from an aggregate view. However, the impact of uncertainty on investment depends on the nature of the investor. Only those companies large enough to diversify their market strategies sufficiently to cover non-tradables, importables and exportables, would benefit from stability in the effective exchange rate. Even standard hedging instruments in financial markets cannot eliminate this risk (Huizinga, 1994). An individual investor, whose access to capital is constrained, so that replicating the macro portfolio is not available for her, will choose to expand market penetration where risk is lowest, given identical profit expectations. Under a basket peg we get the investment function:

$$
\begin{aligned}
I_A^{BP} = F_A(r_A) + F_B\left(r_A + \vartheta m \left[\frac{\alpha_1}{2}\sigma_1^2 - \frac{\alpha_2^2}{2\alpha_1}\sigma_2^2 \right] \right) \\
+ F_C\left(r_A + \vartheta m \left[\frac{\alpha_2}{2}\sigma_2^2 - \frac{\alpha_1^2}{2\alpha_2}\sigma_1^2 \right] \right)
\end{aligned}
\tag{17.8}
$$

and the actual impact of the basket peg depends on the two risk premia, as shown in Figure 17.2. The risk premium $u_B = E[R_B] - r_A$ disappears for $\alpha_1 = \sigma_1/(\sigma_1 + \sigma_2)$ and $u_C = E[R_C] - r_A = 0$ if $\alpha_1 = \sigma_2/(\sigma_1 + \sigma_2)$. Above the $45°$-line in Figure 17.2 the risk premium is positive, below it is negative.

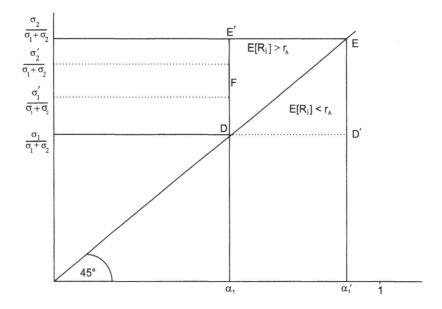

Figure 17.2 Expected and required returns and portfolio shares under basket peg

If we define the exchange rate p_1 with country B by $\sigma_1^2 < \sigma_2^2$, we find that investment in C requires a positive risk premium as long as $E[R_B] = r_A$, i.e. as long as $\alpha_1 = \sigma_1/(\sigma_1 + \sigma_2)$. This is equivalent to the bloc-floating situation and shown in Figure 17.2 by point D and E'. However, under a basket peg, if country A continues to extend its economic ties with B, so that α_1 increases to α_1', the risk premium on C investment falls until it reaches zero at E, while simultaneously the premium on B becomes negative up to point D'. The consequence is a further integration of A's and B's economies with expanding investment and growth and increasing specialization in trade with the less volatile currency zone.

The assumption of exogenous bilateral exchange rate volatilities may apply in the case of small countries with fully liberalized capital markets and no central bank intervention. However, to the degree that a shift from bloc floating to basket pegging implies an increase in σ_1 (authorities intervene less to keep p_1 stable), it is likely to produce reverse effects.

At the given portfolio share α_1, $E[R_B]$ must exceed r_A as shown by point F. Simultaneously, $\sigma_2/(\sigma_1 + \sigma_2)$ might fall to point F', thereby reducing the risk premium in $E[R_C]$. The required expected return on B investment rises and falls for C. This is likely to reduce investment related to B and expand investment to C, reducing therefore α_1. Thus, given that Asia is pegging to the US dollar, switching to a basket peg as recommended by Williamson and Dornbusch/Park would reduce its trade shares with the dollar zone and presumably extend them with Japan and Europe.

The net effect on aggregate investment and growth depends on the specific investment functions $I_B(F_{K_B} - E[R_B])$ and $I_C(F_{K_C} - E[R_C])$. It can, however, not be excluded that the switch from a single currency peg to a basket peg might narrow growth opportunities if the marginal investment functions are unequal, such as $I'_B > I'_C$, which is likely to be the case if B is a large country (like the USA) and C is small (like Japan). On the other hand, if C is the same size or larger than B (say euro zone versus dollar zone) the basket peg might improve capital accumulation in A (Asia). Thus, both Asia and Europe would benefit directly from Asia adopting a basket peg, while the USA and Japan would profit from derived income effects.

Ultimately what matters is how exchange rate regimes affect volatility. Under a basket peg the determinants are (σ_1 and σ_2. However, in the small country case, where A cannot influence p_3, both bilateral exchange rate volatilities (σ_1^2 *and* σ_2^2) are a function of the variance of the exchange rate between the two international currencies, σ_3^2 (see Table 17.2). Therefore, exchange rate stability and capital accumulation in a small Asian country will depend ultimately on the volatility of key currencies. If, however, currency blocs congeal around key currencies as a consequence of bloc floating, the capacity of anchor countries to use exchange rates as an adjustment tool in case of fundamental disequilibria will be restrained. The next section will demonstrate that bloc floating will increase the volatility of the equilibrium exchange rate of key currencies as a trade-off to lower volatility within monetary blocs.

3   The consequences of bloc floating for equilibrium exchange rates in a bloc-floating regime

The fundamental equilibrium exchange rate is defined as the rate at which external and internal balances are simultaneously achieved. As in the previous section, we will model bloc floating by keeping one exchange rate (P_1) fixed and given with $\sigma_1 = 0$, the other (P_2) flexible and bearing the thrust of adjustment.[22]

3.1   *External balance*

A world of three countries (A, B, C) has the trade matrix shown in Table 17.3.

AB (Y_B, P_1) describes the volume of exports (denominated in domestic currency) by country A to country B as a function of income in B (Y_B) and the relative price (P_1) between the two countries.

We obtain the following equation for A's trade balance:

$$T^A = AB(Y_B, P_1) + AC(Y_C, P_2) - P_1 \cdot BA(Y_A, P_1) - P_2 \cdot CA(Y_A, P_2)$$

$$(17.9)$$

Table 17.3 Trade matrix in a three-country world

Exports by	Imports to A	B	C	Σ
A	–	AB (Y_B, P_1) $++$	AC (Y_C, P_2) $++$	X_A
B	BA (Y_A, P_1) $+-$	–	BC (Y_C, P_3) $+-$	X_B
C	CA (Y_A, P_2) $+-$	CB (Y_B, P_3) $+-$	–	X_C
Σ	M_A	M_B	M_C	

The relative import shares are assumed to be identical with our previous foreign wealth portfolio shares in equation 17.5:

$$\alpha_1 = \frac{P_1 \cdot BA}{M_A}; \quad \alpha_2 = \frac{P_2 \cdot CA}{M_A} \quad \alpha_1 + \alpha_2 = 1 \tag{17.10}$$

Marginal imports are distributed in the same proportion as total imports and the marginal propensity to import is equal to the average propensity and the degree of openness:

$$m = \frac{M_A}{Y_A} = \frac{\partial M_A}{\partial Y_A} = \frac{\alpha_1 M_A + \alpha_2 M_A}{Y_A} = \alpha_1 \frac{\partial M_A}{\partial Y_A} + \alpha_2 \frac{\partial M_A}{\partial Y_A} \tag{17.11}$$

Writing for $\partial BA / \partial Y_A = BA_Y$, we have

$$P_1 \cdot BA_Y = \alpha_1 m \quad ; \quad P_2 \cdot CA_Y = \alpha_2 m \tag{17.12}$$

Thus, adjustment in the trade balance depends on two relative price variables. Ordinary textbook models take the effective exchange rate as the adjustment instrument. Exchange risk would then appear as the variance of the effective exchange risk and under an ideal basket peg ($\sigma_1 = 0$) the model becomes deterministic. However, we are here interested in analysing the effects of bloc floating for the determination of equilibrium exchange rates. Bloc floating implies that A pegs its exchange rate to the anchor currency, so that its relative prices (say P_1) are fixed (domestic prices are assumed constant). The exchange rate to the third country (P_2) remains flexible and will become the sole instrument for exchange rate adjustment.[23] It is clear that the impact of a variation of P_2 is small when the share of trade denominated in the flexible exchange rate (α_2) is small. This implies that in order to obtain a given adjustment effect from the variation of the real effective exchange rate, the flexible price has to vary by the factor of $1/\alpha_2$.[24] Given that $0 < \alpha_2 < 1$, P_2 will need larger variations than if $\alpha_2 = 1$. In other words, the larger the regional currency zone (α_1) the larger will be the required change in the flexible bilateral exchange rate (P_2).

The volatility of the effective exchange rate will fall with the extension of a currency bloc around country A, i.e. with rising α_1 because σ_1 and σ_{12} are low (in our model equal to zero). In order to show the impact of bloc floating on the economies' equilibrium, we will now determine the response of the trade balance to a change in relative prices. By differentiating 17.9 we obtain:[25]

$$T_{P_2}^A = \frac{\partial T^A}{\partial P_2} = AC_{P_2} - CA - P_2 \cdot CA_{P_2} = \alpha_2 M_A(\varepsilon_{C/A} + \varepsilon_{A/C} - 1)$$

$$(17.13a)$$

A rise in the relative price of imports from country C, i.e. a depreciation of A's currency, will improve the trade balance provided the Marshall–Lerner condition ($\varepsilon_{C/A} + \varepsilon_{A/C} - 1 > 0$) is fulfilled. However, the impact depends also on the trade weight α_2.

Assuming income in countries B and C constant (no repercussion effects), we also have the import propensity in country A which is, given our assumptions, reflecting the economy's degree of openness as from equations 17.5–17.5b):

$$T_Y^A = \frac{\partial T^A}{\partial Y} = -m$$

$$(17.13b)$$

The fundamental equilibrium exchange rate is defined as the simultaneous achievement of *internal* and *external balance*. In its simplest form, assuming no foreign assets, external balance implies $T^A = 0$. Williamson (1991) objects to this on the grounds that countries may benefit from exporting or importing capital over long periods. External balance then represents a target value T^* for long-term sustainable current accounts. As we will see, this is relevant for the position of the external balance equilibrium curve, but not for its slope. Thus, under bloc floating, the required adjustment by P_2 to an exogenous demand shock in A is:

$$\left.\frac{dP_2}{dY}\right|_{EB} = -\frac{T_Y^A}{T_{P_2}^A} = \frac{m}{\alpha_2 M_A(\varepsilon_{C/A} + \varepsilon_{A/C} - 1)}$$

$$(17.14)$$

As is well known, the depreciation required to keep the current account in balance after a demand shock is larger, the larger the degree of openness, i.e. the larger the import propensity (m), and the lower the import and export price elasticities. But in addition to these textbook results, the required price adjustment must increase with the extend of bloc floating, for the larger the trade zone with fixed exchange α_1, the smaller will be α_2 and only P_2 is free to adjust. Thus, a small open economy with a large degree of bloc floating will require very large changes in the flexible exchange rate in order to achieve external balance.

3.2 Internal balance

Internal balance represents the equilibrium in the domestic goods market when planned spending by domestic residents (absorption) plus net exports equals the highest level of activity consistent with continued control of inflation (Williamson, 1991).

Given that equilibrium output is:

$$E(Y) + T^A(P_1, P_2, Y_A) - Y = 0 \qquad (17.15)$$

with the marginal propensity to spend: $1 > \partial E / \partial Y = 1 - s > 0$, and defining the target income compatible with NAIRU as Y^*, we obtain the internal balance equation

$$E(Y) + T^A(P_1, P_2, Y) - Y^* = 0 \qquad (17.15a)$$

with the slopes:

$$\left.\frac{dP_1}{dy}\right|_{IB} = -\frac{1 - s - m}{\alpha_1 m_A(\varepsilon_{B/A} + \varepsilon_{A/B} - 1)} = 0 \qquad (17.16)$$

which is equal to zero under bloc-floating and

$$\left.\frac{dP_2}{dy}\right|_{IB} = -\frac{1 - s - m}{\alpha_2 m_A(\varepsilon_{C/A} + \varepsilon_{A/C} - 1)} > 0 \qquad (17.16a)$$

which takes all the load of adjustment. Again bloc floating amplifies the required price adjustment effect, although a high degree of openness (m) mitigates this impact.

3.3 Fundamental equilibrium

Figure 17.3 shows the locus of points compatible with internal balance on the IB line. It is downward sloping as a lower (less competitive) real exchange rate reduces net exports and has to be offset by higher spending to keep output constant. External balance is drawn by the EB line. It is upward sloping for higher net exports resulting from real depreciation to be compensated by higher domestic spending and imports to keep the trade balance constant (Williamson, 1994: 189).

300

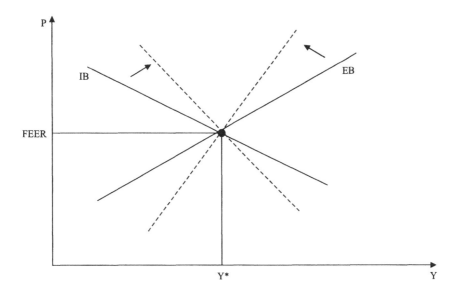

Figure 17.3 Fundamental equilibrium

Full macroeconomic balance is achieved at the intersection of both curves, determining the fundamental equilibrium exchange rate (FEER) at the equilibrium income level. In Williamson's interpretation of normative FEERs, the IB curve would shift with changes in the NAIRU-compatible activity level (Y^*) and the EB line with a change in terms of trade or current account targets (T^*).[26] Consequently, FEERs are not constant or equal to one, as postulated by purchasing power parity.[27] This is relevant for our model of bloc floating. Equations 17.14 and 17.16a show that as the slopes of the IB and the EB lines become steeper, the smaller the trade share α_2. If P_1 is fixed and only P_2 is free to adjust, the latter has to move more to produce the same effect. Thus, any change in non-inflationary equilibrium income, terms of trade or current account targets will require a higher rate of change in the FEER. This is formally shown by the simultaneous satisfaction of the internal and external balance equilibrium conditions.

Internal balance : $E^A(Y_A) + T^A(P_1, P_2, Y_A) - Y^* = 0$

External balance : $T^A(P_1, P_2, Y_A) - T^* = 0$ (17.17)

Both equations having continuous derivatives, the system satisfies the conditions of the implicit-function theorem with the Jacobian[28]

$$J = \begin{vmatrix} 1 - s - m & \alpha_2(\varepsilon_{A/C} + \varepsilon_{C/A} - 1) \\ -m & \alpha_2(\varepsilon_{A/C} + \varepsilon_{C/A} - 1) \end{vmatrix} = (1 - s) \cdot \alpha_2(\varepsilon_{A/C} + \varepsilon_{C/A} - 1) > 0$$

After totally differentiating both equations in 17.17 and keeping either Y^* or T^* constant we obtain the two sets of solutions:

$$\left.\frac{dP_2}{dT^*}\right|_{Y^*=constant} = \frac{1-s-m}{(1-s)\alpha_2(\varepsilon_{C/A}+\varepsilon_{A/C}-1)} \; ; \; \left.\frac{dY}{dT^*}\right|_{Y^*=constant} = \frac{1}{1-s}$$

$$(17.18a)$$

$$\left.\frac{dP_2}{dY^*}\right|_{Y^*=constant} = \frac{m}{(1-s)\alpha_2(\varepsilon_{C/A}+\varepsilon_{A/C}-1)} \; ; \; \left.\frac{dY}{dY^*}\right|_{T^*=constant} = \frac{1}{1-s}$$

$$(17.18b)$$

Thus, not surprisingly, an increase in the two target variables for NAIRU income (Y^*) or the desired current account (T^*) will raise equilibrium income (Y) by the multiplier effect $1/(1-s)$. However, the price effect depends on the degree of openness (m) and on the size of currency bloc ($\alpha_2 = 1 - \alpha_1$). *Ceteris paribus*, if m is low, an increase in the current account target (T^*) requires a higher increase in P_2 (a higher devaluation) than if A imports and exports a large part of its income: given the small volume of foreign trade, the price channel would have to work harder in order to achieve the same numbers. By contrast, an increase in NAIRU-compatible income requires larger appreciations if the degree of openness is high, in order to keep fundamental equilibrium. However, in either direction the price effect of bloc floating ($\alpha_2 < 1$) is clearly higher than in an ordinary two-country model with fully flexible exchange rates (where $\alpha_2 = 1$). This proves formally that bloc floating renders the fundamental equilibrium exchange rate more volatile. The increased exchange rate stability *within* the currency bloc comes with the trade-off of higher instability *between* the currency blocs. One may call this the '*enlargening effect*' of bloc floating on the equilibrium exchange rate.

The literature on foreign exchange rates has focused on overshooting and magnification effects. *Overshooting*, first formalized by Dornbusch (1976), describes a temporary deviation by the nominal exchange rate from the long-term equilibrium exchange rate which is due to rapid adjustment in financial markets and sticky goods prices. The *magnification effect* (Bilson, 1979) shows that the nominal exchange rate will respond more than proportionately to a change in money supply if today's monetary policy stance creates expectations of further increases in money supply in the future. The *enlargening effect* described here in a bloc-floating model is of a different order: it enlarges the effect of the variation in the *equilibrium* exchange rate, rather than the observed exchange rate.

Referring back to equations 17.4 and 17.4a we find that the volatility in equilibrium exchange rates directly affects the level of required returns. By inserting equation 17.18a and 17.18b into 17.4 and given Note 8 we obtain the required excess return (risk premium):

$$
\begin{aligned}
E(u_C) = r_C - r_A &+ \frac{1 - s - m}{(1 - s)\alpha_2(\varepsilon_{C/A} + \varepsilon_{A/C} - 1)} \cdot \frac{dT^*}{P_2} \\
&+ \frac{m}{(1 - s)\alpha_2(\varepsilon_{A/C} + \varepsilon_{C/A} - 1)} \cdot \frac{dY^*}{P_2} = \mu_C
\end{aligned}
\tag{17.19}
$$

Given that α_2 tends towards zero with increasing currency blocs, the expected mean value for u_C increases for given shocks dT^* and dY^*. In other words, bloc floating drives an increasingly large wedge between the real returns in the two currency areas and reduces investment.

What about uncertainty? If market participants use all available information and on average predict the fundamentals of the necessary exchange rate adjustments correctly, then $u_C = \mu_C$ and the expected forecasting error is zero $E[\varepsilon_C] = 0$. However, the variance of the required excess return, which depends on the variance of the real exchange rate would increase with bloc floating. If market participants base their expectations on information available in the previous period such that $E(u_t|\Omega_{t-1})$ and given that $\alpha_{2_{t-1}} \subset \Omega_{t-1}$, then $E(u_t|\Omega_{t-1}) < u_t$ for $\alpha_{2_t} < \alpha_{2_{t-1}}$. Even if the mean forecast error $E(\varepsilon)$ is zero in the long run, we obtain short-run error persistence measured by $(u_t - E[u_t])^2 = \varepsilon_t^2 > 0$ being autocorrelated. However, given that $E(\varepsilon) = 0$, we have $var(\varepsilon_t) = E(\varepsilon_t^2) = h_t = \sigma_t^2 > \sigma_{t-1}^2$. Thus, uncertainty measured by the conditional variance also rises with bloc floating.

Changes in the fundamental equilibrium therefore have a direct consequence for the level of 'safe' domestic returns, which are compatible with the risky required returns from investing in tradables. But the nature of the currency peg matters. For example, a higher current account target will require a devaluation of A's currency. This will either push $E[R_N]$ up[29] (small country case) or allow A to accept investment in C which is less profitable in local currency, but achieves the necessary return via the appreciation of C's currency (large country). Because of the arbitrage this extends to $E(R_B)$. If A has pegged to a 'large' anchor currency, the currency bloc remains unaffected by the new foreign exchange objective and its local $E[R_N]$ and $E[R_B]$ returns stay constant. But investment (and trade) would increase with C because of the premium resulting from C's currency appreciation (as long as expectations last!). Finally, if A has pegged to a basket of small currencies which are unable to impose their domestic return as the international standard, then both $E(R_N)$ and $E(R_B)$ will increase. Investment will then fall within the currency bloc ($I_N + I_B$), but increase towards C (I_C). The net effect for growth is a priori uncertain. A higher level of non-inflationary income (Y^*) has a similar effect. The net impact of changes in the fundamental

303

objectives of internal and external balance depends, of course, on the respective policy objectives.

Thus, ignorance about bloc floating increases risk and required excess returns. We may conclude that the phenomenon of bloc floating has negative repercussions all over the world by raising required returns due to greater exchange rate uncertainty and lower investment and growth. The paradox is that the larger the uncertainty, the larger is the incentive to reduce it by choosing to peg one's currency to an anchor, which will further increase uncertainty in the world.

The negative consequences of bloc floating do not depend on whether we assume rational expectations or 'limited rationality'. From a 'fundamentalist' point of view, exchange rates reflect volatility in fundamentals and bloc floating would translate into excess returns (u_i). For example, during the 1980s it would have taken increasing amplitudes in the DM/dollar exchange rate in order to correct the growing American balance of payments deficit and the German trade balance surplus. Investors would have taken this into account when forming opinions on their returns ($E[R_N], E[R_C]$). Alternatively, taking a 'limited rationality' approach, more volatile fundamental equilibrium exchange rates would increase uncertainty about the 'right' exchange rate, leading to adjustment inertia and serial correlation in ε_c. We would observe the well-known clusters of exchange rate volatility with heteroskedasticity in the error term of excess returns. In this case it is the equilibrium that 'drifts away' from the spot rate until the adjustment gap becomes sufficiently important. The spot rate would increasingly resemble a random walk.

What conclusions can we derive from our model for the emerging currencies in Asia and Europe?

The economic development of Asia's high-performing countries has been supported by integration into the world economy on the basis of a dollar peg. There are signs of decreasing returns from this strategy. The negative American trade balance and protectionist pressures make further penetration of the US market more difficult. Economies of scale could be reaped by Asian countries from diversifying into other currency blocs. Williamson and Dornbusch/Park therefore suggest a basket peg. As we have seen, a basket peg can give some partial protection against exchange uncertainty, provided certain conditions are met. Even if most East Asian countries are economically 'small', capital markets are not fully liberalized, and the competitiveness of exchange rate *levels* (rather than volatility) takes an important role in policy strategies. It is therefore doubtful that the requirements for increased investment under a basket peg are met. But even if they are, it is uncertain that they would translate into higher investment, given the trade-off between the internal and external balance requirements. A simulation by Cours *et al.* (1996) confirms this conclusion. Under these conditions it would appear that small European countries had more to gain from pegging to the Deutsche Mark in the past, than Asian countries would benefit today from a common basket peg.

Europe is not an example to be followed by Asia. But the emergence of a European currency bloc has made exchange rates between the three major world currencies more volatile and thereby contributed to the reduction of investment worldwide. How will this situation be affected by the creation of the European Monetary Union?

The first point to retain is the fact that EMU is not a currency bloc: the Euro will be a new and large currency, managed by a single, unified monetary authority. This eliminates exchange risk in Europe. Consequently, the size of the European currency bloc will fall: by integrating intra-European trade under one currency, relative world trade shares change. Intra-EU trade becomes domestic trade, thereby reducing the degree of openness of European economies. While on average this degree was 26.4 per cent in 1992, the non-EU trade share was only 10.7 per cent (Table 17.4). Thus, the parameter m in equations 17.5a and 17.5b would be more than halved for the European Union.

From equations 17.5a and 17.5b we know that a reduction in the degree of openness would reduce excess returns required to compensate for the exchange risk impact. Consequently, expected required returns would fall in Europe and stimulate investment. Given that the euro-market will be large, this should also reduce required domestic returns $E[R_N]$ and launch a new growth process which would then have repercussions in Asia and America.

Table 17.4 Openness of European Union

	Imports from the EC as % of GDP		Imports extra EU as % of GDP		EU Imports as % of total	
	1963	1997	1963	1997	1963	1997
B**	23.0	43.2	11.9	14.5	66.67	74.92
DK	17.6	17.6	9.5	8.2	65.00	68.29
D	6.8	11.7	6.8	9.2	50.00	55.77
GR	9.4	16.5	5.7	6.6	62.50	71.31
E	5.4	14.8	5.4	8.1	50.00	64.74
F	5.0	11.3	5.5	7.3	47.56	60.86
IRL	27.3	30.8	9.1	23.4	75.00	56.91
I	6.2	10.1	7.0	7.5	47.14	57.42
NL	25.2	25.4	13.3	16.6	66.07	60.46
P	9.1	26.5	9.1	9.7	50.00	73.14
UK	4.75	12.3	11.00	11.3	30.16	52.12
EUR 15+	8.3	14.5	7.9	9.5	50.2	62.32
USA			2.8	11.5		
Japan			9.7	8.7		

** shares for Belgium incl. Luxembourg

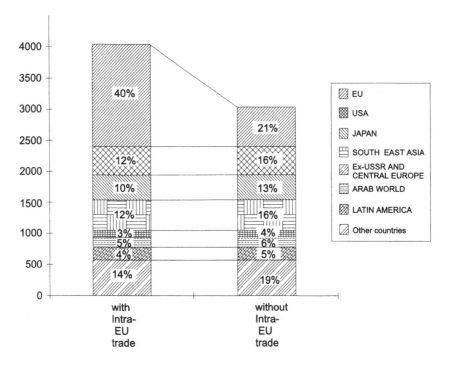

Figure 17.4 World exports and relative export shares with and without intra-EU trade in $ billion (1994)

Source: CHELEM Data Base (1996), CEPII, Paris.

Furthermore, with the subtraction of intra-EU trade from world trade, European relative trade shares (α_1, α_2, ...) will get redistributed (see Figure 17.4). However, for other countries nothing changes: Asia, Japan and the USA will still export the same volumes to the different regions in the world, although their relative shares in total world trade will increase. But now they will deal with an integrated α_{EU} instead of separate portfolio shares for each European country. This would further reduce exchange rate risk for them and open opportunities for increased returns from trade with Europe. These effects from European Monetary Union are unambiguously positive, for they cause a structural reduction of exchange risk in the world economy which is likely to translate into greater growth.

What about shock-induced exchange rate volatility? The impact from changes in the fundamental equilibrium exchange rate on the arbitrage of deterministic returns depends on the respective price elasticities in equations 17.18a and 17.18b: fundamental exchange rate volatility between the US dollar, the yen and the Euro would depend on the net effect of internal and external balance shocks. Their outcome is a priori uncertain. However, a reduction in Europe's degree of openness (m) would require *larger* exchange rate variations for the Euro exchange rate in response to changing current account targets, but *less* variations due to changes in income and growth objectives. Europe would regain a degree of policy autonomy which it has presently lost. In other words, Europe becomes more autonomous from exchange rate movements, and monetary policy would focus more on domestic interest rates. It is therefore possible that the future European monetary authorities will follow an exchange rate policy of 'benign neglect' with respect to the external balance. This could lower required expected returns and stimulate investment worldwide.[30] Given that large Euro financial markets should make it easier to finance external deficits and to lend surpluses, such a policy of benign neglect should become more easily manageable than it has even been for the DM.

4   Empirical evidence of bloc-floating effects

Empirical confirmation for the theoretical considerations in Sections 2 and 3 focus on the questions: is there evidence of currency blocs and can we find indicators for increased exchange rate risk and volatility?

As mentioned in the introduction, the emergence of currency blocs is well documented by Frankel and Wei (1993) and Bénassy-Quéré. It is not only clear that exchange rate variability is lower within regional groupings than across groups, but also that the trade-weighted share of currency blocs has changed. In particular the DM bloc has doubled in size during the existence of the European Monetary System (EMS). Frankel and Wei have shown that international trade is biased towards intra-regional partners which is consistent with the model developed in Section 2. However, based on their cross-country studies they detect only a very limited impact of exchange rate variability on trade volume. Rana (1981) found that volatility had negative effects on import volumes in the case of South Korea, Taiwan and the Philippines. Kenen and Rodrik (1986) used time series to find that in seven out of eleven industrialized countries volatility terms had the expected negative impact on imports, with statistically significant values for the United States, Canada, Germany and the UK, i.e. four currencies that were freely floating. Furthermore, their volatility coefficients were substantially higher than those for domestic activity and in most cases higher than the log of the real effective exchange rate index. We may conclude from this evidence that exchange rate volatility matters to trade, although it is not clear how much.

In this chapter we have taken investment and growth rather than trade as the relevant macroeconomic variable. Also, the relevant group of goods comprises tradables and not trade itself. Given the complexities of determining these variables, we will not pursue the empirical validation of this hypothesis here and focus on exchange rate volatility. Can we detect confirmation of bloc-floating effects in indicators of volatility?

We have put forward the hypothesis that bloc floating increases the volatility in the fundamental equilibrium of the bilateral floating exchange rate and simultaneously reduces the volatility of the effective exchange rate, although not as much or in the same way as a pure basket peg. This falling volatility in the effective exchange rate goes beyond the portfolio effect, as shown by Figure 17.1a. The reason is that shocks to fundamental variables require larger adjustment in the flexible exchange rate. The problem with empirical verification is that we are unable to observe the equilibrium rate directly. Furthermore, as Barrell *et al.* (1998) show, deviations of observable spot rates from FEERs can be rather persistent. We therefore need a theory explaining the link between observable exchange rates and FEERs. This is no easy task, although we have two models: the rational expectation hypothesis and the limited rationality assumption. In the first case we should observe an increase of the variance or standard deviation of the spot rate going in parallel with the agglomeration of currency blocs. In the second case we should find a higher frequency of outlier exchange rates around the mean, i.e. the density function of the exchange rate has increasing probability weights in its tails. They can be measured by excess kurtosis.[31] A third approach, somewhat in between, would accept rational expectations in the long run and limited rationality in the short term. This implies that the mean forecasting error in the effective exchange rate is zero in the long run, but its variance is conditional on the past. If the regional currency bloc is large, the forecasting error in the effective exchange rate should be lower than if it is small, given that the peg conditions expectations. However, if the size of the bloc varies, the conditional variance should rise with rising bloc size. It follows that we must check for possible bloc-floating effects by testing these three hypotheses:

1 Bilateral volatility between anchor currencies must be increasing relative to effective exchange rates (fundamentalist view).
2 The weight in the tails of the probability distribution of exchange rate changes must increase with the trade weight of currency zones in the world economy (limited rationality).
3 The conditional variance of the real effective exchange rates exhibits lower error persistence and higher serial correlation with past variances for countries with large and increasing currency blocs than for those whose exchange rates float freely.

We will proceed as follows: first we will look at some casual, visual evidence for exchange rate volatility. Then we will compare different statistical indicators of volatility. Finally, we will compare conditional volatility coefficients derived from a GARCH model.

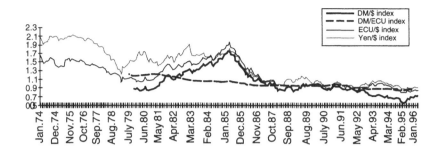

Figure 17.5 Nominal exchange rate indices

Sources: Bank for International Settlements (1996), Electronic Data Base, Basle; International Financial Statistics (1996), International Monetary Fund, Washington, DC.

To start, Figure 17.5. shows the evolution of nominal exchange rate indices for key currencies. Most remarkable is the stability in intra-European exchange rates, reflected by the DM/Ecu rate and the high variability between the key world currencies. The first decade after Bretton Woods appears to be marked by lower short-term volatility but substantial medium-term swings (misalignments). The second decade shows higher short-term volatility, though greater stability in trends, at least after the Louvre Accord in 1987. Both the yen and, to a lesser extent, the DM reveal a long-term trend to appreciate vis-à-vis the US dollar.

Figures 17.6 (a, b, c) show a twelve-month moving average of the standard deviation of real exchange rate changes for the two bilateral as well as the effective exchange rate for each country in real terms. The time series show the familiar cluster pattern around certain periods. Periods of large volatility are followed by periods of relative tranquillity. In Gemany, REER volatility is falling as expected with the emergence of the EMS, although ERM realignments can sometimes (1981/2, 1992/3) have disturbing effects. Not

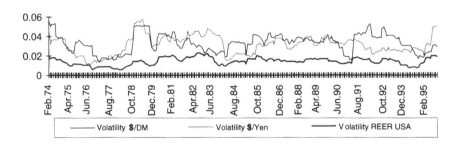

Figure 17.6a Volatility of real exchange rates, bilateral and effective, USA

Sources: As Figure 17.5.

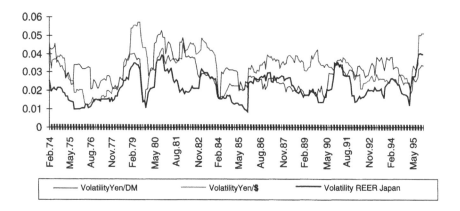

Figure 17.6b Volatility of real exchange rates, bilateral and effective, Japan
Sources: As Figure 17.5.

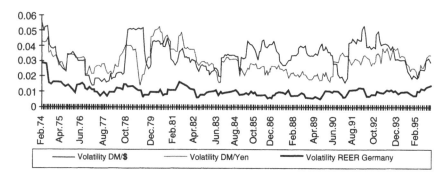

Figure 17.6c Volatility of real exchange rates, bilateral and effective, Germany
Source: As Figure 17.5.

surprisingly bilateral exchange rate volatility in the USA and Germany is always higher than the effective rate's. In Japan, the absence of a currency zone contributes to the higher effective exchange rate volatility. Nevertheless, there seems to be a tendency to privilege stabilization of the yen/dollar over the yen/DM rate. Although the shock absorbing portfolio-effect of the effective exchange rates is observable at certain periods, it is significantly less marked than for Germany and the USA. America finally appears indifferent between exchange rates with Japan and Europe, although the existence of a dollar zone contributes generally to lower real effective exchange rate volatility. We may take this as an indicator of additional intra-bloc exchange rate stability resulting from dollar and DM currency blocs. Given the large DM bloc, the German REER is relatively stable. Without a yen zone, Japan's REER is most volatile. The USA occupies an intermediary position with a smaller and more stable currency bloc (30 per cent) than Germany (up to 47 per cent).

This picture is reinforced by calculating relative volatilities as the ratio of real bilateral rates and the national REER (Figures 17.7 a, b, c). Bilateral

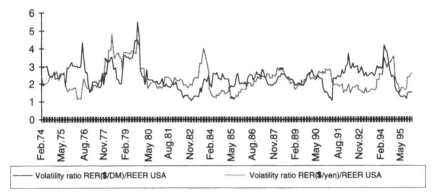

Figure 17.7a Relative volatility of bilateral real exchange rates to REER, USA
Sources: As Figure 17.5.

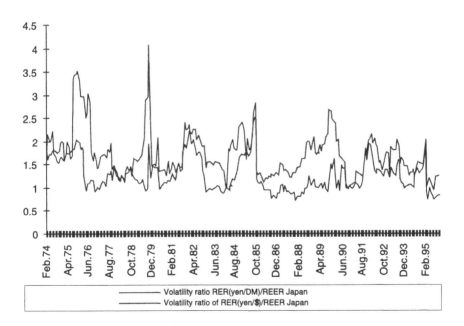

Figure 17.7b Relative volatility of bilateral real exchange rates to REER, Japan
Sources: As Figure 17.5.

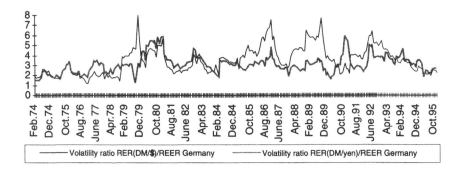

Figure 17.7c Relative volatility of bilateral real exchange rates to REER, Germany
Sources: As Figure 17.5.

volatility is clearly higher than REER volatility in Germany and the USA and it is rising for Germany, as one would expect, given the expansion of the EMS. Only in the EMS crisis-ridden 1990s does this index come down. For the United States, bilateral volatility is greatest in the late 1970s when confidence in the dollar was deteriorating. In the late 1980s, when the dollar zone shrank and the Plaza and Louvre Accords led to exchange rate interventions, bilateral volatility somewhat receded. Finally for Japan, whose currency does not serve as a monetary anchor, bilateral and effective exchange rates vary to a quite similar degree.

These observations are in line with the hypothesis derived from bloc-floating theory, although they are not sufficient to 'prove' positively a bloc-floating effect. It is obvious that other factors, such as monetary policy, central bank interventions and political events can have a significant effect on observed exchange rate volatility.

In order to catch the medium-term effects of these developments and to distinguish between rational expectations and limited rationality, it may be more appropriate to cover larger periods than twelve-month moving averages. I have taken the time intervals defined by Bénassy-Quéré for dollar appreciations and depreciations, and submitted the first differences of the log of the exchange rates to a normality test (see Table 17.5).

In a fundamentalist model, the standard deviation for Germany's REER should fall and for bilateral rates increase, given that Germany's currency bloc doubles in size over the twenty years. Clearly, this is the case for the German REER and the US dollar, but it is less obvious for the DM/yen exchange rate. The limited rationality model, on the other hand, would correspond to increases of kurtosis in the probability distribution of exchange rate changes. It seems primarily to explain German developments in the 1990s when the EMS went through significant turbulences. In the USA, the REER standard deviation remains fairly constant, which corresponds to a stable dollar zone.

Table 17.5 Normality test of monthly variations of logarithmic real exchange rates and REERs ((H 0 = N(0, 1))

Sample size		March 1974–October 1978 56	November 1978–February 1985 76	March 1985–April 1990 62	May 1990–May 1995 61
GERMANY					
d(ln(REER Germany))	Mean	−0.058	−0.288	0.131	0.191
	Standard deviation	1.273	1.014	0.852	0.968
	Excess kurtosis	−0.399	0.274	−0.211	0.279
d(ln(DM/$))	Mean	−1.049	0.613	−1.312	−0.302
	Standard deviation	2.743	3.266	3.551	3.470
	Excess kurtosis	3.683	0.591	−0.500	2.176
Bilateral/effective	Ratio st. deviation	2.155	3.220	4.169	3.583
	Ratio ex. kurtosis	−9.241	2.160	2.370	7.812
d(ln(DM/yen))	Mean	−0.183	0.379	−0.309	0.908
	Standard deviation	2.861	3.484	2.473	3.190
	Excess kurtosis	0.348	0.177	−0.283	−0.663
Bilateral/effective	Ratio st. deviation	2.248	3.434	2.903	3.294
	Ratio ex. kurtosis	−0.872	0.647	1.341	−2.380
UNITED STATES					
d(ln(REER USA))	Mean	−0.307	0.558	−0.556	−0.195
	Standard deviation	1.029	1.580	1.584	1.473
	Excess kurtosis	0.239	0.119	−0.643	0.464
d(ln($/DM))	Mean	1.049	−0.613	1.312	0.302
	Standard deviation	2.743	3.266	3.551	3.470
	Excess kurtosis	3.683	0.591	−0.500	2.176
Bilateral/effective	Ratio st. deviation	2.667	2.067	2.242	2.355
	Ratio ex. kurtosis	15.400	4.958	0.778	4.688

Table 17.5 Contd.

		March 1974– October 1978 56	November 1978– February 1985 76	March 1985– April 1990 62	May 1990– May 1995 61
Sample size					
d(ln($/yen))	Mean	0.866	−0.234	1.003	1.210
	Standard deviation	2.756	3.557	3.576	2.788
	Excess kurtosis	1.745	0.714	−0.625	−0.027
Bilateral/effective	Ratio st. deviation	2.679	2.251	2.258	1.893
	Ratio ex. kurtosis	7.295	5.988	0.973	−0.059
JAPAN					
d(ln(REER Japan))	Mean	0.708	−0.357	0.172	0.797
	Standard deviation	1.857	2.823	2.503	2.328
	Excess kurtosis	−0.119	1.398	0.569	−0.004
d(ln(yen/DM))	Mean	0.183	−0.379	0.309	−0.908
	Standard deviation	2.861	3.484	2.473	3.190
	Excess kurtosis	0.348	0.177	−0.283	0.663
Bilateral/effective	Ratio st. deviation	−1.540	1.234	0.988	1.370
	Ratio ex. kurtosis	−2.910	0.127	−0.497	154.752
d(ln(yen/$))	Mean	−0.866	0.234	−1.003	−1.210
	Standard deviation	2.756	3.557	3.576	2.788
	Excess kurtosis	1.745	0.714	−0.625	−0.027
Bilateral/effective	Ratio st. deviation	1.484	1.260	1.429	1.198
	Ratio ex. kurtosis	−14.605	0.511	−1.099	6.403

Source: Author's calculations based on IMF data.

Limited rationality seems to have been at work during the dollar overvaluation in 1978–85. Finally, Japan suffers from high exchange rate instability without any clear tendency, although this is reflected more in the standard deviation than in excess kurtosis.

These indicators give credit to limited rationality at least at certain periods but not in all. We should be able to detect a more differentiated behaviour by using a GARCH process to model conditional volatility. The hypothesis of bloc floating implies that the expected variance of the next period depends on the size of the currency bloc in this period. If agents behave rationally they would take all available information and therefore they would use the conditional distribution of exchange rate observations for forecasting purposes and consequently for the required return on investment. The historical variance (or standard deviation) would be inconsistent with such behaviour. As discussed in the previous section, we would assume that rational agents avoid systematic errors so that:

$$E_{t-1}[u_t] = E[u_t | \Omega_{t-1}] = \mu_t$$
$$\varepsilon_t = u_t - \mu_t, E(\varepsilon_t) = 0 \text{ and } var\ (\varepsilon_t) = E(\varepsilon_t^2) = h_t$$

$$(17.20)$$

Under a credible currency peg, $E_t(dp_t)$ is equal to the preannounced (fixed or crawling) exchange rate (with $E(\varepsilon) = 0$) and fluctuations will be random and uncorrelated to the past with the variance σ_ε^2. Hence the error process is white noise. If, however, the equilibrium exchange rate responds with larger variances to random shocks (e.g. dT^*, dY^*) because of increasing weights of currency blocs ($\alpha_2 \rightarrow 0$), then the error term becomes autoregressive, as we have seen in the last section. Furthermore, uncertainty is itself increasing and this is reflected in a rising variance for the error term. On the other hand, for countries with a large currency bloc, the exchange rate is less likely to be an adjustment tool. Consequently, forecasting errors should be smaller and less persistent. Hence the GARCH model description would be (Bollerslev, 1986):

$$\varepsilon_t = u_t - \mu_t = \nu_\varepsilon \sqrt{h_t}$$
$$\varepsilon_t | \Omega_{t-1} \sim t(0, h_t, \kappa)$$
$$h_t = a_0 + \sum_{i=1}^{p} a_i \varepsilon_{t-i}^2 + \sum_{j=1}^{q} b_j h_{t-1}$$

The forecast error depends on white noise shocks (ν_t) in this period, presumably dT^*, dY^* or other factors, and the conditional variance h_t, which is a function of squared previous forecast errors and past variances. A t-distribution was chosen as it seemed to fit better than a normal.

The first step consists in formulating the mean equation by choosing the best-fitting ARMA model. In the second step, the GARCH approach of Bollerslev (1986) is implemented. To prevent the coefficients and therefore the variance h from becoming negative we imposed a linearly declining structure on the a-coefficients, following Engle (1982). Past residuals are given less weight the larger the distance to the present period.

If the currency bloc is large, error persistence, i.e. Σa_i, must be low for the real effective exchange rate and the variance impact (Σb_i) large. The opposite applies to REERs of countries with no currency bloc. Given these considerations, we should expect that Germany, forming the largest currency bloc, would have higher b-coefficients for its REER and lowest a-coefficients; the Japanese REER would exhibit the opposite and the USA would stay between these two countries. Table 17.6 gives the results.[32]

Table 17.6 GARCH (p,q) models of real exchange rates (January 1973–April 1996, 268 observations)

Dependent variable	Coefficient	$\Delta REER^{USA}$ (1)	$\Delta REER^{Germany}$ (2)	$\Delta REER^{Japan}$ (3)
Mean:				
constant	α_0	−0.00052	−0.0019	0.00108
		(−0.626)	(−0.304)	(0.766)
Δe_{t-1}	α_1	0.2544	0.2508	0.29397
		(3.7886)	(4.728)	(5.181)
Variance:				
Constant	a_0	0.000015	0.0000031	0.000072
		(0.9406)	(1.162)	(0.9117)
$\sum_{i=1}^{q} \varepsilon_{t-i}^2$	a_1	0.08889	0.02647	0.10383
		(1.3228)	(1.0956)	(1.18)
h_{t-1}	b_1	0.84174	0.9487	0.76432
		(6.9218)	(25.634)	(3.607)
	φ	24.49	45.989	9.91
Loglik		911.58	1007.86	791.8

Notes
t-values are given in parentheses.
Loglik is the value of the log-likelihood-function.

These results are coherent with the hypotheses of bloc floating. They are not die-hard proofs, as we do not have counterfactual evidence. We may, however, conclude that it is likely that the emergence of the DM bloc has contributed to increased worldwide exchange risk and, consequently, lower investment. Asia has tried to protect itself by pegging to the US dollar. However, this strategy has its limits, as is increasingly witnessed.

5 Conclusion

This chapter has shown that the emergence of regional currency blocs can be explained by the combination of risk-averse private investors maximizing their wealth and public authorities maximizing aggregate investment. By pegging their currency to an anchor, they reduce exchange rate risk within the currency bloc and with respect to their effective exchange rate. This will stimulate private investment. However, the conscious policies of *reducing* national exchange rate volatility pursued by many small countries have produced the 'undesigned' result of *increasing* exchange rate risk between the floating key currencies in the world.[33] Our model showed the mechanism which creates the trade-off between intra-bloc stability and inter-bloc volatility. Although 'hard' statistical proofs are difficult to obtain given the lack of counterfactual evidence, empirical evidence does concur with the hypotheses derived from theory. Alternative policy options to bloc floating might involve Asian countries switching to a basket peg, as proposed by Williamson, Dornbusch and Park, but it is uncertain that it would make a big difference. The European Monetary Union, on the other hand, should improve economic conditions by reducing the European currency bloc, thereby lowering exchange risk premia and required returns worldwide, thus stimulating growth.

Notes

1 I will not dwell on the technical methods of how to reduce exchange volatility. For evidence from Taiwan, see R. Dawn and Gang Shyy (1998); for Korea, Yeongseop Rhee and Chi-Young Song (1998). For the European experience see Collignon (1994).

2 Eichengreen and Bayoumi (1998) find that East Asia may fulfil the OCA criteria just as well as Europe. Yet most Asian countries remained dollar pegged, while Europe became DM pegged.

3 For empirical data see World Bank (1993). For the theoretical foundation of this phenomenon see Riese (1986).

4 For simplicity we will abstract from technological progress in this chapter. As Page (1994: 233) observes on the high-performing Asian economies: 'between 60 per cent and 120 per cent of their output growth derives from accumulation of physical and human capital and labour force growth.'

5 The argument is made convincingly by G. Larraín (1998).

6 See also Dixit and Pindyck (1994: 13).

7 For a more comprehensive treatment see Dornbusch (1983).

8 Relative prices are: $P_1 = P_B/P_A e_{A/B}; P_2 = P_C/P_A e_{A/C}; P_3 = P_1/P_2$, where P_A, P_B, P_C are national price indices and $e_{A/B}$ is the nominal exchange rate defined as the price of foreign currency B in terms of A's domestic currency. P_3 results from cross exchange rates. In what follows, we will assume that domestic prices are fixed in the short term, so that variations in $P_i(dP_i = \partial P_i/\partial_t)$ are exclusively due to variations in nominal exchange rates. A rise in P_i implies a

nominal *and* a real depreciation of A's currency and an appreciation of the foreign currency. The rate of depreciation is equivalent to the first difference of the logs of P_i $(dp_i = \partial P_i / \partial_i \cdot \frac{1}{P_i} | i = 1, 2, 3)$.

9 Huizinga (1994) gives a very clear and simple exposition of investment calculus of capital expenditures under uncertainty. Using a fixed rate of discount he obtains volatile revenue. I incorporate the risk factor into the 'required expected return'.

10 Foreign investment means in this context investment undertaken in A in relation to activities (import, export) with B or C and not foreign direct investment. FDI would reduce uncertainty since foreign inputs and outputs would be denominated in the same currency, but also (as a rule) growth generating investment at home.

11 In a Keynesian tradition F_{K_i} is the marginal *return* on capital rather than the marginal *product* as in the neo-classical world. This allows to formulate F_{K_i} as a function of the real exchange rate level (P_i) and, consequently, investment is a function of both the 'competitive' exchange rate level and its variance.

12 In reality there are of course also other risk factors: price, inflation and interest rate volatility or policy risk.

13 This statement implies a market-oriented development strategy. Financial repression may be a method to provide investment funding at low cost, but ultimately it may end in financial distress and lower growth (World Development Report, 1989). Under those circumstances, financial liberalization leading to higher real interest rates would promote growth, as documented by Frey (1988). This would stand in contradiction with our equation 17.3. However, even without financial repression, higher real interest rates may contribute to higher growth if they cause an increase in the productivity of investment $(\partial F_{K_i} / \partial r_i > 0)$ higher than the reduction of investment demand resulting from the increase in the cost of capital. Work by Gelb (1989) shows that this 'efficiency effect' can be substantial, while other work by Edwards (1988) shows a strong negative relationship between real growth and exchange rate variability. McKinnon (1991: 30) concludes: 'Stabilising the domestic price level without resorting to direct price controls and keeping deposit (and thus lending) rates of interest sustainably positive in real terms while limiting variance in the real exchange rate are crucial for successful economic development.' There is, however, some evidence that a mild form of financial repression (while maintaining positive real interest rates) has helped growth in Asia (see Stiglitz and Uy, 1996).

14 The assumption of considering the domestic environment 'safe' (free of stochastic shocks) may seem unusual but is justified by the intention to isolate the exchange risk factor on investment. If exchange rates vary positively with domestic income shocks, diversification into tradables may diversify some risk away and we would have to consider the non-diversifiable risk.

15 For simplicity we assume identical coefficients of risk aversion. Political risk may lead to differentiated νs.

16 Of course, a real devaluation would also help by shifting the marginal efficiency of capital and increasing the range of profitable investment opportunities. But in the long run this strategy implies a permanent distortion of relative prices.

17 Assuming all partial trade balances initially to be zero and trade weights to be represented by import shares, the real effective exchange rate index is: $P = P_1^{\alpha_1} \cdot P_2^{\alpha_2}$ where the import shares are the weights for the respective bilateral real exchange rates and also the elasticity by which the effective exchange rate responds to a change in the bilateral relative prices. Taking logarithms gives: where $p = \alpha_1 p_1, + \alpha_2 p_2$ where p, p_1, p_2 are all logs. In a three-country world it follows that $p_3 = p_1 - p_2$. The variance of the effective exchange rate is: $\sigma_A^2 = var(p) = \alpha_1^2 var(p_1) + \alpha_2^2 var(p_2) + 2\alpha_1 \alpha_2 cov(p_1, p_2) = \alpha_1^2 \sigma_1^2 + \alpha_2^2 + \alpha_2^2 + 2\alpha, \alpha_2 \sigma_{1,2}.$

18 If authorities reduced the volatility of both P_1 and P_2 we return to Bretton Woods.

19 Bénassy-Quéré assumes $\sigma_1 = 0.25\sigma_2$ as a significant criterion.

20 From equation (17.6b) it is clear that bloc floating also reduces the variance of the real effective exchange rate, as demonstrated by Figure 17.1a. How far this stabilization goes depends on the correlation coefficient between the two exchange rates (rho) and the degree of relative volatility.

21 Whether it also rises in absolute terms depends on the impact on p_3. In the next section it will be shown that a fall in α_2 will in any case increase the volatility in the fundamental equilibrium exchange rate between A and C.

22 As before, P_is are relative prices; p_i stands for their logs.

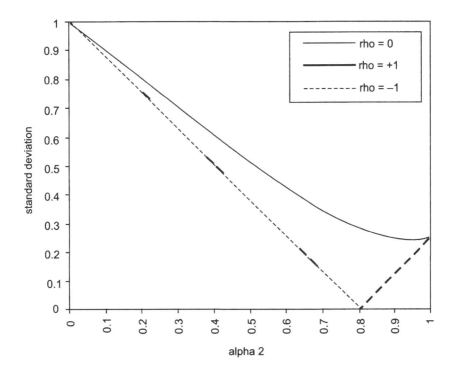

Figure 17.1a Volatility of nominal effective exchange rate

23 Because the third exchange rate is determined by the cross rate of the two others, one can focus on the adjustment process in country A only.

24 Because $\partial p_2/\partial p_A = 1/\alpha_2$.

25 Given that the price elasticity for A's exports $(\varepsilon_{C/A})$ to and imports $(\varepsilon_{A/C})$ from B are $\varepsilon_{C/A} = \frac{\partial AC}{\partial P_1} \cdot \frac{P_1}{AC} = ACp \cdot \frac{P_1}{AC}$ and $\varepsilon_{A/C} = \frac{\partial CA}{\partial P_1} \cdot \frac{P_1}{CA} = ACp \cdot \frac{P_1}{CA}$ and assuming initial trade balance $AC = P_2CA$ we obtain the equivalence 17.13 (see Dornbusch, 1980: 67).

26 We have excluded terms of trade shocks in this model by assuming relative domestic prices constant.

27 Williamson (1994: 190) points out that for very high trade elasticities and flat EB and IB curves, there may be an empirical case for PPP (although this is not borne out by the facts for manufactured goods). Our model shows that in a world with bloc floating, PPP is even less likely to occur.

28 As we assume P_1 as fixed, only α_2 is relevant.

29 If dY^* and u_C equal zero, equation 17.19 can be written as $E[R_N] = r_A = r_C + dP_2/P_2$ which is the classical arbitrage condition.

30 This is not to say that misalignments would not have to be corrected, but simply that the correction would depend less on exchange rates than it does in the open economies of today's Europe.

31 For the difference in risk concepts see Rothschild and Stiglitz (1970).

32 The GARCH models have been calculated by Susanne Mundschenk on RATS, using REER time series provided by the BIS.

33 For an analysis of 'how the independent actions of individuals will produce an order which is not part of their intentions' see Hayek (1979: 70).

References

Barrell, R. Anderton, B., Lansbury, M. and Sefton, J. (1996) 'FEERs for the NICs: Exchange Rate Policies and Development Strategies in Taiwan, Korea, Singapore and Thailand', this volume, pp. 247–81.

Bénassy-Quéré, A. (1998) 'Exchange Rate Regimes and Policies: an Empirical Analysis', this volume, pp. 40–65.

Bergsten, C.F. and Henning, C.R. (1996) *Global Economic Leadership and the Group of Seven*, Institute for International Economics, Washington, DC.

Bilson, John F.O. (1979) *Recent Developments in Monetary Models of Exchange Rate Determination*, IMF Staff Papers 26, Washington, DC.

Bollerslev, Tim (1986) 'Generalized Autoregressive Conditional Heteroskedasticity', *Journal of Econometrics*, 31, 307–27.

Breuer, J.B. (1994) 'An Assessment of the Evidence on Purchasing Power Parity', in J. Williamson (ed.) *Estimating Equilibrium Exchange Rates*, Institute for International Economics, Washington, DC.

Collignon, S. (1994) *Europe's Monetary Future*, Pinter Publishers, London.

Cours, Ph., Delassy, H. and Levais, F., (1996) 'Consequences for Europe of Exchange Rate Policies in Developing Asia: a Macro-Economic Simulation', conference paper, Seoul.

Dawn, R. and Shyy, Gang (1998) 'The Case of Taiwan', this volume, pp. 110–43.

de Grauwe, P. (1989) *International Money. Postwar Trends and Theories*, Oxford University Press, Oxford.

Dixit, A. and Pindyck, R. (1994) *Investment under Uncertainty*, Princeton University Press, Princeton, NJ.

Dominquez, Kathryn and Frankel, Jeffrey A. (1993) *Does Foreign Exchange Intervention Work?*, Institute for International Economics, Washington, DC.

Dornbusch, Rüdiger (1976) 'Expectations and Exchange Rate Dynamics', *Journal of Political Economy*, 84.

―― (1980) *Open Economy Macroeconomics*, Basic Books, New York.

―― (1983) 'Exchange Rate Risk and the Macroeconomics of Exchange Rate Determination' in R. Dornbusch, *Exchange Rate and Inflation*, MIT Press, Cambridge, Mass.

Dornbusch, R. and Frankel, J.A. (1988) 'The Flexible Exchange Rate System: Experience and Alternatives', reprinted in J.A. Frankel, *On Exchange Rates*, MIT Press, Cambridge, Mass., 1995.

Edwards, S. (1988) 'Implications of Alternative International Exchange Rate Arrangements for Developing Countries', in H.G. Vosgerau (ed.) *New Institutional Arrangements for the World Economy*, Springer-Verlag, Berlin.

Eichengreen, B. and Bayoumi, T. (1998) 'Is Asia an Optimum Currency Area? Can It Become One? Regional, Global and Historical Perspectives on Asian Monetary Relations', this volume pp. 348–67.

Engle, Robert F. (1982) 'Autoregressive Conditional Heteroskedasticity with Estimates of the Variance of United Kingdom Inflation', *Econometrica*, 50/4: 987–1006.

Frankel, Jeffrey A. (1995) *On Exchange Rates*, MIT Press, Cambridge, Mass.

Frankel, J.A. and Wei, S.J. (1993) 'Trade Blocs and Currency Blocs', in CEPR, 'The Monetary Future of Europe', conference papers, La Coruña 11–12 December 1992.

Frey, M. (1988) *Money, Interest and Banking in Economic Development*, Johns Hopkins University Press, Baltimore and London.

Friedman, Milton (1953) 'The Case for Flexible Exchange Rates', in *Essays in Positive Economics*, University of Chicago Press, Chicago.

Gelb, A. (1989) *Financial Policies, Growth and Efficiency*, World Bank Working Paper, WPS 202, Washington, DC.

Giavazzi, F. and Giovannini, A. (1989) *Limiting Exchange Rate Flexibility. The European Monetary System*, MIT Press, Cambridge, Mass, and London.

Hayek, F.A. (1979) *The Counterrevolution of Science. Studies on the Abuse of Reason*, Liberty Press, Indianapolis.

Huizinga, John (1994) 'Exchange Rate Volatility, Uncertainty and Investment: an Empirical Investigation', in L. Leidermann and A. Razin, *Capital Mobility: the Impact on Consumption, Investment and Growth*, Cambridge University Press, Cambridge.

Kenen, P. and Rodrik, D. (1986) 'Measuring and Analyzing the Effects of Short-term Volatility in Real Exchange Rates, *Review of Economics and Statistics*, 311–15.

Larraín, G. (1998) 'Industrialization and the Optimal Real Exchange Rate Policy for an Emerging Economy', this volume, pp. 151–86.

McKinnon, R. (1991) *The Order of Economic Liberalization. Financial Control in the Transition to a Market Economy*, Johns Hopkins University Press, Baltimore and London.

Montiel, P. (1994) 'Capital Mobility in Developing Countries: Some Measurement Issues and Empirical Estimates', *The World Bank Economic Review*, Vol. 8, No. 3, 311–50.

Minford, P. (1992) *Rational Expectations Macroeconomics*, Blackwell, Oxford.

Page, J. (1994) 'The East Asian Miracle: Four Lessons for Development Policy', in *NEER Macroeconomics Annual 1994*.

Rana, R. (1981) *ASEAN Exchange Rates: Policies and Trade Effects*, Institute of Southeast Asian Studies, Singapore.

Rhee, Y. and Song, C.-Y. (1998) 'The Case of South Korea', this volume, pp. 69–104.

Riedel, James (1996) 'Intra-regional Trade and Foreign Direct Investment in the Asia-Pacific Region', in D.K. Das, *Emerging Growth Pole. The Asian-Pacific Economy*, Prentice-Hall, Singapore.

Riese, Hajo (1986) 'Entwicklungsstrategie und ökonomische Theorie-Anmerkungen zu einem vernachlässigten Thema', in *Ökonomie und Gesellschaft*, Jahrbuch 4, Campus Verlag, Frankfurt/New York.

Rothschild, M. and Stiglitz, J. (1970) 'Increasing Risk: I. A Definition', in *Journal of Economic Theory*, 2, 225–43.

Stiglitz, J. and Uy, M. (1996) 'Financial Markets, Public Policy and the East Asian Miracle', *The World Bank Research Observer*, Vol. II, No. 2, August.

Stockman, A. (1987) 'The Equilibrium Approach to Exchange Rates', in Federal Reserve Bank of Richmond, *Economic Review*, March/April.

Williamson, John (1991) 'FEERs and the ERM', *National Institute Economic Review*, No. 137, August.

——(1994) *Estimating Equilibrium Exchange Rates*, Institute for International Economics, Washington, DC.

World Bank (1993) *The East Asian Miracle*, Washington, DC.

World Development Report (1989) *Financial Systems and Development*, Washington, DC.

18

DISCUSSION

Rüdiger Dornbusch

Collignon's chapter is a highly simulating, and successful, effort to put forth a theory of why countries peg one rate or another. His answer is that pegging is tantamount to risk reduction and that is good for investment. The argument is very persuasive, the demonstration is flawless and so there is very little to add. Perhaps this is a good place, then, to offer some reflections around the issues raised in the chapter.

What is wrong with flexibility?

The central proposition is that flexible exchange rates are variable exchange rates and variable rates induce risk premia that limit capital formation. Hence governments will look for risk reduction and that leads them to peg rates. They go shopping for an optimal risk reduction – pegging to A or to B – and out of this pursuit by individual countries comes the formation of currency blocs. This is not the traditional optimal currency area nor is it the argument of borrowed stability via nominal anchors. It is an argument based on variance of real exchange rates and risk premia.

At this stage, the reader is entitled to ask a few questions. The most important surely is whether nothing is lost in signing away an exchange rate. When our little country pegs to, say, Germany, there is certainly a reduction in volatility but there is also the loss of a key adjustment instrument. There appears little exploration in the chapter of the cost of giving away an instrument. One answer, implicit perhaps, might be that wage–price flexibility will make up, so that nothing is lost on flexibility and yet there is a reduction in the risk premium because whatever the flexibility of wages and prices contributes to adjustment does not come with the same kind of volatility that is endemic to capital markets and flexible rates. That may well be the argument and it is worth expressing it in detail. If this is not the argument, then we surely must be puzzled. Giving away instruments to secure benefits is a cost benefit issue.

323

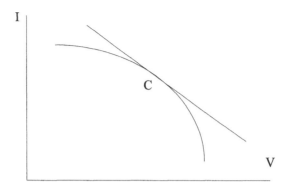

Figure 18.1 Iso-loss function and constraint diagram

We might set up a simple framework in which the authorities have a loss function that includes inflexibility of the exchange rate and volatility as an argument:

$$L = \varphi(I, V) \tag{18.1}$$

Moreover, there is a negative relationship between inflexibility and volatility: fixed rates are stable rates, fully flexible rates are maximally unstable.

$$V = V(I) \quad V' < 0 \tag{18.2}$$

The familiar iso-loss function and constraint diagram (see Figure 18.1) will typically give us the choice of an interior solution of limited exchange rate (in)flexibility and limited volatility. This would be a band float relative to some big brother. Collignon does well in explaining why countries are eager to get rid of volatility, but he pushes us inevitably in the direction of asking why flexibility is valued so little. Does it have to do with a corporatist aversion to markets, the same kind of aversion that in Europe has clipped the role of competition for half a century? As Europe goes to an EMU, the question of how to replace the exchange rate in terms of adjustment tools is more acute than ever. Without a new mechanism, unemployment is bound to be the adjustment variable.

Hubs and clubs

It might also be interesting to ask how we should think of the difference between EMU and the currency association around the dollar. The right answer here is surely a distinction between hubs and clubs. The USA is, of course, a hub. It is the next big thing to a large number of countries each of which looks for reduction in volatility and seeks a plausible hub to tie itself to. Argentina, for example, might peg to the Brazilian currency, to the DM or the dollar. The dollar answer dominates because Germany and even the associated Europe are relatively small, Brazil is explosively volatile and the dollar (and its associates) is the biggest and closest hub.

In Europe that kind of analysis does not naturally come up with a single answer. Portugal and Spain would peg the French franc, and surely Denmark and the Netherlands or Austria would peg the DM. That is not what we observe. One possible answer is that nominal anchor arguments – finding a strong currency – do matter in building a bloc. The other is that a theory of clubs might do better when there is no dominant partner. The dollar bloc and EMU are not the same and we need a good theory of how they come about. The theory might also help us understand why we have neither an Asian currency area nor a yen bloc.

LeChatelier and intra-regional volatility

Collignon offers the result that the creation of currency blocs will increase the volatility of rates between them. This is a very interesting finding. There is certainly a market for results that explain mega swings in the yen/dollar or DM/dollar rates and their co-movement.

It might be interesting to explore this result in a more generic fashion in terms of Samuelson's investigation of constrained economic systems. It will be recalled that in his *Foundations* Samuelson noted the relevance of LeChatelier's principle that the more constrained a system, the smaller its elasticity, the larger the absorption of pressure that must be carried by the adjustable parts. Collignon's finding is reminiscent of this general result.

Where does the volatility come from, where does it go?

In Collignon's chapter, and in much of the literature, volatility of flexible rates is just there. Nobody knows where it comes from. Moreover, when rates are fixed, it just goes away without even leaving footprints. It is troublesome to have models where noise is just a byproduct of an exchange rate system and can be removed plain and simple.

Surely, the volatility of exchange rates must be part of a broader stochastic setting of asset markets. In this perspective, fixing one of the prices might, in principle, reduce the variability of all or some, or it might increase it. I am not aware of an attempt to tackle the wider research problem, but it surely deserves attention.

Benchmarking

Collignon's chapter puts at the centre of discussion the risk premium which results from a country's exchange rate volatility. It is interesting to ask whether there are possible issues of benchmarking that come from club or hublike monetary arrangements. The argument is simply this. A fixed exchange rate area offers a wider and deeper market for securities and that ought to translate into lower yields than are required to persuade portfolio holders to accept securities traded in liquid markets.

The creation of the Euro is about to do precisely that, offering a rival to the dollar security market. The interesting question is whether there might be a conflict between the pull of being in a wide market and the risk reduction that might be better served by being in a different club or hub. It is difficult to see the two separately. When the Euro is introduced, perhaps for the first time countries that would naturally be on the Euro will no longer need to choose between an exchange rate preconditioned by their capital market considerations and one that works best in reducing volatility.

19

THE CASE FOR A COMMON BASKET PEG FOR EAST ASIAN CURRENCIES

John Williamson

This chapter examines the case for a simultaneous change in the exchange rate peg used by a group of East Asian currencies. I assume for the time being that nine economies would be involved: China, Hong Kong, Indonesia, South Korea, Malaysia, the Philippines, Singapore, Taiwan, and Thailand. The reason for picking this group is the impression that they are close competitors to each other; in due course the chapter examines whether this is in fact sufficiently true to make these countries a natural monetary grouping such as the EMS countries are widely agreed to be.

The first section describes the current exchange rate policies of the nine countries. This is followed by a discussion of some of the problems created by those policies. Section 3 describes the advantages of a common peg, and goes on to calculate what a common basket peg for the East Asian countries would look like, both before and after dropping potentially marginal members of the group. The final section of the chapter argues that use of a common peg imposes rather few constraints on other dimensions of a country's exchange rate policy.

1 Exchange rate policies

China still has an inconvertible currency and the mechanism by which its value is determined on the foreign exchange market is opaque, but it certainly does not float freely and its value is certainly not fixed. The renminbi appears to be devalued by a substantial step from time to time, rather as under the old Bretton Woods system, and in between to vary quite a lot but in no very systematic way (although it has been more stable recently). For example, it was devalued by about 50 per cent against the dollar at the beginning of 1994, and then tended to appreciate a bit until mid-1995, since when the rate has been relatively stable in terms of the dollar.

Table 19.1 Relative exchange rate volatility, 1992–5

	Against the dollar	Nominal effective exchange rate	Real effective exchange rate
China	7.55	7.51	9.58
Hong Kong	0.10	1.01	1.08
Indonesia	0.16	1.29	1.37
South Korea	0.58	0.81	0.86
Malaysia	1.54	1.67	1.64
Philippines	2.56	2.71	2.71
Singapore	0.86	1.02	1.13
Taiwan	1.45	1.22	1.65
Thailand	0.47	0.86	0.88
Average of 11 floaters	2.71	n.a.	n.a.

Source: International Financial Statistics, The Republic of China, *Financial Statistics*; Williamson (1996: Table 8.4).

Note:

The eleven floaters are Australia, Canada, Finland, Italy, Japan, New Zealand, Peru, South Africa, Sweden, Switzerland, and the United Kingdom.

The nominal effective exchange rate is calculated using a trade-weighted average of the national currency value, the dollar, the yen and the DM. Trade with the Western Hemisphere is included in the dollar weight, and the rest of the world is divided proportionally among the three currencies.

Volatility is measured by the standard deviation of changes in end-month exchange rates.

Table 19.1 shows three measures of exchange rate volatility for the nine East Asian currencies: the standard deviation of changes in the end-month bilateral exchange rate against the US dollar, and the standard deviation of monthly changes in effective and real effective exchange rates.[1] It can be seen that the volatility of the renminbi is by far the highest of any of the East Asian currencies, measured either against the dollar or in terms of either effective exchange rate index. China is also unusual in that the volatility of the real effective rate is substantially higher than that of the nominal effective rate.

1.1 Hong Kong

The Hong Kong dollar has had a fixed link to the US dollar, backed up by an Exchange Fund that acts effectively as a currency board, since 1983. It is an unambiguous case of a fixed exchange rate, and it is fixed to the US dollar. As a result, its volatility against the dollar is minimal. (One can in fact use a value of 0.1 to calibrate other results in the table; any greater value occurs because policy is not directed at stabilizing the rate in question.) But this stability against the US dollar still leaves the Hong Kong dollar with significant volatility in terms of both the nominal and real effective rates.

1.2 Indonesia

Indonesia describes its system as one of a managed float, although it seems that in practice it is closer to a crawling peg, with the crawl defined against the dollar. Thus in the first eight months of 1995 (the period during which the yen went on its great rollercoaster), the rupiah's bilateral exchange rate against the dollar depreciated between 5 and 10 rupiahs each month, an average of 0.4 per cent, while its effective exchange rate varied from a depreciation of 5.5 per cent in March when the dollar was weak to an appreciation of 6.8 per cent in August when the dollar was recovering. Table 19.1. shows that on a short-term basis the rupiah has been almost as stable against the dollar as the Hong Kong dollar has been,[2] but both nominal and real effective rates have been somewhat more volatile than in Hong Kong. In the last year the authorities have gradually opened a band around the official rate, which has now reached ±4 per cent.

1.3 South Korea

Korea describes its current exchange rate system as a "market average rate system." This means that it has a band with margins of ±2.25 per cent on any day, but today's band is centered on yesterday's average rate. Each day the exchange rate can move within the predetermined band based on the average rate for transactions the previous day, but since those transactions are themselves subject to strong official influence this allows for less impact of the market than might be assumed. The band is defined in terms of the US dollar. As Table 19.1 shows, the rate is in practice quite stable in terms of the US dollar, while both nominal and real effective rates are not that much more volatile than the dollar rate: indeed, they are the most stable in the region.

1.4 Malaysia

The IMF's *Annual Report on Exchange Arrangements and Exchange Restrictions* has since 1991 described the external value of the Malaysian ringgit as

> determined by supply and demand in the foreign exchange market. The Central Bank of Malaysia intervenes only to maintain orderly market conditions and to avoid excessive fluctuations in the value of the ringgit in terms of Malaysia's trading partners and the currencies of settlement.

Although Table 19.1 indicates that the ringgit fluctuates much more than the three currencies shown immediately above it in terms of the dollar, there have been occasional press reports of heavy intervention designed to prevent the ringgit appreciating to a degree that the authorities fear would jeopardize competitiveness, as well as reports of concerns about downward pressure on the ringgit for a brief period in the wake of the Mexican crisis in early 1995. The volatility of the effective rates is only marginally larger than that against the dollar.

1.5   The Philippines

The IMF *Annual Report on Exchange Arrangements and Exchange Restrictions* describes the policy of the Philippines as one of floating, but with the authorities intervening "when necessary to maintain orderly conditions in the exchange market and in light of their other policy objectives in the medium term." Table 19.1 suggests that volatility has been in the same range as other countries with (largely) freely floating rates, but I do not know whether this is because floating has in fact been quite free or because policy has been erratic. Volatility in the effective rates is again marginally larger than that against the dollar.

1.6   Singapore

The IMF *Annual Report on Exchange Arrangements and Exchange Restrictions* states that Singapore

> follows a policy under which the Singapore dollar is permitted to float, and the exchange rate of the Singapore dollar... is freely determined in the foreign exchange market. However, the Monetary Authority of Singapore monitors the external value of the Singapore dollar against a trade-weighted basket of currencies with the objective of maintaining a low and stable domestic inflation rate.

Since Singapore had a current account surplus of about 14 per cent of GDP in 1995, the highest in the world, and much of this was used to acquire reserves (which stood at some $67 billion in September 1995, for less than 3 million people) rather than to finance a capital outflow, it is clear that the float is a far from free one. The statistics in Table 19.1 show that volatility was relatively low in terms of the dollar and of both concepts of the effective exchange rate, although it is not so low as to suggest that policy approximates pegging to a trade-weighted basket.

1.7   Taiwan

Taiwan is another economy with a float that is reputed to be heavily managed, although the statistics in Table 19.1 suggest that it is freer than the majority of other East Asian currencies. Apart from the marginal difference in highly erratic China, Taiwan is the only case where the nominal effective rate is more stable than the dollar rate. Taiwan is also unusual in that, again apart from China, it is the only country where the real effective exchange rate is noticeably more unstable than the nominal effective rate.

1.8 Thailand

The Thai baht was officially pegged to the US dollar until a devaluation in November 1984, at which time it was announced that its value would be determined on the basis of a weighted basket of the currencies of Thailand's major trading partners. The same formula has been repeated ever since in the IMF's *Annual Report on Exchange Arrangements and Exchange Restrictions*. It is therefore somewhat surprising that, despite the gyrations in the value of the dollar, the baht has never varied more than about 5 per cent from a rate of 26 bahts to the dollar. The explanation seems to be that the unpublished basket to which Thailand ties the baht has a dollar weight of about 88 per cent. This results in dollar volatility being fairly low, while volatility in both the effective rates is also relatively low.

This review suggests that the current exchange rate practices of East Asian currencies are quite varied. At one extreme, those of China have, at least until recently, continued to be erratic. At the other extreme, Hong Kong has an almost perfectly fixed exchange rate against the dollar. Several other East Asian countries are also heavily dollar-focused: Indonesia (even though the rupiah depreciates continuously), Thailand, and South Korea, and perhaps (now) China. Singapore also has a fairly stable rate against the dollar, but it is also relatively stable in effective terms, suggesting that the basket has a significant influence. The Philippines seems to float, while the remaining two countries, Malaysia and Taiwan, have intermediate statistics, suggesting heavily managed floats.

2 Evaluation

The first point that has to be acknowledged is that East Asian countries have for some years managed their exchange rates far better than other groups of developing countries. They have not crucified their economies by misconceived attempts to use the exchange rate as a nominal anchor. They have not allowed their currencies to become so overvalued, either by keeping their exchange rates fixed in the face of differential inflation or by allowing them to float up too much, as to jeopardize export growth. The faults that I discuss below are second order as compared to those virtues.

Nevertheless, there remains much room for improvement. China's policy has been undesirably erratic, and in recent years it has run a current account surplus that makes absolutely no sense from the standpoint either of accelerating development or of nurturing harmonious relations with its trading partners and potential fellow-members of the World Trade Organization. Hong Kong has paid for its fixed exchange rate by an unnecessarily high rate of inflation, and it suffered a brief but severe speculative attack during the Mexican panic in early 1995. Korea's "market average rate system" means that if the market suddenly decided that the equilibrium rate was very different to the actual rate, it could in principle drive the rate to the edge of the band for a number of days in succession, and the band and the rate would migrate together at a rate of 2.25 per cent per day until they had moved to the new equilibrium, and in the meantime speculators could make a killing at the expense of the central bank. Malaysia and Thailand have confronted the problem of trying to repel excessive capital inflows without the aid of a wide band such as Chile and Colombia have found helpful,[3] and Thailand has faced speculative pressures both during the Mexican crisis and in the summer of 1996, presumably in part because current account deficits have been so large during the 1990s. The Philippines has suffered the high degree of volatility that one expects to go with floating rates. Singapore, like South Korea and Taiwan in the post-Plaza period (Balassa and Williamson, 1987), has developed an uneconomically large current account surplus.

These are all problems that could be remedied by policy changes on the part of individual countries quite independently of what is done by their neighbors. However, there is another problem that is common to a number of the East Asian countries, which is the instability of the effective exchange rates of the East Asian currencies that has been noted above. Six of the eight currencies are more unstable in nominal effective terms than in terms of the dollar, and in most cases the instability of the real effective rate is (somewhat) greater still. One way of curing this problem would be for each of the East Asian countries to peg its currency unilaterally to a trade-weighted basket. But, since the trading patterns of the East Asian countries differ, the currency baskets would differ between countries. This would mean that a change in the dollar/yen rate would lead to changes in intra-East Asia exchange rates, which is a matter of concern inasmuch as countries not only have to worry about exporting to and competing with imports from the developed countries, but also about their markets, their suppliers, and above all their competitors in other East Asian countries. This problem could be addressed through collective action, specifically in the form of the choice of a common peg. The next section of this chapter explores what that would involve.

3   Selecting a peg

Consider a simple world where there are only three currencies, the dollar, the yen, and an East Asian currency. For the sake of concreteness let us take the South Korean won as our example. Suppose that the dollar and the yen are floating against each other. If South Korea pegs the won to the dollar, then

Table 19.2 Direction of trade of East Asian economies excluding intra-group trade (1994) (%)

	China			Hong Kong			Indonesia			South Korea			Malaysia			Weighted average		
	X	M	Total	X	M	Total	X	M	Total	X	M	Total	X	M	Total	X	M	Total
USA	28.5	18.0	23.2	40.9	17.9	31.0	24.7	14.7	20.2	30.8	24.9	27.4	36.0	24.3	29.7	36.7	21.4	28.6
Japan	28.6	33.9	31.3	9.8	39.0	22.4	45.4	40.1	43.0	20.3	29.2	27.4	20.3	39.0	30.4	20.8	31.0	26.2
Western Europe	21.2	25.4	23.3	28.2	28.9	28.5	25.8	31.0	28.1	16.9	17.1	17.0	24.7	24.2	24.4	22.7	27.7	25.4
Rest of Western Hemisphere	4.9	5.1	5.0	7.8	2.7	5.6	3.0	4.9	3.8	9.7	5.4	7.3	4.2	2.1	3.0	6.4	3.7	5.0
Rest of world	16.8	17.6	17.2	13.2	11.5	12.5	1.1	9.3	4.8	22.3	23.4	22.9	14.8	1.5	12.5	13.4	16.2	14.9
Deviation from weighted average	23.3	11.4	14.9	22.4	18.4	12.5	55.2	27.3	39.2	24.5	24.6	22.9	6.7	21.8	10.6			

	Philippines			Singapore			Taiwan			Thailand		
	X	M	Total	X	M	Total	X	M	Total	X	M	Total
USA	50.4	26.0	35.6	35.2	24.1	29.0	55.1	24.8	37.7	35.4	14.9	23.1
Japan	19.7	34.1	28.4	13.2	3.5	7.7	21.1	34.6	28.9	27.5	40.1	35.1
Western Europe	23.2	16.5	19.2	26.5	53.8	41.7	14.3	24.3	20.0	26.9	23.2	24.7
Rest of Western Hemisphere	3.2	3.6	3.4	4.0	2.0	2.9	9.5	3.9	6.3	3.7	2.8	3.1
Rest of world	3.5	19.8	13.4	21.2	16.7	18.7	0.0	12.4	7.1	6.5	19.1	14.1
Deviation from weighted average	28.4	22.6	18.4	23.1	58.5	41.1	43.7	14.4	26.1	21.6	24.0	17.7

Weights for the common basket	Nine-currency basket	Eight-currency basket	Six-currency basket
US dollar	38.1	39.7	39.3
Japanese yen	32.6	31.0	33.8
Deutsche Mark	29.3	29.3	26.8

Source: IMF, *Direction of Trade Statistics 1995.*
Notes: X = exports; M = imports. Figures for Taiwan are a mix of data reported by Taiwan and its trading partners, and are subject to greater than normal error.

an appreciation of the yen will lead to an effective depreciation of the won, which will increase Korean competitiveness and thus tend to increase output and strengthen the current account, but will also exert inflationary pressure. If the won had previously been at just the right level to balance the claims of competitiveness against those of inflation control, it will now be too weak. (If, on the contrary, South Korea had pegged the won to the yen, then the yen's appreciation would cause the won to be too strong.)

The obvious solution is to replace the dollar by a basket containing both the dollar and the yen, with weights equal to those in the formula for the effective exchange rate. An unchanged peg to that basket will leave the effective exchange rate of the won unchanged whatever may happen to the yen–dollar rate, changes in which will thus have no impact on Korean output, inflation, or the balance of payments. South Korea will have succeeded in insulating itself from the effect of exchange rate fluctuations between the dollar and the yen. Such insulation is, of course, possible only at the macro level: exporters to Japan will still gain, while those who export to the USA will lose, when the yen appreciates.

The real world contains more than three countries, which complicates matters. To some extent this can be addressed by simply adding extra currencies to the basket. Consider, for example, the trade patterns of the East Asian countries as shown in Table 19.2. It is natural to add a representative European currency, which we assume would be the Deutsche Mark, to a currency basket for an East Asian currency. The more difficult issues arise in dealing with the weights of the other three groupings: East Asia other than the country itself, the rest of the Western Hemisphere, and the rest of the world.

Most developing Western Hemisphere countries peg to the dollar, so the trade weights for these countries can perhaps be added to that for the dollar. The rest of the world, which is a disparate group consisting of countries in the Middle East, the economies in transition, South Asia, Australia and New Zealand, and Africa, is primarily an exporter of primary products. Now the price of primary products is determined by demand in world markets rather than by supply conditions in the exporting countries, so it would make more sense to distribute the trade shares of those products over the industrial importing countries rather than to include the currencies of the countries that export them. I accordingly assume that the share of the rest of the world should be distributed in proportion to the shares of the United States, Japan, Western Europe, and East Asia in gross world product (GWP) in order to get a correct estimate of the effective exchange rate (and, therefore, to generate an optimal basket).

Constructing an appropriate basket raises other technical issues. First, should one use trade shares as displayed in Table 19.2, or would it not be more appropriate to use as weights the elasticities that measure how trade responds to exchange rate changes? Answer: elasticity weights are in principle better, but, unless one has some figures that one believes, it is safer to stay with trade weights.[4] Second, should one include the nominal exchange rate of a country with such rapid inflation that this will provide erroneous data on the real exchange rate? Answer: clearly not, though correcting for inflation properly will delay the availability of data so much as to vitiate the object of the exercise, which is to have an index that can guide intervention policy on a real-time basis. However, since most of the high-inflation countries fall in the residual rest of the world category that we have just proposed to redistribute to the industrial countries, this is not in practice a major problem.

One group of countries remains to be dealt with: the other East Asian countries. A unilateral way of dealing with them is to add them also to the basket to which each country would peg. For example, South Korea would add China, Hong Kong, Indonesia, Malaysia, Philippines, Singapore, Taiwan, and Thailand to the United States, Japan, and Germany. This has one advantage: that it would stabilize the effective exchange rate whatever the other East Asian countries did. But it also has three disadvantages. First, it would make a rather large basket with a long tail of currencies with small weights, and experience has shown that such long tails cause more bother than they are worth, given their very limited impact on the behavior of the basket. Second, several of those countries, notably China and Indonesia, have relatively high inflation, so that it is dangerous to ignore the divergence between nominal and real exchange rates. Third, because the trade structures of the East Asian countries differ significantly, the East Asian currencies would still vary arbitrarily against each other as a result of the fluctuations among the industrial country currencies.

An alternative approach would be for each of the East Asian countries to peg its currency to a common basket. Let us assume for the moment that the relevant group of countries does indeed consist of the nine economies that have been discussed in this chapter. To calculate this common basket peg, one would calculate the weighted average of the extra-regional trade of these nine countries, as is done in Table 19.2, and then assign the weights of the rest of the Western Hemisphere to the United States and divide that of the rest of the world proportionately to their shares in GWP among the United States, Japan, and Western Europe, as discussed above.

Are the East Asian economies sufficiently important competitors to each other to justify a common monetary arrangement? For each of the nine East Asian economies, Table 19.3 lists the eight countries with the most similar commodity structure of exports (at the 4-digit SITC level). At the bottom of each column one can find the number of countries out of the eight closest competitors that are among the eight other East Asian economies being considered in this chapter. It can be seen that on average almost five of each country's closest eight competitors come from this group. The hypothesis that they are important competitors to one another thus receives ample confirmation.

Table 19.3 Export similarity indices for nine East Asian countries (1992)

CHINA	HONG KONG	INDONESIA	SOUTH KOREA	MALAYSIA
1 0.641 HONG KONG	1 0.641 CHINA	1 0.400 CHINA	1 0.540 HONG KONG	1 0.502 SINGAPORE
2 0.496 PORTUGAL	2 0.563 TAIWAN	2 0.375 TUNISIA	2 0.492 TAIWAN	2 0.440 TAIWAN
3 0.471 THAILAND	3 0.540 SOUTH KOREA	3 0.373 NORWAY	3 0.481 ITALY	3 0.406 SOUTH KOREA
4 0.646 SOUTH KOREA	4 0.502 THAILAND	4 0.352 VIETNAM	4 0.473 NORTH KOREA	4 0.401 THAILAND
5 0.448 ITALY	5 0.488 ITALY	5 0.338 MALAYSIA	5 0.472 SINGAPORE	5 0.366 JAPAN
6 0.437 YUGOSLAVIA	6 0.462 PORTUGAL	6 0.332 THAILAND	6 0.471 JAPAN	6 0.364 HONG KONG
7 0.434 TAIWAN	7 0.451 SINGAPORE	7 0.323 ALGERIA	7 0.464 CHINA	7 0.358 MALTA
8 0.492 BULGARIA	8 0.410 AUSTRIA	8 0.322 BRUNEI	8 0.443 THAILAND	8 0.338 UK
East Asia in top 8: 4	5	3	5	5

PHILIPPINES	SINGAPORE	TAIWAN	THAILAND
1 0.389 THAILAND	1 0.507 JAPAN	1 0.563 HONG KONG	1 0.503 TAIWAN
2 0.328 AUSTRALIA	2 0.502 MALAYSIA	2 0.503 THAILAND	2 0.502 KONG KONG
3 0.307 SOUTH KOREA	3 0.476 USA	3 0.492 SOUTH KOREA	3 0.471 CHINA
4 0.305 MALAYSIA	4 0.472 SOUTH KOREA	4 0.476 ITALY	4 0.443 SOUTH KOREA
5 0.302 HONG KONG	5 0.467 TAIWAN	5 0.467 SINGAPORE	5 0.425 SINGAPORE
6 0.301 CHINA	6 0.451 HONG KONG	6 0.447 YUGOSLAVIA	6 0.402 ITALY
7 0.299 TAIWAN	7 0.449 UK	7 0.446 JAPAN	7 0.401 MALAYSIA
8 0.289 PORTUGAL	8 0.425 THAILAND	8 0.444 AUSTRIA	8 0.389 PHILIPPINES
East Asia in top 8: 6	5	4	7

Source: From 4-digit SITC codes; Statistics Canada World Trade Dataset.

Table 19.4 Actual and hypothetical exchange rate changes, end 1994 to end April 1995

| | Actual | | Hypothetical | | | | | | | |
| | Against $ | NEER | Unilateral peg Against $ | NEER | 9-currency basket Against $ | NEER | 8-currency basket Against $ | NEER | 6-currency basket Against $ | NEER |
	[1]	[2]	[3]	[4]	[5]	[6]	[7]	[8]	[9]	[10]
China	0.5	−1	7.0	0.0	9.78	−86	9.47	−1.16	9.71	−0.92
Hong Kong	−0.1	−7.7	4.7	0.0	9.78	0.94	9.47	0.63	9.71	0.87
Indonesia	3.5	−11.5	12.9	0.0	9.78	−2.44	9.47	0.51*	9.71	−2.50*
South Korea	−1.2	−4.4	6.9	0.0	9.78	0.81	9.47	0.51	9.71	0.75
Malaysia	3.6	−5.3	6.5	0.0	9.78	−0.24	9.47	−0.55	9.71	−0.30
Philippines	−6.2	−13.3	7.1	0.0	9.78	0.83	9.47	0.52	9.71	0.76*
Singapore	4.9	−2.9	4.7	0.0	9.78	1.24	9.47	0.93	9.71	1.18*
Taiwan	3.3	−4.2	6.0	0.0	9.78	1.22	9.47	0.92	9.71	1.16
Thailand	2.1	−7.8	8.2	0.0	9.78	−1.50	9.47	−1.18	9.71	−1.56

Memorandum items: Japan 19.1; Germany 12.0.

Note

An increase indicates an appreciation.

* Shows the impact of pegging to an East Asian currency basket where calculation excludes the country's own trade pattern.

Table 19.4 compares the two alternative strategies outlined above with what actually happened over a period that witnessed a major convulsion in the foreign exchange markets, namely the first four months of 1995, when the yen appreciated strongly (by 19.1 per cent) against the dollar. Most of the East Asian currencies stuck closely to the dollar (column 1), and in consequence experienced large depreciations in their effective exchange rates (column 2). This had implications that were presumptively unfavorable for them, since if their currency was previously at the optimal level (which is by definition that which balances the benefits of greater competitiveness against the cost of more inflationary pressure), then it must have been too weak afterwards: excess inflation pressure must have emerged. Had they pegged unilaterally to a trade-weighted basket, then by definition there would have been no change in their effective exchange rates. However, as can be seen from column 3 in Table 19.4, this would have involved significantly different moves against the dollar, and hence against each other. In contrast, a common basket peg based on the external trade of the nine countries, as constructed in Table 19.3, whose results are shown in columns 5 and 6 of Table 19.4, would have resulted in an identical 9.8 per cent appreciation against the dollar, but in modestly different changes in the effective exchange rates.

The identical nominal appreciations presuppose that each of the nine countries would have pegged rigidly to the common peg. Since only Hong Kong has a rigid peg these days, this is an improbable assumption: moreover, most of us presumably would regard such a move as retrograde. Once one allows for substantial bands around parity, actual outcomes would depend on the workings of the foreign exchange market: an appreciation of the parity would not automatically imply an equal appreciation of the market exchange rate. But, if the band were credible, the central expectation would be for the market exchange rate to stay at the same position within the band, and therefore to appreciate by as much as the parity did. The existence of a common peg would still suffice to create a strong tendency for the East Asian currencies to stick together in the face of common shocks emanating from exchange rate instability in the outside world.

The nine countries on which attention has so far been focused were selected because of an a priori belief that they were important as competitors to one another. It is now time to examine whether this is a logical group of countries to share a common exchange rate peg. Such a common peg would be attractive if two conditions are satisfied.

The first is that the geographical distribution of trade (excluding intra-trade) of the countries is similar. Table 19.2 permits such a comparison. The last row sums the absolute values of the deviations in the trade shares of each country from the regional average. It suggests that a common peg would be particularly good for China, Hong Kong, and Malaysia; about average for South Korea, the Philippines, Taiwan, and Thailand; but distinctly less satisfactory for Indonesia and Singapore.

The second condition is that the countries are close competitors in world markets. Table 19.3. shows that, with the exception of Indonesia, each of them has at least half its eight principal competitors as other countries of the region. Similarly, each except Indonesia and the Philippines appears as one of the principal competitors of at least four other countries of the region. Other countries that appear as principal competitors more than twice are Italy (five times), Japan (four times), and Portugal (three times). Italy has none of the East Asian countries among its eight principal competitors, Japan has one (Singapore), and Portugal has three (China, Hong Kong, and South Korea). If one sums the number of times that each of our eight countries has, and appears as, a principal competitor of the others, one gets the following result: Thailand fifteen; Hong Kong twelve; South Korea twelve; Taiwan eleven; Malaysia ten; Singapore ten; China nine; Philippines seven; Indonesia three. Analogous figures for the non-East Asian countries are: Portugal six; Italy five; Japan five.

With the exception of Indonesia, the East Asian countries are unambiguously more similar to each other than to any outside countries.

Taking the two criteria together, the extent to which a common peg would be satisfactory and the similarity in their export patterns, it is clear that Indonesia is a marginal candidate for inclusion in the East Asian group. Singapore is a weak candidate on the first criterion, and the Philippines is somewhat marginal on the second. Hence two additional trade baskets were calculated: one for eight countries (excluding Indonesia), and another for the six core countries (excluding Indonesia, the Philippines, and Singapore).

The final columns of Table 19.4. show the impact on the dollar and effective exchange rates of each of the East Asian currencies of a peg to each of those two baskets over the period of dramatic yen appreciation in early 1995. The interesting feature is how little difference it makes to a country whether its own trade is included in the basket or not. Indeed, Indonesia would have been slightly better off with the six-country basket than with the nine-country basket that included its own trade pattern. All of them would still have been vastly better off with the basket than with their actual policy.

It is of course possible that some of the East Asian countries were wanting to increase competitiveness, in which case a common peg would have thwarted what came as a boon to them. But there is another possible explanation of why their appreciations (against the dollar) were weak or non-existent, which is that they were faced with a classic collective action problem. Each of them could quite rationally have felt compelled to stay close to the dollar because they feared that appreciation against the dollar would also have meant appreciation against their regional competitors (as it actually would have done). The solution to this collective action problem is precisely the adoption of a common basket peg. This would provide each of the East Asian countries with some assurance that its competitiveness was not going to be undermined vis-à-vis its peers if it allowed its currency to appreciate against the dollar when the dollar is weak.

To get a summary figure of the relative stability (in terms of effective exchange rates) that would have been yielded by different policies, one can calculate the average absolute value of the changes in nominal effective exchange rates under each of the five policies. These are as follows:

Actual policy	7.4
Unilateral basket pegs	0.0
Nine-currency basket	1.1
Eight-currency basket	1.1
Six-currency basket	1.1

It is evident that the choice between the three baskets is not an issue of much consequence. In contrast, any of the common baskets would have got on average 85 per cent of the benefits of the set of unilateral pegs, even using a measure that attributes zero significance to holding the relative competitiveness of the East Asian countries constant.

4   The constraints imposed by a common peg

The one area of the world that appears to have economies even more competitive with one another than East Asia is Western Europe. Table 19.5 shows export similarity indices for nine core members of the European Union analogous to those for the East Asian countries in Table 19.4, which shows that on average the European countries have 5.8 of their top eight competitors among the other eight countries considered, as against an average of 4.9 in East Asia (or 5.1 excluding Indonesia).

Those close trade interrelations long ago led the European countries to adopt a concerted exchange rate policy. The European Monetary System, and specifically its exchange rate mechanism, was created precisely in order to insulate the European countries from the instabilities that would otherwise have been imposed on Europe by fluctuations in the value of the dollar. The ERM provided for a mutual pegging mechanism among the participating currencies, with narrow bands (±2.25 per cent), and requiring unanimous agreement for any parity changes. However, the failure to realign after 1987 led to growing disequilibria, which in due course fostered the great ERM crises of 1992–3, as a result of which the ERM bands had to be widened to ±15 per cent. It is hoped that the ERM will be replaced by a single money for a number of the core EU countries in 1999.

East Asia appears to have got to the stage where it too could benefit from some concertation in its exchange rate policies, but I doubt whether it is

Table 19.5 Export similarity indices for nine EU countries (1992)

AUSTRIA	BELGIUM-LUX.	DENMARK	FRANCE	GERMANY
1 0.633 GERMANY	1 0.637 GERMANY	1 0.526 NETHERLANDS	1 0.723 FEDERAL GERMANY	1 0.723 FRANCE
2 0.594 SWEDEN	2 0.597 NETHERLANDS	2 0.493 GERMANY	2 0.674 UK	2 0.652 UK
3 0.594 ITALY	3 0.592 FRANCE	3 0.481 ITALY	3 0.645 USA	3 0.645 SPAIN
4 0.581 FRANCE	4 0.579 SPAIN	4 0.478 FRANCE	4 0.614 SPAIN	4 0.642 ITALY
5 0.512 SPAIN	5 0.536 UK	5 0.463 BELGIUM-LUX.	5 0.592 BELGIUM-LUX.	5 0.637 BELGIUM-LUX.
6 0.512 UK	6 0.500 AUSTRIA	6 0.460 UK	6 0.589 ITALY	6 0.633 AUSTRIA
7 0.500 USA	7 0.494 SWEDEN	7 0.447 AUSTRIA	7 0.587 NETHERLANDS	7 0.631 JAPAN
8 0.500 BELGIUM-LUX.	8 0.492 ITALY	8 0.444 USA	8 0.581 AUSTRIA	8 0.620 USA
EU in top 8: 6	6	7	6	6

ITALY	NETHERLANDS	SWEDEN	UK
1 0.642 FEDERAL GERMANY	1 0.597 BELGIUM-LUX.	1 0.610 FEDERAL GERMANY	1 0.718 USA
2 0.594 AUSTRIA	2 0.587 FRANCE	2 0.607 FINDLAND	2 0.674 FRANCE
3 0.592 SPAIN	3 0.578 FEDERAL GERMANY	3 0.594 AUSTRIA	3 0.652 FEDERAL GERMANY
4 0.589 FRANCE	4 0.565 USA	4 0.568 FRANCE	4 0.563 NETHERLANDS
5 0.544 UK	5 0.563 UK	5 0.529 UK	5 0.544 ITALY
6 0.530 YUGOSLAVIA	6 0.562 DENMARK	6 0.525 SPAIN	6 0.536 BELGIUM-LUX.
7 0.516 USA	7 0.503 ITALY	7 0.524 CANADA	7 0.529 SWEDEN
8 0.513 SWEDEN	8 0.495 SPAIN	8 0.522 USA	8 0.528 JAPAN
EU in top 8:5	6	4	6

Source: From 4-digit SITC codes: Statistics Canada World Trade Dataset.

ready to replicate the ERM. One reason is that the foreign exchange markets of some of the prospective members, especially China, have not yet developed to the point where one would expect effective intervention to defend the cross-rates in other participating countries to be possible (not to mention possible political problems in agreeing on how to defend the margins between the renminbi and the New Taiwan dollar). Another reason is that the countries still have too wide a range of preferences as regards exchange rate policy, and of inflation rates, to permit adoption of as tight a system as the ERM, with its presumption against frequent parity changes.

The alternative that I have outlined above is adoption of a common basket peg. This would permit Hong Kong to continue to operate a currency board system, if that is what it wishes to do: it would simply start to trade US dollars for Hong Kong dollars at a price that would vary depending on the value of the US dollar in the foreign exchange markets vis-à-vis the other currencies in the basket (plus or minus the margins), instead of at a fixed rate.[5] Both China and Taiwan could intervene in their own markets quite independently of one another, pretending that the other does not exist. Some countries can operate wide bands if they so wish, while others can defend much narrower margins. Some can have their bands crawl, if that is needed to offset differential inflation, to avoid importing inflation, or to facilitate a desired balance of payments adjustment. If the participants want to get together to concert these policies, they can do so, but it is not essential that they do so.

The object of the change would simply be to create an expectation that, even without any such concertation, variations in the exchange rates among the industrial countries would no longer have major impacts on the relative competitive positions of the East Asian countries. That would be a significant first practical step toward the East Asian monetary cooperation that leaders in the region have begun to call for. It would also have yielded significant benefits over the period 1995–6, inasmuch as one of the reasons for the boom of 1995 and the near-recession of 1996 was the impact on trade flows of the region's effective depreciation in early 1995 and the subsequent appreciation. A basket peg that had kept the region's effective exchange rates roughly constant would have avoided those destabilizing impacts.

Notes

The author is indebted to Molly Mahar for extremely competent research assistance. Copyright Institute for International Economics: all rights reserved.

1   An "effective exchange rate" is the weighted average exchange rate against all other currencies, where the weights are generally chosen to reflect the pattern of trade. (An alternative weighting system, based on trade elasticities, recognizes also the countries that are important competitors, rather than just trade partners.) A "real effective exchange rate" corrects by changes in relative inflation, so that the index does not change if prices increase as much at home as the

weighted average of the country's trading partners. The effective exchange rate indexes used in this chapter were calculated from rates against a limited number of other currencies, as explained in the note to Table 19.1.

2   The definition of volatility employed would result in a measure of zero volatility if a currency depreciated by the same percentage amount each month.

3   See Williamson (1996) for an extended analysis of the policies of Chile and Colombia, and their results. One expects a wide band to help, as long as it is (even partially) credible, because (a) arbitrageurs will allow for the expected return of the exchange rate toward its parity, and deduct an appropriate discount from the local currency yield when they compare with foreign yields; and (b) investors in the tradable goods industries will tend to look at the parity rather than the market rate when assessing whether to go ahead with potential investment projects.

4   These questions are discussed in Williamson (1982).

5   It could easily diversify its reserve holdings to match the currency basket, or cover its dollar holdings forward to provide similar insurance, if it wished to avoid any foreign exchange exposure.

References

Balassa, Bela and Williamson, John (1987) *Adjusting to Success: Balance of Payments Policy in the East Asian NICs*, Washington: Institute for International Economics.

IMF (various years) *Annual Report on Exchange Arrangements and Exchange Restrictions*, Washington, DC.

Williamson, John (1982) 'A Survey of the Literature on the Optimal Peg', *Journal of Development Economics*, 11, reprinted as Chapter 4 in C. Milner, ed., *Political Economy and International Money: Selected Essays of John Williamson*, Brighton: Wheatsheaf, 1987.

——(1996) *The Crawling Band as an Exchange Rate Regime: Lessons from Chile, Colombia, and Israel*, Washington: Institute for International Economics.

20

DISCUSSION

Jean Pisani-Ferry

It is always a great intellectual pleasure to read any work by John Williamson. It is an even greater pleasure to comment on a chapter which is quintessential John Williamson: it starts from a clear setting, provides a forceful discussion and ends up with an innovative proposal.

The topic of the chapter is a stimulating one. It is not about the choice of an exchange rate regime, an issue on which John Williamson remains intentionally vague: what he proposes would apply to a variety of exchange rate regimes, ranging from currency board arrangements to a managed float, only excluding the free float. Rather, he addresses a different issue: the choice of a unit of account for the exchange rate target which is common to all these regimes.

As documented in Chapter 3 by Agnès Bénassy-Quéré and pointed out in several other chapters in this book, the exchange rate vis-à-vis the US dollar is for most East Asian countries a major external target, which results in what can be termed a common implicit dollar peg. There are obviously significant differences, both in the exact weight of the dollar vis-à-vis other currencies in the (frequently implicit) basket of currencies which is being used as a reference for exchange rate policy, and in the degree of flexibility of the exchange rate vis-à-vis this reference, but there is strong enough evidence of a dollar peg behaviour to investigate whether this choice is the more appropriate one.

As John Williamson points out, the common implicit dollar peg has a merit, which is to act as a coordination device for stabilizing relative real exchange rates among the East Asian countries, thus preventing wide variations in their relative price competitiveness. It also has a drawback, which is to lead to excessive volatility of each country's real effective exchange rate vis-à-vis its main export markets. Fluctuations in the dollar/mark and dollar/yen exchange rates directly impact on the relative price of the region's goods on the European and Japanese markets, thereby resulting in significant shocks to the volume or the profitability of exports. This volatility was hardly consequential as long as each of the East Asian countries could be seen as a small open economy exporting to North America. This is no longer the case. Nowadays, the US market is no longer the main market for the region's exports. Its

344

role has been taken over by the regional market. However, as John Williamson points out, the move to a basket peg raises a typical collective action problem: by making this choice, a country of the region would have to trade higher real effective exchange rate stability vis-à-vis its main export markets for higher volatility in its competitiveness vis-à-vis the other countries in the region; however, a collective move to a basket peg that would give roughly similar weights to the dollar, the yen and European currencies would result in lowering real effective exchange rate instability vis-à-vis the export markets, without affecting relative competitiveness. Hence the proposal for a common basket peg (or, more precisely perhaps, a common basket reference).

Some of the merits of adopting such a common reference do not need to be discussed at length. First, John Williamson's proposal would preserve the individual countries' freedom to choose their exchange rate regime. Second, it would not require complicated institutional arrangements. Third, it would not demand strong political commitments towards cooperation within the region. It is thus much more realistic than more elaborate options that would immediately raise significant political difficulties. However, the strategy of adopting a common reference needs to be compared to an alternative: a coordinated move to basket pegs reflecting each country's trade structure. This would require even less coordination and commitment, as 'coordinated' here only means simultaneous. This would have the advantage that, for example, Thailand, whose exports to Japan represent almost 30 per cent of total exports, would pay more attention to the exchange rate of the yen than Hong Kong, which sells less than 10 per cent of its total exports to Japan. As John Williamson's Table 19.2 confirms that the East Asian countries' geographical patterns of trade are quite diverse, this choice warrants examination.

The costs and benefits of adopting unilateral basket pegs versus a common one arise from a trade-off between stabilizing the real effective exchange rate and maintaining competitiveness vis-à-vis the other East Asian exporters. Table 20.1 gives in both cases the effect of a 10 per cent depreciation of the Deutsche Mark or the yen. As John Williamson points out, differences are minor for some countries, but this is not the case for all: for Singapore, adopting the common basket peg would mean accepting that the yen–dollar exchange rate impacts on its exchange rate vis-à-vis the dollar and the Deutsche Mark, although Japan is a minor trade partner and the USA and Europe are major ones. Whether or not this choice would benefit Singapore depends on the relative effects of a loss in price competitiveness vis-à-vis the other East Asian exporters or vis-à-vis the USA and Europe. This in turns depends on whether Singapore's producers mainly compete with other East Asian producers or with US, European and Japanese producers; in other words whether the elasticity of substitution between Singapore's and the other East Asian nine's products is higher than between Singapore's products and the G-3's products. It is likely that countries like Singapore, Korea and Taiwan, whose production structure increasingly resembles those of advanced industrial countries, are thus led to pay more attention to their exchange rate vis-à-vis the major industrial countries. Summing up, it is not obvious that all countries in the region would gain from adopting a common basket peg rather than a specific one, and for some countries the difference could be significant.

Table 20.1   Hypothetical effects of exchange rate changes

	10% yen depreciation				10% (Deutsche Mark depreciation)			
	Own basket peg		Common basket peg		Own basket peg		Common basket peg	
	NEER / G-3*	Compet / EA9**	NEER / G-3*	Compet / EA9**	NEER / G-3*	Compet / EA9**	NEER / G-3*	Compet / EA9**
China	0	0.8	0.5	0	0	0.0	−0.1	0
Hong Kong	0	−0.7	−0.7	0	0	0.5	0.3	0
Indonesia	0	1.4	1.3	0	0	0.1	0.0	0
South Korea	0	0.1	0.0	0	0	−0.7	−0.7	0
Malaysia	0	0.3	0.2	0	0	0.0	−0.1	0
Philippines	0	0.1	0.0	0	0	−0.6	−0.7	0
Singapore	0	−2.5	−2.3	0	0	2.6	2.2	0
Taiwan	0	−0.1	−0.1	0	0	−0.8	−0.8	0
Thailand	0	0.9	0.8	0	0	0.1	−0.1	0

Source: Author's calculations.

Notes

* Change in the nominal effective exchange rate vis-à-vis the USA, Europe and Japan.
** Change in the price competitiveness vis-à-vis the other East Asia nine.

There is, however, a strong political economy argument in favour of John Williamson's proposal. Adopting a common basket peg would greatly increase the transparency of exchange rate policies within the region. As the East Asian countries would retain flexibility in the definition of their policy vis-à-vis the common reference, it would provide a benchmark against which these policies could be assessed by their trade partners and multilateral organizations like the IMF. This is important because without binding rules on monetary and exchange rate policies, adopting a basket peg would not prevent external shocks, giving rise to uncoordinated reactions. The kind of low-key coordination envisaged by John Williamson would not eliminate 'beggar-thy-neighbour' exchange rate policies. With a common basket peg, it would at least make them observable and facilitate their monitoring. This would be no small benefit.

21

IS ASIA AN OPTIMUM CURRENCY AREA? CAN IT BECOME ONE?

Regional, global, and historical perspectives on Asian monetary relations

Barry Eichengreen and Tamim Bayoumi

The conference "Exchange rate policies in emerging Asian countries", on which this book is based, is one sign of increased interest in collective or cooperative exchange rate arrangements for East Asian countries. A more concrete indication is the announcement in November 1995 by the Hong Kong Monetary Authority and the central banks of Malaysia, Indonesia, and Thailand of repurchase agreements designed to provide one another with exchange market support. In February 1996 Hong Kong and Singapore agreed to intervene for the account of the Bank of Japan to help the latter manage the dollar/yen rate. In March the Bank of Japan joined the network of repurchase arrangements (as had Singapore and the Philippines sometime earlier). Against this background it is not surprising that the apostles of European monetary integration have chosen this time to bring their message to Asia.

The importance of these arrangements should not be exaggerated. The network of repurchase agreements is best thought of as a regional analog to the General Arrangements to Borrow, which gave G-10 countries quick access to international reserves but did not otherwise limit their pursuit of independent monetary and fiscal policies. Support under the Asian arrangements is limited to the value of the US treasury securities of the borrowing governments. One can imagine how these resources had proved to be insufficient to repel an all-out attack on an Asian currency comparable to the Mexican or ERM crises, and how this gave rise to arguments for collective support. And to make collective support politically palatable, its proponents might be led to advocate surveillance, conditionality, and a common peg.

The case for a common peg has been made by Williamson (1998). Williamson argues that the stewards of nine East Asian currencies (China, Hong Kong, Indonesia, South Korea, Malaysia, the Philippines, Singapore, Taiwan, and

347

Thailand – henceforth in this chapter the EA9) should adopt a common basket peg, surrounded by fluctuation bands of plus-and-minus 10 percent. In his words, these countries comprise "a natural monetary grouping such as the EMS countries are widely agreed to be." The counter-argument is that East Asia is less of an optimum currency area than Western Europe. Economic and financial conditions differ significantly across Asian economies. Some financial markets in the region are very open, while others remain highly regulated and restricted (contrast Hong Kong and China). Some East Asian countries compete with Japan in international markets, and their currencies follow the yen up and down; others which import from Japan but compete less with it prefer to depreciate their currencies when the yen strengthens to offset the recessionary impact of higher import prices. Thus, different countries with different economic structures will prefer different monetary-cum-exchange rate responses to common shocks like a change in the yen/dollar rate.

As experience with the European Monetary System and the drive for European Monetary Union have shown, political solidarity can overcome deviations from the ideal of the optimum currency area. But in Europe, the requisite links and institutions have grown up only as a result of a unique process of political and monetary integration that has unfolded over many decades. In East Asia, in contrast, institutionalization is weak. Countries lack the political links and traditions needed to support a concerted exchange rate policy. Historical experience suggests that more than a few years will be needed to develop them.

We argue these points in four sections. Section 1 provides brief background on Asian exchange rate arrangements. Section 2 adopts a regional perspective, asking how East Asia compares with other regions on standard optimum-currency-area grounds. Section 3 adopts an historical perspective, showing how much time has been required historically to develop the political institutions and solidarity needed to support a collective peg. Section 4 concludes.

1 How have Asian exchange rate arrangements evolved?

Table 21.1 shows the exchange rate arrangements reported by the IMF for the EA9 and the world as a whole. (Because the number of East Asians is limited, the panel for all IMF members breaks country totals into percentages, while that for East Asia reports numbers of countries in each category. We have added information for Taiwan, which is not an IMF member, from independent sources.) Clearly, the trend toward greater exchange rate flexibility evident in the world as a whole is also apparent in Asia.

In 1995 Asian currency arrangements spanned the range from fixed to floating rates. The Hong Kong dollar is pegged to the US dollar under a currency board. The remaining eight currencies were also managed. Generally, the intensity of their management has declined over time, a trend associated

Table 21.1 Exchange rate arrangements
(a) IMF member exchange rate arrangements (%)

Classification status	1980	1985	1990	1995
Currency pegged**	67.6	63.3	55.8	37.6
Cooperative arrangements[†]	5.6	5.3	6.5	5.5
Adjusted according to indicators[‡]	2.8	3.3	3.2	1.7
Other	23.9	28.0	34.4	55.2
Flexible limited[§]		(3.3)	(2.6)	(2.2)
Managed float		(14.0)	(14.9)	(21.0)
Independent float		(10.7)	(16.9)	(32.0)
Total	99.9	99.9	99.9	100.0

(b) East Asian[¶] countries exchange rate arrangements

Classification status[*]	1980	1985	1990	1995
Currency pegged**	5	4	3	2
Cooperative arrangements[†]	–	–	–	–
Adjusted according to indicators[‡]	–	–	–	–
Other	4	–	–	–
Flexible limited[§]	–	–	–	
Managed float		2	3	4
Independent float		3	3	3
Total	9	9	9	9

Notes:

* For IMF members with dual or multiple exchange markets, the arrangement shown is that in the major market. Excluding the currency of Cambodia, but including the currencies of Hong Kong and Taiwan.

** Currencies pegged to US dollar, French franc, Russian ruble, Other currency, Special Drawing Rights, or other currency composites (currencies which are pegged to various "baskets" of currencies of the IMF members' own choice, as distinct from the SDR basket).

† Refers to the cooperative arrangement maintained under the European Monetary System.

‡ Includes exchange arrangements under which the exchange rate is adjusted at relatively frequent intervals, on the basis of indicators determined by the IMF member countries concerned.

§ Flexibility limited vis-à-vis a single currency. Exchange rates of all currencies have shown limited flexibility in terms of the US dollar.

¶ East Asian countries are Japan, Hong Kong, Indonesia, South Korea, Malaysia, Philippines, Singapore, Taiwan, and Thailand.

with rising exchange rate variability. The frequency of management ranges from Indonesia, where the authorities intervened continuously, to Malaysia, where intervention was episodic although when it occurred it was often quite substantial. The South Korean authorities had announced a gradual widening of their intervention margins with the intention of moving to a free float by the end of the decade. China's currency is difficult to place on this continuum, since it remains inconvertible; it appears that the renminbi is held within a wide fluctuation band against the dollar and significantly realigned from time to time.

Frankel and Wei (1994) attempt to disentangle the weight of different reference currencies in the Asian authorities' implicit basket pegs by regressing each currency against the US dollar and the Japanese yen. They find that even in the 1990s most currency baskets have been dominated by the dollar. In the early 1990s the only currencies to weight the yen significantly were the Hong Kong dollar, the Singapore dollar, the Malaysian ringgit, and the Thai baht. And even in those countries, the weight of the dollar relative to the yen was more than four (in Singapore), more than five (in the case of Malaysia), and more than six (in the case of Thailand). In Hong Kong, with its dollar-based currency board, the yen has no explanatory power. The weight on the yen has in many cases increased over time (most clearly in the cases of the Indonesian rupiah, the Thai baht, and the New Taiwan dollar). While the yen is increasingly used to invoice intra-Asian trade, and while the Asian countries have slowly shifted the composition of their external debt away from the dollar and toward the yen, the dollar retains its dominant role in East Asian exchange rate management.

Limiting his analysis to periods when the Japanese currency fluctuated sharply against the US dollar, Takagi (1996) attaches higher weights to the yen. While his findings for Indonesia, the Philippines, and Thailand do not differ much from those of Frankel and Wei, he emphasizes the tendency for the Korean won and the Malaysian ringgit to follow a depreciating yen (suggesting that these countries regard Japan as a close competitor in international markets), and for the Singapore dollar to follow closely an appreciating yen (as the authorities ward off imported inflation). These asymmetric responses, reflecting different national priorities attached to export competitiveness and price stability, would clearly complicate efforts to design a collective currency peg.

Benassy-Quéré (1998) has analyzed the relative importance of the dollar and the yen in Asian currency pegs by comparing the volatility of nominal exchange rates against the dollar with their volatility against the yen. Volatility against the dollar is uniformly lower than volatility against the yen, but the relative importance of the yen in Asian currency pegs (as reflected in the declining relative volatility of that currency) has grown between the second half of the 1980s and first half of the 1990s for Singapore, Malaysia, and the Philippines. The opposite is true for Indonesia, South Korea, and Thailand. Regression analysis similar to Frankel and Wei's suggests a role for the yen in basket pegs only in Malaysia, Thailand, and Singapore.

One interpretation of these trends is that East Asia is paralleling the tendency toward greater exchange rate flexibility evident in other parts of the world. That tendency can be resisted only where governments are prepared to repress the domestic financial system and impose capital controls. In East Asia (and most especially Hong Kong and Singapore, which have set themselves up as international financial centers), the scope for such controls is limited. From this perspective, it is no coincidence that China, the one country in the region which retains very significant controls, is also the only one that holds its currency within bands that are realigned periodically. Given the infeasibility of controls, by this interpretation, East Asia is inevitably transiting toward greater exchange rate flexibility. Even Hong Kong, which had previously resisted greater flexibility, is having to contemplate it since the resumption of Chinese control in 1997.

Others might argue instead that East Asia is following in Europe's footsteps. Following the breakdown of Bretton Woods, European governments were torn between pegging to the dollar, the traditional anchor currency issued by what was still the world's leading commercial power, and pegging to their regional anchor, the Deutsche Mark. In the short run they responded by allowing their currencies to fluctuate more widely. But with the passage of time, the costs of this strategy became clear. The growth of intra-European trade increased the costs of uncontrolled intra-European exchange rate variability. The authorities responded by institutionalizing a sequence of collective pegging arrangements, the Snake and the EMS.

One can imagine a similar response in Asia. Oscillations in the exchange rate linking the EA9's two principal trading partners, the USA and Japan, have led governments to move away from rigid dollar pegs. But with the growth of intra-Asian trade and finance, large fluctuations in intra-EA9 rates have grown increasingly uncomfortable. One can imagine that Asia, like Europe before it, will respond with the adoption of a common or collective peg.

Whether this scenario is desirable or feasible is the subject of the remainder of this chapter.

2 Regional perspectives

The obvious framework for analyzing the costs and benefits of a common peg is the theory of optimum currency areas. Indeed, the motivation for Mundell's (1961) seminal article was to ask whether there was any justification for greater exchange rate variability between Canada and the USA than between regions within the two countries. Subsequently, insights from this literature have been utilized to explain observed exchange rate variability across countries.

In a recent paper (Bayoumi and Eichengreen, 1996) we sought to operationalize optimum currency area (OCA) theory and apply it to data for European countries. We related exchange rate variability to four country characteristics that OCA theory suggests increase or reduce the desirability of stable exchange rates and monetary unification. First are 'asymmetric' output disturbances (affecting different countries differently), which we measure as the standard deviation of the change in the log of relative output in the two countries. Second is the dissimilarity of the composition of the exports of a pair of trade partners, also a proxy for asymmetric shocks. This variable should be particularly relevant for Asia, where, according to Kwan (1994) and Takagi (1996), the similarity of trade structures vis-à-vis Japan should be a powerful determinant of the weight countries attach to the yen in their basket pegs. (In particular, Kwan argues that the higher the share of manufactures in total exports, and hence the more similar a country's export structure with Japan's, the larger should be the weight on the yen in a basket peg.) Third is the importance of commercial links between each pair of countries, which we measure using data on bilateral trade. Fourth is economic size, since the costs of a common currency, in terms of macroeconomic policy independence forgone, should be balanced against the benefits, which will be greatest for small economies where there is least scope for utilizing a separate national currency in transactions. We measure this as the arithmetic average of (the log of) real GDP in US dollars of the two countries.

The estimating equation is therefore:

$$SD(e_{ij}) = \alpha + \beta_1 SD(\Delta y_i - \Delta y_j) + \beta_2 DISSI\ M_{ij} + \beta_3 TRADE_{IJ} + \beta_4 SIZE_{IJ}$$

$$(21.1)$$

where $SD(e_{ij})$ is the standard deviation of the change in the logarithm of the end-year bilateral exchange rate between countries i and j, $SD(\Delta y_i - \Delta y_j)$ is the standard deviation of the difference in the logarithm of real output between i and j, $DISSIM_{ij}$ is the sum of the absolute differences in the shares of agricultural, mineral, and manufacturing trade in total merchandize trade, $TRADE_{ij}$ is the mean of the ratio of bilateral exports to domestic GDP for the two countries, and $SIZE_{ij}$ is the mean of the logarithm of the two GDPs measured in US dollars. In each case, variables are measured as averages over the sample period.

We estimated this equation for Japan and its nineteen leading trading partners over the period 1976–95. This sample includes eight of the EA9 (we lack data for China). It includes the United States and Germany, the two countries in addition to Japan whose currencies feature in most proposals for EA9 pegs. The basic result is as follows (with t-statistics in parentheses):

$$SD(e_{ij}) = \quad -0.01 \quad + \quad 0.79\ SD(\Delta y_i - \Delta y_j) + \quad 0.01\ DISSIM_{ij}$$
$$\qquad\qquad (0.27) \qquad (3.61) \qquad\qquad\qquad (1.64)$$

$$\qquad - \quad 0.34\ TRADE_{ij} + \quad 0.01\ SIZE_{ij}$$
$$\qquad\quad (7.57) \qquad\qquad\quad (5.24)$$

$$R^2 = 0.36 \quad S.E. = 0.028$$

The signs of all the coefficients are as predicted, and three of the four differ significantly from zero at high levels of confidence. (The fourth, the measure of the dissimilarity in the composition of exports, approaches significance at the 10 percent level.) Countries that trade more heavily have more stable exchange rates, as do smaller economies, countries whose GDPs generally fluctuate together, and countries with a more similar composition of exports. Thus, the theory of optimum currency areas does a credible job of explaining the exchange rate policies of Japan's principal trading partners.

Next, we use the estimated coefficients and values of the independent variables in 1995 to predict the dependent variable. The predicted level of exchange rate variability can be thought of as an "OCA index," with smaller values suggesting that countries better approximate an optimum currency area. Table 21.2. suggests, not surprisingly, that the very small, very open economies of the region, Hong Kong and Singapore, would find it most appealing to peg to other East Asian countries. The cases where the value of the OCA index approaches West European levels are Singapore–Malaysia, Singapore–Thailand, Singapore–Hong Hong, Singapore–Taiwan, and Hong Kong–Taiwan. These are the country pairs for which the argument for a common external peg is strongest. In contrast, the case for Indonesia, South Korea, and the Philippines is weaker. Furthermore, any attempt to encourage the adoption of a common peg by the first five East Asian countries would be complicated by the fact that Malaysia and Thailand have relatively little economic incentive to adopt the same external peg.

Then there is the question of what that common external peg should be. In Bayoumi and Eichengreen (1996), on European exchange rate policy, we not only considered OCA indices for each pair of countries but also constructed these indices for each country vis-à-vis a common external anchor, Germany. The problem with applying this approach to Asia is that no single currency plausibly offers an attractive external peg. In Table 21.3 we therefore report values of the OCA index for each Asian country vis-à-vis Japan, the United States, and Germany, and construct a basket peg, following Williamson

Table 21.2 Optimum currency area indices for Asian countries

	Japan	USA	Germany	Basket
Hong Kong	0.086	0.025	0.093	0.063
Indonesia	0.106	0.121	0.112	0.114
South Korea	0.090	0.099	0.096	0.095
Malaysia	0.093	0.077	0.113	0.093
Philippines	0.094	0.076	0.101	0.089
Singapore	0.063	0.016	0.081	0.050
Thailand	0.090	0.095	0.103	0.096
Taiwan	0.087	0.077	0.100	0.087

Table 21.3 OCA indices for bilateral relationships

	Hong Kong	Indonesia	Korea	Malaysia	Philippines	Singapore	Thailand
Hong Kong							
Indonesia	0.12						
Korea	0.08	0.11					
Malaysia	0.11	0.11	0.11				
Philippines	0.09	0.11	0.09	0.10			
Singapore	0.04	0.09	0.07	−0.06	0.06		
Thailand	0.10	0.11	0.10	0.09	0.08	0.03	
Taiwan	0.06	0.11	0.08	0.11	0.08	0.06	0.09

(1998), by imposing weights of 0.3, 0.4, and 0.3 for the yen, dollar, and Deutsche Mark.

Table 21.3 suggests that a common basket peg with these weights works nearly as well as choosing between the yen, dollar, or Deutsche Mark countries in the sense that most of the figures in the column headed 'Basket' are only a little larger than the smallest of the three other columns. The principal exceptions are Hong Kong and Singapore, both of which would clearly prefer to peg to the dollar. While Indonesia, South Korea, and Thailand might marginally prefer the yen, and Malaysia, the Philippines, and Taiwan might marginally prefer the dollar, a basket peg in fact does almost as well for all these countries.

The preceding analysis takes a reduced form approach to operationalizing the theory of optimum currency areas. It employs simple proxies for the arguments of that theory. An alternative is to consider in more detail each of the factors pointed to by the theory. For example, in Bayoumi and Eichengreen (1994) we provide a detailed analysis of asymmetric disturbances, using the structural VAR methodology of Blanchard and Quah (1989). Analyzing time series for prices and output, we identify disturbances with temporary and permanent impacts on output, which we interpret as aggregate-demand and aggregate-supply shocks. Again, we discuss the cases of both Europe and Asia, since Europe provides an obvious metric for the Asian economies, the EU having opted to proceed with monetary union.

Asia compares well with Europe in terms of the magnitude of disturbances. Aggregate-demand disturbances were about twice as large in Europe as in Asia over the sample period 1972–89, confirming the impression of relatively good macroeconomic management in Asia. In contrast, there is little to choose between the continents in terms of the magnitude of aggregate-supply shocks (Table 21.4).

The demand shocks of Hong Kong, Indonesia, Malaysia, Singapore and Thailand are relatively highly correlated with one another (as shown in

Table 21.4 Size and speed of adjustment to disturbances

	Supply disturbances		Demand disturbances	
	Size	Speed	Size	Speed
Germany	0.022	1.193	0.015	0.659
France	0.034	0.243	0.014	0.101
Netherlands	0.033	0.692	0.019	0.511
Belgium	0.028	0.668	0.020	0.508
Denmark	0.022	1.104	0.017	0.135
Astria	0.018	0.999	0.017	0.415
Switzerland	0.031	0.997	0.016	0.858
Italy	0.030	0.427	0.036	0.380
UK	0.018	0.425	0.019	0.016
Spain	0.057	0.083	0.015	0.123
Portugal	0.061	0.426	0.026	0.367
Ireland	0.021	1.222	0.038	0.382
Sweden	0.030	0.261	0.012	0.419
Norway	0.031	0.651	0.034	0.704
Finland	0.018	0.875	0.027	0.684
Average	0.030	0.684	0.022	0.417
Japan	0.012	1.670	0.017	0.270
Taiwan	0.021	1.470	0.049	0.673
South Korea	0.029	0.890	0.038	0.115
Thailand	0.026	1.380	0.042	1.279
Hong Kong	0.023	1.590	0.044	1.190
Singapore	0.032	1.350	0.028	1.072
Malaysia	0.032	1.040	0.063	1.607
Indonesia	0.130	1.240	0.071	1.335
Philippines	0.089	0.590	0.081	1.475
Australia	0.011	0.920	0.017	0.910
Newzealand	0.060	0.650	0.031	0.291

Table 21.5). The make-up of this grouping is not surprising. Malaysia, Singapore, and Thailand trade heavily with one another. With the possible exception of Singapore, they have all followed what Williamson calls 'dollar-focused' exchange rate policies over the sample period. This reinforces the presumption that the correlation of demand disturbances reflects exchange rate policy and should not be regarded as invariant with respect to the exchange rate regime.

From the perspective of policy options, the correlation of supply shocks is more informative, since it should be less sensitive to choice of exchange rate arrangement. Table 21.6 reveals two groups of Asian countries among which aggregate-supply shocks are significantly correlated: Japan, South Korea, and

Table 21.5 Correlations of demand disturbances across different geographic regions

(a) Western Europe

	Germany	France	Nether-lands	Belgium	Denmark	Australia	Switzer-land	Italy	UK	Spain	Portugal	Ireland	Sweden	Norway	Finland
Germany	1.00														
France	0.30	1.00													
Netherlands	0.21	0.34	1.00												
Belgium	0.36	0.53	0.52	1.00											
Denmark	0.34	0.32	0.20	0.30	1.00										
Australia	0.32	0.50	0.29	0.56	0.30	1.00									
Switzerland	0.18	0.42	0.37	0.28	0.22	0.45	1.00								
Italy	0.22	0.62	0.24	0.49	0.06	0.44	0.32	1.00							
UK	0.09	0.20	-0.05	-0.03	0.00	-0.15	-0.08	0.05	1.00						
Spain	-0.10	0.53	0.11	0.26	0.25	0.30	0.04	0.49	0.23	1.00					
Portugal	0.24	0.47	0.05	0.45	0.30	0.60	0.36	0.63	0.24	0.32	1.00				
Ireland	0.06	0.09	0.39	0.00	0.34	-0.12	0.19	-0.08	0.25	0.02	-0.01	1.00			
Sweden	0.10	0.18	0.29	0.36	0.18	0.02	-0.07	0.25	0.18	-0.01	0.08	0.30	1.00		
Norway	-0.24	0.01	-0.14	-0.24	-0.11	-0.16	-0.11	-0.30	0.13	0.14	-0.19	-0.20	-0.11	1.00	
Finland	0.10	0.47	0.32	0.60	0.36	0.53	0.30	0.65	0.16	0.40	0.54	0.17	0.33	-0.21	1.00

(b) East Asia

	Japan	Taiwan	Korea	Thailand	Hong Kong	Singapore	Malaysia	Indonesia	Philippines	Australia	New Zealand
Japan	1.00										
Taiwan	-0.01	1.00									
Korea	0.19	0.33	1.00								
Tailand	-0.04	0.54	0.32	1.00							
Hong Kong	0.23	0.22	0.05	0.43	1.00						
Singapore	-0.09	0.44	0.27	0.70	0.37	1.00					
Malaysia	0.12	0.41	0.43	0.58	0.54	0.67	1.00				
Indonesia	0.16	0.17	0.17	0.36	0.62	0.64	0.58	1.00			
Philippines	0.29	0.09	0.16	0.15	-0.19	-0.05	-0.11	0.04	1.00		
Australia	0.22	0.20	0.46	0.32	0.32	0.34	0.50	0.05	-0.01	1.00	
New Zealand	0.00	-0.39	-0.41	0.10	0.43	0.13	0.06	0.09	-0.06	0.21	1.00

Table 21.6 Correlations of supply disturbances across different geographic regions

(a) Western Europe

	Germany	France	Netherlands	Belgium	Denmark	Australia	Switzerland	Italy	UK	Spain	Portugal	Ireland	Sweden	Norway	Finland
Germany	1.00														
France	0.52	1.00													
Netherlands	0.54	0.36	1.00												
Belgium	0.62	0.46	0.56	1.00											
Denmark	0.68	0.54	0.56	0.37	1.00										
Australia	0.41	0.28	0.38	0.47	0.49	1.00									
Switzerland	0.38	0.25	0.58	0.47	0.36	0.39	1.00								
Italy	0.21	0.28	0.39	0.00	0.15	0.06	-0.04	1.00							
UK	0.12	0.12	0.13	0.12	-0.05	-0.25	0.16	0.28	1.00						
Spain	0.33	0.21	0.17	0.23	0.22	0.25	0.07	0.20	0.01	1.00					
Portugal	0.21	0.33	0.11	0.40	-0.04	-0.03	0.13	0.22	0.27	0.51	1.00				
Ireland	0.00	-0.21	0.11	-0.02	-0.32	0.08	0.08	0.14	0.05	-0.15	0.01	1.00			
Sweden	0.31	0.30	0.43	0.06	0.35	0.01	0.44	0.46	0.41	0.20	0.39	0.10	1.00		
Norway	-0.27	-0.11	-0.39	-0.26	-0.37	-0.21	-0.18	0.01	0.27	-0.09	0.26	0.08	0.10	1.00	
Finland	0.22	0.12	-0.25	0.06	0.30	0.11	0.06	-0.32	-0.04	0.07	-0.13	-0.23	-0.10	-0.08	1.00

(b) East Asia

	Japan	Taiwan	Korea	Thailand	Hong Kong	Singapore	Malaysia	Indonesia	Philippines	Australia	New Zealand
Japan	1.00										
Taiwan	0.61	1.00									
Korea	0.46	0.54	1.00								
Thailand	0.32	0.59	0.36	1.00							
Hong Kong	0.29	0.28	0.05	0.31	1.00						
Singapore	-0.10	0.25	0.02	0.29	0.63	1.00					
Malaysia	-0.02	0.06	-0.03	0.35	0.47	0.71	1.00				
Indonesia	0.14	-0.03	-0.10	0.13	0.53	0.55	0.52	1.00			
Philippines	0.10	0.37	-0.11	-0.06	0.05	0.05	-0.03	0.03	1.00		
Australia	0.12	0.21	0.19	0.14	-0.16	-0.22	0.03	0.09	0.23	1.00	
New Zealand	0.01	0.19	-0.25	0.15	-0.12	0.13	-0.11	0.01	-0.06	-0.41	1.00

Taiwan; and Hong Kong, Indonesia, Malaysia, and Singapore. Again, the patterns are intuitive. Japan, South Korea, and Taiwan were among the first East Asian countries to industrialize, and they compete with one another in the American market. Industrialization began later in Indonesia, Malaysia, Hong Kong, and Singapore. Compared to South Korea and Taiwan, these countries import less from Japan (Kwan, 1994).

Financial disturbances are an increasingly prevalent source of asymmetric shocks. They provide the strongest argument against a common peg. The argument is that Asia's emerging economies need exchange rate flexibility and monetary independence to cope with financial disturbances. A widely held lesson of the Mexican crisis is that emerging markets with weak banking systems and heavy dependence on foreign capital should not peg their exchange rates. When banks run into trouble, a government seeking to maintain an exchange rate peg will have limited ability to inject credit into the banking system; since currency traders know that the authorities will find themselves between a rock and a hard place, banking problems inevitably spill over into the foreign exchange market.

These problems are especially prevalent in emerging markets. The capacity for prudential supervision tends to be less than in advanced industrial countries. Even capital and reserve requirements stricter than those of the Basle Accords may not avert this danger, since emerging markets experience immense capital inflows and outflows, which tend to be intermediated by the banking system. In many developing countries, governments are reluctant to allow nonfinancial firms to fail, either because they hold a financial stake or because the firms in question have disproportionate political power; hence, the authorities will be disinclined to allow bank credit to contract when global interest rates rise or the banking system is otherwise forced to retrench. Governments in this situation, forced to choose between injecting credit into the banking system and defending the exchange rate, cannot credibly commit to the latter, and the markets, knowing this, have an incentive to run on their reserves.

Historically, banking problems have not been as pervasive in East Asia as in other emerging markets. Banks in the region have been tightly regulated; their access to offshore funds has been strictly controlled. The question, as Dornbusch and Park (1998) put it, is whether Asian banking systems will acquire Latin American features as liberalization proceeds. There was already some evidence of this kind of instability in Thailand in 1996. Moody's has noted the appalling opaqueness of Thai banks' published balance sheets, illustrating the difficulty noted above of applying First World standards of regulation and supervision to emerging markets. The revelation in parliamentary debate of the insolvency of the Bangkok Bank of Commerce (BBC), Thailand's ninth largest, led to a generalized run on deposits in the summer of 1996. These events had a predictable impact on the foreign exchange market. When the government made clear that it was prepared to create the liquidity needed to bail out BBC, this contributed to a run on the baht. The IMF reportedly recommended that the government widen the band in which the currency is allowed to move against the dollar.

To summarize, problems of financial fragility, insofar as they impact different countries at different times, provide perhaps the strongest economic case against schemes for a common currency peg. The other side of the OCA equation is speed of adjustment to shocks.

Our own estimates (again from Bayoumi and Eichengreen, 1994) suggest that adjustment in Asia is relatively fast. Almost all of the change in output and prices in response to a shock takes place in the first two years. (In Europe, by comparison, at most half of the change occurs in the first twenty-four months.) The fastest adjustment to supply shocks is (in descending order) in Japan, Hong Kong, Taiwan, Thailand, and Indonesia, the slowest in the Philippines. These results would appear to be consistent with the general impression that labor markets are more flexible in East Asia than in Western Europe.

Labor mobility is relatively high in Asia. Goto and Hamada (1994) note the extent of migration between the less and more developed East Asian economies and emphasize its responsiveness to changing economic conditions. The share of the labor force accounted for by foreign workers can be large. In Singapore, for example, workers from Malaysia, Thailand, Indonesia, and the Philippines accounted for fully 10 percent of employment in the 1980s. The elasticity of supply of Chinese workers to Hong Kong is notoriously high. Emigration has been as much as 2 percent of the labor force of the sending countries. This is a high level of labor mobility by European standards, reflecting extensive experience with migration and the existence of networks of overseas Chinese.

Having considered the costs of a harmonized monetary policy, we turn now to the benefits. By European standards, the structural characteristics of the EA9 are consistent with relatively large savings in transactions costs from the adoption of a common currency peg. Several, but not all, of the economies in this group are relatively small. All are relatively open, some exceptionally so; the export/GDP ratio in 1993 ranged from 84 percent in Singapore to 19 percent in China. Intra-EA trade is high and rising. Goto and Hamada compute trade intensity indices, which normalize bilateral trade by the relative share of the countries in question in total world trade, eliminating size effects. Those indices, computed for 1990, show higher values for East Asia than for Western Europe. While there are a few instances – Ireland and the UK, the Netherlands and Belgium-Luxembourg, Spain and Portugal, and Greece and Italy – where intra-European trade is exceptionally intensive, a substantial number of bilateral links in East Asia are at least as intense: Japan–Korea, Japan–Indonesia, Japan–Thailand, Hong Kong–Taiwan, Singapore–Malaysia, Singapore–Indonesia, Singapore–Thailand, and Malaysia–Thailand. Cross-border investment is also extensive. Flows of direct foreign investment into

Indonesia, Malaysia, and Thailand, joined more recently by China, have been especially pronounced since the mid-1980s. Japan has traditionally been the main source of direct foreign investment in the region, but its share of the estimated DFI stock of the EA9 has declined from 28 percent in 1982 to 21 percent in 1993. This reflects very different movements in the relative importance of Japanese investment in the NICs and ASEAN four: Japan's share in the NICs rose from 24 to 32 percent over the period, while its share in ASEAN fell from 30 to 22 percent. By some estimates, the NICs themselves supply a larger share of the total stock of DFI in East Asia than either Japan or the United States, reflecting heavy investment by Singapore and Hong Kong in Indonesia, Malaysia, and Thailand.

On standard optimum currency area grounds, then, the economies of East Asia would seem to be more or less as plausible candidates for internationally harmonized monetary policies as the members of the European Union. While they do not satisfy all the standard OCA criteria, neither does Europe. Some countries in the region, notably those with smaller, more open economies, may find a collective peg more attractive than others, but the same is true in Europe. As in Europe, the problems created by remaining deviations could in principle be overcome by sufficient political solidarity. The next section asks whether this is a realistic prospect.

3 Historical perspectives

In this section we consider whether the political preconditions exist in Asia for the successful operation of a collective currency peg. As the last section has shown, different countries will generally prefer different weights on the yen, dollar, and Deutsche Mark. A common peg will involve compromises and costs, just as the harmonization of monetary policies has involved compromises and costs in Europe. Side-payments and trade-offs across issue areas will be required to compensate the losers, and political means for providing them must be in place.

Moreover, establishing a common peg is easier than defending it. Successful defense may require collective support, and more support than is available under the existing network of repurchase arrangements presupposes surveillance and policy conditionality. A clear lesson of European experience is that strong-currency countries will be reluctant to support the exchange rates of their weak-currency counterparts without leverage over the latter's policies, for fear that the common monetary policy will be thrown off course and that their loans will not be paid back. The political preconditions for making that leverage effective should not be underestimated.

In Western Europe, the debate over monetary integration has gone hand in hand with discussions of political integration and the creation of a supranational entity empowered to override previously sovereign national governments. Efforts to create collective currency arrangements have entailed formal institutionalization, starting with the Treaty of Rome, an international treaty signed by six countries that cited exchange rates as a matter of "common concern," proceeding to the creation of the EMS Act of Agreement, and culminating with the Maastricht Treaty. At each stage, national governments delegated a growing range of powers to the collectivity and elaborated progressively more detailed governance structures. As Paul-Henri Spaak put it when discussing the creation of the EEC, "Those who drew up the Rome Treaty . . . did not think of it as essentially economic; they thought of it as a stage on the way to political union."

The point should not be exaggerated: there has been resistance in Europe to the creation of supranational authority and the construction of institutional restraints on national policy every step of the way. Where the Werner Report, an early 1970s landmark on the road to EMU, saw the strong centralization of fiscal functions in the hands of the European Commission as a prerequisite, national governments refused to surrender their powers. Where some of the founders of the EMS anticipated the pooling of countries' international reserves and the creation of a European Monetary Fund to oversee their utilization, countries like Germany resisted this attempt to abrogate their monetary sovereignty. The debate over EMU, especially in Denmark and the UK, is very much a debate over whether or not to accept further compromises of national sovereignty. But the nature of the debate itself, and the profound transfer of national powers to the European Commission and the European Central Bank foreseen in the Maastricht Treaty, are themselves indicative of how far Europe's political dialogue has come.

Why did the political preconditions for this assignment of powers to a supranational entity and the extensive institutionalization of governance develop in Europe? One answer is the continent's unique socio-political history. Economic integration has a path-dependent character which can operate in strongly self-reinforcing ways. In Europe, initial conditions and chance events along the transition path have worked to strengthen integrationist tendencies to the point where the political preconditions for monetary union are in place. In Asia, in contrast, neither initial conditions nor subsequent events have been conducive to the development of the requisite political cohesion.

Some may object that Europe has taken only fifty years to develop the necessary support for monetary integration; after all, as recently as 1944 Germany and France were at war. But this is to overlook the deeper roots of the integrationist agenda. Proponents of European integration trace their antecedents back to Pierre Dubois, a jurist and diplomat in the French and English courts, who in 1306 proposed a permanent assemblage of European princes working to secure a lasting peace. The English Quaker William Penn proposed a European parliament and a supranational European government in 1693. Jeremy Bentham advocated a European assembly, Jean-Jacques Rousseau a European federation, Henri Saint-Simon a European monarch and parliament. By the middle of the nineteenth century intellectuals like Victor Hugo spoke of a United States of Europe. We could go on, but the point is clear: in Europe, the ideal of integration is intimately connected with the liberal and democratic principles of the Enlightenment and has roots in centuries of history.

Interwar developments further suggest that post-World War II initiatives were an incomplete break with the past. Belgium and Luxembourg established an economic union in 1922. The Low Countries and Scandinavia agreed to harmonize their tariffs as part of the 1930 Oslo Convention. The Pan-European Union, founded by the Austria Count Richard Coudenhove-Kalergi in 1923, lobbied for a European federation and attracted the support of Aristide Briand and Edouard Herriot, who were later premiers of France. In 1924, Herriot, then French prime minister, spoke out for the creation of a United States of Europe. In 1929, Briand proposed to the League of Nations the creation of a European confederation. Konrad Adenauer and Georges Pompidou were also members of the Pan-European Union.

One can thus say that by 1945 the intellectual preconditions for European integration were in place. It was only necessary to add to this combustible mix the spark of the Marshall Plan. Under the terms of US aid, the recipient governments were required to decide among themselves on the distribution of the transfer. In response, they established the organization that quickly evolved into the OEEC and then the OECD. The USA provided political cover and financial resources for the European Payments Union. It supported the creation of the European Coal and Steel Community, an entity singled out by its historian as the first true instance of "supranationality" (Gillingham, 1992). The point is that these concrete economic steps took place in an environment with important political preconditions in place.

Katzenstein (1996) makes similar points, albeit in different terms. He speaks of powers and norms in the international system and of the character of domestic state structures as determining the scope for regional integration. In discussing international power and norms, he singles out US foreign policy for establishing the principle of multilateralism in Europe after 1945. By domestic state structures conducive to integration, he means states which recognize the legitimacy of international law and institutions, features of European politics that can ultimately be traced back to the Enlightenment. East Asia, in contrast, lacks the political solidarity and cohesion to institutionalize a durable system of collective currency pegs. Post-World War II resistance to a strong institutional structure for European integration was overcome partly by the intervention of an outside agent, the United States, which provided financial and political incentives to pursue this route. In East Asia, in contrast, the post-World War II period saw a very different geopolitical dynamic. The USA guaranteed the security of Japan, South Korea, and other countries bilaterally; SEATO (the Southeast Asia Treaty Organization, an attempt to create a regional analog to NATO) did little except on paper. There was no Asian Marshall Plan to impel the governments of the region to establish collective governance.

Nor does East Asia's history feature a Jean Monnet or Paul-Henri Spaak to speak out for regional integration. Before World War I, many countries were under the dominance of colonial powers which provided little scope for self-determination. The military governments that emerged after the war discouraged cross-border rapprochement for fear that this would undermine their domestic political control. Some go so far as to argue that most East Asian governments are actively hostile to autonomous international bureaucratic structures. Then there is the fact that ideological distance between China's communist government and market-oriented regimes elsewhere in East Asia is so great (in contrast to Western Europe, where after World War II variants of the social market economy were embraced by virtually all the members of the present-day European Union). It is hard to believe that Beijing would permit other East Asian countries to mandate a change in Chinese macroeconomic policy as a quid pro quo for intervention in support of the renminbi, or that other countries would entrust Beijing with this authority in return for its support.

At a deeper level, East Asia lacks a Benthamite/Rousseauan/Saint-Simonian heritage of collective democratic governance through integration. As Katzenstein puts it, "the notion of unified sovereignty... central to the conception of continental European states, does not capture Asian political realities." As in China today, the regions resist the attempts of the center to exercise its politics through the operation of political and legal institutions. The idea of a centralized state with a monopoly of force that regiments its citizens through the superimposition of a common set of institutions is a European conception, not an Asian one. Asian civil society is structured by ritual, ceremony, and economic networks more than by military force or the rule of law. The notion of strong, cohesive nation-states in the Western mold being foreign to Asia, it is unrealistic to speak of pooling national sovereignties which do not exist.

Consequently, integrationist initiatives in Asia have proceeded not through the creation of strong supranational institutions but by establishing loose networks of cooperation. It is revealing that Asia-Pacific Economic Cooperation (APEC), which is essentially just a consultative forum, has succeeded where initiatives to create smaller, more cohesive Asian analogs to the EEC or European Free Trade Area have not.

This predisposition to rely on loose networks rather than formal institutions is clearly evident in the monetary domain. Where the EU has created the Committee of Central Bank Governors, the Monetary Committee, the European Commission, the European Monetary Institute, and, prospectively, the European Central Bank, Asia has created SEANZA, under whose auspices seventeen countries hold biennial central bank training courses, SEACEN, a grouping with ten members which holds annual meetings of governors and also provides training courses, and the Executives' Meeting of East Asia and

Pacific Central Banks (EMEAP), an eleven-country grouping whose functions are limited to information sharing. Even the advocates of a new, encompassing regional institution suggest as a model the BIS rather than the EU's Monetary Committee or European Monetary Institute (EMI).

It is not surprising, then, that the most recent international monetary initiative in East Asia takes the form of a network of repurchase arrangements limited in geographical and financial coverage. Only seven of the EA9 participate, and credit lines are limited to those which can be fully collateralized by the borrowing country's holdings of US treasury securities. Practical experience as well as political analysis thus creates doubts about whether the EA9 would agree to establish a common currency peg encompassing the entire region and to create an institutional framework for extensive operations in support of those pegs.

4 Conclusion

We have analyzed the economic and political prospects for monetary integration in East Asia. We find that the region satisfies the standard optimum currency area criteria for the adoption of a common monetary policy about as well as Western Europe. Its small, open economies would benefit from the reduction in uncertainty that would result from the creation of a durable common peg. Intra-Asian trade and investment have reached relatively high levels. Adjustment to shocks is fast, and supply and demand disturbances are small and symmetric by European standards.

The strongest argument against even a limited sacrifice of monetary autonomy is that domestic financial systems are less well developed than in Western Europe. The legacy of financial repression and capital controls continues to limit financial depth, as emphasized by Dornbusch and Park (1998). Currency pegs, whether unilateral or collective, are risky where governments are required to intervene in support of their banking systems. Proponents of collective pegging may object that this freedom would not be sacrificed if the fluctuation of currencies was limited to, say, plus or minus 10 percent, if the band was allowed to crawl, and if realignments were undertaken as appropriate. The sceptical rebuttal is that this is precisely the kind of arrangement under which Mexico was operating in 1994, and look what happened.

Even if one decides on economic grounds in favor of a common basket peg, there remains the question of whether Asia possesses the political wherewithal to operate it successfully. Asian economic and political relations are based on loose interlocking networks. The notion that the governments of the EA9 would all agree to a common basket peg assumes a uniformity and a reliance on consultation and institutionalization that may be realistic for Europe but which are quite foreign to Asia. Moreover, pegs are resilient to shocks only when they receive collective support. Unilateral pegs can be successfully operated only under exceptional circumstances; even Argentina's convertibility plan required $8 billion of external support to survive the Tequila Effect in 1995. As European experience has shown, governments are willing to commit significant financial resources to other countries' currency pegs only when there exist institutional guarantees of leverage over those countries' domestic policies. And in Europe, decades of work to create supranational institutions, in turn building on a centuries-long integrationist tradition, have been required to approach that point.

The danger, then, is that putting the economic cart so far ahead of the political horse will create an Asian analog not to the EMS but to the Snake, an unstable and unsatisfactory arrangement. It could set back the cause of exchange rate stability and regional economic cooperation for years to come.

References

Bayoumi, Tamim and Eichengreen, Barry (1994) "One Money or Many? Analyzing the Prospects for Monetary Unification in Various Parts of the World," *Princeton Studies in International Finance* 76.

——(1996) "Ever Closer to Heaven? An Optimum-Currency-Area Index for European Countries," *European Economic Review* (forthcoming).

Bénassy-Quéré, Agnès (1998) "Exchange Rate Regimes and Policies: an Empirical Analysis," this volume, pp. 40–64.

Blanchard, Olivier and Quah, Danny (1989) "The Dynamic Effects of Aggregate Demand and Supply Disturbances," *American Economic Review* 79, pp. 655–73.

Calvo, Guillermo A. (1996) "Capital Flows and Macroeconomic Management: Tequila Lessons," *International Journal of Finance and Economics* 1, pp. 207–24.

Corden, W. Max (1972) "Monetary Integration," *Princeton Studies in International Finance* 32.

Crone, Donald (1993) "Does Hegemony Matter? The Reorganization of the Pacific Political Economy," *World Politics* 45, pp. 501–25.

Dooley, Michael P. (1996) "Capital Controls and Emerging Markets," *International Journal of Finance and Economics* 1, pp. 197–206.

Dornbusch, Rüdiger and Park, Yung Chul (1998) "Flexibility or Nominal Anchors?," this volume, pp. 3–34.

Frankel, Jeffrey A. and Wei, Shang-Jin (1994) "Yen Bloc or Dollar Bloc? Exchange Rate Policies of the East Asian Economies," in Takatoshi Ito and Anne O. Krueger (eds), *Macroeconomic Linkage: Savings, Exchange Rates and Capital Flows*, Chicago: University of Chicago Press, pp. 295–334.

Fraser, Bernie (1995) "Central Bank Co-operation in the Asian Region," unpublished manuscript, Reserve Bank of Australia.

Gillingham, John (1992) *Coal, Steel and the Rebirth of Europe*, Cambridge: Cambridge University Press.

Goto, Junichi and Hamada, Koichi (1994) "Economic Preconditions for Asian Regional Integration," in Takatoshi Ito and Anne O. Krueger (eds), *Macroeconomic Linkage: Savings, Exchange Rates and Capital Flows*, Chicago: University of Chicago Press, pp. 359–85.

Katzenstein, Peter J. (1996) "Regionalism in Comparative Perspective," *Cooperation and Conflict* 31, pp. 123–60.

Kohsaka, Akira (1996) "Interdependence Through Capital Flows in Pacific Asia and the Role of Japan," in Takatoshi Ito and Anne O. Krueger (eds), *Financial Deregulation and Integration in East Asia*, Chicago: University of Chicago Press, pp. 107–46.

Kwan, C.H. (1994) *Economic Interdependence in the Asia-Pacific Region*, London: Routledge.

Leiderman, Leonardo and Bufman, Gil (1995) "Searching for Nominal Anchors in Shock-Prone Economies in the 1990s: Inflation Targets and Exchange Rate Bands," unpublished manuscript, Tel Aviv University.

Mundell, Robert A. (1961) "A Theory of Optimum Currency Areas," *American Economic Review* 51, pp. 657–65.

Sachs, Jeffrey (1995) "Alternative Approaches to Financial Crises in Emerging Markets," unpublished manuscript, Harvard University.

Tagauchi, Hiroo (1994) "On the Internationalization of the Japanese Yen," in Takatoshi Ito and Anne O. Krueger (eds), *Macroeconomic Linkage: Savings, Exchange Rates and Capital Flows*, Chicago: University of Chicago Press, pp. 335–55.

Takagi, Shinji (1996) *The Yen and its East Asian Neighbors, 1980–1995: Cooperation or Competition?*, NBER Working Paper 5720, Cambridge, Mass.

Tavlas, George and Ozeki, Yuzuru (1992) *The Internationalization of Currencies: An Appraisal of the Japanese Yen*, Occasional Paper No. 90, Washington, DC: International Monetary Fund.

Tower, Edward and Willett, Thomas D. (1976) "The Theory of Optimum Currency Areas and Exchange Rate Flexibility," Special Papers in *International Economics No. 11*, International Finance Section, Department of Economics, Princeton University, Princeton, NJ.

Urwin, Derek W. (1996) *The Community of Europe*, London: Longman.

Wickham, Peter (1985) "The Choice of Exchange Rate Regime in Developing Countries," *Staff Papers* 32, pp. 248–88.

Williamson, John (1998) "The Case for a Common Basket Peg for East Asian Currencies," this volume, pp. 327–43.

Woo, Wing Thye and Hirayama, Kenjiro (1996) "Monetary Autonomy in the Presence of Capital Flows: And Never the Twain Shall Meet, Except in East Asia," in Takatoshi Ito and Anne O. Krueger (eds), *Financial Deregulation and Integration in East Asia*, Chicago: University of Chicago Press, pp. 307–34.

22

DISCUSSION

Adriaan Dierx

Eichengreen and Bayoumi will perhaps be surprised to hear that one of the 'apostles of European monetary integration' agrees with their chapter's conclusion that for political reasons, the emerging Asian countries are unlikely to introduce a formal common basket peg in the near future. Most Asians appear to agree as well: 'Monetary cooperation will move forward at a pace comfortable to all.'

This raises the key question of the timing of the chapter. On the one hand, one might argue that the chapter was appropriately timed in order to offer an immediate response to Williamson's proposal that the Asian currencies be pegged to a common currency basket including the US dollar, the Japanese yen and the Deutsche Mark. On the other hand, that proposal, first made by John Williamson at the Seoul conference (see Chapter 19) and supported by Rüdiger Dornbusch and Yung Chul Park (Chapter 1), risked being dead on arrival due to the immediate criticism expressed by Eichengreen and Bayoumi (Chapter 21).

This dilemma is also reflected in the arrangement of the chapter. In Section 2, on regional perspectives, economic arguments in favour of a common currency peg are stressed to arrive at the conclusion that 'the economies of East Asia would seem to be more or less as plausible candidates for internationally harmonized monetary policies as the members of the European Union'. It is necessary to make this argument, because prior to the conference no established literature in favour of a common currency peg in Asia appears to have existed. In the section on historical perspectives, the authors then proceed by tearing down the structure that they just finished building. They conclude by saying that a common basket peg in Asia 'could set back the cause of exchange rate stability and regional economic cooperation for many years to come'.

The strongest (economic) argument provided against a common currency peg is that in Asia domestic financial systems are less well developed than in Western Europe: 'Asia's emerging economies need exchange rate flexibility and monetary independence to cope with financial disturbances.' This argument is not very persuasive, however, because – as the authors note themselves – 'banking problems have not been as pervasive in East Asia as in other emerging markets'. The example of Thailand is used to illustrate Asia's problems, but no other Asian country is mentioned.

The political arguments against a common currency peg I find very convincing in general terms, even if at times the historical perspective goes quite far back in time. However, a couple of statements in this section seem rather inappropriate. Discussing the European experience, the authors state that: 'strong-currency countries will be reluctant to support the exchange rates of their weak-currency partners ... for fear that ... their loans will not be paid back.' And, after identifying the European countries as 'states which recognize the legitimacy of international law and institutions', the authors go on: 'East Asia, in contrast, lacks the political solidarity and cohesion to institutionalize a durable system of collective currency pegs', which seems a little tough on the Asian countries.

Finally, would it not be interesting to add a geographical argument to the economic and historical arguments made? In Europe, economic and political integration is advocated more strongly on the continent than in the UK or the Nordic countries. In Asia, the continent (i.e. China) is already fully integrated. The other Asian countries are either island nations or located on a peninsula. From the geographical perspective, one could argue that it would be natural for the Asian countries to peg their currency to the Chinese yuan. From a political and economic perspective, however, this idea clearly remains unrealistic.

If indeed the emerging Asian countries are unlikely to introduce a formal common basket peg, the policy relevance of Chapter 21 is doubtful. However, as the authors point out, the march towards European integration was not completed in a single day, but rather by a slow step-by-step approach. Assuming that there is general agreement on the basic objective of Asian monetary cooperation, a gradual approach might be more productive than the forced establishment of a common basket peg.

In practice, the Asian countries have opted for such a gradual approach. The Asian central banks are engaged in a regular exchange of views on monetary matters, including reserve management, bank supervision, payment and settlement systems, etc. Bilateral agreements on securities repurchase arrangements were signed by seven Asian countries, with a view towards maintaining the stability of their currencies in case of crisis. Suggestions on how to advance this gradual process of monetary cooperation further would surely be very welcome.

Note

The views expressed here do not necessarily reflect the opinion of the European Commission.

23

ROUNDTABLE DISCUSSION

Prospects for regional monetary cooperation

Jean Pisani-Ferry

Jean Pisani-Ferry

The purpose of this roundtable discussion is to take up two major issues that have arisen in the presentation of the papers and to introduce a third one into the picture. The two major issues are the absence, or at least the low degree, of monetary coordination among East Asian countries and the very limited international role of the yen. Several rationales have been given for this situation, which strikingly contrasts with that of Europe. They may deserve further discussion. But more importantly, we should look ahead and discuss whether cooperation among central banks could develop and whether the yen could take a larger role in Asia. These perspectives could also gain from being discussed in the context of the third issue: the transformations in international monetary relations that will arise from the introduction of the Euro and the possible competition between the Euro and the dollar on the international scene.

To address these topics, the participants in this roundtable discussion are Masahiro Sugita, director of the international department of the Bank of Japan; In June Kim, professor at the Seoul National University and member of the Monetary Board of the Bank of Korea; André Icard, Deputy Director-General of the Bank for International Settlements; Toru Kusukawa, chairman of Fuji Research Institute; and Adriaan Dierx, administrator in the Monetary Affairs Directorate of the European Commission.

Masahiro Sugita

Although there are many areas in which Asian monetary cooperation can be found useful, let me start with exchange rate regimes. I take up this issue simply because it has been the main theme of this seminar, and not because I believe it is the most pressing issue in Asian monetary cooperation. Asia is different from Europe, and I don't think we will see anything similar to the European monetary system among us in the near future. Diversity among

East Asian countries, in terms of size of territory, number of population, stage of economic development and historical background, just to give a few examples, makes a regional currency union highly unlikely.

That said, the enormous economic changes that this region is undergoing have brought about some modification to the overall picture of diversity. Trade relations are changing. As a result of industrialization, trade in this region is no longer exclusively integrated vertically. Days when some countries exported manufactured goods while others concentrated on raw material exports have passed. A new network of production is being formed in which parts manufactured and processed in a number of countries make up a final product. In this emerging pattern of division of labour, countries in the region compete with each other in efficiency and cost. Rivalry in manufacturing in the region has strengthened our interest in relative exchange rate relations among us. Asian countries had for a long time maintained relatively stable exchange rates vis-à-vis the US dollar, through fixing their currencies to it, according a relatively high weight to it in a currency basket, or simply conducting discretionary operations. Stability of exchange rates among most Asian countries had thus been secured indirectly through stability of each currency against the US dollar. Japan was an exception and wide dollar/yen fluctuations have led to wide gyrations between Asian currencies and the yen. The problem has most acutely been felt since 1995, as a sharp correction of the high exchange rate of the yen eroded the competitiveness of other Asian countries, resulting in some moderation of their export growth. Faced with this situation, East Asian countries might wish to have more stable exchange rate relations vis-à-vis the yen than before. Countries with debt denominated in yen would derive additional benefit from stability vis-à-vis the yen.

I am not preaching or even suggesting linkage to the yen to our neighbours. I am merely identifying economic changes bearing on regional exchange rates to draw policy implications on our part. If neighbouring countries pursue exchange rate policies paying more attention to the yen exchange rate, then the need may arise for them to hold more yen reserves. Also important in this connection will be the Japanese policy on the use of the yen for international reserves as well as the depth and breadth of the market of short-term money market instruments.

Here, I would like to mention some changes in our policy over the past decade. Traditionally, Japan's policy towards the use of the yen as a reserve currency was not very accommodating. However, the policy shifted to a less restrictive one than before, and we no longer resist the yen's natural trend towards internationalization, including its use as a reserve currency. Also, heightened concern about the Tokyo financial markets' loss of competitiveness has recently generated momentum within Japan for the deregulation of financial markets. In November 1996, Prime Minister Hashimoto took the initiative to conduct a comprehensive review of financial policies with the aim of creating a free, fair and global financial market in Japan. Such a move will eventually result in expanding the list of short-term monetary instruments available and in facilitating transactions in those instruments, encouraging further the international use of the yen.

Now let me turn to other areas where monetary cooperation can more readily be made. Here I would like to touch upon EMEAP (Executives' Meeting of East Asia and Pacific Central Banks). It was launched in 1991 as a forum for regional central banks to get together and exchange views, and now consists of eleven central banks. It kept a rather low profile until 1995, when a call by Mr Bernie Fraser, then Governor of the Reserve Bank of Australia, for an Asian version of the Bank for International Settlements suddenly cast a spotlight on it. EMEAP has come to be seen as a possible embryo of such an institution. I might just note in passing that certain developments in international finance in 1995, including the Mexican financial crisis and a sharp fall in the US dollar, provided momentum for strengthening the cooperation among Asian and Pacific central banks. In any event, partly influenced by Bernie Fraser's call, EMEAP held its first meeting at governors' level in July 1996 in Tokyo. The meeting established two working groups and one study group for promoting further cooperation; one of the working groups was on central banking operations, the other on financial market development, and the study group was on bank supervision.

These groups have started their work by collecting information regarding institutional frameworks and activities in pertinent fields with a view to compiling data books for the reference of participating central banks. How the work of these groups will proceed from there and what fruits of cooperation they will bear are beyond conjecture at this stage.

I therefore would like to discuss only a few areas of possible regional cooperation which some of my Asian central bank colleagues have suggested and express my own personal views on them.

One such area is the provision of a joint safety net in case of emergency. Bilateral repo agreements on US securities had been in place among nine monetary authorities in East Asia and Oceania. Whether or not there is any further need to expand safety nets hinges critically upon the development and stability of the future international financial system. In any event, keeping close contact and consultation with US monetary authorities in matters involving dollar reserves is essential.

Another important area in which some of the Asian monetary authorities are interested is reserve management. Monetary authorities having US dollar assets amounting to $500 billion face an enormous task of managing them efficiently, profitably and prudently. Whether that task could more effectively be handled through a BIS-like institution is a question not easily answered, particularly when the cost involved in such a joint enterprise is taken into account. Nevertheless, in view of the highly sophisticated financial techniques available today, there should be ample room for monetary authorities to cooperate in learning about new investment tools and methods.

The third possible area of cooperation is bank supervision. Strengthening banking systems in emerging markets has become an important issue in various international financial fora in the wake of the Mexican crisis in 1995. Particularly in East Asia, the rapid growth of banks at a time of technological innovation requires the matching development of a sound bank supervisory framework. The similarity of problems and challenges facing bank supervisors in this area is likely to make cooperation in this field highly rewarding.

Finally, financial infrastructure in Asia needs to be further developed and solidly built in order to facilitate the rapid growth of transactions reliably and efficiently. Monetary authorities, while competing with each other, realize that linkage of well-developed markets and solid payment and settlement systems in the region is a precondition of efficient financial intermediation and further economic development.

In June Kim

Before discussing the plausibility of regional monetary cooperation in East Asia and the possible international role of the yen and the Euro in the region, let me briefly review the exchange rate policies of South Korea over the last two decades and talk about a desirable exchange rate system for it to pursue in the future. If this kind of system can be applied to other East Asian countries, this would naturally foster cooperation in the region.

During much of the 1970s, South Korea pegged its currency to the US dollar. Since domestic inflation was not under control, occasional devaluations were necessary to maintain price competitiveness and purchasing power parity. When the dollar became overvalued in the early 1980s, South Korea's exchange policies shifted to a managed basket peg to avoid the won appreciating automatically by being pegged to the dollar.

In the late 1980s, South Korea enjoyed a large current account surplus for the first time in history, due to three favourable external factors, the so-called 'three lows': low oil prices, low world interest rates and depreciation against the Japanese yen. In face of this new development, the government did not know what to do at first. The possibility of allowing the Korean won to appreciate in order to maintain price competitiveness and reduce the external surplus never came to the mind of the country's policy makers. Since the won was depreciating in effective real terms, South Korea at one point was accused of manipulating exchange rates. However, the large current account surplus did not benefit the national economy, either. The sudden increase in the money supply caused by the current account surplus resulted in speculative bubbles, overconsumption and a subsequent balance of payment deficit. Therefore, the government decided to make major reforms in its exchange rate policies.

In 1990, the government adopted a new exchange rate policy, called the 'Market Average Exchange Rate System'. In this system, the exchange rate is allowed to float freely within a daily fluctuation band, above or below the prevailing rate of the previous day, to reflect the foreign exchange market. The daily fluctuation band was initially set at 0.4 per cent below or above the prevailing rate, but was subsequently widened to the current 2.25 per cent. South Korea also opened its capital market in 1992 and allowed foreign direct and portfolio investment.

Even after having reformed its exchange rate policies, South Korea still had two major problems to resolve. First, it needs to establish how to maintain the price competitiveness of the won in the face of wild fluctuation of exchange rates between the Japanese yen and the American dollar. Second, it will somehow need to control the impacts of foreign capital flows on the exchange rates within a desirable range after opening the capital market. I believe most Asian countries face or will face the same problems.

After opening its capital market, South Korea experienced an appreciation of its currency in spite of current account deficits, since these were outweighed by foreign capital inflows. Since the country is still in the stage of rapid economic growth, it is quite natural that the rate of return on investment there is much higher than in advanced countries: I believe that there is a real interest gap of more than 4 per cent between South Korea and the USA. There is a limit to lowering interest rates in South Korea through foreign capital inflows, since most foreign capital inflows have to be sterilized through open market operation in order to maintain price stability. In the last several years, Korean output has been close to its potential. Additional increases in the money supply would have raised the inflation rates instead of lowering real interest rates. I believe that the real interest rate gap between South Korea and the USA will remain to a large extent intact until the former becomes a mature industrial economy.

In 1996, the South Korean won began to depreciate, mainly because of the large current account deficits. An abrupt drop in the semiconductor price and the depreciation of the Japanese yen vis-à-vis the US dollar were responsible for the sudden increase in the current account deficits, which reached almost 5 per cent of GDP in 1996. The size of capital inflow was affected not only by the interest gap, but also by the size of the current account deficits. If the current account deficit to GDP ratio of a small open economy reaches some critical level, it will discourage capital inflow even if there are substantial interest advantages. This is why capital inflows in 1996 did not work toward appreciating the Korean won.

In the long run, it is desirable to let the nominal won–dollar exchange rate move in the direction of maintaining the price competitiveness of South Korean products in world markets. In other words, it is desirable to maintain multi-country purchasing power parity. In the short run, however, it is desirable for exchange rates to be determined freely in the foreign exchange market. If deviations of exchange rates from competitive exchange rates (which maintain the real effective exchange rate constant) have a stable relationship with current and capital account imbalances, it will not be difficult to maintain the deviation of exchange rates from a competitive exchange rate within a desirable range. Under this exchange rate regime, we can set up a target for the exchange rate at a level which would maintain the real effective exchange rate constant and let the exchange rate fluctuate freely within a wide band to reflect the current and capital account balance.

As international capital mobility increases, speculative activities become more prevalent, causing the exchange rate to deviate from the level that best reflects economic fundamentals. The central bank then needs to make a skilful intervention in the foreign exchange market. As liberalization and internationalization of the financial sector proceed, the linkage between interest rates and exchange rates will strengthen. Financial liberalization increases the volatility and unpredictability of interest rates and exchange rates. The Korean monetary authority faced the important but difficult tasks of keeping the money supply at an appropriate level and of harmonizing monetary, interest rate and foreign exchange policies.

Let me now turn to the prospects for regional policy coordination. Liberalization and globalization of financial markets have heightened the international dimension of monetary policy making, and opened the way for greater cooperation among East Asian countries. With growing capital mobility and the potential for financial shocks spilling over into Asian markets, economic coordination for responding to such shocks could be attractive.

There is no doubt that we need some kind of forum where monetary experts meet and consult in a very informal way and monitor the development of the market situation. At least in the first stage, it will be very important for monetary and exchange rate policy coordination to have a forum that is flexible and accessible. As we all know, EMEAP was established in 1991 to meet the growing demand for policy coordination in the region, and the Governors' Meeting and Working Groups were begun after the Governor of the Bank of Australia proposed an 'Asian BIS' in September 1995.

There are four areas in which EMEAP central banks might cooperate more closely:

1 information and experience sharing on macroeconomic policies in the face of rising and potentially volatile cross-border capital flows, and on managing exchange rates;
2 information and experience sharing in the area of supervision of the banking and financial systems;
3 development of contingency plans to deal with crises which might arise from shocks either inside or outside the region;
4 provisions for reserves management and other central banking services to member central banks.

After the Mexican crisis of December 1994, the central banks of Asian countries have looked for ways to secure liquidity in case of financial crisis. As a contingency plan to deal with financial crisis, a large number of bilateral repurchase agreements have been signed between EMEAP central banks. Repurchase agreements are essentially collateralized loans. When the objective is to borrow cash, the collateral is securities. These repurchase agreements allow participating countries to secure liquidities by selling securities held as reserve assets to the other central banks. These securities could then be subject to repurchase at some future date. The repurchase agreements will enhance the liquidity available to central banks in time of need.

In my opinion, South Korea should contract this kind of bilateral arrangement with major Asian countries, even though we have not yet agreed to sign this agreement. It is also desirable for South Korea to expand swap arrangements with major industrial countries. By doing so, it could finance the liquidity needed in a currency crisis and help neighbouring countries when they lack liquidity in their currency crises.

Could we envisage the formation of a yen bloc in East Asia? Let me briefly evaluate whether the Japanese yen has comparative advantage as an international currency. In order to serve as an international currency, it is often said that a currency should meet three criteria. First, it should have a stable value. Low inflation in the issuing country will probably ensure this. Second, it must be a convenient instrument to use. To meet the condition, the issuing country needs to have a well-developed financial market: the market must be large, liquid and free of restrictions so that the participants can borrow and lend in that currency freely and in large amounts. Third, the currency needs to be sufficiently supplied in world markets.

If we apply these criteria to major currencies today, the dollar still enjoys a comparative advantage over the Japanese yen and the Deutsche Mark in playing the role of key international currency even in the East Asian region. The following are often cited as unfavourable factors for forming a yen bloc in the Asia-Pacific:

1   high dependence of Asian countries on the US market;
2   Japan's limited capacity and willingness to absorb Asian imports;
3   prolonged appreciation of the Japanese yen over the last decade;
4   unwillingness of the Asian countries to lose monetary autonomy;
5   difference in stages of economic development among the Asian countries;
6   concern among the Asian countries that monetary union could pave the way for political union.

But with the growing use of the yen in the invoicing of trade in the Asia-Pacific, in the denomination of regional capital flows, and in the reserve holdings of the central banks of Asian countries, the Japanese yen had become a very important currency alongside the dollar in this region. Whether the yen can play a more important role in the future will depend on Japan's own efforts to internationalize its currency. In order to make the yen more important as an international key currency, Japan should make its financial market more open, more efficient and more liquid. At the same time, Japan should absorb more imports from this region. If Japan succeeds in these efforts, the market could come to accept the yen as an international currency.

What role can we envisage for the Euro? If European monetary union is successful, then the Euro will be very important, particularly in Europe. Its impact on the dollar will depend on how both European and non-European countries adjust their reserve holdings. Central banks hold reserves for two reasons: first, as a cushion to meet temporary shortages in foreign currencies which are needed to pay current account deficits; and second, as a means of supporting the value of their currencies if the need arises.

After EMU is completed, the need for participating countries to hold reserves will decline. Consequently, European central banks will dump dollars both to trim their reserves and to diversify into other currencies such as the Japanese yen and the Swiss franc. This will tend to weaken the dollar against the Euro. Monetary union will also help to make European capital markets broader and more liquid, hence more of a match for America's. If the European central bank can establish its anti-inflationary credibility, then the dollar could face a competitor of equal might.

What about the impact of the Euro outside the EU? The creation of a single European currency will undoubtedly boost the Euro's attractiveness as an international currency for invoicing trade, as foreign reserves, as a tool of intervention, and as an investment. In the future, we will see the dollar still used as an international key currency, particularly in the Western Hemisphere. It will also be used alongside the Japanese yen in the Asia-Pacific region. In Europe, however, the Euro will be the dominant currency.

André Icard

It is natural that central banks in geographical regions should wish to exchange information and to cooperate closely on a range of central banking matters. For example, such cooperation takes place in Europe within the European Monetary Institute and in Latin America within the Centre d'Études Monétaires Latino-Américaines (CEMLA). As far as Asia is concerned, an embryo of monetary cooperation exists, but is spread mainly among three international groups with, until now, limited scope and activity. This situation prompted Mr Fraser's proposal for an 'Asian BIS'. However, the reference to the BIS, which carries on its banking activity worldwide and which aims at developing mechanisms for cooperation at the global level, appears to be somewhat confusing.

Let me try to clarify the debate, first by describing the membership and the activity of the three existing forces for monetary cooperation in Asia; second, by analysing what the different degrees and forms of 'monetary cooperation' are; third, by briefly examining what the role of the BIS is and the part it could play in regional cooperation.

The oldest central bank group in Asia is South East Asia New Zealand and Australia (SEANZA). It was founded in 1957 by the central banks of five countries, which were formerly part of the British Empire: Australia, India, New Zealand, Pakistan and Sri Lanka. Later on, the group was expanded to thirteen other countries[1] including Iran and Papua New Guinea. SEANZA provides training facilities to its members and organizes one meeting a year at governor level.

The second Asian central bank group, South East Asia Central Banks (SEACEN), was created in 1966. It has ten members: Indonesia, Korea, Malaysia, Nepal, Philippines, Singapore, Sri Lanka and Thailand; also Myanmar and Taiwan which, unlike the others, are not members of any of the two previous groups. Like SEANZA, SEACEN provides training facilities and a yearly meeting at governor level.

EMEAP is both the most recent and the most active Asian central bank group. As already mentioned, it was set up in 1991 at the initiative of the Bank of Japan and comprises eleven central banks, Australia, China, Indonesia, Japan, Hong Kong, South Korea, Malaysia, New Zealand, Philippines, Singapore and Thailand. EMEAP organizes several high-level meetings per year, at least one at governor level. It set up two working groups on financial markets and central bank operations, as well as a study group on banking supervision. The question of appointing a permanent secretary is currently under discussion.

From this short description, several characteristics emerge, which express the extreme diversity of the area:

- only six countries (Indonesia, South Korea, Malaysia, Philippines, Singapore and Thailand) are members of the three groups;
- all EMEAP members are also SEANZA members;
- while SEANZA covers the whole Asian area (and even stretches somewhat beyond it), SEACEN is a sub-regional group.

As for EMEAP, its membership is based on the criterion of size (population, production or financial activity). As it comprises East Asian and Pacific central banks, it does not include India. Recent developments clearly show that EMEAP is becoming the most dynamic group of the three and in future could become a core of monetary cooperation in the region. However, due to the extreme diversity of Asian countries, a single and standardized approach would most probably not cover all the needs in the area. On that account, my personal belief is that there is room for a pragmatic and diversified approach where different groups with diverse levels of organization, membership involvement and geographical representation could coexist and cooperate.

Let me now discuss the various degrees and forms of regional cooperation. A distinction can be drawn between 'technical' cooperation and 'financial' cooperation. In the most advanced cases, these two aspects of cooperation are covered by the same institution. This is the case, for example, of the European Monetary Institute (EMI), which was the centre for cooperation among the European Union central banks in all aspects concerning the functioning of the European Monetary System (EMS). It was preparing monetary union in Europe, and it managed the credit lines set up in the EMS framework. This is also the case of the BIS which by statute is a bank focusing on monetary cooperation among central banks and as such provides all banking and financial services requested by central banks; it is a major centre of reflection and meeting at the level of governors, senior officials and specialists. At an earlier stage of development, however, technical and financial cooperation can be envisaged separately and realized to different degrees.

The first degree of technical cooperation is training. We saw that both SEANZA and SEACEN provide facilities of this kind for their members, but training programmes for central banks can also be granted by external bodies (the IMF, World Bank, Regional Development Bank and other international institutions).

The second degree of cooperation among central banks is the exchange of information at governor and senior official level. The yearly meeting organized by SEANZA and SEACEN and the meetings held in the EMEAP framework are mainly devoted to this kind of cooperation.

A big step forward is achieved when meetings at governor or top official level are devoted not only to sharing information, but also to political and technical discussion on matters of common interest (monetary policy, the economic situation, market development, financial supervision, payment systems and so on). In order to be effective, such cooperation generally needs groups of technicians and a permanent secretariat able to prepare reports and analyses to be considered and discussed by the governors. We saw that EMEAP is moving towards developing this kind of cooperation among its members.

The most advanced stage of monetary 'technical' cooperation is of an institutional nature. It implies, in general, the creation of a new structure or body with statutes or at least a set of formal rules, a board or a committee of governors to manage the system and staff or at least a significant permanent secretariat. This of course implies a strong political will and in general includes the definition of common foreign exchange policies or principles and a certain degree of monetary policy coordination and understanding. Such an advanced degree of cooperation needs to develop and grow over time.

Financial cooperation among central banks starts when they have agreements to offer each other financial support in the event of pressure in the foreign exchange market. These agreements can present different degrees of involvement. Indeed, it is important to distinguish between liquidity facilities, credit facilities (which can be bilateral or multilateral) and common reserve funds.

Liquidity facilities like repo lines allow assets to be liquefied by other central banks, with little or no loss. These procedures present the advantage of speed and discretion in comparison to market operations which, for large amounts, may need to be staggered to some extent, and will provide information to market participants on the need of the central bank for liquidity.

The 'repo' agreement passed in November 1995 between Hong Kong, Indonesia, Malaysia and Thailand and extended in early 1996 to Japan, Singapore and the Philippines is of this nature (repurchase agreements lead in essence to fully collateralized loans upon activation). Another form of liquidity facility could take the form of central bank swaps between two reserve currencies by which, for instance, an Asian country could convert assets in Deutsche Marks without market operation in assets in US dollars. These liquidity facilities must be distinguished from credit facilities which involve no collateral or only partial collateral.

Credit facilities generally take the form of swaps between a strong foreign currency and the currency of the debtor, which in this way receives a net expansion of its foreign exchange reserves available for intervention. These swap agreements can be bilateral or made by several central banks in order to create a cross-swap network, as was the case at the early stage of the European 'Snake'. At a more advanced stage, this swap 'network' can be transformed into a multilateral facility of credit by which the debtor country is supported by all the members of the system. Of course, this multilateral facility can be complemented by bilateral credits on an *ad hoc* basis, as has been the case on a few occasions in the EMS.

The most advanced degree of financial cooperation is the setting up of a common reserve fund able to intervene on behalf of the members or to complement their own interventions. This needs a significant institutional set-up similar to the one already discussed for the last stage of 'technical' cooperation.

I would now like to discuss the role that the BIS could play in this regional context. The BIS is supportive to regional central bank cooperation, and sees it as an important complement to cooperation on a global scale. With the growing importance of financial markets in Asia and the links between them, it is natural that central banks in the region wish to cooperate more closely.

The BIS commenced its activities in Basle in May 1930 and is thus the world's oldest global financial institution. It is the only central banking institution at the international level. It is owned and controlled by central banks and provides a number of highly specialized services to central banks and, through them, to the international financial system more generally. The BIS's predominant tasks are 'to promote the cooperation of central banks and to provide additional facilities for international financial operations'.

The BIS is a major international bank and the regular meeting place of the world's senior central bankers. As such, it fulfils several roles, as:

- *a forum for international monetary cooperation*: the services offered by the BIS in hosting meetings of central bankers and in providing facilities for various committees make a significant contribution to international monetary cooperation and mutual understanding;
- *a bank for central banks*: the BIS plays an important role in providing central banks with a broad range of financial services for managing their external reserves;
- *a centre for monetary and economic research*: the BIS's research economists contribute to a better understanding of international financial markets and the interaction of national monetary policies;
- *agent or trustee*: the BIS facilitates the execution of various international financial agreements.

The BIS provides a forum for cooperation, essentially between central banks of major countries, i.e. those whose economic and financial developments can have an important influence on others. Until recently only two central banks of the Asia-Pacific area were shareholders of the BIS: the Bank of Japan, the governor of which has been a board member since 1994, and the Reserve Bank of Australia. However, the BIS has long-standing banking relationships with practically all the Asian central banks. Furthermore, over the last decade, in line with the globalization of financial markets, the economic and financial weight of a number of countries has increased substantially, especially in Asia, and their central banks have progressively participated in BIS activities.

In September 1996, the board of the BIS invited nine major central banks to subscribe to BIS shares. Five of these central banks are located in Asia: China, Hong Kong, India, South Korea and Singapore, the four others being Brazil, Mexico, Russia and Saudi Arabia. The selection of new members was based on economic and financial criteria, as well as those central banks' involvement and contributions to global economic and financial cooperation. But, of course, this enlargement of membership to five Asian central banks will not influence the close relationships already maintained with many other central banks in the region.

As regards the possible contribution of the BIS to monetary cooperation in Asia, a clear distinction should be made in this respect between 'financial' and 'technical' cooperation. In the first domain, the BIS already provides all the financial services that a central bank or a group of central banks could ask of an international body. The bank's capital strength, which corresponds to an AAA+ rating, its adaptability to market changes and to the needs expressed by consumers, its specialization in liquidity support, its long tradition of efficiency, safety and discretion are advantages open to all central banks, in Asia as in other parts of the world. Creating a regional bank to cover the same field of activity would certainly be a long, difficult and costly process for an uncertain advantage. Furthermore, confronted by already globalized markets, central banks need globalized international bodies to help them in their reserve management and access to market operations. In such an environment, regional institutions do not seem to be the appropriate answer to current problems.

By contrast, the situation is totally different on the grounds of technical cooperation, as the BIS cannot substitute local or regional arrangements. If, as is likely, one or several of the existing Asian monetary cooperation group decides to organize technical committees and a permanent secretariat and wants to determine a place for meetings, this certainly has to be located in Asia. The facilities located in Basle will be of little help. Certainly the BIS, if requested, can help in the development of regional initiatives and can support regional cooperation according to its experience; furthermore, it is already used to organizing regional meetings on technical topics such as bank supervision, payment systems, monetary policy, reserve management, etc. However, such a contribution to regional monetary cooperation can only be a complement to local initiatives.

Basically, the BIS is a forum for central bank cooperation at the global level and is focused on issues that cannot be tackled in a satisfactory manner in regional fora. The recent expansion of the membership of the BIS is a reflection of and a reaction to the globalization of markets, complementary to regional cooperation. There is neither incompatibility nor substitutability between strengthening regional cooperation and developing mechanisms for cooperation at the global level.

Toru Kusukawa

As a practitioner in the market rather than a scholar, I do not pretend to be scholastically or theoretically compatible with other participants in the discussion. My presentation therefore is a humble one by a former international banker. The question I would like to focus on is: why is the yen not more widely used as an anchor currency? The simplest answer is that whatever Japan does for its own currency, it is up to the rest of the East Asian countries to decide whether it has value as an anchor currency or not. Up to now, the yen has not proved very suitable for a number of reasons.

The first reason is that the yen has fluctuated by 40 per cent in the past two years. Is this fluctuation a thing of the past or will it happen again? If such volatility is deemed to be inevitable in the future, nobody will use the yen as an anchor currency.

In these past violent fluctuations, we can trace some unfortunate instances when the yen–dollar rate was left as it was, not reflecting the change in economic fundamentals for several years. Therefore, when the adjustment was made, it was necessarily a violent one. Unfortunately, this adjustment was accompanied by political intervention to use the exchange rate as a lever in US–Japan trade negotiations. Continuous interventions to talk up the yen were made by many American politicians and officials. Intervention by the Bank of Japan in such circumstances naturally did not produce any noticeable results. The result was an overshooting of the yen rate to the dollar. Three lessons are to be drawn from this experience: (i) changes in economic fundamentals must be reflected in the exchange rate more vividly and regularly; this in turn means that the obstacles to such changes must be taken away; (ii) politicians should not meddle in the market; and (iii) intervention must be a joint effort with the blessing of all central banks concerned.

If political intervention, such as we have witnessed in the past, is kept to a minimum, the rate will probably, in the long term, settle with the gradual appreciation of the yen, reflecting the inflation rate differential between Japan and the USA (about 2 per cent per year). This will have the effect of stabilizing the international exchange rate regime as a whole.

The Japanese current account surplus will remain at around $60 to 70 billion for the time being. The surplus may decline in the future, but it will not turn into deficit. The trade surplus with the USA will remain, mainly due to the structure of trade between the two countries. Recycling of the surplus must therefore be intensified. As Japanese investors have burnt their fingers in the past when investing in dollar-denominated securities and real estate, it is difficult to resume recycling along the former patterns. One of the ways to solve this deadlock is to let foreigners use the Tokyo market more actively. The endeavour to increase the new issues in Tokyo markets by foreign borrowers should be intensified.

There are also a number of basic limitations that prevent a larger role for the yen. It is a fact that even many Japanese prefer to use the dollar instead of the yen for their international transactions. I once had a heated discussion with Mr Akio Morita, then Chief Executive Officer of Sony Corporation, when the yen was soaring every day in the market. His argument was that even if he did his utmost to meet international competition by saving here and there, by reforming his organizational structures, and by increasing his company's productivity through rationalization and so on, perhaps he might finally, after twelve months' effort, succeed in reducing his costs by 5 per cent only to find that his endeavours had been annulled by a 5 per cent appreciation of the yen in the exchange market. He felt that something must be terribly wrong with foreign exchange markets and those who work in them. I asked why he had stuck to the dollar instead of using the yen. I did not get a convincing answer from him on this point, but his indignation obviously did not dissipate.

However, since then, many things have happened in Japan. The relocation of production facilities to foreign countries has increased and exports are being replaced by products made at such relocated factories. Moreover, many exporters are combining their exports with imports of whatever they can lay their hands on – parts, raw materials and other overseas products – thus safeguarding against the risk of exchange rate fluctuation.

The attitude of the central bank is important if the currency is to become an anchor currency. The experience of the Bank of England in the 1960s, when the pound sterling was slipping from its position as a key international currency, still influences central bankers. Bundesbank, for instance, has a clear understanding that outside elements should not disturb it in the smooth execution of its duty, namely maintaining the value of the DM. Any central bank will prefer to be left alone as far as its domestic monetary policies are concerned. This parochial attitude is why currencies do not become anchor currencies.

The magnitude of economic integration in the Asian region would have to be further enhanced for the yen to achieve key currency status. Although intra-regional trade has increased remarkably, and economic interdependence in trade and investment has intensified, further development of the so-called horizontal division of labour among the region's countries is necessary.

The tendency of East Asian countries to link their currencies to the US dollar is still strong. However, with the increase of intra-regional trade, countries are bound to calculate their competitive power against Japanese products by translating into yen. Simply ignoring the yen will not be possible if these countries wish to compete in the region. Finally, an additional encouraging sign is that the yen is more positively used for capital transactions and its function as reserve currency is increasing.

Adriaan Dierx[2]

The establishment of the European Monetary Union (EMU) and the introduction of the Euro as the sole currency within it will have important implications for the International Monetary System (IMS). The economic weight of EMU, on its own, should make the Euro a major currency. As we will see, however, it is very unlikely that the introduction of the Euro will have a disruptive effect on the IMS. It must be seen in the context of a changing international economic order, that has already moved towards a multi-polar system. The central question that I will address is whether the Euro will be an important currency outside EMU and, in particular, in the emerging Asian countries.

I will first focus on the prospects for the internationalization of the Euro. As the dollar currently plays a predominant role, the main issue is whether and how the emergence of the Euro as an international currency will affect the dollar. I will then investigate how EMU will change international monetary relations. The key question is whether the IMS will become more or less stable with the Euro's arrival. I will next focus on the consequences for the Union's trading partners, in Asia and elsewhere, of the possible emergence of the Euro as an international currency. What role, if any, can the Euro play in Asia and what will be the impact on relations between the emerging Asian countries and the European Union?

The US dollar is currently the most important international currency. Even in Asia, the dollar continues to play a dominant role, while the role of the Japanese yen remains very limited. As demonstrated at this conference, the yen, for example, does not function (explicitly or implicitly) as an anchor currency for any other Asian currency.

The dollar is pre-eminent both as a unit of account and as a store of value. At the world level, 48 per cent of total world trade was denominated in dollars in 1992, 15.5 per cent in Deutsche Marks and only 5 per cent in Japanese yen. In addition, the dollar was used in 83 per cent of all foreign exchange transactions in 1995, while the shares of the Deutsche Mark and the Japanese yen were 37 per cent and 24 per cent, respectively (world total over all currencies: 200 per cent). The dollar's share in the private financial wealth portfolio declined from 67 per cent in 1981 to 40 per cent in 1995, but remained well above those of the Deutsche Mark and the Japanese yen. In 1995, these last two currencies had shares of 16 per cent and 12 per cent respectively. In the emerging Asian countries, however, the share of foreign debt denominated in yen was much higher. The 1993 figures for Malaysia, the Philippines, Indonesia and Thailand range between 38 per cent and 52 per cent.

The share of the US dollar in official reserves has been declining as well (from 71 per cent in 1983 to 61.5 per cent in 1995). The Deutsche Mark's share, on the other hand, has been rising (from 12 per cent in 1983 to 14 per cent in 1995), and the yen's share has been increasing as well (from 5 per cent in 1983 to 7 per cent in 1995). This movement can be explained by the yen's appreciation and by the rise in the share of Asian holdings in the world total. In addition, some Asian countries have started to diversify their official reserves away from the dollar. On average, the share of the yen in the foreign exchange reserves of emerging Asian countries has increased from 15 per cent at the beginning of the 1980s to around 20 per cent in the early 1990s. Asian countries have the incentive to hold more yens for several reasons: first, to protect their foreign currency reserves against dollar weakness; second, to hedge against exchange rate risk in general; and third, to expand their yen assets as a means of offsetting yen liabilities.

The emergence of the Euro as the single currency of EMU is expected to reinforce the trend towards greater diversification of international currencies. While it may be true that the Euro will develop to become an important international currency, this evolution will be gradual for two main reasons. First, economic agents will seek to be convinced in practice of the intrinsic qualities of the Euro. Second, the use of international currencies involves important economies of scale: the wider the circulation of a particular currency, the lower the transaction costs associated with its use. These economies of scale explain inertia effects that prolong the international role of the dollar, despite the decline in weight of the United States in the international monetary system.

The Euro has considerable potential to develop internationally. First, its role as an invoicing currency should be important given the Union's weight in world exports (21 per cent in 1996 excluding intra-Community exports). The comparable weights of the USA and Japan are 20 per cent and 10.5 per cent respectively. It is less likely that the Euro will develop as a vehicle currency on exchange markets or as a currency for quotation of primary products because the inertia effects due to information and transaction costs are high for these functions. However, the Euro may develop more rapidly as a currency for denominating international assets following the unification of European financial markets and in view of the guarantees of stability offered by the European central bank. On the other hand, diversification needs of European investors could play in the opposite direction, increasing the demand for non-Euro assets. Finally, the role of the Euro as a reserve currency and as an anchor currency (in particular, in the East European and Mediterranean countries) might increase.

The international role of the Euro will probably first show itself in the European zone of influence, where economic and trade links with the EU are strong: the introduction of the Euro will reinforce a shift already taking place away from the dollar (mainly towards the DM) in areas such as the Central and East European countries. Its role will also grow at world level, but there are strong factors of inertia that will make this development very gradual.

The US dollar's role as an international currency might be more affected if the introduction of the Euro were accompanied by a simultaneous internationalization of the yen. However, it is not very likely that the yen will take over the role of the US dollar as the international currency of choice in Asia. The United States remains the key trading partner for most Asian countries and, excluding Japan, intra-regional trade denominated in dollars is buoyant. But even a continuation of the recent rise in the international use of the yen would diminish the dominance of the US dollar.

Within a narrower market, the dollar's advantages in terms of externalities and user networks would diminish. However, the changing pattern of trade and capital flows in Europe and Asia, together with the prospects for monetary integration, explains why the yen is less likely to be adopted as a regional anchor currency in the Asian region than is the Euro in Europe. The prospects for the internationalization of the yen in Asia are limited and it is quite likely that both economic and political obstacles will continue to hamper them. Nonetheless, the international role of the Euro will be influenced by the behaviour of Asian investors. If these were to diversify their assets, the vast bulk of which is invested in American securities, in favour of the Euro, the latter's use would extend beyond its regional zone of influence.

The establishment of EMU and the internationalization of the Euro will have numerous repercussions for international monetary relations.

The introduction and further development of the Euro as an international currency may first give the European Union a weight in international monetary matters that is equivalent to its weight in economic or trade issues. On the monetary side, however, the Union's weight is much less important, in view of the dollar's central role. US monetary policy action has on several occasions triggered global interest rate movements that were not in line with cyclical requirements in other countries, causing distortions and diverting economies from their medium-term growth paths (e.g. the sudden tightening of US monetary policy in 1994 contributed to disrupting the recovery in Europe). Monetary policy in EMU – particularly under the assumption of a synchronized European business cycle – would certainly have an impact on global interest rate constellations, both due to the sheer size of the European economy and to the importance of the Euro in international portfolios.

The degree of openness of the European Monetary Union will become more similar to that of the United States (8 per cent) and Japan (9 per cent), reducing the impact of exchange rate fluctuations on the individual member states. In addition, changes in the value of the dollar will no longer cause disruptions in intra-Union trade relations (as happened a number of times in the past). Some of the drawbacks of the old system were caused by the fact that diversification away from the dollar had detrimental effects: DM assets were the major beneficiaries, with the consequence of emerging tensions within the EMS aggravated by the relative narrowness of DM capital markets. Both factors will be substantially reduced, which could result in a more stable relationship among the major currencies. All of this does not necessarily imply that European industry will become less interested in exchange rate developments, particularly in relation to the US dollar.

The exchange rate of the Euro may also be affected by its internationalization. Some depreciation of the dollar/Euro rate could stem from the reallocation of international portfolios and from the excess of dollar reserves in the European system of central banks. On the other hand, diversification needs might prompt European investors to move into dollar-denominated assets, something that would have the opposite effect. On the whole, the magnitude and net effects of such movements are difficult to ascertain. However, as these factors operate in different directions, one can expect that their overall effect will remain modest.

In spite of this, developments in the Euro exchange rate will continue to have an important impact in the context of the expansion of external economic and trade relations. These developments depend not only on the monetary and fiscal policies enacted within the Union, but also on the macroeconomic policies of other countries. With this in mind, the Union will remain interested in a broadening of international policy coordination with the aim of limiting the variability of the Euro exchange rate.

More generally, the introduction of the Euro should increase the symmetry in the international monetary system, which should be in the interests of the Asian countries as well. The greater monetary weight of the European Union will also permit a more efficient distribution of the benefits derived from the international coordination of monetary and exchange rate policies.

The consequences in Asia of the emergence of the Euro as an international currency are likely to be limited. However, if the Euro were to be used to a greater extent in the emerging Asian countries, the benefits of exchange rate stability between the Euro and the various Asian currencies would become more evident as well. With the expansion of trade between the emerging Asian countries themselves and also with European countries, the benefits of exchange rate stability within the East Asian region and relative to the Euro will become greater. In addition, a growing use of the Euro in invoicing international commercial transactions should reduce transaction and hedging costs for importers from and exporters to the European Union.

The growing share of the European Union in Asian external trade could also be reflected in a growing Euro share in official reserves. In addition, the arguments given above for holding yen as a significant part of official reserves could be used in favour of holding Euros as well. The inclusion of Euros in a country's official reserves would give protection against dollar weakness and exchange rate risk in general. The Asian countries might gain from portfolio diversification as well. The sharp rise of the Japanese yen in the 1980s and early 1990s significantly increased the debt service burden of some emerging Asian countries. If their debt portfolio had been more diversified, this would not have happened to such an extent. The introduction of the Euro in 1999 could provide the opportunity for such a diversification.

The importance of exchange rate stability has been recognized within the region itself and has resulted in a series of initiatives aiming to increase monetary and foreign exchange cooperation in the East Asian region. These initiatives constitute a first step towards a new approach to international monetary relations within the region, a prerequisite for a larger use of the yen.

History has shown that changes such as the ones described above will occur only very gradually. The process of diversification away from the dollar has been going on for some time and has not had any disruptive effects. The establishment of the European Monetary Union is a natural continuation of the on-going process of European integration. Ultimately, the European Union will have a weight in international monetary matters that will be equivalent to its weight in economic or trade issues. However, the additional impact of EMU will only gradually become apparent, as markets come to be fully convinced of the stability of the Euro.

Still, it is useful to reflect on the possible consequences of the European Monetary Union for the International Monetary System. First, EMU will create a pole of monetary stability, that could serve as a point or reference for countries with which the Union has close economic and trade relations.

This would be primarily the case for East European and Mediterranean countries. However, the emerging Asian countries might benefit as well, because a stable Euro would reduce the risk of holding Euro-denominated assets in private portfolios and official reserves.

Second, EMU will lead to an increased symmetry in international monetary relations, with the European pole able to exercise an influence consistent with its weight in the international economy, and other players more influenced by events in Europe. The development of a more balanced international monetary system should be in the interests of the emerging Asian countries as well.

Third, the establishment of EMU and the increased importance internationally of the Euro will provide incentives for policy makers in the United States, Asia and Europe to cooperate on monetary and exchange rate matters. The monetary weight of the Euro and the size of international trade relations will make it impossible to ignore these matters. The participation of a number of Asian countries in the BIS and the recent entry of South Korea in to the OECD are useful first steps.

The advent of the Euro thus provides an opportunity to think together about how to improve international monetary relations. Current arrangements leave room for improvements, with cases of damaging misalignments and macroeconomic imbalances undermining growth and giving rise to protectionist pressures. There is no blueprint on how to achieve this. It is a long term process of reflection with our partners in international macroeconomic cooperation.

Notes

1 Bangladesh, China, Hong Kong, Indonesia, Iran, Japan, South Korea, Malaysia, Nepal, Papua New Guinea, Philippines, Singapore and Thailand.

2 Contribution prepared in cooperation with Fabienne Ilzkovitz, unit head in the Monetary Affairs Directorate, Directorate-General for Economic and Financial Affairs, European Commission. The views expressed here are those of the author and do not necessarily reflect the opinion of the Commission.

24

THE CURRENCY CRISIS IN THAILAND

Toshiyuki Kobayashi

The Bank of Thailand, the Thai central bank, announced its surprise decision to move to the managed float of the baht on July 2, 1997, sending the currency spiraling downward 15.4 percent the same day. Prior to that date, the baht had been pegged to a dollar-dominated basket of currencies for nearly thirteen years. The Thai baht's slide continued thereafter and its crisis spread rapidly to its neighboring currencies.

The currency turmoil has had a serious impact on Thailand's domestic economy. Particularly, the heavy interventions by the Bank of Thailand in the currency market caused a significant drain of the country's foreign exchange reserves. The total volume of interventions, including those in the forward exchange markets, is said to have amounted to as much as $30 billion. Under these circumstances, the Thai government decided to accept a $17.2 billion emergency international financing package put together by the International Monetary Fund and a group of Asian countries led by Japan. At the same time, the government announced on August 5 a sweeping package of economic reform measures, including an increase in the value added tax from 7 percent to 10 percent and setting a macroeconomic target of reducing the current account deficit from 8 percent of gross domestic product in 1996 to 5 percent in 1997.

Thailand's move to float the baht on July 2 immediately sent shock waves throughout other South-East Asian countries. The Philippine peso and the Malaysian ringgit came under intense selling pressure and were forced to devalue, followed by the Indonesian rupiah, which fell sharply later in the month in a cycle of speculative contagion. The central banks of the various countries have since tried to defend their currencies mainly by raising domestic interest rates but, at the time of writing, August 21, 1997, the slide of the currencies concerned does not seem to have been halted.

Thailand used to be an excellent performer among the fast-growing South-East Asian economies. The country has enjoyed an average annual growth rate of over 8 percent in the last decade. The Japanese business presence in the country is substantial, with, for instance, as many as 1150 Japanese subsidiaries registered with the Bangkok Chamber of Commerce and Industry.

Why then did the currency crisis happen? What impact did it have, or does it still have, on the Thai domestic economy, Japanese subsidiaries in Thailand, and the rest of the countries in South-East Asia? In order to sustain high economic growth, the Thai government had tried very hard to preserve the stability of the baht by effectively pegging it to the dollar. But the recent currency crisis has forced the government to reconsider its conventional policy of putting a higher priority on economic growth. Will the Thai economy be able to return to its steady growth in the near future?

This chapter was written in light of these questions. With the cooperation of the Fuji Bank people stationed in Bangkok, I had the chance to interview personally a number of executives and financial officers of Japanese subsidiaries there toward the end of July on the impact that the effective devaluation of the baht had on the Thai economy as well as on their own companies. This chapter will also include the result of the survey.

1 The prelude to the currency crisis and the present state of the Thai economy

1.1 Characteristics of economic growth in Thailand

Since the mid-1980s, the annual real growth of Thailand's gross domestic product has averaged more than 8 percent. Figure 24.1 shows the contribution to the overall growth of Thai GDP over the period 1990 through 1995 by three types of inputs, or factors of production – labor, capital, and technology – on the basis of so-called "growth accounting," which calculates how much growth is due to each input – say, capital as opposed to labor. The figure shows that much of the growth in the Thai economy during the first half of the 1990s was driven by an increase in the stock of physical capital. If the growth due to an increase in labor and capital inputs is classified as the "growth achieved by increases in quantitative inputs" and the growth due to a more efficient use of technology as the "growth made by a rise in qualitative input," then the growth of the Thai economy during the period under review was achieved almost predominantly by an increase in quantitative inputs, particularly capital input.

In order to maintain a phenomenal growth of over 8 percent, Thailand needed and, as a matter of fact, successfully attracted vast inflows of foreign money. The surge in capital inflows, which started in 1993, has sustained the high economic growth of the country over the past few years.

1.2 Exchange rate policy

Prior to the Thai government's decision to float the baht on July 2, 1997, the Thai baht had been pegged to a particular basket of foreign currencies – a

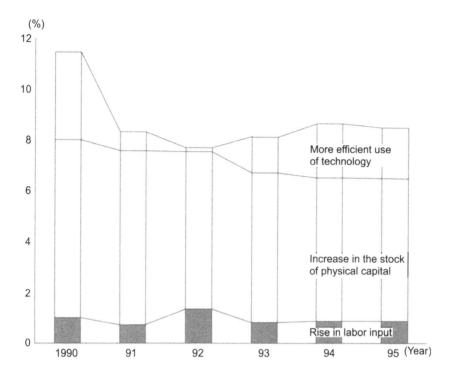

Figure 24.1 Contribution to the growth of Thai GDP based on "growth accounting"
Source: Data Stream.

quasi-fixed currency regime which started in November 1984. In the early days of the regime, which happened to coincide with the end of the first term of the Reagan administration, the dollar was very strong and Thailand was suffering from a balance of payments deficit. At that time, the Thai government wanted to bring the value of the baht down by giving reduced weight to the dollar in the currency basket. In order to let the baht effectively depreciate, the government introduced a scheme to determine the currency mix on a so-called "trade-weighted basis," or in other words in proportion to the share of trade with Thailand. The degree of the Thai dependence on trade with the United States was approximately 15 percent in 1984.

However, because of the sharp depreciation of the dollar after the Plaza Accord in September 1985, the baht tended to appreciate on the trade-weighted basis. The Thai government, therefore, decided to change the method of calculating the currency basket from the trade-weighted to a currency-weighted basis. The basket of foreign currencies to which the baht was pegged was dominated by the US dollar – estimated at about 80 percent – on the new currency-weighted basis. Figure 24.2 shows that the baht remained in a narrow range of 25–25.5 baht to the dollar during the seven years

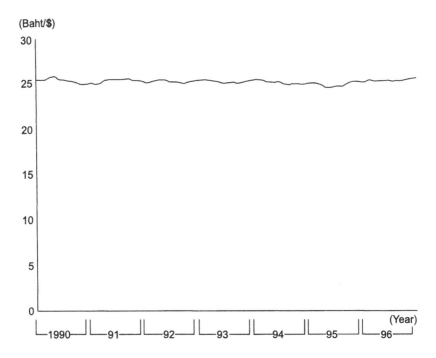

Figure 24.2 The exchange rate of the Thai baht against the US dollar
Source: Data Stream.

between 1990 and 1996, underlying the fact that the baht was virtually pegged to the US dollar. This rigid exchange rate mechanism continued until July 2, 1997, when the Thai government abandoned the currency peg and moved to a managed float.

1.3   Political and economic circumstances since 1996

Thailand's economic growth, which had averaged about 8 percent a year for ten years until 1995, began to slow in 1996. The major factor behind the slowing of growth was poor export performance, which, in turn, was attributed to: (1) a loss of competitiveness overseas in Thailand's major export items such as clothing and footwear, which faced considerable competition from such countries as China and Vietnam; and (2) an upward pressure on inflation caused by vast inflows of foreign capital and a resultant appreciation in the real exchange rate of the baht.

After mid-1996, Thailand suffered from a series of unpropitious political and economic events summarized in Table 24.1. In September, Moody's, the US credit-rating agency, downgraded Thailand's short-term sovereign debt ratings to Prime-2 from Prime-1. At about the same time, mounting pressure

Table 24.1 Major political and economic events in Thailand over the last twelve months

Month/Year	Major events
August 1996	Rumors abound that the baht may be devalued.
September	Moody's downgrades short-term sovereign debt. Banharn Silpa-archa, prime minister, resigns.
November	Gen. Chavalit Yongchaiyudh is elected as prime minister.
January 1997	The authorities order Thai financial institutions to disclose the amount of their non-performing loans biannually.
February	Somprasong Land & Development, the large real estate developer, defaults on an interest payment of its $80 million convertible Eurobonds.
March	The government unveils ten finance companies with liquidity problems.
April	Moody's downgrades long-term sovereign debt and deposits of five commercial banks.
May	The baht comes under heavy selling pressure. The Central Bank of Thailand and three other neighboring countries jointly intervene in the market to support the weakened baht (May 13). The central bank separates offshore and onshore markets (May 15).
June	The authorities suspend sixteen finance companies with liquidity problems.
July	The central bank shifts the currency regime from a fixed exchange rate to a managed float (July 2). The government seeks an IMF loan.
August	The government announces its economic reform measures (August 5). A $17.2 billion emergency financing package is put together by the IMF and a group of Asian countries led by Japan.

Source: Fuji Research Institute Corporation.

from his political opponents and allies forced Mr Banharn Silpa-archa, Thailand's embattled prime minister, to resign. The business community blamed him for mismanaging a slowing economy after many years of high economic growth. Early in 1997, a property crisis emerged, leaving banks and finance companies highly exposed to the collapsing property market. In March, financial authorities unveiled ten of the country's ninety-one finance companies as having liquidity problems. Toward the end of June, the Thai authorities suspended the operations of sixteen ailing finance companies, including the ten with liquidity problems unveiled in March, and urged them to come up with merger plans.

1.4 Move to a managed float of the baht

As evidenced by falling stock prices, Thailand's economic conditions have been gradually worsening since 1995. Periodic speculative attacks on the baht, which started in mid-1996, had been fought off by the central bank's interventions in the currency market. However, intensified speculative pressure on the Thai currency made it impossible for the Thai central bank alone to resist it and the central banks of Thailand and its neighboring countries stepped in jointly for the first time on May 13, 1997, in an attempt to prop up a weakened Thai baht by way of coordinated intervention. Furthermore, the central bank prohibited financial institutions in Thailand from selling baht to foreigners and subsequently from buying it from them as well, producing the confusing two-tier baht market, whereby domestic and foreign purchasers of baht are treated differently.

Eventually, the Bank of Thailand had to sever the baht's link to a dollar-dominated basket of currencies on July 2 to free the Thai currency in a managed float. Figure 24.3 illustrates very stable movements in the value of the

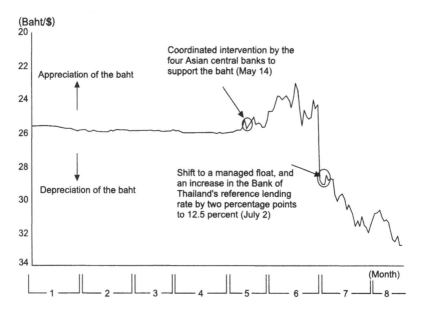

Figure 24.3 The Thai baht against the US dollar (January to August 1997)

Source: Data Stream.

Note

The baht effectively devalued by 25.8 percent between the end of April and August 20, 1997.

394

baht until May, its volatile fluctuations in June, and its steep decline after July 2.

1.5   Speculative contagion

No sooner had Thailand floated the baht than the currencies of neighboring countries began to come under heavy speculative pressure one after another. Early in July, the Philippine peso and the Malaysian ringgit fell victim to speculative threats, followed by the Indonesian rupiah later in the month. Currently, regional currencies appear to be still in the midst of turmoil.

Monetary authorities in a number of ASEAN countries other than Thailand responded to this currency turmoil by altering their exchange rate policies and also by raising their domestic interest rates. Figure 24.4 shows the fluctuations in short-term interest rates in Thailand, Indonesia, Malaysia, and the Philippines since the beginning of 1997. Interest rate fluctuations in those countries, excluding Malaysia, were particularly volatile after the start of the currency upheaval in Thailand early in July.

For exchange rate policies, the Philippine central bank decided on July 11 to allow the peso to move within a new wider range consistent with significantly changed market conditions. Bank Indonesia, the Indonesian central bank,

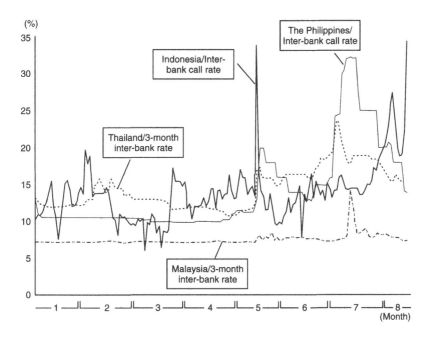

Figure 24.4 Short-term interest rates in the ASEAN-4 countries in 1997
Source: Data Stream.

first responded with a preemptive move to widen its intervention band from 8 percent to 12 percent early in July but had to abandon altogether in the middle of August its attempt to hold the rupiah even within its newly expanded trading band. Malaysia was reluctant to surrender to the speculative threat and did not change its exchange rate policy specifically by simply allowing its currency to fall in the foreign exchange market. Instead, in mid-August the Malaysian government urged importers to defer their imports as long as they could in an attempt to bring down the country's rising trade deficit.

2   Factors behind Thailand's currency turmoil

2.1   Factors leading to the currency crisis

The recent currency crisis in Thailand can be attributed broadly to two factors: (1) its conventional policy of attracting foreign capital, and (2) its inappropriate macroeconomic policies. Figure 24.5 summarizes a sequence of events leading to the currency crisis.

After World War II, Japan and South Korea initially severely restricted inflows of foreign capital and achieved industrialization by allocating the limited amount of funds and production resources to state-designated industries such as coal and steel. Conversely, Thailand made its miraculous economic growth possible by freeing its financial markets to foreigners and, at the same time, by attracting capital aggressively from overseas. In order to attract foreign capital, the Thai government decided to adopt two major policies: (1) to peg the baht effectively to the dollar, allowing foreign investors to invest in Thailand without incurring currency risk; and (2) to establish in 1993 an offshore banking market in Bangkok called the Bangkok International Banking Facilities (BIBF, to be detailed later), which facilitated vast inflows of foreign capital into Thailand.

Massive inflows of foreign capital contributed greatly to an increase in supply capacity in the economy and hence rapid economic growth, which was driven mainly by a rise in investment, particularly since 1993. However, the surges in capital inflows have had three negative effects on the Thai economy.

First, large capital inflows into Thailand, whose currency was effectively pegged to the dollar, naturally created an upward pressure on inflation, which in turn pushed up the real exchange rate of the baht. In addition, because Japan has been the largest trading partner of Thailand over the past several years, with, for instance, a 23.8 percent share in 1995, a sharp decline in the value of the yen against the dollar since mid-1995 has caused a rise in the effective exchange rate of the baht. Currency overvaluation was one of the major reasons for the deterioration in Thailand's current account.

Second, volatility in the balance of Thailand's external accounts increased. As mentioned above, the current account deficit expanded sharply due in part to currency overvaluation. On the other hand, the establishment of the BIBF

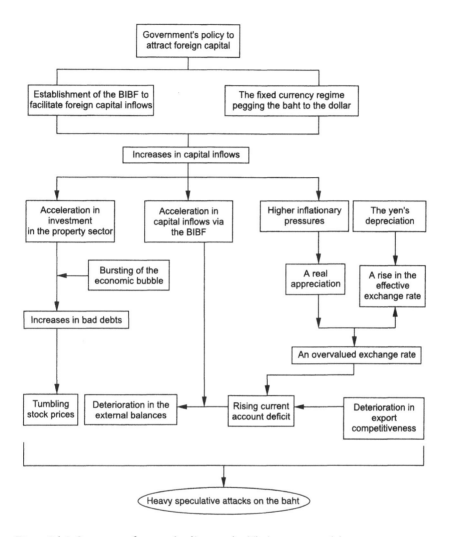

Figure 24.5 Sequence of events leading to the Thai currency crisis
Source: Fuji Research Institute Corporation.

facilitated inflows of foreign capital as borrowers could take advantage of a stable exchange rate and also of the interest rate differential between the Unitied States and Thailand. Stability in the balance of Thailand's external accounts decreased because of the situation in which the expanding current account gap was financed in effect by volatile capital inflows through the BIBF.

Third, not all the capital inflows were used for the improvement of economic productivity in Thailand. Part of the money went into speculative property investments, like luxury condominiums and golf courses, creating a bubble in the economy. The subsequent bursting of the economic bubble left local banks and finance companies with huge amounts of bad debts. As a result, the SET stock index fell sharply, with financial stocks declining particularly.

These three negative effects on the economy were increasingly felt as the economy slowed, and finally provoked the currency crisis. To recapitulate, the government's policy of attracting foreign capital and its inappropriate macroeconomic management following the vast inflows of foreign capital into Thailand were the major reasons for the crisis. In order to achieve high economic growth, the Thai government maintained the exchange rate in effect at a level higher than it should have been and opted for a type of growth driven by quantitative inputs by attracting huge amounts of foreign capital into Thailand. As a result, the economy entered a vicious spiral of an increasingly overvalued exchange rate, a rising current account deficit, vast inflows of foreign capital, and failing financial institutions exposed heavily to the collapsing property market. All these factors together created the currency crisis starting on July 2, 1997.

2.2 The BIBF and an increasing volatility in the external balances

2.2.1 The Bangkok International Banking Facilities (BIBF)

The Bangkok International Banking Facilities (BIBF) is an offshore banking market established in March 1993. Originally, the market was expected to develop into a regional financial center, but it appears that its aim right from the outset was to facilitate steady inflows of foreign money into Thailand in order to meet its increasing domestic investment needs. As Figure 24.6 shows, so-called "out–in" transactions – lending through the BIBF to domestic borrowers – expanded rapidly from the start of the market in 1993.

Only those banks, either Thai or foreign, that are granted licenses from the central bank can participate in the BIBF. The source of funds of the "out–in" transactions via the BIBF is overwhelmingly short-term borrowing by licensed banks from their overseas branches, their parent institutions or other banks in foreign countries, while the investment of the funds by such banks is made by way of normal commercial and industrial loans to businesses in Thailand. As the funds are converted into baht by the borrowers for use in Thailand, foreign exchange risk is on the domestic borrowers.

2.2.2 Capital inflows into Thailand in recent years

Table 24.2 shows the components of the Thailand's capital account over the period 1991 through the third quarter of 1996. Net inflows of foreign capital into Thailand began to increase significantly from 1993, the year the BIBF was established. Moreover, the proportion of inflows through the BIBF

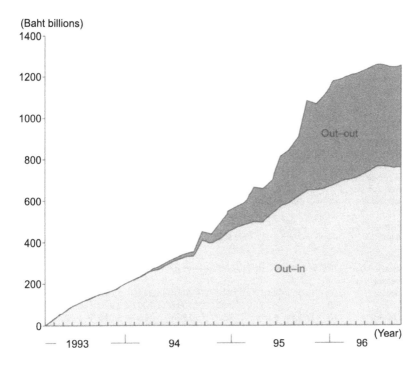

Figure 24.6 Outstanding balance of loans via the BIBF
Source: Bank of Thailand.

occupied the largest share of all net inflows of capital into Thailand from 1993. Net inflows through the BIBF increased from \$7.7 billion in 1993 to \$10.5 billion in 1994 before slightly declining to \$8.7 billion in 1995. However, net inflows of general foreign currency loans to Thailand's private borrowers were negative both in 1993 and 1994, suggesting that those inflows were largely substituted by loans through the BIBF in the first two years after its establishment. It is considered that, excluding these substitutions, net capital inflows through the BIBF had been on a rising trend at least until 1995. At the same time, Figure 24.7 shows that the share of loans via the BIBF of the total foreign debt of Thailand had been rising steadily, to 35 percent in 1996. In this way, within a few years the volume of capital inflows through the BIBF expanded to proportions which could have important bearings on the economy as a whole.

The principal reason for the massive inflows of foreign capital was the existence of interest rate differentials between the United States and Thailand. Back in 1993, US short-term interest rates ranged from 3 to 4 percent, while the three-month inter-bank offered rate in Thailand was on average slightly over 10 percent. The interest rate differential narrowed somewhat in

Table 24.2 Thailand's capital account ($ million)

	1991	1992	1993	1994	1995	1996/ Q1	1996/ Q2	1996/ Q3	1996/ Q1-Q3
Foreign direct investment	1,846	1,968	1,572	872	1,181	455	252	249	955
Equity investment	36	453	2,680	−404	2,119	548	148	73	770
Government bonds	0	299	301	670	246	267	0	−70	198
Bank debentures	0	75	144	573	744	0	−132	−117	−248
Corporate bonds	−4	96	2,331	1,628	966	586	706	935	2,226
Total of investment in bonds	−4	470	2,777	2,871	1,956	853	574	749	2,176
Loans to the government	174	−432	−250	−486	−156	29	37	−64	2
Commercial banks	216	1,755	−1,127	3,812	4,486	−1,244	1,016	−1,622	−1,850
BIBF	0	0	7,700	10,500	8,700	1,700	2,000	−100	3,600
Loans to banks	216	1,755	6,573	14,312	13,186	456	3,016	−1,722	1,750
General loans	6,514	3,139	−2,200	−5,429	2,671	1,005	1,848	1,915	4,768
Total of loans	6,904	4,463	4,123	8,398	15,702	1,490	4,901	130	6,521
Currencies and deposits	2,055	1,753	2,679	2,034	3,377	3,647	2,490	−1,198	4,939
Others	455	372	−3,330	−1,609	−2,460	−1,116	−2,676	3,602	−190
Balance of capital account	11,293	9,478	10,501	12,161	21,875	5,876	5,688	3,605	15,170

Source: The Bank of Thailand, *Quarterly Bulletin*, and others.

Note: Q = quarter.

1994 because of a surge in US interest rates, but widened again to 5 to 6 percent in 1995. However, the exchange rate of the baht against the dollar barely changed throughout those years. In these circumstances, companies in Thailand could comfortably borrow foreign currencies uncovered, in other words without hedging in the options or forward exchange markets.

2.2.3 Expansion of capital inflows via the BIBF and financing of the current account deficit

Figure 24.8 shows the balance of Thailand's current and capital accounts as well as its current account deficit as a percentage of gross domestic product

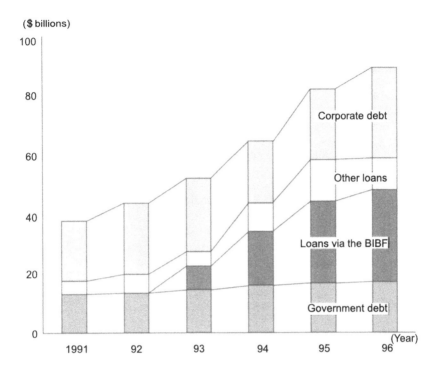

Figure 24.7 Foreign debt of Thailand
Source: Bank of Thailand.

over the period 1991 through 1996. This figure is designed to show how the current account deficit was financed by net inflows of foreign capital, of which the inflows through the BIBF occupied a significantly large proportion. To view the matter from a different angle, Table 24.3 shows the ratios of the inflows of foreign direct investment to total current account deficits of the so-called ASEAN-4 countries – Malaysia, Thailand, the Philippines, and Indonesia – over the period 1990 through 1995. The particular ratio for Thailand remained extremely low in 1994 and 1995 compared with the other three countries.

How, then, should the inflows of foreign capital via the BIBF be assessed in the light of balancing Thailand's external accounts? As mentioned previously, the principal reason for the massive inflows of foreign capital was the existence of interest rate differentials between the United States and Thailand. Whether or not the inflows will continue depends, therefore, very much on the future movements in interest rates in the two countries. However, now that a fixed exchange rate policy has been abandoned in favor of a managed float, the financial incentive for increased foreign capital inflows through the BIBF is no longer the nominal interest rate differentials between the

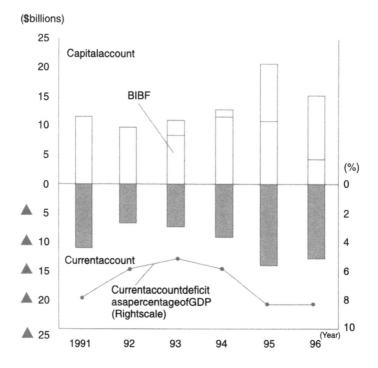

Figure 24.8 Thailand's capital and current accounts

Source: Bank of Thailand, *Quarterly Bulletin*.

Notes
Figures for the 1996 capital and current accounts are represented by the first three-quarters of the year, while the current account deficit as a percentage of GDP is based on the figures for the full year.

United States and Thailand, but a differential between the effective cost of foreign currency borrowing by Thai businesses, including the cost of hedging, and their cost of borrowing in the baht from local banks in Thailand.

Table 24.3 Ratio of FDI inflows to current account deficit (%)

	1990	1991	1992	1993	1994	1995
Malaysia	268.0	95.6	239.2	178.2	104.8	56.1
Thailand	31.6	24.4	31.0	21.4	1.7	8.8
Philippines	19.7	52.6	22.8	23.2	65.5	57.2
Indonesia	36.6	34.8	63.9	95.2	75.6	60.2
Total	45.2	46.2	74.4	60.8	46.5	36.0

Source: Asian Development Bank, *Key Indicators*.

Taking this factor into consideration, steady inflows of foreign capital via the BIBF are not expected to continue over the coming years.

Meanwhile, financing the current account deficit by capital inflows via the BIBF has endangered, rather than improved, the stability of Thailand's external accounts. Originally, the minimum amount of a single loan through the BIBF was $500,000, so that even medium and small-sized companies in Thailand could gain easy access to the market. In addition, the licensed banks are given preferential treatment of taxes. Corporate income tax for the licensed banks, for instance, is 10 percent as against the normal 30 percent, and they are exempted from paying specific business tax and municipality tax. Moreover, many of the BIBF-licensed foreign banks tried very hard to build up their loan portfolio in order to be eligible for a full-branch banking status in Thailand. Activity through the BIBF has in effect undermined the stability of the country's external accounts and has had negative effects on the economy as a whole.

2.3   The end to a pegged exchange rate policy

2.3.1   Economic impact of capital inflows under the fixed exchange rate regime

If there is a vast flow of foreign money into a country that maintains a fixed exchange rate, as Thailand used to do, the monetary authorities of that particular country normally intervene in the foreign exchange market, selling its own currency for US dollars, to stabilize the exchange rate – an unsterilized intervention. This intervention results in an equal rise in foreign exchange reserves and the monetary base, which, in turn, puts upward pressure on inflation.

In such circumstances, the monetary authorities try to counter this inflationary effect of the intervention by conducting offsetting open market operations in the government bond market – a so-called sterilized intervention. Aggressive sterilization through open market sales, however, will have an effect of both containing inflationary pressures and at the same time putting upward pressure on domestic interest rates by supplying a huge amount of government bonds to the market. This upward pressure on domestic interest rates tends to keep rates at high levels, as it is likely to more than offset the downward pressure on market interest rates, which is caused normally by the growth in the money supply stemming from unsterilized interventions.

On the other hand, inflationary pressures caused by unsterilized interventions will push up the real exchange rate. If a rise in the price of domestic goods in Thailand is higher relative to a weighted average of the prices in the United States, the value of the baht tends to decline. However, if such a currency is pegged to the dollar, the real exchange rate of such a currency should appreciate, causing a deterioration in the current account balance.

The two effects caused by inflationary pressures – sustained high domestic interest rates and an expansion in the current account deficit caused by a real appreciation of the currency – normally show up in tandem. If sterilized interventions meet with success in containing inflation to levels comparable with that in the United States, a real appreciation will not occur. However, if the growth of the money supply stemming from unsterilized intervention more than offsets the effects of sterilized intervention, then inflationary pressures will bring about a real appreciation of the currency, which in turn will cause currency overvaluation. Since government bond markets in the ASEAN economies are not fully mature yet, open market sales by sterilized intervention are likely to cause a surge in interest rates and are, therefore, less likely to contain inflationary pressure.

2.3.2   Real and effective exchange rates of the baht

Figure 24.9 shows the changes in the US and Thai consumer price indices (CPI) over the period 1990 through to early 1997 (January 1990 = 100). During most of the period under review, the Thai CPI was higher than the US counterpart and the disparity between the two tended to expand gradually, particularly from 1993 when foreign capital inflows through the BIBF started to pick up.

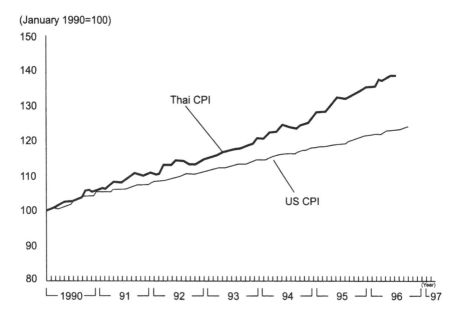

Figure 24.9 The US and Thai consumer price indices (CPI)
Source: Data Stream.

404

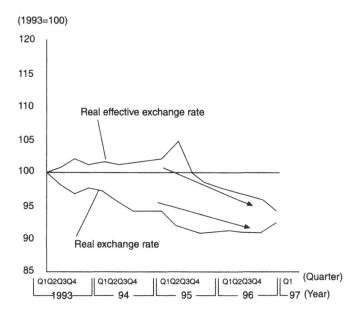

(1993=100)

Figure 24.10 The real exchange rate of the Thai baht and its real effective exchange rate

Source: Data Stream.

Notes
The real exchange rate is the rate that has been adjusted for relative changes in the United States and Thailand. The real effective exchange rate is the real value of the baht in terms of a basket of trade-weighted currencies. The basket includes the currencies of the top nine trading partners of Thailand, covering about 70 percent of all Thai trade. The nominal decline in the index indicates appreciation of the exchange rate.

Furthermore, as mentioned before, Japan has been the largest trading partner of Thailand for a number of years (Japan's share of all Thai trade was 28.3 percent in 1995). Therefore, a sharp depreciation of the yen against the dollar since mid-1995 has caused a rise in the effective exchange rate of the baht. This factor may well have intensified the extent of overvaluation of the Thai currency. Figure 24.10 shows the movements of the real exchange rate of the baht against the dollar and the baht's real effective exchange rate since the beginning of 1993 (January 1993 = 100). The real exchange rate began to appreciate from the start of 1993 and the real effective exchange rate from mid-1995.

2.3.3 Selling pressure on the baht?

Who in the world could have launched a series of attacks against the Thai baht since May 1997, when renewed pressure on the currency began to mount? For the following three reasons, it seems unlikely that sudden and massive outflows of capital, or capital flight, occurred in the recent currency crisis in Thailand as it did at the time of the Mexican financial crisis in 1994.

First, a significant part of Thailand's foreign debt over the past several years consisted of inter-bank borrowing while an astounding 80 percent or so of the net inflows of capital in Mexico in 1993, the year before the crisis, was accounted for by inflows of speculative portfolio investment, which reversed in a large scale in 1994.

Second, the size of interventions by the Bank of Thailand this time around is said to have amounted to about $30 billion, which was much larger than the net inflows of portfolio investment (equity plus bonds) into Thailand in 1995 – about $4.1 billion.

Third, if a serious bout of capital flight from the baht took place, there would have been a jump in domestic interest rates in Thailand, which, however, did not occur until after April 1997 (see Figure 24.4).

Considering that a sudden reversal of short-term capital inflows was unlikely as a factor leading to the run on the Thai baht, I think it was triggered by an expanded forward sale of the currency. According to treasury managers, currency traders sold Thai baht heavily for US dollars in the forward exchange market after mid-May 1997. Those forward short positions in the Thai baht were evidenced by a sharp rebound in the offshore baht after the Thai government separated offshore and onshore markets on May 15. This rebound in the offshore baht took place because currency traders scrambled to buy baht in the offshore markets to offset their forward short positions in the baht.

2.4 Ailing financial institutions with huge bad debt

Beginning in the 1990s, construction of luxury condominiums and golf courses flourished in Thailand. Figure 24.11 shows that the total number of golf courses more than doubled during the three years ending in 1994. Aggressive lending by financial institutions, particularly by finance companies, to the property sector has turned into bad debt after the booming property market collapsed.

Massive inflows of foreign capital through the BIBF had a strong bearing on the creation and bursting of speculative property bubbles in Thailand. Many financial institutions, finance companies in particular, are already in serious difficulty and have to contend with a mountainous pile of non-performing loans to the property sector. According to Moody's, financial institutions in Thailand have an outstanding balance of loans to the property sector totaling $32 billion, of which $13 billion of loans, or approximately 40 percent of all, is bad debt. With their total annual earnings of $3.6 billion, the Thai financial institutions will need nearly four years to write off the bad debt they have now.

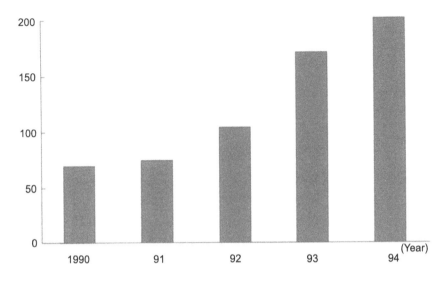

Figure 24.11 Total number of golf courses in Thailand

Source: Institute of Statistical Research, *The Comparative Studies of the Thai and Japanese Bubble Economies*.

The details of non-performing loans at Thai financial institutions have not been disclosed officially. However, ten out of the ninety-one finance companies in Thailand were unveiled in March as having liquidity problems. Toward the end of June, operations of sixteen ailing finance companies, including the ten revealed in March, were suspended by the Thai authorities. Furthermore, the operations of an additional forty-two finance companies were suspended in August, raising the total of suspended companies to fifty-eight, or nearly two-thirds of all the non-bank lenders in Thailand. The ailing financial system drove Thailand's equity market down and triggered a further decline in the baht.

2.5 Restructuring of Thailand's economic growth policy

One of the principal goals of Thailand's economic growth policy was to attract as much foreign money as possible into the country. This goal was achieved successfully by the establishment of the BIBF and also by the government's rigid exchange rate regime. On the other hand, vast inflows of foreign capital were conducive to a rising current account deficit, an overvalued exchange rate, and a greater imbalance of Thailand's external accounts, all of which undermined Thailand's macroeconomic stability.

The abandonment of the currency peg on July 2 was triggered by speculative attacks on the Thai baht, which was caused by Thailand's inappropriate macroeconomic policy of putting a higher priority on economic growth.

The Thai government was thus forced to restructure its traditional high economic growth policy. The government was also forced to restrict the inflows of foreign capital via the BIBF from July 1996. The two major policies of the Thai government – the currency peg and facilitation of foreign capital inflows through the BIBF – have thus undergone a drastic revision, suggesting that Thailand's future economic growth policy needs to be given a thorough overhaul.

3 Impact of Thailand's currency crisis

3.1 Economic reform package by the Thai government and the rescue plan led by the IMF

After a series of talks with the International Monetary Fund, the Thai government announced a package of economic reforms on August 5, 1997. The details of the package are shown in Table 24.4.

Table 24.4 Pledges by the Thai government on 5 August 1997

---

1. Maintain foreign currency reserves of at least $25 billion ($32.4 billion at the end of June 1997)
2. Reduce the current account deficit from 8 percent of gross domestic product in 1996 to 5 percent in 1997 and to 3 percent or less in 1998
3. Keep economic growth to no more than 4 percent in 1997 and 1998
4. Contain the annual inflation rate to 8 to 9 percent (4.9 percent in July 1997)
5. Aim to balance the budget and to maintain sound fiscal management
6. Stabilize the nation's financial system
7. Raise value added tax to 10 percent from 7 percent
8. Cut the charges for public utilities
9. Maintain the currency regime of a managed float

Source: Fuji Research Institute Corporation.

Responding to this plan by the Thai government, a $17.2 billion emergency international financing package was put together by the IMF and a group of Asian countries led by Japan. The details of this loan package are shown in Table 24.5. Funds provided by the IMF and the parallel disbursements from bilateral lenders are to be used exclusively to replenish Thailand's international reserves and cover a potential balance of payments shortfall.

3.2 Impact on the economy

The impact of the currency crisis on the Thai economy is expected to be both far-reaching and serious in view of the three problems detailed below.

Table 24.5 The IMF financing package for Thailand

Total package: $17.2 billion
Of the total: $4 billion from the IMF (the stand-by credit)
$4 billion from Japan (an untied loan by the Export and Import Bank of Japan)
$1.5 billion from the World Bank
$1.2 billion from the Asian Development Bank
$5 billion provided equally by Australia, Hong Kong, Malaysia, Singapore, and China
$1.5 billion provided equally by South Korea, Indonesia, and Brunei

Source: Fuji Research Institute Corporation.

3.2.1 Restrictive economic management

The successful implementation of the economic reforms unveiled on August 5 will necessitate structural adjustment in the Thai economy and a higher degree of economic austerity. Currently, Thailand is suffering from a significant economic slowdown because of the deterioration in its fiscal positions, sluggish construction demand, and weak consumer spending. In addition, the package of reforms set macroeconomic targets including a reduction in the current account deficit from 8 percent of gross domestic product in 1996 to 3 percent or less in 1998 and an increase in the value added tax from 7 percent to 10 percent from August 16, 1997. In these circumstances, a pick-up in economic growth can hardly be expected.

3.2.2 The risk of stagflation

De facto devaluation of the baht since July 2 has been putting upward pressure on inflation because higher import prices due to depreciation of the baht are having repercussions on the prices of general merchandise made in Thailand. Higher rates of inflation coupled with the slowdown in economic growth mentioned in 3.2.1 above could tip the economy into a situation known as stagflation.

3.2.3 Ailing financial institutions

The Thai government's package of economic reforms included a new plan to deal with troubled financial institutions. However, while early shedding of non-performing loans and strengthening of the deposit insurance system are being talked about, there is no clear-cut blueprint for stabilizing the nation's financial system. For example, the government aims to encourage the fifty-eight finance companies, whose operations have been suspended, to merge with foreign financial institutions. But there are not so many foreign financial institutions that are interested.

The Thai government set up a new company in March 1997 jointly with local financial institutions with substantial exposure to property developers and plans to let the new company purchase non-performing loans from ailing finance companies. But it is feared that the new company may not function well because of the difficulty it faces in raising funds. In any event, confidence in the baht will not recover unless the bad debt problems of the Thai financial institutions are solved. If inflows of foreign capital tail off in the future, the nation's economy may possibly lapse into a deflationary spiral.

3.3   Impact on Japanese subsidiaries in Thailand

Toward the end of July, I had the chance to interview a number of financial managers of the Japanese subsidiaries in Bangkok on the impact that the recent currency crisis had on their own companies. The impact can be classified into the following three categories:

3.3.1   Foreign exchange losses arising from uncovered foreign debt

Many of the Japanese subsidiaries in Bangkok seem to have a substantial amount of foreign currency debt. As the Thai baht had been pegged to the dollar for many years, not all of their foreign debt was hedged by the options or forward exchange agreements. With the sharp depreciation of the baht after the crisis occurred on July 2, those companies, whose foreign debt remained uncovered, faced the risk of foreign exchange losses.

There is, however, a considerable divergence between companies on how the hedging issue was dealt with. Some of them, particularly large companies, which had an expert financial officer, started to hedge their foreign currency debt in mid-1996, when a rumor of the baht's devaluation against the dollar arose, and successfully finished hedging most of their debt by the time the baht was actually devalued on July 2, 1997. Many of the export-oriented companies had no need at all to hedge because their foreign currency liabilities were matched by their foreign currency assets. However, the potential foreign exchange losses posed a serious problem for the vast majority of smaller companies, which were simply not equipped with the expertise of hedging.

3.3.2   Profitability of Japanese subsidiaries set to decline

While growth in equipment investment and consumer spending in Thailand has been leveling off, Japanese subsidiaries there are now finding it increasingly difficult to boost their domestic sales. In the meantime, they are meeting with very strong requests from their domestic suppliers to allow them to raise the prices of raw materials and other goods as the upward pressure on inflation has intensified since the currency crisis occurred on July 2. Under these circumstances, profitability of Japanese subsidiaries in Thailand is set to decline for the time being. What they are concerned with most is how a price rise on raw materials can be passed on to increases in the selling price of their products. They are also concerned about how to cut costs, particularly labor costs.

3.3.3 Currency risk management

The management of currency risk has emerged as a primary goal for most of the Japanese subsidiaries in Thailand since the new foreign exchange regime of a managed float, not a one-off devaluation of the currency, was introduced. Some of the large companies began to ask a number of local commercial banks to offer their swap rates and to choose a bank capable of offering the most competitive pricing. Those companies which are not equipped with the expertise of hedging have started aggressively to shift their foreign currency debt to borrowings denominated in the baht.

3.4 Impact on neighboring countries

Since Thailand announced its shift to a managed float early in July, speculative contagion spread to its neighboring countries – the Philippines, Malaysia, and Indonesia. The currencies of these countries came under intense selling pressure one after another. This speculative contagion among the four countries can be explained in part by the existence of the common features described below, which foreign speculators used to their advantage.

- All of these four countries have been suffering from a current account deficit at least from the beginning of the 1990s. The current account deficit as a percentage of gross domestic product for Thailand was 8.1 percent in 1996, for Malaysia 6 percent, for the Philippines 4.5 percent, and for Indonesia 3.8 percent.
- Although the foreign exchange regimes differed from one country to another, the currencies of the four countries were broadly pegged to the US dollar. Table 24.6 displays the degree of volatility of the currencies concerned against the US dollar and Japanese yen expressed in standard deviation of monthly percentage changes in the exchange rate of the four currencies during the period between January 1991 and August 1996. The degree of volatility of the four currencies against the dollar was much smaller than that against the yen. Therefore, the negative effect of the currency peg could be found in the countries other than Thailand as well.

Table 24.6 Volatility in ASEAN-4 currencies (January 1991 to August 1996)

	Against US dollar	*Against Japanese yen*
Thai baht	0.00420	0.0236
Malaysian ringgit	0.01235	0.0267
Philippine peso	0.01420	0.0332
Indonesian rypiah	0.00240	0.0291

Source: Data Stream.

Note:
The volatility of a currency is expressed in standard deviation of monthly percentage changes in the exchange rate of the relevant currency.

- The real exchange rates of the three currencies other than the Thai baht and their real effective exchange rates all started to appreciate significantly from 1993 (see Figure 24.12). An overvalued exchange rate was, therefore, a common feature among the four East Asian currencies.
- There were fears that the speculative bubbles in the overheated property sector of the other countries would burst as they had in Thailand.

After Thailand abandoned the pegged exchange rate on July 2, neighboring ASEAN countries started to allow a significant depreciation of their currencies. The Philippine central bank decided on July 11 to allow the peso to move within a new wider range consistent with significantly changed market conditions. On August 14, Indonesia abandoned its attempt to keep its currency within the conventional intervention band and expressed its intention no longer to support the rupiah in the foreign exchange market. In the meantime, the Malaysian central bank abandoned its support of the ringgit on July 14 at a level it had defended for the preceding two months. These movements were brought about because any further intervention in the market could drain away dwindling foreign exchange reserves. But more basically, each of the neighboring ASEAN countries tried to prevent their export competitiveness from being seriously undermined by the sharp fall of the Thai baht relative to their currencies. For the time being, as long as the Thai baht continues to weaken, the pressure of competitive devaluation will remain.

In these circumstances, the stability of the value of the Thai baht seems to be absolutely necessary for the value of the neighboring currencies to stabilize. However, in order for the baht to stabilize, the currency markets must be assured of the implementation of the economic reforms and also of the government's resolve to tackle the bad debt problems of Thai financial institutions. Stabilization of the baht, therefore, is expected to take some more time.

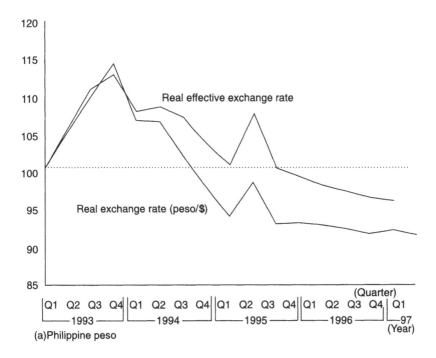

(a) Philippine peso

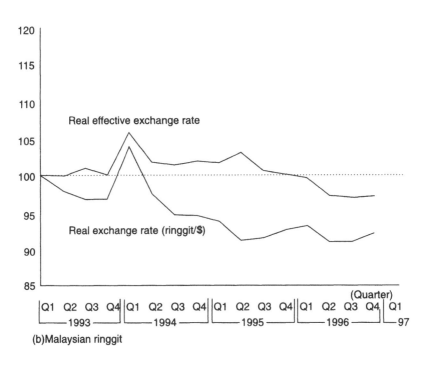

(b) Malaysian ringgit

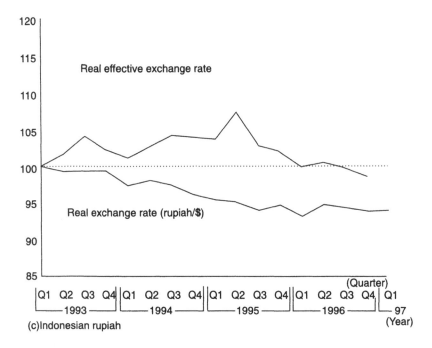

Figure 24.12 The exchange rates and real effective exchange rates of the ASEAN-4 currencies other than the Thai baht

Source: Data Stream.

Note
Calculations of the real effective exchange rates were made on the same basis as in Figure 24.10.

4 Conclusions

Once the Thai government moved from its thirteen-year virtual peg with the US dollar to a managed float of the baht, the currency turmoil spread rapidly to the neighboring South-East Asian countries. The recent currency crisis in Thailand raised a number of serious questions about the economic policies of the ASEAN countries, particularly Thailand.

The first question was about the exchange rate regimes. The exchange rate closely linked to the US dollar facilitated vast inflows of foreign capital at an early stage of economic development. However, with the ASEAN countries' dependence on trade with Japan averaging as high as 20 percent, their export competitiveness tended to be affected by fluctuations in the dollar/yen rate. During the first half of the 1990s, when the dollar was weak vis-à-vis the yen, the real effective exchange rates of the dollar-pegged currencies remained depressed, boosting the export competitiveness of the countries concerned.

On the other hand, a sharp appreciation of the dollar against the yen after 1995 caused their real effective exchange rates to rebound significantly, with the result that export competitiveness of many of the ASEAN countries was seriously undermined. Future exchange rate policies of the affected countries should, therefore, be more flexible by setting, for instance, trade-weighted trading ranges of respective currencies.

The second question was about exchange rate policies and macroeconomic management. The recent currency crisis in East Asian countries was triggered by heavy speculative attacks on the Thai baht in the foreign exchange market. The Latin American debt crisis in the 1980s was caused by defaults on loans to a number of countries in the region. Mexico's financial crisis of 1994–5 occurred when massive inflows of hot money were reversed all of a sudden. For a few years before the financial crisis, Mexico had used volatile short-term financing rather than long-term direct investment to fund its current account. In the recent East Asian currency crisis, neither defaulting on debts nor large-scale capital flight occurred. It was rather macroeconomic management that was conducive to speculative attacks on the baht. Therefore, in a larger sense, there would be no other way to avoid a serious currency crisis than to employ appropriate foreign exchange and macroeconomic policies.

The third question was about the nature of economic development. Neither economic growth achieved by quantitative inputs nor a macroeconomic policy of putting a higher priority on growth than on stability served useful purposes. Now that the importance of macroeconomic stability has been realized only too well after the recent currency crisis, the Thai government will find it difficult to pursue economic growth only through increases in quantitative inputs. In other words, economic growth resulting from rises in qualitative inputs should now be pursued. Rises in qualitative inputs may include such things as improvement in productivity or industrial development due to better management or better economic and monetary policies. They would also include building an infrastructure in services such as an efficient financial system.

The focus of the Thai government's economic policy on growth should shift away from a quantitative to a qualitative approach in implementing the economic reform measures announced on August 5. If this fundamental shift in approaches can be made satisfactorily, the Thai economy should return to its steady growth in the not too distant future. Thailand can then provide valuable suggestions to its neighboring East Asian countries by capitalizing on its recent experience in the currency crisis and the process of its rehabilitation.

INDEX

Adenauer, Konrad 362
Aghelvi, B. 23
Allais, M. 222
Amsden, A. 152, 168, 248
Anderton, Bob 245–79
Argentina 162, 173
Asea, P. 224
Asia: imported inputs 162; supra-national banking organizations 363–4
Asia Pacific Economic Cooperation (APEC) 110
Association of South-East Asian Nations (ASEAN): capital flows 51–2; and currency crisis in Thailand 395–6; exchange rate, choosing 49; Japanese investment in 360; trade flows 51
Athukorala, P. 254
Australia 235–6, 355, 356, 357
Austria: adjustment to disturbances 355, 356, 357; purchasing power parity 235–6

balance of payments: and development policies, South Korea 259–60; and exchange rates, South Korea 88; and industrial development 189; Taiwan 114
Balassa, B. 152, 161, 163, 223–7, 259
Balassa-Samuelson effect 223–7; deviations from 225, 234; extended model 227–30; and industrialization 166–7; weaknesses of 225–6
band-basket-crawl exchange rates (BBC) 16–23, 37–9; band feature 18; band width 18–19; basket feature 17–18; and free floating rates 22; target zone scheme 18–20; transparency of 22
Bangkok International Banking Facilities (BIBF) 396, 398; expansion of capital inflows 400–3

Bangladesh 235–6
Bank for International Settlements (BIS) 379–1
Bank of Korea (BOK) 69, 72; credibility of 97; intervention by 89–91, 96; sterilization by 90–1, 92–3
Bank of Thailand, and currency crisis 389
banks: impact on foreign exchange markets 358; international liabilities 52
Barrell, R. 223, 237, 239, 245–79, 280, 282, 308
basket currencies: dollar dominated 350; Taiwan 116–17; see also common basket peg
Bayoumi, Tamim 347–66
Belgium: adjustment to disturbances 355, 356, 357; imports 305; purchasing power parity 235–6
Benaroya, François 222–42
Bénassy-Quéré, Agnès 40–64, 105–8, 237, 288, 289, 307, 312, 344, 350
benchmarking 325–6
Bentham, Jeremy 361
Bergsten, C.F. 285
Bhagwati, J.N. 154, 186, 225
Bhutan 40, 42, 44, 46, 50
Blanchard, Oliver 354
bloc floating: consequences of 297–307; definition of 287–8; effects, evidence of 307–16
Bolivia 235–6
Bollerslev, Tim 315–16
Bradford, C.I. 152
Brahmatt, M. 233
Branson, William H. 80
Brazil 162, 173, 235–6
Bretton Woods system 40, 109
Breuer, J.B. 250, 286

417

Briand, Aristide 362
Busson, F. 225, 238, 239

Canada 235–6
capital account, Thailand 400, 402
capital controls on exchange rates 21–2
capital flows: exchange rate policies in
  Asia 51–3; and New Taiwan dollar 130;
  South Korea 86–89; into Thailand
  398–400, 403–4
capital inflows and currency crisis in
  Thailand 398–400, 403–4
capital market: and flexible exchange
  rates 16
Central Bank of Taiwan 114; credit
  controls 138; and exchange rate
  regimes 112–14; monetary policy
  132
central banks: cooperation of 363–4, 377–8;
  technical cooperation 378–9
Chenery, H. 152
Chile: consumption 172; exports 175; and
  flexible exchange rates 16–17; imported
  inputs 162; industrialization,
  comparisons with South Korea 167–76;
  investment 171, 176; manufacturing
  exports 177; manufacturing value
  added 177; per capita growth 171; R&D
  sources 173; real effective exchange
  rates 19; real exchange rate 169; real
  wages 172; relative export prices 153
China: Balassa–Samuelson model, deviations
  from 234, 238; bank liabilities 52;
  currency arrangements 4; currency
  composition 53; currency life cycle 205;
  domestic saving ratios 246; East Asian
  trade, share of 8; exchange rate
  arrangements, evolution 350; exchange
  rate regime 40; exchange rate
  volatility 42; export similarity
  indices 336; external trade 59–60;
  imported inputs 162; inflation rate 17;
  macroeconomic indicators 50; managed
  floating system 30–1; manufacturing
  exports 9–10; manufacturing
  output 247; manufacturing sector
  changes 226; nominal basket pegs 44,
  46; relative volatility 328; trade, direction
  of 333; trade patterns 8
Cho, Dongchul 87
Coeuré, Benoît 280–2
Collignon, Stefan 285–321

common basket pegs 327–43; constraints
  on 340–2; costs and benefits 351–4;
  exchange rate policies in Asia 327–32;
  selection 332–40
competitiveness: and band-basket-crawl
  rates 16–17
consumer price index: Asia 50; Taiwan 116,
  120, 122
consumption: and industrialization 172
convertibility 11–12, 36; in Asian
  economies 4; restrictions on 11
Corbo, V. 168
Corden, W.M. 49
Costa Rica 235–6
Coudenhove-Kalergi, Richard 362
Coudert, Virginie 219–21
Cours, Ph. 304
currency: and balance of payments
  crises 189; and industrial
  development 188–218; life cycle model of
  see life cycle model of currency
currency blocs: emergence of 289–7; yen
  as 14
currency crisis in Thailand 389–415; and
  capital inflows 398–400, 403–4; currency
  risk management 411; and economic
  growth 390; economic reform
  package 408; and exchange rate
  policy 390–2; factors behind 396–408;
  financial institutions, ailing 406–7,
  409–10; impact of 408–14; and Japanese
  subsidiaries 410–11; managed float, move
  to 394–5; pegged policy, end of 403–6;
  political and economic circumstances
  392–4; prelude to 390–6; pressure on
  currency 405–6; real and effective
  exchange rates 404–5; restrictive
  economic management 409; restructuring
  economic policy 407–8;
  speculation 395–6, 397; stagflation 409;
  volatility, increasing 398–403
currency risk management, Thailand 411
current account: Asia 50; deficit,
  Thailand 400–3; and development
  policies, Taiwan 265–6; and development
  policies, Thailand 268; of NICs 49; and
  real exchange rates 20; South Korea 80–6

Dadush, U. 233
Dawn, Ray B. 109–42
de Grauwe, P. 287
de Gregorio, J. 224

debt, and currency crisis in Thailand 406–7
Denmark: adjustment to disturbances 355, 356, 357; imports 305; purchasing power parity 235–6
Devarajan, S. 237
Diaz-Alejandro, C. 152
Dickey, David A. 80, 139
Dierx, Adriaan 367–8, 383–8
Dollar, D. 150, 225, 233, 237
dollar peg, for Asia 304
domestic demand and FEERs 251
domestic prices and FEERs 256
domestic saving ratios 246
Dominguez, Kathryn 91
Dornbusch, Rüdiger 3–34, 87, 192, 238, 280, 286, 294, 302, 317, 322–5, 358, 364, 367
Dubois, Pierre 361
Dunnett, A. 252

econometric models using FEERs 252–7, 271–8
Ecuador 235–6
Eichengreen, Barry 347–66
Engle, R.F. 58, 139
equilibrium exchange rate models 287; see also fundamental equilibrium exchange rates
Euromoney 25
Europe: exchange rates 40; imported inputs 162; political integration, historical development 361–2
European Coal and Steel Community 362
European Monetary Institute 364, 378
European Monetary System (EMS) 351
European Monetary Union (EMU) 305, 348, 361; importance for International Monetary System 383–8
European Union: export share 306; openness to imports 305
exchange rate clubs 324–5
exchange rate policies in Asia: and capital flows 51–3; choosing 49–50; cointegration analysis 58; current policies 327–31; equilibrium 249–52; evaluation of 331–2; foreign anchors 50–3; long-run estimates, computing 57; movements, South Korea 70–80; nominal pegs 41–6; rationale for 49–56; real pegs 46–8; in Thailand 390–2; and trade flows 9–10, 50–1; unit root analysis 57–8

exchange rate volatility 285–321; blocs floating, consequences of 297–307; currency blocs, emergence of 289–97; and currency crisis in Thailand 412; external balances 297–300; fundamental equilibrium 300–7; internal balances 300; intra–regional 325; of nominal rates 288; relative against dollar 42; shock–induced 306–7
exchange rates: band-basket-crawl see band-basket-crawl exchange rates; fixed see fixed exchange rates; flexible see flexible exchange rates; floating see floating exchange rates; foreign see foreign exchange rates; real effective see real effective exchange rates; real see real exchange rates; round–table discussion on 369–88
Executive's Meeting of East Asia and Pacific Central Banks (EMEAP) 363–4, 371
exogenous shocks and exchange rates 48; adjustments to, speed of 354–5
export-oriented industrialization: in Asia 49; high value-added 191; labour-intensive 190; rising value-added 190–1; Singapore 261
exports: and GDP, Asia 50; and industrialization 175; orientation of, Asia 59; of services and FEERs 255–6; share, European Union 306
external balances and FEERs 280–1
external trade, Asia 59–60

Ffrench-Davis, R. 174
financial deregulation, Taiwan 114
financial institutions, ailing in Thailand 409–10
financial liberalization period, Taiwan 114–16
financial risk premia, Asia 292
Finland 355, 356, 357
fixed exchange rates 12–15, 36–7; in Asian economies 4; and inflation 12
flexible exchange rates 15–16; intervention 16; problems with 323–4; pure float 16
floating exchange rates 37–9; in Asian economies 4; managed see managed floating system; Singapore 262
foreign anchors for exchange rate policies 50–3; and exchange risk reduction 294; model for 53–6

foreign debts: Asia 50; Thailand 401
foreign direct investment: intra-Asian 359–60; ratios, Thailand 402; Taiwan 128–9
foreign exchange rates: and bloc floating 302; and currency crisis in Thailand 410; and interest rates, Taiwan 138–40; intervention, South Korea 89–99; and NTD fluctuations, Taiwan 117
France: adjustment to disturbances 355, 356, 357; Balassa-Samuelson model, deviations from 234, 238; imports 305; R&D sources 173
Frankel, J.A. 40, 45, 51, 65, 91, 238, 286, 288, 307, 350
Fraser, Bernie 371, 377
free–floating exchange rates: transition to 22–3
free-marketeer approach to industrialization 152–4
Friedman, Milton 15, 285
Froot, K. 224, 225
Fuller, Wayne A. 80, 139
fundamental equilibrium 300–7
fundamental equilibrium exchange rate (FEER) 245–79; and development policies 257–70; econometric models using 252–7, 271–9; and life cycle of currencies 192
Funke, N. 15

Gan, W.–B. 250
Gereffi, G. 152
Germany: adjustment to disturbances 355, 356, 357; currency and economic performance 196; currency life cycle 205; foreign exchange turnover 75; imports 305; R&D sources 173; real exchange rate volatility 310, 312, 313, 316
Gillingham, John 362
Goldfajn, I. 224, 225
Goldstein, M. 253
good trade volumes and FEERs 252–4
Goto, Junichi 359
Granger, C.W.J. 58, 139
Greece 235–6, 305
Guatemala 235–6

Hamada, Koichi 359
Helleiner, G.K. 152

Henning, C.R. 285
Herriot, Edouard 362
Heston, A. 224, 225, 226, 230, 232
Hong Kong: actual and hypothetical rates 337; adjustment to disturbances 355, 356, 357; Balassa-Samuelson model, deviations from 234, 238; currency arrangements 4; current exchange rate policies 328; exchange rate arrangements, evolution 348–9, 351; exchange rate regime 40; export similarity indices 336; external trade 59; foreign exchange turnover 75; inflation rate 17; macroeconomic indicators 50; manufacturing exports 9–10; optimum currency indices 353, 354; purchasing power parity 235–6; real effective exchange rates 5, 7; relative volatility 328; trade, direction of 333; trade patterns 8
Hseih, D. 224
Huang, Juann H. 94
hubs 324–5
Hugo, Victor 362
Huizinga, John 295

Icard, André 35–9, 376–81
Iceland 235–6
import substitution policy: and exchange risk reduction 293; and industrialization 153; Taiwan 111–12
imports: European Union openness to 305; orientation of, Asia 59–60; of services and FEERs 255–6
income and price level 224
income distribution and industrialization 174
India: bank liabilities 52; cointegration analysis 58; currency composition 53; exchange rate regime 40; exchange rate volatility 42; external trade 59–60; imported inputs 162; macroeconomic indicators 50; nominal basket pegs 44, 46; purchasing power parity 235–6; real basket pegs 48; unit root analysis 58
Indonesia: actual and hypothetical rates 337; adjustment to disturbances 355, 356, 357; Balassa-Samuelson model, deviations from 234, 238; cointegration analysis 58; currency and economic performance 196; currency appreciation and stability 195; currency arrangements 4; currency

composition 53; and currency crisis in
Thailand 395–6; currency life cycle 200,
202, 204, 205, 208, 209; currency
ranking 211; current account ratios 402;
current exchange rate policies 329;
exchange rate arrangements,
evolution 350; exchange rate regime 40;
exchange rate volatility 42, 412; export
similarity indices 336; external trade 59;
financial risk premia 292; inflation
rate 17; linked exchange rate system
25–7; macroeconomic indicators 50;
managed floating system 24–5;
manufacturing exports 9–10;
manufacturing sector changes 226;
nominal basket pegs 44, 46; optimum
currency indices 353, 354; purchasing
power parity 235–6; real basket pegs 48;
real effective exchange rates 5, 7; relative
volatility 328; short term interest rates
(1997) 395; trade, direction of 333; trade
patterns; unit root analysis 58
industrial development: and balance of
payments 189; and currency 188–218;
stages of 189–93
industrialization: approaches to 152–4; and
entrepreneurial effort 159–61; and
exports 175; and income
distribution 174; and investment 171,
176; optimal policies 154–5; optimal real
exchange rate policy 161–7; political
support for 159; and price incentives
155–9; and public sector intervention
153–4; and real exchange rates 149–84;
role of state 152; targeting principle 154
inflation: and currency crisis in
Thailand 403–4; and fixed exchange
rates 12; restraining, Singapore 263
inflation rates 17; Taiwan 120
Intal, P.S. 259, 269
interest rates: and currency crisis in
Thailand 395; differentials, Taiwan 125;
and foreign exchange rates, Taiwan
138–40; parity, Taiwan 120; policy,
Taiwan 138
international Fisher effect (IFE) 120
International Monetary Fund (IMF) 21, 40,
110; and currency crisis in Thailand 409
interventionist approach to
industrialization 152–4
investment: and exchange risk
reduction 289–97; and

industrialization 171, 176; risk, and
currency performance 192
Ireland: adjustment to disturbances 355,
356, 357; imports 305; purchasing power
parity 235–6
Israel 16–17
Italy: adjustment to disturbances 355, 356,
357; imports 305

Janci, Didier 222–42
Japan: adjustment to disturbances 355, 356,
357; Balassa-Samuelson model, deviations
from 234, 238; banks, role of 52;
currency and economic performance 196;
currency arrangements 4; and currency
crisis in Thailand 410–11; currency life
cycle 197, 198, 205; East Asian trade,
share of 8; export share 306; external
trade 59; foreign exchange turnover 75;
as foreign investor 53; inflation rate 17;
manufacturing sector changes 226; real
effective exchange rates 5, 7; real exchange
rate volatility 310, 311, 314, 316; as
reference currency 14–15
Johnson, H.G. 154, 186

Katseli-Papaefstrayiou, Louka, T. 81
Katzenstein, Peter J. 362
Kawai, M. 65
Kenen, P. 307
Khan, M. 253
Kim, E. Han 80
Kim, Jin Chun 72
Kim, Joon-Kyung 87
Kim, Seung Jin 72
Kobayashi, Toshiyuki 389–415
Kohsaka, A. 120
Krugman, Paul 185
Kusukawa, Toru 381–3
Kwack, Sung Y. 72
Kwan, C.H. 51, 352, 358

labor mobility, Asia 359
Lafay, G. 222, 225, 237
Lansbury, Melanie 245–79
Larraín, Guillermo 149–84, 281
Latin America: export share 306
law of one price (LOP) 223, 226;
relaxing 229–30
LeChatelier's principle 325
Lee, J.-W. 258
Lee, Jang-Young 65–8

Lee, J.W. 168, 169
Levasseur, V. 43
Lewis, Arthur 190
liberalization, South Korea 168
life cycle model of currency 191–211;
  cross-section data 204; implications
  211–12; and industrial development
  191–3; medium term outlook 204–11;
  methodology 193–204
linked exchange rate system 25–7
Lo, Andrew 80
long-term debt service, Asia 50
Lowell, J. 40
Luxembourg 305, 341

MacKinlay, A. Craig 80
macroeconomic balance-FEER approach to
  life cycle of currencies 192, 193
macroeconomic indicators, Asia 50
macroeconomic policies: Taiwan 132–8
magnification effect 302
Malaysia: adjustment to disturbances 355,
  356, 357; Balassa-Samuelson model,
  deviations from 234, 238; currency and
  economic performance 196; currency
  appreciation and stability 195; currency
  arrangements 4; currency composition
  53; and currency crisis in Thailand 396;
  currency life cycle 205, 206, 208;
  currency ranking 211; current account
  ratios 402; current exchange rate
  policies 329–30; exchange rate
  arrangements, evolution 350; exchange
  rate regime 40; exchange rate
  volatility 42, 412; export similarity
  indices 336; external trade 59; financial
  risk premia 292; inflation rate 17;
  macroeconomic indicators 50; managed
  floating system 28–9; manufacturing
  exports 9–10, 177; nominal basket
  pegs 44, 46; optimum currency
  indices 353, 354; purchasing power
  parity 235–6; real effective exchange
  rates 5, 7; relative volatility 328; short
  term interest rates (1997) 395; trade,
  direction of 333; trade patterns 8
managed floating system: Indonesia 24–5;
  Malaysia 28–9; Singapore 27–8; South
  Korea 31–2; Taiwan 29–30; Thailand,
  move to 394–5
manufacturing: and development policies,
  Thailand 267–8; exports 9–10, 177, 246;
output 247; sector changes 226; in trade
  flows, growth of 9; value added 177
manufacturing exports 9–10, 177, 246
manufacturing output 247
manufacturing sector, changes in 226
market average exchange rate system (South
  Korea) 73–6, 82; exchange rate
  movement 76–80
Marquez, J. 254
Maswood, S.J. 51
Mathieu, C. 225
McKinnon, R. 40
McNeilly, C. 254
Meller, P. 174
Mendoza, E. 224
MERCOSUR 168
Mesquita-Moreira, M. 153
Mexico 173, 195, 235–6
Mimosa 54
Minford, P. 292
Ministry of International Trade and Industry
  (MITI, Japan) 52
monetary aggregates: growth, Taiwan 121
monetary cooperation, Asia: round-table
  discussion 368–87
monetary policies, South Korea 259
monetary policies, Taiwan 133–5;
  decision–making process 135;
  instruments and goals 133; transmission
  process and effectiveness of 134
money supply, Taiwan 120
Monnet, Jean 363
Montiel, P. 291
Morandé, F. 172
Morita, Akio 382
Morocco 235–6
multiple currency basket peg system: South
  Korea 70–3; Thailand 24
Mundell, R.A. 40, 351
Mundell-Fleming model 120
Murphy, K. 150, 151, 155, 156, 158, 159
Muscatelli, V. 254

National Wages Council, Singapore 262
Netherlands: actual and hypothetical
  rates 341; adjustment to
  disturbances 355, 356, 357;
  imports 305
New Five–Year Economic Plan (South
  Korea) 259
New Taiwan dollar, and US dollar 110;
  correlations of 126, 128; exchange rate

movements 111, 124; fluctuations, consequences 128–32; means and standard deviations 113, 115; REER index 116–17, 118, 119, 127

New Zealand 355, 356, 357

newly industrialized economies: East Asian trade, share of 8; external balances and FEERs 280–1

newly industrialized countries (NICs): capital flows 52; currency performance 206–7; exchange rate, choosing 49; Japanese investment in 360; trade flows 51

nominal basket pegs 44, 46

nominal exchange rates: indices 309; Taiwan 120; volatility of 288

nominal pegs 41–6; implicit, estimates of 44, 46; volatility of 42

non-tradable sector, productivity and exchange rates 223, 224; in Balassa-Samuelson model 227–30; wages and prices 228

Norway 355, 356, 357

Nurkse, Ragnar 15

Obstfeld, M. 15

oil price shock: on Singapore 262; on Thailand 268

oil share in external trade, Asia 60

one price, law of 223; in Balassa-Samuelson model 227, 229–30

open market operations: Taiwan 136

optimum currency area, Asia as 347–66; adjustments to disturbances, speed of 355; bilateral relationships 354; demand disturbances, correlations of 356; exchange rate arrangements, evolution 347–50; historical development 360–4; indices 353–4; and political integration 360–3; regional variation 351–60; supply disturbances, correlations of 357

ordinary least squares method of estimation 212–14

Organization for Economic Cooperation and Development (OECD): and capital account commitment 12; domestic saving ratios 246

Oum, Bongsung 72, 87

overshooting 302

Pacific Economic Cooperation Council (PECC) 110

Pain, N. 250

Pakistan: bank liabilities 52; currency composition 53; exchange rate regime 40; exchange rate volatility 42; external trade 59–60; macroeconomic indicators 50; nominal basket pegs 44, 46; purchasing power parity 235–6; unit root analysis 58

Pakko, M. 233

Panama 235–6

Paraguay 235–6

Park, Yung Chul 3–34, 87, 280, 294, 317, 358, 364, 367

Penn, William 361

Philippines: actual and hypothetical rates 337; adjustment to disturbances 355, 356, 357; Balassa-Samuelson model, deviations from 234, 238; currency appreciation and stability 195; currency arrangements 4; currency composition 53; and currency crisis in Thailand 395; currency life cycle 205, 208, 209; current account ratios 402; current exchange rate policies 329; exchange rate arrangements, evolution 349; exchange rate regime 40; exchange rate volatility 42, 412; export similarity indices 336; external trade 59–60; financial risk premia 292; inflation rate 17; macroeconomic indicators 50; manufacturing exports 9–10; manufacturing sector changes 226; nominal basket pegs 44, 46; optimum currency indices 353, 354; purchasing power parity 235–6; real basket pegs 48; real effective exchange rates 5, 7; relative volatility 328; short term interest rates (1997) 395; trade, direction of 333; trade patterns 8; unit root analysis 58

Pisani-Ferry, Jean 344–6, 369

political integration, Asia 360–3

Pollard, P. 233

Pompidou, Georges 362

Popper, H. 40

portfolio balance approach to life cycle of currencies 192–3

Portugal: adjustment to disturbances 355, 356, 357; imports 305; purchasing power parity 235–6

price incentives in industrialization 155–9, 169

price levels: and exchange rates 228–9; and income 224

price stability, Singapore 263–4
prices: domestic, and FEERs 251, 256
private sector demand and FEERs 256–7
privatization, Chile 168
probit/logit method of estimation 214–15
purchasing power parity 222–42;
  Balassa-Samuelson effect 223–30;
  econometric estimates 230–4; and
  exchange rate levels 234–8; and exchange
  rates, Taiwan 120; and life cycle of
  currencies 192, 193

Quah, Danny 354

Ramaswami, V.K. 186
Rana, R. 307
real basket pegs 48; and exchange risk
  reduction 294–5
real effective exchange rates (REERs) 5–6;
  correlations 7; movement, Taiwan 118,
  119, 127; and New Taiwan dollar
  116–17, 118, 119; stability of 7;
  Thailand 404–5
real exchange rates: appreciation in rer
  policy 151, 161; and current account 20;
  depreciation in rer policy 151; flexibility
  of 20–1; indices, and industrialization
  169; and industrialization 149–84;
  volatility of 7–8, 46, 309–10
real pegs 46–8; implicit, estimates of 48
real wages: and industrialization 172
redeposit requirement policy: Taiwan 138
regional monetary cooperation, prospects
  for 369–88
Reinhardt, Carmen 10
relative return on capital and currency
  performance 192
research and development: and
  industrialization 173
reserve requirement policy: Taiwan 136, 137
Rhee, Yeongseop 69–104
Ricardo-Balassa effect 161
Riedel, J. 254, 289
risk: and currency performance 192;
  financial premia, Asia 292; and
  investment 289–97
Robinson, Joan 15
Rodrik, D. 149, 150, 152, 154, 166, 168,
  186, 248, 307
Rogoff, K. 15, 224, 225
Rose, A. 238
Rousseau, Jean-Jacques 361

Sachs, J. 168
Saint-Simon, Henri 361
Samuelson, Paul A. 223–7, 325
Samuelson–Balassa–Komyia effect 12–13, 16
savings: domestic ratios 246
Sefton, James 245–79
selective credit controls: Taiwan 138
Serranito, F. 43
services: exports and imports and
  FEERs 255–6
Shyy, Gang 109–42, 243–4
Silpa-archa, Banharn 393
Singal, Vijay 80
Singapore: adjustment to disturbances 355,
  356, 357; Balassa-Samuelson model,
  deviations from 234, 238; cointegration
  analysis 58; currency and economic
  performance 196; currency appreciation
  and stability 195; currency arrangements
  4; currency life cycle 197, 199, 205,
  206; currency ranking 211; current
  balance 264; current exchange rate
  policies 330; domestic saving ratios 246;
  econometric model of 252–7; economic
  growth of 245–9; exchange rate
  arrangements, evolution 350, 351;
  exchange rate regime 40; exchange rate
  volatility 42; exchange rates and
  development policies 260–4; export
  similarity indices 336; export-oriented
  industrialization 261; external trade
  59–60; FEER and import prices 263;
  financial risk premia 292; floating
  exchange rates 262; foreign exchange
  turnover 75; industrial restructuring
  261–2; macroeconomic indicators 50;
  managed floating system 27–8;
  manufacturing exports 9–10, 246;
  manufacturing output 247;
  manufacturing sector changes 226;
  nominal basket pegs 44, 46; optimum
  currency indices 353, 354; purchasing
  power parity 235–6; real basket pegs 48;
  real effective exchange rates 6, 7; relative
  volatility 328; trade, direction of 333;
  trade patterns 8; unemployment 261,
  unit root analysis 58
Smithsonian Agreement (1971) 109
Snake 351, 379
Song, Chi-Young 69–104
South East Asia: East Asian trade, share of 8;
  export share 306

South East Asia Central Banks
(SEACEN) 363, 377
South East Asia New Zealand and Australia
(SEANZA) central bank group 363, 377
South Korea 69–104; adjustment to
disturbances 355, 356, 357; balance of
payments 88, 259–60; Balassa-Samuelson
model, deviations from 234, 238; bank
liabilities 52; capital flows 86–89;
cointegration analysis 58;
consumption 172; convertibility in 12;
currency and economic performance 196;
currency appreciation and stability 195;
currency arrangements 4; currency
depreciation 257; currency life cycle 200,
201, 205, 206, 207; currency
ranking 211; current account 80–6;
current account deficits 88–9; current
balance 260; current exchange rate
policies 329; domestic saving ratios 246;
econometric model of 252–7; economic
growth of 245–9; effective exchange rate
ratios 170; exchange rate arrangements,
evolution 349–50; exchange rate
movement 76–80, 372–3; exchange rate
regime 40; exchange rate system 70–80;
exchange rate volatility 42; exchange rates
and development policies 257–60;
exchange rates with dollar 71, 84;
exchange rates with non-dollar
currencies 74; export similarity
indices 336; exports 175; external
trade 59–60; FEER and import prices
260; financial risk premia 292; foreign
capital inflows 86; foreign exchange
market intervention 89–99; foreign
exchange reserves 83; foreign exchange
turnover 75; industrialization,
comparisons with Chile 167–76; inflation
rate 17; intervention, effectiveness of 93–
9; intervention, mechanics of 89–91;
intervention, trends in 91–2;
investment 171, 176; macroeconomic
indicators 50; manufacturing exports 9–
10, 177, 246; manufacturing output 247;
manufacturing sector changes 226;
manufacturing value added 177; market
average exchange rate system 73–6;
monetary policy, tight 259; multiple
currency basket peg system 70–3;
nominal basket pegs 44, 46; optimum
currency indices 353, 354; per capita

growth 171; R&D sources 173; real
basket pegs 48; real effective exchange
rates 5, 7; real exchange rate indices 169;
real wages 172; relative deflator 13;
relative export prices 153; relative
volatility 328; stabilization
programme 259; sterlization trend
in 92–3; trade, direction of 333; trade
patterns 8; trade surplus 73; unit root
analysis 58; wage increases and
development policies 258
Spaak, Paul-Henri 361, 363
Spain: adjustment to disturbances 355, 356,
357; imports 305; purchasing power
parity 235–6
speculation: and flexible exchange rates 15;
in Thailand 395–6
spot rate, NTD 114
Sri Lanka: currency composition 53,
exchange rate regime 40; exchange rate
volatility 42; macroeconomic
indicators 50; nominal basket pegs 44,
46; purchasing power parity 235–6; unit
root analysis 58
stagflation in Thailand 409
Statute for the Administration of
Foreign Exchange (SAFE, Taiwan) 110
Sterdyniak, H. 225
stock market volumes, Taiwan 131
Stockman, A. 287
Sugita, Masahiro 369–72
Suh, S. 168
Summers, R. 224, 225, 230, 232
supra–national banking organizations,
Asia 363–4
Swan, T. 192
Sweden: adjustment to disturbances 355,
356, 357; purchasing power parity 235–6
Switzerland: adjustment to disturbances
355, 356, 357; foreign exchange turnover
75; purchasing power parity 235–6

Taiwan 109–42; actual and hypothetical
rates 337; adjustment to
disturbances 354, 355, 356; Balassa-
Samuelson model, deviations from 232,
236; bank liabilities 52; bubble economy,
bursting 129; consequences of currency
fluctuations 128–32; CPI, WPI in 122;
credit controls 138; currency and
economic performance 196; currency
appreciation and stability 195; currency

Taiwan (cont'd)
fluctuations 117–28, 130; currency life cycle 207; currency ranking 211; current balance 267; current exchange rate policies 330–1; econometric model of 252–7; economic growth of 245–9; exchange rate regime 40; exchange rate regime, review 111–16; exchange rates and development policies 264–7; export similarity indices 336; external trade 59; FEER and import prices 266; financial liberalization period 114–16; fixed rates period 112; foreign direct investment 128–9; inflation rate 17; interest rate policy 136; macroeconomic indicators 50; macroeconomic policies 132–8; managed floating rates period 112–14; managed floating system 28–9; manufacturing exports 10, 246; manufacturing sector changes 226; monetary aggregates, growth 121; monetary policies 133–5; movement of REER 116–17, 118, 119, 127; multiple rates period 111–12; open market operations 136; optimum currency indices 353, 354; real effective exchange rates 6, 7; real interest rate differentials 125; redeposit requirement policy 138; relative export prices 153; relative volatility 328; reserve requirement policy 136, 137; selective credit controls 138; stable price level. 129–32; stock market volumes 131; trade, direction of 333; trade balance 123; trade patterns 8
Takagi, Shinji 350, 352
taxation: and capital controls on exchange rates 21–2; Chile 168
Taylor, Mark P. 120
Thailand: adjustment to disturbances 355, 356, 357; Balassa-Samuelson model, deviations from 234, 238; banking instability 358–9; capital account 400, 402; cointegration analysis 58; currency and economic performance 196; currency appreciation and stability 195; currency arrangements 4; currency composition 53; currency crisis in *see* currency crisis in Thailand; currency life cycle 203, 204, 205, 206, 208; currency ranking 211; current account ratios 402; current balance 270; current exchange rate policies 331; domestic saving ratios 246;

econometric model of 252–7; economic growth of 245–9, 390; exchange rate arrangements, evolution 350; exchange rate policy 390–2; exchange rate regime 40; exchange rate volatility 42, 412; exchange rates and development policies 267–70; export similarity indices 336; external trade 59–60; FEER and import prices 270; financial risk premia 292; foreign debts 401; foreign direct investment ratios 402; industrialization strategy 268; inflation rate 17; macroeconomic indicators 50; manufacturing exports 9–10, 177, 246; manufacturing output 247; manufacturing sector changes 226; multiple currency basket peg system 24; nominal basket pegs 44, 46; optimum currency indices 353, 354; purchasing power parity 235–6; real basket pegs 48; real effective exchange rates 6, 7; relative volatility 328; short term interest rates (1997) 395; trade, direction of 333, trade patterns 8, unit root analysis 58
Thatcher, Margaret 25–6
Tornell, A. 154
tradable sector, productivity and exchange rates 223, 226; in Balassa-Samuelson model 227–30; and wages 227
trade balance: and bloc floating regimes 297–9; Taiwan 123
trade flows: exchange rate impact on 10–11; and exchange rate policies in Asia 50–1; intra-Asia 359; manufacturing, growth of 9
trade prices: and FEERs 254–5
trade volumes and prices 250

unemployment, Singapore 261
United Kingdom: adjustment to disturbances 355, 356, 357; currency and economic performance 196; currency life cycle 205; foreign exchange turnover 75; imports 305; R&D sources 173
United States: Balassa-Samuelson model, deviations from 234, 238; currency and economic performance 196; currency life cycle 205; export share 306; foreign exchange turnover 75; as hub 324–5; R&D sources 173; real exchange rate volatility 309, 311, 313–14, 316
universal banking, Taiwan 114

Veld, J. 249
Venables, A. 154, 157
Vietnam 4
Villa, P. 225, 238, 239
volatility of exchange rates *see* exchange rate
    volatility

Wade, R. 152, 248
wages: in Balassa-Samuelson model 227–8;
    costs and exchange rate policies 251;
    increases and development, South
    Korea 258; Singapore 262
Warner, A. 168
Weale, Martin 141–6
Wee, Ai Ning 188–218
Wei, S.J. 40, 45, 51, 65, 288, 307, 350
Werner, A. 238
Werner Report 361
Whitley, J. 250
wholesale price index: Taiwan 116, 120, 122
Wickham, Peter 81

Williamson, A. 299, 300
Williamson, J. 18, 22, 185–7, 192, 230,
    249, 259, 280, 294, 300–1, 327–43, 347
    353, 355, 367
Winograd, C. 153
Wolff, E. 150
World Bank 150, 152, 168, 174, 230, 249
    289
World Trade Organization 155
Wren Lewis, S. 249, 280, 282

yen: as anchor currency 381–2; fluctuations
    against dollar 370; as reserve
    currency 370; role of 53
yen bloc 14, 45
Yeoh, Lam Keong 188–218
Yoo, J. 253, 258
Young, A. 150, 152, 163

Zambia 235–6
Zimbabwe 235–6

For Product Safety Concerns and Information please contact our EU representative GPSR@taylorandfrancis.com Taylor & Francis Verlag GmbH, Kaufingerstraße 24, 80331 München, Germany

T - #0008 - 270225 - C0 - 234/156/25 [27] - CB - 9780415178525 - Gloss Lamination